CW00762649

An oasis settlement on the edge of the
Kumtagh Desert in eastern Xinjiang provides
a lush contrast to the huge, encroaching
sand dunes (Guo Xiao Dong).
Previous page: The multicoloured,
variegated patterns of
aidelaixi, or Atlas silk
make it one of Xinjiang's
most renowned products
(Sun Jiabin).

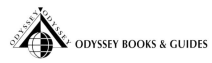

ODYSSEY BOOKS & GUIDES

Odyssey Books & Guides is a division of Airphoto International Ltd.
1401 Chung Ying Building, 20–20A Connaught Road West, Sheung Wan, Hong Kong
Tel: (852) 2856 3896; Fax: (852) 3012 1825

E-mail: magnus@odysseypublications.com; www.odysseypublications.com
Follow us on Twitter—www.twitter.com/odysseyguides

Distribution in the USA by
W.W. Norton & Company, Inc, 500 Fifth Avenue, New York, NY 10110, USA
Tel: (800) 233 4830; Fax: (800) 458 6515; www.wwnorton.com

Distribution in the United Kingdom and Europe by
Cordee Ltd, 11 Jacknell Road, Dodwells Bridge Industrial Estate, Hinckley, Leicestershire LE10 3BS, UK
Tel: (1455) 611 185; info@cordee.co.uk; www.cordee.co.uk

Distribution in Australia by
Woodslane Pty Ltd, Unit 7/5 Vuko Place, Warriewood, NSW, 2102, Australia
Tel: (2) 9970 5111; Fax: (2) 9970 5002; www.woodslane.com.au

Xinjiang: China's Central Asia
ISBN: 978-962-217-790-1

Copyright © 2012 Airphoto International Ltd.
All maps Copyright © 2012 Airphoto International Ltd., except pages 80–81 Copyright © Orchid Press; and inside front and back cover base maps Copyright © Ladder Information Company, Urumqi (English text Copyright © Airphoto International Ltd)

Library of Congress Catalog Card Number has been requested.

All rights reserved. No part of this book may be translated, reproduced or transmitted in any form or by any means, electronic, mechanical, photocopying or otherwise, without the prior permission of the publisher, except for brief passages for inclusion in critical articles or reviews.

Although the publisher and author(s) of this book have made every effort to ensure that all information was correct at the time of going to press, the publisher and author(s) do not assume and hereby disclaim any liability to any party for any loss or damage caused by errors, omissions or misleading information. The publisher has made every effort to obtain express permission of all copyright holders and to give proper accreditation wherever possible; any omission of credit in whole or in part is unintentional.

Grateful acknowledgment is made to the following authors and publishers; all materials remain the property of their respective copyright owners as indicated:

Nicholas Roerich Museum, New York for *Heart of Asia* © Nicholas Roerich 1930; Little, Brown, and Company for *High Tartary* © Owen Lattimore 1930; Little, Brown and Company for *Pivot of Asia: Sinkiang and the Inner Asian Frontiers of China and Russia* © Owen Lattimore 1950; University Press of America for "The Father's Last Three Wishes", taken from *Uighur Stories from Along the Silk Road* © Cuiyi Wei and Karl W. Luckert 1998; the Random Century Group for *An Adventure on the Old Silk Road* © John Pilkington 1989; Hodder & Stoughton Publishers for *The Antique Land* © Diana Shipton 1950; Random Century for *From Heaven Lake* © Vikram Seth 1983; HarperCollins Publishers for *In Xanadu* © William Dalrymple 1989; National Geographic Image Collection for "Journey to Shipton's Lost Arch", taken from the December 2000 issue of *National Geographic* magazine © Jeremy Schmidt/National Geographic Image Collection; HarperCollins Publishers for *Shadow of the Silk Road* © Colin Thubron 2007; Northwestern University Press for *News from Tartary* © Peter Fleming 1936.

Managing Editor: Jeremy Tredinnick
Design: Alex Ng Kin Man
Cover Design: Au Yeung Chui Kwai
Maps: On the Road Cartography, Ladder Book Information Company, Professor Bai Liyiang, Louise Taylor-Pearse, Christoph Baumer

Front cover photography: Guo Xiao Dong
Back cover photography: Sun Jiabin (left) and courtesy of the Asian Art Museum, Museums in Berlin (right)

Production by Twin Age Ltd, Hong Kong, email: twinage@netvigator.com
Manufactured in Hong Kong

A Uygur face melds Central Asian and Oriental features – the epitome of Xinjiang in all its rich complexity (Peter Hibbard).

The Gongnaisi Grasslands in the Ili Valley's Narat Scenic Area, deep in the central Tien Shan. With lush pasture, pristine forest and a backdrop of mighty mountain peaks this picturesque region is home to nomadic Kazakhs, who summer here in yurts (Pei Hong Bin).

XINJIANG
CHINA'S CENTRAL ASIA

JEREMY TREDINNICK

WITH

CHRISTOPH BAUMER & JUDY BONAVIA

Opposite: One of the Idkah Mosque's minarets plays host to white doves. Located in the centre of Kashgar, this mosque is the heart of Islam in China (Jeremy Tredinnick).

Uygur musicians perform a section of the Twelve Muqam, a vibrant musical art form that is central to Uygur cultural identity (Huan Yong Zhong).

EDITOR'S NOTE

As is so often the case, one's preconceptions of a region and its inhabitants – even one of which you think you have reasonable knowledge – are dashed as soon as you delve beneath the superficial trappings of tourism-related travel. Xinjiang is just such a place: renowned through history as a harsh land of extremes and ordeals, its modern-day tourist industry developed – quite justifiably – around the wealth of archaeological and cultural treasures relating to its Silk Road legacy.

However, Xinjiang is much more than simply a few stops along a Silk Road tour. Its complicated, intriguing history, its hugely diverse geography, its complex network of ethnic groups, its rich artistic, musical and gastronomic heritage, all these factors combine to invite deeper exploration and investigation by the intrepid, imaginative and plain curious. Modern conveniences in travel, technology and accommodation have blunted the worst travails of a Xinjiang sojourn, and the sheer breadth of experiences now possible in this land of parched deserts and lush mountains, of succulent fruits among green oases, of melodic song and ebullient dance, make it more worthwhile than ever to visit.

A note on spellings: The majority of place names follow the official Chinese pinyin spelling, with Uygur names in brackets. However, there are instances where we feel that common usage within a specific location or area should be reflected within our pages; examples are the use of Tien Shan (phonetically more accurate in its use by Central Asian peoples) instead of Tian Shan, and the use of the Uygur name Kashgar instead of the Chinese Kashi for that city.

A note on dates: In deference to Xinjiang's religious demographic, the traditional use of BC (Before Christ) and AD (Anno Domini) has been replaced with the equivalent but more neutral BCE (Before the Common Era) and CE (Common Era), whereby "Common" simply pertains to the most frequently used timeline reference, the Gregorian Calendar.

ACKNOWLEDGEMENTS & THANKS

During the course of research for this book I was the beneficiary of generous advice, assistance and support from a fittingly broad range of people. Grateful thanks are due to the following: Nisagul Imin and Parhat Ahunjan in Urumqi, Kamil Zunun and Alip at Xinjiang Caravan International Travel Service (www.caravantravel.cn), Chiu Chan Pong of the Crown Inn in Tashkurgan, Susan Whitfield of the British Library and International Dunhuang Project (http://idp.bl.uk), Lilla Smith of the Asian Art Museum, National Museums in Berlin, The Roerich Museum in New York (www.roerich.org), James Millward at Georgetown University, and Bill Bleish (formerly) of Flora & Fauna International (www.fauna-flora.org).

Jeremy Tredinnick, 2012

Two Keriyan Uygur women share a quiet joke at the dastarkhan, or meal table, where delicious nan bread and green tea are offered to guests (Sun Jiabin).

A quintessential Xinjiang scene: trekking by camel through the deep desert of the Taklamakan (literally "go in, and never come out") is now popular with tourists, although historically this was one of the most feared sections of the Silk Road (Sun Jiabin).

Snow-capped mountains are reflected in Sleeping Dragon Bay on the Kanas River in Xinjiang's far north. Kanas Lake and its surrounding alpine scenery are fast becoming one of the region's most popular destinations for nature lovers (Li Xue Liang).

Contents

The Land and its People   28

Geography: Topography &
  Trade Routes   33
  Physical Features and Climate   33
  The Concept of Trade Routes   38
  Xinjiang's Trade Corridors   40

Wildlife: Dwellers of Desert
  and Mountain   41

History: Migrations through
  Time   45
  Prehistory   49
  Farmers and Nomads   49
  Xiongnu and Han Struggles   51
  Sogdians and the Silk Road   53
  Tang, Turks and Tibetans   55
  Uygurs, Karakhanids and
    Kara-Khitan   56
  The Golden Horde   57
  The Rise of Islam   58
  Junggar and Qing Struggles   61
  Imperial Designs   65
  Provincial Status & Warlord Rule   72
  The East Turkestan Republics   74
  Part of the PRC   76
  Modern-day Xinjiang   78

Administration and Economy   92

Environmental Issues   96

Ethnic Diversity   98
  Uygurs   98
  Kazakhs   101
  Hui   102
  Mongols   103
  Kyrgyz   106
  Tajiks   106
  Uzbeks   107
  Russians   108
  Tatars   109
  Manchus   109
  Daur   110
  Xibe   110

Sports and Games   111

Musical Traditions   113
  Uygur Music   113
  An Ethnic Musical Kaleidoscope   115

Literature   117

Religion and Art   122

Food and Drink   128

Language   132

Urumqi (Wulumuqi)   133
  History   133
  Getting Your Bearings   138
  Sights   139
    Shaanxi Mosque   140
    Yanghang Mosque   140
    Khantengri Mosque   140
    Erdaoqiao Market   141
    International Grand Bazaar   142
    Central Jade Market   142
    Parks   144
    Confucian Temple   145
    Xinjiang Uygur Autonomous
      Region Museum   146
  Urumqi Practical Information   152
  Around the City   156
    Heaven Lake (Tianchi)   156
    The Southern Pastures   162
    The "Centre of Asia"   163
    The Road to Turpan   163

Turpan and the East   166
Turpan (Turfan or Tulufan)   166
  History   166
  Sights   169
    Turpan Prefecture Museum   174
    Emin Minaret   175
    Miyim Haji Karez Museum   176
    Grape Valley   179
    Ancient City of Jiaohe   182
    Sand Therapy Health Centre   183
    Flaming Mountains   183
    Bezeklik Thousand Buddha Caves   186
    Astana Tombs   187
    The Ancient City of Gaochang   189
    Tuyoq   191

MOON LAKE (AIDING HU)   194
TURPAN PRACTICAL INFORMATION   194
SHANSHAN   198

HAMI   199
HISTORY   199
SIGHTS   201
  TOMBS OF THE HAMI KINGS   201
  GAI SI'S TOMB   202
  THE HAMI CULTURAL OFFICE
    MUSEUM   202
  LAFUQUEKE (LAPUQIAOK) RUINS   203
  WUPU (WUBAO) ANCIENT TOMBS   203
HAMI PRACTICAL INFORMATION   203
THE BARKOL (BALIKUN)
  GRASSLANDS   208
  XINJIANG'S FAR EAST – GANSU'S
    GATEWAY TO THE WEST   212

NORTH XINJIANG AND THE ILI
VALLEY   213
THE ROAD TO THE ALTAI   216
  THE BEITING RUINS   216
  QITAI GHOST CITY   217
  DINOSAUR VALLEY AND PETRIFIED
    FOREST PARK   217
  KARAMAY NATURE RESERVE   222
  THE COLOURFUL CITY SCENIC AREA   223
  FUHAI COUNTY   224
ALTAY CITY AND THE NORTH   229
  STONE MEN   230
  BUERJIN (BURQIN)   230
KANAS LAKE NATIONAL PARK   231
KANAS LAKE PRACTICAL INFORMATION   235
  HABAHE COUNTY AND BAIHABA   235
THE ROAD SOUTH   236
  URYHE GHOST CITY   237
KARAMAY (KELAMAYI)   243
KARAMAY PRACTICAL INFORMATION   243
TACHENG   244
CHANGJI, SHIHEZI AND KUYTEN   244
BORTALA MONGOL AUTONOMOUS
  PREFECTURE AND THE JUNGGAR GATE   248
SAYRAM LAKE AND FRUIT VALLEY   254

THE ILI VALLEY   255
YINING (KULJA)   262
SIGHTS   263
  ILI KAZAK AUTONOMOUS PREFECTURE
    MUSEUM   265
  MUSEUM OF LIN ZEXU   266
YINING PRACTICAL INFORMATION   267
EXPLORING THE ILI VALLEY   270
  QAPQAL (CHABUCHAER)
    XIBE AUTONOMOUS COUNTY   270
  HUOCHENG COUNTY   270
  TEKES AND ZHAOSU COUNTIES   271
  THE NARAT GRASSLANDS   273
  MOUNTAIN HIGHWAYS AND THE
    BAYANBULAK GRASSLANDS   278

THE ROAD TO KASHGAR AND
THE SOUTHWEST   282
SOUTH TO KORLA   282
  BOSTEN LAKE   284
KORLA   285
SIGHTS   286
KORLA PRACTICAL INFORMATION   287
LUNTAI AND THE TARIM HIGHWAY   288
KUCHA (KUQA)   290
SIGHTS   295
  KUCHA GRAND MOSQUE   297
  MOLENA ASHIDIN HODJA'S TOMB   297
  ANCIENT CITY OF SUBASHI   298
  KIZIL KARA BUDDHIST CAVES AND
    THE KIZILGAHA BEACON TOWER   298
  KUMTURA CAVES AND SIMSIM CAVES   299
  KIZIL THOUSAND BUDDHA CAVES   299
KUCHA PRACTICAL INFORMATION   303
AKSU   306
AKSU PRACTICAL INFORMATION   307
ARAL AND THE DESERT ROAD TO
  HOTAN   307
AKSU TO KASHGAR   310
  ARTUSH   310
  THE KYRGYZ   311
KASHGAR (KASHI)   313

Lined by golden-topped poplars, the Tarim River meanders through the northern Taklamakan Desert, a lifeline for the region's inhabitants as well as the caravans of old (Yan Xian).

HISTORY   313
SIGHTS   315
  THE SUNDAY BAZAAR AND LIVESTOCK
    MARKET   319
  IDKAH MOSQUE   320
  ABAKH KHOJA'S TOMB   322
  THE BRITISH AND RUSSIAN
    CONSULATES   326
  TOMB OF YUSUF HAS HAJIB   327
KASHGAR PRACTICAL INFORMATION   327

AROUND KASHGAR   334
  THREE IMMORTALS BUDDHIST CAVES
    (SANXIAN DONG)   334
  ANCIENT CITY OF HANOI   334
  OPAL (WUPOER)   335
  SHIPTON'S ARCH   335
  TOUR COSTS   343

THE KARAKORAM HIGHWAY   343
  OYTAGH   344
  KARAKUL LAKE AND MUZTAGATA   345

TASHKURGAN   346
TASHKURGAN PRACTICAL
  INFORMATION   351
THE KHUNJERAB PASS   351

THE SOUTHERN SILK ROAD   355
YENGISAR   357

SHACHE (YARKAND)   358
SHACHE PRACTICAL INFORMATION   364

ZEPU (POSGAM)   364

YECHENG (KARGHALIK)   364

HOTAN (KHOTAN OR HETIAN)   367
  HISTORY   372
  ENTER THE ARCHAEOLOGISTS   374
  SIGHTS   379
    HOTAN MUSEUM   381
    SHATUO SILK FACTORY   382
    THE TOMB OF IMAM ASIM   384
    ANCIENT CITY OF YOTKAN   384
    ANCIENT CITY OF MELIKAWAT   385
    ANCIENT STUPA OF RAWAK   385
    RIVER RAFTING   389
  HOTAN PRACTICAL INFORMATION   389

BEYOND HOTAN   390
  MAZAR TAGH   391
  DANDAN OILIK   392

YUTIAN (KERIYA)   398
  KARADONG AND YUAN SHA   399
  LIUSHUI   400

MINFENG (NEW NIYA)   400
MINFENG PRACTICAL INFORMATION   402
  NIYA   402

MINFENG TO QIEMO   404
  ENDERE   405

QIEMO   407
  ZAGHUNLUK   407
  WHERE IS ANCIENT QIEMO?   408
  TRIPS FROM QIEMO   408
QIEMO PRACTICAL INFORMATION   412

RUOQIANG (CHARKHLIK)   412
RUOQIANG PRACTICAL INFORMATION   415
  ARJIN MOUNTAIN NATIONAL NATURE
    RESERVE   415
  MIRAN   416

LOP NOR AND LOULAN   417
SITES ALONG THE KONCHE RIVER
  (KURUK DARYA)   430
  QÄWRIGHUL   430
  XIAOHE   431

A–Z FACTS FOR THE
  TRAVELLER   434
  ACCOMMODATION   434
  AIRLINES AND AIR TRAVEL   434
  ALCOHOL   436
  BARGAINING   436
  CLIMATE AND CLOTHING   436
  CRIME   438
  CURRENCY AND CREDIT CARDS   438
  CUSTOMS AND CULTURE   440
  DINING ETIQUETTE   440
  ELECTRICITY   441
  EMBASSIES AND CONSULATES   441
  FOOD AND DRINK   441
  HEALTH AND ALTITUDE   444
  INTERNET   444
  MAPS AND BOOKS   445
  POST AND TELECOMMUNICATIONS   445

POTENTIAL DANGER OF ILLEGAL PASTIMES 445
PUBLIC HOLIDAYS 445
RED TAPE 448
ROADS 448
TIPPING 449
TIME 449
TOURS AND TOUR AGENCIES 449
Xinjiang-based Agencies 449
China-based Online Agencies 451
International Agencies 451
TRAVEL TO AND WITHIN XINJIANG 452
By Air 452
By Rail 452
By Road 453
USEFUL WEBSITES 456
Regional Government Sites 456
News Sites 456
Silk Road-related 456
General 456
VISAS AND CUSTOMS 457
THE CHINESE LANGUAGE 460

RECOMMENDED READING 467
INDEX 471

SPECIAL TOPICS
Xinjiang Superlatives 48
Chronology of Periods in Chinese History 50
Two Early Western Travellers 59
The Great Game 66
Foreign Exploration in Xinjiang 79
Indo-European Mummies 148
The Karez: Wellspring of Life in the Desert 177
Karakhoto: the Black City of the Tanguts 204
The Importance of Horses 209
The Ancient City of Beiting (Besh Balik) 219
Carved in Stone: Rock Art and Turkic
    Tombs in the Altai 226
Toll waves and Speed Traps on Today's
    Silk Roads 246
The Rock Sanctuary of Kangjia Shimenzi 250
Highways Across the Sand 292
The Silk Secret 369

Islam Akhun 375
Paper Manufacturing in Hotan 377
Lop Nor: the Riddle of the Wandering Lake 420
Loulan: Lost City of the Gobi 424

LITERARY EXCERPTS
Nicholas Roerich on *the heart of Asia* 39
Owen Lattimore on *Qing rule in Xinjiang* 64
Owen Lattimore on *what's in a name* 70
Cuiyi Wei and Karl W. Luckert on
    a father's final wishes 118
Alice Thorner on *Xinjiang's artistic importance* 123
Owen Lattimore on *Turpan's cleanliness* 170
Nicholas Roerich on
    old believers and ancient inhabitants 238
Owen Lattimore on *Sayram Lake and the
    Ili Valley* 258
Owen Lattimore on *Xinjiang's princely ponies* 274
John Pilkington on *the importance of blood ties* 309
Diana Shipton on *Kashgar through the seasons* 318
Vikram Seth on *a common language* 322
William Dalrymple on *a trip to the cinema* 330
Jeremy Schmidt on *rediscovering
    Shipton's Arch* 336
Diana Shipton on *an excursion to Oitagh* 346
Colin Thubron on *a side trip to Rawak* 386
Peter Fleming on *reaching an oasis* 410
Colin Thubron on *crossing the Altun* 414

MAPS
Xinjiang (Political) **Inside front cover**
Silk Road Routes **80–81**
Urumqi **136–137**
Turpan City **171**
Turpan Area **195**
Yining **263**
Kucha **295**
Kashgar **316**
The Five Great Passes Route from Yarkand
    to Leh **365**
Xinjiang (Physical) **Inside back cover**

A camel driver leads his beasts of burden along the shores of Karakul Lake in southwestern Xinjiang's High Pamirs (Sun Jiabin).

The ancient Uygur city of Gaochang in the Turpan Depression, its ruins glowing gold in the late afternoon sun in imitation of the Flaming Mountains that tower over it to the north (Li Xue Liang).

THE LAND AND ITS PEOPLE

The enormous area today known as the **Xinjiang Uygur Autonomous Region** (commonly referred to simply as Xinjiang) came to the attention of the wider world more than two millennia ago with the rise of the various trading routes collectively known as the "Silk Road", a major section of which crossed its barren wastelands, skirted its hellish deserts, and hugged the foothills of its majestic mountain ranges, bridging the distant power centres of a newly unified China and the expansive Roman empire.

Known in those times simply as the "Western Regions" by the nascent Han Dynasty, Xinjiang was initially considered to be nothing more than a vast wilderness populated mainly by unsophisticated barbarians, but this errant view was soon amended as explorers, soldiers and merchants began to blaze a trail into the west, discovering that fertile oases around the desert edges had already been peopled by migratory tribes from farther west, and these complex communities paid tribute to powerful nomadic tribes populating huge swathes of lush grassland in the north.

Over the centuries these nomadic peoples and city-states were subject to both religious and economic influences from India, Greece, Persia and, of course, China, resulting in a land that today is rich with archaeological and cultural treasures. But after the decline of the fabled land routes between Asia and the West, Xinjiang faded from global consciousness until the turn of the 20th century brought new explorers and newfound interest.

However, modern Xinjiang's appeal encompasses much more than its Silk Road legacy, rich and fascinating though that is. Occupying one-sixth of China's territory, it is home to 13 distinct nationalities (including the Han), one of the world's harshest but most bewitching desert regions, lush oases producing a cornucopia of delectable fruits and nuts, and a selection of little-explored mountain ranges to delight the most seasoned traveller.

Geographical comparisons clearly illustrate Xinjiang's immense dimensions: occupying 1.66 million square kilometres (more than 600,000 square miles), it is larger than Alaska and well over twice the size of Texas, while in European terms you could fit France, Germany, Spain and the UK into its borders with space to spare. Xinjiang's international borders include – from northeast to southeast – Mongolia, Russia, Kazakhstan, Kyrgyzstan, Tajikistan, Afghanistan, Pakistan and India, a total boundary line stretching 5,600 kilometres (3,480 miles); its domestic borders are also lengthy, abutting on the Tibet Autonomous Region and the provinces of Qinghai and Gansu.

This is a region of stunning contrasts, ranging from the Turpan Depression, the lowest point in China, to some of the highest in the Tien Shan, or Heavenly Mountains. Xinjiang's many natural sights offer pine-studded mountain pastures, wind-rippled sand dunes, icy jagged peaks, pocked limestone pinnacles, and clear-blue fresh- and saltwater lakes. This geographical diversity in turn plays host to

A magnificent specimen of Xinjiang's most iconic animal, the doughty Bactrian camel, at the Uryhe Ghost City (Jeremy Tredinnick).

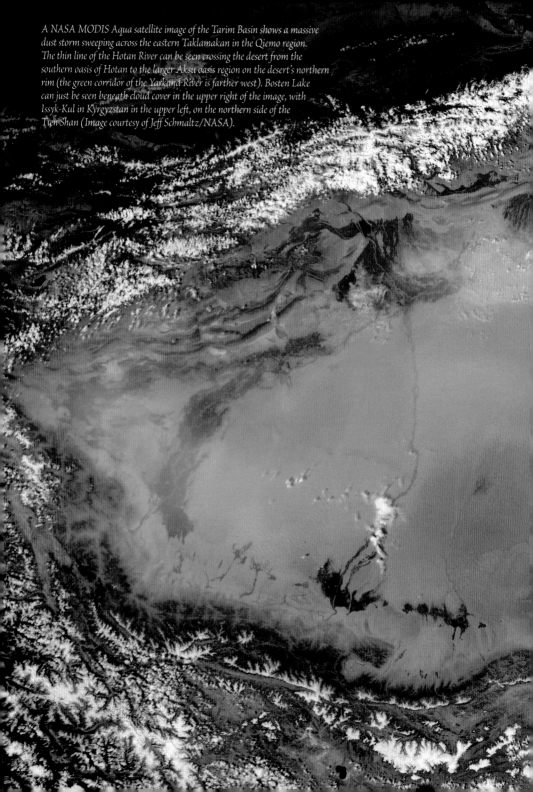

A NASA MODIS Aqua satellite image of the Tarim Basin shows a massive dust storm sweeping across the eastern Taklamakan in the Qiemo region. The thin line of the Hotan River can be seen crossing the desert from the southern oasis of Hotan to the larger Aksu oasis region on the desert's northern rim (the green corridor of the Yarkand River is farther west). Bosten Lake can just be seen beneath cloud cover in the upper right of the image, with Issyk-Kul in Kyrgyzstan in the upper left, on the northern side of the Tien Shan (Image courtesy of Jeff Schmaltz/NASA).

an array of cultures, from the pastoral nomadism of the northern grasslands of the Junggar Basin to the prosperous agricultural oases of the south that surround the fearsome **Taklamakan Desert**, which in Uygur translates as "enter and never return". The infamous Taklamakan has been feared and cursed by travellers for more than 2,000 years. In his book *Chinese Central Asia* Sir Clarmont Skrine, British consul-general at Kashgar in the 1920s, described it thus:

> To the north in the clear dawn the view is inexpressively awe-inspiring and sinister. The yellow dunes of the Taklamakan, like the giant waves of a petrified ocean, extend in countless myriads to a far horizon with, here and there, an extra large sand-hill, a king dune as it were, towering above his fellows. They seem to clamour silently, those dunes, for travellers to engulf, for whole caravans to swallow up as they have swallowed up so many in the past.

But in truth it was the extreme nature of this reputation, the hidden possibilities of its lost cities and the romantic image of its necklace of lush, shady oases that first drew adventurers and explorers, then appealed to a new wave of travellers in the latter half of the 20th century: tourists.

They came predominantly to explore the ancient sites of the "Silk Road", a term created in the 1870s by the German geographer Ferdinand von Richthofen, which conveniently categorizes what was perhaps the greatest East–West trade route and conduit for cross-cultural exchange the world has ever seen. However, this title is essentially a misnomer in both its parts, for there was never one single "road" – rather a multitude of shifting trails that crisscrossed the territory of modern Xinjiang – and although silk was certainly an important and precious trade product, it was but one of myriad commodities that were transported between kingdoms, as well as the arguably far more important abstract concepts of religious and cultural beliefs.

As Xinjiang's greater potential has been realized – its pristine mountain splendour, wealth of natural resources and rich cultural legacy – it has begun to develop along international lines: its urban centres are growing fast, fuelled by an influx of migrant workers from the east; industry and agriculture is booming as exploitation of mineral deposits is ramped up and land is opened to farming through increased irrigation; and both adventure and cultural tourism is being promoted by the private and government sectors.

injiang's population now stands at nearly 22 million, and will in all likelihood continue to grow at above national averages. With all this change come the same risks and concerns to be seen in multicultural regions undergoing rapid development throughout the world. There are as many different views of Xinjiang's potential, its problems and the course of its future as there were trading routes through the trackless sands and mountain passes during its early heyday. This book does not seek to provide a comprehensive insight into the realities of Xinjiang's social and political landscape; those wanting to study these aspects of this most fascinating and complex region are advised to use the Internet as well as the plethora of print publications available (see the Recommended Reading section for a starter's list).

The focus of this guidebook is to take the reader on a journey that crosses mountain and desert, moves from city skyscraper to rug-strewn yurt, enters mosque, temple and natural forest cathedral, embraces encounters with nomadic herdsmen, wily market carpet-sellers and serene pilgrims, all the while highlighting the breadth and depth of the experience awaiting the intrepid traveller. In essence, Xinjiang still offers today what it did 2,000 years ago: a chance for adventurous souls to explore a faraway land filled with natural and man-made wonders.

GEOGRAPHY: TOPOGRAPHY & TRADE ROUTES   — By Raynor Shaw

The defining characteristics of any geographical region are primarily a function of its underlying geology – which determines the topography and soils – and of its latitude, which (together with the topography) determines the climate and vegetation. These factors influence the distribution of population through their control of a number of vital features: the availability (springs and rivers) or lack (rain shadow or continental deserts) of water resources; the dimensions of rivers and their valleys (water and land routes); the character of river or mountain crossing points (fords and passes); the extent and fertility of arable and grazing land (favourable topography and suitable soils); and the location of settlement sites and defensive positions (level areas and natural fortresses). Together, these factors control the settlement patterns and population density of a region, which constitute the markets that determine the trade routes within and through that region.

PHYSICAL FEATURES AND CLIMATE

Most of China's mountain ranges, and hence the intervening valleys and their rivers, are oriented east to west, clearly favouring east-west travel along the grain of the topography. This is especially true of Xinjiang: the cloud-enveloped peaks of the **Tien Shan**, the Heavenly Mountains, are aligned in parallel ranges that strike across the centre of the region, separating the Junggar Basin (to the north) from the Tarim Basin (to the south). During the Early Palaeozoic period, about 500 million years ago, the sites of the Junggar and Tarim basins were the only landmass in the area that is now Xinjiang, the remainder of the region being covered by a sea. Later earth movements compressed the area, folding the marine sediments and creating belts of mountains adjacent to the former landmass.

Today, the Tien Shan is 250–300 kilometres wide, and generally between 3,000 to 5,000 metres above sea level (a.s.l.). The highest peaks, which exceed 7,000 metres a.s.l., are located in the west near China's border with Kazakhstan and Kyrgyzstan, while the range declines in altitude towards the east, finally disappearing into the desert northeast of Hami. Enclosed within its spur ranges are the **Ili Valley** – exceptionally fertile because of abundant water and mineral-rich soils, but isolated from the rest of Xinjiang by the very mountains that nurture it – and the **Turpan** (Turfan) and **Hami** depressions in the east. Air currents from the Arctic Ocean deposit rainfall preferentially on the northern and western slopes of the Tien Shan, which are important pastoral

Clockwise from top left: Picturesque Moon Bay on the Kanas River snakes through rich alpine forests in northern Xinjiang (SC Keung); fringing sheet ice rims Karakul Lake with Muztagata looming in the background (Jeremy Tredinnick); a layer of snow sits incongruously on sand dunes in the Gurbantunggut Desert (Yang Hong).

areas. In contrast, the southern slopes, which are in the rain shadow, are much drier. Consequently, the Turpan and Hami depressions are arid. Due to the province's hot and dry continental climate, the living conditions are very harsh.

The **Turpan Depression**, a 50,000-square-kilometre downfaulted geological block, is enclosed on all sides by branches of the Tien Shan. Surrounding the basin, the impressive peaks of the **Bogda Shan** rise to 5,400 metres a.s.l. to the north, while the smaller 1,500-metre ridges of the **Kuruk Tagh** border it to the south. These summits contrast with the surface of **Aiding Lake** in the basin's midst, which at 154 metres below sea level is the lowest point in China. The red sandstone "Bogda Mountains" run parallel to the main range as a barren ridge of deeply eroded hills approximately 100 kilometres long but an average of only nine kilometres wide. These are the fabled "**Flaming Mountains**" of historical texts.

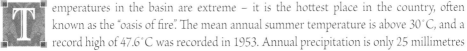

Temperatures in the basin are extreme – it is the hottest place in the country, often known as the "oasis of fire". The mean annual summer temperature is above 30°C, and a record high of 47.6°C was recorded in 1953. Annual precipitation is only 25 millimetres – thunder and lightning do occur, but rain evaporates before it reaches the ground. Rivers are small and short, and most seep into the ground; consequently, subterranean water is plentiful and is used for irrigation through *karez*, underground channels that support crops of wheat, cotton, melons, seedless grapes and other fruits.

North of the Tien Shan lies the broadly triangular **Junggar (Dzungarian) Basin**, with the **Gurbantunggut (Kurban-Tungut) Desert** occupying the floor of the basin. The 2,000-metre-high mountains of the **Tarbagatai** range rise on the western edge of the basin, with several lakes at their foot. The Junggar Basin terminates to the north at the **Altai Mountains**, which are generally over 3,000 metres a.s.l. in the northwest, but decline in height towards Mongolia in the southeast. There are few rivers in the basin, the largest being the **Irtysh River** that flows along the foothills of the Altai Mountains, and is the only river in China to empty into the Arctic Ocean. Air masses from the northwest penetrate the basin through several passes, which results in an annual precipitation of between 150–300 millimetres. These moist air currents deposit more rainfall in the northwest reaches of the mountains – which are covered with lush coniferous forests and meadows – than at the southeast end, which supports vast grasslands. The Junggar Basin is significantly colder than the Tarim Basin to the south, being subjected to cold northwest winds in winter.

South of the Tien Shan lies the irregular, diamond-shaped **Tarim Basin**. China's largest inland basin, it is 1,500 kilometres from west to east and 600 kilometres from north to south, with an area of 530,000 square kilometres and an average elevation of 1,000 metres a.s.l. The Tarim Basin is bordered by the **Kunlun Mountains** to the south, and the **Pamirs** to the west, which together exclude oceanic moisture and create an arid climate. Thus, the outer edge of the basin receives only 50–100 millimetres of rainfall, which drops to a paltry 10 millimetres in the centre. The result is a series of concentric belts, comprising the outer ring of mountains (the snow-capped peaks of the Tien Shan and Kunlun mountains), a zone of *gobi* (a sparsely vegetated stone desert with blackened, mineral-coated rocks), and a ring of oases (vast tracts of crops and networks of irrigation canals nurturing wheat, maize, rice, apricots, pears, apples, long-staple cotton and silk), with the formidable **Taklamakan Desert**, a vast area of sand and salt lakes that make up the largest desert in China, at the centre.

Temperature ranges in the Tarim Basin are extreme, with summer-winter differences of 50–60˚C, and day-night differences of 15–20˚C. The eastern edge of the Tarim Basin once contained the famous "wandering" **Lop Nor** (Lake), China's biggest shifting salt lake, complete with large surrounding reed swamps. Although it was roughly 2,000 square kilometres in size as recently as the 1950s, increases in irrigation and dam projects upstream on the Tarim River (its main feeder) in recent decades have reduced its flow to such an extent that today the river peters out in the desert long before it reaches the Lop Nor, which is now no more than a dry, salt-encrusted lakebed, with little chance of revival.

The **Tarim River** flows west to east through the Taklamakan, and is the longest inland river in China with a total length of nearly 2,100 kilometres. "Tarim" means "converging rivers" in Uygur, and it is indeed formed from the union of a network of rivers that cross the desert from the south and west – the Kashgar, Yarkand and Hotan rivers – or emerge from the Tien Shan to the north, such as the Aksu and Muzat rivers. Many of these rivers have only seasonal surface flow, but water occurs about 1–2 metres below the surface of many dry riverbeds, issuing as springs and feeding small lakes around which settlements have grown up. Another important tributary of the Tarim River is the Konche (Konqe) River, which flows out of **Bosten (Baghrash) Lake**, itself fed by the Kaidu River that collects snowmelt from the high grasslands of the Tien Shan. Situated south of Urumqi near Korla, Bosten Lake is China's largest inland freshwater lake, more than 1,000 square kilometres in area and holding eight billion cubic metres of water (though its size and volume fluctuate).

The world's second-highest mountain, 8,611-metre **K2** (called Qogir Peak by the Chinese) lies on the border between Xinjiang and Pakistan in the **Karakoram** range, which is separated from the Kunlun Mountains by the high-altitude valley of the upper Yarkand River. From the formidable peaks and high-altitude plateaus of the Karakoram and Pamir ranges in the far west, the **Kunlun Mountains** extend eastwards into Qinghai Province, forming Xinjiang's southern border with Tibet. The summits are relatively even, reaching over 5,000 metres a.s.l., although a few approach 7,000 metres. There are many glaciers in the moister west, whereas the eastern section is more continental, and so is drier. Towards the east, the Kunlun Mountains branch, the northern spur becoming the **Altun Mountains (Arjin Shan)** that form the southeastern border with Qinghai. A remote area of high-altitude plateau forms the southeastern corner of Xinjiang, and encompasses the **Arjin Mountain National Nature Reserve**, representing the northernmost limit of typical Tibetan Plateau habitat for wildlife species such as yak, wild ass and Tibetan antelope.

The Concept of Trade Routes

Following initial settlement, the economy of a region expands and prospers both by trading with other areas, and by facilitating trade between adjacent regions (by serving as a trade corridor, or as an entrepôt). Traders always seek the easiest, shortest – and consequently cheapest – routes along which to transport their goods. Historically, traders also favoured routes that were safe from attack, and were well supplied with food and water, both for themselves and for their pack animals.

Over the years, geographers have studied the factors that determine land settlement patterns and trade networks, historians have observed the rise and fall of towns and cities, and explored the impetus for the recorded changes, and economists have studied how investment, costs and market fluctuations have affected competing trade corridors. Consequently, there is a rich body of literature on trade patterns, with an associated terminology.

Trade corridors are pathways along which goods move between two or more **nodes**. Cities form the nodes, and competing modes of transportation infrastructure form a network of links. Some nodes are regarded as **hubs**, serving at least two major corridors. Hubs have a circular hinterland and radiating trade corridors. Other nodes are classified as **gateways**, being dependent on only one major corridor, which may be topographically or politically defined. National boundaries create classical gateways, because goods and carriers must stop for inspection and documentation at a limited number of border crossing points. The importance of node cities is also dependent upon whether they lie at the extremes of, or in the interior of, their geographical regions. Within a region, a

The Heart of Asia

*I*s the heart of Asia beating? Or has it been suffocated by the sands?

From the Brahmaputra to the Irtysh, from the Yellow River to the Caspian Sea, from Mukden to Arabia – everywhere are terrible, merciless waves of sand. The cruel Taklamakan is a threatening extreme of lifelessness, deadening the central part of Asia. Under moving sands, the old Imperial Chinese road hides itself. Out of sandy hills, trunks of a once mighty forest lift their seared arms. Like deformed skeletons, the age-devoured walls of ancient cities stretch along the road.

Perhaps near this very spot passed the great travelers, the migrating nations. The eye, here and there, glimpses isolated kereksurs, menhirs, cromlechs, and rows of stones – silent guardians of ancient cults.

The extremities of Asia, to be sure, wage a gigantic struggle with the ocean tides. But is Asia's heart alive? When a Hindu yogi arrests his pulse, his heart still continues its inner functions. So, too, the heart of Asia. In oases, in yurts, in caravans, dwells an unusual thought. The masses of people, entirely isolated from the outside world, who receive some distorted message of outside events only after a lapse of months, do not die. Each sign of civilization, as we shall see, is greeted by them as a benevolent, long-awaited message. Rather than reject possibilities, they try to adapt their religions to the new conditions of life. This is apparent when we see what the

Karakirghizes, a 1932 tempera on canvas painting by Nicholas Roerich (Courtesy of the Nicholas Roerich Museum, New York)

people in the most remote deserts say of the leaders of civilization and humanitarianism.

The name of Ford, for instance, has penetrated into the most remote yurts and provinces.

*A*mid the sands of the Taklamakan, a long-bearded Moslem asks: "Tell me, could a Ford negotiate the old Chinese road?"

And near Kashgar they ask: "Can a Ford tractor plough our fields?"

In Chinese Urumchi, on the Kalmuck steppes, throughout Mongolia, the word "Ford" is used as a synonym for motive power.

A gray-bearded Old Believer in the wild Altai Mountains, or a youth of the cooperative, says enviously: "In America, you have a Ford. But unfortunately we have none..."

Nicholas Roerich, Heart of Asia, 1930

Opposite: An aerial view of desert dunes near Qiemo shows the wind's effect on the Taklamakan topography, with ripple-like ridges and wave-like mountains of sand flowing towards the horizon (W. Ewig).

hierarchy of trade corridors develops, depending upon the size of the region and the prevailing trade patterns (for example political conditions, or changing consumer demand). However, history has shown that enterprise, bold leadership, and technological advances can also direct the development of trade patterns, disregarding the importance of geography and population density, and influencing the location of cities in the economic hierarchy of a region.

XINJIANG'S TRADE CORRIDORS

Xinjiang's fluctuating economic prosperity over the millennia reflects the changing importance, and the shifting location, of the ancient Silk Road. This major network of trade routes, which ran through some of the world's most inhospitable territory, migrated northwards and southwards over the almost 3,000 years of its existence in response to changing political systems, shifts of national boundaries, and fluctuating climate. The vast deserts and arid plains of Xinjiang, which extend for thousands of kilometres before terminating abruptly against high mountain ranges, presented particular challenges to the early travellers. However, signs of the prosperity that once accompanied intensive trading along the route are clearly seen in the lines of abandoned Buddhist cities, such as **Gaochang** – a moated and walled garrison town founded in the seventh century CE – and **Jiaohe**, which lie ruined in the desert near Turpan, and **Niya**, **Endere** and **Miran**, which remain buried. Trade along the Silk Road has defined the history of Xinjiang.

The Silk Road began in northern China, in Chang'an (Xi'an), and later Beijing, two important hub cities that were the focus of feeder routes that radiated in all directions. Heading westwards to Central Asia and Europe, after passing through Lanzhou the route was confined to the **Hexi Corridor** (between the Gobi desert to the north and the Nan Shan mountains to the south) in Gansu Province. From the third century BCE, the Great Wall protected the northern side of the Silk Road from attack. However, passing through the Yumen (Jade Gate), caravans left the protection of the Great Wall and entered the deserts of Central Asia. About 3–4 weeks after leaving the Jade Gate, travellers were first confronted by the challenges of the Lop Nor depression, and then by the fearsome Taklamakan Desert.

The Taklamakan Desert is one of the most inhospitable places on Earth, a vast area of shifting sand dunes that support no visible forms of life, create taunting mirages, and generate strange sounds that mislead travellers from the trodden path. Among the many other problems of the desert were finding sufficient drinking water for people and animals, locating the trail in the shifting sands, and surviving the hot sun by day. Eventually, the daytime heat was avoided by travelling at night, and by employing sailors who could navigate by the stars.

There was a choice of two possible routes around the Taklamakan Desert. Initially, because of the threat of attack from the warring northern tribes, most caravans used the southern route, a confined corridor that ran along the foothills of the Altun and Kunlun mountains, through the oases of Miran, Cherchen and Khotan to Yarkand (the latter two are still important Uygur centres).

These desert towns were important gateways along this trade corridor. However, this southern route was dry with little or no food or water. In contrast, the northern route, though another confined corridor, followed the line of the Tien Shan first past Lop Nor and the kingdom of Loulan, then through the oases of Karashahr and Kucha to Yarkand or Kashgar. These gateways were watered by numerous streams and provided better grazing for animals, although the route was susceptible to raids by northern tribes. However, by the third century CE, the route curved further to the northwest through Turpan, and later, as the area became more peaceful under the Tang Dynasty (a golden age for three centuries), another route developed north of the Tien Shan that took it into the Kazakh steppe, away from the confines and rigours of the desert corridors.

WILDLIFE: DWELLERS OF DESERT & MOUNTAIN — *By John Hare and William Bleisch*

With its high mountains, inhospitable, partially explored deserts and unique plants and animals, Xinjiang has for long remained a little known part of China for naturalists. For political and military reasons, access to Xinjiang has been difficult for foreigners and enabled nature to keep many of its secrets hidden.

In the centre of the vast deserts of the Taklamakan, the Desert of Lop and the Gashun Gobi – which occupy nearly 80 percent of the province's land area – there is no fresh water; the only water available is salt-water slush which bubbles up from below the ground. In such an inhospitable environment it would seem most unlikely that any large animal could survive, but incredibly the **wild Bactrian camel**, which lives in the heartland of all three deserts, is able to do so because it can safely drink saline liquid that has a higher salt content than seawater.

There are estimated to be only 600 wild Bactrian camels left in China and 90 percent of these are in Xinjiang. Not only does the wild camel have a higher salt-tolerant system than any other mammal in the world – including the domestic Bactrian camel – but between 1955 and 1979 it also survived 43 atmospheric nuclear tests. During this period, its habitat in the Desert of Lop was the designated epicentre of China's nuclear test area. However, it appears not to have suffered from exposure to radiation in any way.

If one looks at the week-old embryo of a Dromedary or single-humped camel, one can see the remains of a second hump. So it is quite possible that the Dromedary of the Sahara, Africa and the Middle East evolved from the double-humped Bactrian camel, making the Bactrian the ancestor of all camels, whether single or double-humped. In addition, the wild camel has a consistently wide genetic difference from the domestic Bactrian camel. Little wonder that the Xinjiang provincial government has chosen this amazing creature as its provincial emblem. In March 2007, the Zoological Society of London launched a programme called EDGE to highlight wild mammals that are on the edge of extinction. The wild Bactrian camel was listed as the eighth most critically endangered mammal in the world.

The other mammal to venture into the extremes of the desert is the black-tailed or **goitred gazelle**. This hardy beast manages to survive on water trapped in the roots of plants. The point

where the plants themselves can no longer survive marks the extent of the gazelle's range. Where conditions are milder, it may be joined by the **Asiatic wild ass** or **kulan**, which looks like an over-sized, skewbald donkey. The kulan's primary habitat is Mongolia, but it occasionally wanders over the international border into Xinjiang, and there have been sightings in the Kuruk Tagh mountains south of Turpan, and in the Karamay (Kalamaili) Nature Reserve in the eastern Junggar Basin, where **Mongolian gazelles** and **saiga antelope** are also found.

Other large mammals exist on the periphery of the deserts, near and in the mountain ranges that encircle the deserts – the Kunlun Shan, Arjin (Altun) Shan, Kuruk Tagh, Altai Mountains and Tien Shan. These include two wild relatives of goats, the **long-horned ibex** and the **bighorn Argali wild sheep**, and their chief predators, the **snow leopard** and the **Eurasian wolf**. In the mountains to the south of the province, the **blue sheep** replaces the ibex and serves as the chief prey for snow leopards.

All these animals are hunted and consequently are extremely timid and fearful of man. The bighorn Argali wild sheep, whose ram carries magnificently curved horns, can usually only be seen as a dark dot on top of a mountain, and one has to venture into the highest elevations in the Altai and Pamir Mountains to spot them (the Pamir argali is also known as the Marco Polo sheep). They also occur in the extreme south of Xinjiang in the Kunlun and Arjin mountains. Beyond these barrier ranges rises the Tibetan Plateau, where the **Tibetan wild ass**, the **Tibetan antelope** or **chiru**, and the massive **wild yak** still roam in huge herds. The range of the **Tibetan brown bear** also spills into

Above: Wild Bactrian camels are one of only very few species capable of surviving in Xinjiang's harsh desert environment (Huang Wei Guo). Opposite top: The chiru, or Tibetan antelope, a resident of Xinjiang's high-altitude plateaus on the border with Tibet (William Bleisch). Opposite bottom: The magnificent snow leopard – Xinjiang's top predator (Photo by Milan Trykar, courtesy of the Snow Leopard Trust).

Xinjiang from Tibet. A subspecies, the **Gobi bear**, of which there are thought to be only about 35 left in the world, has entered into neighbouring Gansu Province from Mongolia but at the moment there has been no recorded sighting in Xinjiang.

The range of the **Przewalski's horse**, or *takhi* (the common Western form Przewalski is the Polish spelling of Nikolai Przhevalsky, the Russian general who discovered a number of the region's animals), is also primarily centred in Mongolia, but for many years before it became extinct in the wild in 1969, there was a herd in northern Xinjiang close to the Mongolian border. The successful reintroduction programme currently under way in Mongolia and in the Karamay Nature Reserve should ensure that the takhi reoccupies its former territory in Xinjiang.

The snow leopard, a magnificent animal equipped to withstand conditions of extreme cold, is extremely rare and very difficult to sight even with a skilled guide. Although greatly threatened by herdsmen and hunters, the numbers in Xinjiang are not as desperately low as is sometimes thought and are believed to have slightly increased. In the Arjin and Kunlun mountains, many stories are told of the sightings of the "wild man", or **yeti**. Even professional Chinese naturalists are known to believe in their existence, but none have ever been photographed.

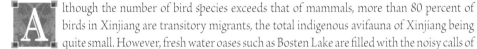 lthough the number of bird species exceeds that of mammals, more than 80 percent of birds in Xinjiang are transitory migrants, the total indigenous avifauna of Xinjiang being quite small. However, fresh water oases such as Bosten Lake are filled with the noisy calls of shorebirds and waders (**egrets**, **terns**, **red-billed gulls, widgeons** and other ducks), especially during spring and autumn, when they stop at these critical way-stations along their migratory routes; and in the Tien Shan during the summer months a large number of species can be seen, including **red-billed** and **Alpine choughs**, **redstarts**, **black storks**, **kestrels**, **hobbies**, **golden eagles**, **Himalayan griffon vultures** and **lammergeyers** (these last three can be found in all Xinjiang's mountain regions). At the Bayanbulak Swan Reserve large numbers of **whooper** and **wart-nose swans**, **bar-headed geese, larks, mallard ducks**, various types of **tern**, **crane** and **shovellers** congregate.

The vertebrate group of birds does not play a significant role in desert conditions, easily accounted for from an ecological point of view by the extreme environmental fluctuations and in particular the poor plant cover and monotonous stony landscapes. The diversity of bird fauna over desert areas is very limited, the most common species being **Pallas's sand-grouse, Henderson's ground jay**, the **Houbara bustard**, the **desert wheat ear, desert warbler, pale rosefinch, great grey shrike, Kozlov's accentor** and of the diurnal birds of prey, the **black vulture**, **long-legged buzzard** and **black kite**. In the high mountains of the Kunlun and Pamirs, **Himalayan** and **Tibetan snowcocks** still play hide and seek with those who try to see them.

Reptile fauna is also limited. This is due to the severe climatic conditions, particularly the significant length of time when temperatures are below -40 degrees Celsius in the depths of winter. However, Xinjiang's reptile population is unique, comprising 14 species in all, including **Przewalski's skink**, a large nocturnal lizard, the **Gobi gecko** and the **common agama** – a very large lizard with a bright-yellow throat. **Horned lizards** are quite numerous, and there are four species of snake: the **sand snake**, **Pallas's copper snake**, the **sand boa** and **rat snake**. The **green toad** is the only species of amphibian.

Other mammal species are the **red fox**, **Tibetan fox**, **stone marten**, **alpine weasel**, **marbled polecat**, **Eurasian lynx** and **Pallas's cat**. Their prey includes many different members of the jerboa (gerbil) family: Xinjiang contains 11 species including the **Gobi jerboa**, **pigmy five-toed jerboa**, **Kozlov's jerboa**, **long-eared jerboa**, **Mongolian jerboa**, **small five-toed jerboa**, **northern three-toed jerboa**, **big-toed dwarf jerboa**, **common jerboa** and **Siberian jerboa**. Importantly, Xinjiang is also home to a small but vital population (less than 1,000) of **Asiatic beavers**, an endangered species found along mountain river systems on the Xinjiang-Mongolia border in the northeast.

The **Ili pika** (hamster), which was only identified as a new species in 1983, was discovered on high cliff habitat within a restricted area in the Tien Shan mountains. Further expeditions to monitor the pika undertaken in 2002 and 2003, found that the colony had been almost wiped out. The reasons for a decline in pika populations is complex but, as with other pika species around the world, a consensus among researchers is emerging. Pikas are notoriously sensitive to an increase in temperature and could easily be affected by an abrupt rise. The Ili pika could be the first documented victim of global warming and human-induced climate change.

The Tarim River creates a unique habitat of desert forests rising from sand dunes. Here, unique forms of **wild hare** and **red deer** survive, and occasional grassy marshes are sometimes still home to **wild boar**. This area once also supported the **Caspian tiger**, a subspecies that is now extinct throughout its range. It disappeared during the political turmoil in the province in the 1930s.

Though not blessed – like Mongolia to the north – with large amounts of wildlife, Xinjiang is nevertheless the habitat for some fascinating species. Every effort must be made to ensure that they survive, thrive and do not go the way of the tiger.

[John Hare is the founder and chairman of the Wild Camel Protection Foundation, a UK-based charity dedicated to the conservation of the wild Bactrian camel and its fragile desert habitat (www.wildcamels. com). Dr William Bleisch has been working on wildlife conservation in China since 1987. He was the China Programme Manager for Flora and Fauna International (www.fauna-flora.org) from 2002 to 2007.]

HISTORY: MIGRATIONS THROUGH TIME

Xinjiang's history is an epic saga of monumental proportions, a convoluted tale involving mysterious origins, myriad nations, the ebb and flow of migrating tribes and conquering armies. What follows is merely a broad outline of the complex interweaving of cultures through the centuries that has culminated in the fascinating region as we see it today. If you are tempted to delve deeper into Xinjiang's past, *Eurasian Crossroads: A History of Xinjiang* by **James A. Millward** (see Recommended Reading section) is a recent and accessible historical narrative, an erudite and enthusiastic account that impartially tells Xinjiang's story in great detail.

拔達山汗納
款入礮渠逃
寒風情知三
寒已逞窮嘉
荒識早斂戳
順贺彼悔遲
跛庭雄和衆
亦秀兩部宮
成功速在五
年中
天恩如此昭
優既保泰彌
殷慎勅躬
己卯長至月作
御筆

This superb artwork by Qing Dynasty court painters depicts Emperor Qianlong's battlefield court in the Ili (Yili) Valley at the end of his campaign against the Junggars in the late 18th century. Nomads' yurts can be seen in the upper right of the

painting, while supplicants prostrate themselves before the emperor's dais in the centre (The Palace Museum, Beijing).

XINJIANG SUPERLATIVES

Xinjiang is a land of extremes, of desolation but also of bounty. The following list will give you some idea of the unique combination of accomplishments and outstanding facts and figures that the region boasts:

- Urumqi is the farthest city from the sea in the world, a distance of 2,250 kilometres from the nearest ocean.

- Xinjiang boasts the most sunshine in China, with 2,550–3,300 hours of sunlight each year. Kucha County is China's sunniest, averaging 180 cloudless days per year.

- Turpan County is China's driest, averaging 299 rainless days per year.

- On 25 July 1962, Turpan recorded a ground temperature of 76.6°C – making it the hottest place in China.

- On 27 January 1969, Yining registered 94 centimetres (37 inches) of snowfall in a day.

- The highest road in the world (averaging more than 5,000 metres above sea level) is the Xinjiang-Tibet Highway that runs from southern Xinjiang over the Kunlun Mountains into northern Tibet – its highest point is 6,035 metres.

- The Taklamakan Desert is the largest desert in China, with an area of 320,000 square kilometres.

- On average, each person in Xinjiang eats more than 100 kilogrammes of fruit and sweet melons per year – the highest consumption of fruit per capita in China.

- China's only wild camel reserve, 65,000-square-kilometre Lop Nur Wild Camel National Reserve, is located in the region surrounding the ancient lake of Lop Nor.

- Xinjiang's Bayanbulak Swan Natural Reserve is the only one of its kind in China, with an area of over 1,000 square kilometres.

- The Altai Region of Xinjiang has the only beaver natural reserve in China.

- China's only natural reserve for four-clawed tortoises is in Xinjiang's Huocheng County.

- Aiding Lake in the centre of the Turpan Depression is the world's second lowest depression (after the Dead Sea), at 154 metres below sea level. The gerbils that build their burrows there live in the lowest habitable place in China.

- Bosten Lake is the largest inland freshwater lake (over 1,000 square kilometres) in China.

- Xinjiang has China's highest production of lavender oil – an important source of this precious medicinal product.

- Xinjiang boasts the highest quality and highest output of hops (for beer production), sweet grapes and walnuts in China.

- The earliest examples of cotton cloth were found in an Eastern Han Dynasty (25–220 CE) tomb in Turpan's Minfeng County in 1959 – today Xinjiang boasts the best quality and largest production of long-staple cotton in China.

- The Idkah Mosque in Kashgar is the largest mosque in China.

- Xinjiang has China's largest reserves of petroleum, totalling an estimated 200–400 hundred million tons, a third of the country's total.

- Xinjiang has China's richest coal resources, with a total reserve of 2.19 trillion tons.

PREHISTORY

The earliest clues of the existence of man in Xinjiang come from simple stone tools discovered near Hotan (Khotan) and along the northern rim of the Kunlun Mountains, dating to around 20,000–15,000 years ago, a time when there was more water runoff from the mountains than is seen today, and consequently greater wildlife. These early settlers were most likely hunter-gatherers; excavation of Mesolithic sites (c. 10,000 BCE) all around the Tarim Basin reveal arrowheads, scrapers and more refined stone tools commensurate with a hunter-gatherer culture.

Neolithic sites (10,000–4,000 BCE) are numerous; these fixed settlements show a low level of cultivation was taking place, although most likely only as a supplement to hunting and gathering, and at this point there was no animal husbandry. Archaeological exploration today is serving up rich pickings from the second to first millennia BCE, most sensationally in the form of human remains and artefacts that show that Xinjiang cultures developed alongside those of western Central Asia and central China. Silk, lacquer and seashells illustrate that trading was already taking place, while jade from the Hotan region was coveted by early Chinese rulers, as proven by the many jade items excavated from the tomb of Fu Hao of the Shang Dynasty (1600–1027 BCE) at Yinxu.

FARMERS AND NOMADS

 ittle is known for sure, and no doubt much is yet to be revealed through ongoing research, but the generally accepted theory at present is that Xinjiang was populated from around 2000 BCE onwards by waves of migrant peoples from western Central Asia and Siberia, and it is likely that the bronze metallurgy they brought (starting in the early second millennium BCE) predated that in central and eastern China. These migrating Bronze Age tribes were animal herders, mobile through use of chariots (a significant cultural leap forward) and advanced in many ways – early use of animal husbandry is in evidence in sites such as Tashkurgan, Loulan and in the Turpan region, as well as woven materials, ornaments, ceramics, grains and farming tools.

Research by Victor Mair and J.P. Mallory, two leading Western experts on human history in the Tarim Basin, points to the earliest of these groups being **Tokharian** speakers – Tokharian is one of the earliest Indo-European languages, originating from the linguistic stock of early peoples based around the Black Sea. These Tokharian migrants moved into and spread around the Tarim Basin, bringing with them agrarian technologies most probably from the region of Bactria (northern Afghanistan and modern Iran), since barley, wheat and domesticated sheep all originate from the west, while a medicinal herb used in Bactria and India – ephedra – has been found alongside mummies from the late first millennium BCE.

Iron items appeared around 1200 BCE – again, predating central China, not surprisingly given that the Iron Age began in the west – and it is the Iron Age that is associated with the rise of pastoral nomadism and the migration of increasingly powerful tribes across Central Asia, most significantly the **Scythian** cultures that dominated a huge swathe of Central Asia and moved into the mountains and steppes of the Junggar Basin and Turpan Depression. The settled areas in these locations show signs of early contact and influence with the Scythian tribes, but rather than destroying each other, as James Millward puts it in *Eurasian Crossroads*, "prehistorical evidence from Xinjiang shows a relationship characterised by complex interactions of herders and farmers and mixed agricultural and pastoral land use".

From around 650 BCE and through the latter half of the first millennium BCE the **Saka** began moving into the mountains around Tashkurgan, north to the Ili Valley and as far as the Altai Mountains. The Saka were horse nomads of Iranian descent who buried their dead in huge barrows

CHRONOLOGY OF PERIODS IN CHINESE HISTORY

NEOLITHIC	7000—2100 BCE
HA	2100—1600 BCE
SHANG	1600—1046 BCE
WESTERN ZHOU	1045—771 BCE
EASTERN ZHOU	770—256 BCE
SPRING AND AUTUMN ANNALS	722—481 BCE
WARRING STATES	475—221 BCE
QIN	221—207 BCE
WESTERN (FORMER) HAN	206 BCE—8 CE
XIN	9—24
EASTERN (LATER) HAN	25—220
THREE KINGDOMS	220—265
WESTERN JIN	265—317
EASTERN JIN	317—420
NORTHERN AND SOUTHERN DYNASTIES	386—589
SIXTEEN KINGDOMS	317—439
FORMER ZHAO	304—329
FORMER QIN	351—383
LATER QIN	384—417
NORTHERN WEI	386—534
WESTERN WEI	535—556
NORTHERN ZHOU	557—581
SUI	581—618
TANG	618—907
FIVE DYNASTIES	907—960
LIAO	916—1125
NORTHERN SONG	960—1127
SOUTHERN SONG	1127—1279
JIN (JURCHEN)	1115—1234
YUAN (MONGOL)	1279—1368
MING	1368—1644
QING (MANCHU)	1644—1911
REPUBLIC OF CHINA	1911—1949
PEOPLE'S REPUBLIC OF CHINA	1949—PRESENT

called *kurgans* and prized metal objects, especially in gold, usually crafted in animal-style motifs. Around the second century BCE, however, the Saka were displaced in the Ili Valley and Junggar Basin by the **Wusun**, a Turkic-speaking tribal group who, under pressure from a neighbouring tribe, the **Yuezhi**, had moved south and west from the Siberian steppe in and around the Yenisey River basin (located in modern-day Russia and Mongolia).

he exact origin of the Yuezhi is uncertain, but it seems most likely that they were a nomadic confederation also from the Siberian-Mongolian steppe who moved south into present-day Gansu and Xinjiang's Tarim region to escape attacks by the **Xiongnu**, a Mongol or Turkic tribal group (also sometimes referred to as Huns) who grew into the dominant nomadic power in the second century BCE. In the Tarim Basin the Yuezhi encountered, and perhaps partially merged with, the Tokharian oasis dwellers, but as the Xiongnu grew in power and extended the boundaries of their control, the majority of the Yuezhi were forced to move farther west, first to the Ili, where the Wusun had settled, then across Zhetisu (modern-day Kazakhstan), following the northern foothills of the Tien Shan, until they reached the Oxus River (the Amu Darya on the border of Aghanistan and Uzbekistan). Here they founded the **Kushan Empire**, which expanded quickly and by the first century CE was controlling the westernmost oases of the Tarim Basin.

XIONGNU AND HAN STRUGGLES

Xinjiang now entered a classical period defined by nomadic groups to the north and west of the Tien Shan interacting with and exerting control over the sedentary oasis communities of the Tarim Basin. The Xiongnu built an empire that stretched from northeast China across the Mongolian steppe to the Junggar Basin, and by 162 BCE they had constructed a permanent command post near Lake Baghrash (Bosten Lake). Supplied by levies from the resource-rich oases, and benefiting from the vast grasslands north of the Tien Shan, the Xiongnu grew strong enough to challenge the newly formed Han Dynasty to the southeast.

The Han Dynasty (206 BCE–220 CE) was the first of China's truly great dynastic empires; based on the immensely rich agricultural resources of central and southern China, its power grew and its borders were extended simultaneously with those of the Xiongnu: it was inevitable that the two powers would clash. However, initially it was the Xiongnu who held the upper hand, and it was Emperor Wudi (ruled 141–87 BCE) who sent the first Chinese official into the "Western Regions" in search of allies.

Ambassador **Zhang Qian** was charged with finding and recruiting the Yuezhi, who had recently been defeated by the Xiongnu and driven west to the fringes of the Taklamakan Desert and beyond. Since the Warring States period (475–221 BCE), the "Huns" (a generic term given to confederations of nomads of both Turkic and Mongol descent) had been launching aggressive raids into Chinese territory – indeed, this had prompted Emperor Qin Shihuangdi of the Qin Dynasty (221–207 BCE) to build the Great Wall. Eager to defeat the Xiongnu, who represented the latest wave of powerful marauders, Wudi heard that the Yuezhi were seeking revenge on the Xiongnu and would welcome help with retaliation from any ally.

Zhang, with a caravan of 100 men, set out in 139 BCE from the Chinese capital of Chang'an (present-day Xi'an), only to be captured by the Xiongnu as he passed through the Hexi Corridor in northwest Gansu. The surviving members of the caravan were treated well; Zhang married and had a son. After 10 years, he and the remainder of the party managed to escape and continue their journey west along the northern trade routes to Kashgar and the Ferghana Valley. Upon reaching the Yuezhi, Zhang found them to have settled prosperously in the various oases of Central Asia and to be no longer interested in avenging themselves on the Xiongnu. Zhang stayed one year gathering valuable military, economic, political and geographical information and returned via the southern Tarim Basin oases, only to be captured again, this time by Tibetan tribes allied with the Xiongnu; once again he escaped. In 126 BCE, 13 years later, he returned to Chang'an. Of the original party only he and one other completed the trail-blazing journey – the first land route between East and West and one that would eventually link Imperial China with Imperial Rome.

Zhang reported on some 36 kingdoms in the Western Regions, delighting Emperor Wudi with detailed accounts of the previously unknown kingdoms of Ferghana, Samarkand, Bokhara and others in what are now the CIS, Pakistan and Iran as well as the city of **Li Kun**, which was almost certainly Rome. Zhang recounted stories he had heard of the famous Ferghana horse, rumoured to be of "heavenly" stock. Tempted by this fast and powerful warhorse, seemingly far superior to the average steed and having the potential to defeat the marauding Xiongnu, Wudi dispatched successive missions to develop political contacts – the first of which Zhang led in 119 BCE – and return with foreign envoys, and of course horses, from the courts of Ferghana, Sogdiana, Bactria, Parthia and northern India. Now extinct, these horses were immortalized by artists of both the Han and the Tang (618–907 CE) dynasties. Zhang continued seeking allies against the Xiongnu, travelling in 115 BCE to the Ili Valley territory of the Wusun, but again he was unable to enlist support.

The Han court soon realized the importance of the Xinjiang region as a supply source for the Xiongnu, and a strategy was developed to "cut off the right arm of the Xiongnu" by forcing them out of the Tarim Basin and Turpan regions. A series of military successes by Han generals resulted in the establishment of the Protectorate of the Western Regions in 60 BCE at Wulei, near modern-day Luntai, and thus the Tarim Basin as far as the Pamirs came under Han control, while the Xiongnu split into Southern and Northern confederations, the former allying with the Han, the latter retreating north of the Tien Shan.

Over the next 200 years Xinjiang was the setting for much warring between the Han and Xiongnu, as well as rebellious city-states, with the various protagonists in turn holding sway. A number of Han military expeditions had to march into the region to re-establish the protectorate, most notably under the command of the great military tactician **General Ban Chao**, who between 70 and 102 CE brought the city-states in the Turpan region and along the northern rim of the Taklamakan back under Han control through a combination of strategic manipulation, merciless trickery and guile.

As part of their efforts to control the region, the Han government developed the *tuntian* system, setting up agricultural colonies populated by soldiers, who effectively supplied themselves (lessening the drain on the imperial coffers) and brought a significant level of security to the region. This relative peace allowed the blossoming of the already well-worn trade routes and opened the doors to unprecedented levels of commerce along the "Silk Road". The empires of Rome and Han China had developed almost simultaneously in the second century BCE, but had only the vaguest consciousness of each other. From Zhang Qian the Chinese knew of a country called Ta Ts'in or Li Kun, which historians believe was Rome, while the Romans knew of Seres, the Kingdom of Silk. But with the thrust of the Han Dynasty into Central Asia, trade developed between the two distant powers. It is interesting to note, however, that the development and extension of trade routes was never a motive in Han China's conquest of the Western Regions; rather it was a need to cut off the supply lines to the Xiongnu aggressors of the north and lessen its ability to harass or invade Han territory that forced the Han to move west into Xinjiang.

SOGDIANS AND THE SILK ROAD

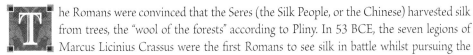 he Romans were convinced that the Seres (the Silk People, or the Chinese) harvested silk from trees, the "wool of the forests" according to Pliny. In 53 BCE, the seven legions of Marcus Licinius Crassus were the first Romans to see silk in battle whilst pursuing the Parthians, a rough warlike tribe, across the Euphrates. They became the victims of the first "Parthian shot", which broke the Romans' front line formation and was quickly followed by a tactic that both terrorized and amazed the Romans: the Parthians waved banners of a strange, shimmering material that towered above the defeated soldiers, blinding them in the brilliant heat of the desert. The Romans managed to obtain samples of this marvellous silk from the victorious Parthians, who had traded it for an ostrich egg and some conjurers with a member of Emperor Wudi's early trade missions.

The Parthians, along with the Sogdians, Indians and Kushans, soon became prominent middlemen in the trade of silk and other exotic merchandise, reaping tremendous profits, bartering with Chinese traders who escorted their goods beyond the Great Wall as far as Loulan (capital of the Shanshan kingdom located near Lop Nor Lake in the heart of the Lop Desert), and carrying the trade on to Persian, Syrian and Greek merchants. Each transaction increased the cost of the end product, which reached the Roman Empire in the hands of Greek and Jewish entrepreneurs. Silk garments became all the rage in Roman society, so much so that in 14 CE men were no longer permitted to wear them, as they were perceived to contribute to an already decadent society. Despite the disapproval of the Empire's moral superiors and its high cost, silk was widely worn amongst even the lowest socioeconomic classes. The silk trade flourished up until the second century CE, when it began to arrive in Rome via the sea trade routes.

Silk actually composed a relatively small portion of the trade along the Silk Road: eastbound caravans brought gold, precious metals and stones, textiles, ivory and coral, while westbound caravans transported furs, ceramics, cinnamon bark and rhubarb as well as bronze weapons. Very few caravans, including the people, animals and goods they transported, would complete the entire route that connected the capitals of these two great empires. The oasis towns that made the overland journey possible became important trading posts, commercial centres where caravans would take on fresh merchants, animals and goods.

The oasis towns of the Tarim Basin and Turpan Depression prospered considerably in the centuries after the decline of the Han Dynasty, extracting large profits on the goods they bought and sold. In the far west and south the towns of Kashgar and Yarkand, among others, were under the control of the Kushan Empire, while those on the northern rim and in the east, although nominally still answering to dynastic China (Han, Three Kingdoms and Jin dynasties), grew into distinct and powerful city-states who ruled themselves. Regardless of who held political power, however, it was the **Sogdians** who became the dominant figures in commerce from the third to eighth centuries CE, spreading all the way from their homelands in Transoxiana (between the Amu and Syr rivers, historically known as the Oxus and Jaxartes) across Xinjiang and Gansu, and even into northern China. Benefiting from an invaluable network of connections, the *lingua franca* of trade became Sogdian and the script used for documentation was **Kharoshthi**, a Gandharan script used by the Sogdians.

arge Sogdian communities were found in every major trading town along the interweaving routes – indeed, the Sogdian connection is probably the strongest linking factor between the many routes and types of commerce grouped under the umbrella term "Silk Road". In *Eurasian Crossroads* Millward even suggests that, "'The Soghdian network' would perhaps be a better, if less romantic, term".

But while trade in merchandise flowed in ever increasing volume along the caravan routes north and south of the Taklamakan, more significant was the simultaneous movement of religious ideas and beliefs, in particular Buddhism, that entered the Tarim from Gandhara via the Kushan Empire during the second and third centuries CE. On the Southern Silk Road the **Khotan kingdom** was a devout centre of Mahayana Buddhism, and the northern Tarim city-state of **Kucha** became one of the most important Buddhist centres in Central Asia in the third and fourth centuries, home to a sophisticated culture and the birthplace of **Kumarajiva**, the famous Buddhist monk and translator of Buddhist texts into Chinese. Cave and temple art in Buddhist centres around the Tarim Basin reached new heights of skill and beauty during this time, showing heavy Gandharan, Indian, Persian and even Greek influences.

By the middle of the fourth century the Xiongnu empire had collapsed, to be replaced by another nomadic group from Mongolia, the **Ruanruan**, who took over Jungaria (Dzungaria) and exacted tributes from kingdoms south of the Tien Shan. Only a century later, however, the Ruanruan lost their foothold in the Tarim Basin to the **Hephthalites**, who inherited the territories of the fading Kushan empire and moved in from the west, subduing the Tarim Basin cities as far as Gaochang in the Turpan region, and sending delegations to the Northern Wei Dynasty (386–534) in China.

But Hephthalite dominance was destined to be short lived too; in 560 yet another nomadic steppe confederation arose in Mongolia and spread out to encompass the Ruanruan's former territory. These were the **Kök Türks** (Göktürks), but they remained as a single unity for less than 25 years, before splitting to form the **Eastern and Western Turkic Khaganates**, the latter ruling Jungaria and much of modern-day southern Kazakhstan, Kyrgyzstan and the Ferghana Valley, eventually extending its empire as far as the Caspian Sea and opening relations with Byzantium.

During this period, the oases city-states of southern Xinjiang (Gaochang, Kucha, Yarkand and Shanshan, etc) were left to rule themselves, although they still paid tribute either to the khaganates in the west or the Sui Dynasty in the east, who were regaining footholds in Hami and the southeast rim of the Tarim Basin. But with the succession of the Tang Dynasty in 618, more change was in the air.

TANG, TURKS AND TIBETANS

In the seventh century the **Tang Dynasty** united central China once again as a great and powerful state. Wary of the power of the Turkic khaganates, the Tang followed the same strategy that the Han had used, inexorably extending their sphere of political and military control first to Hami and the Turpan Depression, then on to the Kuchean kingdom and beyond, wresting control of the Tarim Basin from the Western Turks and denying them valuable resources, thereby reducing their power, and at the same time widening the flow of commerce and cultures to China.

Prosperous and highly artistic, the Tang court eagerly sought out the exotic and beautiful from far away, and consequently the Silk Road flourished. Chang'an, the capital, a large cosmopolitan centre, was the departure point and final destination for travellers on the Silk Road. The city in 742 had a population of nearly two million, including over 5,000 foreigners. Numerous religions were represented and the city contained the temples, churches and synagogues of Buddhists, Nestorian Christians, Manichaeans, Zoroastrians, Hindus and Jews, to name but a few. Foreigners from Byzantium, Iran, Arabia, Sogdia, Mongolia, Armenia, India, Korea, Malaya and Japan lived in Chang'an (some Tang tomb murals depict foreigners in the imperial court), and the music and dance forms of the Kuchean kingdom were welcomed and heavily influenced these art forms in China.

In 670, however, a new power entered the fray, as the **Tibetan empire** sought to extend its territory into southern Xinjiang. They quickly forced the Tang out of the Tarim Basin, and for the next 50 years it was the subject of a violent tug of war between the Tang, Turks and Tibetans. In 730 the Tang regained control of the Tarim region and drove the Western Turkic Khaganate from Jungaria; pushing west they moved into the region that became known as Semireche, but in 755 disaster struck when they were defeated by a coalition of Turkic and Arab armies at the Battle of Talas River. This precipitated a general retreat from both northern and southern Xinjiang, coinciding with a rebellion lasting from 755 to 763 by **An Lushan**, a half-Sogdian, half-Turk general who nearly destroyed the Tang Dynasty but for timely assistance from the new **Uygur khaganate** based in the Orkhon Valley in Mongolia. The Tang survived, but a new offensive by the Tibetan empire forestalled any possibility of continued Tang dominance in the west, and Tibetans once again occupied the Tarim Basin from 790 until around 850 – indeed, it would be almost 1,000 years before China exerted direct rule over Xinjiang again.

By the end of the eighth century, the sea routes from the southern coastal city of Canton (Guangzhou) to the Middle East were well developed, while the Tibetan occupation of the Tarim Basin often disrupted the overland trade routes. The art of sericulture had also been mastered by the Persians and Byzantines, and the heyday of the Silk Road was over. However, this did not mean the end of trade, and caravans continued to carry merchandise between cities, although many of these were disappearing as glacier-fed rivers began to dry up or shifted their courses, forcing communities to move to new locations and form new towns and settlements.

Uygurs, Karakhanids and Kara-Khitan

The **Uygur Empire** rose from the ashes of the Eastern Turkic Khanate in the eighth century, aided by their friendly relations with the Chinese. During this imperial period the Uygur Empire stretched from Manchuria to the Caspian Sea, with its capital, Ordu Baliq, in present-day Mongolia. However, the empire did not last long, and between 840 and 844 the powerful **Kyrgyz** tribe drove the Uygurs from their lands, and the tribes divided. Some settled in the Hexi Corridor of Gansu Province, and established kingdoms at Dunhuang and Zhangye; others moved westwards into the oases south of the Tien Shan, then occupied by the Indo-European Tokharian speakers. At this time the Tibetan empire was crumbling, and the Uygurs eventually gained control of the Silk Road trade routes, supplying horses to the Chinese and establishing independent kingdoms. They still utilized Sogdian middlemen, but slowly the use of Turkic languages and Uygur script broke the Sogdian monopoly. The Uygurs abandoned shamanist beliefs, and first adopted Manichaeism, then Buddhism and finally, from the 10th century on, Islam.

The Uygur states in eastern Xinjiang, such as Kumul (Hami), Khocho (Gaochang) and as far west as Kucha formed a loose confederation known as the **Khara-Khoja**, but in the southwest the **Karakhanid (Qarakhanid) Khanate** grew, based around its capital at Kashgar. The Karakhanids were remnant nomadic tribes from the Uygur Empire who had moved west from Jungaria as it was taken over by Kyrgyz and Karluk tribes and formed a new power base in Semirech'e, Transoxiana and Kashgaria.

Thus by the 10th century the entire Tarim Basin was effectively under the control of ruling clans with common roots traced back to the Uygur Empire. At this time the Karakhanids converted to Islam – this was the time of the literary luminaries **Mohammed Kashgeri** and **Yusuf Has Hajib** – and subsequently invaded the Buddhist kingdom of Khotan on the Southern Silk Road, forcibly converting its population to Islam. However, the Kara-Khoja states remained Manichaean and Buddhist, and were tolerant of other religions such as Christianity. The kingdom of Khocho enjoyed a golden period, its agriculture booming – it exported cotton, grapes and wine to China, and a surplus of grain made it affluent, allowing for the construction of opulent temples.

The 12th century saw the continuation of what had become a familiar pattern in Xinjiang's history, with a new wave of nomadic usurpers invading the rich lands of Jungaria and the Tarim Basin. These were the **Kara-Khitan** (Kara-Kitai or Qara Khitay), a Mongolian speaking people who had formed the Liao Dynasty (916–1125) in northeast China, but who were driven from their lands in 1132 by the Jurchens of Manchuria (who in turn created their own Jin Dynasty). The Kara-Khitan Khanate conquered and claimed overlordship over both the Kara-Khoja and Karakhanid states, and ruled as far west as north Afghanistan and Transoxiana. The Kara-Khitans were Buddhists, but tolerated and permitted other religions to exist within their realm. Having ruled northern China as the Liao Dynasty they brought to the Xinjiang region new, sophisticated methods of administration, although they too left individual city-states to govern themselves.

t the beginning of the 13th century, as Genghis Khan was uniting the tribes of Mongolia and defeating his enemies, the Naiman and Merkit, a Naiman chief named **Kuchluk** fled west and found refuge with the Kara-Khitans. A treacherous but cunning man, he managed to usurp and take control of the khanate in 1211, but his appalling policies of oppression against the Muslims of Kashgaria only served to hasten his demise, and when Genghis Khan's forces swept across the Junggar steppe and down the Tarim caravan routes they were, by and large, welcomed by the populace.

THE GOLDEN HORDE

You could smell them coming, it was said, even before you heard the thunder of their hooves. But by then it was too late. Within seconds came the first murderous torrent of arrows, blotting out the sun and turning day into night. Then they were upon you – slaughtering, raping, pillaging and burning. Like molten lava, they destroyed everything in their path. Behind them they left a trail of smoking cities and bleached bones, leading all the way back to their homeland in Central Asia. "Soldiers of Antichrist come to reap the last dreadful harvest" one 13th-century scholar called the Mongol hordes.

Peter Hopkirk, Foreign Devils on the Silk Road

The **Mongol Empire** comprised the largest land empire in history, stretching from the Sea of Japan to the Caspian Sea. Between 1218 and 1253 these "barbarians" conquered all of Central Asia and Russia, up to the borders of Eastern Europe. The Mongols, whose empire spanned a relatively short period of time, were led out of the grasslands by Temujin (1162–1227), later known as **Genghis Khan** (Chinggis Khaan or Jenghis Khan), an illiterate political and military genius. He unified and organized the scattered nomadic tribes of Mongolia, Manchuria and Siberia into a disciplined and highly effective military force. After first testing his mounted troops with the conquest of the Xixia Kingdom (comprising much of modern-day Qinghai and Gansu, and controlled by the **Tanguts**, a Tibeto-Burman people), Genghis Khan moved south across the Gobi Desert one spring; four years later, in 1215, most of northern China had been subdued by the Mongol fighting machine, which then turned its energies towards Central Asia.

Xinjiang was subdued between 1216 and 1218 – the eastern Uygur states had wisely offered allegiance to Genghis Khan in 1209, and thus survived the Mongol advance, retaining control of their kingdoms in return for supplying troops and taxes – and the cities of Bokhara and Samarkand were completely destroyed in 1220. With the death of Genghis in 1227 the empire was split as per his wishes into *ulus* or separate khanates for each of his four sons: his second son **Chaghatai** inherited the majority of the Kara-Khitan territory, including the Tarim region and the Ili Valley, where he made his capital, while third son **Ogedei** controlled central Siberia and the Junggar Basin, including the lush grasslands of the Irtysh River and Altai and Tarbagatai mountains.

nevitably tensions mounted and turned violent, but it was **Mongke**, the son of Genghis's youngest son Tolui, who eventually seized control of all Xinjiang and the Great Khanship. It was Mongke who came to agreement with **Batu**, son of Genghis's eldest child Jochi, and khan of the Golden Horde in the west of the Mongol empire (today's Kazakh steppe and beyond), to divide the great steppe following a line from the Altai through the Tarbagatai to the Ili Valley, splitting Semireche and foreshadowing future delineations between the lands of Russia and China many centuries later.

Kublai Khan (1216–1294), the grandson of Genghis and Mongke's younger brother, completed the conquest of China in 1279 and founded the Yuan Dynasty, establishing his capital at Khanbalik (present-day Beijing). Kublai had many contenders for power in the Xinjiang region, and waged war with pretenders of both Chaghatayid and Ogedeid descent, in particular **Khaidu** (Qaydu), who although a member of the house of Ogedei, controlled much of the Chaghatai Khanate until the beginning of the 14th century.

Less ruthless and more tolerant than his grandfather, Kublai permitted a certain degree of religious freedom, resulting in the conversion of many Mongols to Islam. Since the Mongols controlled much of the territory of the old Silk Road, overland trade was re-established with Europe and a cosmopolitan culture flourished. Marco Polo's father and uncle, visiting the empire in the 13th century, were asked to bring 100 Christian priests to China on their return journey so that the Mongol ruler could learn more about the Western religion.

Within the Mongol government Uygurs proved invaluable, using their administrative skills to facilitate the empire's growth. But the Mongols proved to be poor and corrupt administrators. A Chinese adviser to the court remarked, "you may conquer a great empire on a horse, but it cannot be ruled from the back of the horse". The Mongol Empire began to disintegrate in the late 1200s and fell apart completely with the death of Kublai.

THE RISE OF ISLAM

After the fall of the Mongol Yuan Dynasty, Xinjiang split up into khanates, with a great deal of fighting between small feudal rulers, mainly of Chaghatayid descent but controlled by powerful Mongol **Dughlat** emirs. In the 1330s the **Chaghatai Khanate** was divided into two, one half covering

TWO EARLY WESTERN TRAVELLERS

Marco Polo (1254–1324): The most famous Western foreigners to make the great overland journey were the Polo family. Around 1263 the Venetian traders, Nicolo and Maffeo Polo (Marco's father and uncle), set off to sell their luxury goods in the Volga River region. Unable to return home due to a war, they joined a Mongol tribute mission to Khanbalik, Kublai Khan's capital at Beijing. The Great Khan took a liking to the Polos and through them asked the Pope to send "a hundred men learned in the Christian religion, well versed in the seven arts, and able to demonstrate the superiority of their own beliefs."

In 1271, Marco, then 17, joined the Polo brothers on their return journey, which carried blessings and credentials from the Pope. They took the overland route via Persia and Central Asia to the Oxus River, across the Pamirs into present-day Xinjiang, and along the Southern Silk Road to Dunhuang, finally arriving at the Great Khan's court of Shangtu in 1275. The Polos were to remain in China for about 17 years, and Marco, who became something of a court favourite, is believed to have held an official post. They left in 1292 by sea, escorting a Mongol princess to Persia and arriving back in Venice in 1295.

Benedict de Goes (1562–1607): Even as late as the early 17th century, the debate continued whether or not Marco Polo's Cathay and the Empire of China were one and the same. In 1602, Benedict de Goes, a lay Jesuit from the Azores, was chosen by his order to follow in Marco Polo's footsteps. He set off from India disguised as an Armenian trader. He was haunted by the constant fear of being exposed as a non-Muslim but managed to join a caravan of 500 merchants bound for Kabul. There, he joined another caravan, which in spite of great caution was attacked, and its remnants struggled over the Pamir passes to reach Yarkand (Shache) in 1603. A year later, he joined an eastbound merchant caravan and, from travellers along the way, learned that Jesuits had found favour at the Ming Court. This convinced him that Cathay was indeed China. While his caravan waited in Jiuqian for permission to continue, de Goes became impoverished through dealings with Muslim merchants. Despondent at not hearing from the Jesuits in Beijing, he soon fell ill. The Jesuits' emissary arrived in 1607, just in time to watch de Goes die.

Transoxiana, an area which had converted mostly to Islam, the other half known as **Moghulistan** (the Persian name for Mongols was "Moghuls"), comprising shamanistic, Buddhist and Christian peoples based around Issyk-Kul and the Ili Valley, and controlling Jungaria, and the Turpan and Tarim basins.

Power in the western half devolved into the hands of several tribal leaders, most notably the Qara'unas, who appointed khans who were mere puppets. However, in the Ili Valley the Dughlats chose one **Tughluq (Telug) Timur** to be the khan of Moghulistan, and this proved to be a momentous decision. Timur was no figurehead ruler; he quickly established himself as a capable and forceful khan. Soon after his ascension he converted to Islam, and this resulted in the emirs of Moghulistan doing the same, although the general population of the region was slower in converting.

During his reign (1347–63), Tughluq Timur twice invaded and conquered Transoxiana in the hope that he could reunify the Chaghatai Khanate, and during this time he met with a young **Tamerlane** (1336–1405). But his dream was not to last, and within half a dozen years of his death in 1363, Tamerlane had come to power and begun his conquest of large parts of Central Asia, including an incursion into the Tarim Basin in 1389, when he penetrated as far as Karashahr. Tamerlane had grand plans to re-create the Mongol Empire, but he died whilst preparing an invasion of Xinjiang.

In Moghulistan after Teghluq Timur's death a Dughlat emir named Qamar ad-Din had seized control, having all but one of Timur's family killed. The surviving son, **Khizr Khwaja**, was raised in hiding but emerged to claim the throne after Qamar fled from Tamerlane's army into the Altai mountains. Khizr made a pact with Tamerlane, and then in the 1390s proceeded to attack the Khara-Khoja kingdom in Turpan, known as **Uyguristan** and still Buddhist. Khizr is credited with forcing the population of Uyguristan to convert to Islam, although Buddhism survived until well into the 15th century before Islam finally achieved domination.

Since the 13th century the oases to the south of the Taklamakan had been ruled by Dughlats, ostensibly answering to the Chaghatai khans, but often rebelling – Kashgar managed to be independent from Moghulistan between 1416 and 1435. In 1465 a Dughlat named **Mirza Abu-Bakr** founded an independent kingdom at Yarkand, successfully repelling attacks by the ruler of Moghulistan at the time, Yunus Khan. He extended his sphere of control to Kashgar and Khotan and remained in power for 48 years, finally being deposed in 1514 by Yunus Khan's grandson, Sultan Said Khan.

As a Chaghatai Khan, **Sultan Said (Saiyid) Khan** was seen by the general populace as an eminently acceptable replacement to the tyrannical Abu-Bakr. Said Khan set himself up in Kashgaria, also using Yarkand as his capital, and reached a peaceful agreement with his brother Mansur, who ruled Aksu, Kucha, Karashahr, Turpan and the Ili Valley, thus establishing the **Yarkand Khanate**, which would last until 1682.

Meanwhile, elsewhere in Xinjiang other significant developments were taking place. The **Ming Dynasty** (1368–1644), which took little interest in the violent power struggles in the remote west, nevertheless had tried to keep an element of control in the Turpan region until Yunus Khan reunited it with Moghulistan, and maintained a military stronghold in eastern Xinjiang at Hami. This was a source of conflict between the Ming and Chaghatai rulers, and there were many attacks and much plundering in this region until the mid-1500s.

More important however was the emergence in northern Xinjiang of a new nomadic confederation made up of Mongols from western Mongolia (unrelated to Genghis Khan), the **Oirats** (including the Eleuths and Kalmyks or Kalmuks), who had caused the Ming problems before being forced west into the mountains and steppes of Jungaria. A sub-group of the Oirat confederation called the **Junggar** would create the final great nomadic empire in Central Asia, thereby putting in motion events that would define Xinjiang – and all the vast lands across its western borders – as we know them today.

JUNGGAR AND QING STRUGGLES

B y the 16th century, the entire Taklamakan region was thoroughly entrenched in Islam; Buddhist stupas and temples were either destroyed or left to crumble. The Ming Dynasty, nearing the end of its hold on power, had virtually shut China off from the outside world, effectively ending the centuries-old influx of foreign ideas and culture. Islam brought a whole new mix of religion, art and architecture that today is the root of Uygur culture in Xinjiang, and this linked it to the states of Central and South Asia rather than to China in the east.

Sufis – Islamic mystics – began to proselytize their version of Islam throughout Xinjiang, from the mountains of the Pamirs to the desert oases and the Kazakh grasslands of the north, where they encountered the Buddhist **Junggar Empire**, which was growing in power and beginning to exert control over the northern Tarim Basin. Sufis of the **Naqshbandiyya** order (*tariqa*) were particularly successful in Moghulistan and Kashgaria, and in the late 16th century Khoja Ishaq Wali moved from Transoxiana to the Tarim Basin and set up the **Ishaqiyya** Sufi order based in the Kashgar region ("Khoja" was a Persian title meaning "lord").

Chinese Soldier, 1793, by William Alexander, an English artist who accompanied Earl Macartney, Britain's envoy to China.

n the early 17th century another Sufi master arrived from the west, **Khoja Muhammad Yusuf**, but such was his success preaching in the oasis cities of the Tarim and Turpan basins that jealous members of the Ishaqi order poisoned him. Yusuf's son, **Khoja Afaq**, continued his work, and his branch of the Naqshbandiyya became known as the **Afaqiyya**. The two branches grew powerful, effectively gaining secular power over the region, but all the while despising each other. Khoja Afaq initially found favour with Khan Abdullah of the Yarkand Khanate, but when the ruler went on Hajj to Mecca, his son, Ismail Khan, who was in league with the Ishaqis, drove Afaq out of Kashgar.

Afaq went first to Kashmir, then Tibet, where he asked for assistance from the Fifth Dalai Lama in regaining power in Kashgaria. The Tibetan ruler agreed, and sent a message – effectively an order – to **Galdan**, chief of the Tibetan Buddhist Junggar confederation, to help Afaq. This he gladly did, sweeping south and conquering the Tarim Basin, in return for an annual levy from the Afaqis. (The Abakh Khoja Tomb in Kashgar is the resting place of Khoja Afaq.) Conflict between the two Sufi sects continued from oasis to oasis for some time, but other events would soon overshadow Xinjiang.

The Ming Dynasty had by now been replaced by a ruling house from northern China, the Manchus, themselves with a nomadic background. The **Qing Dynasty** (1644–1911), like the Tang and Han before it, faced serious opposition from a powerful nomadic empire to the north that drew on a rich source of agriculture and livestock in the western region encompassing Xinjiang. The Junggar Empire had grown throughout the 17th century, forcing the Kazakh tribes west and exacting tribute from the Tarim Basin states, and by the early 18th century its threat to Qing China was considerable.

Decades of conflict between the two powers had resolved nothing, but when, in the 1750s, arguments over succession caused problems among the Junggar clans, **Emperor Qianlong** (ruled 1735–1796) decided to take advantage of the instability, allying himself with defecting Oirat tribes and launching a full-scale attack on the Junggar. The Qing's huge agricultural tax base, advanced technology and logistical strength, combined with the fact that its steppe background allowed it a greater understanding of Junggar strengths and weaknesses, gave its army the advantage, and it swept through the eastern regions and conquered Jungaria easily, capturing Kulja (Ghulja, on the site of modern-day Yining) and the Ili Valley in 1755.

When his erstwhile Oirat allies rebelled against Qianlong's plans to split up Jungaria, the emperor was merciless in reprisal, ordering his troops to systematically wipe out the Junggar nation. This was done so successfully that all that remains of this once great tribal confederation is the name given to the lands where it once thrived.

In Kulja Qianlong had found two brothers of the Afaqi sect, kept by the Junggars as hostages. He decided to support them in a campaign to take control of the Tarim Basin, thus ensuring a position of influence there, but in typically treacherous style the Afaqis reneged on their deal, refused to recognize any allegiance to Qianlong and slaughtered his envoys. Thus, although he had not originally intended to invade the southern desert lands, Qianlong was forced to retaliate and take each oasis city one by one, until by 1759 the entire Tarim Basin was under Qing control.

Qianlong placed this vast new dominion under the direct control of a single military official, known as the **General of Ili**, who was headquartered at the fort of Huiyuan, 30 kilometres west of Kulja. The massacre of the Junggars had left much of Jungaria's rich grasslands and mountains empty of people, and the Qing repopulated the region with "**banner troops**", military forces who were self-sufficient and able to develop the land around them. The idea was to form an effective security blanket over a volatile region without draining imperial resources in the east. At this time the **Torghut Mongols** returned from the west and were welcomed and given land in and around the Tien Shan.

he late 18th century saw the first use of the term "Xinjiang", or "**New Territory**". To minimize the risk of revolt the Qing left government of the southern oases in the hands of local Muslim leaders known as *begs*, while another system used *jasaks*, or princely rulers, who governed over important areas but answered to the Qing government and could be removed at any time – **Emin Khoja**, the ruler of Turpan, was one such trusted jasak. Unfortunately many instances of egregious abuse of these systems by local rulers often resulted in unrest, rebellion and retribution.

However, life under the Qing was in many ways less dangerous and more productive than it had been for centuries. They introduced a new monetary system, and actively encouraged agricultural development throughout the region. By the early 19th century they were permitting large-scale colonization of eastern and northern Xinjiang by Han Chinese, who were given prime lands previously held by Uygurs and Kazakhs and exempted from certain taxes. Inevitably this was to cause friction between the colonists and indigenous populations.

The Qing had 50,000 troops stationed in Xinjiang by the mid-19th century, and to supply them the ***tuntian* (state military farm)** model was used. This was the predecessor of the Xinjiang Production and Construction Corps that was to come in the latter half of the 20th century, but even these farms could not fully supply the military government, which was forced to request regular large stipends from the Qing court, something it could ill afford at that time.

The rise of the **Khokand kingdom** to the west of Kashgar in the Ferghana Valley, and the invasion of Kashgaria by **Jahangir Khoja** allied with Kyrgyz troops, resulted in a period of vicious warfare, with cities sacked and plundered, only to be recaptured and plundered once again. Jahangir was captured and executed, but his brother, **Muhammad Yusuf Khoja** carried on the conflict, backed by the Khokand rulers. Attempts to make peace with Khokand were only partially successful, and bloody rebellions continued, the last and most awful led by **Khoja Wali Khan** in 1857. The level of pillaging and appalling acts of reprisal left the local populace disgusted and filled with antipathy for both the Khojas and Chinese troops.

QING RULE IN XINJIANG

*T*he traditional Chinese policy in the administration of Chinese Turkestan and Zungaria, since the decisive conquests under the Manchu Empire, now nearly three hundred years ago, has been straightforward. After establishing practicable frontiers, based on the mountain ranges dividing these far outer territories from the sphere of Russian power and influence, every effort was made, so far as the physical difficulties of great distance and intervening deserts would allow, to identify the province with China. The alien Ta Ch'ing dynasty created by the conquering Manchus merged their interests in those of China, and directed their policies toward fortifying an integral Chinese civilization, which should be rooted in the heart of China and overshadow all the frontiers.

To this end, the westward frontiers of what is now Hsin-chiang were closed, but from the side of China trade was encouraged and the development of wealth and civilization was fostered as far as was commensurate with keeping the subject races militarily impotent. The North Road and the South Road were, in still more momentous epochs, channels leading on to the still remoter West; but from this time the flow of wealth in these channels was controlled in a new sense. The province was no longer an intermediate region, but a terminal area into which flowed exports of men and manufactures, and those more imponderable exports, arts and civilization. From it, as if in tribute, returned the produce of the less civilized subject races, raw materials of all kinds and jade and precious metals. Yet, until the end of the nineteenth century, China derived no substantial revenue from this remote dominion. Motives of policy demanded that the Chinese, both in Mongolia and Chinese Turkestan, should concern themselves above all with the maintenance of the buffer territories between themselves and the countries of the West, and with preventing any undue increase of strength among the subject races of those territories. True commercial exploitation depended on the later appearance of new commercial interests.

*B*y the beginning of our century [the 20th century], traffic became more important. The development of foreign trade on the coast of China stimulated the demand for raw materials. Though the foreigners could not trade in the interior, away from the Treaty Ports, the Chinese traders who dealt with the foreigners were encouraged to go farther and farther into the hinterland, in search of cheap raw materials. The trade of Mongolia and Hsin-chiang, especially, woke to a new importance. The demand for wool and camel hair became one of the standards of commerce, and in return for the wool sold to the foreigners the Chinese merchants were able to buy and transport increased quantities of cloth, tea, and manufactured articles for sale among their distant fellow-subjects.

Owen Lattimore, **High Tartary**, 1930

IMPERIAL DESIGNS

Throughout Xinjiang's various insurrections and the Qing's implementation of development strategies in the late 18th and 19th centuries, the government in Beijing kept a close eye on major events beyond its borders, specifically the aggressive expansion into Central Asia by **Tsarist Russia** and, in retaliation to this, the **British Empire**'s increased interest in southern Xinjiang and other Central Asian kingdoms contiguous with its sphere of control on the Indian subcontinent. This was the beginning of the covert struggle between powers that came to be known euphemistically as the **Great Game**. Qing China looked on with concern as Russia took control of the Central Asian steppe and mountains along Xinjiang's western border, massing troops within easy reach of Qing territory. The Qing court's concern was well founded – Xinjiang's economic frailty, the degeneration of the military farms and widespread misrule by those in power had left it poorly defended.

For some time trade between China and Russia had been an important source of supplies and revenue, and in 1851, after much tricky negotiation, the **Treaty of Kulja** was signed, opening Kulja (Yining) and Chuguchak (Tacheng) to Russian commerce. The treaty allowed Russian merchants to trade for 8.5 months a year, and Russian consuls were permitted to live in both towns. Thus Russian trade flourished and Russian influence grew in the north and Ili Valley in particular.

In 1862 uprisings in Gansu and Shanxi by **Tungans** (the name given to Chinese Muslims today known as Hui) put even more pressure on the increasingly beleaguered Qing Dynasty, and in 1864 a **Tungan rebellion** erupted in Xinjiang as well, beginning in Kucha but quickly spreading throughout the region. Where Uygurs outnumbered Tungans – such as Hotan – they too rebelled against the Qing authorities, but the idea that this was a united independence movement is erroneous: within a matter of months Xinjiang had become a fragmented region where petty warlords ruled and inter-ethnic rivalries caused distrust and hatred.

Into this cauldron of discontent came the infamous character **Yakub Beg**, who was to figure large in inner-sanctum discussions in Beijing, London and St Petersburg for a decade or more. In 1865 the ruler of Khokand sent an army led by Khoja Buzurg and Yakub Beg to assist the Kyrgyz who had taken Kashgar's Muslim town. Beg quickly took Yengisar, displaced Buzurg, made a pact with the Tungans and drove the Chinese out of Kashgar, establishing himself as the Emir of Kashgaria in 1867. Claiming to be a descendant of Tamerlane, he proceeded to conquer all of southern Xinjiang, breaking relations with the Tungans and taking Kucha, then moving east as far as Urumqi, Turpan and Hami, recruiting local minorities along the way.

Most Muslims disliked Beg as much as they disliked the Chinese – he was not Uygur but a Khokandi, and his dictatorship was characterized by bloody massacres, the rape and pillage of towns, secret police and high taxes. Attempting to carve out his own kingdom but surrounded by potential enemies, Beg trod a fine line of foreign diplomacy, signing commercial treaties with both

The Great Game

In the early 19th century, Russian troops began a great expansion south through the Caucasus Mountains (now in Georgia) towards Persia. Initially, when Napoleon Bonaparte temporarily aligned himself with Tsar Alexander I and planned to march across Persia and Afghanistan into British India, London was not alarmed. But Britain was immediately alert to the vulnerability of the no-man's land north of the subcontinent and its strategic importance to both Britain and Russia. Although nothing came of Napoleon's elaborate plan, Russia continued its drive through the khanates of the former Silk Road in Central Asia for the next 50 years.

Until the early 20th century, the two rival imperialist powers were locked in an often subtle, sometimes overt struggle for control of the region, stretching from the Caucasus in the west through Central Asia to Chinese Turkestan and Tibet in the east. Russia was determined to gain access to the fabled riches of India – the source of Britain's power and wealth – through the uncharted mountain passes of the Pamir and Karakoram Mountains, while Britain fought to keep the Russians out by maintaining a loyal string of buffer states along the Indian borders. Power in this remote area rested more upon gathering intelligence and surveying the uncharted mountain passes than on high-level diplomacy. Despite the dangers involved, mostly from hostile tribes and khanates in the region, adventurous and patriotic British officers eagerly volunteered to map the region, report on Russian movements

and try to entice the suspicious khans into aligning themselves with Britain. Explorations were carried out under the guise of "shooting expeditions" or "geographical surveys" by the British, and "scientific expeditions" by the Russians. They ventured into dangerous and unknown territory, often in clever disguises; many never returned and lie in unmarked graves throughout the dry mountain passes of Central Asia.

Pundits, Indian explorers highly trained in secret surveying techniques, were employed by Captain Thomas Montgomerie of the Indian Survey, a mammoth agency in charge of providing the government with maps of the subcontinent and surrounding regions. It was politically sensitive for British officers to travel into the dangerous regions of Afghanistan, Turkestan and Tibet, beyond India's borders. Their deaths could not be avenged if they were accused of spying and murdered by suspicious khanates, wary of foreign threats to their power. Pundits, as native Indians, were less likely to be detected and could be more readily disowned if they were caught or killed. Disguised as Buddhist pilgrims, they mapped unknown regions, keeping track of their paces per day, counting them on prayer beads to measure distances, and noting these measurements on scroll paper hidden inside hand-held prayer wheels. A compass was concealed in the lid of the prayer wheel, and thermometers, for estimating altitudes, were hidden in the lid of the stave. Although the pundits were rarely rewarded for their bravery and cunning, this dangerous work was immortalized in Rudyard Kipling's *Kim*.

The theatrics and intrigue of this Great Game, as it was called (*bolshaya igra* in Russian), was as exciting for armchair strategists as it was for the players. Volumes of books, articles, pamphlets and editorials written about the perceived threat of the enemy's position in Central Asia dictated official foreign policy, and intrigued the public with stories about politics and adventures in the exotic kingdoms of Ladakh, Bokhara, Khokand and others.

A Russian secret mission reached Kashgar in 1858, and in the 1860s Russia occupied Tashkent (one of the richest cities in Central Asia), Samarkand and Bokhara. At the same time, Yakub Beg established himself as ruler in Kashgar and played Russia and Britain against each other, establishing treaties with both powers in an effort to gain international recognition for his kingdom (which neither would do publicly for fear of angering the Chinese government). Yakub Beg's control spread, and soon threatened the Yili (Ili) region with its strategic access to the southern Russian frontier and rich minerals. In 1871, to the consternation of the Chinese government, the Russians occupied Yili. Six years later, a Chinese army under the command of General Zuo Zongtang finally defeated Yakub Beg and restored Chinese command in the region.

In the 1870s, the Russians took Khiva and Khokand. In 1884, Russia's annexation of Merv near the Persian border gave them access to Persia and Afghanistan. Strategically close to British India, they were blocked only by the formidable High Pamirs and Karakoram ranges; Britain and Russia came close to war. By the end of the 1880s the Russians were sending intelligence-gathering sorties into the Pamir region. British Indian forces subdued the unreliable tribes along the Indian frontier in an attempt to block Russian encroachment.

In 1888, Captain Gromchevsky, a Russian explorer, entered the remote Kingdom of Hunza (now in Pakistan) and was favourably received by the volatile khan in an area considered to be within the British sphere of influence. Worse, Hunza raiders, later discovered to be envoys of the khan himself, were using a secret pass to attack trade caravans in the mountains between Leh and Yarkand (Shache). Determined to find this important pass before the Russians, Lt (later Col Sir) Francis Younghusband set out for Hunza. He ran into Gromchevsky high up in the Karakorams and shared a meal of vodka and blinis with him while discussing the rivalry between their two countries. The next day, Younghusband proceeded on to Hunza to secure British interests there. According to Younghusband, the notorious Khan of Hunza, Safdar Ali (who had seized power by killing his mother and father and throwing his two brothers over a cliff) was "under the impression that the Empress of India, the Tsar of Russia and the Emperor of China were chiefs of neighbouring tribes".

With the establishment in 1890 of a British Indian Agency in Kashgar, the city became a crucial listening post for the British. George (later Sir George) Macartney spent 26 years here as the British consul-general, creating a vast intelligence-gathering network that kept a particularly wary eye on the Russians while forging closer ties with the Chinese governor. Relations with the all-powerful Russian consul, Nikolai Petrovsky, were tenuous. Petrovsky also had a network of spies whose tentacles spread everywhere. Younghusband came to Kashgar with the young Macartney to persuade the Chinese to occupy the Pamir region directly west of their territory, thereby filling in the gap between China and Afghanistan. The Russians learned of this plan (via Petrovsky) and moved in first.

The easy defeat of Tsar Nicholas's navy by the Japanese in 1905 so demoralized the Russians and crushed their dreams of a Far Eastern Empire that they signed the historic Russo-British Convention in 1907, which ended the first round of the Great Game. The terms of this treaty give a good indication of the imperialist manner in which both countries managed their international affairs. Both Britain and Russia agreed to stay out of Tibet except officially through China; Afghanistan was considered to be within Britain's sphere of influence, but she agreed not to interfere in Afghanistan's domestic politics; and lastly, both agreed to leave the territory that was to become Pakistan independent but divide it in two, the north and centre to Russia, the south and Arabian Gulf access to Britain.

The Russian Revolution of 1917 began the second phase of the Great Game. The Russian eastern front collapsed and the Bolsheviks tore up the landmark treaty. Lenin planned to subdue the East with Marxism and stated bluntly: "England is our greatest enemy. It is in India that we must strike them hardest... The East will help us to conquer the West."

The White Russian armies retreated westwards, setting up resistance fortifications in Central Asia, where Muslims were trying to throw out the Russians altogether. The fabulously wealthy Emir of Bokhara approached Colonel Percy Etherton in Kashgar with a plan to secretly deposit his fortune of some £35 million in gold and silver for safekeeping in the Consulate-General.

Etherton could not accommodate so great a treasure but did assist in the escape of the emir, whose treasure fell into the hands of the Bolsheviks. Etherton widened his network of spies and his propaganda efforts were formidable; the Russians in Tashkent put a price on his head.

By the mid-1930s Russia and Britain were preoccupied with the growing threat of fascism in Europe, and at the end of World War II Britain faced the disintegration of her empire, including the loss and partition of India in 1947. In China, the Communist Party came to power two years later, completing the turnover of players and inaugurating a new phase in the Great Game. With the disintegration of the Soviet Union and the creation of the Commonwealth of Independent States (CIS) in 1991, China suddenly found itself bordering on three new countries – Kazakhstan, Kyrgyzstan and Tajikistan – and dealing with three nascent governments. Today, rather than a power struggle over control of geographic regions, the "Game" continues through jockeying for control and influence over Central Asia's huge energy reserves – as well as its vital water resources.

the British and Russians, as both powers wanted to establish strong relations with local rulers in an effort to extend their own area of control. But Beg's greatest fear was reprisal by the Qing, despite its declining power, and sure enough in spring of 1877 a carefully prepared, well-supplied and well-armed force of 60,000 soldiers moved into Xinjiang from Gansu under the command of **Zuo Zongtang** (Tso Tsung-t'ang), a brilliant Hunanese general. Zuo quickly and methodically retook the region, town by town, first dealing with the Tungan defenders of Hami, Turpan and Urumqi, and after Yakub Beg's sudden death in Korla in May moving swiftly south to capture Kashgar by the end of the year.

With the fall of Hotan in 1878 the Tarim Basin and southern Junggar Basin were once again firmly under Qing control; the Ili Valley, however, was an entirely different matter. In 1871, ostensibly to protect the lives and livelihoods of its citizens, Russian forces had advanced up the Ili River and taken over Kulja and the entire valley. Russia would dearly have loved to keep it, but having assured the Qing court at the time that it would relinquish control as soon as the political situation had stabilized, and more importantly with Zuo's battle-hardened army on the doorstep, it was forced to enter negotiations for the Ili region's return to Chinese control. After a farcical attempt at a settlement (the Treaty of Livadia in 1879) was quashed by the Qing court for its scandalous concessions to Russia, a skilled diplomat, Zeng Jize, was sent to negotiate an acceptable agreement. The result was the **Treaty of St Petersburg**, signed in February 1881, by which China paid a sum of nine million roubles for the return of the Ili Valley east of the Horgos River, and Russia was granted customs-free trade rights in Xinjiang and Mongolia.

With the Ili Valley situation settled, the Qing's focus returned to the region as a whole. Xinjiang was in a poor state on all fronts, with little semblance of proper governance visible, many ethnic communities decimated or displaced, and much agricultural land ruined. Many advisers at the Qing court lobbied for Xinjiang to be discarded and the country's resources used instead to bolster its coastal defences and the island of Formosa, or Taiwan, against the threat from Japanese expansionism; others argued that Xinjiang remained vital as a buffer between China and the Russian Empire. First Zuo and then **General Liu Jintang** put forward the case for Xinjiang to be given provincial status, arguing that in the long run this would be the cheapest and safest way to ensure stability in the region.

In the end the Qing court agreed, and in 1884 Xinjiang Province was officially created. From this point on the name "Xinjiang" would officially replace the many and various historical names by which the region had been known (the Western Regions, Jungaria, Chinese Turkestan, Uyguristan, Kashgaria, Moghulistan and Altishahr, among others). For the first time, the vast lands to the north and south of the Tien Shan would be grouped together as a single geopolitical and administrative entity.

WHAT'S IN A NAME?

*T*he use of the name Uighur has been revived in Sinkiang only in recent years. Historically it first appears in the records of the T'ang Dynasty (618–907) as the name of a tribal confederation of pastoral nomads living along the Selega River, in what is now the northern part of the Mongolian People's Republic. From 745 to 840, warriors of this confederation penetrated into Inner Asia north and south of the Tien Shan. In 840 the Uighur power in Mongolia was destroyed by Kirghiz from the Lake Baikal-Yenisei area. Some of the Uighur warrior class succeeded in withdrawing southwest, where they took over the oases north of the Tien Shan, infiltrated in large numbers into the oases south of the mountains, and made themselves the rulers of a settled population. From Chinese transcriptions of the name Uighur, like Hui-hu and Wei-wu-erh, there was eventually formed the name "Hui" or "Hui-hui," the popular Chinese term for all Moslems.

The people or peoples among whom the Uighurs were absorbed but to whom they gave their name had for half a millennium or so enjoyed flourishing civilizations. From the oases of easternmost Sinkiang have been recovered documents dating from the first century A.D., written in the Sogdian script. The language of these documents has been identified as belonging to the Indo-Iranian group; the main centers of the Soghds were Samarkand and Bokhara, but their language was widely used in Inner Asia, especially by traders. The Khotan oasis has given up documents in the Tokharian

language and also in the Saka language, also belonging to the Indo-Iranian group, which date from 200–400 A.D. and are written in the Karoshthi script, which came from India. The Saka civilization was related to the Kushan culture in northwestern India, and like it showed marked Hellenistic influences. In the same period there flourished in the Kucha and Turfan oases a civilization which also used the Tokharian language. What is most interesting about this language is that it belongs, like the Indo-Iranian languages just mentioned, to the larger Indo-European family, but unlike them has more affinity with languages of the "Kentum group" spoken in western Europe than with those farther east.

Besides speaking Indo-European languages the pre-Uighur peoples were distinguished by their devotion to Buddhism and Greco-Buddhist art, and to Manichaeism. The most important literary and artistic treasures from the Tarim Basin are connected with these religions.

When the Uighurs penetrated to the Tarim area, they had already felt the influence of Manichaeism through Sogdian traders. After their contact with the settled population, numbers of the Uighurs were converted to Buddhism. In turn they established their own language among the indigenous people. Both groups were also influenced at an early period by Nestorian Christianity.

Subsequently Islam became the dominant religion in the whole area. The Kashgar region was first converted in the tenth century, but

Islam spread slowly and did not completely drive out Buddhism until the sixteenth century.

The period of Uighur domination was brought to an end in the first quarter of the twelfth century by the invasion of the Khara Khitai, who at the beginning of the thirteenth century were in turn overthrown by Jenghis Khan. Mongol Khans continued to rule over the area even after the Mongol (Yuan) Dynasty was overthrown in China. The period of Mongol ascendancy was marked by a dual system of administration in which native princes, ecclesiastical leaders, and commune elders retained a considerable degree of authority. With the weakening of the Mongol hold the Moslem prelates, called khojas, were able to take over complete control in 1566 and establish what was virtually a theocratic state. Their influence continued to some extent even after the invasion by the Jungar Mongols in 1650 and the replacement of Jungar rule by the Manchus in 1756.

*I*n the checkered history of Sinkiang the Uighurs appear as only one of many invading peoples. Despite the fact that in the process of amalgamating with the indigenous population the Uighurs were able to impose their own language on the other peoples, the total importance of their influence should not be exaggerated. Physically the present population of the Tarim Basin is more akin to the Alpine than to the Mongoloid type. The culture, way of life, and other aspects of the present population also owe little to the Uighurs who rode out of Mongolia in the ninth century.

*T*he revived use of the name Uighur in Sinkiang, though justified by the fact that the Uighur language is used by the people who now once more call themselves Uighur, is primarily political in motivation...

...During the Manchu period the population of the Tarim Basin was generally referred to in documents as Ch'an Hui, or Turbaned Moslems, and in the Chinese spoken language as Ch'an-t'ou, or Turbaned Heads. When foreigners first began to penetrate the area in numbers in the nineteenth century, they referred to the population either as "Turkis" or as "Sarts" and to the region as Turkistan... though the term has never had any administrative significance there...

At a meeting held in Tashkent in 1921 a small number of emigrants from the Tarim Basin living in Soviet Central Asia demanded that the name Uighur be revived. In 1934 the Provincial Government of Sinkiang accepted a resolution from the Association for the Promotion of Uighur Education for a formal change to this name. A resolution adopting the new name was promulgated in that year under the signature of Sheng Shih-ts'ai and Khoja Niaz, a nationalist leader who had been instrumental in setting up the abortive East Turkistan Republic in the Turfan area in the early thirties. The growing use of the name Uighur is a measure of increasing national consciousness among people who for several centuries had referred to themselves only as Kashgarliks, Turfanliks, and so on – that is, as inhabitants of a particular oasis.

Owen Lattimore, Pivot of Asia: Sinkiang and the Inner Asian Frontiers of China and Russia, 1950

PROVINCIAL STATUS AND WARLORD RULE

injiang's status as a province marked a significant change in China's policy within its borders. Gone was the military government, and with the creation of counties and prefectures governed by civil officials of almost exclusively Han descent – an administrative system known as *junxian* – local ethnic rulers were stripped of their powers or marginalized. **Liu Jintang**, the new province's first governor, began an agrarian reclamation programme designed to rejuvenate Xinjiang's agriculture-based economy, attracting migrants from eastern China with subsidized loans and land. He also began a sweeping educational programme, opening Confucian-style schools for Uygurs, a move that was not received well in southern Xinjiang, where schooling followed a religious style of *maktaps* (local schools) and *madrasas* (colleges attached to shrines and mosques).

Interestingly, at this time many Uygurs were relocated to the Ili Valley and Junggar Basin to repopulate areas that had suffered a depletion of ethnic groups and communities during the chaos of the previous decades. Where in centuries past the Uygur population had been almost exclusively distributed around the Tarim and Turpan basins, by the beginning of the 20th century Uygurs had spread throughout Xinjiang and almost doubled in numbers (though they remained concentrated in southern Xinjiang, where they comprised the vast majority of the local populace in the oasis towns).

The Boxer Rebellion of 1900 in northern China spelt the beginning of the end for the Qing Dynasty, but more important to Xinjiang was the completion of Russia's **Trans-Siberian Railroad**, which opened up even greater trading possibilities between Xinjiang and Russia. Xinjiang exported brick tea and cotton in large amounts, in return for hides and furs, livestock and manufactured goods from Russia. Russian merchants gained more and more influence over commerce in Xinjiang, their produce considerably cheaper than equivalent items from China because of the easier supply routes from the west.

With the fall of the Qing Dynasty in 1911 and the creation of the **Republic of China** in 1912, Xinjiang was effectively left to self-rule. Revolutionary elements in the Ili Valley and the mainly Hunanese army that had reconquered Xinjiang tried to take control, but after Xinjiang's last governor, Yuan Dahua, recognized the Republic of China then retired and fled the province, one of his subordinates, a judiciary official named **Yang Zengxin**, took control of Urumqi, and through cunning political manoeuvring proceeded to neutralize his Ili and Hunanese opponents, eventually gaining overall power throughout Xinjiang until his death in 1928.

Yang was a mandarin from Yunnan Province who ruled through a combination of shrewd governance, wily negotiation and brutal enforcement. He maintained control over his vast territory by placing other Yunnanese, as well as family members, in strategically important positions, creating a conduit of reliable information that kept him fully aware of unrest and potential rebellion. Yang was merciless when crossed: on one particularly memorable occasion he invited a group of Yunnanese military officers to a Chinese New Year banquet; having been tipped off that they were conspiring against him, Yang drank congenially with them, then suddenly signalled to his guards, who beheaded three of the officers at the table, leaving Yang, unruffled, to languidly finish his meal.

Xinjiang's continuing fiscal troubles were made worse by the cessation of the annual stipend from the Qing coffers. When revolution swept away the Russian Empire and paved the way for the new Soviet Union, Yang was forced to navigate a political minefield as White Russian armies retreated into northern Xinjiang to escape from Bolshevik forces. Trade with Russia was vital to Xinjiang's economy, so in spite of China's frosty official relationship with the Soviets, Yang allowed the Bolsheviks to enter Xinjiang and drive the remnants of the White army into Mongolia. He then made trade agreements with the Soviets that allowed more consulates to be opened in the north, further increasing Xinjiang's dependence on Russian commerce.

Fittingly, Yang's death in 1928 came at a dinner banquet, when he was assassinated by soldiers loyal to a disaffected official named Fan Yaonan. Although Fan tried to seize control of the province he was quickly caught and executed by Yang's second in command, **Jin Shuren**, who was then granted the governorship of Xinjiang by the Kuomintang (KMT) government in Nanjing, to whom Xinjiang still nominally owed allegiance.

However, where Yang had, for all his brutality and wheeler-dealing, administered Xinjiang in a manner that kept it from implosion or subsumption by the Russians, Jin Shuren was unable to maintain equilibrium. A less than competent ruler, he tried to combat fiscal deficits by raising taxes and printing money in absurd amounts. He also treated local ethnic groups so badly, appointing Han officials to "manage" them, that within a few years the region was ripe for revolt.

I n 1931 the **Hami Rebellion** was set off by a Han tax collector named Zhang, who forced a Uygur to give his daughter to him as a wife. Jin had recently abolished the Hami khanate, which had traditionally enjoyed special privileges because of its loyalty to the Qing rulers. This was an unwise move; the local Uygur population had for years begrudged Han settlement and preferential treatment, and the mob who attacked Zhang's wedding celebration and killed him, sparked off a wide-ranging rebellion that called for the return of the khanate. Reinforcements from Urumqi moved in to quell the rebel forces, who sought help in Gansu from a young Hui warlord named **Ma Zhongying**.

Ma was a charismatic and able military leader, and his successes led to independent uprisings of Uygurs, Huis, Kazakhs and Kyrgyz throughout Xinjiang in the winter of 1932–33. A coalition of Hui and Uygur forces moved in on Urumqi from the south and north, taking it in early 1933. However, a government military commander named **Sheng Shicai**, an experienced soldier from Liaoning Province who had trained in Japan, retook the city with a force of Chinese Manchus who had been repatriated into Xinjiang after retreating into Russia from invading Japanese forces in northeast China.

Jin Shuren alienated too many of his allies and was forced out of office in April 1933, and Sheng was made commander-in-chief and *de facto* ruler of the provincial government. He appealed to the Soviets for assistance in beating Ma's forces, and with two Soviet brigades (including planes that dropped chemical bombs), he defeated the Hui-Uygur armies in January 1934 and forced Ma Zhongying to retreat southwest towards Kashgar.

THE EAST TURKESTAN REPUBLICS

Meanwhile, Uygur rebellion in southern Xinjiang had followed a different path. Beginning in Khotan (Hotan), where an Islamic government was formed by **Muhammad Emin Bughra**, it had spread east and west, sacking Chinese-controlled Yarkand in spring 1933 with the help of Kyrgyz forces, then advancing on Kashgar, which throughout that year was to change hands frequently as various Hui, Uygur and Kyrgyz armies fought viciously over its Muslim town (Kashgar's walled Chinese city remained under Chinese-Hui control). In November 1933 **Sabit Damulla**, a writer and publisher from Artush, declared the foundation of an independent state, the **East Turkestan Republic** (ETR), with Kashgar as its capital even though a Hui army held out in the fortress-like Chinese city. **Khoja Niyaz**, a veteran Uygur commander of the Hami Rebellion who was on his way south with a Uygur army at the time, was named president for life, and he entered Kashgar to great fanfare in January 1934. However, the republic was to be short-lived; in April 1934, after only five months, Niyaz and the government of the ETR were forced to retreat to Yengisar when the main Hui army, led by Ma Zhongying, entered Kashgar, uniting with Huis in the Chinese city and slaughtering thousands of civilian Uygurs in the Muslim city.

Curiously, Ma claimed authority in the name of the Nanjing government, but only three months later in July, he mysteriously disappeared across the border into Soviet territory, ostensibly to train with the Soviet army, and although his bemused officers received letters purportedly from him, he was never seen again, and the truth of his demise is not known. In his absence the Hui army maintained control of the Southern Silk Road oases, based around Khotan.

K hoja Niyaz in the meantime had made contact with Soviet agents in the Pamirs, and subsequently arrested Sabit Damulla and other ETR ministers, handing them over to the Soviets who had by this time advanced from Urumqi as far south as Aksu. Niyaz cut a deal with Sheng Shicai, and was made vice-chairman of the Xinjiang Provincial Government, while his colleague Mahmud Muhiti was made commander of Uygur and Chinese forces in southern Xinjiang, based in Kashgar. However, after an uneasy truce of a few years between the independent Huis and the untrustworthy Muhiti, a new uprising in 1937 gave Sheng enough reason to use Soviet troops again and put down all rebellion, regaining total control of Xinjiang for the provincial government. The Soviets were only too happy to help in stamping out any possibility of an Islamic state in Xinjiang, since this would have caused a ripple effect in its own Muslim-dominated territories across the border to the west (today's Kyrgyzstan, Uzbekistan and Kazakhstan).

Sheng instituted agricultural reforms, religious freedom and recognition of distinct ethnicities; he built roads, schools and increased trade with the Soviet Union, but for this he had to rely heavily on Soviet advisers and huge loans from Moscow, which left him open to suspicion from the KMT government in Nanjing. Of course Sheng's dictatorship, although resulting in some positives for the people of the region, was far from harmonious; he implemented Soviet-style security policies, and ordered a series of savage purges against any perceived "enemies of the people"; during his 10-year rule it is estimated that between 50,000 and 100,000 people were killed.

Sheng played a dangerous political game, switching allegiance between the Soviets and KMT depending on who he thought would best serve his ambitions. While still under Soviet influence he invited a group of Chinese Communists to Xinjiang, including Mao Zedong's brother Mao Zemin, but in 1942, with Germany attacking the Soviet Union and Xinjiang's economy healthier than it had been for some time, Sheng closed the province's Soviet borders and began courting Chiang Kai-shek's Nationalist government. He had the Chinese Communists jailed and eventually executed (including Mao Zemin), oversaw the complete withdrawal of Soviet military forces, technical staff (including oil technicians for Xinjiang's nascent oil industry) and advisers from the province, and allowed KMT forces to move into Xinjiang from the east. When in 1943 the tide of World War II shifted and the Soviet Union prevailed over Germany, Sheng attempted to switch sides again, this time incarcerating Urumqi's KMT representatives, but Stalin rebuffed his attempts at reconciliation. He turned back to Nanjing, but they had had enough of him and in 1944 he was removed from office and relocated to a minor position in Chongqing (a large bribe spared him from execution).

rom 1944 to 1949 the KMT followed a familiar strategy of developing and populating Xinjiang with migrants and officials from the east, but Nationalist policy was to consider all ethnicities living in Xinjiang as essentially Chinese, and Sheng's recognition of distinct ethnic groups was quashed. Taxes were raised but the cessation of trade with Russia had a disastrous effect on the economy, and once again rebellion was in the air. The Kazakhs of northern Xinjiang had been in a state of semi-revolt since the Russian border was closed, and under a local chief, **Osman Batur**, Kazakh forces took control of the Junggar Basin region, and civil unrest spread to the Ili Valley.

In late 1944, what came to be known as the **Three Districts Revolution** (after the Ili, Altai and Tarbagatai districts of northern Xinjiang) broke out in towns around Yining (Kulja). The city was stormed and both KMT troops and local Han Chinese massacred, and on 12 November the rebellion's leader, **Ali Khan Tore**, declared the creation of a second **East Turkestan Republic**, exactly 11 years after the Kashgar ETR had been founded. The second ETR was backed by the Soviets, who had a history of influence in the Ili Valley, and Osman Batur joined forces with the Ili ETR government. From this position of strength, the second ETR fought successfully against the KMT, but encouraged by the Soviets, the Ili ETR government negotiated a ceasefire with the KMT and formed a coalition government in 1946, agreeing to abandon its claim as an independent Turkic state and accept designation as an autonomous geographic region called "Eastern Turkestan" (actual independence from China would inevitably have led to dependence on, and *de facto* control by, the Soviet Union).

Under a new KMT governor, **Zhang Zhizhong**, many positive reforms took place, but the two sides never trusted each other, and Zhang resigned in 1947, frustrated by a lack of progress. The coalition soon fell apart and more instability followed, and when in 1949 the KMT finally fled mainland China, leaving the **Chinese Communist Party** (CCP) victorious and the People's Liberation Army (PLA) ready to enter Xinjiang, many of the province's Muslims welcomed the coming change of government.

PART OF THE PRC

The first task for **Mao Zedong** and the government of the new **People's Republic of China** (PRC) was to bring the second ETR firmly back into the China fold. Mao invited the top five leaders of the ETR government to a conference in Beijing in the summer of 1949, and they travelled to Alma-Ata (today's Almaty) in Kazakhstan to board a plane to Beijing. They never arrived – the Soviets informed the PRC government that the plane had crashed, killing everyone on board. Many conspiracy theories have since been put forward, but the truth remains hidden. Regardless of how they died, the consequence for the Ili ETR was that without its leaders the remaining government officials quickly agreed to abandon calls for autonomy in northern Xinjiang. (Osman Batur was caught and executed in 1951.)

The PLA effectively governed Xinjiang for the first few years after "liberation," while political and administrative infrastructure was set up. While Han Chinese held most high-level positions of authority, non-Han were encouraged to join the CCP and take an active role in the region's development. Perhaps the most successful of these was **Saypidin Azizi**, a Uygur who had studied in the USSR and was a committed communist; he had been a member of the Ili ETR government and became Chairman of the Xinjiang Nationalities Committee, and eventually Chairman of the Xinjiang Uygur Autonomous Region's People's Council.

Implementing some of the CCP's collectivization policies in remote Xinjiang, with its vastly differing cultures – in particular the nomadic Kazakh, Mongol and Kyrgyz herdsmen – proved extremely difficult. Concessions and adaptations to environmental and cultural conditions were necessary; unsuccessful attempts to create large cooperatives among Kazakh nomads in northern Xinjiang had to be rethought, and a more careful approach of bringing the *auls*, or family groups, into a semi-nomadic state reaped better results.

Nevertheless, there was inevitable dissent and resistance as the PRC government tried to mould Xinjiang to fit its plans for the future. Significant sectors of the Muslim population remained volatile, and to stabilize the region and reduce the threat of Muslim uprisings, throughout the 1950–70s the Beijing government settled Han Chinese there, most significantly through the formation in 1952 of the **Xinjiang Production and Construction Corps (XPCC)**. This comprised a collection of huge state farms, or *bingtuans* – mainly in the southern Junggar Basin – structured in military style and populated initially by demobilized soldiers from the KMT army that had been stranded in Xinjiang in 1949, the Ili National Army (from the second ETR) and the Communist First Field Army, and later by convicts and migrants, especially young people from the Shanghai region, which had formed a close connection with Xinjiang.

On 1 October 1955, Xinjiang Province was renamed the **Xinjiang Uygur Autonomous Region**, bringing it in line with the PRC's system of self-rule for non-Han peoples at local and regional level, but under the overriding control of the CCP. However, while Saypidin Azizi headed the People's Council, **Wang Enmao**, a seasoned campaigner from the Long March years, was made commander of the Xinjiang Military Region, and as such held the real power in Xinjiang.

The **Great Leap Forward** (1958–60) was as disastrous for Xinjiang as elsewhere in China, with famine sweeping the region and increased tension between Muslims and Han Chinese after anti-Islamic policies were ramped up and collectivization drives were more aggressively pursued. Relations between China and the Soviet Union soured, and when in 1962 an estimated 60,000 Kazakhs and other ethnic peoples fled across the border into Soviet Kazakhstan, Mao closed the borders again. The **Cultural Revolution** (1966–76) resulted in greater intolerance of ethnic cultural and religious differences, and violent clashes erupted periodically across the region, from Hami to Yining, Kashgar and Hotan.

Little is known for sure about the realities of life in Xinjiang in the late 1960s and 70s, but a major blow to its economy was the collapse of the XPCC farms, with as many as a million disillusioned young labourers giving up and heading back east. When the Cultural Revolution ended and Deng Xiaoping came to power, restrictions on Islam and many of the most oppressive policies were relaxed or rescinded. From 1980 a change in the government's outlook led to official documents stating that Xinjiang's government hierarchy should contain at least 45 percent Uygur representation – 60 percent in the Uygur-dominated south – as well as at least 15 percent representation for other ethnicities. Deng actively promoted the local-autonomy model and encouraged freedom of ethnic cultures, including languages.

There was still dissent, of course. Under the more relaxed policies of the 1980s Islamic fervour made a revival and a resurgence of activism saw student demonstrations in 1985 and 1988, calling for greater religious and ethnic freedom. In 1986, China's first anti-nuclear protests were held in opposition to nuclear tests in the desert near Lop Nor, which had been carried out since 1967. In 1990, a dozen or more members of a resurgent independence movement known as the **Islamic Party of Turkestan**, who were plotting a series of terrorist attacks in Xinjiang to pressure Beijing for independence, were discovered in the town of Baren in the Kashgar region. The **Baren Incident** saw government troops besiege the town for nearly three weeks before finally overcoming the 300 or so Uygur sympathisers fighting with the insurgents, who were either captured or killed.

But the final decade of the 20th century was to see Xinjiang change so drastically that in the heady rush of a revitalized economy, improved relations with its western neighbours and the consequences of the Internet revolution, the prospects for all its inhabitants were imbued with a new vigour.

MODERN-DAY XINJIANG

The 1990s were a pivotal period for Xinjiang, with events outside its borders catalyzing change within. The collapse of the Soviet Union in 1991 and subsequent creation of the Commonwealth of Independent States (CIS) had immense significance for the region, with the potential for a renewed commercial land bridge easy to imagine. Equally, the incredible economic reforms sparked by Deng Xiaoping's 1992 "To get rich is glorious" tour of southern China led to an influx of eager entrepreneurs searching for a way to make their fortune. The result was a 32 percent increase in the number of Han Chinese in Xinjiang, to 7.49 million, between 1990 and 2000, according to an official census.

Xinjiang's oil and gas resources were known to be huge, and expansion of the petrochemical industries went ahead at great speed, as did mining and agriculture – the bingtuan farms were back in business in a big way. Inevitably the region's major towns and cities underwent a process of modern urbanization that caused a degree of culture shock for much of the local populace – the steroidal skylines of today's Urumqi and Korla bear almost no resemblance to their sprawling, low-rise panoramas in 1990.

aving been considered little more than a backwater buffer by the central government for 40 years, suddenly Xinjiang was seen as a valuable source of energy and raw materials – which the Chinese economic juggernaut craved – as well as a hugely significant conduit to Central Asia and Europe. When in 1990 **Alashankou Port** was opened, finally creating a contiguous rail line connecting Urumqi to the Turk-Sib Railway line in Kazakhstan, the "**Eurasian Continental Rail Bridge**" was declared open with great fanfare. More trading ports and free-trade zones followed, and the economy boomed.

Separatist groups still worked behind the scenes, however, fuelled in their fervour to create an independent Uygur homeland by the creation of the eponymous states of Kazakhstan, Kyrgyzstan and Tajikistan to the immediate west. A police roundup of suspected separatists during Ramadan in Yining resulted in large demonstrations that turned violent in February 1997, with at least nine deaths, an episode subsequently known as the **Kulja Incident**. The resulting bus bombings in Urumqi, which killed nine and injured 68, were perhaps a response to the crackdown that followed the Kulja Incident.

In 2000 Beijing launched its **Great Development of the West** programme, designed to develop the economies of China's western provinces and raise the standard of living of its peoples – the gap between the eastern coastal regions and the west having grown hugely disparate as rampant capitalism took hold in cities throughout central and southern China. Billions of renminbi were pumped into Xinjiang in order to improve infrastructure, expand irrigation for more agriculture, and provide homes, jobs, etc for both its residents and the continuing influx of migrants – a process that continues to this day.

continued on page 92

FOREIGN EXPLORATION IN XINJIANG

By Susan Whitfield

PIONEERS OF THE EASTERN SILK ROAD

Three thousand years ago Xinjiang was populated by Indo-Europeans and Turkic peoples who had as much or more contact with civilisations to their south, north and west than with the Chinese to the east. The route into China from Xinjiang is through a relatively narrow strip of traversable land bounded by mountains and steppe, the Hexi Corridor, and this was often controlled by nomads. Being outside their political control, the area west beyond the corridor, present-day Xinjiang and western Gansu — in ancient times called "The Western Regions" — remained a largely mythical place in the Chinese imagination during the first millennium BCE. An early legend tells of King Mu who, in the 10th century BCE, travelled there encountering the "Queen Mother of the West", a quasi-Daoist deity. The story mentions mountains and deserts, suggesting at least some knowledge of the region's topography.

Towards the end of the first millennium BCE China's jade mines ran out and the rulers were forced to look elsewhere for this precious stone, valued more highly than gold or diamonds. Khotan in today's southern Xinjiang provided an alternative supply. Silk was probably also traded and exchanged with the kingdoms of the Western Regions during this period and the earliest finds date from before 1500 BCE in today's northern Afghanistan, but there is little evidence of sustained trade between China and the lands further west before the Han Dynasty. Lapis mines in present-day northeastern Afghanistan had, for example, been sending their product westwards as far as Egypt since the time of the Pharaohs, yet they do not seem to have been able to develop a market over the Pamir Mountains and through the Western Regions and the Hexi Corridor eastwards to China.

All this changed in the last two centuries of the first millennium BCE when the establishment of strong political regimes across Eurasia ensured the stability and infrastructure to enable sustained long-distance trade: the start of the Silk Road. The rise of the Parthians in present-day Iran controlling the land routes to Rome, and the Kushan Empire straddling the Pamir and the heart of Central Asia and reaching southwards into northern India, were essential elements in this. To the east it was the expansion of Han Dynasty China into the Western Regions that was crucial; this was owing both to the adventures of the diplomat Zhang Qian, sent on various missions to the Western Regions by the Han emperor, and the subsequent military efforts of General Ban Chao who drove out the nomads who controlled the Hexi Corridor, thus opening China's way westwards. These men were the Chinese pioneers of the Eastern Silk Road.

ZHANG QIAN 张骞 (195–114 BCE)

Zhang Qian's first foray into China's Western Regions lasted far longer than he expected. Sent in 139 BCE by the Chinese Han emperor to elicit the support of the Yuezhi – peoples who formerly occupied the area but who had been displaced westward by the encroaching nomadic Xiongnu – his large entourage was soon captured by the Xiongnu. He was held for several years, during which he acquired a Xiongnu wife and son. However, he retained loyalty to his original mission and finally escaped, continuing westwards as bidden. The Yuezhi, by now happily settled beyond the Pamir, were not interested in fighting a war against the Xiongnu and Zhang Qian started homewards. He was captured again, although this time managing to escape in less than a year. It was 126 BCE when he finally re-entered the Chinese capital.

Zhang Qian's travels did not stop here. He reported in detail on the geography, cultures and economies of 36 kingdoms of the Western Regions and, despite his experiences, he agreed to other missions. After failing to find a route to Central Asia via Southeast Asia – the so-called cotton route through the tropical rainforest-covered mountains of Vietnam and Burma – he returned to the Western Regions in 119 BCE. He died in 114 BCE two years after his final return.

Zhang Qian started a tradition: over the next two millennia thousands of diplomats followed in his footsteps into Central Asia, seeking intelligence and alliances, continuing up to the British and Russian envoys and spies who sought to control the Western Regions in the late 19th and early 20th centuries – the Great Game.

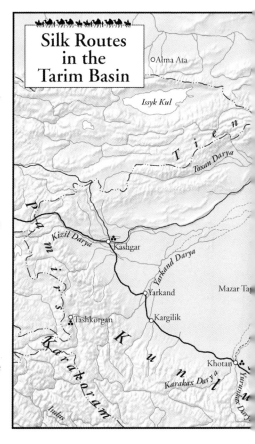

Silk Routes in the Tarim Basin

BAN CHAO (32–102 CE)

Diplomats after Zhang Qian depended on their soldiers to maintain safe passage and the pioneering Chinese general of the Western Regions was Ban Chao. He first succeeded in defeating the Xiongnu, Zhang Qian's captors, and drove them out of the Hexi Corridor. His initial campaigns were around Hami, in today's northeastern Xinjiang, but then the independent kingdoms of the Western Regions, including Khotan, Kroraina (Loulan) and Shule (Kashgar),

allied with the Xiongnu against the Chinese. Ban Chao led a long campaign against them, finally subduing them into alliances and installing pro-Chinese rulers. His campaigns took him over the Pamirs into Central Asia as far as Merv and he dispatched envoys further west. In 97 CE he sent Gan Ying to Rome, but the envoy was misled by false information given by the Parthians as to the length and difficulty of the journey and turned back. It was owing to Ban Chao and his soldiers'

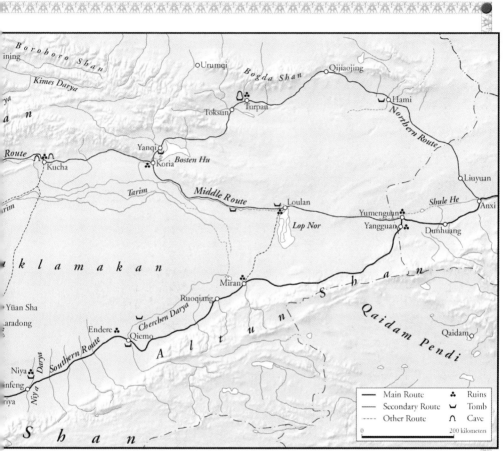

From Southern Silk Road: In the Footsteps of Sir Aurel Stein and Sven Hedin; *Orchid Press, Bangkok 2004 reproduced by permission of Orchid Press.*

long campaigns in alien territory far from home that China was able to move into the Western Regions.

We know about these early campaigns because of the Chinese imperial histories, which kept records of major events, including military campaigns, and also contained chapters on the Western Regions. Ban Chao's father, brother and sister were the historians responsible for the *Hanshu* (History of the Han).

THE SILK ROAD: TRAVELLERS THROUGH TWO MILLENNIA

From the end of the 2nd century BCE, present-day Xinjiang became a key section of the Silk Road and over the next two millennia tens of thousands of travellers passed through its testing terrain. Few left written records and only a handful of names are known to history, but many were pioneers in their own ways and helped create the culture of the Western Regions, with its unique ethnic, political and religious mix.

From the start, the Chinese used their imperial princesses as diplomatic bargaining chips. The chosen women were sent to marry rulers of distant lands to cement alliances. Some left poems and letters telling of their homesickness and one is credited with smuggling the secret of silk technology out of China in the early centuries CE. Many of these princesses were Buddhist and at least they would have found a thriving Buddhist community in the Western Regions. The resident community was swelled by travelling monks, on their way to proselytize in China or collect scriptures from India. Fa Xian (c.337–c.422) and Xuanzang (c.602–664) are the best known of the Chinese clergy, both having left accounts of their journeys, but hundreds more are recorded in Chinese books. We also know the names of Indians and monks from the Western Regions itself, including the famous translator Kumarajiva (344–413). Born in Kucha of an Indian father, he is commemorated by a statue at the Kizil Caves. But there were undoubtedly hundreds, if not thousands more who made the often hazardous journey in search of scriptures and enlightenment.

Not all the religious travellers were Buddhist. Manichaeism, Nestorian Christianity, Judaism and Islam all found their way to Xinjiang and the oasis kingdoms of the Taklamakan. An eighth century stone inscription in China, for example, records the arrival of a Nestorian Christian named Adam at the gates of Chang'an in 635 and an 8th or 9th century Judaeo-Persian document on the trade of sheep was found at a Khotanese site suggesting the presence as well of Jewish traders alongside the dominant Sogdians. We know little of these merchants from further afield who enabled the Silk Road to thrive in the first millennium, but by the Mongol period we learn more through Marco Polo and Ibn Battuta.

Alongside these other travellers, was a constant stream of diplomatic envoys, officials and soldiers. China was not alone in recognizing the importance of the Western Regions and continued to try to control the land, with varied success, up until the Mongol period. The empire sent officials to administer the region and relocated farmers from central China to establish agricultural colonies to provide supplies for the armies. Envoys passed through to China from the empires and kingdoms on the other sides of the Western Regions. With the reestablishment of Chinese rule in China in 1368, however, the rulers of the Ming Dynasty decided control of the Western Regions was no longer viable and the garrisons were withdrawn. By this time the Silk Road trade had already switched largely to the sea routes. It was four centuries before China turned its attention westward again, conquering lands north and south of the Tien Shan in the 1750s and administering them under the name "Xinjiang" or "New Territory". Over the next two centuries other powers were again to realize the strategic importance of this region, namely the Russian and British empires. Their power struggle, the Great Game, led to a new generation of pioneers of the Western Regions.

MAPPING AND EXPLORATION IN THE MODERN ERA

The Russians had routes into Xinjiang from the north to Kulja, present-day Yining in the Ili River Valley, which proved a focus of contention between Russia and China for two centuries. The Russians were the first modern European explorers of Xinjiang, with recorded visits by envoys of the Tsar as early as the 1650s, but with a peak of exploration in the 18th and especially the 19th centuries as Siberia and northern Central Asia came under Russian control. Scores of Russian explorers covered the geology, flora and fauna of the Tien Shan and the plateaus of Dzungaria (Junggaria) on the borders of Mongolia. Following the signing of the Sino-Russian treaty in 1851 and the establishment of Russian Turkestan, Russian attention turned to mapmaking as they sought to define the eastern borders of the Russian Empire.

Mapmaking was also on Chinese minds after their establishment of this "New Territory". The Chinese court had commissioned Jesuits to prepare maps of China and they surveyed Xinjiang between 1750–60 with a new survey between 1768–73 following their westward expansion. Xinjiang became a convenient place to exile disgraced officials, a practice which continued into the 20th century. Some exiles put their time there to good use. For example, the Military Governor Songyun (in office 1802–9) used exiles for the compilation of a gazetteer of Xinjiang, including the official Xu Song (exiled 1813). Following an expedition in 1815–16 to collect information, he noted numerous local sites and published several essays and books on the region.

Like the Russians and Chinese, the British also concentrated on mapmaking, a precursor to controlling territory. In 1857 the three Schlaintweit brothers, Prussian scientists but employees of the British Government in India, crossed the Karakoram and travelled through Xinjiang. Despite one brother (Adolph) being executed by the local ruler in Kashgar, the other two returned with at least one map and reports that the Jesuits' positioning of Kashgar and Yarkand was inaccurate. The death of Adolph showed that travel in these parts was not without risk, despite the Treaty Of Tsientsin in 1858 in which Europeans were allowed to travel in China. The British decided to train Indians – "pundits" – to go in disguise as locals carrying compasses in the top of their walking sticks, and recording their steps – and thus the distance travelled – by counting rosary beads. The first such pundit to reach Xinjiang was Mohammed-i-Hamed who, in 1864, made it to Yarkand. As well as his mapping activities he reported back on cities buried by

desert sands. Just a year later William Johnson reached Khotan and Keriya, also telling of buried cities and taking his own surveys. Other British explorers and diplomats followed, including the Forsyth Mission of 1873. In 1886 Dalgeish managed a circumambulation of the Taklamakan and produced a new map, although at great cost: he was murdered on his way back.

Meanwhile the Russians continued their activities, sending a team to Kulja to check the Jesuits' maps in 1859. There were over a dozen Russian expeditions in the following decades, especially when the Russians took control of the Ili Valley between 1871 and 1881. One of the most successful was Przewalski, who made five expeditions between 1872 and 1891, including across the Taklamakan and to the Lop Desert in search of the wild horse which was to bear his name.

Apart from Przewalski, among the most famous – and infamous – of the scores of travellers of these last decades of the 19th century were the geographer Ferdinand von Richtofen, who travelled as far as Lop Nor and who is now best remembered for coining the term "Silk Roads" (*Seidenstrassen*); Ney Elias, who in 1872 travelled from Beijing to Hami and Kulja; Csoma de Koros, searching for the antecedents of his native Hungarian peoples in Yarkand, but who was sidetracked by Tibet and eventually died in Darjeeling on a final attempt to reach Yarkand; the American diplomat in Russia, Eugene Schuyler, who made it to Kulja; Regel who in 1879 reached Turpan, the first recorded visit by a European since the Jesuits; the Grum Grijimalo brothers, who went on four expeditions to Xinjiang, the last in 1888, also reaching Turpan and Lop Nor; and Dutreuil de Rhins and Grenard, mapmakers who in 1890 went along the Southern Silk Road and then across the mountains, reaching Tibet in 1893 where de Rhins was murdered.

By the late 19th century, after Yakub Beg's short-lived independent kingdom was suppressed and Xinjiang was firmly under Chinese control, Russian and British presences were established in Kashgar. The Russians, headed by Petrovsky, were allowed a Consulate, but this status was denied George Macartney for many years in retaliation for the British meeting with Yakub Beg. Both men welcomed travellers: for much of their stay the two diplomats were not on speaking terms and there was an extremely small group of other foreign residents. Travellers provided welcome company and news of home.

The time and circumstances were ripe for archaeologists to follow up the explorer-spies accounts of ruined desert cities. Their appetite had also been whetted by the discovery of manuscripts written in Indian scripts. A few had been brought back by Grenard after his companion's murder; another, a birch bark book found in a site near Kucha, was given to Captain Hamilton Bower, who had originally been on a hunting trip in the Pamirs but had been diverted to track down Dalgeish's murderer. He took the manuscript back to Calcutta, where it was published by the Calcutta-based scholar Rudolph Hoernle. The scholarly world took note, among them a Swedish student of von Richthofen, Sven Hedin.

SVEN HEDIN (1865–1952) – SPANNING THE ARCHAEOLOGICAL ERA

With his scientific training and his desire always to be on the move, the Swede Sven Hedin belongs with the explorer-scientists of the 19th century, but his desultory diggings at the buried cities only mentioned by previous explorers marks Hedin's expeditions as the start of the imperial archaeological age in Central Asia. His final expedition, from 1926–35, sees its end.

As a young scholar, Hedin had already travelled to Central Asia in the 1880s, but decided to return to Europe to pursue the studies necessary for future travels. These were punctuated by a visit to Kashgar in 1890, but it was 1893 before he set out on his first expedition, first exploring the geology and fauna of the Pamirs. In spring 1895 he left Kashgar on an infamous attempt to cross the Taklamakan, recalled replete with rhetorical flourishes in his popular book *Through Asia.* His account made no attempt to deny that this was a badly managed expedition fated by his own ambition and lack of planning. The expedition failed to take enough water for the journey and two of his men and many of his animals died.

Hedin's writing reads like fiction, recounting the adventures of a brave European battling in a faraway, alien land replete with loyal and scheming natives, "prowling wild animals" and "Tangut bandits". This is not surprising given that he admits his own childhood was spent devouring the writings of Fenimore Cooper, Jules Vernes and "the long line of heroes and martyrs of Artic exploration". For a generation accustomed to Rider Haggard's tales of derring-do, his books fired the popular imagination.

This initial encounter with the Taklamakan was not to deter him, and it was his subsequent less dramatic travels around Khotan and Lop Nor that were to excite budding archaeologists. Although not carrying out any systematic digging, his short forays to Dandan Oilik and Karadong near Khotan, and then to the ancient settlements of Loulan yielded Buddhist murals, sculptures and other objects as well as manuscript fragments. His book appeared in 1898 in Swedish and English editions and was soon reprinted.

Hedin's second expedition, co-financed by the King of Sweden and the millionaire Emmanuel Nobel, started in 1899. Surveying was one of Hedin's primary aims. He had already mapped over 6,500 miles on his first expedition, and on returning to the Taklamakan he decided to chart the course of the Tarim River, travelling over many months in a boat before the river froze over. He then returned to more discoveries in the Lop Desert.

Hedin shared with many of his contemporaries a desire to explore Tibet and reach Lhasa. He attempted this on both these expeditions, but without success. He got further on a third visit, between 1905 and 1909, but still failed to reach the capital. It was then many years before he returned to Central Asia. His 1926 visit was at the invitation of Lufthansa Airlines to help map a route from Berlin via Urumqi to Beijing. But the distrust by Chinese scholars and officials of foreign archaeologists forced him to revise his initial plans and to make the expedition a collaborative effort between the Chinese and Swedes.

Hedin was remarkable in managing to transcend the growing distrust that Aurel Stein and others encountered from Chinese scholars and authorities by negotiating this joint Sino-Swedish expedition. It could have been the start of a new era of collaboration, but it was many years before this happened. However, in the interim, one expedition member – Huang Wenbi (1893–1966) – went on to become the foremost archaeologist of the Western Regions.

As well as being a great explorer and mapmaker, Hedin was a born publicist and his racy accounts of his Taklamakan crossing and Lop Nor discoveries were to inspire a generation. The first part of his final expedition was filmed, providing unique early footage of the steppe route out of Beijing to Karakhoto and thence to Urumqi. If Hedin were alive today he would undoubtedly have been fronting television programmes of his travels. As it was, his popularity proved his downfall, as his public support of the German regime led to him being ostracized by many former colleagues and supporters.

Among those inspired by his early travels was a man similar to him in age and physical stature, also a linguist, mapmaker and a brave and intrepid explorer, but completely different in temperament from the flamboyant Hedin. This was the Hungarian Aurel Stein, who came to dominate this brief age of imperial archaeology.

AUREL STEIN –XINJIANG ON THE WORLD MAP

Stein was not the first to explore the ancient cities of Xinjiang, but he deserves credit as the greatest, whether assessed in terms of the numbers and duration of his expeditions, the distances covered, sites explored, finds acquired or his indefatigable documentation. Travelling around Xinjiang today with good transport, sealed roads, guidebooks and maps, shops stocking almost everything, mobile phones and GPSs, it is difficult to imagine the logistic skills, energy and foresight required to organize a three-year expedition when almost all the supplies for this whole period – medicine, food, clothing and shelter – had to be bought in advance and transported on yak and horseback over the high mountain passes of the Hundu Kush, Karakoram and Pamirs from Kashmir. Then they had to be repacked in the orchard of Macartney's residence in Kashgar for transport by camel along the old routes skirting the Taklamakan. Hedin had shown the perils of desert travel. Stein's own understated accounts of his expeditions could not be more different from those of Hedin, and his organization was always meticulous. His own desert crossing was achieved without losing any men or animals, despite some sticky moments.

Stein was neither a young nor a rich man, but he had an excellent education, a breadth of knowledge and was already well travelled. Born in Budapest and educated in Germany, he then spent a period in England, becoming a confirmed

Anglophile. He returned to Hungary for his military service, during which he learned surveying skills. On return to London he sought out the scholars who lived around Earls Court – referred to as "Little India" – and came to the attention of Sir Henry Yule, author of books on Marco Polo and medieval travellers to China and a member of the Indian Council. He recommended Stein for the joint post of Principal at the Oriental College in Lahore and Registrar of Punjab University. Stein arrived in Kashmir in 1888 and it was to remain his home until his death, bar a brief period in Calcutta as Hoernle's successor. Unlike Hedin he had no family wealth or rich sponsors and had to work. In his periods of leave he went on explorations of Indian sites with a colleague, Fred Andrews, and learned from him the basics of photography and, from those travels, a thirst for archaeological discovery. When he read reports of the Taklamakan cities and heard of the manuscript finds, he immediately drew up a proposal for an expedition and applied to his employers for leave. This was finally given and he left Kashmir in 1900 on his first expedition to Xinjiang. Unlike most of the other imperial archaeologists, Stein travelled without any fellow countrymen, his closest companion being a succession of fox terriers, the first named Dash and the remainder following in the line as Dash 2, Dash 3, etc, up to Dash 7.

Stein's initial focus was Khotan where, he believed, he might find an interesting mix of Indian, Iranian and Chinese cultures. He was not to be disappointed. Khotan was a semi-autonomous Buddhist kingdom with an Iranian language and Chinese and Indian foundation myths. It survived until conquered by the Karakhanids in 1006 and left behind rich archaeological remains preserved by the desert sand. These included sites already recorded by Hedin, as well as new ones. From Khotan he moved eastwards to the ruins of the ancient kingdom of Kroraina – or Loulan – which thrived in the 3rd and 4th centuries CE. Niya was on its western border and here he uncovered hundreds of manuscript archives from abandoned houses, telling of tax collections and land disputes among the residents of this once prosperous land. Written in the Gandharan language in Kharoshthi script, they attested to the links with lands farther west. He continued eastward through the territory of ancient Kroraina, including Miran and then, like Hedin, on to the Lop Desert.

Stein was to return to these oasis cities of the southern Taklamakan on all his further three expeditions to China, and his finds changed our understanding of Central Asia. Among these cities he discovered over 30,000 manuscripts and thousands of textiles and artefacts, now in the British Library, the British Museum, the Victoria and Albert Museum, the National Museum of India and museums in Calcutta and Lahore. Yet he is most famous – or infamous – not for his explorations in Xinjiang, but for his acquisition of a cache of manuscripts from a Buddhist cave temple site at Dunhuang in neighbouring Gansu Province. There is no doubting the importance of the Dunhuang manuscripts, but his excavations in Xinjiang, especially along the Southern Silk Road, were equally important and revealed just as many treasures.

Stein's fourth expedition was aborted by the Chinese authorities and his finds confiscated. His photographs remain the only record of the few manuscript finds (some of which were forgeries, by this time becoming more common). But, despite this setback and his age, Stein did not stop his explorations. During the 1930s, well into his 70s, he made four expeditions to Iran and Iraq, and numerous sorties to what is now northern India and Pakistan and more of the Near and Middle East. He finally reached Kabul in his 81st year at the invitation of the American Consul with a plan for a year-long archaeological tour, accompanied

296. MY COMPANIONS AND MYSELF AT ULUGH-MAZAR, IN THE DESERT NORTH OF CHIRA.
From left to right, sitting : Chiang-ssŭ-yeh, myself with ' Dash,' Rai Bahadur Lal Singh.   Standing : Ibrahim Beg, Jasvant Singh, Naik Ram Singh.

Aurel Stein (centre) with his faithful terrier "Dash", pictured with field companions in March 1908 in the southern Taklamakan east of Khotan (Photograph courtesy of the British Library).

by Dash 7. But he caught a chill and was dead within a week. His grave can still be visited at the British Cemetery in Kabul. The fate of Dash 7 is unknown.

RUSSIAN EXPEDITIONS: KLEMENTZ, KOZLOV, OLDENBURG AND DUDIN

The Russians, who had led the way in 19th century exploration, continued to be among the pioneers of Xinjiang archaeology. The report delivered by the Keeper of the St Petersburg Museum of Anthropology and Ethnography, Dmitri Klementz (1848–1914), to the 1898 Congress of Orientalists in Rome created great excitement among European scholars in this distant region. Under the auspices of the Eastern-Siberian Department of the Russian Geographical Society, Klementz and his wife had visited sites around Turpan and collected manuscript fragments, broken-away fragments of wall paintings and other artefacts. He showed these to German scholars

on his way to Rome and they readily agreed to collaborate on a future expedition. However, this did not happen and the two empires sponsored separate expeditions over the next two decades. Both concentrated on the northern Silk Road, especially around Kucha and Turpan. This was to lead to some competition despite agreements to excavate at different sites, and the early promise of collaboration soon faded when both realized the scholarly riches to be found.

However, it was several years before the Russians followed up on Klementz's finds. A member of Przewalski's final two expeditions, Pyotr Kozlov (1863–1935), led two expeditions but it was on his second (1907–9) that he made his greatest find. This was the ruined city of the almost forgotten civilization of the Tanguts or Western Xia, peoples who controlled an empire reaching from present-day northern Tibet to the Mongolian border from the 10th to 13th centuries. Karakhoto – or "Black City" – was on the Etsin-Gol River near the present-day Mongolian border. A stupa outside the city walls yielded thousand of manuscripts and printed documents in Tangut, Tibetan and Chinese along with Buddhist paintings to rival those found at Dunhuang. They now grace galleries in the Hermitage Museum.

Russian explorations along the Silk Road in Xinjiang itself were led by Sergei Oldenburg (1863–1934), director of the Asiatic Museum in St Petersburg. His two archaeological tours (1909–10 and 1914–15), known as the Russian Turkestan expeditions, led him to the northern Silk Road sites around Turpan and then Kizil. Unlike Stein, who preferred to travel without any fellow countrymen and who took his own photographs, the Russians travelled in groups with a dedicated photographer. This was Samuil Dudin, and he is responsible for an extensive and excellent photographic archive. Another traveller under Russian sponsorship, the Finn Baron Mannerheim, was also an excellent photographer, although many believed his travels had more to do with political and economic rather than historical and archaeological gain.

Oldenburg's second expedition led him to Dunhuang, where he acquired hundreds of scrolls and thousands of fragments from the Library Cave, although the Chinese government had sent an official to clear it in 1909–10. The debate about how many forgeries were then being traded on the Silk Road continues to this day.

GERMAN EXPEDITIONS: GRUNWEDEL AND LE COQ COMPETE FOR GLORY

L ike the Russians, the Germans sent teams to the Western Regions over the next two decades, with Albert Grunwedel and Albert von Le Coq alternating as leaders. Very different in background and personality, the two men took varying approaches to Silk Road archaeology. Grunwedel, who had met Klementz, was a scholar and Head of the Indian Section of the Museum of Ethnography in Berlin. He led the first expedition in 1902 after struggling to raise funds. He set out with the Orientalist Georg Huth and a museum technician, Theodor Bartus, a former sailor. The expedition reached its chosen destination, the oasis of Turpan, at the beginning of December 1902. Turpan was to lend its name to all four German expeditions and to the collections comprising their discoveries, even though investigations and excavations were also carried out in neighbouring areas, including around Kucha. Grünwedel was a great believer in documentation; he regarded it

Albert von Le Coq, 1860–1930 (picture courtesy of the Asian Art Museum, National Museums in Berlin).

as his primary task to prepare accurate plans and to keep records of the find sites of the excavated objects. This is invaluable for being able to study the funds in context and be assured of their provenance. Grünwedel was second only to Stein in this but, unfortunately, he was prevented by illness from directing a second expedition and his place was taken by Le Coq, who was far less concerned with full documentation. By this time Huth had died, probably owing in part to the privations of the first expedition.

Le Coq, son of a businessman and trained in London and America, set out with Bartus determined to make his name. He ignored Grunwedel's counsel of caution and worked frantically with Bartus to secure crateloads of spectacular wall paintings from the Bezeklik caves. Grunwedel's recovery and arrival in Kashgar prevented Le Coq and Bartus making a trip to check out the Dunhuang discoveries. Grunwedel took over, but returned to Bezeklik for more finds.

Le Coq then led the fourth and final expedition, finishing just before World War II threw Europe – and scholarly activity there – into turmoil.

It is often recorded that Berlin's wonderful collection of wall paintings from Bezeklik, Kizil and other sites was completely destroyed when the museum was bombed during World War II. In fact, most of the collections had been removed by then for safekeeping to salt mines and was returned to Berlin after the war (although missing quite a few crates, also thought lost until the Hermitage admitted German curators to view them in its storerooms a few years ago!). The paintings destroyed by the bombing were those that were fixed to the walls and could not be removed. The sandbags piled up against them by the desperate curators did little to protect them against the direct hit.

Japan Enters the Fray: The Otani Expeditions

Next to the material acquired by Stein during his expeditions to the Western Regions during this period, one of the largest collections was recovered by members of the Otani expeditions. These three expeditions between 1902 and 1914 were organized and sponsored by the Buddhist Count Otani Kozui, the 22nd Abbot of the Nishi Honganji branch of the Jodo Shinshu sect, the largest religious organization in Japan at the time. Prior to inheriting the abbotship from his father in 1903, the young Otani had spent two years (1900–1902) in England and other parts of Europe with the aim of learning about Western theology and religious practice. He met Hedin and Stein, and decided to send young monks on expeditions to explore the journey of Buddhism along the Silk Road. Others attributed his monks with less spiritual aims: Macartney was distinctly distrustful of their true motives. However, they travelled widely and acquired significant collections of archaeological objects and manuscripts, as well as plant specimens.

Unfortunately the Otani expeditions resulted in no published expedition reports, although the monks' diaries give useful information. Nor did the young monks have any training in archaeology or documentation. More problematic for studying the collection is the fact that, unlike those from all other expeditions, it became part of the private collection of Count Otani. He experienced financial difficulties and much was dispersed. Large parts are now in the National Museum of Korea in Seoul and in China, both at Lushun and the National Library. Smaller parts are scattered at institutions throughout Japan.

Huang Wenbi and Chinese Archaeology in Xinjiang

After the curious and intrepid exiles of the 18th century, there is little in Chinese works on Xinjiang, apart from political reports, until after the time of the European and Japanese explorers. One Chinese explorer who deserves mention was the official Jiang Xiaowan (Jiang Siye, d. 1922), originally from Hunan, who was sent to Xinjiang in 1883. He acted as interpreter, secretary, Chinese teacher and companion on Aurel Stein's second expedition (1906–8).

It was not until 1926 that the Chinese started systematic excavation of the Western Regions. The Sino-Swedish expedition (1926–35) was led by Sven Hedin and Xu Xusheng and sponsored by the German government and the airline Lufthansa. Huang Wenbi (1893–1966), who was one of the first Chinese scholars to make a name in archaeology, was an expedition member. The expedition, the largest of its kind at the time, concentrated on the Lop Nor area. Huang excavated Han Dynasty fortifications, the oases around the Tarim Basin as well as the Turpan Basin. Swedish archaeologist Folke Bergman (1902–1946) discovered the Xiaohe tombs, as well as excavating around the southern Lop Nor, Qiemo farther west, and around Urumqi and Turpan. These excavations yielded finds from the Han to Tang dynasties, as well as pre-Han artefacts.

Huang, a member of the Institute of Archaeology at the Chinese Academy of Sciences, led further archaeological missions to the region from the 1950s and unearthed numerous important artefacts, as well as discovering new sites. The results of these and other Chinese archaeological expeditions in the region were brought together in 1983 by the Archaeological Research Institute of the Xinjiang Academy of Social Sciences in *Xinjiang kaogyu sanshinian* ("Thirty years of Xinjiang Archaeology").

A NEW ERA OF COLLABORATION

From the 1980s onwards, excavation in Xinjiang has been extensive, and has yielded large numbers of artefacts from a range of periods. The past decade has also seen Sino-Japanese and Sino-French archaeological collaborations. As a result of these, along with later gifts and purchases, there are extremely rich collections of manuscripts, artefacts and textiles from Xinjiang in institutions throughout China, but especially in the National Museum, the Xinjiang Uygur Autonomous Region Museum and Institute of Archaeology. Collaboration has also started between holders of the material from the earlier expeditions with the formation of the International Dunhuang Project (see opposite). Images of tens of thousands of artefacts are now freely available online, along with information about the sites and the explorers. Perhaps now these wonderful sites and their artefacts will start to get the scholarly attention they deserve and it will finally be possible to reconstruct a full history of the Silk Road kingdoms of the Western Regions.

An exquisite woollen wall hanging shows a distinctly Hellenistic detail of a warrior's head. Dated to the 3rd–2nd centuries BCE, it was discovered at the Shanpula site near Hotan (image courtesy of the Xinjiang Uygur Autonomous Region Museum).

IDP: THE SILK ROAD ONLINE

Little was known of the remarkable heritage of the Silk Road until explorers and archaeologists of the early 20th century uncovered the ruins of ancient cities in the desert sands, revealing astonishing sculptures, murals and manuscripts. One of the most notable discoveries was the Buddhist cave library near the oasis town of Dunhuang on the edge of the Gobi desert in western China. The cave had been sealed and hidden at the end of the first millennium CE and only rediscovered in 1900. Forty thousand manuscripts, paintings and printed documents on paper and silk were found in the cave itself. Tens of thousands more items were discovered at other Silk Road sites, mainly in Xinjiang. These unique items have fascinating stories to tell of life on this great trade route from 100 BCE to 1400 CE. Yet most were dispersed to institutions worldwide in the early 1900s.

The turmoil of the 20th century meant that conservation and cataloguing were delayed, further hindering access. The International Dunhuang Project (IDP) was formed in 1994 out of a desire by the holding institutions to work together to rectify this by reuniting all these artefacts through the highest quality digital photography, coordinating international teams of conservators, cataloguers and researchers to ensure their preservation and cataloguing, and pushing the limits of new web technologies to make this material accessible to all. This is an immense task, but thanks to IDP's continuing work, the voices of the people who once lived in these ancient cities, worshipped in the cave temples and traded goods along the Silk Road can now be heard.

Over 150,000 images of manuscripts, paintings, textiles and artefacts along with catalogues, translations, historical photographs, site plans and much more are freely available to all on IDP's multilingual website, hosted by IDP's members in Britain, Germany, France, Russia, China, Japan and Korea.

To find out more visit **http://idp.bl.uk** – *"promoting the study and preservation of the archaeological legacy of the Eastern Silk Road through international cooperation."*

fter the 9-11 attacks in the US and the US-led invasion of Afghanistan, there was more talk of separatism and terrorism in Xinjiang. In January 2007 the Chinese Public Security Bureau raided a terrorist training camp belonging to the **East Turkestan Islamic Movement (ETIM)** in the Tashkurgan region of the Pamirs, with 18 terrorists reported killed and 17 captured.

Then, in August 2008 just before the Beijing Olympics, two Uygur men attacked a group of police officers in Kashgar, killing 16. ETIM was blamed for this incident, but in July the following year violent riots broke out in Urumqi. More than 1,000 Uygurs were protesting the death of two Uygurs in southern China a few days earlier, but the protest escalated out of control as ethnic Han Chinese were targeted and attacked. Two days later, hundreds of armed Han Chinese clashed with Uygurs and police in retaliation. Official reports gave a total of 197 people dead and 1,721 injured, though many claimed higher figures. Over 1,000 young Uygur men were subsequently arrested and detained, and by February 2010 26 had been given death sentences. In August 2010 a bomb attack on a group of police and paramilitary guards by a Uygur man in Aksu resulted in seven deaths and 14 injuries, though many of these were in fact Uygurs.

At the time of writing in early 2012 a veneer of calm existed on the streets of Urumqi, but inter-ethnic tensions undoubtedly remain in the region – it would be stretching credibility too far to imagine that a history such as Xinjiang's would enable easy solutions to its many and complex problems. Certainly there exists a general dissatisfaction among Uygurs because of a perceived strategy by Beijing to "swamp" Xinjiang's ethnic cultures under continuing waves of Han immigrants, and it is true that on the whole social interaction between Uygurs and Han Chinese remains rare or superficial, but actual popular support for terrorist groups such as ETIM is minimal. The new face of Xinjiang, with its slick roads, skyscrapers, fast-food chains, Internet cafés and cell phones has animated its entire population – regardless of ethnic group – and heralded its resurgence as a vital and vibrant region of global interest.

[Acknowledgement and thanks go to James A. Millward, whose book on Xinjiang's history – credited on page 45 – was referenced and proved invaluable during the compiling of this History section.]

ADMINISTRATION AND ECONOMY

injiang Uygur Autonomous Region is the largest provincial-level administrative region in China. It is divided into prefecture-, county- and township-level divisions: there are two prefecture-level cities (Urumqi and Karamay); five autonomous prefectures (Ili Kazakh, Bortala Mongol, Changji Hui, Bayingolin Mongol and Kizilsu Kirghiz); and seven prefectures (Turpan, Hami, Aksu, Kashi, Hotan, Tacheng and Altay – the last two under the jurisdiction of the Ili Kazakh Autonomous Region). These prefectures are subdivided into 11 districts, 62 counties, six autonomous counties and 20 county-level cities (four of which – Shihezi, Aral, Tumshuke and Wujiaqu – are outside prefecture jurisdiction, and are directly administered by the Xinjiang

Production and Construction Corps); in turn, the districts and counties are subdivided into more than 1,000 towns, townships, ethnic townships and subdistricts or neighbourhoods.

In autonomous prefectures and counties, a significant percentage of government positions must be filled by those of ethnic extraction, to ensure fair representation for ethnic groups that form the majority in that particular area. In reality, however, Xinjiang is of such economic and political importance to Beijing that the central government keeps an eagle eye on administrative affairs throughout the region, maintaining close control through trusted officials in high-ranking roles everywhere.

The **Xinjiang Production and Construction Corps** (also known as the XPCC or *Bingtuan*) is a unique quasi-military and economic governmental organization that has administrative authority over several medium-sized cities (see above) as well as settlements and farms throughout the region. The XPCC has its own administrative structure, and fulfils all governmental functions (healthcare, education, etc) for areas under its jurisdiction, with almost no interference from the regional government, answering ultimately to Beijing.

ormed in 1954 under orders from Mao Zedong, the XPCC's stated mission was to develop frontier regions, promote economic development, ensure social stability and ethnic harmony, and act as a deterrent to any independence movements. Over the past 58 years it has built farms, towns and cities, and settled millions of Chinese migrants into Xinjiang – primarily in the foothills and lowland areas north of the Tien Shan, where vast tracts of arable land were created from semi-desert through impressive irrigation projects. Under the name **China Xinjian Group** [sic] it wields significant economic clout, with a number of publicly traded subsidiaries. The XPCC and its place in the region's recent history provokes wildly disparate opinion both within Xinjiang and farther afield; by some it is praised as a cornerstone of stability in a previously troubled region and a major contributor to its current prosperity; by others it is seen as no more than a blatant vehicle of colonization and sinicization.

Xinjiang is an economic treasure trove for China, both in terms of agriculture and industry. Its high mountains and glaciers provide abundant water for irrigation of its vast pastures, farmland and oasis agricultural hotspots: in 2005, 51.2 million hectares of natural forage grassland (20 percent of China's total) and 4.1 million hectares of cultivated land (twice as much as the national per capita average) were in use, allowing an astonishing range of agricultural produce. Leading products are cotton, grain, sugar beet, hops, tomato sauce, livestock such as sheep and cattle, and numerous fruits, in particular melons, grapes and pears. In 2005 the total value of agriculture, forestry, animal husbandry and fisheries amounted to more than Rmb83 billion, a 7.4 percent increase on the previous year.

As well as its agricultural wealth, Xinjiang is replete with mineral resources, and most importantly has huge potential oil reserves in both the Tarim and Junggar basins. There are also rich deposits of natural gas, coal, gold, copper, nickel, rare metals, saline minerals and nonmetals. Coal reserves are estimated at 2.19 trillion tons (40 percent of China's total reserves); oil reserves are calculated to be 20.86 billion tons (30 percent of the country's land-based resources); and 10.3

trillion cubic metres of natural gas are reckoned to await exploitation in the region. In 2004 the **West-East Gas Pipeline** came into operation after two years of construction. This 4,000-kilometre-long natural gas pipeline starts in southern Xinjiang's Lunnan Oilfield and runs across the breadth of China to Shanghai, providing power for the Yangtze River Delta region. A **Second West-East Pipeline** began construction in 2008, part of an even longer pipeline: China has funded a huge Central Asia-China natural gas pipeline that extends from Turkmenistan, through Uzbekistan and Kazakhstan to Horgas Port, where it now links with the new West-East pipeline, whose main trunk line initially runs parallel with the first West-East pipe, but then turns south and runs all the way to Guangzhou – with eight branch line offshoots – thereby providing China with an extra, much-needed injection of energy to help fuel its growing needs.

The presence of significant oil deposits in the Karamay region has been known since the mid-20th century, but Sino-Soviet tensions kept Xinjiang's export-import potential unrealized until the 1990s, when the collapse of the Soviet Union and the creation of the new Central Asian CIS states in 1991 suddenly opened the door to border trade once again. Private entrepreneurs and state organizations in Xinjiang were able to export Chinese goods to Central Asian countries, filling the gap left by the collapse of the Soviet economy. Steel, raw materials and technical expertise in turn have been imported since then, and the last 20 years has seen explosive trade growth, especially since the turn of the century. While petrochemicals are inevitably the leading industrial sector, textiles, steel, building materials and food-processing industries are also growing fast – witness the speed of growth in industrial output in Xinjiang, which in 2005 increased by Rmb96.2 billion, 15.6 percent up from the previous year, and in 2010 had resulted in a GDP of RMB543.7 billion, an overall economic growth of 10.5 percent.

Above: "Green corridors" bordering Xinjiang's cross-desert highways are designed to protect it from encroaching sand dunes (Jeremy Tredinnick). Opposite top: Oil derricks in the centre of the Taklamakan (Sun Jiabin). Opposite bottom: Urumqi is now a thoroughly modern city with the requisite Western trappings (Sun Jiabin).

Xinjiang's economic boom has been facilitated by an ongoing commitment to the development of its transportation network. The opening of the **Tarim Highway** in 1995 allowed access to the oilfields of the Taklamakan but was also part of a strategy to upgrade Xinjiang's road system. This has been highly successful, and continues with a number of new projects, such as the 2007 cross-desert highway linking Aksu with Hotan, and the section of Highway 312 from Sayram Lake across the Tien Shan to Horgas Port, Xinjiang's largest and most important trade post, which was reopened to commerce in 1983, and was made a full free-trade zone in recent years. (Streamlined customs procedures at this and other international trading ports have also helped no end in facilitating cross-border trade.)

Xinjiang's completion of its rail line from Urumqi to Alashankou Port to link up with a spur of the Turk-Sib Railway in Kazakhstan in 1990 was hailed as the opening of the **Eurasian Continental Rail Bridge** (a grand notion previously discussed by China and the Soviets but sidelined during their disputes). While it didn't quite live up to its promise, this was nevertheless a pivotal moment in Xinjiang's economic resurgence. In 2000, the Nanjiang Railway to Kashgar was completed, and in June 2011 it was extended south and east along the Southern Silk Road as far as Hotan. The Urumqi-Alashankou route also had an additional electric rail line opened in 2010, linking Jinghe to Yining and Horgas on the Kazakh border, and there are plans for the northern Junggar Basin also to be opened up to rail transport. The quality of Xinjiang's improved transport infrastructure has been an important factor in its economic success.

It is clear that the central government's specific policy to develop its western territory has garnered significant returns, both for Xinjiang and China as a whole. The statistics are impressive: figures for 2010 showed total exports for Xinjiang – predominantly to Central Asia – of just under US$13 billion, with imports standing at more than US$4 billion. In 2010 Xinjiang's GDP was Rmb543.7 billion (US$86 billion) – up from Rmb220 billion (US$28 billion) in 2004. The per capita GDP in 2010 was Rmb25,057, up 9.3 percent from 2009.

But statistics cannot illustrate the grander and more appealing truth of this region's re-emergence on the global economic stage. Once a vital passageway on the trading routes of the Silk Road, Xinjiang has now become the bridgehead for a new Eurasian land link, a fresh and exciting commercial route that instead of silk transports oil, electronic goods and new cultural ideologies between East and West.

Environmental Issues

Looming large over Xinjiang's environmental concerns is the overarching issue of water. This is not a new phenomenon; since the start of human habitation in the Tarim and Junggar basins, a regular supply of water has been paramount in determining where, and in what numbers, mankind could survive and prosper. The fact that Xinjiang encompasses three great mountain ranges, all of which provide huge volumes of water to its lowland and desert areas via numerous rivers fed by rainfall and meltwater from enormous glaciers and snowcaps, has been a key factor in its history. But over the past century, and in particular in the last two decades, Xinjiang's explosive population increase has put its water resources under serious pressure.

Since the mid-19th century Xinjiang's population has grown sixfold, boosted not only by Han migration but by significant growth in non-Han numbers as well, particularly Uygurs. The consequence of this has been a tenfold increase in land under cultivation, with the bingtuan farms in the vanguard as they diverted water from rivers for irrigation and turned semi-desert into farmland. Water is also now being diverted to maintain green corridors protecting the cross-desert highways that allow produce, both agricultural and industrial, to be transported out of the region.

The massive drain on the rivers and groundwater sources such as desert aquifers is most visible in the disappearance of Lop Nor and the Tarim River many hundreds of kilometres upstream of its historical watercourse. To combat this problem, water has been repeatedly redirected from the Konque River and Bosten Lake into the Tarim River, but that in itself can lead to an imbalance in the ecology of the lake. Other large water diversion projects have been undertaken in northern Xinjiang, with channels redirecting water from the Irtysh River to the Karamay region and new farmland up to 300 kilometres to the south.

Desertification is also a major worry in the region. In 2004 alone the Taklamakan Desert expanded by 400 square kilometres; surprisingly, this has happened even as volumes of water in Xinjiang's rivers have been historically higher than normal, due to increased runoff from melting glaciers and snowcaps as the effects of global warming start to become more obvious. It is estimated that two-thirds of each of China's glaciers will have melted away by 2050, and by the 21st century they may have completely disappeared. The consequences of this for Xinjiang's water-needy agrarian economy will be catastrophic – tapping the significant underground water reservoirs known to be beneath Xinjiang's deserts would help, but as these are finite reserves it would only be putting off the inevitable.

Other environmental concerns include a loss of pastureland to cultivation, coupled with an increase in livestock, which has led to serious overgrazing. Forests are on the retreat as a result of excessive cutting and falling water tables, and an increase in the size and ferocity of sandstorms has a damaging effect on agriculture on the desert fringes. In addition, underground fires in coalfields within Xinjiang emit monstrous amounts of carbon dioxide into the atmosphere.

If the previous paragraphs leave you wondering how Xinjiang will survive, remember this: similar or even worse litanies of potential woes can be found in environmental literature on regions throughout the world, from developing countries to First World superpowers. Many problems are global in their scale and require a collective and highly motivated commitment to find solutions. Within Xinjiang in recent years awareness has grown of its many and various environmental challenges. Tree-planting campaigns and efforts to improve the efficiency of water use show that there is a slow but steady increase in understanding of the region's problems. Xinjiang certainly faces testing times in the future – but in this it is hardly alone.

Ethnic Diversity

Xinjiang is home to 12 ethnic nationalities (not including the Han): **Uygur**, **Kazakh**, **Hui**, **Mongol**, **Kyrgyz**, **Uzbek**, **Tajik**, **Xibe**, **Manchu**, **Russian**, **Tatar** and **Daur**. Uygurs and Han Chinese can be found throughout the region (though in general the majority of Uygurs live in the south, while Han communities are mostly concentrated in urban centres), and combined make up more than 85 percent of Xinjiang's total population. The much smaller populations of the other ethnic groups are often centred around specific locations, but Xinjiang's historical legacy as a conduit of trade and culture has meant that today small communities of most ethnic nationalities are scattered across the region.

Uygurs

The largest ethnic group in Xinjiang are the **Uygurs** (also spelt Uyghur, Uighur or Uigur, and pronounced "Weega"), a Turkic-speaking people who number approximately 9.3 million. Followers of Islam, they give their name to the Xinjiang Uygur Autonomous Region but live, for the most part, south of the Tien Shan, in the cities and farmlands of the Tarim Basin oases.

The word *Uygur* means "confederation of nine tribes", and the Uygurs' origins can be traced back to a group of nomadic Turkic tribes, the Gaoche, whose homelands lay south of Lake Baikal and around the upper Yenisey River in present-day Russia and Mongolia. Legend tells that the Turks are descended from the union between a boy and a she-wolf. Enemy soldiers killed the boy, and the she-wolf took to the mountains near Turpan, where she gave birth to 10 boys. One of the wolf-boys married a human woman and produced the forebears of the Turkic tribes. In fact, the Uygurs of Xinjiang today are genetically a mixture of both eastern and western Eurasian lineages, a product of the migration of northern nomadic Turkic tribes into the Tarim Basin, where they mingled with the existing Indo-European peoples already resident there, as well as with migrant Han populations from the east. Because of this hugely varied genetic pool, Uygurs' facial features can range from the aquiline, swarthy look common in Iran and the Middle East to the flatter, moon-faced appearance of the Han Chinese and Mongols. All are authentically Uygur, and most importantly, all are connected by strong cultural tradition.

The traditional square, mud-brick Uygur home is comfortable and quite spacious. Rooms are heated in winter by a brick *kang*, a platform for communal sleeping. It is covered at all times by colourful wool and felt rugs, as are the walls, which have decorated niches for food and utensils. Villagers use their flat roofs for drying melon seeds and grain, and the many families who tend vineyards have an open brick-work drying room for grapes, either on the roof or in nearby fields. In an open courtyard fronted by a colourfully painted porch and frequently shaded by grapevine trellises, or in a deep cellar under the house, families relax during the intense heat of the day.

The majority of non-urban Uygurs tend fields of wheat, maize, vegetables and melons, orchards of apricots, peaches, pears and plums as well as vineyards. Many engage in the sideline production of silk and carpets. In the cities they work as traders, restaurateurs, factory workers and civil servants – unsurprisingly the entrepreneurial spirit runs strong within their blood. All schools and universities today teach solely in the Chinese language, with Uygur language used only in history and "mother tongue" classes specifically for Uygurs (Han Chinese do not attend Uygur-language classes). Where once schools taught Islamic studies, these are now non-existent except at the Islamic University.

Muslim religious festivals are widely celebrated: in particular, the month-long Ramadan fast, which culminates in several days of festivities known as the **Bairam** or "Minor" festival, and **Korban** or "Major" festival. Korban is the celebrated Muslim New Year. In Kashgar, early morning services (6am Xinjiang time) can mean up to 10,000 people flooding the Idkah Mosque, its courtyard and the central square, where spontaneous dancing moves throughout the day to the rhythms of the drummers and horn players perched on the rooftops. Children roam the streets in packs, the youngsters with handfuls of candy and noisemakers, the older ones with water pistols. Families who can afford it buy a sheep to be slaughtered on this festive day, and the whole family gathers for hours of feasting and celebration. This is the **Meshrep** (see "Uygur Music" on page 113), the rambunctious "get-together" or party that involves singing, dancing and music playing, storytelling and games. Any celebration is reason to have a meshrep, be it a festival, wedding, birthday or public holiday.

Weddings are merry occasions with plenty of music and dancing; an imam usually officiates and reads from the Koran. National minorities were exempt from the one-child policy of the Chinese government, but efforts have been made to introduce a limit of two children per family, being born at least three years apart – an extremely unpopular policy. Once polygamous, the Uygurs now conform to Chinese marriage laws but divorce is quite common in the countryside, as is early marriage.

Uygur dress is still quite traditional in the southern cities of Kucha, Kashgar and Hotan, and to a degree in Turpan. Here, you are most likely to see the men wearing three-quarter-length coats or **chapan** (tied at the waist with a sash) over trousers tucked into high leather boots. The women wear full, flowing dresses of beautifully variegated colours, often of homespun **aidelaixi** (Atlas) silk, with heavy brown stockings. The more devout Muslim women still wear veils outside the house, but many women either cover their hair with a scarf or don the colourfully embroidered square **dopa** (cap), which is also worn by men and children.

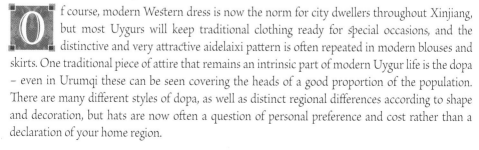 f course, modern Western dress is now the norm for city dwellers throughout Xinjiang, but most Uygurs will keep traditional clothing ready for special occasions, and the distinctive and very attractive aidelaixi pattern is often repeated in modern blouses and skirts. One traditional piece of attire that remains an intrinsic part of modern Uygur life is the dopa – even in Urumqi these can be seen covering the heads of a good proportion of the population. There are many different styles of dopa, as well as distinct regional differences according to shape and decoration, but hats are now often a question of personal preference and cost rather than a declaration of your home region.

Uygur women enjoy wearing jewellery and make-up to match their highly colourful festival dresses; an unusual custom is to use eyeliner to link their eyebrows together in a single line, considered a more alluring appearance. Long hair kept in plaits was once common, and unmarried girls traditionally wore their hair in 10 or more braids.

Great importance is attached to etiquette. Upon entering a home you are expected to rinse your hands three times from water poured by the host from a ewer. In partaking of the *dastarkhan* – a cloth placed on the floor and laid with fruits and nan – you should stand with the family with hands together, palms uppermost, as if holding the Koran, then pass them over your face in a downwards motion, a religious gesture of thanks and blessings. Forms of address are respectful and accord with the individual's status within the family. Older men stroke their beards in the Muslim sign of courtesy. The traditional greeting is *Es Salaam Aleikum* ("May peace be upon you"), the response being *Wa Aleikum Es Salaam* ("And upon you").

Uygurs have a rich tradition of storytelling, music and dance (see page 113). Their dancing is elegant, full of twirling and delicate hand movements. Their folk songs include themes of exile, poverty and love as well as humour. A popular folk hero, about whom numerous stories are invented, is the character Effendi (a Turkish creation) and his donkey. The tales are satirical and amusing; for instance one has Effendi setting out on his donkey to talk with Chairman Mao.

Manuscripts and treatises on Uygur medicine, which date back to at least the eighth century, include over 400 commonly used herbs and more than 200 prescriptions. A centre for Uygur medicine in Kashgar has been particularly successful in the treatment of skin diseases, especially vitiligo, known as "the white wind sickness". One treatment for this condition is a mixture of sugar, raisins, bird blood, mutton, grapes and Chinese medicine. Indeed, in the 10th century Chinese medicine benefited hugely from an exchange of medical knowledge and practices with the Uygur kingdoms of the Tarim Basin.

Kazakhs

Like the Uygurs, Kazakhs are the descendants of a number of different ethnic groups, including the early Indo-Iranian Scythians, the Wusun and later tribes of Turkic and Mongol stock such as the Kypchaks, Kara-Khitans and Naimans. They came into being as a distinct nationality under the name "Kazakh", meaning "free" or "independent", around the 16th century. Nomadic pastoralists, they

Opposite top: Old and new forms of transport meet in Hotan on the Southern Silk Road (Jeremy Tredinnick). Opposite bottom: At a traditional Uygur wedding the bride is carried to her new home in a carpet. Above: Some Uygurs however go for a more modern ceremony (Guo Xiao Dong x2).

occupied the vast grasslands of Central Asia, but when Russia and China came to agreement on their mutual border, a large number of Kazakhs found themselves officially part of the Chinese nation.

Today, around 1.5 million Kazakhs call Xinjiang home, the majority living in the Junggar Basin and its surrounding mountain ranges, as well as in the Ili Valley. Livestock herding is still their main livelihood, and although there are reasonable numbers of Kazakh urban dwellers in cities such as Urumqi, Yining, Altay City and Tacheng, and a few settled farmers in the Altai foothills and Ili Valley, their cultural connection to the nomadic life keeps many of them roving between high mountain summer pastures and lowland winter settlements.

Horses are intrinsic to the Kazakh way of life, and one of their most important cultural symbols. All Kazakhs are at home on horseback, often learning to ride before they can walk; on their steeds they protect and move their herds of sheep, cattle, horses and camels from one pasture to another. The Kazakh's traditional home is the yurt – a portable lattice-framed circular tent covered by thick felt, able to be assembled or packed away in a surprisingly short time, but sturdy and offering excellent shelter from the excessive heat and cold of the steppe and mountain environments. Inside, a yurt's floor and walls are decorated with hand-woven rugs in bold, colourful geometric designs or using floral motifs influenced by the natural beauty of the surrounding landscape.

Kazakhs are extremely hospitable people and will often invite visitors into their homes; they are great meat eaters, horsemeat being a delicacy, with mutton the main staple. Dairy products such as hard cheeses are popular, and *kumis* – fermented mare's milk (mildly narcotic) – is the traditional drink of choice. Music and song is another important part of Kazakh identity, traditionally used to transmit cultural and religious beliefs between communities (see page 115). It is not uncommon to happen upon a shepherd on horseback with a *dombra* (lute) singing happily as he minds his herd. At communal gatherings, Kazakhs dress in all their finery – beautifully embroidered, flared dresses and hats with bird feathers on the crown for the women, regal open-fronted robes (also embroidered in bold patterns) and *kalpaks*, black-and-white felt caps with upturned brims, for the men. As well as feasting, music and dancing, they enthusiastically participate in sports and games such as *kokpar* (known farther south as *buzkashi*), the riotous rugby-like horseback competition using a goat or sheep carcass instead of a ball; wrestling – both on horseback and on the ground; picking a silver coin or weighted handkerchief from the ground whilst at full gallop; and *kyz-kuu*, or "catch the girl", where a young man on horseback tries to catch and kiss a similarly mounted girl within a set distance – failing this, she is entitled to whip him for the return leg, to much laughter from onlookers. Eagle hunting and falconry are also very popular – a tradition shared with the Kyrgyz and Tajiks.

HUI

The Hui are ethnically Chinese Muslims of uncertain origin – they probably grew as a distinct ethnic nationality from a combination of Persian traders, Mongol and Turkic immigrants who settled in China, intermarried and assimilated into the surrounding culture over time. Known historically as the **Hui-he**, and during the Qing Dynasty as **Tungans** (Dungans), they are most numerous in the provinces of Ningxia and Gansu, but also a significant presence in Xinjiang, where around 900,000 now live, mostly in the Changji Hui Autonomous Prefecture, Turpan, Shanshan and Yanji Hui Autonomous counties, and the cities of Urumqi and Yining.

In many ways similar to Han Chinese, the Hui differ in a few noticeable ways: Hui men usually wear small white caps, and the women cover their heads and shoulders with plain scarves tied around the neck. As Muslims, the Hui do not eat pork, but they have developed a number of distinctive dishes to compensate, from cooked sheep and cow entrails, fried sheep's tail, bean jelly and fried cakes (*youxiang*) to the famous hand-pulled noodles that can be used in delicious hot soups (lamb and tomato noodle soup is a favourite) or fried, ring-shaped noodles called *sanzi*. Sweet foods are popular, and honey or brown sugar is often added to a savoury dish to change its flavour.

The Hui are conservative in their day-to-day living, follow the precepts of Islam carefully and celebrate Islamic festivals with fervour. They are family-oriented – a visitor will be greeted by the entire family, served fragrant tea, fruits and sweets, and treated with great respect – and renowned for their business sense. In Xinjiang, many Hui work in the catering and handicrafts industries, and of course in a range of trading businesses.

Mongols

 injiang's Mongol population of approximately 173,000 is mainly located in the Bortala Mongolian Autonomous Prefecture, the Bayinguolin Mongolian Autonomous Prefecture, and in the Hoboksar Mongol Autonomous County near Tacheng. They are all descended from the Oirat Mongols who migrated from western Mongolia in the 15–16th centuries, but while some represent the remnants of the Junggar tribes who were crushed by the Qing armies, the majority are descendants of the Torgut Mongols who returned to China-controlled territory from the Volga River region of Russia during the 18th century (see page 249).

Like the Kazakhs, Mongols are nomadic pastoralists, and the similarity between these two ethnic groups' lifestyles and environments means that their cultures also follow comparable, if not identical, patterns. Mongol food is broadly the same as that of Kazakhs' – mutton, beef, dairy products and bread making up the bulk of their diet; fermented mare's milk is drunk with gusto, but called *airag* rather than kumis; and the Mongolian *ger* is almost identical to the Kazakh yurt. Music and poetry is also an important aspect of Mongol culture – like Kazakh music, it reflects the natural world of the mountains and grasslands in which they live, and often has a heroic warrior fighting evil as a central theme, such as in the folk epic "Jianger". Important events such as the **Nadaam** (in July or August) and **Nawruz** (Spring) festivals are celebrated with huge gatherings during which games, poetry recitals, music and dancing take place, and competitions in horseback and standing archery, horse racing and wrestling are contested fiercely.

Clockwise from top left: Exuberant dancing at a meshrep, or Uygur party (Bao Di); a young Mongol woman in festival finery; a Kazakh boy at ease on his horse (Sun Jiabin x2); a colourfully painted traditional Uygur cradle (Peter Hibbard); members of a Kazakh aul congregate in a yurt; the meticulous crafting of the dopa, an intrinsic element of Uygur clothing (A Gai/Odyssey x2); a Uygur girl dressed in typically colourful clothing (Sun Jiabin).

Mongols do differ from their Turkic neighbours in some fundamental ways, however: they have their own distinct written and spoken language, and they practise a form of Tibetan Buddhism that is heavily influenced by the shamanistic beliefs that preceded it (look for the *obo* stone cairns hung with silk scarves printed with prayers at mountain passes in Mongol areas within the central Tien Shan). Mongol clothing often utilizes silk in its festival finery, with red and blue the most common colours, decorated by either ethnic swirling patterns or intricate circular designs. Headwear is varied, with girls often wearing scarves or embroidered bandana-style coverings, while men's hats can have a tall central spike reminiscent of a mini stupa.

KYRGYZ (KIRGHIZ)

The Kyrgyz number around 172,000 in Xinjiang, and are located primarily in the southwestern Kizilsu Kirghiz Autonomous Prefecture, although small numbers also make their home in the high border range of Aksu Prefecture, and the Tekes and Zhaosu counties south of the Ili Valley. A mountain-loving people, the Kyrgyz originated in the upper Yenisey River region of Russia/Mongolia, but as a powerful tribe moved southwest and destroyed the Uygur Empire in the ninth century. They in turn were driven west into modern-day Kazakhstan, where they mingled with tribes in the northern foothills of the Tien Shan, before gradually moving south into the heart of the Heavenly Mountains and Pamirs, settling among the mighty peaks and valleys, and converting to Islam.

There are close historical, cultural, linguistic and religious connections between the Kyrgyz and Kazakhs – indeed, for a long time imperial Russia did not distinguish between the two, and termed both groups "Kyrgyz". Because of these affinities, their customs, beliefs, eating habits and clothing are very similar. However, the geographic distinction of their homelands and a strong sense of tribal unity clearly defines the Kyrgyz identity, perfectly encapsulated in the epic poem "Manas", sections of which are recited at festivals and other celebrations; like comparable Kazakh gatherings, these are excuses for much eating, music, singing and dancing, and sports and games such as horseback wrestling and swinging on high wooden swings.

The Kyrgyz treat guests with great respect and ceremony. An important visitor will be honoured with a feast featuring a boiled sheep, and will be served the sheep's head (as per Kazakh custom) as a sign of highest respect. Kyrgyz felts are exquisitely embroidered and of high quality, and their traditional clothing at festivals is stunning; normal headwear for women is a colourful headscarf but festival hats are fur-lined, pointed and topped with balls of bird feathers. Milk tea with added salt is a popular Kyrgyz drink.

TAJIKS

The Tajiks occupy the high-altitude plains and valleys of the Pamirs in Xinjiang's far southwest, their population of 44,000 mainly concentrated in the Tashkurgan Tajik Autonomous County, although small communities live in southern oasis towns such as Shache, Zepu, Yecheng and Pishan. Muslim and semi-nomadic, they have much in common with the nomadic cultures of the Kyrygz, Kazakh and Mongol ethnic groups, but the Tajiks come from Persian stock, and speak an entirely separate language of Indo-Iranian origin (though they write using the Uygur script).

Historically the Tashkurgan region was home to the Sarikol kingdom, and in fact the people who live here belong to a Tajik sub-group whose dialect is distinct from the language spoken in Tajikistan. Living at heights of 3,000 metres or more, theirs is a semi-nomadic lifestyle: they plant barley, wheat and other cold-resistant crops in the spring, move their herds of horses, sheep and yaks to high summer pastures and return in autumn to harvest their fields, ready for the long, cold winter. Tajik homes are roughly square, flat-roofed, low-ceilinged, and constructed from stone and wood (yurts or mud huts are used in the summer pastures), with a clay oven in the main room.

Tajik women wear distinctive "pillbox" hats usually covered by a white scarf, colourful dresses, jackets and skirts (all intricately embroidered) and smart leather boots; men use thick sheepskin hats for protection from the elements, with long sheepskin jackets belted at the waist, and equally practical high leather boots. A love of colour (especially red) makes Tajik festivals kaleidoscopic affairs, in particular weddings, which can last for three days of almost non-stop dancing and celebration. The most famous Tajik dance is a simulation of the flight of the eagle – their national symbol – with arms outstretched, graceful movements and twirling. A unique instrument is used, a short flute made from the wing bone of an eagle, called a *nay*.

s well as the horse-related sports common to all Central Asian peoples, Tajiks hold yak races and hunt with birds of prey. Tajik greetings are interesting and carefully observed: two women will kiss each other lightly on the lips, two men will clasp hands and simultaneously kiss the back of the other's hand, while a woman will greet a man by lowering her head to kiss his palm, while he blesses her by lightly touching her head. Etiquette is strictly observed – a visitor to a Tajik home should always remember not to remove their hat, not to tread on any food or salt, and to remain at the table until the food has been cleared away.

Uzbeks

Xinjiang's Uzbek population of around 15,000 is scattered throughout the region, mainly to the north and south of the Tien Shan, some practising agriculture but the majority city dwellers engaging in trade and handicraft businesses – Uzbeks are renowned for their skill with embroidery and needlework. A Turkic-speaking, Muslim people, it is difficult for visitors to distinguish Uzbeks from the more numerous Uygurs, since they share so many cultural, religious and social beliefs. Uzbeks trim their caps, collars, sleeves and hems with intricate embroidery, and their rich cuisine has influenced Xinjiang food heavily, in particular the many different types of *plov*, known in the region as *poluo*. On special occasions a dish called *narren* – mincemeat cooked with pepper, buttermilk and broth – is eaten with tasty nan bread, and the ravioli-like *manty*, filled either with meat, potatoes and onions or pumpkin, is also very popular.

Xinjiang's ethnic Russians often retain their own distinct customs (Ma Zhong Yi).

RUSSIANS

Approximately 11,200 ethnic Russians reside in Xinjiang today, predominantly living in the northern cities of Yining, Tacheng, Altay City and Urumqi, though in rural areas they also farm, and practise market gardening and bee-keeping. Russians began migrating into Chinese-controlled territory in large numbers during the 18th century, fleeing the strictures of Tsarist Russia, but more arrived at the end of the 19th century, and after the October Revolution of 1917 many White Russians escaped the Bolsheviks by crossing into Xinjiang.

Chinese Russians are mostly followers of the **Orthodox Eastern Church**, and thus celebrate the traditional festivals of Easter and Christmas. Their music and dance is different to many of Xinjiang's other ethnic groups – tap dancing is popular, and guitars, balalaikas and accordions are used to make lively music. Traditionally they speak Russian – a Slavic language – and use Cyrillic script, but in official and business activities they all speak putonghua and use Chinese characters. Indeed, there has been so much intermarriage with Han Chinese over the years that many ethnic Russians now use Han names.

Some cultural traditions remain, such as eating three meals a day, a love of soup, bread and cakes, and beef and vegetable stews, accompanied by cucumbers and tomatoes. Russian men also have a penchant for wine, and many make their own at home. Yellow is the colour of betrayal, so nothing yellow is given as a gift – blue represents friendship and is therefore the favoured colour.

TATARS

The Tatars (Tartars) are a Turkic-speaking people of confused origin. Most historians agree that they can be traced back to the Ta-ta tribe of the Lake Baikal region, who joined and mingled with the Mongol Golden Horde of Genghis Khan, spreading across the Eurasian steppe as far as the Volga and Crimean regions. Land grabbing and persecution in 19-century Tsarist Russia forced many to flee, and the early 20th century saw many Tatar merchants and intellectuals migrating across China's borders and settling in the towns and cities of northern Xinjiang.

Tatar Women sing at a local event (Sun Jiabin).

Today around 4,700 Tatars live in Xinjiang; they mainly practise Islam and are comparatively well educated, occupying significant positions in trade and industry. As a small minority they have mixed freely with Uygurs and Kazakhs, and most speak either of these languages in preference to their own. Traditionally Tatar men wear embroidered white shirts and caps under black waistcoats or robes, while the women wear pleated skirts and a small cap with a veil covering the back of the head and neck. This clothing is still worn on special occasions, but Western dress is the common apparel these days.

Tatars celebrate the **Saban (Plough) Festival** each spring, as well as all the Islamic festivals; their music is lively and cheerful, made using accordions, two-stringed violins, the *kunie* (a wooden flute) and *kebisie* (a type of harmonica), with themes harking back to their steppe origins. Tatar pastries are very popular throughout Xinjiang, including the *gubaidiai* and the *yitebailixi*, whose crisp crusts contain delicious soft centres of cheese, dried apricots and rice, and pumpkin, meat and rice, respectively. Tatars are known for their orderliness and cleanliness – their houses are quiet havens, and their dining rooms and kitchens kept spotless.

MANCHUS

Xinjiang's Manchu population are descendants of the Qing Dynasty's "eight banner battalions", large groups of soldiers (and subsequently their families) transferred from northeast China to populate and safeguard the region. Today, there are approximately 24,000 Manchus concentrated in Urumqi and the Ili, Changji and Hami areas. Prior to the 1911 revolution, Manchu men wore their hair in a queue and dressed in short jackets over long belted gowns, while women coiled their hair high on the heads and wore the classic *cheongsam* and small, embroidered shoes. However, after the revolution the queue was abolished and cheongsams became the standard Han dress, and as the 20th century progressed Manchu clothing and customs became virtually the same as the Han Chinese.

Manchus are predominantly farmers, and like the Han celebrate the Spring and Mid-Autumn festivals, but the **Banjin Festival** is a specifically Manchu tradition, celebrating their official self-naming as "Manchu" in 1635. It falls on the 13th day of the 10th lunar month, and traditional clothing (minus the queues) is still worn – the women look spectacular in gorgeous silk cheongsams and high, flat headdresses decorated with flower motifs. Manchu food is based around wheat and millet dishes, with mutton the favoured meat. Dumplings, steamed buns and candied rice "cookies" are popular.

Daur

ike the Manchus, the Daur were brought to Xinjiang as part of the Qing's "eight banner" system in the 18th century. A tribe of Mongol origin from modern-day Heilongjiang Province, they were stationed first in the Ili Valley on the Horgas River, then relocated to the Tacheng area, where they are centred today, and number around 6,700. Although they retain their own language, the Daur also speak any of the prevailing necessary languages required, from putonghua to Kazakh, Mongolian or Uygur. They are predominantly farmers and livestock breeders, and dress in similar fashion to Mongols, wearing long, vividly coloured and embroidered robes, belted for men.

Millet or buckwheat noodles form the Daurs' staple food, together with dairy products and plenty of meat, including mutton, beef, fish and chicken. They are renowned for their bravery, and enjoy riding, shooting and wrestling sports, as well as a type of field hockey. The Daur religion is based on shamanism, while some are Tibetan Buddhists.

Xibe

Numbering 42,000, the Xibe (historically known as the Sibo) are an ethnic group originating from central Manchuria in northeast China (near present-day Shenyang). Distinguished from the Manchus by their own distinct dialect, Xinjiang's Xibe population have preserved their native tongue and many traditional customs, while the Xibe who remained in their homeland have lost them and become fully assimilated into Han Chinese culture.

Like the Daur and Manchu groups, the Xibe were translocated by Emperor Qianlong as a reinforcement measure to guard against insurrection or incursions in remote Xinjiang during the mid–late 18th century. They were settled in the Ili Valley, where they consolidated their position and made a home for themselves in the Qapqal region of the Ili River. Today, the majority still live here, mainly in Qapqal Xibe Autonomous County and to a lesser extent Huocheng and Gongliu counties. Their religion is a mixture of shamanism, Tibetan Buddhism and ancestor worship.

Xibe traditional dress is similar in many ways to that of the Manchus, but is only worn during festivals by the older folk – Western-style clothing is now the usual attire, as with the majority of Xinjiang's ethnic groups, especially in or near major cities. The Xibe are fond of pickled vegetables, milk and butter tea, and a traditional dish made from an entire sheep, all its parts chopped up and made into a soup. As well as the Spring Festival and other regional celebrations, the Xibe have their own special event, the "**April 18th Festival**", commemorating the end of their long journey to Xinjiang, and the founding of their new home.

Festival sports and games follow the usual pattern, with horseracing, wrestling and much singing and dancing going on; however, the Xibe are particularly famous for their skill as archers – they are regularly represented at national and international events. They are also renowned for their language skills, often mastering all the major ethnic languages in Xinjiang and working in high-level positions in business and government.

SPORTS AND GAMES

 injiang's array of ethnicities has resulted in a wide range of exciting and fascinating ethnic sports and games played throughout the region. Some cross ethnic boundaries and are played by many different groups: the horseback team sport involving violent "tussling" for a sheep or goat carcass known variously as **kokpar** or **buzkashi** is enjoyed by Kazakhs, Kyrgyz, Tajiks and even Uygurs; **wrestling** is hugely popular with Mongols, Kazakhs, Xibe and other groups; **horse races**, or *baiga*, are intrinsic to all the nomadic cultures, as is **archery**, both standing and from horseback.

Hunting with birds of prey, including eagles, hawks and falcons is practised from the Altai to the Kunlun mountains; the Kyrgyz, Tajiks and Kazakhs use eagles to hunt large animals in the mountains such as wolves, wild sheep and foxes, and falcons for birds and smaller prey like hares, but the Uygurs of the southern Tarim oases also enjoy **falconry**. Racing of various domestic animals is popular, from **camel and donkey races** in the desert oases communities to **yak racing** in the high mountain plateaus. Traditionally Uygurs enjoy pitting animals in contest against one another; at festival times **ram fights** are watched enthusiastically, and **cock fighting** is also practised.

Swinging games are a favourite pastime for many ethnic groups; Kazakhs and Kyrgyz use logs suspended between double A-frame structures, on which two or more girls stand and swing back and forth until the log is almost vertical, inducing squeals of excitement. Another form of this game caters to more participants, whereby a thick central pole is raised and rooted firmly in the ground, and multiple ropes tied to a revolving wheel at its apex; participants spin around the pole holding a rope and swinging as high as possible as the collective speed increases.

The most famous traditional Uygur festival game, however, is the *Dawaz* (tightrope walking), a high-wire act involving feats of heart-stopping derring-do, with both children and adults walking ropes strung between poles at heights of 10–15 metres above ground – there is no safety net – whilst performing various balancing tricks with cups, steel hoops, etc. The Dawaz is performed in front of

major sites such as the Emin Minaret in Turpan, the Idkah Mosque in Kashgar – where there is an annual Dawaz Festival – and from one rooftop to another across the International Grand Bazaar square in Urumqi. The most famous Dawaz performer is **Adili Wuxor**, a Uygur who crossed the Yangtze River on a highwire in record time in 1997.

MUSICAL TRADITIONS

Xinjiang's numerous ethnic groups boast rich and varied musical traditions that, in some cases, are traceable far back into recorded history. During the Western Han Dynasty (206 BCE–8 CE) the music of Yutian (the ancient name for the modern-day Hotan region) had already reached its capital, Chang'an, and by the Northern and Southern Dynasties (386–589 CE) the music of the famed kingdom of Qiuci (Kucha) had become popular in the east. During the artistic "golden age" of the Tang Dynasty (618–907), distinct music types from Qiuci, Gaochang and Shule influenced the development of music and dance at the Chang'an court – and even as far as Japan and Korea. The Uygur music of today claims inheritance from those ancient traditions.

UYGUR MUSIC   —by Fausto Caceres (http://compound-eye.org/rogc)

Xinjiang's musical landscape is as fertile as its oases and mountain pastures. While influenced by Central Asian sounds recognizable across a huge area of central Eurasia, travel to different areas in Xinjiang and you will notice an obvious variety of regional Uygur styles. The complexity of cultural histories woven into its many communities has resulted in a diverse musical spectrum worthy of note; one could say that listening to the range of styles that have been cultivated in the different oases are in and of themselves a small historical tour of ancient traditions, introduced and influenced by connection through routes of trade while evolving regional characteristics by geographical isolation. Throughout the vastness of Xinjiang, unique stylistic qualities are apparent in the regions of Kashgar, Hotan, Aksu, Hami (Kumul) and Ili.

The most prestigious and celebrated genre of Uygur music is the **Muqam** (Mukam), the Uygur art form that was declared a "masterpiece of the oral and intangible heritage of humanity" by UNESCO in 2005. There are essentially four main regional Muqam styles, namely the Twelve Muqam, Dolan Muqam, Turpan Muqam and Qumul Muqam. The most renowned of these is the

Above: Music has been an important element in cultural tradition among Uygurs – and all Xinjiang's other ethnic groups – for millennia (Sun Jiabin). Opposite top: A Uygur acrobat performs the Dawaz in front of the Emin Minaret in Turpan during a festival (Yan Xian). Opposite bottom: A game of kokpur or buzkashi in full flow (Sun Jiabin).

Twelve Muqam (*On Ikki Muqam*), a complex suite of 12 widely dynamic sections regarded as the classical music of the Uygurs. Each intricate symphonic section varies wildly within the muqam.

In the mid-16th century, Amanisa Han (Aman Isa Khan, 1526–1560), an imperial concubine of the Yarkand Khanate who was also an accomplished musician and poetess, worked to collate and preserve the rich resources of Uygur folk music that were then scattered among Uygur-populated areas to the north and south of the Tien Shan mountains. Aided by other musicians, she ultimately arranged and standardized 12 lavish, entertaining compositions from existing music, now collectively known as the Twelve Muqam; each consists of a *Muqäddimä* (introduction), a suite of elaborate named pieces, the *Chong näghmä* (great music), *Dastan* (narrative songs), and the faster section of the muqam which includes dancing – the *Meshrep* (*Mäshräp*, or "gathering"). As this collection in essence unified groups of people spread over an immense territory, to many it has come to be thought of as an anchor of Uygur identity.

However, other distinct musical traditions – also referred to as muqam – exist in Xinjiang, such as the music played by the Dolan Uygurs in the region between Aksu and Kashgar. While the Twelve Muqam are regarded as Uygur classical music, music of the Dolan region can be thought of as Uygur "soul-rock" with its wild, wailing falsettos and heavy rhythms. Dolan instruments are also quite distinct although they generally share the same names as the most popular Uygur instruments.

The most common Uygur instruments are:

- **Dutar** – a long-necked, two-stringed (usually nylon) lute with a bulbous body. The dutar is used in folk songs and in the muqam. It is also the most common instrument found in Uygur homes.
- **Rawap** – a plucked, metal-stringed lute with a small, bowl-shaped body covered with skin, and distinctive ornamental horns.
- **Dap** – a frame drum lined with metal rings covered with donkey skin. It plays a key role in folk songs and instrumental muqam music.
- **Tämbür** – a long-necked lute similar in general shape to the dutar but notably thinner and with five metal strings.
- **Sunay** – a small, double-reed wind instrument with a wooden body, finger holes and metal bell.
- **Naghra** – iron kettledrums covered in skin and played with a pair of wooden sticks. Sunay and naghra are usually played together in groups. They can be found signalling wedding processions or in cities signalling the opening of new businesses.

Other instruments include the *chang* (hammered dulcimer), **satar** (long, bowed lute) and **sapaya** (paired percussive sticks with metal rings – often played by beggars and Sufis).

In addition to muqam and traditional folk styles, Xinjiang is home to its own vibrant pop music scene, the most popular music being contemporary adaptations of traditional folk songs. Songs most often infuse traditional as well as modern instrumentation for a sound that remains very much culturally tied to the region and its indigenous peoples.

O n arriving in Xinjiang for the first time, an initial sampling of Uygur music can be found – and heard – on Sheng Li Lu just south of the International Grand Bazaar in Urumqi, where the cacophony of sound creates a virtual walking mix-tape of some of the most infectious local pop music you will hear anywhere in China. Along this strip a dozen or more CD shops are lined up within a block; indeed, if you have an ear for Uygur music recordings – both classical muqam, folk and pop, or recordings by artists of the Central Asian countries to the west and south – this is where you can begin sampling CDs.

The same and more will be found as you head to the cities of the south, and you may very well encounter impromptu outdoor performances in parks and bazaars, or meshreps under shaded grape trellises during the summer months. Popular performers of folk and pop of recent years include: Abdullah Abdurehim; Momenjan; Abdurehim Heyt (king of the dutar); Shahridzoda; Abdukadir Yar Eli; Arzigul Tursun; and Dilnaz (a Uygur performer from Kazakhstan), to name but a handful.

It is worth paying attention to the richness of Uygur music, this "music farthest from the sea". So tightly woven is musical tradition within the tapestry of Uygur culture – and indeed that of all Xinjiang's ethnic groups – that it may just serve the listener as a gateway to a deeper understanding of the spirit of the region.

AN ETHNIC MUSICAL KALEIDOSCOPE

While you are most likely to be exposed to Uygur music during your travels, each of Xinjiang's other ethnic groups have their own distinct musical traditions, using similar styles and instrumentation but still recognizably their own.

Kazakh music is based around their nomadic culture, and is very similar to both Kyrgyz and Uzbek folk music forms (unsurprising, given the close ethnic backgrounds of these three groups). It is said that, "a good horse and a song are the wings of the Kazakhs". Travelling bards known as *akyns* move around between communities, singing either unaccompanied or with a long-necked string instrument such as the *dombra* or *kobyz* (lute-like instruments, the former plucked, the latter played with a bow); they spread songs telling of legend and myth, of folk tales, religious beliefs and amusing everyday activity, simple, gracefully melodious and narrative in nature with frequent changes of rhythm. The lack of a written language in Kazakh and Kyrgyz history was compensated for by the development of music and poetry that could travel with and between the herds and mobile communities of the nomads. During festivals and get-togethers contests known as *aytis* take place between akyns, who battle through song, improvising witty lyrics that can be social or political, with the audience deciding the winner.

Kyrgyz travelling musicians are called *manaschi*, and their folk music is characterized by the use of long, sustained pitches, rich harmonious chords blended with sprightly tunes and free rhythms, with Russian elements also distinguishable. Their most popular musical instrument is the *komuz*, a plucked three-string instrument, and the musical subject matter is typically heroic sagas, in

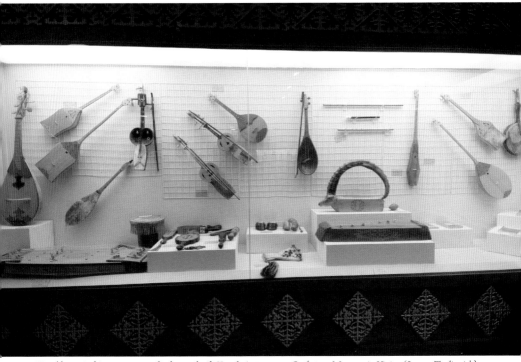

Kazakh musical instruments on display at the Ili Kazak Autonomous Prefecture Museum in Yining (Jeremy Tredinnick).

particular the Manas epic (20 times longer than Homer's *Odyssey*), the patriotic tale of the warrior Manas and his descendants, who fought the Kara-Khitan and Kalmyk nations. Other Kyrgyz folk instruments include the *kyl kiak*, a two-stringed bow instrument, the *sybyzgy*, a side-blown flute, and the *temir ooz komuz* (mouth komuz), also known as the jew's harp in some countries.

The music of the **Mongols** follows either the "long song" or "short song" format, with the former used for epic song and using changing rhythms that can be a strict beat structure or freeform, depending on the singer, and the latter quick and lively, often humorous and dealing with the everyday world – herding, man's connection with nature and the animal kingdom, horses, women, etc. The classic Mongol instrument is the *moriin khuur* or *matouqin*, a two-stringed fiddle with a trapezoidal soundbox, played with a bow. The three-stringed, lute-like *shanz* is also used, as well as a table zither with 14 strings called a *yootchin*.

A highly distinctive and now quite famous musical treat can be seen in Xinjiang near Kanas Lake, where a few of the **Tuva** people still practise **throat singing**, a diphonic form of song where the singer can produce two or even three separate tones at the same time. Tuvans also use the *limbe*, a long flute with a rich, deep tonal quality.

The folksongs of the **Tajiks** in the high mountains of the Pamirs are centred around the harsh but beautiful natural world that surrounds them. The melodic tunes are often sung in chorus, accompanied by hand drums, a rawap and the unique Tajik *nay*, a short flute made from the wing bone of an eagle.

The **Xibe**, **Manchu** and **Daur** peoples, whose origins lie in far-off northeastern China, have preserved their own ancient folk music. To the untrained ear their songs may sound similar to that of the Mongols, but the melodies and song structures of each are unique. Sadly, their small populations and ongoing integration into a homogenized mainstream Xinjiang society mean the chances for visitors to encounter them are small.

The music of the **Tatars** and **Russians** is lyrical, with easy rhythms, usually played using accordions, mandolins and guitars. Tatar folksongs like "The White Swan Shakes its Wings" are melodic and popular throughout northern Xinjiang in particular. **Uzbek** classical music is known as *shashmaqam*, and is similar to the Uygur muqam, but modern Uzbek folk and rock music, using elements and instruments of the past but infused with Western forms, are extremely popular throughout Xinjiang today.

LITERATURE

The early communities and nomadic tribes that populated Xinjiang in ancient times relied on oral traditions such as storytelling, poetry and song to express and pass down their cultural, religious and social heritage. The Sogdians who effectively "managed" the commerce along the trade routes through Xinjiang used a written language to detail their business but also their religious practice. Most of the early Uygur literary works were translations of Buddhist and Manichaean religious texts, such as the *Sutras of the Golden Lustre*, translated in the 10th century from Sanskrit into the Uygur script that was itself derived from Sogdian. However, there were also narrative and poetic works, for example the epic of *Oghuznama*, a tale common in northwestern Turkic-speaking areas. Some of these early Uygur texts have been translated into English, Russian, German and Turkish.

Howewer, with the coming of Islam to Kashgar and the south of Xinjiang in the 11th century, Uygur literature flourished. Among hundreds of important works surviving from that era are the *Kutadgu Bilig* (*The Knowledge of Happiness*) by **Yusuf Has Hajib**, *Divan-i Lugat-it Türk* (*A Dictionary of Turkic Dialects*) by **Mohammed Kashgeri**, and **Ahmed Iagnaki**'s *Atabetul Hakayik* (*The Gift of Reasons*) of the late 12th or early 13th century. Many of these works were written in Chaghatai, a Turkic language written in script derived from Arabic.

Medieval Uygur literature encompassed both Islamic religious works – such as the 14th-century *Tales of the Prophets* by Rabghuzi – and tales based on legend, like *Oghuzname* (*The Legend of Oghuz Kagan*), dating to the 15th century. At the same time, the Timurid Turkic poet and philosopher Alishir Nowai based epic poems on the Irano-Central Asian love stories of Leyla and Majnun, and Farhad and Shirin.

THE FATHER'S LAST THREE WISHES

*O*nce upon a time there lived an old man who had three sons. After years passed he became confined to bed. One day he called his children to him so that he could tell them his last will.

"Please go to the garden, and each of you bring me two sticks as thick as your fingers and as long as your arm."

They did as he requested and then kneeled by the bed of their mortally ill father.

"My sons," the father said, making his last will, "I will not remain with you much longer. I will pass away as soon as Fate calls. Now I am going to leave with you my last three wishes. First, each of you break one of the sticks you picked up."

Dutifully they did what they were asked. The sticks broke quite easily.

"Now put all the remaining sticks together in a bundle and break them," he instructed.

The three sons bundled together the three remaining sticks, and none of them could break them.

"Now, working together, the three of you try to break them."

The three sons exerted their energy together, and the sticks broke.

"Aha, do you understand the point? Strength comes from unity. That is my first wish. After I die, please hold together in love for each other. If you continue to unite as one man, you will be courageous and strong for the remainder of your lives.

"My second wish is this," the old man continued, "always eat your bread with honey. Do not eat a piece of tasteless bread. I am not going to tell you my third wish right now. Please fulfill the two that I have told you, and you will see the results. Whenever you meet with difficulties that you cannot resolve, just ask your mother about my third wish. Then you will be alright."

Soon afterward the old father died. As he had instructed, the three sons lived together in perfect harmony. Devotedly they cared for one another, but lived in idleness.

In addition, according to their father's second wish, they always ate honey with their bread. This required that they sell all the furniture from their family home, to pay for the honey. Their standard of living rapidly deteriorated. Then, finally, they came to their mother to ask about their father's third wish.

"My sons," said the mother, "there is a bag of golden ingots buried in the garden. Your father provided it for just such a contingency. But he did not say where it is. It seems to have been buried around one of the fruit trees. Take your hoe and spade with you, and try to dig it up."

The three sons immediately began to dig up the garden. They worked through the morning and became tired and hungry. The mother brought them bread and water for lunch. Her children ate these as if they had never tasted such a delicious meal. After they finished working that evening, they once again enjoyed the same bread-and-water meal.

They worked in this manner for about two months, until all the soil in the garden had been loosened.

Even though the golden ingots were never found, the trees that had been neglected for some years were bearing fruit again. The mother called her sons together and said:

"Do not try to find the golden ingots anymore, my sons. Let me tell you what your father's second and third wishes mean. To eat bread with honey means to eat by working. Your bread tasted like honey after your tiring work. That is what you have experienced. Now, listen to your father's third wish. Actually, there are no golden ingots buried in the garden. In order to obtain the treasure you have loosened the soil of the orchard. The fruit-bearing branches are the golden ingots that your father meant."

Cuiyi Wei and Karl W. Luckert, Uighur Stories from Along the Silk Road, *1998*

Worshippers leave Kashgar's Idkah Mosque after midday prayers, some checking in on business or friends by cell phone, others attracted to makeshift stalls in the square outside, which sell shoes, dopas and other day-to-day items (Magnus Bartlett).

In the 17th–18th centuries, lyric genres such as the *ghazal* (love poems) and *gasida* (long couplet-formed odes) flourished. Romantic imagery blossomed, as did the perennially popular theme of heroism. Famous poetic works of this era include *"Gul we Bulbul"* (*"*The Rose and the Nightingale"*) by Shah Yari, *"Muhabbatnama we Mihnetkame"* ("Love and Bitterness Intertwined") by Hirkit, and *"Muhbbatnama"* ("Love Letter") by Molla Abdureyim.

By the 19th and 20th centuries, elements of unrest began to appear in Uygur literature, with resistance a theme existing uneasily alongside tales of love. Uygur scholars, poets and writers were often caught up in the struggles of the times. **Ziya Samedi** (1914–2000) was a Kazakhstan-born Uygur intellectual who promoted Uygur education and nationalism in the Ili Valley in the 1930s and was arrested and imprisoned for seven years as a result. Upon his release and the demise of the republic, however, he occupied various important roles within the PRC's new Xinjiang Government, as regional director of education, director of culture and chairman of the writer's association, but in 1958 was convicted as an "ethnic nationalist" and sentenced to two years in a re-education camp. After this he fled Xinjiang and settled once again in Kazakhstan, from where he wrote a number of famous historical novels, including *Ehmet Ependi* (*Mr Ehmet*), *Mayimhan* and *Yillar Siri* (*Secret of the Years*), none of which are legally permitted in Xinjiang.

Among the most famous and well-loved pieces of modern Uygur literature are *Iz* (*The Track*) and *Uyghanghan Zemin* (*The Awakened Land*), by **Abdurehim Otkur** (1923–1995), a Hami-born author and poet who over the years worked as a newspaper editor, government interpreter, and finally as a scholar of Xinjiang's Institute of Literature Studies of the Academy of Philosophy and Social Sciences. **Zordun Sabir** (1937–1988) is another popular Uygur author, most famous for his historical novel *Anayurt*.

RELIGION AND ART

he most significant innovations carried along the trade routes to China were the belief systems and religious arts of India, Central Asia and the Middle East – but before they reached and began influencing dynastic China they had already found a home in the oasis kingdoms of the Tarim Basin. Buddhism began its evolution as a religious doctrine in the sixth century BCE, and was adopted as India's official religion in the third century BCE. When Buddhism, and to a lesser extent Manichaeism and Nestorianism arrived in China, their art and creed revolutionized its culture – but their impact on the kingdoms of the Western Regions was equally profound. Thanks to the climatic conditions and forbidding geography of the region, many of the structures in Xinjiang housing ancient religious manuscripts, beautiful frescoes and statuary– built from the first century BCE to the end of the Tang Dynasty – lay hidden under centuries of sand until their rediscovery at the turn of the 20th century.

A Unique Artistic Oasis

"*Between the early murals of Miran and the latest work in the Turfan area lie almost a thousand years. Throughout this millennium a characteristic form of temple art flourished in the oasis kingdoms and reached occasional heights of outstanding excellence. This remarkable stream of creative production brings into question previous references to the area as no more than a highway connecting the ancient Eastern and Western Worlds, and to its civilization as the culture of the Silk Road. Considering the relatively small dimensions of international trade in ancient times, it would seem extremely unlikely that several dozen or even several hundred camel caravans a year could have supplied the economic foundations for such extensive artistic and religious enterprise. On the other hand the region abounds in evidences of much wider areas of cultivation supporting a much larger population in former periods than today. This agricultural prosperity, based on the known richness of the soil when properly irrigated, would go much further than the commerce of the silk route to explain not only why the Tarim Basin could afford so many monasteries and temples, but why it attracted a continuous stream of invaders.*

Western scholars have generally approached Sinkiang as a peripheral area, a sort of transmission belt through which classical Greek forms, motifs, and techniques were passed on to China and Japan. Later on recognition was granted to Persian and Indian influences, and even traces of contact with Byzantium. Attention has also been devoted to the westward expansion of elements of Chinese civilization. The accumulated archaeological evidence, however, suggests the need for revision of these older attitudes. At first (as at Niya and Miran), a mere outpost of the Hellenistic world of western Asia, the Tarim Basin later developed a unique synthesis of alien and indigenous cultural elements. The Kyzyl tableaux and mountainscapes, the Rustam from Dandan Oilik, the goddesses and friars of Shorchuk, the Uighur nobles of Bezeklik – to cite only a few examples – could have been created nowhere else in the world. On grounds of the distinctive character and the intrinsic value of its productions, Buddhist Central Asia clearly ranks as an art center of international importance."

Alice Thorner, in an Appendix to Pivot of Asia, by Owen Lattimore, 1950

According to legend, the Han Emperor Mingdi, who had already heard of **Buddhism**, dreamt of a golden figure floating in a halo of light – perhaps a flying *apsara* (Buddhist angel) – that was interpreted by the Emperor's wise men to be the Buddha himself. Consequently, an envoy was sent to India to learn about the new religion, returning with sacred Buddhist texts and paintings as well as Indian priests to explain the teachings of the Buddha to the Emperor. Monks, missionaries and pilgrims began travelling from India to Central Asia and then on to China, bringing Buddhist writings and paintings, while converts followed the Silk Road west. The new Buddhist art that emerged in the Tarim Basin, now known as **Serindian** art, absorbed different styles and forms along the way, including those popular in the Kingdom of Gandhara (in what is now the Peshawar valley of northwest Pakistan), where indigenous Indian art forms had already been mixed with those of the Greeks and Persians in the early sixth century BCE.

This Graeco-Indian or Gandharan art was considered revolutionary for its depiction of the Buddha in human form, the temporal earthbound personality of Sakyamuni. Since Sakyamuni had achieved nirvana, escaping the cycles of birth and rebirth, he had essentially ceased to exist. He had previously been symbolized by a footprint, a wheel, a tree, a stupa or Sanskrit characters. The Greek (Hellenistic) influence on traditional Buddhist painting was obvious: instead of a loincloth the Buddha wore flowing robes, had a straight chiselled nose and brow, full lips and wavy hair. Some of the Indian influences that remained were the heavy eyelids and elongated ear lobes, stretched long because of Sakyamuni's former life as a heavily jewelled and worldly prince, a symbol of the life he renounced for the ascetic spiritual life.

As a result of rushed and highly unprofessional excavations in the cities and temples of Gandhara (which were already in extremely poor condition), most of the wall paintings and frescoes were destroyed and sculptures are all that remain of this exquisite art form. Nonetheless, it was this art form that travelled across the Pamirs, establishing itself in the oasis towns of the Taklamakan and beyond, where it was again to absorb new influences. Concurrently with the school of Gandhara, the school of Mathura also began to show the Buddha in human form, and its influence is noticeable in figures found in Rawak on the Southern Silk Road.

With the rapid spread of Buddhism along the Silk Road, elaborate cave complexes and monasteries were built in and around the oasis towns, generously supported by powerful local families and merchants to ensure the safe passage of their caravans. Many of the cave frescoes

Above: A ninth-century mural detail showing Tokharians offering gifts of money to the Buddha, from Cave 20 in the Bezeklik complex – this piece disappeared from the Museum für Indische Kunst, Berlin, in 1945. Below: A mural from the Cave of Statues in the Kizil complex near Kucha, showing celestial musicians in an Indo-Persian style (Courtesy of the Asian Art Museum, National Museums in Berlin). Opposite: The Bezeklik caves are situated in a stunning location in a steep gorge within the Flaming Mountains near Turpan (Jeremy Tredinnick).

portray these benefactors in pious positions, sometimes by name, since these gifts were believed to help them in their quest for nirvana. Pilgrims from China continued to travel west searching for original manuscripts and holy sites, over the Karakoram range to Gandhara and India.

The first Chinese pilgrim to actually reach India and return with extensive knowledge of Buddhism was **Fa Xian** (337–422 CE), a monk who travelled the southern route in 399, through Dunhuang and Khotan and over the Himalayas to India. He studied Buddhism under various Indian masters in Benares, Gandhara and Ceylon (Sri Lanka), and went as far as Sumatra and Java in Indonesia; altogether he visited over 30 countries, returning to China in 414 via the sea route. The Buddhist monk **Xuanzang** (600–664) is perhaps the most well known of all Chinese travellers on the Silk Road, and one of the four great translators of Buddhist texts. His lasting fame is primarily due to the humorous 16th-century novel *Journey to the West* (also known as *Monkey*), a fictional account of his pilgrimage that includes the various escapades of an odd assortment of characters who accompany the monk on his journey.

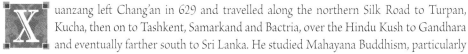

uanzang left Chang'an in 629 and travelled along the northern Silk Road to Turpan, Kucha, then on to Tashkent, Samarkand and Bactria, over the Hindu Kush to Gandhara and eventually farther south to Sri Lanka. He studied Mahayana Buddhism, particularly the Yogachara school, at various monasteries for 14 years and became a renowned scholar, winning many debates against Hinayana Buddhist scholars. He returned to China in 645 via the Southern Silk Road and wrote *Records of the Western Regions*, an excellent account of his travels and the state of Buddhism in the seventh century.

With a disciple he co-founded the **Fa Xiang school**, the Chinese form of Yogachara, which was popular during the Tang Dynasty. The central tenet in this belief is that the external world is a product of our consciousness, things exist only as far as they exist in our minds, and nirvana (Buddhahood) is achieved after working through several complex levels of spiritual development and detachment. The Fa Xiang school denies that Buddhahood is possible for everyone, in direct opposition to other Mahayana schools, and it actually contributed to the latter's decline after the Tang Dynasty. Xuanzang translated over 75 Sanskrit works into Chinese, and translated the teachings of the Taoist philosopher Laozi into Sanskrit as well. His translations were known for their high literary content and he was instrumental in creating an extensive Buddhist vocabulary in Chinese.

The religions of **Manichaeism** and **Nestorian Christianity** were also introduced, accepted and assimilated along the Silk Road and found solid bases in many Tarim kingdoms, although neither reached the popularity enjoyed by Buddhism. Manichaeism was started by Manes of Persia in the third century BCE and is a religion based on the opposing principles of light and dark (spirit and flesh). Followers of Manichaeism, persecuted by the Sassanian kings in the third to sixth centuries CE, began arriving in Central Asia and flourished during the Sui (581–618) and Tang dynasties. Until the discovery of Manichaean libraries and wall paintings at Kharakhoja (Gaochang, near Turpan), little was known of this religious sect, believed by most scholars to have no literature or art. It sustained a substantial following into the 10th century, but then quickly disappeared with the advent of Islam in the West and Buddhism in the East. However, Manichaeism survived in southeastern China until the 17th century.

One of the essential beliefs of Nestorian Christianity is that Christ is fully human as well as fully divine, both natures being complete side by side. This belief was condemned in 431 by the Council of Ephesus and hence forbidden in the Roman Empire. The Independent Church of the East, based in Seleucia-Ctesiphon near today's Baghdad, retained this belief. Unable to expand westwards, the Persian Church sent its missionaries east towards China in the seventh century. Nestorian manuscripts were discovered in the Turpan and Khotan regions and Marco Polo found thriving Nestorian communities in cities along the Silk Road as late as the 13th century, even though all foreign religions had been heavily persecuted in 843–845. Eventually, under pressure from Islam these religions disappeared from northwestern China.

Islam was first introduced to China by Arab traders and missionaries travelling along the Silk Road during the Tang Dynasty. In Xinjiang, Islam pervades almost every facet of society: the *muezzin's* call to prayer from the minarets of the many mosques spread throughout the oasis towns, the ubiquitous skull caps worn by all men, the copies of the Koran and other religious material piled up in front of the mosques, the veiled women in the bazaar – all are constant reminders of the devotion and pervading existence of this belief.

Islam – Arabic for "submission to God" – was founded by the Prophet Muhammad, born in the city of Mecca (Saudia Arabia) in 570 CE. Muhammad declared that there was but one God, that he was God's messenger, and preached a universal brotherhood in which all men were equal. As an able statesman and commander, he unified the Arab nations. The people of the Middle East were ready to accept Muhammad's new religion after centuries of fighting and wars between khanates. Islam flourished, and within a century it had stretched from Persia to Spain.

Every Muslim has five fundamental religious duties, known as the Pillars of Islam. He must recite the creed, *La illaha illa 'llah Muhammad Rasulu llah* ("There is no God but Allah, and Muhammad is his prophet"), pray five times a day facing Mecca, fast during the month of Ramadan, give alms to the poor and make a pilgrimage to Mecca. The Koran is the holy book of Islam, consisting of written and oral records compiled during Muhammad's lifetime and in the years immediately following his death. It contains the philosophy and moral code of Islam and is considered the true word of God as revealed to Muhammad; it is the supreme authority to which every Muslim looks for guidance. The teachings of Islam were first revealed at Creation but since then man has continually erred and God's prophecy has become obscured with false interpretations. Prophets are periodically sent to Earth by God to reaffirm his word; they are considered divine and include the Hebrew patriarchs Abraham and Moses, as well as Jesus. Muhammad was sent by God to restore purity. He was the last prophet; the next will be the Messiah. Muslims call the followers of prophets – including Jews and Christians – *ahl-e-kitab*: "People of the Book".

Islam suffered a major split immediately after the death of Muhammad in 632. Since he had not clearly named a successor, there were violent power struggles and two main sects emerged: the Sunnis, the larger sect – to which the Uygurs belong – who follow elected leaders; and the smaller sect, the Shias (or Shiites), led by hereditary leaders called "imams", direct descendants of Muhammad through his daughter Fatima. The Ismailis, the followers of Aga Khan (an offshoot of the Shias), include the Tajiks of western Xinjiang.

The spread of Islam from the Middle East was a critical factor in the disappearance of Buddhist civilizations along the Silk Road, and perhaps the most destructive element in the loss of Serindian art. To Muslims, the portrayal of "the almighty" in human form was intolerable, and since many of the Buddhist cave frescoes, silk paintings and statues exemplified the Gandharan figurative style, they were unceremoniously destroyed or defaced. With a few exceptions, only those caves and monasteries that had been swallowed by the sands centuries before survived mutilation by the followers of Allah.

Of course, the discovery and subsequent removal of much of Xinjiang's greatest ancient art by the likes of Sven Hedin, Aurel Stein, Albert von Le Coq, Paul Pelliot, Pyotr Kozlov and Count Otani was labelled destruction, vandalism and theft by the Chinese government once the true wealth of treasures hidden within the deserts and barren wilderness became apparent. There is no doubt that much damage was done, and the region's plethora of sites are in a sorry state compared to their original glory, but many argue that if the foreign archaeologist-explorers had not spirited away most of the greatest remaining pieces, they would not have survived local vandalism or the turbulent decades of the 20th century that followed.

FOOD AND DRINK

"Turfan for grapes,

and Hami for melons;

The girls of Kucha are all like flowers."

—Ancient Chinese proverb

For many, an abiding memory of their Xinjiang experience will be the rich, juicy flavour of a slice of Hami melon slurped up at a street-side stall, or the explosion of taste from a plump grape popped into the mouth under a Turpan trellis. Not for nothing is Xinjiang famous throughout China – and beyond – as the producer of the best melons and grapes in Asia. Its plentiful sunshine, low rainfall but abundant supply of water, long frost-free growing season and significant variance in daytime and night-time temperatures create perfect conditions for growing fruit with a high natural sugar content and great taste.

Clockwise from top left: Plump, juicy grapes hang heavy on the vine in a family's courtyard in Turpan; a barrow of Ili peaches tempt passers-by in a Yining market; pomegranates are particularly popular along the Southern Silk Road; a variety of melons on offer outside the Khantengri Mosque in Urumqi (Jeremy Tredinnick x4).

Although a range of fruits are grown throughout the region's communities, different areas are famous for producing the juiciest and best of a particular type: the sweet, pale-fleshed **musk melons** of Shanshan are considered the "king of melons" (and in fact are commonly known as Hami or honeydew melons, though there are many varieties), while Turpan **grapes** and **raisins**, Hami **dates**, Korla **fragrant pears**, Ili Valley **apples**, Yarkand **pomegranates**, Kashgar **peaches**, Artush **figs** and Kucha **mulberries** all enjoy reputations as the best of their kind. The ubiquitous **watermelon**, larger than musk melons, red-fleshed and refreshing, is eaten throughout the year, with thick-skinned winter melons stored underground to keep them juicy. **Dried fruit and nuts** are also a major part of the culinary landscape, always present on the table at meals and filling stalls at markets; dried apricots, figs, dates and light-green, red or black raisins (air-dried from the green, red and purple grape varieties all grown in Xinjiang) can all be found, while **walnuts** from Hotan, **almonds** and **pistachio** nuts are also very popular for their nutritious and medicinal value.

A lthough Uygur cuisine is less varied and complex than that of Sichuan, Yunnan and other parts of China, it maintains a spicy edge that blends well with the selection of meat and vegetables available. *Laghman* is found everywhere – a mutton stir-fry with fresh eggplant, string beans, tomatoes and hot green peppers served over thick noodles. Rice is most often eaten on special occasions and on Sundays at the bazaar when small restaurants prepare *poluo*, a tasty fried rice pilaf prepared with pumpkin or mutton, accompanied by *manty*, a thin-skinned dumpling filled with mutton and onion. Despite the intense heat, the most common midday meal is *chushira,* a hearty wonton soup spiced with red peppers and herbs. Night markets and bazaars are never without *kebab* vendors – offering a choice of grilled mutton, fat or liver skewers – and clay bread-making ovens that make a wide variety of *nan*, flatbreads that are patterned and sprinkled with delicious herbs and spices. Another product of these ovens, popular with tea in the morning, is *samsa*, a small square packet of dough filled with mutton fat and onions, and baked like bread. *Apke* is hard to miss in the bazaar; roughly translated as goat's head soup, it consists of a large cauldron with the goat's head prominently displayed atop a coil of intestines that have been cleaned, stuffed with meat, flour, eggs and oil, and then reunited in a simmering broth with the remaining entrails.

To drink, Uygurs prefer a rough, broken black *chai* (tea), sold in bricks that are indistinguishable from pressed sticks and twigs. A popular summer drink (best in Turpan) is made from the juice of rehydrated peaches or apricots, known by its Chinese name *bingshui*, literally "cold water". *Durap* – a refreshing mixture of chipped ice, fresh yoghurt and sweet honey – and hand-churned vanilla ice cream, *maroji*, are extremely popular in Kashgar and along the Southern Silk Road.

Top left: A roadside melon and gourd seller outside the Kashgar Livestock Market. Top right: Nan bread of varying size is on sale wherever you go in Xinjiang, and makes a tasty snack as well as a useful plate for food (Jeremy Tredinnick x2). Bottom: Noodle dishes stand heaped on large platters in a busy market (Sun Jiabin).

LANGUAGE

Uygurs speak a Turkic-Altaic language influenced over time by various Central Asian dialects; many do not understand Mandarin and they are delighted to hear foreigners make an attempt at their language. Kazakhs speak a separate but very similar language, and the two ethnic groups can often communicate. The following word list, with no excuses for the transliteration, is only a start:

Es salaam aleikum—Peace be upon you   **Wa aleikum es salaam**—And upon you

Yakshee musiss?—How are you?   **Yakshee**—Good

Yakshee emess—No good   **Harashor**—Great

Haah—Yes   **Emess**—No

Kanche pul?—How much?   **Kanche kilomitir?**—How many kilometres?

Rakmet—Thank you   **Kechurung**—Excuse me/sorry

Kosh—Goodbye   **Posh**—Get out of the way

Sen ismim nema?—What is your name?   **Sen naden kelding?**—Where are you from?

Tamaka—Tobacco   **Mohorka**—Xinjiang blend rolled in newspaper

Bazaar—Market   **Ash**—Food

Autobuz—Bus   **Ashkana**—restaurant

Meschit—Mosque   **Mazar**—Tomb

Bilhet—Ticket   **Biket**—Bus station

bir—one   **ikki**—two   **yuetch**—three   **tut**—four

bash—five   **alte**—six   **yete**—seven   **sekiz**—eight

tokuz—nine   **on**—ten   **on bir**—eleven   **on ikki**—twelve

yigrime—twenty **ellik**—fifty   **yüz**—one hundred   **ikki yüz**—two hundred

URUMQI (WULUMUQI)

Urumqi is the capital of the Xinjiang Uygur Autonomous Region, and its political, economic, scientific and technological centre. The city's industrial plants, educational institutes and commercial activities are the hub of Xinjiang's economy, while it is the regional centre for road, rail and air communications. Little surprise therefore that each year its numbers swell as immigrants both from the surrounding region but also from many of China's eastern provinces arrive in search of a new, prosperous life. Current figures show Urumqi's metropolitan population at around 2.7 million people – and rising fast. It is, by some distance, the most modern city in Xinjiang, with the prerequisite forest of city-centre skyscrapers expanding annually, as befits any regional Chinese capital. It is also, according to the *Guinness Book of Records*, the most remote large city from any sea in the world, 2,250 kilometres from the nearest coastline.

Given this fact, it is somewhat ironic that in 1992 the Beijing government officially decreed Urumqi a land "port", with all that title's attendant tax incentives – a move designed to lure capital investment and industry, and indicative of how important Xinjiang is considered to be in terms of China's economy as a whole.

Situated just north of the **Tien Shan** (**Heavenly Mountains**), at the entrance of a gap between the main Tien Shan range to the southwest and the Bogda Shan spur to the east, and facing the Junggar Basin to the north, early settlements in the Urumqi area were strategically placed to control traffic between the Tarim Basin oasis cultures in the south and the great grasslands of the nomadic tribes in the north. However, Urumqi itself was settled only recently in historical terms, and did not play a major role in early Silk Road trade, when the main trade routes passed far to the south.

HISTORY

Although it is almost impossible to visualize the connection today amidst the city sprawl, the name Urumqi actually means "Beautiful Pastures" in Mongolian, and must once have fit that description perfectly, with rolling grasslands backed by snow-capped peaks. During the Western Han Dynasty (206 BCE–8 CE), Chinese troops were garrisoned in the vicinity of present-day Urumqi in a concerted effort to open the grasslands to agriculture. During the Tang Dynasty small towns and military barracks were established in the area to encourage the development of the new northern Silk Road – an alternative to the southern routes that were coming under pressure from Tibetan incursions. In 648 CE Emperor Zhenguan created the town of **Luntai**, 10 kilometres south of present-day Urumqi's city centre at the site of an ancient settlement known as Urabo. From this seat of local government, taxes were collected from caravans on the northern trade route.

However, it wasn't until 1763 that a city was established on the east bank of the Urumqi River, settled by Chinese soldiers and exiles, and given the name **Dihua**. "*Dihua*" in Chinese means

Urumqi's modern cityscape, with the mighty Bogda Shan as a backdrop (Sun Jiabin).

"to enlighten and civilize", which appeared to be the attitude of the Qing Dynasty rulers towards the local minorities. The town grew in importance with the opening of silver and lead mines as well as Emperor Qianlong's military expansion into the Junggar region. An independent Muslim rebellion swept through the city in 1864, led by Tuoming, who declared himself the "Pure and True Muslim King", but was soon defeated by Yakub Beg's Kashgarian troops moving north from Kucha.

Dihua was declared the capital of Xinjiang Province in 1884. It became a city of spies and intrigue, where the governors were virtual warlords and succession to the post was frequently contested with violence. Dinner parties were infamous stages for overthrowing contenders for power. In 1916, Governor Yang Zengxin invited all whom he suspected of disloyalty to a banquet and while he ate heartily and the military band played on, a number of his dinner guests had their heads severed one by one. At another banquet in 1928, the governor himself and several officials were executed in a hail of bullets. The new governor and the Russian consul rode through the city in an open carriage escorted by 40 mounted Cossacks. Soviet Russian influence became all pervasive.

Peter Hopkirk, in his book *Foreign Devils on the Silk Road* (an excellent account of the race for buried archaeological treasures in the early 20th century), records Albert von Le Coq's first experience in Urumqi in 1904:

> One of the first things they witnessed on arrival was a particularly cruel form of execution in progress in the town's main street. The victim was incarcerated in a specially built cage known as a *kapas*. His head, firmly secured, stuck out of the top, while his feet rested on a board. The latter was gradually lowered, day by day, until on about the eighth day his neck finally broke. The traffic went on as usual past this barbaric apparatus. A melon dealer sits surrounded by his fruit, totally unperturbed by his neighbour's dying agonies.

T he city (also called Hongmiaozi or "Red Temple" by locals) was divided into three in the early 20th century: a Chinese walled city, a native walled city, and a Russian refugee settlement in the aftermath of the Russian Revolution. The latter was home to poverty-stricken refugees – their houses clustered around the Russian Consulate-General and an Orthodox church – and was a hive of intrigue between Red and White Russian factions. Rain turned the rubbish-strewn streets into mud pits so deep that, according to Sven Hedin, writing in the 1920s: "During our stay two horses were drowned and even children are said to have perished."

Like China's customs office, in those days the postal service was run by foreigners. Mail took 45 days to get to Beijing but only 28 days to London, carried first by couriers and then by Russian trains. Urumqi was linked to Beijing by telegraph, but the Muslim rebellion that enveloped Xinjiang in the 1930s destroyed the line. The rebellion also frustrated the attempts of the Eurasia Air Line (a Sino-German enterprise) to run regular flights from China to Europe via Urumqi.

In 1935, in a political gambit aimed at maintaining his dictatorial control over Xinjiang, Governor Sheng Shicai invited Soviet troops to cross the Sino-Soviet border and help quell Ma Zhongying's Muslim rebellion: Soviet aid included a five-million-rouble loan, weapons (including airplanes, which had a devastating effect on the rebel forces) and advisers. In exchange the Russians were granted exclusive trading, mineral and petroleum rights; there followed a period of strong Russian influence until the Sino-Soviet split in 1960.

Left: The Hetan Expressway passes the sheer cliff of Hongshan, with Zhenglong Pagoda perched on top. Above: A (not so) old photograph displayed in Hongshan Park's Viewing Pavilion – visibile in the picture at top right – shows the same area before the advent of the expressway and the construction boom (Jeremy Tredinnick x2).

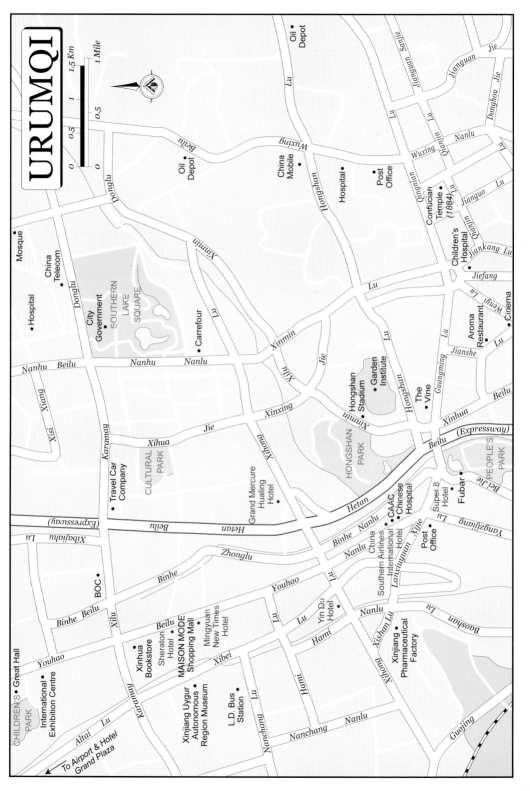

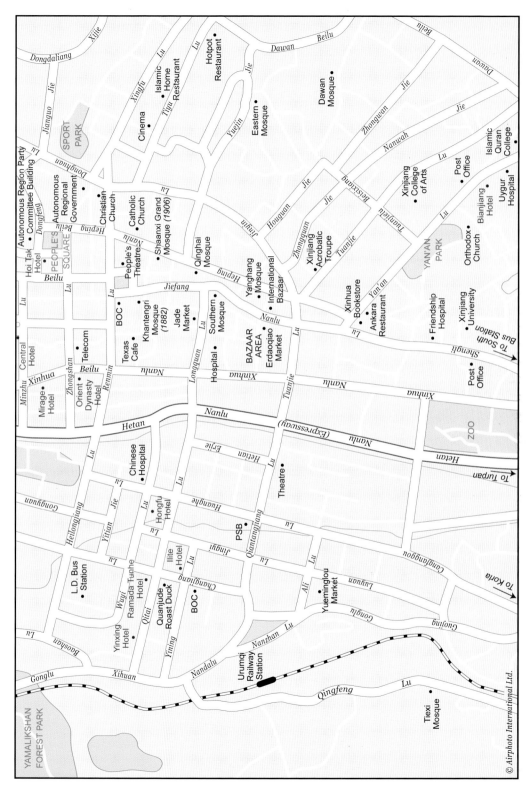

The next few decades saw Urumqi grow slowly as the region's industrial centre, although it remained very much "out of sight" as a backwater during the tumultuous Mao years and the post-Mao Chinese search for identity and vision. The city was opened to foreigners once again in the 1980s, and has been central to the development strategies of Beijing's "Go West" programme since its inception in 2000. Huge influxes of migrant workers and entrepreneurs have arrived from the east, attracted – along with international investors – by Xinjiang's wealth in natural resources, its petrochemical and manufacturing industries, and its rising significance in China's plans to create a new economic bridge between the Middle Kingdom and Central Asia.

GETTING YOUR BEARINGS

Urumqi lies at an average of 800 metres (2,626 feet) above sea level, close to the northern foothills of the Tien Shan. The snow-clad **Bogda Peak** (5,445 metres), 70 kilometres (40 miles) to the east, dominates the skyline on clear days, although these are not as frequent as they once were – air pollution from factories and the burning of "coal bricks" during winter in the growing residential areas is a problem familiar to most Chinese cities.

More than 75 percent of Urumqi's population is Han, with Uygurs accounting for only around 13 percent, eight percent Hui, 2.3 percent Kazakh, and a smattering of Manchu, Mongol, Xibe, Tatar, Uzbek and Russian minorities. As such it does not exhibit the ethnic flavour of other large Xinjiang cities such as Kashgar, Turpan or Yining; nevertheless, it buzzes with an energy typical of a frontier town – make no mistake, Urumqi very much suits that title – and the busy city streets teeming with businessmen from all parts of Asia and beyond give a good idea of the hopes and aspirations of both the regional and municipal governments, as well as the populace in general.

The city is developing rapidly, with giant skyscrapers now dominating the skyline in the city centre, which can be roughly delineated as stretching from **Hongshan (Red Hill) Park** in the north to **Erdaoqiao Market** and the **International Grand Bazaar** in the south, and from **People's Square** in the east to **Urumqi Railway Station** in the west. Most visitors will concentrate their attention on this downtown area, even though today the modern city sprawls far to the north and south.

Splitting the city in half from north to south is the **Hetan Expressway**, a huge six-lane motorway that follows the course of the Urumqi River through the city; leaning right up alongside it is Urumqi's main landmark, the rocky bluff of Red Hill, from whose summit panoramic views of the city can be seen. The main north-south thoroughfares in the city centre are Xinhua Lu and Jiefang Lu, which are crossed east-west by Minzhu Lu, Zhongshan Lu and Renmin Lu. This is the commercial centre of Urumqi, with everything from high-end brand stores and car showrooms to huge department stores and vibrant markets.

Where Jiefang Bei Lu is more Chinese in feel, the southern section of the street, Jiefang Nan Lu, has a more distinctive Uygur atmosphere, with mosques and traditional markets. This is the

Locals fish in Mirror Lake in People's Park, with the Jian Hu Pavilion on its far side, and city skyscrapers towering on its flanks, reminiscent of New York's Central Park (Jeremy Tredinnick).

best area in town to experience Uygur city life – here you will see carpet sellers displaying vividly coloured wool rugs and felt mats, and boot makers labouring on the knee-length leather boots worn by Uygur men and Kazakh women. The delicious aroma of fresh-baked nan bread emanates from bakeries, milliners display the embroidered *dopa* skullcaps that are an indispensable item in every Uygur's outfit, while animal skin traders and black-market moneychangers bargain along the street.

North of the city centre Youhao Lu and Xibei Lu are your main points of reference, boasting some of the city's top hotels as well as the **Xinjiang Uygur Autonomous Region Museum**.

SIGHTS

Urumqi's main streets are wide and tree-lined, many with open water channels that help cool the air. High-rise construction has generally made the skyline indistinguishable from any other Chinese city, but in recent years an emphasis has been placed on Uygur-style architecture for some grand edifices, notable examples being the **Great Hall** (People's Hall) opposite the Kunlun Hotel (Youhao Bei Lu) and the **International Grand Bazaar** on Jiefang Nan Lu. A few handsome Russian-style buildings remain, with green corrugated-iron roofs, stucco facades painted blue, yellow and white, and classically columned porticoes dating from the 1950s. A particularly attractive example is the Western Region Military Hospital on Youhao Lu, while the **People's Theatre**, on Nanmen Square where Renmin Lu crosses Jiefang Lu, mixes Eastern and Western architectural styles to good effect with its golden dome and colonnaded façade.

People's Square is a large, open, concreted area surrounded by government buildings, hotels and office blocks; inevitably used by early morning t'ai chi practitioners, at its centre is a columnar monument to Xinjiang's integration into the Chinese nation. Around its plinth are carved scenes of Chinese soldiers marching to the relief of the region's beleaguered ethnic groups, with Uygur men, women and children singing and cheering them on. A few small weekend carnival rides for children line the square's periphery, and a more modern accoutrement is an enormous TV screen that flashes news, events and who knows what else for much of the day.

SHAANXI MOSQUE

Urumqi has well over 100 mosques, many built after 1978, when the Communist Party adopted a more relaxed attitude towards religion. The largest is the **Shaanxi Mosque**, on Heping Nan Lu, just southeast of the People's Theatre. Built during the Qing Dynasty with money contributed by Hui Muslims in Shaanxi Province, this Chinese-style mosque is a brick and wood structure with an elaborate, green-tiled roof topped with the Islamic crescent. The prayer hall, with large red pillars and painted eaves, can accommodate up to 500 for religious services. Outside the mosques, vendors offer copies of the Koran and holy commentaries printed in Arabic.

YANGHANG MOSQUE

Also known as the **Tatar Mosque**, and standing at the southern end of Jiefang Lu, this huge complex of 3,000 square metres was built in 1897 with private donations from the Tatar community. The dome is a Tatar-style octagonal pyramid adorned with a crescent and wood-and-brick geometric carvings, since Islam strictly prohibits the use of idols or animal figures in its religious artwork. This mosque is the main centre of worship for Muslims in Urumqi, containing classrooms for teaching the Koran and dormitories for the imam.

KHANTENGRI MOSQUE

Originally known as the Southern Mosque, this picturesque wood-brick structure was first built in 1864 and expanded in 1882, but when its condition deteriorated it was relocated to the northern end of Jiefang Nan Lu, just south of Nanmen Square, in 1919. Renovated again in 1984, it was then renamed the **Khantengri Mosque**, after a mountain in the Tien Shan.

While outside the three gold-domed minarets attract admiring gazes, the convex-shaped prayer hall offers more eye-catching workmanship, with two layers of raised eaves covered with glazed tiles above a colourfully painted panel. A separate washroom allows the faithful to wash before prayers, and the passageways leading to the prayer hall are decorated with carved orchids, plums, bamboo and lotuses. The

mosque covers an area of about 4,000 square metres, and can accommodate 1,100 worshippers, the majority lining up outside the mosque in its shady grounds. Interestingly, the grounds also serve as a shopping market, stalls being set up in front of the mosque's two spiral staircases to sell fruit, drinks and other popular items.

ERDAOQIAO MARKET

Traditional covered markets are found all over the city, but the largest and most famous is **Erdaoqiao Market** on Jiefang Nan Lu, a bustling, vibrant melée of traders and shoppers. Inside the gaily fronted market, stacks of colourful silver and gold filigree gauze cloth from Pakistan, traditional Uygur *aidelaixi* (Atlas) silk and Chinese cotton are sold from small, privately owned stalls. Uygur families bargain for wall or *kang* (heated sleeping-platform) carpets, and Pakistani traders bustle around yelling and making deals. Food stalls sell yellowish chunks of fatty lung served with a piquant sauce, cold spicy noodles with dried beancurd, *samsa* dumplings, boiled sheep heads and roasted meats. *Shashlik* vendors have a constant stream of customers for spicy sticks of barbecued mutton, fat or liver. Tinkers make kettles, boxes, moulds and water holders, colourful stalls are lined with traditional Yengisar knives, and through it all modern dance music blares from CD players.

Outside the market facing Jiefang Nan Lu stands a model of a bridge, flanked by bronze statues depicting traders and merchants. This is a reference to Erdaoqiao's beginnings, when this area was nothing more than a wooden bridge over a flood-control ditch, around which the market grew. In summer real camels sit and stand beside the bridge, draped in Uygur-style cloth, while their owners cajole passers-by into photo sessions next to the bored beasts.

During summer and autumn months melon vendors set up shop on the street-side, doing brisk business amidst enormous piles of mouthwatering Hami and watermelons. Shoppers stand shoulder to shoulder as they bite into slices of the juicy fruit for Rmb2 or more per segment (prices change according to the time of season), slurping and smacking their lips in time-honoured tradition – there is no better way to slake your thirst on a hot day. Alongside the melon hawkers, itinerant merchants lay out their wares on the ground; wandering around can mean picking your way between piles of walnuts and pistachios, skirting barrows buried beneath stacks of spiced nan bread, and manoeuvring around small crowds drawn by teams of men hawking the latest miracle medicine cure-all.

Left: Fruit stalls line the alleys around the Khantengri Mosque. Above: Traders lay out piles of nuts on the street in front of Erdaoqiao Market – the main building is merely the hub of a sprawl of market stalls that spread out to the north and south (Jeremy Tredinnick x2).

INTERNATIONAL GRAND BAZAAR

Immediately south of Erdaoqiao the **International Grand Bazaar** stands massive and impressive, despite its slightly faux feel. Sandwiched between Jiefang Nan Lu and Heping Nan Lu, Urumqi's modern take on Central Asia's rich trading heritage claims to be the biggest bazaar area in the world. Two huge buildings in distinctly Islamic style are separated by a square dominated by an enormous minaret reminiscent of the Kalyan Minaret in Bokhara, Uzbekistan. Carved around the base is a scene of Uygurs dancing joyfully, and regular displays of real ethnic dance and song take place in the square. In the evening the bazaar is lit up to resplendent effect, and on festival days you might even see tightrope walking – the *Dawaz*, a Uygur favourite – across the square between the two roofs. Inside the bazaar buildings, which, in contrast to many covered markets are surprisingly light and airy, all the usual Central Asian fare can be browsed and bought, from carpets to dried foodstuffs, musical instruments to knives. Admittedly, much of what is on offer here is simply tourist bric-a-brac, and a Carrefour supermarket (one of a number in Urumqi) and KFC outlet inside one of the buildings are particularly incongruous, but nevertheless the Grand Bazaar's imposing style makes it satisfying and rewarding for most visitors.

CENTRAL JADE MARKET

Another huge new structure built to showcase Xinjiang's Uygur heritage is located north of Erdaoqiao near the junction of Jiefang Nan Lu and Longquan Jie. Pale yellow in colour, with eight slender minaret-like columns framing its entranceways, this four-storey building houses shops dedicated to the sale of jade, the precious stone that was probably Xinjiang's very first claim to fame during the earliest dynasties of central China. Everything from huge, rough-looking raw nephrite rocks to perfectly polished statuettes of exquisite craftsmanship can be found, while outside at the back makeshift stalls groan under the weight of more rocks, brought to the city from the faraway rivers and mountains of the Southern Silk Road oases by opportunistic traders trying to cut out the middleman. As with the markets elsewhere in the city, the side streets around the jade market are also packed with food stalls selling noodle dishes, bowls of *poluo* (fried rice pilaf style), nan breads, milk tea and pomegranate juice.

Above: A new mosque is part of the International Grand Bazaar complex – to the left is the bazaar's central minaret.
Opposite: The Zhenglong Pagoda is popular with domestic tourists (Jeremy Tredinnick x2).

Parks

Urumqi's most well known public oasis of greenery is **Hongshan (Red Hill) Park**, which at 910 metres (3,000 feet) provides a panoramic view over the city. Located on the east bank of the Urumqi River, this reddish-brown, forested hill is dotted with small pavilions and winding walkways, as well as exercise machines and children's carnival rides on its less precipitous eastern side, where there is an entrance gate opposite the Hongshan Stadium.

Tourists and locals alike make good use of the shady trees and peace away from the city noise, but the main focus for out-of-towners is the nine-storey red-brick **Zhenglong Pagoda (Pagoda to Suppress Dragons)**, which figures prominently in the folklore of Urumqi. In 1785 and 1786 the city suffered from severe river flooding caused, it was rumoured, by a large red dragon that had settled here, turned into a mountain and was clawing its way towards Yamalike Hill, which rises to the west of the city. If the two mountains joined, the Urumqi River would be blocked and drown the city, so in 1788, Governor Shang An built two pagodas to placate the dragon, one on the dragon's head, Red Hill, the other on Yamalike Hill. The latter pagoda has long since collapsed, but the one in Hongshan Park still stands right on the edge of a sheer cliff that looks down on the river – and now also the Hetan Expressway, which hugs the sheer walls as it channels traffic north and south. The pagoda is small but attractive, and the protective fence around its base is covered with linked padlocks, placed there by romantic couples as signs of their mutual love, or supplicants with secret wishes they hope will come true with the help of the dragon. An amusing sign near the pagoda reads: "Strictly prohibit from abandoning stones bottles of wine and minglement" [sic] – an attempt to control the parties that often develop among park-goers.

Numerous other pagodas were built on Hongshan, which became a holy Buddhist centre; however, many were burnt down by the warlords who later ruled the city. Most recently a three-storey, Chinese-style **Viewing Pavilion** (entry Rmb5) was built on the hill's highest point. Ornate and picturesque, with wall-mounted photographs inside of Urumqi old and new, the views from its upper level are spectacular – when the haze holds off. Sadly pollution too often means the horizon fades quickly into grey smog. A square next to the Viewing Pavilion has regular displays of Uygur dancing, which draws crowds of Chinese tourists who happily join in with the paid performers. Although not the most authentic of shows – the Uygur women are dressed up in festival finery but their long braids are nearly all false – it is a joyful and entertaining experience, with everyone dancing together to music played by an enthusiastic orchestra.

At the base of the hill, near the southern entrance gate, a small and rather grubby "lake" sports paddleboats and water birds, and a landscaped garden is glorious in spring bloom and when autumn colours the trees golden. Entry to Hongshan Park costs Rmb10.

Also very popular among locals is **People's Park**, a long, thin stretch of greenery immediately west of the Hetan Expressway with its main northern entrance on Youhao Lu. Large shady trees and

Left: The classical Chinese-style Viewing Pavilion on the crown of Hongshan Park. Top right: The People's Theatre in Renmin Square is fronted by grand columns and statues of dancing Uygurs. Bottom right: The entrance to the Confucian Temple (Jeremy Tredinnick x3).

ornamental pavilions and open corridors make this a cool, pleasant spot to stroll around, and close to the northern gate is **Mirror Lake (Jian Hu)**, an elm- and willow-banked haven in the middle of the city where fishermen trade stories and families of three or four generations come to boat and have lavish picnic feasts on Sunday afternoons. By the lake stands the **Jian Hu Pavilion**, a pretty two-storey structure with green roof tiles built in 1878 by an exiled minister of the Qing Dynasty (he had been part of the Reform Movement) who loved the lake. In 918 a Xinjiang Warlord added the "Hall of the Red Phoenix Crying in the Morning Sun" nearby, modelled after the Palace Museum in Beijing. People's Park also has a small zoo and a children's amusement park at its southern end near Heilongjiang Lu.

Half a dozen kilometres east of the city centre is **Water Mill Ditch Park**, in a narrow valley boasting hot springs that maintain a temperature of 28–30°C, and whose curative effects on arthritis and skin diseases draw plenty of visitors. In summer this is a favourite picnic spot among cityfolk.

Confucian Temple

Hidden away on a quiet street to the northeast of People's Square is the **Confucian Temple**, a low, classically constructed Qing Dynasty temple with sweeping eaves, courtyards filled with roses and halls dominated by colourful statues of Chinese gods and guardians. More than 1,000 square metres in area, it offers a completely different atmosphere to that of the city's mosques and markets. Originally called the Zhaozhong Temple, it was built to commemorate the soldiers who died during the Qing's reconquest of Xinjiang in the 18th century.

XINJIANG UYGUR AUTONOMOUS REGION MUSEUM (XINJIANG BOWUGUAN)

ocated on Xibei Lu, Xinjiang's biggest museum was previously called the Xinjiang Regional Museum, but in 2000 its attractive main building, a mix of Uygur and Russian styles, was torn down and a larger complex was constructed, a process that lasted five years. In 2005 the new **Xinjiang Uygur Autonomous Region Museum** opened its doors; its modern architecture is not to everyone's taste, with arched façades on either side of a curving concrete and blue-glass main

lobby. Although it will be a disappointment to those expecting a museum like those in Xi'an or Beijing, this is a must-visit destination for anyone in Urumqi, as it is the best place to get a detailed overview of Xinjiang's many millennia of human civilization. The museum's central domed entrance hall contains a 3D relief map of the region that immediately gives an insight into the importance of its topography in determining where and how humans could live and prosper.

The two-storey building is split neatly into four sections: on the ground floor are the "Silk Road" and "Ethnic Minorities" displays, while upstairs a large room is devoted to Xinjiang's famous "Mummies", and another concentrates on enforcing the idea that Xinjiang is part of the "Motherland". It is best to visit the galleries in chronological order, so first turn right and enter the "Silk Road" down a tunnel-like corridor, walking on a Perspex layer over a sandy "desert" floor.

This section actually covers a much greater time frame than its name implies – the first exhibit is an 8,000-year-old skull from Artux City, followed by pottery, wool and felt hats, and a dyed, corduroy-style trouser leg from 1,000 CE. A host of Bronze Age implements, colourful clothing and weapons are all in amazingly good condition and show excellent craftsmanship, but it is when you move on to the collection of items from the Western Han Dynasty (206 BCE–220 CE) onwards that the incredible wealth of ancient artefacts becomes apparent. The dry desert conditions helped to preserve an amazing array of items that detail life in the oasis kingdoms: fragments of silks, brocades, embroideries and wool carpets, wooden utensils and simple pottery are displayed (Han Dynasty pieces taken from the sites of **Loulan** and **Niya**) as well as copper seals,

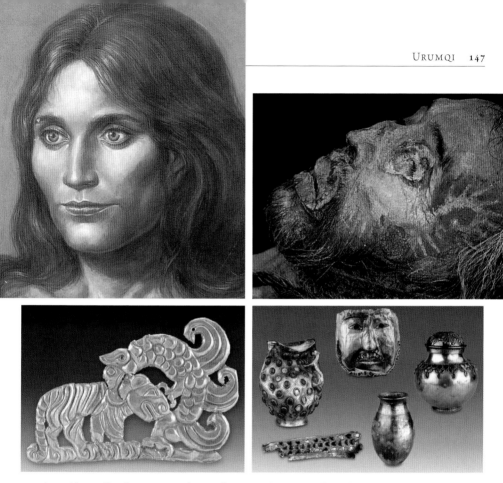

wooden tablets, official paper records, Buddhist mural paintings from the Wei and Jin dynastic period when **Kucha** was an advanced, independent kingdom, and even 1,500-year-old cakes and twisted dough sticks.

From the Northern and Sui dynasties are samples of silk weaving from **Hotan** and **Turpan**, using Central Asian tree and animal patterns, as well as wooden slips with rare Buddhist scriptures written in early Uygur Mongolian characters, Brahmani and Qiuci scripts, and a large clay Buddha head from the **Kizil** caves. A pair of brocade shoes, exquisite silks and hemp cloth documents from the **Astana Tombs** near Kharakhoja (Gaochang) date from the Tang Dynasty, as do specimens of grains, nuts, dried fruits, and nan (stamped with the same patterns used today), painted wooden figures, pottery tomb guards, Buddha heads in the Gandharan style, and a pair of metal eye shades ingeniously designed for protection from sandstorms.

Clockwise from top left: The main entrance to the Xinjiang Uygur Autonomous Region Museum (Magnus Bartlett); an artist's impression of the "Loulan Beauty"; a closeup of the male mummy discovered at the Zaghunluk site near Qiemo (Christoph Baumer); gold was used extensively by the early nomadic cultures of northern Xinjiang, including masks and finely wrought containers; a solid gold plaque discovered at Jiaohe shows a monster attacking a tiger; a superb brocade arm cover from Niya, sporting both animal motifs and Chinese characters (Liu Yu Sheng x3).

INDO-EUROPEAN MUMMIES

By Christoph Baumer

Today, the majority of Xinjiang's inhabitants are Uygurs – of Turkic stock – and Chinese. But members of these two ethnic groups are relative newcomers, for the Chinese only began to migrate there from the third century BCE onwards, while the Uygurs came from Mongolia to Xinjiang in the eighth century CE. So who lived in southern and eastern Xinjiang before and between those times?

Sensational finds of mummified bodies made since 1979 provide the surprising answer: over 4,000 years ago, two waves of Indo-Europeans settled not only in Xinjiang but also in western Mongolia and southern Siberia. These Indo-Europeans were cattle-raising equestrian nomads, who invented the stirrup, caused the spread of sheep-breeding and wool processing, and presumably passed on to China the art of metalworking. It seems that they were a warlike people, subjugating the agricultural populations they met during their migration eastwards. Only two millennia later were they mixed and mingled with Mongols and Chinese.

The initial immigrants were members of Indo-European peoples from the Caucasus, the Caspian region and the Ukraine, who took possession of the steppes of Eurasia during the fourth millennium BCE. From them emerged the 4,500-year-old Afanasievo culture in the Russian Altai Mountains and the valley of Minusinsk in southern Siberia. Around 2000 BCE, groups of these Indo-Europeans moved south and settled in the Tarim Basin, at the beginning of the Bronze Age. **Tokharian**, the language of these people called "**Proto-Tokharians**", which died out only in the ninth century CE, was clearly of Indo-European origin, and shows remarkable linguistic connections with European languages

such as Greek, Celtic, and Germanic and Slavonic languages. The more superficial similarities with Iranian languages occurred a thousand years later when the Proto-Tokharians mingled with people from a second wave of Indo-Europeans, namely the **Saka** (or Sak) of Persian stock. In the final centuries BCE, the Tokharian language split into three major dialects: the oldest was Tokharian A, which was already extinct in the first century CE and was thereafter only used in religious texts; Tokharian B served religious as well as administrative purposes and was mainly used along the northern Silk Road, particularly in the Kingdom of Kucha, wherefore it is also called "Kuchean"; while Tokharian C spread into the southeastern region of the Tarim Basin, to places such as Loulan.

About 800 years after the Proto-Tokharians, a second wave of immigration from the west began. These were the ancestors of the Saka, who penetrated into the Tarim Basin over several centuries from northern and eastern Persia and mingled with the Proto-Tokharians. Two of their largest and richest graveyards are found at Zaghunluk, near Qiemo, and Shanpula, near Hotan. Their most important dialect was Hotanese, which is related to Old Persian. As of the second century CE, Hotanese was written in the Indic script called Brahmi.

This unexpected discovery is based on the analysis of 302 mummies and skulls from nine different sites in and around the Tarim Basin dating from the Bronze Age (roughly 2000–900 BCE) and the Iron Age (900–200 BCE). The investigation showed that only 11 percent of the corpses examined displayed Sino-Mongolian characteristics, while 89% had Indo-European

A superb example of a desertified mummy within a typical boat-like coffin (Liu Yu Sheng).

attributes. After the second century BCE, the proportion of Sino-Mongolian people found among mummies increases slowly and more corpses with mixed Indo-European and Sino-Mongolian characteristics have been identified.

Unlike the ancient mummies of Egypt, those found in the Taklamakan were not artificially mummified prior to their burial. However, thanks to four preconditions, the corpses were naturally mummified and almost perfectly preserved – on numerous mummies even the eyelashes remain. First, the climate within the Tarim Basin, and especially in the desert, is extremely arid. There are few other places in the world where the relation between extremely rare precipitation, which takes place at most every second or third year in the form of light snowfall, and the degree of evaporation is so extreme. In the eastern portion of the desert, average precipitation is less than 10mm a year, with an evaporation potential of 2,900mm. There is even a phenomenon known as "devil's

rain", when the few raindrops that fall evaporate before reaching the ground. Second, there is a high accumulation of salt in the desert soil. The rivers that reach the desert move salt from the surrounding mountains into the basin, and the evaporation triggered by the arid environment causes the salt to concentrate on the desert surface. In such a saline environment, most bacteria and microbes that cause the decomposition of bodies cannot survive or, at least, cannot grow. Third, there is clear evidence, based on the specific garments the dead were wrapped in, that the best-preserved mummies were buried in winter. In such a cold environment the microbes buried with the dead had the least chance of survival.

The fourth precondition for the natural mummification of the Tarim mummies was man-made. While the dead were indeed sometimes placed in coffins, these had no bottom and simply lay in the sand. As the coffins were not tightly sealed and the tombs shallow, the existing ventilation inside the graves allowed any remaining moisture to evaporate, accelerating the dehydration of the corpses. When bodies were simply put on a reed mat without the use of a coffin, the dehydration of the dead was further accelerated. Since wooden coffins were only used in the earlier periods, not in the later, it is possible that the people understood this and learned from their experiences with previous burials. Or perhaps there were already restrictions in place on cutting trees (see below).

While global awareness of the rather sensational discovery of Indo-European mummies in northwest China only spread in the 1990s, the two great pioneer explorers of the Southern Silk Road and of Lop Nor, **Sir Aurel Stein** and **Sven Hedin**, had in 1914 and 1934 respectively already advanced the hypothesis of Indo-European traces in some of the ancient cultures they discovered. Both found, in the northern Lop Nor Desert along the former riverbed of the Kum Darya, several mummies bearing distinctly Indo-European traits rather than Chinese features. Stein observed, in his book *Innermost Asia*, "that the dead belonged to the autochthone [native] and not the Chinese race would have been adequately proved by the manners of the burial alone. But a look at the dead man's head sufficed to show that this racial type was distinctively non-Mongolian. The face was narrow across the cheeks, the nose high and aquiline, the eyes straight. The head was dolichocephalous [long]. The whole appearance of head and face suggested the Homo Alpinus."

Both, Hedin and Stein brought the hypothesis forward that former cities such as Loulan could have been founded by Indo-Europeans. Even before them, the French explorers Jules Dutreuil de Rhins and Ferdinand Grenard, who had explored parts of the Southern Silk Road between 1891 and 1893, suggested that the oldest population of the southern Tarim Basin were Indo-Europeans of Eastern Iranian stock who had arrived in the seventh century BCE.

The most important graveyards containing Indo-European bodies were found at the following sites: **Qäwrighul (Gumugou)** and **Töwän (Tieban)** in the northern Lop Nor region along the riverbed of the former Konche Darya (Peacock River), also called Kuruk Darya (Dry River) or Kum Darya (Sand River). These Indo-European people lived about four millennia ago, mainly through animal husbandry and small-scale agriculture. Most of their dead were buried with small bags of ephedra twigs placed on the chest. The therapeutic effect of its bioalkaloid – ephedrine – was probably already known, for it helps cure colds, bronchitis and asthma. At Qäwrighul, around the tomb seven circles of large wooden posts were driven into the ground, creating the impression of a radiating sun (and at the

same time stabilizing the sand). However, such tombs required much timber from dozens of trees that might have led over centuries to local deforestation. Interestingly, the earliest legal ban on felling trees in China was implemented later in the Kingdom of Shanshan, in the southwestern part of the Tarim Basin. An inscription found in Kharoshthi dating from the third century CE stipulated: "It is prohibited to fell trees casually. Whoever fells a tree together with its roots will be fined one horse. It is forbidden to fell trees in their growing period; offenders will be fined a cow."

A third Indo-European graveyard dating from the Bronze Age was located at **Xiaohe** near a side river of the Konche Darya in the northwestern Lop Nor Desert. A fourth, large necropolis with hundreds of Indo-European mummies from the second and first millennia BCE was discovered at **Zaghunluk,** near Qiemo, and a fifth, even larger with thousands of tombs dating from 900 to 100 BCE, at **Shanpula**, east of Hotan. The corpses were mostly buried lying on their backs with knees raised. Almost of the same size as Shanpula is the sixth graveyard of **Charwighul** near the ancient city of Karashahr, with more than 1,000 tombs dating from 500 to 100 BCE. Here the tombs are marked with stone heaps, with the larger ones covered by four to five stone plates, around which round stones are arranged in circles. As at some other Indo-European graveyards such as Zaghunluk, small children, horses and bullocks were sometimes sacrificed.

A few of the famous Tarim mummies can be seen in the Xinjiang Uygur Autonomous Region Museum in Urumqi, and in the small but worthwhile Museum of the Xinjiang Archaeological Institute in Urumqi (by appointment only). Mummies are also on display in the district museums of Turpan, Korla, Hotan and on the site of Zaghunluk.

There are superb examples of Yuan Dynasty horse halters, coins, gold figures and porcelain from central China, while the final section of the Silk Road display shows Qing Dynasty items such as jade and silver carvings, stone stelae and beautiful multicoloured silks, again from Hotan.

Above the "Silk Road" display on the first floor of the museum lies Xinjiang's highlight display and its signature exhibits. A sign at the entrance to the temperature-regulated room says: "Passed Away but Amaze the World Immortally [sic]"; this is your introduction to the famous **Xinjiang mummies**, and the first glass case you come to is the prize exhibit, the "**Loulan Beauty from Tiebanhe Riverside**". Excavated from Tieban River north of Lop Nor in 1980, the smooth, black-skinned corpse is a 45-year-old woman of Indo-European origin, with red hair, a thin, aquiline nose, and covered with a red-brown, rough wool blanket. Dated by Chinese archaeologists to 1800 BCE, her features are delicate, her lips drawn back in a tiny, enigmatic smile, while fur-topped, leather-soled shoes cover her feet, and a feather, comb and woven basket are arranged around her exactly as they were when she was found.

Other mummies include a child, a boy of 4–5 years swaddled in a wool blanket fastened with 16 wooden pins, a long-haired adult female from 1800 BCE discovered in the desert at the Xiaohe Graveyard and wearing a pointed felt hat with weasel skin trim, and the desiccated corpse of one Zhang Xiong (583–633), whose feet retain incredible detail in the skin and toenails. Some of the mummies were excavated from the Astana tombs, Tang Chinese governors or military staff buried with bows and arrows alongside them, while a beautifully caparisoned male and female Indo-European couple were exhumed from Qiemo in southern Xinjiang, buried alongside each other and dating to 800 BCE. Some of the mummies occasionally go on international exhibition tours, but there are always alternatives available to display from the museum's store vaults.

After this emotive insight into Xinjiang's past, the "Being with Homeland Forever" hall is a somewhat confusing collection of archaeological, environmental, political and socioeconomic displays aimed at reinforcing China's soveriegn right to Xinjiang, though in truth it does little to educate foreign visitors about the province. Also on the second floor, where once a well-stocked shop was located with everything from jewellery to books and carpets, there now stands the "Display of White Jade" room – essentially a less interesting shop filled with extravagant jade carvings and less expensive but still pricey jade jewellery and trinkets.

The final gallery, back on the ground floor and titled "Ancient Costume of Western Regions Exhibition Hall", is well worth exploring in full, as it devotes space for each of Xinjiang's 12 ethnic groups (not including the Han): you enter into a replica of a Uygur courtyard and house, with a wonderful display of Uygur musical instruments, then pass through rooms highlighting each nationality's unique dress and customs, from Kazakh yurts to dummies of Mongolian wrestlers, Kyrgyz livestock and Xibe archers, from Russian iron-and-brass beds to Daur hanging cradles.

Photography is not allowed anywhere in the museum. Entrance to the Xinjiang Uygur Autonomous Region Museum costs Rmb30 (entry is free on Sundays, but watch out for the crowds

– during the winter months entry is free every day). It is located at 581 Xibei Road (tel: (0991) 453 6436), one block west of the Sheraton Urumqi Hotel, and is open 10:30am–6pm daily, last ticket sold at 4:30pm. To get there take bus No. 7 from Xinhua Lu or bus No. 51 from the main train station, although a taxi would probably be a better option.

URUMQI PRACTICAL INFORMATION

Urumqi is a sprawling, industrial Chinese city, with all the energy, vitality... and difficulties that come with that categorization. Pollution can be a real problem, with dust in the air getting into your eyes and throat, making walking around town a thirsty and eventually irritating affair. Luckily there always seems to be a stall within easy reach selling a refreshing drink or fruit snack of some kind. Local buses are convenient – all bus fares, regardless of distance, cost Rmb1 – but figuring out the route network can be frustrating. Taxis are also cheap and generally easy to find – a fare across town will cost no more than Rmb10–15, while a taxi from the airport into the city costs Rmb50–80.

In August 2011 three new BRT bus lines opened, boasting modern, double-length articulated buses accessed at covered bus stops and still costing only Rmb1 per trip. This new bus system cost Rmb930 million and the three routes span the city via its main thoroughfares – though even locals are still confused by the colour-coded system and where each bus actually goes (they are numbered 1, 2 and 3, but bus No 1, for example, often takes different routes to its destination).

Wandering in the market areas is interesting and enjoyable, but be careful of pickpockets, especially in the International Grand Bazaar – in Urumqi this type of stealing has been raised to an art form, with some thieves using surgical tongs to "fish" in passing people's pockets and bags. Also be on the lookout for cars... on the pavements! In Urumqi it is normal for vehicles to park on the pavement and they often drive at considerable speed through pedestrian crowds looking for a space.

Normal business hours are 10am–2pm and 4–8pm, Beijing time – remember that official times are always stated in **Beijing time**, but locals usually think in "**Xinjiang time**", ie two hours behind, meaning for them their day starts at 8am and finishes at 6pm, which in practical terms fits in with actual daylight hours more accurately.

TRANSPORTATION

rumqi Diwopu International Airport (Airport Code: URC) is situated 20 kilometres northwest of the city centre, and has become a busy travel hub in recent years. **Flights within Xinjiang** include daily schedules to Aksu and Kashgar, Yining and Korla; four flights per week to Hotan and two or three flights a week to Altay City, Tacheng and Qiemo. Domestically, Urumqi is now connected through regular schedules (from daily flights for major cities to 3–4 flights per week or once-weekly) to Beijing, Changsha, Chengdu, Chongqing, Dalian, Dunhuang (seasonal), Guangzhou, Hangzhou, Jinan, Kunming, Lanzhou, Sanya, Shanghai, Shenzhen, Shijiazhuang, Qingdao, Xiamen, Xi'an, Xining, Yinchuan and Zhengzhou.

International flights have blossomed as well: Urumqi now serves Almaty and Astana in Kazakhstan; Moscow, Khabarovsk and Novosibirsk in Russia; Bishkek and Osh in Kyrgyzstan; Dushanbe in Tajikistan; Tashkent in Uzbekistan; Kabul in Afghanistan; Islamabad in Pakistan; Baku in Azerbaijan; Ashgabat in Turkmenistan; Tehran in Iran; Sharjah in the UAE; and Jeddah in Saudi Arabia, as well as Seoul in South Korea (*see* A–Z Facts for the Traveller section on page 434 for relevant airline websites).

Daily **trains** operate to/from Lanzhou, Xi'an, Beijing and Shanghai (and points in between), as well as to Kashgar via Korla, Kucha and Aksu on the Nanjiang Railway, which was completed in 2000. Prior to that, the opening of the Urumqi–Moscow rail link in 1991 meant that the city was no longer simply a railhead station but was now a stop-off point for westbound travellers on potentially exciting overland trips into the CIS and on to Europe. Trains operate between Almaty and Urumqi via Aktogay–Dostyk (Kazakh border post) and Lankol (Chinese border post), a journey of 40 hours plus; the railway line passes through the Junggar Gate into Kazakhstan and between Alakol Lake and Lake Balkhash before linking up with the Turk-Sib Line running north-south between Almaty and Semey (Semipalatinsk).

Two new rail lines have opened Xinjiang up further to train travel. In July 2010 the electric Jingyihuo Railway began passenger service from Jinghe (on the route from Urumqi to Alashankou) south to Yining (in the Ili Valley) and thence to the Kazakh border at Horgas (Khorgas). Then in June 2011 a single-track line began transporting passengers between Kashgar and Hotan along the southern rim of the Taklamakan, stopping at Yengisar, Shache, Yecheng and Pishan in between. A dedicated Urumqi-Hotan train leaves daily in each direction, taking approximately 35 hours.

Daily **long-distance buses** depart to/from Korla (10 hours); Kucha (15 hours); Aksu (19 hours); Kashgar (24 hours) and Hotan (via the cross-desert highway and Minfeng, between 20 and 26 hours) from the **Southern Bus Station** at the junction of Shengli Lu and Xinhua Nan Lu. There are also many buses every day to Turpan (2–3 hours) from here. The **Northern Bus Station** on Heilongjiang Lu serves routes to Yining in the Ili Valley (via Sayram Lake, 11–14 hours); Horgas Gate (the border crossing from the Ili into Kazakhstan, from where buses can take you to Almaty, 14 hours to Horgas, up to 26 hours to Almaty); Karamay (6 hours); Tacheng (12 hours) and Burqin (Buerjin, 13 hours), as well as Hami in the east (8–10 hours). There are also sleeper buses to Lanzhou, a journey of up to 40 hours – though the train is by far the better option.

ACCOMMODATION

Urumqi's hotel options have come on in leaps and bounds over the last decade – although upmarket travellers will still notice a gap in service quality when comparing them to same-level hotels in Beijing, Xi'an or Shanghai, for example. However, there is now a full range of offerings, from five-star establishments through mid-range business hotels to cheap and cheerful hostels. In a big city, though, experienced travellers know it pays to stay in comfort. Following is a selection of some of the city's top hotels, and some good cheaper alternatives:

Sheraton Urumqi Hotel

9 Youhao Bei Lu. Tel: (0991) 699 9999; fax: (0991) 699 9888;

email: urumqi.sheraton@sheraton.com, website: www.starwoodhotels.com/sheraton

A stylish international-brand hotel with good views from the upper floors. Located in the most upmarket shopping district, with the new Maison Mode pedestrianized shopping mall right next door where all the top international brands have outlets.

Yin Du Hotel

179 West Xihong Lu. Tel: (0991) 453 6688; fax: (0991) 451 7166;

email: yindu@yinduhotel.com; website: www.yinduhotel.com

An excellent five-star hotel north of the city centre in a busy business district, with 253 rooms and all modern facilities. Popular with coach tour companies because of its large forecourt parking space.

Grand Mercure Hualing (formerly Hua Ling Grand Hotel)

9 Xihong Dong Lu. Tel: (0991) 518 8888; fax: (0991) 518 9666; email: hotel@mail.hualing-grand-hotel.com; website: www.hualing-grand-hotel.com

This venerable Chinese five-star was taken over in 2012 by the Accor hotel group and is being fully renovated as a Grand Mercure class international four-star business and leisure hotel that will provide competition for the likes of the Sheraton. The brand's mission is to "express the spirit of a region" within a fully modern setting. It is situated in the northeast of the city between Nanhu Square and Hongshan Park, and has excellent views south over Hongshan to the city's skyscrapers and beyond to Bogda Shan – when the weather and pollution allow.

Hoi Tak Hotel, Xinjiang

1 Dong Feng Lu. Tel: (0991) 232 2828; fax: (0991) 232 1818;

email: xjbc@mail.hoitakhotel.com; website: www.hoitakhotel.com

Located directly facing People's Square, this is a central five-star hotel that gets good online reviews.

Hongfu Hotel

160 Wuyi Lu. Tel: (0991) 588 1588; fax: (0991) 582 3188;

email: reservations@hongfuhotel.com; website: www.hongfuhotel.com

A respected Chinese five-star hotel with 302 rooms and all luxury amenities located in the city business district between the railway station and the Hetan Expressway.

China Southern Airlines Pearl International Hotel

576 Youhao Nan Lu. Tel: (0991) 638 8888; fax: (0991) 638 8666;

email: reservations.urumqi@kempinski.com

A modern luxury hotel within easy walking distance of Hongshan Park.

Mirage Hotel

5 Xinhua Bei Lu. Tel: (0991) 293 7888; fax: (0091) 284 6666;

email: mirage@mirage-hotel.cn; website: www.mirage-hotel.cn

A gleaming five-star occupying a large block in the centre of the downtown shopping district.

Orient Dynasty Hotel

17 Xinhua Nan Lu. Tel: (0991) 233 5678; fax: (0991) 233 5888; email: xj_dfwc@126.com

A busy four-star in the heart of the main shopping centre, on the corner of Xinhua Nan Lu and Zhongshan Lu.

Ramada Tunhe Hotel

52 Changjiang Lu. Tel: (0991) 587 6688; fax: (0991) 587 7070;

email: thhotelgrace@hotmail.com; website: www.ramada.com

A four-star hotel managed by Ramada, located close to the railway station.

Mingyuan New Times Hotel

7 Youhao Bei Lu. Tel: (0991) 481 8688

A four-star hotel north of the city centre, close to the Xinjiang Uygur Autonomous Region Museum and next to new exclusive shopping mall Maison Mode.

Super 8 Urumqi Ba Yin He

3 Gongyuan Bei Jie. Tel: (0991) 559 8899; website: www.super8.com

One of a branded group of three-star Chinese hotels that offers free wifi and breakfast in a great central location beside People's Park.

Central Hotel

177 Minzhu Lu. Tel: (0991) 293 6666; website: www.pengren.cn (Chinese only)

A three-star business hotel located in an old, rather attractive building on the Minzhu Lu roundabout next to the People's Cinema. An excellent location.

FOOD AND DRINK

Small Muslim restaurants clustered around the markets serve authentic Uygur cuisine like *laghman*, *chushira*, poluo, kebabs, nan and *apke*. The lanes around Erdaoqiao are packed with people crowded around tables in the evenings; the area in front of the People's Theatre has a night market buzz, and the **Red Flag Covered Market** (Hongqi Lushi Chang) that connects Renmin and Zhongshan Lu is a lively fruit and vegetable market lined with restaurants. Sichuanese and other Chinese restaurants can be found on Renmin Lu and Xinhua Lu, around the bus station and opposite the Red Flag Covered Market, as well as in all the better hotels. Grapes from Turpan, melons from Hami and Ili peaches begin to arrive in July, and tasty nan bread is on sale everywhere – flat like a pizza base with curling patterns and a sprinkling of herbs or spices on top, it makes a very tasty snack and costs only Rmb2 for a mid-sized nan. In summer, freshly squeezed fruit juices, savoury milk tea and ice cream are sold on every corner.

For those yearning for international food other than the Western restaurants in the top hotels, there are some surprising options. On the right just up Jianshe Lu from the cinema on Minzhu Lu roundabout is a new Maltese restaurant called **Aroma** (2/F, 196 Jianshe Lu, tel: 283 5881) that serves great Mediterranean cuisine and has free wifi. The popular restaurant called **The Vine** (20/F Times Square, Xi Daqiao) that is run by a Caribbean couple and features excellent Caribbean dishes, steaks and salads, fruit shakes and delicious cakes, was originally located in an alley near Minzhu Lu, but has now moved to the 20th floor of a new skyscraper that is part of the Times Square complex on Guangming Lu near the northern end of Xinhua Beilu and the bridge over the Hetan Expressway. At the northern end of Yan'an Lu, five minutes' walk south of the International Grand Bazaar, is the cheap but excellent **Ankara Turkish Restaurant**.

Also in an alleyway off Renmin Lu (near Nanmen Square and behind the Khantengri Mosque) is the **Texas Café** (tel: 281 0025), a Tex-Mex style restaurant offering great steaks, burritos, etc, in a very Western setting, with a selection of books at the back and large TV screen. The American-run **Rendezvous** (958 Yan'an Lu, tel: 255 5003) is another option, while Gongyuan Beijie, a lane that runs down the west side of People's Park, is home to a number of bars, most popular of which is **Fubar** (40 Gongyuan Bei Jie, tel: 584 4498, email: info@fubar.com.cn), owned and operated by an Irishman. Imported beers, pizza and fish and chips are on the menu, and a dartboard, table football and pool tables make this a home from home for many expats. (This street is rumoured soon to be demolished by the authorities, meaning all the bars will need to move.) Nightclubs and more pricey bars can be found in all the top hotels, but beware the attentions of the ubiquitous "hostesses".

AROUND THE CITY

HEAVEN LAKE (TIANCHI)

Nestled into the northern slopes of the Bogda Shan, a three-hour road journey of 120 kilometres (74 miles) east of Urumqi, lies the beautiful azure lake known as **Tianchi**, the **Heavenly Lake**, 1,940 metres above sea level and surrounded by steep hills blanketed in forests of spruce, pine and fir. Originally called Yaochi, or Jade Lake, it was renamed in 1783 by Ming Liang, a Qing Dynasty military commander in charge of the Urumqi region. Tianchi's crystal-clear waters are fed by snow meltwater and the runoff from the massive glaciers that descend from Bogda Feng or Peak (5,445 metres), which towers over its southern end. The crescent-shaped lake averages 40 metres deep but is 105 metres at its deepest point; it is 3.4 kilometres long and 1.5 kilometres across at its widest point, covering an area of around five square kilometres. (Sadly, these figures may be optimistic since in recent years water levels have begun

Right: The serpentine road that ascends to Tianchi, which lies just under 2,000 metres above sea level (Hao Pei).

Heaven Lake presents a picture-postcard scene in winter (Sun Jiabin).

to drop.) Legend has it that in 985 BCE Emperor Mu of the Zhou Dynasty attended a banquet at Jade Lake as the guest of the fairy goddess Wang Wu, the Queen Mother of the West, and here they fell in love. (Some sources, however, place this meeting in the Kunlun Mountains far to the south.)

It's certainly a romantic spot. The road that ascends to Tianchi snakes up through picturesque hills to the lakeside, where Kazakh families pitch their yurts in summer and graze their herds of horses, sheep and cattle in the lush alpine meadows. Amidst fields of wildflowers grow morrel mushrooms, wild peppermint and rhubarb, while higher up the mountain are edelweiss and the rare, creamy **Snow Lotus** (*Saussurea involucrata*), which blooms in

Clockwise from below: Herding sheep in the lush Southern Pastures; the "Geographic Centre of Asia" as per the calculations of Chinese scientists; traditional Kazakh dancing in the mountains, with Kazakh yurts in the background (Sun Jiabin x3); a Kazakh woman lays lumps of cheese out to dry near Heaven Lake (Peter Hibbard).

July. Larger than a normal lotus flower, the plant grows from rock crevices and is believed to have magical powers, which often figure in Chinese kung-fu stories. Its dried pistils, marinated in wine, are popularly believed to relieve arthritis, rheumatism and menstrual cramps.

In fact, in 1990 this area, covering 128,690 hectares from Bogda Peak down to the rim of the Junggar Basin (460 metres above sea level), was designated the **Bogeda Biosphere Reserve** by UNESCO, because of its huge range of ecosystems and the wealth of plants and wildlife that inhabit them. The local government controls the area as the Tianchi Nature Reserve, but significant increases in tourist numbers have affected its appeal for many. In 2006, a four-year, Rmb800 million (US$100 million) "restoration" plan was implemented, involving an increase of the tourism area around the lake from 158 to 548 square kilometres, and the addition of electric vehicles and a cable car.

Nevertheless, it's understandable that people flock here in great numbers during the summer months – the mountain views are truly stunning. Most tourists just go for the day, take a boat ride on the lake, have lunch at the lakeside restaurant and ride or walk along the mountain paths. However, it is much more rewarding to stay overnight, since the area is significantly more quiet and calm after the tour group crowds leave in the late afternoon. It is possible to hike or ride on horses up to the snowline or glaciers, where the wilderness is pristine and vistas spectacular.

Travellers can stay on the western side of the lake in one of the many yurts owned by locals, with a mat on the floor and a bowl of hot fresh milk in the morning. The farther away you go, the less likely you are to see other tourists. Be forewarned that the yurts do not have washing or toilet facilities. The Tianchi Hotel has small chalet-like rooms overlooking the lake, which are quite expensive (book through a travel agent in Urumqi). Buses leave daily at 9am (Rmb50) from the bus station and outside the north gate of People's Park in Urumqi, but all vehicles now stop at a new entrance gate down near the main road from the city. Entry to the lake area costs Rmb100 (visiting is also allowed during the winter months but is dependent on road and weather conditions), and a Rmb70 return shuttle bus takes you up the winding road to the lake shore.

THE SOUTHERN PASTURES (NAN SHAN)

While Tianchi claims top spot as the most touted day trip out of the city, locals generally prefer to head south to the beautiful valleys of the **Southern Mountains** (**Nan Shan**), which begin about 30 kilometres south of the city. This mountainous area is the northern tip of the Kalawucheng range of the Tien Shan, and is a natural summer pasture for Kazakhs. A combination of precipitous peaks, thick forests and meadow-filled valleys with rushing streams and ribbon-like waterfalls, there are many valleys to explore, but the most popular is **White Poplar Gully (Baiyang Gou)**, 75 kilometres (46 miles) from Urumqi. Through this narrow, verdant gully, framed by snow-capped peaks and dotted with tall dragon-spruce trees, runs a mountain stream, and at the far end is a 20-metre waterfall which sprays clouds of refreshing mist around it. Between May and October, Kazakh families move their yurts into the area to graze their herds. Horsemen offer rides to tourists, and you can visit their yurts, drink milk tea, watch horseracing and traditional Kazakh dancing. Buses leave People's Park in the morning and return late in the afternoon.

Other sites worth visiting are **Gangou Chrysanthemum Terrace**, located in the west of Shuixi Valley, a pastureland of wildflower-strewn meadows at 2,000–2,400 metres; **Miao'er Gully**, which also boasts a waterfall, and **Daxi Gully**, where five glaciers descend from the mountaintops, the longest 2.4 kilometres long, an average of 500 metres wide, and at an altitude of 3,800 metres – though as with so many glaciers worldwide these are shrinking fast.

Unsurprisingly, in recent years rampant development has come to this area. In 2009 the **Silk Road Ski Resort** was renovated and extended to become a huge complex with eight kilometres of slopes covering a vertical drop of 610 metres and catering to thousands of skiers (it is popular mostly with Russian ski tourists). Another massive four-season ski and leisure centre, **PingTian Resort** (www.pingtianresorts.com) is also in the works. The foreign-owned village complex will feature 27 ski runs with state-of-the-art lifts, as well as golf courses, horseback riding activities and a dude ranch in summer. Construction began in November 2008 and will go ahead in phases, with an emphasis on "preserving and enhancing the landscape and making sure the facilities still fit into the natural environment with a sense of balance and harmony".

However, this and other tourism development in Nan Shan's valleys means that the Kazakh families and their yurt communities have had to retreat deeper into the mountains, so more walking is required if you want to meet them – and the benefits to them of all this change is highly debatable.

THE "CENTRE OF ASIA"

About 25 kilometres southwest of Urumqi, at the village of **Baojiacaozi** in Yongfeng County, a tall pyramidal structure topped by a metal globe marks the "Geographic Centre of Asia", officially measured by Chinese experts as lying at the coordinates 43° 40' 50" North, 87° 19' 52" East. Stand here and you will be farther from the sea than anywhere on the planet. It takes only 30 minutes to get here by car, and the monument can be visited as part of a day trip to the Nan Shan area.

THE ROAD TO TURPAN

With a major highway now open between Urumqi and Turpan, buses and cars can make the journey in two hours or less. The rail line and motorway, Highway 312, criss-cross each other through a flat landscape of low shrubs and pebbles, with Bogda Peak to the north and a lower spur to the south. Forty kilometres outside Urumqi they pass two large salt lakes, one four square kilometres in size, the other much bigger at 17 square kilometres – a small hydrotherapy tourist industry has built up here.

Farther south is the town of **Dabancheng** – the ladies of old Dabancheng were made famous by a Uygur folksong praising their beautiful long plaits. Beyond the town are the ruins of a fort built in 1870 by Yakub Beg and destroyed soon after by the Qing Dynasty army that was sent to put down

The motorway between Urumqi and Turpan is a top-class highway, allowing smooth, rapid transit through the forest of wind turbines that make up the "Dabancheng Wind Power Factory" (Magnus Bartlett).

the rebellion. However, today the area around this town is famous for a very different reason – it is the site for the "**Dabancheng Wind Power Factory**", a corridor of hundreds of towering wind turbines 80 kilometres long and 20 kilometres wide, placed strategically in the gap between spurs of the Tien Shan that channels air between the huge desert regions to the north and south of the mountains, generating consistent levels of wind. The turbines make an impressive sight as you drive through them, especially when they are all spinning their huge blades – they produce an estimated power-generating capacity of 100 megawatts, and more are being added.

The road winds through a barren gorge before emerging to a stark, open expanse and descending gradually into the Turpan Depression, leaving the railway at Daheyan. Across the *gebi* desert (meaning stony and not to be confused with the Gobi Desert of Mongolia) run the famous underground water channels or *karez* that irrigate the rich oasis of Turpan. Traceable by the mounds of earth at their openings, these lines of connected wells stretch from the mountains to the oasis like trail markers for an army of giant moles. Through this ostensibly empty landscape the road shoots, an amazingly smooth, well-maintained four-lane motorway that puts to shame many similar highways in the US or UK. Before you know it, you've arrived at the northern fringes of Turpan.

Harvesting grapes in Turpan; perfect growing conditions result in bountiful crops of the juiciest grape varieties – little wonder that this region is renowned throughout Asia for its grapes and grape products (Yan Xian).

Turpan and the East

Turpan (Turfan or Tulufan)

One of the earliest names of this town, Huozhou ("Land of Fire"), was derived from the intense summer temperatures, which reach over 40°C (104°F) between June and August. Yet another appellation, the "Storehouse of Wind", refers to the blustering winds that often whip through the streets for several hours in the afternoons. Influenced by an extreme continental climate, the winters here are also extreme, often dropping to -15°C (5°F), while annual precipitation is a mere 20mm (0.9 inches). **Turpan** is principally an agricultural oasis, famed for its grape products: seedless white raisins (which are exported) and wines (mostly sweet). Ironically, add the benefits provided by the ingenious *karez* irrigation, and it is actually the extreme aridity and scorching heat – that would otherwise make this a lifeless hell – that allow for such great productivity of high-quality fruits.

The city is located on the northern rim of the **Turpan Depression**, which averages some 80 metres (260 feet) below sea level (Turpan city itself is 30 metres above sea level). Nearby **Aiding Hu (Moon Lake)**, at 154 metres (505 feet) below sea level, is the second lowest continental point in the world after the Dead Sea. Along with some southern Xinjiang cities, Turpan claims longevity records, with many people over 100 years of age. Locals believe that the climate, drinking milk and eating grapes are the main factors. More than 70 percent of Turpan's population of 260,000 is Uygur, and this results in a very different feel to the more Chinese cities to the north. The cultural influence of Islam is immediately more apparent, while the overt manner in which Mother Nature makes her presence felt gives Turpan its own unique atmosphere.

History

In 108 BCE, Turpan was inhabited by farmers and traders of Indo-European stock who spoke a form of Tokharian, a now extinct Indo-Persian language. Whoever occupied the Turpan oasis commanded the northern trade route and the rich caravans that passed through annually. During the Han Dynasty control over the route swung back and forth between the Xiongnu and Chinese; then, until the fifth century CE, the capital of its kingdom was at **Jiaohe** (Yarkhoto).

During the Northern Wei Dynasty (386–534) the capital of **Gaochang (Kharakhoja)** was established to the east of Jiaohe by the Loulan people, who sent tribute to the Tang court in Chang'an, maintaining diplomatic relations with 24 sovereign states. The House of Qu, a Buddhist Han dynastic family, ruled Turpan from the beginning of the sixth century. Qu Wentai was so aggressively hospitable to the Buddhist monk Xuanzang, and so eager for him to stay and teach the people of Gaochang that after a month's delay, the monk resorted to a three-day hunger strike to secure permission to continue his pilgrimage to India.

The Khan of the Western Turks later urged Qu Wentai to prevent Silk Road merchants from travelling eastwards, which prompted Emperor Taizong to send an expeditionary force to Gaochang. Its approach caused Qu Wentai to die of fright, and it was left to his son to surrender in 640. In their campaign to pacify the west, the Chinese established a protectorate-general to watch over the region. Turpan's cotton cloth, *alum* (used in paper making), Glauber's salt and fresh "mare's-nipple grapes" were traded in Chang'an. During the Tang Dynasty Turpan introduced China to the art of making grape wine.

When the northern Uygur Empire disintegrated, the nomadic tribes dispersed, and some established an independent kingdom at Gaochang in the mid-ninth century. The Indo-European natives were assimilated by the Uygurs and a rich, intellectual, highly artistic, religious culture developed. Buddhists, Manichaeans and Nestorians lived together harmoniously and religious art flourished in the cities and monastic caves; religious literature was translated into the numerous languages and scripts used at that time. The Gaochang state continued to exist well into the 13th century, when the Mongols swept through Central Asia. After the death of Genghis Khan (Chinggis Khaan), Turpan became part of the Chaghatai Khanate known as Uyguristan.

Marco Polo observed in the 13th century that the people of Turpan "declare that the king who originally ruled over them was not born of human stock, but arose from a sort of tuber generated by the sap of trees, which we call *esca*; and from him all the others descended. The idolaters [Buddhists] are very well versed in their own laws and traditions and are keen students of the liberal arts. The land produces grain and excellent wine. But in winter the cold here is more intense than is known in any other part of the world."

At the end of the 14th century, the Uygurs in the Turpan area were forcibly converted to Islam by an heir to the Chaghatai Khanate loyal to Tamerlane the Great. During Turpan's period of aggression towards the neighbouring oasis of Hami, the Chinese refused entry to all trade caravans from Uyguristan and expelled Uygur traders from Gansu Province. However, the Ming Dynasty maintained good relations with Turpan, which supplied a special dye vital to the production of the famous blue-and-white Ming porcelain.

The Islamic inhabitants of Turpan rebelled against the domination of the Buddhist Oirat Mongols to the north, and with Hami, joined in the Qing Dynasty's Junggar campaign against the Oirats (also known as the Junggars). However, in 1861 Turpan rebelled against the Chinese garrison troops and joined in Yakub Beg's revolt.

Sir Francis Younghusband, journeying through Turpan in the 1880s, noted that it "consists of two distinct towns, both walled – the Chinese and the Turk, the latter situated a mile west of the former. The Turk town is the [more] populous, having probably twelve or fifteen thousand inhabitants, while the Chinese town has not more than five thousand at the outside."

Above: An image of the Turpan Depression created by Landsat 7's Enhanced Thematic Mapper plus (ETM+) sensor highlights its mix of sand dunes, salt lakes, oases and the rugged mountains from which its life-giving streams emerge (Image provided by the USGS EROS Data Center Satellite Systems Branch as part of the Earth as Art II image series). Opposite: A happy couple head homeward with a cartload of firewood along one of old Turpan's poplar-lined tracks (Jeremy Tredinnick).

In the early 20th century, many Western explorers and archaeologists were attracted to Turpan's ancient cities and Buddhist caves. The German Albert von Le Coq's first expedition in 1902–1903 yielded nearly 2,000 kilogrammes of treasure, which he transported back to Europe; on his second expedition a year later, he shipped off 103 crates. The other two German expeditions yielded 128 and 156 boxes respectively. The British archaeologist, Sir Aurel Stein, mopping up after von Le Coq in 1915, loaded over 140 crates onto 45 camels and dispatched the antiquities to Kashgar. Of what was left, incalculable damage was done to these archaeological monuments by the Uygurs themselves, who had by now become ardent Muslims and defaced most of the beautiful artwork that remained.

The main crops grown in Turpan are wheat, sorghum, cotton, grapes, peanuts, melons and vegetables. There are several communally owned industries, the main ones being coal and chemical production; smaller ones include dried fruit, wines and fruit juices.

SIGHTS

Turpan's verdant growth of poplar and fruit trees, vineyards and lush cultivated fields form a striking contrast to the surrounding desert. Cable and French wrote in the 1930s: "Turpan lies like a green island in a sandy wilderness, its shores lapped by grit and gravel instead of ocean water."

The town centre is relatively small and compact, and can be explored on foot, with frequent stops for refreshments, of course – never underestimate the dehydrating power of the sun here. One of the main north-south thoroughfares, Qingnian Lu, is pedestrianized and has walkways covered by grape trellises, a blessed relief from the hammer-like heat of the summer sun. This street passes the eastern edge of the main public square, on the other side of which is Gaochang Lu; the Turpan Prefecture Museum was once located at its northern end (but has now moved to the eastern edge of town), while to the south it meets Laocheng Lu and the bazaar area.

THE CLEAN OASIS

"*You are going to Turfan?*" an old Turki yamen-runner and interpreter on the North Road had asked me. "Ah, Turfan! It is a good place. Clean, clean! I left it when I was a boy and have never saved the money to go back. But it is clean, clean. The streets of the bazaar are cleaner than the k'ang of the Chinese. There not even the horse of a traveler can leave anything in the street without someone rushing up to tidy it." He had no higher praise. As usual, however, we found that the inn of the big town was more filthy, more smelly, and in the hands of people more impudent, lazy, and thievish than the inns of tiny halting places by the road; but even while we were lamenting the evil prospect, there sought us out a Russian Tatar. He was a merchant I had met in Urumchi, and having seen us pass through the streets he had come to rescue us and install us in a cool Turki room, with thick clay walls and arched windows opening on a private court. Then, our lodging settled, we went to "open our eyes," which is the admirable Chinese phrase for staring, in the bazaar or trading quarter.

The walled city, in vivid contrast with the open country, is cool and green. Over the central streets, which are at once passageways and marketplaces, are trellises, covered with mats, gourd-vines, and the branches of willows and poplars. In the chequered shade the people step softly, loose-robed and barefooted or slipper-shod; and as they chatter in Turki, guttural but soft, the eyes of women flash under stenciled eyebrows and the teeth of men flash from black beards. From wells and ditches at the city gates of battlemented mud, little boys drive innumerable donkeys carrying water pannier-wise in wooden butts, to be splashed over the streets. From the time that the struggle against the heat begins in the morning until it slackens at dusk, the whole population flings water on the walls and floors of houses, on the streets, and on the vegetables for sale in little booths or spread out on the clean streets. Although we splashed water copiously on the walls of our room, it dried in a few minutes. The streets, thus constantly moistened and patted with bare feet and slapped with slippers, do indeed become beautifully smooth and clean...

...The shopping hour is over by nine in the morning. After that, riding along the empty streets, one may see only in the recesses of the shops figures seated cross-legged, magnificently set off by the muted glow of carpets and bright wares in dark corners; poised in that most commanding sloth which goes by the name of Oriental dignity. Through deserted gateways one gets a glimpse here of the carved wooden galleries and plaster domes of mosques and there of caravanserais, with courtyards walled about with bales of cotton and populated by somnolent donkeys.

Owen Lattimore, **High Tartary**, 1930

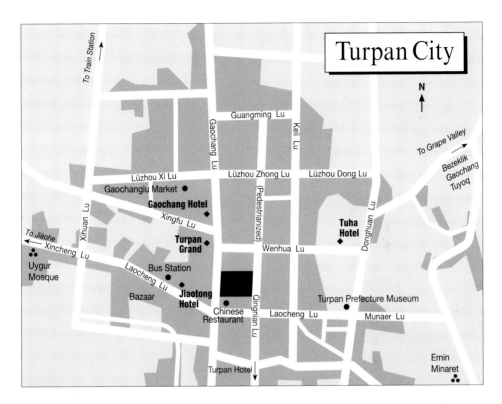

imply wandering out of the town centre in the general direction of the Emin Minaret will transport you back in time, to the dust roads of the town's more traditional suburbs, where spacious houses with ornately painted front doors, shady courtyards and cool underground rooms for sleeping or storing produce accommodate the large Uygur families. Either attached to the house or in nearby vineyards are high open mud-brick rooms (called *yinfang* in Chinese and *liangjie* in Uygur) used for drying grapes: after 40 to 50 days the grapes have become raisins and are ready for market, where they are sold for better prices than fresh grapes.

The **Turpan Bazaar** has a two-storey covered section with stalls selling *dopa* hats, clothing, boots and shoes, Yengisar knives, bright embroideries and bolts of cloth. Around and behind the covered bazaar the streets teem with vegetable and fruit sellers, dried fruits and nuts, carpet dealers, bakers and small private food stalls. A thirst-quenching, cold summer drink made up of cold water and the juice of rehydrated peaches or apricots (known as *bingshui*) is ladled from refrigerated tins; an ice slush, sold in small shot glasses, is also popular. Sunday is the busiest market day but the rest of the week is active as well.

Clockwise from opposite page: An eighth-century tomb guardian from the Astana Tombs sits behind glass in the Turpan Prefecture Museum; floral embroidery on a Gaochang-era boot (Jeremy Tredinnick x2); Sogdian script on a document discovered at Bezeklik (Liu Yu Sheng); young Uygur women sport traditional waist-length braided hair and colourful aidelaixi-style clothing (Sun Jiabin); one of the Turpan Prefecture Museum's mummies, displayed as it was found, with legs bent at the knees (Jeremy Tredinnick).

On the south side of the main street, a short walk west of the bazaar, is the **Uygur Mosque (Green Mosque)**, built in 1983, its six minarets surmounting a green-and-white mirrored facade. Opposite stand several new Islamic-style buildings, including the hospital and the teacher's training college. The annual **Turpan Silk Road Grape Festival** takes place over one festive week in late August; the streets are lined with grapes from all over the county, and people from over 30 cities in the northwest provinces serve regional delicacies and wear traditional clothing – although often the full colourful festival scene only materialises on one or two days, so it's best to check with the locals or a reputable tour company for the best day to attend.

Turpan Prefecture Museum (Tulufan Zìzhìqu Bowuguan)

Many visitors never make it to the Turpan Prefecture Museum, heading instead straight out of town to the many attractions in the vicinity. Though these are all worth visiting, of course, the reality is that very little remains within the sites themselves, so the museum represents your best opportunity of seeing artefacts unearthed from nearby locations, including paper fragments, porcelain, weapons, daily implements, silks, and earth and wooden figurines.

The old museum was a neat and tidy building on Gaochang Lu, but the entire collection has been moved to a new location on the corner of Donghuan Lu and Laochang Lu (on the way to the Emin Minaret). It is now housed in a beautiful building constructed in Islamic style, and covers three floors, though its various sections follow basically the same format as was found in the old museum.

Visitors start their tour up a staircase on the second floor, which is split into four sections. On the right as you enter is a Video Room where a 30-minute introduction to the Turpan area runs in both Chinese and English (when it is actually working). The "Dinosaur Fossil Hall" contains a number of huge skeletons, the main one comprising the actual bones of a 24-million-year-old creature named *Paraceratherium tienshanensis*, discovered by railroad workers in 1993. The geographical change of the Turpan Basin from lush swampy jungle 20 million years ago to dry desert today, and the consequent evolution of life, is explained imaginatively. There are teeth from the Miocene era, including ancestors of elephants, rhinos and giraffes from 15 million years ago, a sabre-tooth skull, and interesting displays showing the development of both horses and humans.

Also on the second floor is the "Culture and History" hall with exhibits from archaeological digs at the major local sites of Jiaohe, Astana and Gaochang (Karakhoja or Khocho). There are flints dating back 40,000 years, gold ornaments from 475 BCE, and 2nd century BCE relics from Jiaohe such as bows and arrows, wood carvings and weaving tools. Intricate pottery and wooden figures of servants and animals come from Astana in the 4th–5th centuries CE, while ancient scrolls, eye protectors, a baby coffin (from Tuyoq) and an impressive tomb guardian date to a couple of centuries later, at the start of the Tang Dynasty. Items from this period include scripts in Chinese, shoes and wooden carvings of carts and food. The Gaochang Uygur period from the 9th to 14th centuries is represented by superb silk fragments and beautifully embroidered boots – the delicate flower patterns are still popular today, and can be seen on modern shoes in the town's markets.

Further down is another small hall displaying old scripts and coins excavated from Jiaohe, Astana and Gaochang, providing a fascinating comparison of the different languages used in each period.

On the third floor is a temperature-regulated gallery containing "The Ancient Corpses of Turpan", discovered only in the last few decades. This section is a great improvement in layout from the previous museum. There are 12 mummies in total (including two infants); a husband and wife couple discovered in Astana cemetery in 1972 had documents buried with them showing dates (502–640 CE) and their family name – they are very well preserved, with the man's thin moustache still clearly visible. An interesting touch are the model replicas of the couple standing next to the corpses in lavish Tang clothing, illustrating how they looked in life.

A lift brings you to the exit on the first (ground) floor where there is one final room, used as an exhibition hall for a regularly changing collection of items such as bronzes from the Qing Dynasty (on show in 2011). All sections of the museum now have boards and signs with clear English explanations, and computer screens in each hall provide more information and details. When you arrive at the museum you must register with your passport/ID. Bags must be left at the ticket office and no water is allowed inside the museum. Photography is permitted throughout the museum but no flash should be used, and it is still wise to ask the museum staff in each hall before taking pictures (on occasion they may not allow photography). The museum is open daily from 10am to 6:30pm, closed on Mondays and there is no entrance charge (website: www.turfanological.com).

Emin Minaret (Su Gong Ta)

he striking **Emin Minaret** stands two kilometres (just over a mile) east of the city and is one of the architectural gems of the Silk Road, its unusual conical shape the only tall structure in the area. Construction of the minaret began in 1777 at the behest of the ruler of Turpan, **Emin Khoja**, who had gained power by assisting the Qing army in its campaign to defeat the Junggar hordes of the northwest, but it was completed in 1778 by his son Suleyman, for whom it is also called the Sugong (Prince Su) Minaret. The tower is 37 metres high and 10 metres wide at its base; the plain yellow sun-dried bricks taper skywards in attractive geometric, wave and floral patterns. It was designed by a Uygur architect called Ibrahim, and uses no timber in its walls, instead being structurally supported by the 72-step, spiral brick staircase that ascends within.

Tourists are not permitted to climb the minaret, but there is a good view of the surrounding area from the second-storey balcony above the mosque entrance. The complex is encircled by broad, verdant vineyards, the tall liangjie drying houses and vegetable plots, a beautiful setting with the Flaming Mountains as a dramatic backdrop. The mosque, which adjoins the minaret, has a beamed ceiling supported by simple wooden pillars, with a domed sacred area, and side halls that were used as madrasahs until the 1950s. It was renovated in 2000 (the minaret was left untouched); a stone tablet inside the mosque tells its history in Arabic and Chinese, but a recent addition is another rough stone tablet above it showing two dragons – the symbol of Chinese power – a peculiar statement to make in an Islamic religious building, where traditionally any figurative representation is forbidden.

Left: A Statue of Emin Khoja stands near the entrance to the Emin Minaret complex. Right: The 37-metre-high minaret is a stunning piece of architecture, constructed entirely of brick with intricate geometric and floral patterns (Jeremy Tredinnick x2).

A t the entrance to the complex gardens another new figure now also contradicts normal Islamic practice: a large stone statue of Emin Khoja stands facing east and holding what appears to be a scroll. Add to this the Chinese dance music blaring from souvenir stalls at the entrance, the concrete-framed grape arbours, gazebos and viewing platforms, and it is obvious that this site has been chosen for development as a highlight tourist destination in the region. Consequently the atmosphere loses something of its authenticity, although it remains an impressive and worthwhile stop on the Turpan itinerary.

The mosque is only used by locals for prayer on Fridays, Saturdays and Sundays, but during festivals it comes alive, its grounds filling up with pilgrims and picnickers full of festive cheer, creating a carnival atmosphere. Entrance for tourists costs Rmb30.

MIYIM HAJI KAREZ MUSEUM

Although the ingenious underground irrigation system known as *karez* is used in many regions of Xinjiang, including Hotan, Artush, Kucha, Hami and Urumqi, it is most famous – and most highly concentrated – in the Turpan Depression. A number of karez wells and semi-open channels can be visited around Turpan city, but in 2007 a new museum opened in the western suburbs of town, constructed above a functioning karez. The **Miyim Haji Karez Museum** was created by a wealthy local businessman and is linked to the Xinjiang Karez Research Association, which is partially funded

THE KAREZ: WELLSPRING OF LIFE IN THE DESERT

The ancient *karez* irrigation system is an ingenious method of providing water in large quantities to an area of arid land that otherwise would not be fit for large-scale human habitation. A karez is comprised of a series of wells and linking underground channels that tap subterranean water and use gravity to bring it to the surface at a destination lower than the source. By this means water can be transported long distances in hot, dry climates without losing a large proportion of the source water to seepage or evaporation.

Karez means "well" in Persian (the Arabic word is *qanat*), and examples of this type of irrigation are known from Xinjiang in the east, through the Iranian and Arabic world to Morocco in western North Africa. However, nowhere in the world has this system been used so extensively, and to such productive and significant effect, as in the Turpan Depression.

Records of the karez system of Turpan and Hami date back more than 2,000 years to the Han Dynasty (206 BCE–220 CE), but it is likely that they extend far beyond that, to the time when Indo-European Tokharians migrated into the Tarim Basin from the region of Bactria (modern-day Iran and Afghanistan), where the earliest examples of karez have been found.

Although many oases at locations all around the Tarim Basin employed karez technology to carve out a good living on the edge of the desert, the area around Turpan

contains by far the greatest concentration of wells and channels, and this is because its geography is perfectly suited to karez. The glaciers of the Tien Shan's eastern Bogda Mountains feed into streams and rivers, providing a plentiful supply of water. This surface runoff runs out from the base of the mountains and forms an aquifer at the Flaming Mountains, an uplifted rocky ridge blocking its route into the Turpan Depression. Where the water finds its way through the Flaming Mountains – especially at the gorges that split them north to south – the Turpan karez builders are able to easily locate and collect the precious liquid, taking advantage of the

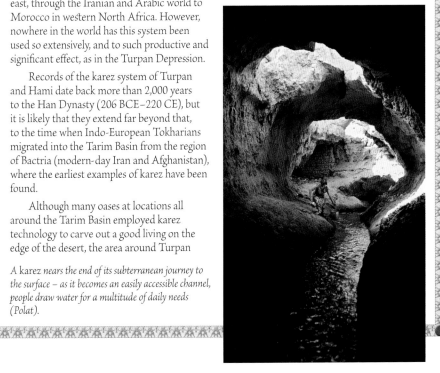

A karez *nears the end of its subterranean journey to the surface – as it becomes an easily accessible channel, people draw water for a multitude of daily needs (Polat).*

downward sloping nature of the depression and the consequent current provided by gravity. The result is a stable water source year-round, independent of season.

Digging and maintaining a karez is no easy feat. It requires skill at divining the best place to dig, and monumental effort in harsh conditions. Wells generally begin at the base of the mountains, dug down to the water table where hopefully a good volume of subterranean water can be tapped. The tunnel is then dug, but skill is required in making sure that while continuing to descend, it slopes at a lesser gradient than the contours of the land, so that the water reaches the oasis close to ground level, where surface canals can distribute it to small ponds and reservoirs. Wells are dug at regular intervals along the tunnel's route – hence the distinctive line of "mole hills" that mark a karez – to access water and for maintenance purposes. Keeping the underground channels unclogged is an ongoing task, as the mounds of earth beside each well shaft indicate. Two men and a draught animal work as a team: one man is lowered down the shaft to clear the tunnel and the buckets of mud are hoisted to the surface by a rope pulley system using the haltered animal (though modern technology means mechanized pulleys are often used now).

Generally the underground tunnels are 1.5–1.7 metres in height and less than a metre wide, and can run for 5–20 kilometres. The first, and deepest, well nearest the mountains can be up to 80 metres deep. Traditionally, every karez was named, usually after the village or person who made it. Karez makers occupied a position of high standing within the community, while those who paid for a successful karez (not every well found what it was looking for) could live comfortably on the revenue from fees for water rights.

The ancient oasis towns of the Tarim and Turpan basins depended heavily on karez irrigation for survival, and if the wells and tunnels were neglected or abandoned, the desert would quickly reassert itself and the towns would dry up and die. Also critical, but not within man's control, was climate change; over the centuries the Xinjiang region became drier, the glaciers gradually shrank, and the rivers they fed likewise diminished, resulting in less or no water flowing to the dependent settlements. Many oasis towns, including Yotkan, the original site of Hotan, were abandoned because their life-support system had disappeared.

At its height, the total number of karez in Xinjiang reached 1,784, with 172,367 vertical wells and 5,272 kilometres of underground canals, providing an annual water output of 858 million cubic metres. Today there are only 614 left, providing 301 million cubic metres. Of these, 404 are in the Turpan area (231 million cubic metres) and still provide the bulk of irrigation and drinking water for the population. Modern trends have seen plastic flooring being used in some karez, but open channels are also used now – they are quicker and easier to make and maintain, but of course very inefficient in that huge amounts of water are lost to evaporation. History provides the lesson: the old ways are best.

The Turpan karez system ranks alongside the Dujiangyan Irrigation System (built in 256 BCE during the Warring States Period) and Grand Canal (whose earliest sections date back to the fifth century BCE) as one of China's three great water projects, displaying an astonishing level of engineering innovation and heroic human endeavour. It is highly probable that without the life-giving attributes of the karez, the civilizations of the Tarim Basin could never have reached the size and sophistication that allowed the Silk Road to flourish.

by the museum's ticket sales. Its grounds comprise pleasant, shady gardens with the ubiquitous grape trellises. The path to the museum building passes a set of life-size models showcasing the traditional techniques used to dig the wells and maintain them – no modern machinery here, everything was done by hand using wood and rope winches, buckets and work animals such as donkeys.

nter the museum and you face a map of Xinjiang showing the karez as coloured lines – the green lines are working channels, the blue lines show karez that are not working but are reparable, while the red lines are dried up and beyond repair. There were once more than 1,700 karez in Xinjiang (comprising more than 5,000 kilometres of underground canals) but now only around 600 remain in active use, while most of the rest are collapsing – constant maintenance is needed or they quickly become useless. The Xinjiang Karez Research Association is beginning to maintain select karez again, but funds are in short supply. There is a possibility that this amazing system, whose history stretches back more than 2,000 years in Xinjiang, could disappear in the next few decades unless a concerted effort is made to preserve it.

The museum contains a large diorama showing a cross-section of land from the Tien Shan to the Flaming Mountains and into the Turpan Depression, which clearly explains how the karez work, and why the geological peculiarities of this area have allowed such a blossoming of agricultural land to be centred in this arid landscape. The sandstone ridge of the Flaming Mountains is uplifted rock that blocks the water runoff from the Bogda Shan range, creating underwater reservoirs that then find their way through in only a few places to the southern side – it is this relative ease of locating significant subterranean watercourses that have allowed the region's communities to so successfully utilize the karez system.

Visitors then descend a sloping walkway to an underground tunnel where a real karez channel flows, following it downstream until it emerges as an open channel from where locals can tap its water to irrigate the surrounding fields and vineyards. Finally, after negotiating a mini-mart of souvenir stalls, a liangjie drying house can be explored, where grapes are draped over wooden racks that reach up to the building's ceiling, the open brickwork letting hot air flow through to dehydrate the grapes and create Turpan raisons, considered by many to be the world's juiciest and best. Entrance to the museum is Rmb40.

GRAPE VALLEY (PUTAO GOU)

Grapes were introduced to Turpan over 2,000 years ago, including the green, elongated "mare's-nipple" (*manaizi*) variety. Together with Turpan melons and wines, they formed an essential part of the kingdom's tribute to the Tang imperial court at Chang'an, where the fruit arrived fresh and tender, transported in lead-lined boxes packed with snow from the Heavenly Mountains.

Lying at the base of the western end of the Flaming Mountains, 12 kilometres northeast of the town, **Grape Valley** is eight kilometres long and 0.5 kilometres wide, covering 400 hectares, and is the most popular place to visit vineyards during the summer season. A large entrance gate on

Clockwise from top left: Jiaohe's impressive city ruins are best viewed late in the afternoon, when the harsh glare of the sun softens and shadows lengthen (Jeremy Tredinnick); an aerial view of Jiaohe reveals the strength of its strategic and defensive location; drying grapes to create Turpan's renowned raisins (Sun Jiabin x2); a last vestige of Buddhism can be seen at Jiaohe's main temple, where two headless seated Buddhas occupy high niches in the inner wall (Jeremy Tredinnick).

the road is where you pay the entrance fee (Rmb15), and farther on there is a pleasant public park surrounded by vineyards and fruit trees. There are trellised walkways overhung with bunches of grapes, and patios with tables for relaxing and eating the grapes and melons. The small, tart *suosuo* grape first comes out in mid-July, followed by the "mare's-nipple" and the red and black grapes in August. Their sugar content is 24 percent for fresh grapes and 75 percent for raisons. Mulberry, fig, apple and pear trees also bear fruit in season, and running at the foot of the mountains is a spring; the cool water is safe to drink and refreshing. There is also a winery located in the valley. The trip to Grape Gorge is a good day trip by bicycle if you leave early enough to avoid the intense afternoon sun, but it can get crowded and it is a favourite with tour coaches.

ANCIENT CITY OF JIAOHE (YARKHOTO)

The ruined city of **Jiaohe** is probably the most visually rewarding site of all Turpan's outlying tourist attractions. It is situated 10 kilometres (six miles) west of Turpan in the Yarnaz Valley, perched atop a narrow terrace like an island above two rivers – the city's Chinese and Uygur names both mean "confluence of rivers". The cliffs rise more than 30 metres above the riverbeds, forming a formidable natural defence.

Jiaohe was the capital of the State of South Cheshi, one of the 36 kingdoms of the Western Regions during the Han Dynasty. The city was developed by a general appointed to administer the entire Turpan area, and proved to be an effective fortress when troops and peasants took refuge from raiding bands of Xiongnu horsemen. From the Northern Wei (386–534 CE) to the Tang (618–907) dynasties, Jiaohe was under the jurisdiction of the Gaochang Kingdom. Between the mid-eighth and mid-ninth century the city was occupied by Tibetans, but was subsequently brought under Gaochang's control again. Jiaohe reached its cultural peak under the Uygurs in the ninth century. The city was largely destroyed by Mongol invasions in the 13th century, and was gradually abandoned after the Yuan Dynasty.

The ruins date to the Tang Dynasty, a period when the population numbered more than 5,000. They stretch for 1,700 metres from north to south; a central watchtower overlooks the 300-metre-long main street, and a Buddhist monastery complex stands in the city centre. Inside the monastery are the remains of several headless Buddha statues in niches, a dagoba and monks' cells. The west side of the main road was the residential area, and to the east were government buildings and a prison. At the far northern end stand the walls of a large Buddhist stupa surrounded by the remains of 25 minor stupas, though visitors are restricted to a point in front of the main stupa and cannot venture farther.

The layout of the city is still clear among the dusty ruins. High adobe walls, once enclosing private homes, face the street and side-lanes. Like the streets, the courtyards were dug below the surface, the living quarters hollowed out of their sides. Little wood was used except for doors, windows and ceilings. Among the eroded remains to be seen are bread ovens and wells. The view over the steep gorges through which the rivers run is breathtaking, and the green valley below contrasts with the brown ruins of the city. Jiaohe was partly excavated in the 1950s, and brought under the protection of the state in 1961. In 1994, 55 ancient tombs of the Cheshi period were excavated, revealing many valuable artefacts, including a beautiful golden plaque showing a scaled monster biting a tiger, a rare bone sculpture of a deer head, and many pieces of pottery.

Today, wide wooden boardwalks and paved paths protect the ruins from damage – in many areas signs warn visitors not to stray off the designated paths (CCTV cameras are strategically placed to ensure no transgressions are made). A large viewing platform has been built in the central area, giving an excellent panorama of the extensive ruins. Early morning or late afternoon are definitely the best times to come, both for the soft, golden hues imparted to the ruins by the sun's low position in the sky, and also because it can get extremely hot here in the middle of the day. Entrance to Jiaohe is through the South Gate and costs Rmb40.

SAND THERAPY HEALTH CENTRE

From June to August each year, hordes of people come from all parts of Xinjiang to "take the sands" – a traditional Uygur treatment for rheumatism, lumbago and arthritis. At the Sand Therapy Health Centre 16 kilometres northwest of town, patients lie under makeshift tents and umbrellas, covering themselves with the hot desert sand several times a day to relieve their aches and pains (some endure temperatures of up to 80°C, or 170°F, though less than 48°C is more sensible). Treatment is supervised by a local Uygur medical centre; entrance costs Rmb10.

FLAMING MOUNTAINS (HUOZHOU SHAN)

The red sandstone hills that run along the northern edge of the Turpan Depression, beginning just northeast of Turpan, were immortalized as the "**Flaming Mountains**" in the famous 16th-century Chinese allegorical novel *Journey to the West* by Wu Cheng'en, in which the Buddhist pilgrim-explorer Xuanzang and his bizarre companions, Pigsy, Monkey and Sandy, attempted to cross them but could not penetrate the flames. As the story goes, Monkey procured a magical palm-leaf fan from Princess Iron Fan, wife of the Ox Demon King, and waved it 49 times, causing heavy rains to fall and extinguish the fire. The locals now add that, while attempting to cross the Flaming Mountains, Monkey burnt his tail, and ever since then all monkeys have had red bottoms.

The range is 100 kilometres long and about 10 kilometres wide; it averages 500 metres high, with its highest point 851 metres above sea level. Eight gorges cut through it – the legend goes that the mountains are what remains of a dragon from the Tien Shan who preyed on the people of the oases. The military commander Karakhoja fought the dragon for three days and nights, finally dealing it eight fatal wounds; its body fell and instantly turned into the Flaming Mountains, the canyons appearing where the hero's sword cuts had hewn it.

In reality the Flaming Mountains are composed of mainly arenaceous rock, conglomerate and mudstone, and were uplifted during tectonic movement. Devoid of plant life, and scored by innumerable shallow gullies – the result of lava flows during the mountains' nascent volcanic

The Flaming Mountains are the stuff of legend, a land of fire and death. Yet, strangely, it is their hidden reserves of water that allowed the rich oasis kingdoms of this area to flourish (Li Xue Liang).

activity – when the sun's fierce rays beat down in mid-afternoon, the hillsides actually do appear to be engulfed by tongues of fire, and the reflected heat is intense. Any trip east of Turpan will take you past the mountains; there are many spots to stop and appreciate their phenomenal appearance.

Bezeklik Thousand Buddha Caves

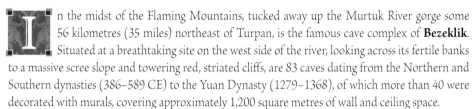

In the midst of the Flaming Mountains, tucked away up the Murtuk River gorge some 56 kilometres (35 miles) northeast of Turpan, is the famous cave complex of **Bezeklik**. Situated at a breathtaking site on the west side of the river, looking across its fertile banks to a massive scree slope and towering red, striated cliffs, are 83 caves dating from the Northern and Southern dynasties (386–589 CE) to the Yuan Dynasty (1279–1368), of which more than 40 were decorated with murals, covering approximately 1,200 square metres of wall and ceiling space.

Bezeklik was an important centre for Buddhist worship under the fifth century Xizhou Huigu government of the Gaochang Kingdom, which built the royal temple of the King of Huigu at the site. The caves are well hidden, stretching almost 1,000 metres along the cliff side on a long ridge overlooking a valley where the monastery was located. Originally access was via a winding pathway to the cliff top, and a steep stairway leading down to the monastery 10 metres below. Some of the temples were hewn into the rock face, others constructed of sun-dried bricks – a unique feature of Bezeklik.

In the Uygur language Bezeklik means "place where there are paintings" or "beautiful decorated place", depending on who is translating. The caves were excavated at the beginning of the 20th century by the German archaeologists Albert von Le Coq and Albert Grunwedel, who found them filled with sand. They first dug away at the entrance and found six huge portraits of Buddhist monks. The thousand-year-old murals inside the caves were in superb condition, their colours rich and fresh; some showed Indian monks in yellow robes, their names inscribed in Brahmi script; others were clad in the violet robes of East Asia. They found huge portraits of Buddhas at different periods throughout history, and figures of foreigners presenting gifts to the Buddha, including Indian princes, Brahmins, Persians, and a stranger with red hair and blue eyes. The central shrine had frescoes depicting the legends of Indian gods and mythical demons; in each corner of this temple was one of the Guardians of the World. The Germans also found life-size painted stucco statues of Buddhas, disciples and guardians.

Von Le Coq and his associate, Theodor Bartus, set to work removing as many of the best murals as they could, sawing through the stucco and straw surfaces. Crated and transhipped to Europe, the murals were housed in the Ethnological Museum in Berlin. Allied bombing during World War II destroyed some of them, and the remainder are on display in the Asian Art Museum (previously called the Museum of Indian Art) in Berlin. A few large, beautiful murals from Bezeklik are kept in the Hermitage Museum in St Petersburg.

Sadly, at the site itself most of the remaining cave paintings are in poor shape and very little is visible in complete form. Von Le Coq and other explorers took the best of what had not already been defaced by Uygur Muslims after their conversion to Islam in the 14th century, and more defacing occurred in the half-century before Chinese archaeologists realized the huge significance and value of the caves' murals. However, a few caves do still harbour good fragments that give a glimpse of the splendour for which Bezeklik must once have been renowned. Most of these caves are locked, so an attendant must be found to unlock them for you – photography is strictly forbidden.

Caves 16, 17, 28 and 69 are representative of the Tang period, and include multiple images of the Buddha in classical Tang style, the faces calm and beatific, as well as images of donors of Turkic origin. The caves filled with paintings from the height of the Uygur period in the late ninth and early 10th centuries must have been glorious to behold in their heyday – even now the artistry of the painters' work can be seen in what remains. Cave 20 originally held a sleeping Buddha, and a passage around it allowed circuits to be made by pilgrims. Von Le Coq took virtually all its contents to Berlin, and now all that remains of the sleeping Buddha are the feet (clad in Indian-style sandals), but you can still get an idea of the sculptor's skill from their detail and faded colour. Photos of the superb paintings of three Uygur princes and two princesses taken from this cave have been placed on its walls – they now reside in Berlin.

ave 27 originally contained seven Buddha statues; all that remain are their auras and lotus petals, but the thousand Buddha murals at the back of the cave are in quite good condition, despite having had their faces scratched off (a common form of defacement by Muslims). Plexiglass walls in front of these and a number of other cave sections protect them from further damage. Caves 31 and 33, dating to the 11th century, also once contained horizontal Buddha statues – the murals in cave 33 in particular are very emotive, the faces on the many devotees clearly displaying great sadness as they mourn the earthly death of the Buddha. Cave 39 contains 1,000 Buddha images on its arched ceiling (their features have been defaced) and worshipping bodhisattvas on the walls.

Entrance to Bezeklik costs Rmb20; despite the relatively sad condition of the caves, it is a must-see destination, if only for its spectacular setting amid the Flaming Mountains. A giant sand dune rises behind the caves, and camels are on hand to take people for mini-treks through the stark terrain. On the way to the caves, a few kilometres south of its entrance a bizarre attraction has been set up. Across the gorge here the mountainside is a very steep sand slope; zigzagging steps have been built high up the mountain, and from the top, for a fee of Rmb20, tourists are given a mat with which they shoot down a gigantic sand slide, screeching and hollering as they go. Even closer to the cave complex what can only be described as a Buddha theme park has been built to cater to the growing domestic tourism market. Near the mouth of the valley are the **Shengjinkou Thousand Buddha Caves**, but nothing of interest remains.

ASTANA TOMBS

A predominantly Tang Dynasty burial ground, the **Astana Tombs** are 40 kilometres (25 miles) southeast of Turpan and measure five kilometres long and two wide; here, the imperial dead of

Top: Most of the Bezeklik caves were cut out of the sheer walls of the Murtuk River gorge, and looked down on the coursing water (Liu Yu Sheng). Above left and right: Cut from Cave 9 of Bezeklik by von Le Coq, these famous murals show Uygur princes (59.5 x 62.4cm, MIK III 6876a) and princesses (57 x 66cm, MIK III 6876b) making offerings to the Buddha (courtesy of the Asian Art Museum, National Museums in Berlin).

Gaochang were buried. The dry climate preserved the bodies and artefacts perfectly, and the custom of wrapping corpses has yielded a rich variety of silks with Chinese and Middle Eastern designs. The Xinjiang Uygur Autonomous Region Museum in Urumqi has a fine collection of relics from Astana. Painted stucco figurines have revealed such aspects of daily life as traditional costumes, customs and riding accoutrements. Samples of grains, breads, pastries and dumplings placed in the graves give insight into their diet. Von Le Coq excavated the site in the early 1900s and found a buried box of

Russian matches made in 1890 – proof that a tsarist expedition had been there before him. He was followed by Sir Aurel Stein in 1915. The Chinese carried out extensive excavations in 1972 and 1973, collecting in total around 10,000 burial items.

Three of the tombs are open to the public. A steep, narrow passage leads down about five metres into a small dark chamber. Two contain faded, simple paintings: in one, auspicious birds; in the tomb of the Tang Dynasty General Zhang Xun and his wife (now encased in the Turpan Prefecture Museum), four murals depicting Jade Man, Gold Man, Stone Man and Wooden Man – all symbols of Confucian virtues. The third tomb contains the mummies of a woman and a man, in whose mouth a Persian coin was found. These well-preserved bodies have extremely long hair and fingernails. Entrance to the tombs costs Rmb20.

THE ANCIENT CITY OF GAOCHANG (KHARAKHOJA/KHOCHO)

The extensive ruins of the ancient city of **Gaochang** lie 47 kilometres (29 miles) southeast of Turpan. Built in the second century BCE as a garrison town, it became the capital of the Kingdom of Gaochang under the Han house of Qu. By the seventh century it held sway over 21 other towns. The practice of Buddhism led to the establishment of many monasteries, temples and large

Above right: An aerial view of Gaochang shows the city's outer wall and the rectangular temple area, which is undergoing extensive renovation (Sun Jiabin). Right: A Buddha mural from Cave 31 of the Bezeklik complex (Liu Yu Sheng).

religious communities, and the monk Xuanzang taught in this city for several months amidst paintings and statuary in Graeco-Buddhist Gandharan style. A Confucian college taught the classics of Chinese ethics. In the ninth century, the Uygurs established their Kharakhoja Kingdom here, bringing with them Manichaeism, which flourished alongside Buddhism and the Nestorian faith. Manuscripts have been discovered here, including beautifully illuminated Manichaean scriptures. The city was destroyed around the 14th century, during a period of warfare lasting 40 years.

Gaochang consisted originally of three parts: the outer and inner cities, and a central palace complex, totalling two square kilometres in area. The palace, which was guarded by 900 soldiers, had 12 gates. Nothing remains of it today, but inside the huge city walls, amongst the acres of ruins, are the Bell Tower and the temple area, and a few traces of Buddhist paintings are still visible in the niches and on the walls. The 5.7-kilometre-long city wall is mostly intact, and is roughly rectangular in shape. Made of rammed earth and mud, it is 12 metres thick and 11.5 metres high. At the height of its power Gaochang was probably home to 30,000 people including 3,000 monks.

Grunwedel and von Le Coq dug extensively here and found superb floor mosaics, frescoes, statuary and manuscripts. A Nestorian church was discovered outside the walls of the old city, containing a Byzantine-style mural possibly depicting a Palm Sunday service. The Germans also discovered an underground room with the thousand-year-old corpses of more than 100 violently murdered Buddhist monks, thought to be the victims of religious persecution.

on Le Coq's discovery of a two-metre-high fresco depicting Manes, the founder of Manichaeism, proved that Gaochang had been a flourishing Manichaean community in the mid-eighth century. This ancient religion was founded by Manes around 242 CE in Sassanian Persia, but met with intense hostility from Zoroastrians and later Christians in Northern Africa. Manes died in jail in 274 or 276 and his converts were heavily persecuted; consequently, there are no written records or religious texts of this faith anywhere else. Some 500 Manichaeans fled east to Samarkand and founded a community. The religion and its art were subsequently transported along the Silk Road, assimilating Buddhist influences (particularly those from Persia and Gandhara) by the time it reached Gaochang. Von Le Coq's discoveries included Manichaean manuscripts written on leather, silk, paper and parchment, frescoes, and hanging paintings created on cloth, all revealing strong Persian influences. The manuscripts helped illuminate facets of this little known faith.

Much of Gaochang has been destroyed by locals and the site only vaguely resembles a town. The soil of the old walls is rich, and peasants have carried off large quantities over the centuries to fertilize their fields (farmers believed that the bright pigment of the wall paintings was excellent fertilizer). Beams and wood were carted off to be used as fuel. Cable and French noted: "Destruction of the buildings had been going on for a long time, and we saw farmers at work with their pickaxes pulling down the old ruins and probably destroying many relics in the process." Anti-Buddhist feeling was another cause of the destruction. Many wall paintings of the Buddha in human form were slashed and the eyes picked out by fearful Muslims. "For the belief still exists," wrote von Le Coq, "that painted men and animals, unless their eyes and mouths at least have been destroyed, come to life at night, descend from their places, and do all sorts of mischief to men, beasts and harvest." One tragic story relates how a Muslim peasant came across a library of illustrated manuscripts and simply threw them into the river, worried that his mullah would find him with blasphemous material.

t the entrance to the city (entry fee Rmb40), young boys offer horse and donkey cart rides to the inner temple (for a fee of Rmb100) in the southwestern corner, roughly two kilometres down a track that winds through indistinguishable dirt mounds and the remains of the inner city wall. The temple, which covers 10,000 square metres, is now undergoing extensive renovation, its collapsing walls being shored up and in some cases encased in modern brickwork – a somewhat dubious form of preservation.

Tuyoq (Tuyugou)

This peaceful, ancient village is situated 70 kilometres east of Turpan in a lush gully carved into the Flaming Mountains (it is actually located within Shanshan County). It is surrounded by vineyards and famous for its oval-shaped seedless grapes, the raisins of which are well known in Beijing. The infamous von Le Coq discovered the ruins of Buddhist cave temples here in 1905, "clinging like a swallow's nest to the almost perpendicular slope of the mountainside". These caves are thought to be the oldest in the Turpan area and date from the fourth century. Part of the monastery perched atop one of the cliffs fell into the gorge in 1916 during an earthquake. Von Le Coq found a monk's cell, with Persian architectural influences, containing numerous eighth- and ninth-century religious texts and beautiful embroideries.

The famous Uygur legend of Tuyoq concerns five pious Muslims – the first to bring Islam to this region – who came east to preach their faith. In Tuyoq they made their first conversion, a shepherd; according to myth, when an imposter tried to pose as Allah the six men, who were determined to test the power of this supposed deity, witnessed his fear upon meeting a black cat on the way to the mosque and knew immediately that he could not be their true god. The denounced Allah tried to kill the faithful Muslims but they fled to the caves of Tuyoq and a spider spun a web in the doorway to conceal the cave while two pigeons stood guard. Afterwards, they remained in Tuyoq to continue their mission.

Because of the extreme piety of the six men, a trip to pray at the village's mosque and the **Tuyugou Hojamu Tomb**, which commemorates the six Muslims and stands on the hillside above the village, is considered necessary before making the Haj pilgrimage to Mecca; those who make the journey here are rewarded with the title of "half a hadji". The tomb has a gleaming green-tiled dome, and is surrounded by a three-metre-high wall, while many new tombs have been built on the hillside close to the wall, erected by contemporary Muslims who wish to be buried near the region's original proselytizers of Islam. A new metalled road passes next to it on its way through the gorge to the north of the Flaming Mountains.

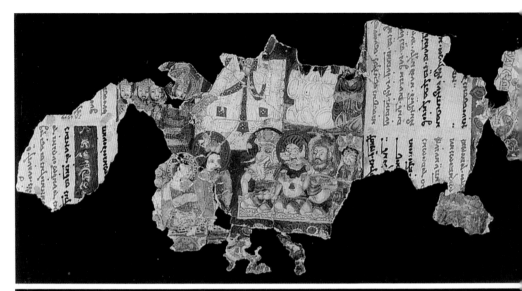

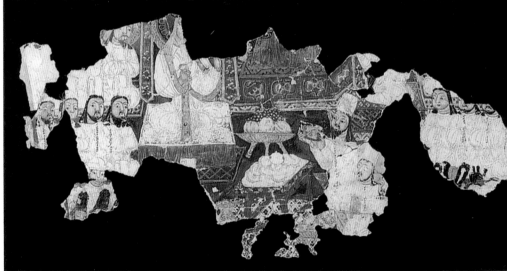

Above: A leaf from a Manichaean book from Gaochang (Khocho), dating to the 9th–10th centuries, showing Persian-Manichaean gods facing Hindu gods (including Ganesh) on one side, and on the other a feast commemorating the death of Mani (Colours and gold on paper, 25.5 x 12.4cm, MIK III 4979, Courtesy of the Asian Art Museum, Museums in Berlin). Opposite: The house in Tuyoq where Albert von Le Coq based his operations during the exploration and excavation of the many archaeological sites in the Turpan region (Jeremy Tredinnick).

Tuyoq is a charming, timeless village with a friendly community who have preserved their culture and living style more successfully than most. However, these days the village residents have begun to realize the potential for tourist dollars as more and more visitors traipse through their streets and peer into their courtyards, so there is now an entry fee (Rmb30, plus Rmb20 extra to visit the mazar). The mosque sits attractively on the village's main street, its whitewashed façade and four green-tiled minarets making it easy to distinguish among the red brick of the village houses. Behind the mosque is a stream where children swim and yell while old men stroke their long beards and eat melons in the shade. By the side of this stream is a 'typical mud-brick house with a sign over its door stating that this was where Albert von Le Coq stayed while he scoured the countryside around for valuable archaeological sites. Simply strolling around the village is a fascinating and enjoyable experience, but care should be taken not to offend its residents by prying or invasive camera-wielding. Uygurs are by nature a hospitable people, and showing respect will open doors that might otherwise be closed.

Tuyoq's own "thousand Buddha caves" are located one kilometre upriver in the gorge. Over 40 were carved into the soft dirt and rock surrounding the gully, amidst verdant vineyards and the rugged backdrop of the Flaming Mountains. Only nine caves contain traces of frescoes, three of which are locked. Wooden walkways and steps now ascend to the caves (ropes and ladders used to be the only way to access them), but the bridge to the caves is in a state of disrepair, and few people actually make the trip, preferring the tranquillity and shade of the village.

MOON LAKE (AIDING HU)

This salt lake 55 kilometres (34 miles) southeast of Turpan, in the heart of the Turpan Depression, lies at the bottom of the second lowest continental basin in the world, 154 metres (505 feet) below sea level. The surface of the lake is completely encrusted with an ice-like layer of salt, and its shores are like quicksand. Glauber's salt – used in detergents and as a diuretic – is manufactured here in a factory employing 3,000 people. In the winter the lake freezes over, and trucks move out onto the surface collecting frozen salt to dump into troughs beside the lake; there it melts in the searing summer temperatures, which can reach horrifying temperatures. Many of the workers were sent here during the Cultural Revolution (1966–1976) from the rich, green provinces of Zhejiang, Sichuan and Guangdong and have been here ever since. Several Han Dynasty beacon towers loom over the lakeside, but despite its geological credentials, this is not a pleasant place to be for long, and most tourists leave it off their already packed itinerary.

TURPAN PRACTICAL INFORMATION

Although many of Turpan's streets are trellised with grapevines, providing welcome green-dappled shade, do not make the mistake of picking the enticing grapes that hang in large bunches just a few feet above your head – if you are caught you will be slapped with a Rmb15 fine. Within town the bazaar and museum are within easy walking distance; even the Emin Minaret can be reached on

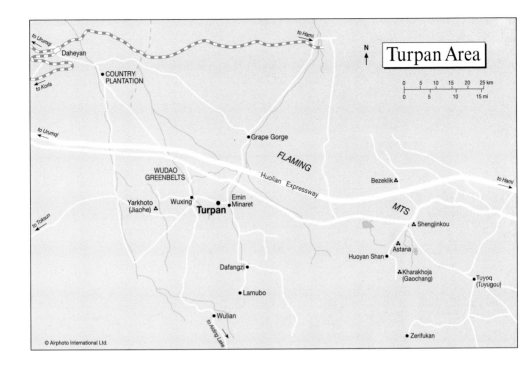

foot through the old town, although hiring a bike is a better way to get there if you do not have a car available, and Grape Valley and Jiaohe are also possible to visit by bicycle. However, all the sites farther afield than these require motorized transport, and by far the easiest way to see them is on guided tours arranged through local tour companies. There are many offering daily sightseeing tours to Turpan's various sites and prices are rated according to the number of people signed up.

Regardless of your mode of transport, an essential item to take is adequate water – this cannot be stressed enough. Whether it's bottles of water, milk tea, fruit juice, sliced watermelon or any of a number of local refreshments, it's vital to keep yourself hydrated throughout the day.

Transportation

Turpan's main bus station is opposite the bazaar on Laocheng Lu. There are hourly buses to/from Urumqi (2.5 hours, Rmb40) and **Daheyan**, the closest railhead on the Lanzhou-Urumqi and Urumqi-Kashgar lines about 58 kilometres northwest of town. Arriving in Daheyan by train, outside the station minibuses, taxis and private cars vie to bring you to Turpan in under an hour, and depending on how many people are in your vehicle this can cost as little as Rmb15. Daily buses also operate to/from Hami (5–6 hours) and three times a week to/from Kashgar (Rmb170), Kucha (Rmb100) and points in between – sleeper buses are best for the longer journeys.

The main mosque in the picturesque village of Tuyoq, at the base of the Flaming Mountains (Jeremy Tredinnick).

ACCOMMODATION

Water is often rationed during the dry summer and hotels are forced to limit its use (showers) to a few hours in the afternoon or evening. Turpan now has a few new accommodation options to add to the old favourites – although one of those, the **Silk Road Turpan Oasis Hotel** that was for many the best combination of culture and comfort until it fell on hard times, is currently closed, its attractive Uygur-influenced facade standing empty and increasingly decrepit behind locked gates on Qingnian Lu's pedestrianized street section. (Check www.the-silk-road.com to see if it has opened again.) As with all oasis towns, discounts are available during the low season – these can be anything from 25–50 percent off rack rates.

Turpan Tuha Petroleum Hotel

230 Wenhua Lu. Tel: (0995) 866 6666; fax: (0995) 866 6668; email: tlftuhahotel@yahoo.com.cn; website: www.hoteltuha.com

This four-star hotel in the east of town is owned by the combined oil concerns of Turpan and Hami (hence "Tuha"), with 143 rooms, four restaurants, a swimming pool, gym and even a bowling alley. Rooms start from Rmb880, suites from Rmb1,680.

Turpan Grand Hotel

422 Gaochang Lu. Tel: (0995) 855 3918; fax: (0995) 855 3908

A good clean three-star hotel that sees few tourists because of a lack of Uygur influence, but its location is convenient and rooms are spacious and good value. An outdoor café shaded by grape trellises at the back is a pleasant respite from the dust of the city.

Xizhou Hotel

Corner of Qingnian Lu and Wenhua Lu. Tel: (0995) 855 4000; fax: (0995) 855 4068

A 56-room Chinese-style three-star hotel 100 metres south of the old Silk Road Turpan Oasis Hotel. Caters to mostly Chinese tourists (little English spoken), but the location is excellent.

Turpan Hotel (Tulufan Binguan)

2 Qingnian Lu. Tel: (0995) 852 2301; fax: 852 3262

This old guesthouse at the southern end of Qingnian Lu has been spruced up with new wings, and has Uygur singing and dancing nightly during the tourist season. An extremely relaxed atmosphere, especially in the social beer garden; bicycle rental and tours available.

Jiaohe Manor Hotel

9 Jiaohe Road. Tel: (995) 768 5799; fax: (995) 768 5699

Another three-star hotel boasting 108 rooms but built in a graceful, traditional style. It is set back from the road on the way to Jiaohe 2km west of town. Standard rooms start at around Rmb500.

Jiaotong Binguan

Laocheng Lu, next to the bus station.

A good budget option in a great location opposite the bazaar, although it can be a little noisy. Rooms start at Rmb280 for a double.

FOOD AND DRINK

Tasty Uygur dishes can be found in many of the small restaurants and teahouses throughout the bazaar and around the Public Square – *laghman, chushira, samsa,* kebabs and nan as well as the Sunday treat of *poluo* and *manta.* Chinese restaurants are also plentiful these days, and many have English menus. Cold flat rice noodles in a garlic/vinegar sauce make for a particularly satisfying meal during the intense midday heat. In the mornings, fresh milk and yoghurt is sold on the streets and in the bazaar. Aside from *chai,* liquid refreshment includes *bingshui,* fruit juices (manufactured in Turpan) and a sweet ice slush; ice cream and popsicles are eaten all day long. Xinjiang *pijiu* is of fairly poor quality, more like soda water with a barley aftertaste (try the watermelon cider). One of the local specialities is salt fish, a dried fish encrusted with mud and salt harvested from the beds of the surrounding lakes once they begin to evaporate in early summer. **John's Information Café** at the Turpan Hotel serves Western fare and refreshing iced drinks.

Fresh fruit is always available in the markets and along the streets: apricots, grapes, peaches, mulberries, pears, pomegranates, etc. Aside from the common watermelon, some of the more popular varieties of sweet melons, or *gua,* include the exportable Hami *gua* (a large netted green melon with orange meat resembling a cantaloupe in taste and a watermelon in texture), the sweet Minzu *gua* (a smooth-skinned melon with green meat like a honeydew), and the fragrant Tang *gua* (a black-striped yellow melon; the inside is green with an orange tint to the pulp). Hand-sized bags of raisins are sold everywhere, and make great snacks during long day trips. However, be warned that the sugar content of Turpan's grapes, raisins and melons is very high, so wash your mouth out with water or tea regularly, or your teeth may suffer the consequences.

SHANSHAN

Drive 90 kilometres east of Turpan on Highway 312 and you reach the town of **Shanshan**, perched on the edge of the mighty **Kumtagh Desert**. "Kum" means "sand" and "tagh" means "desert" in Uygur; thus this desert area literally translates as "Sand Mountain", and it is easy to understand why, for the southwestern corner of the county is occupied by 2,500 square kilometres of gigantic sand dunes rolling like waves off towards the heat-hazed horizon. This is classic desert terrain as most people envision it, and hence a favourite activity is camel trekking.

Shanshan is considered the true place of origin of the honeydew melon, despite its "Hami" moniker. In reality these melons have been cultivated widely throughout the Xinjiang region since the Yuan Dynasty, but when the king of Hami presented the juicy, fragrant melons as tribute to

Emperor Kangxi in the 17th century, he found them delicious and asked his officials their name. Knowing only that they had been sent by the king of Hami, they were given that name and it stuck. From Shanshan the highway covers 316 kilometres through sun-baked red-brown mountains and across barren landscapes before arriving in the oasis of Hami.

HAMI

The city of **Hami** is the capital of **Hami Prefecture**, which includes the **Barkol (Balikun) Kazakh Autonomous County** and **Yiwu County** and totals 143,000 square kilometres in area. The city's population of 330,000 comprises numerous minority groups, including Uygur, Kazakh, Hui and Mongol, but the majority are Han Chinese. Hami is the eastern gateway to Xinjiang, the first stop by rail within the region coming from Gansu. It is a rich agricultural oasis fed by more than 100 karez, the underground irrigation channels bringing cold water from the melting snows of the most easterly peaks of the Tien Shan. As in Turpan, during the summer months Hami produces its famous melons, hops and many other kinds of fruit, grains and pulses.

More than 30 types of Hami gua (melon) are grown here as well as watermelons, although the Chinese consider those grown in adjacent Shanshan County the best. The fields around the city are devoted to the cultivation of these melons, of which more than 40,000 tons are produced annually. They ripen from late June, when they begin appearing in the markets, but are sweetest in September.

The district has natural resources of coal, iron, gold, rock salt, titanium and tungsten. Industrial output includes carpets, cement, clothing, plastics, beer and canned fruits. Like Turpan, Hami is in a fault depression over 100 metres below sea level, and temperatures are extreme, from a high of 43°C (109°F) in summer to a low of -32°C (-26°F) in winter. In 1986, archaeologists excavated more than 80 tombs in the area and discovered 50 well-preserved corpses, complete with fur hats, leather boots and colourful woollen clothing, said to be more than 3,000 years old.

HISTORY

Perhaps the earliest reference to Hami (or Yiwu, Yizhou, Qomul or Kumul, as it was variously known) was in a book made of bamboo slips and bound together with white silk, found in a second-century BCE tomb in Henan Province. This record, discovered in the third century, is an account of the quasi-mythical travels of Emperor Mu, the fifth emperor of the Zhou Dynasty, who, on returning from his visit to the Queen Mother of the West, stayed in Hami for three days and received gifts of 300 horses and 2,000 sheep and cattle from the local inhabitants.

Hami was considered by the Chinese the key to access to the northwest, but they were not always successful in keeping the city free of nomadic incursions. In 73 CE, the Han general Ban Chao wrested the area from a Xiongnu army and established a military and agricultural colony. In the sixth and early seventh centuries, Hami was incorporated in turn into the empires of the Eastern and

Western Turks, which at their peak stretched from Manchuria westwards to beyond the Aral Sea. But with the assertive military posture of the Tang emperor Taizong, Hami and many other Central Asian oases had come under the protection of a military protectorate-general by 640. The Buddhist monk Xuanzang spent several weeks in Hami recuperating from his near-fatal desert crossing.

Marco Polo, who traversed the "province of Kamul" on his way to the court of Kublai Khan in the 13th century, rejoiced at a most hospitable local custom: "I give you my word," he wrote, "that if a stranger comes to a house here to seek hospitality he receives a very warm welcome. The host bids his wife do everything that the guest wishes. Then he leaves the house and goes about his own business and stays away two or three days. Meanwhile the guest stays with his wife in the house and does what he will with her, lying with her in one bed just as if she was his own wife; and they lead a gay life together. The women are beautiful and vivacious and always ready to oblige." This adulterous behaviour was frowned upon by one of the Mongol khans, who prohibited its practice. For three years the people of Hami obeyed; then, laden with gifts, they begged the khan to allow them to return to their age-old tradition, "for their ancestors had declared that by the pleasure they gave to guests with their wives and goods they won the favour of their idols and multiplied the yield of their crops and their tillage." The perplexed khan replied sternly: "Since you desire your own shame, you may have it."

During the Ming Dynasty, Hami sent tribute missions to the emperor and found itself invaded from time to time by its powerful oasis neighbour, Turpan. In 1681 it was annexed by the Oirat (Junggar) Mongols, who had displaced the Chaghatai rulers in their growing Kashgarian Empire.

rom 1697 to 1930 a succession of Uygur Hami kings held nominal sway over Hami, first sending tribute to the Qing Dynasty, then becoming embroiled in the various Muslim revolts that swept through Xinjiang. In 1880 the brilliant Chinese general Zuo Zongtang, after defeating the rebel ruler of Kashgar, Yakub Beg, set up his headquarters in Hami in anticipation of a military confrontation with the Russians, who had occupied the Ili Valley region in the west. He contributed to the rebuilding of Hami following a Muslim uprising. In 1887, Sir Francis Younghusband, British explorer, soldier and mystic, noted that the environs of Hami were strewn with ruins and that there were only about 6,000 inhabitants. Younghusband and Colonel M. Bell had journeyed overland from Beijing by separate routes, planning to meet up in Hami before travelling on to India together. Younghusband was late and described his eventual meeting with Bell, months afterwards at the end of his journey, as follows: "Colonel Bell told that he really had waited for me a whole day in Hami – this place in the middle of Central Asia, nearly two thousand miles from our starting point – and, astonished at finding I had not turned up to date, had proceeded on his way to India."

Sven Hedin and Albert von Le Coq both met the last Hami king before his death in 1930. Von Le Coq was entertained at a banquet accompanied by large quantities of Russian liqueur and French champagne, which the king, though Muslim, had no qualms about drinking. The rooms of the palace

The mausoleums of the Hami kings are the city's highlight attraction (Fan Shucai).

were furnished with jade, porcelain, fine carpets and silk embroideries, and, incongruously, a cuckoo clock. Hedin described the king as "a portly little man of 70 years, with a reddish complexion, friendly eyes, aquiline nose, and snow-white beard". Northeast of the city the king had a summer palace, an amalgam of Chinese and Persian architecture, with a beautiful garden encompassing the ancient ruins of a Buddhist temple.

Upon the king's death, "princely state" status gave way to Chinese bureaucracy, characterized by overbearing tax "reforms" and insensitive Han officials, resulting in a rebellion that spread across Xinjiang under the leadership of the young Muslim, Ma Zhongying. Hami at that time consisted of three walled towns – old, new and native Uygur – but a traveller passing through soon after the rebellion wrote: "Ruins lay everywhere, and most of the native city had been reduced to rubble."

SIGHTS

TOMBS OF THE HAMI KINGS

Situated in the leafy, mud-walled suburbs two kilometres south of the town centre, these are Hami's most important remaining monuments. Only two or three of the nine kings appear to be buried here with their families. The tombs are said to have been built by King Boxier, the seventh Islamic king of Hami (assisted by the Qing government, which contributed 20,000 taels of silver) and completed around 1840, after more than 20 years' construction. However, the royal tombs may date from the early 18th century: a stone tablet, dated 1706, was erected at the palace (no longer extant), stating that carpenters had been invited from Beijing to construct a number of large-scale buildings for the beautification of the city.

The tomb complex is 1.3 hectares in size, with a gate at the north entrance and another gate in the east. It comprises three sections: the main mausoleum, constructed from mud bricks and completely Islamic in style, square with a domed roof, its high walls and façade decorated in blue, turquoise and white tiles. Inside are packed the blanket-shrouded tombs of the seventh and eighth kings, their wives and other family members, and the interior walls are painted in a beautiful blue-and-white floral design. Stairs in the western corner of the mausoleum lead to the roof, where you have a panoramic view of the city. Beside this building are two very different mausoleums (originally there were five), constructed in wood, with Islamic domes surmounting multi-tiered, Chinese-style eaves. A large mosque completes the complex; built at the end of the 17th century, its four walls are inscribed with religious scriptures and colourful designs. At 60 metres by 38 metres it covers 2,280 square metres and can hold 5,000 worshippers. It was renovated with government funding in 1983. Entry to the tomb complex costs Rmb20. Nearby stand the remains of the old city wall, extending for about 100 metres, which once protected the palace. Further west is an ancient poplar tree called the Nine Dragon Tree and a tiny mosque used by the local villagers.

GAI SI'S TOMB

This *mazar*, or holy tomb, lies on the same road, closer to the city – a simple mud-brick hall with a wooden verandah and 10-metre-high, green-tiled dome. It is dedicated to the memory of Gai Si, one of the three Muslim missionaries believed to have come from the Middle East during the seventh century. Gai Si died at the border town of Xingxingxia to the east, where the Hami kings later erected a simple memorial to him. In 1945, local Hami Muslims collected money to build the present mazar, and his remains, scattered during the military occupation of Xingxingxia in 1939, were gathered here. A large number of people participated in the reburial ceremony; the holy man's beard was, it is said, miraculously still intact. The tomb has a Rmb10 entrance fee.

THE HAMI CULTURAL OFFICE MUSEUM

Situated on Jianguo Lu, Hami Museum houses a number of corpses and other finds from the 3,000-year-old graves excavated at **Wupu (Wubao)**, 70 kilometres (44 miles) southwest of Hami, in the latter decades of the last century. Coloured cloth, pottery and daily utensils show what life was like for the region's inhabitants at the time of the Western Zhou Dynasty (1027–771 BCE).

Other items include an interesting carved "stone man" figure from a burial site dating to the sixth century CE. Many of these anthropomorphic rocks (some several metres high) can be found scattered about the grasslands of northern Xinjiang, marking the graves of the Eastern and Western Turkic Khaganate period, and are primitively but powerfully carved. There are also samples of Neolithic rock carvings from the northern part of the Hami region, depicting camels, wild goats and scenes of hunting and warfare. These are similar to carvings on rock faces in the northern Altai Mountains and in Hunza, Pakistan. Entrance to the museum costs Rmb5.

Lafuqueke (Lapuqiaok) Ruins

One of a number of ancient city ruins in the Hami area, **Lafuqueke** (Lapuqiaok) lies 60 kilometres (40 miles) west of Hami, and is thought to have been the Nazhi county seat during the Tang Dynasty, and possibly be the site of ancient **Yiwu City** dating to the Eastern Han Dynasty (25–220 CE). The extensive ruins, some 600 metres long and half as wide, include remains of a Buddhist temple (with traces of frescoes), a dagoba, barracks and watchtowers, though all are in a state of poor repair. The site is unexcavated and lies partly under cultivated fields and a graveyard. Entrance costs Rmb10.

Ten kilometres away are the ruins of the **Baiyanggou Temple** (entry Rmb5), and built into the mountainside are 10 Buddhist caves with damaged murals. North of here along the Baiyang Gully about 10 beacon towers stretch out at intervals of one or two kilometres.

Wupu (Wubao) Ancient Tombs

eventy kilometres southwest of the city is the 3,000-year-old burial site of **Wupu**, comprising a 5,000-square-metre area containing multiple graves dating to the 11th century BCE. The graves were excavated first in 1978 and again in 1986; 50 corpses were unearthed, along with large quantities of brightly coloured striped woollen cloth, a full-length cloak in excellent condition, pottery, bone and wooden utensils, as well as leather clothes, sandals and bronzeware, some of which are on display at the site's showroom. Research on the corpses is ongoing at museums in Urumqi, Shanghai and Beijing. The tomb complex charges a Rmb15 entrance fee.

About 30 kilometres from Wubao village is an area of bizarre rock formations. Surrounded by the sandy desert, the **Hami Ghost City** was formed by severe wind erosion of clay rock (the process that forms the famous *yardang* features of the Lop Nur region to the south), creating strange shapes that with a little imagination appear to be man-made structures like castles and towers in the desert landscape. There are a number of similar locations in Xinjiang, including the Qitai Ghost City and Uyrhe Ghost City in the Junggar Basin.

Hami Practical Information

Today, Hami's inner city is all modern Chinese architecture, centred around the large, open Times Square – only the southern part of town contains more traditional Uygur architecture and mud-brick housing. Most visitors only overnight in Hami before continuing on to either Turpan or Dunhuang, depending on their direction of travel, but its less tourist-oriented atmosphere can result in a rewarding experience, and this is the stopping-off point for trips north to Barkol Lake, the eastern extremity of the Tien Shan and the lush grasslands inhabited by Kazakhs who see far fewer foreigners than farther west in the Ili Valley or in the Altai region. The best time to visit Hami is July–September, when the melons are ripe and the grasslands filled with life. The Hami District Travel Bureau (tel: 0902 236 0438) produces an excellent, comprehensive guide to the region titled *Discover Hami* (published by the Shanghai People's Fine Arts Publishing House).

KARAKHOTO: THE BLACK CITY OF THE TANGUTS

By Christoph Baumer

Although the ancient city of Karakhoto, whose Mongolian name means "Black City", actually lies in the northwestern corner of Inner Mongolia rather than in Xinjiang, historically its closest cultural links were with East Turkestan. The ancient city of Karakhoto lies southeast of the two dried-out lakes of Gaxun Nor and Soghun Nor, and to the east of the (also desiccated) delta of the Etzin Gol river. Its history followed a similar pattern to the city of Beiting (see page 219), as its ownership was disputed by Mongol, Turkic, Tibetan and Chinese groups.

During the Han Dynasty (206 BCE–220 CE) the Turkic-Mongol people of Xiongnu fought for control of it with the Chinese; less than 20 kilometres to the south and west of Karakhoto, dozens of ruined watchtowers and small forts – which formed the fortified boundary built by the Han to guard against attacks from the Xiongnu – can still be seen today. This boundary line, researched by Sir Aurel Stein in 1914, follows the Etzin Gol southwards almost to Jiuquan, from where it runs westwards to Hami.

After having been part of the Turkic Khaganate, China reconquered the Etzin Gol in the seventh century and built the fortress of Tungsheng, which would later become the northeastern corner of Karakhoto. But like Beiting, the oasis of Tungsheng also fell to the Tibetans at the end of the eighth century, before passing into the hands of the Uygurs of Gaochang around 850. Less than two centuries later it was conquered by the new regional power, the Tanguts.

The **Tanguts** were of Tibetan stock, belonging to the Qiang tribal group and speaking a language related to Tibetan. Their land was called **Minyak** by the Tibetans, and **Xi Xia** (Western Xia) by the Chinese. The Tanguts had fled their homeland, located at Songpan in the northwest of today's province of Sichuan, during the seventh century after constant Tibetan attacks, and moved to the Ordos. They were vassals of Tibet from 750 to 822 and later had to recognize the Uygurs and the Chinese Song Dynasty as their overlords. But in the year 982 the Tangut leader Jixian declared his independence and founded the Tangut Empire

Siddha (*fragment*), *mineral pigments on canvas, 12th century.*

Greeting the Soul of the Righteous Man on the Way to the Pure Land of Amitabha, *mineral pigments on linen, late 12th century.*

(982–1227). In 1035 the Tangut ruler Yuanhao absorbed Karakhoto into his empire after having annexed Western Gansu, including Dunhuang. In 1038 Yuanhao declared himself emperor.

The capital of the Tangut Empire was Xingzhou (today's Yinchuan in the Ninxia Autonomous Region), but Karakhoto, called Etzina by the Tangut and Heishuicheng by the Chinese, soon became the second most important town in the empire. At the same time, in 1038, Buddhism, which was already widely spread among the Tangut, was elevated to the status of state religion, but Nestorian Christianity and Islam remained well tolerated, as we know from the narrative of Marco Polo. For the translation of the Buddhist teachings into Tangut, and contrary to Tibet, which had adopted an Indic script, the rulers chose Chinese characters to develop a writing system of their own. To ensure a fast spread of the Buddhist texts they were printed using wooden printing blocks. In the second half of the 12th century, movable types were also used.

The Tanguts proved to be one of the strongest and toughest adversaries of Genghis Khan, for they managed to beat off his attacks three times, in 1205, 1209 and 1217. They only succumbed to his fourth campaign after he commanded it personally. Karakhoto fell in 1226 and the capital Xingzhou in 1227. Since Genghis Khan had died a few days before the conquest of the capital – probably due to a fall from his horse – the Mongols unleashed a ferocious slaughter campaign among the Tangut population. Although the Tangut Empire – the last Buddhist empire in Central Asia – disappeared, it left behind a rich cultural heritage. Not only were they generous sponsors of Tibetan monasteries and of the Buddhist Mogao Caves at Dunhuang, but the Tanguts also developed a Buddhist visual art that was a unique synthesis of Central Asian, Chinese and Tibetan influences. They were also a strong bulwark against Muslim armies, which were wiping out Buddhism and destroying Buddhist cultural relics throughout Central Asia and East Turkestan.

The city of Etzina was rebuilt after the Mongol attack of 1226 and regained some prosperity. Today's visitor sees occasionally traces

(All images copyright The State Hermitage Museum, St Petersburg)

Portrait of a Monk, *mineral pigments on canvas, late 12th–13th century.*

Kubera (Vaisravana), *canvas, 95.5 x 64cm, 13th–14th century.*

An unusual double-headed Buddha, clay, mineral paints and gilding, 62cm, late 13th century.

of this renewed life under the Sino-Mongol Yuan Dynasty (1279–1368) when finding shards of blue-and-white porcelain lying on the ground inside the city. The importance of Etzina in those days is further highlighted by Marco Polo's description in *The Book of Ser Marco Polo* (edited by Sir Henry Yule, 1926), although Polo didn't see Etzina himself but passed through Jiuquan and Zhangye around 1273 or 1274: "When you leave the city of Campichu [Zhangye] you ride for twelve days, and then reach a city called Etzina, which is towards the north on the verge of the Sandy Desert; it belongs to the province of Tangut. The peoples are Idolaters [Buddhists], and possess plenty of camels and cattle. The inhabitants live by their cultivation and their cattle, for they have no trade."

Etzina's end came with the fall of the Yuan Dynasty. In 1372, the Ming general Feng Shen attacked the city but failed to conquer its strong fortifications, which are still visible today. According to local tradition, he then laid siege to it and diverted the course of the nearby river so that Etzina had no access to water. When the wells inside the city dried up, the situation became hopeless for its defenders. Finally, the last prince of Karakhoto, named **Kara Bator** (black hero), sank all his treasures in the deepest well, ordered a breach to be made in the defensive walls and attacked the besiegers in despair. All the Tanguts died, but their hidden treasure was never found (a legend tells that Kara Bator cast a spell over it so that it would never be discovered). This second conquest of Karakhoto, the encroaching desert and possibly also climatic changes, brought urban life in the Etzin Gol region to an end. No scroll paintings dated later than 1378 or texts later than 1361 have ever been found.

The site of Karakhoto was discovered and excavated by the Russian officer and explorer **Pyotr Kuzmich Kozlov** (1863–1935). Prior to making his historic discovery, Kozlov had accompanied the famous Russian explorer Nikolai Przhevalsky (1839–1888) in 1883 on his last two expeditions through Central Asia and northeastern Tibet, and also led two expeditions of his own into Mongolia, Eastern Tibet and the Lop Nor region. In 1905, as a special envoy of Tsar Nicholas II, Kozlov met the 13th Dalai Lama in his exile in Urga, today's capital of Mongolia Ulaan Baatar.

In December 1907, Kozlov started his next expedition to the Etzin Gol and Eastern Tibet, and on 19 March 1908 discovered Karakhoto, after following up on an unconfirmed report by the Russian explorer GN Potanin, who had heard rumours about it in 1886 from local tribesmen, but had been unable to locate the ruins. Kozlov was overwhelmed and wrote: "I couldn't have been happier. Ever since reading about the ruins in Potanin's book, Karakhoto had been always on my mind." After less than 10 days of excavation, Kozlov sent his rich findings of *thangkas* (Buddhist scroll paintings or embroideries), manuscripts in various languages such as Tangut, Chinese, Tibetan, Mongol and Persian, coins and pottery to St Petersburg, and left Karakhoto to head southwards to Tibet.

One year later, on the way back to Russia, Kozlov resumed his excavation at Karakhoto on 22 May 1909, and enjoyed even more fruitful results than before. Inside the city he not only discovered fragments of Buddhist murals and smaller statues, manuscripts, coins and bank notes from the Yuan Dynasty, but he uncovered a real treasure when he opened a funerary stupa located west of the city. In his book *Mongolia, Amdo and the dead city Karakhoto*, he recorded his find with obvious glee: "We discovered in this ruin a full library with books, scrolls, manuscripts, more than 2,000 pieces, 300 Buddhist scroll paintings on fine silk and paper as well as very interesting statues in metal and wood. I will never forget these happy moments." All of Kozlov's finds are now kept in the Hermitage Museum in St Petersburg.

In the centre of the stupa, Kozlov not only found the mortal remains of the person buried inside, but also about 20 life-size clay statues "resembling lamas, conducting a religious ceremony in front of hundreds of manuscripts in Tangut script, stacked one upon the other". However, Kozlov was unable to carry so many large and very fragile clay statues back to St Petersburg. He had to leave the bigger ones behind, and carefully concealed them to fetch them later. But he hid them too well, for when he returned in June 1926, he was unable to find the hiding place. "A huge sand dune is covering the place where I hid the statues. Although in 1909 I had made a very careful sketch of the hiding place of these interesting statues, we could no longer find them."

After only one day's fruitless search, Kozlov left Karakhoto and never returned. The priceless statues were either lost under the drifting sand or they had been destroyed by ignorant local people, as still happens today in Xinjiang. The only visual proof of these huge statues is Kozlov's photograph taken in 1909. As well as Kozlov, Sir Aurel Stein briefly visited Karakhoto in 1914, and Folke Bergman, the archaeologist of Sven Hedin's Sino-Swedish Expedition (1927–1935), conducted further excavations there in 1931.

The present ruins are definitely worth a full day's visit. The 6–8 metre defensive walls are very well kept and create a rectangle measuring 435 x 372 metres. A few hundred metres south and west of the ruins, two ancient riverbeds are to be found. Starting a circumambulation of the ruins clockwise at the southwestern corner, first you see a Muslim shrine and then pass the strong bastions of the western gate before reaching a group of small stupas outside the city at the northwestern corner. Small *tsa tsas*, minute sacred Buddhist clay figures, lie on the ground or in the broken stupas. Five stupas stand here painted in white. Following the northern side of the route, after 50 metres you reach a breach in the wall from which, the legend tells, the last defender of Karakhoto led his hopeless counterattack against the Chinese besiegers. As on the western side, strong bastions guard the eastern city gate. In numerous places the sand has piled up to the top of the walls and flooded the city, so that it is possible to cross the walls by climbing the dunes. The few ruins left inside convey an impression of devastation. The ruins of several stupas and temples are left as well as traces of the main streets. On the ground lie broken millstones, shards of blue-and-white porcelain and more coarse red and brown pottery.

In the modest nearby town of Ejin Qi there is a small museum. If you have a 4WD, it's worth hiring a local guide in order to explore the countless ruins in the surrounding area, although none is particularly impressive. To the east are the ruins of Lücheng Si, the "green city" named after the countless green tiles lying on the ground. It corresponds to Kozlov's Boro Khoto and has a huge graveyard. To the north of Karakhoto are the ruins of the fortress Dzun Khure and only five kilometres to the northwest of the black city is the Tang Dynasty fortress of Adune Khure. Farther northwest are the ruins of the large monastery of Kara-Beishing and of the Mu Durbeljiin fort, which is part of the ancient Han Dynasty boundary line. (There is a second fort called Ulan Durbeljin 165km south of Karakhoto, north of Tarangin Durbeljin.)

Karakhoto is reached most easily by road from Jiuquan in Gansu Province (360 kilometres away) – the direct northern route from Hami via Mingshui is rougher and often closed to foreign travellers. In any case, a special permit issued by the Public Security Bureau in Lanzhou is required to visit Karakhoto and stay in the nearby town of Ejin Qi.

TRANSPORTATION

Although there is an airport (variously called Hami Airport, Kumul or Komul Airport), virtually all transport is by road or rail. The railway station is at the northern end of town; several trains run daily either way on the Lanzhou-Urumqi line. There are daily buses to/from Turpan (five hours) and Urumqi (seven hours), also on the popular route to/from Dunhuang in Gansu Province (seven hours). From Hami frequent buses head north through the mountains to Barkol and Yiwu (both journeys take about two hours).

ACCOMMODATION

By far the nicest place to stay is the **Hami Hotel Hami** (Hami Binguan), a large three-star hotel located south of Times Square at 4 Yibin Lu, tel: (0902) 223 3140, fax (0902) 223 9206. Comfortable rooms start from around Rmb340, and there is a business centre in the hotel. Other hotel options include the centrally located **Shangye Hotel** (95 Zhongshan Bei Lu, tel: (0902) 223 1768, fax: (0902) 223 1767) and the **Jiageda Hotel** (8 Aiguo Bei Lu, tel: (0902) 223 2140, fax: (0902) 223 5070).

FOOD AND DRINK

The Nong Mao night market is a large outdoor food bazaar behind the bus station off Binghe Lu. It is lined on both sides with small Chinese and Muslim restaurants; kebabs and nan, cold and fried noodles with mutton and vegetables, local fruit and Hami *pijiu* is all plentiful.

THE BARKOL (BALIKUN) GRASSLANDS

North of Hami the foothills of the Tien Shan rise towards peaks that, while not reaching the awe-inspiring heights of the range's western ramparts, still present a picturesque backdrop to the desert through which the road passes. It soon ascends to 2,000 metres, where a gigantic white stone near the town of **Baishitou**, 63 kilometres from Hami, stands guard over vast prairies of grass.

Once on the northern slopes of the mountains, the road splits, heading west to Barkol, and east to the small town of Yiwu, passing a pretty salt lake on the way. The scenery is wonderful, with desert surrounded by peaks and ridges in all directions. **Yiwu** town boasts an impressive mosque for its size, square shaped with four minarets, one at each corner, and a pointed, curving central dome, but there is little else of note – the attraction of this corner of Xinjiang is in its remoteness and the hiking possibilities coupled with the potential for cultural interaction with local nomadic groups. Yiwu itself is reputed to have the best lamb in the region, so bear this in mind when hunger bites. Accommodation is available at the modest **Yiwu Binguan** (tel: 0902 672 1210). Yiwu came under the spotlight in 2008 when it was identified as the optimum location in China to view a total eclipse of the sun on 1 August; hordes of tourists descended briefly on the area, staying in yurts just north of the town to experience 2mins 1sec of total eclipse – a rare occurrence in a location as pristine as the Gobi Desert – before heading east to Beijing for another phenomenon: the 2008 Olympic Games.

THE IMPORTANCE OF HORSES

China's ability to maintain control over Central Asia and the lucrative Silk Road trade rested, ironically, on trade with the same nomadic barbarian tribes that presented the most serious threat to Chinese rule. One of the most sought-after commodities of this trade was horses.

The growing power of nomadic peoples occupying vast stretches of forest, tundra and desert lay in their horsemanship and manoeuvrability. The introduction of the stirrup, in the third century BCE (if not earlier), which freed the riders' hands, gave the nomadic warriors a superiority in the saddle recorded to this day in the English expression "a Parthian shot", initially a reference to the Parthians' ability to turn in the saddle and discharge arrows at pursuers.

The building of the Great Wall was the reaction of China's sedentary, agricultural society to attacks from the mounted, roving Xiongnu armies that threatened Han Dynasty territory in the second century BCE. From far-off Ferghana (in present-day Uzbekistan), 5,000 kilometres northwest of Chang'an, news came of divine "blood-sweating" horses renowned for their stamina and speed. Anxious to improve the stock of his military mounts, the Han emperor Wudi in 102 BCE dispatched an army of 40,000 men to demand a supply of these mounts from the Ferghana court. The

Han forces were defeated, and a second army of 60,000 troops had to be dispatched to smooth negotiations before 3,000 of these highly prized horses could be brought back along the Silk Road to the Chinese capital. The horses did in fact appear to sweat blood, but this seems to have been caused by a mundane skin bacteria rather than any special genetic trait.

From Kucha there were stories of a breed of "dragon horses", the alleged progeny of lake dragons and wild mares. From Kushan came "heavenly horses", said to be able to take one up among the celestial realm. Arabian steeds came from Bokhara and Samarkand in Transoxiana. The short, sturdy Mongolian pony was a comparatively common breed in China, but capable of travelling long distances under adverse conditions.

Successive Chinese dynasties used imaginative methods to ensure a steady supply of war chargers and post-route horses to stock the imperial stables. The more devious strategies included political intrigue, marriages of Chinese princesses to distant rulers, and the detention of sons of chieftains for "education" in the Chinese capital. In the mid-seventh century, a marriage was arranged between a Turkish khan and a Chinese princess for the price of 50,000 horses as well as numerous camels and sheep.

During the Sui and Tang dynasties, special frontier towns became centres of barter trade, where Chinese silk was exchanged for Central Asian horses. The Song and Ming courts even created a government monopoly on tea (an important barter item) to guarantee the means to meet the ever-growing demand for horses.

During the Tang Dynasty, Uygurs and Tibetans were the main suppliers. In the mid-eighth century there was a minimum requirement of 80,000 cavalry horses to serve the 490,000 frontier troops, not to mention the number of steeds to combat domestic uprisings within China proper. When the Tibetans overran the Tang capital of Chang'an in 763 and occupied the main imperial pastures in western Gansu, the Tang government was forced to beg for assistance from the powerful Uygur Turks, shrewd businessmen who demanded 40 bolts of silk for one poor-quality horse. In the late Tang, China had to barter one million bolts of silk for 100,000 horses annually, a heavy financial burden on a country already plagued with internal strife. The Tibetans slowly replaced the Uygurs as the sole horse suppliers.

Horses as well as the spoils of war were inevitably part of any tribute mission to China. Horse hides and tails – even the penis of a white horse –were highly valued gifts (mixed with honey and wine, the dried penis of a white horse was said to restore virility). Hides were made into saddlecloths, coracle-boats and even armour. Decorative horsetails were affixed to sword sheaths or, as with the Mongols, to military banners and standards.

The finest animals were assigned to the imperial stables near Chang'an to be groomed as mounts for royal hunting forays, palace guards or for courtiers as a form of political favour. Polo had been introduced from Central Asia during the Tang Dynasty and was a popular sport among aristocrats. During the reign of Xuanzong (713–742) exquisitely caparisoned horses were trained to dance to music and perform for the emperor's birthdays.

Chinese literature, sculpture, painting and music glorified the beauty and stamina of these invaluable beasts. A renowned painting shows the legendary exploits of the Eight Bayards of Emperor Mu of the Zhou Dynasty, which carried him a thousand *li* (500 kilometres) a day on his visit to the sacred Kunlun Mountains in southern Xinjiang, where the emperor had his legendary encounter with the goddess Queen Mother of the West. The grace and strength of the Han Dynasty chargers were commemorated in stone sculptures placed before the imperial tombs. Poems and songs were composed to the Six Steeds of Emperor Taizong (627–650) that bravely carried him into battle, especially his famed red roan, which survived five arrows in a charge.

During the Yuan Dynasty, the insatiable Mongol demand for horses, needed for maintaining their fast and efficient pony express system serving all of Central Asia, was easily met within the wide expanses of the Mongol Empire. The succeeding Ming Dynasty, however, was forced to establish a special Horse Trading Office in Shaanxi Province, with branches in Hami and Dunhuang.

Barkol (Balikun) town is 120 kilometres northwest of Hami, and is the county seat of the **Barkol (Balikun) Kazakh Autonomous County**. It is situated within a picturesque landscape, the surrounding snow-capped mountains (some over 4,000 metres high) providing water to lush grasslands. An ancient city wall still remains around the town, bearing witness to its legacy as an important staging post in the ongoing wars between the Xiongnu and the armies of the Han Dynasty 2,000 years ago.

Barkol remained a vital stop on one of the Silk Road trade routes right into the 20th century, when caravans shifted north from the Hexi Corridor route due to revolution and general unrest in that area. This route began far to the east in Baotou, in Chinese Inner Mongolia, then arced through the gobi of Mongolia itself before crossing back into Chinese-controlled territory northeast of Barkol, stopping there to resupply, then heading west through the Tien Shan's northern foothills – today the **Mori Kazakh Autonomous County** of Changji Hui Autonomous Prefecture – to reach Urumqi.

The Barkol region has been famous since the Han Dynasty for its camels – its nickname is "the county of 10,000 camels" – and in particular for the quality of its horses, who are renowned for their hardiness (see special topics on pages 209 and 274). For travellers today, the small **Hotel Barkol (Balikun Binguan**, tel: (0902) 682 6677) provides acceptable rooms, but don't be surprised if you are paid a visit by officers of the local PSB – all foreigners should be registered, as this area, close to the Mongolian border, is militarily sensitive.

Around 20 kilometres before Barkol on the road from Hami, at an elevation of 2,000 metres, is the **"Singing Sand Mountain"**, or **Mingsha Dunes**, Xinjiang's own version of the more famous Mingsha Dunes in Dunhuang. Five kilometres long, up to 100 metres high and covering an area of 25 square kilometres, the quartz sand dunes make a rumbling sound as the tiny particles move across the dune faces, giving rise to the name. A river flows at the base of the dunes, creating a marshy green mass of meadows to contrast with the golden sand. Aligned in a northwest-southeast direction, the eastern slopes are steep while the western side is far more gentle in gradient. Barkol's Mingsha Dunes are far less frequently visited than Dunhuang's, but even so log sleds can be hired for tourists to toboggan down the dune faces. A legend tells that during the Han Dynasty an officer and his troops did battle with the Xiongnu hordes here, sacrificing their lives to a man. Ancient weapons have indeed been dug up from within the dunes in recent years, giving credence to the story.

Ten kilometres west of town lies **Barkol Lake**, an alpine salt lake once known as Puleihai; 1,585 metres above sea level, three kilometres wide and 10 kilometres long, the lake is split by a gravel and sand levee stretching from north to south. The western segment of the lake gives off a silvery sheen when viewed from afar, but the eastern lake has a more azure countenance, and is bordered by marshland that gives onto superb pastureland.

This area has been a favoured camping site for pastoral nomads for millennia; during spring and summer Kazakhs set up their yurts by the lakeside and enjoy great gatherings during which

Aken performances take place, contests of improvisational singing, music and poetry. This is one of the strongest traditional links between Kazakhs whether they live in Mongolia, China, Kazakhstan or Kyrgyzstan. Historically poetry and song allowed nomadic peoples to express and communicate their thoughts and knowledge of religion, creation, nature and history, and therefore *akyns*, or travelling minstrels, were revered by the people. At these grand party-like performances, the people listen avidly while each aken wages a battle of word and song in an attempt to silence his opponent with his knowledge, wit and improvisational virtuosity. If a performance is planned when you are in the vicinity, be sure not to miss it.

Loayemiao Port is a Class A Highway Port 150 kilometres north of Barkol, crossing the border to Altai Province in Mongolia. The border was opened in 1992, allowing 30,000 tons of goods and 10,000 people to cross in both directions annually. A seasonal border crossing, it is unfortunately open only to Chinese and Mongol citizens, and there are no current plans to open it to tourists.

XINJIANG'S FAR EAST – GANSU'S GATEWAY TO THE WEST

For most of its history as a trade route, the journey along the first leg of the northern Silk Road from Anxi (the last major town in Gansu Province) to Hami was by camel or cart, and took two weeks. Cable and French called the desert along this stretch a "howling wilderness", the monotony broken only by changes in the difficult desert surface. The water at each stop was, by turns, muddy, brackish or sulphurous. Even the indefatigable Xuanzang, crossing this stretch of desert and finding himself lost and without water, turned back briefly before gathering his determination to continue, half-dead, towards Hami.

Even during the first decades of the 20th century, access to Xinjiang was difficult and time-consuming, requiring passports, permits and frequently the personal approval of the governor many hundreds of kilometres away in Urumqi. Caravans and travellers were required to stop at a very inhospitable rocky ravine known as **Xingxingxia**, where soldiers manning the frontier checkpoint rigorously investigated all-comers. Delays were long and tiresome, and the area was infested with murderous bandits.

Today, Xingxingxia is the easternmost sizeable town in Xinjiang, the last on Highway 312 before it passes into Gansu, and for modern-day road users heading west, their first stop in the Xinjiang Uygur Autonomous Region. However, few will stop for long as there is nothing to see, and the harshness of the surrounding desert has not been tempered much since Xuanzang's day.

NORTH XINJIANG AND THE ILI VALLEY

s yet relatively few international tourists have discovered the natural wonders of northern Xinjiang. While the extensive **Junggar Basin** (also spelt Zhungar or Dzungar) – 777,000 square kilometres of desert, semi-desert and steppe – comprises the bulk of its land area, in the north and northeast the lush **Altai Mountains** are home to one of the world's greatest areas of taiga biodiversity, while its western border with Kazakhstan is marked by the relatively unexplored **Tarbagatai** range and the infamous **Junggar Gate**, the broad mountain gap that throughout human history has allowed migrations and conquering armies access to the Great Steppe of Central Asia and beyond. The Junggar Basin's southern boundary is the mighty Tien Shan, within whose majestic barrier ranges sits the fertile **Ili Valley** with its endless grasslands and pristine forests.

The Junggar Basin slopes generally from east to west, from approximately 1,000 metres above sea level on the border with Mongolia to around 500 metres in the Karamay region. Its central area is the **Gurbantunggut Desert**, the second largest desert in China (after the Taklamakan). In prehistoric times the basin was a rich tableland of lakes, marshes and forest filled with life, but climatic and geological changes have left it an immense, barren landscape that nevertheless provides treasures we humans cherish. Chief among these are the oil and natural gas deposits that have only begun to be extracted in the last century, but more appealing to the leisure-oriented visitor to this region are its bizarre wind-eroded "ghost city" landscapes, and the incredible wealth of fossils to be found here, both dinosaur bones and the petrified remains of prehistoric forests. The Junggar Basin gets more moisture than the Tarim Basin due to winds that blow through the mountains from Siberia. This allows more vegetation to survive, mostly scrub desert varieties and saxaul, tamarisk, poplar and willow near its rim, in turn creating habitat for wildlife from tiny jerboas to wild ass and gazelles.

The Altai Mountains – Altai translates as "Gold Mountains" in both Turkic and Mongolian – are more than 2,000 kilometres long, straddling Russia, Kazakhstan, China and Mongolia (Xinjiang's northern edge demarcates the southern slopes of the range). The second highest mountain in the Altai is **Khuiten Peak**, 4,374 metres high and lying on the border between China and Mongolia, just 2.5 kilometres south of the actual point where those two countries and Russia all come together. The tri-point peak is called **Nairamdal** (4,180 metres), the second of five closely packed summits collectively known as the Tavan Bogd massif – indeed, the Chinese name of **Youyi Feng** or **Friendship Peak** is commonly used for both Nairamdal and Khuiten. Generally, though, the Altai lies around 3,000 metres above sea level, with 400–800mm of annual rainfall – unlike so much of Xinjiang, water resources are plentiful here.

Forests of larch, fir and spruce occupy elevations of 1,200–2,300 metre; below these are pasture meadows and deciduous trees such as birch and poplar. In spring and summer glorious carpets of wildflowers fill the meadows, and in autumn nature puts on a show of blazing glory as leaves turn to gold – this region is a hiker's dream come true. Thick snow covers the mountains in winter, and

The Junggar Basin is delineated by the Altai Mountains in the north and east and the Tien Shan in the south. Its sandy centre is the Gurbantunggut Desert, the rockier southeastern sector is the Jiangjun Gobi, while from the Altai Xinjiang's western border with Kazakhstan bisects the Irtysh River plain (before it enters the large, elongated Zaysan Lake in the upper left of this image) and follows the Tarbagatai range south to the Junggar Gate (the light-blue lake is Kazakhstan's Alakol). The triangular Ulungur Lake can be clearly seen in the north of the basin – while the deep-blue blob in the bottom left of the image is Sayram Lake, with the fertile Ili Valley stretching east-west beneath it. The irrigated farmland of Urumqi and other cities near the northern slopes of the Tien Shan can be easily distinguished at bottom centre (satellite image by Jacques Descloitres, MODIS Rapid Response Team, NASA/GSFC).

even in summer temperatures can drop low, so warm clothing is always necessary. The colours of the forest in spring and autumn are superb, and consequently the tourist season here is mid-May until the end of September or early October, depending on the vagaries of the weather – winter can descend on the Altai very suddenly, cutting off access to the mountain valleys. The Altai is rich in nonferrous metals such as copper, lead, tin and zinc, as well as the gold that gave it its name.

The northern segment of the Junggar Basin is drained by two main rivers and their many tributaries. The upper **Irtysh** (**Ertis** or **Ertix**) **River**, whose source is deep in the eastern Altai, courses out of the mountains and waters a wide, grassy plain, flowing northwest into Kazakhstan where it enters Zaysan Lake, before continuing on to the Arctic Ocean – a distance of almost 4,000 kilometres in total, 596 kilometres of which flow through Xinjiang. Its name means "rushing water", and more than 20 tributaries emerge from the mountain range within Xinjiang to feed it. The **Ulungur River** also begins in the eastern Altai in Qinghe County, but it never reaches any sea, instead flowing into **Ulungur Lake**, the Junggar Basin's largest remaining open body of water.

Where the northern foothills of the Tien Shan slope down to the southern Junggar Basin, mountain streams once emerged and ran into the semi-desert, disappearing in vast marshlands of reed. Nomadic Kazakhs and Mongols drove their herds from pasture to pasture, and towns developed as staging posts for the northern trade route into Central Asia that was used in conjunction with the more renowned routes south of the Tien Shan. Today, the water is used for irrigation by huge farming concerns, and the cities along the major motorway running west from Urumqi are blossoming along with the agriculture and petrochemical industries. South of these booming towns, separated from them by towering snow-capped peaks, the Ili Valley presents a picture of abundance that is very different from the desert regions to the north and south. Its evergreen valleys, bright, rushing rivers and expansive pastures and fields are picturesque and invite exploration, while the valley's protective ring of mountains has resulted in a strong cultural identity for the Kazakhs who have historically made this a stronghold of their lifestyle.

In contrast to the south, much of north Xinjiang is blessed with richly forested mountains and fertile pastures (Sun Jiabin).

Indeed, the majority of Northern Xinjiang comes under administrative control of the **Ili Kazakh Autonomous Prefecture**, and outside the Han Chinese-dominated cities, the influence of Kazakhs and the nomadic way of life centred around livestock remains strong. Kazakhs are distant descendants of the ancient Wusun tribes and of other Turkic peoples; their language is a Turkic language of the Kipchak branch. Today they total about one million in the entire Ili Kazakh Autonomous Prefecture, outnumbered two to one by the Han Chinese out of a total population of four million (there are 650,000 Uygurs, 70,000 Mongolians, 350,000 Huis and lesser numbers of all Xinjiang's other ethnic groups).

Northern Xinjiang is also home to the **Tuvan** people, who live in the valleys around Kanas Lake. A sub-group of Mongolian extraction, they speak a language similar to Kazakh but are related to the ethnic Tuvans of Russia's Tuva Republic. Around 2,500 Tuvans live mainly in the villages around Kanas Lake, and in the Hemu and Baihaba valleys. Most visitors to northern Xinjiang either fly straight to Altay City or Kanas Lake for a quick-hit Altai experience, or embark on a multi-day circular driving route around the rim of the Junggar Basin on Highways 216 and 217.

THE ROAD TO THE ALTAI

In the early 1990s construction of **Highway 216** finally opened an easy route around the eastern rim of the Junggar Basin to the rich mountains of the Altai range. Far from being devoid of attractions, however, the journey north passes a number of fantastic natural sites boasting unusual phenomena.

Leaving the Urumqi metropolis behind, the highway runs parallel to the Tien Shan, with Bogda Peak and its surrounding massif framed in your vehicle's south-facing windows in all its massive glory. The highway is an excellently maintained motorway punctuated by frequent tollbooths, but before reaching the town of Jimsar it leaves the jagged ridge of mountains behind and turns north along the eastern rim of the vast Junggar Basin, the Jiangjun Gobi to the east, the Gurbantunggut Desert to the west.

THE BEITING RUINS

Eight kilometres north of the town of **Jimsar**, not far west from the point where Highway 216 turns and heads for the Altai, lie the ruins of Beiting City. This puts it at a strategic point on the historical northern trade route from Hami, Barkol and Qitai in the east to Fukang, Urumqi and ultimately the Ili Valley or Junggar Gate to the west. The rectangular city's huge, rammed-earth outer walls measured 1,500 metres from north to south, 1,000 metres from east to west and up to 10 metres thick, with turrets at each corner – Beiting had to be a major fortress since this region was the centre of constant conflict. The city in fact changed hands many times, falling variously under the control of the Xiongnu, Han Dynasty troops, the Western Turkic Khaganate, Tibetans and Uygurs. Less than a kilometre west of the city are the ruins of a stupa complex known by locals as *Xidasi*, or "Big West Temple", which are in better condition than the rather dilapidated city. Beiting only became a state-protected cultural relic site in 1988 (*see* special topic on page 219 for more on this site).

QITAI GHOST CITY

One hundred kilometres north of Qitai town, on the eastern edge of the Junggar Basin in the area known as the **Jiangjun Gobi**, are 84 square kilometres of fascinating wind-formed "yardang" landscape. The **Qitai Ghost City**, although smaller than the more famous Uryhe Ghost City near Karamay on the western side of the Junggar Basin, is renowned for its more unusual shapes on a smaller scale. For the imaginative viewer, the rock formations appear to be shaped like tigers, camels, gigantic mushrooms, etc, while others look like enormous palaces and pavilions. Wind channelled between the rocks creates a low, moaning effect, resulting in the superstitious naming of the site as a dwelling place of ghosts. As with all these sites, the best time to visit is early morning or late afternoon, when the sun is low in the sky, the rocks are coloured gold and the shadows are long.

DINOSAUR VALLEY AND PETRIFIED FOREST PARK

The Jiangjun Gobi is renowned for fossil excavation, and Qitai County in **Changji Hui Autonomous Prefecture**, 370 kilometres northeast of Urumqi, has been a hotspot for palaeontologists since 1928, when Yang Chung-chien, a member of an expedition led by Sven Hedin, discovered the fossilised remains of a sauropod named *Tienshanosaurus chitaiensis* near Jiangjunmiao. Subsequent discoveries of fossilized shells and corals, turtles and crocodilians proved that this basin once held an enormous inland lake. A particularly rich source of dinosaur fossils is the area commonly called **Dinosaur Valley**, where in September 1987 a Sino-Canadian research team unearthed what was at the time Asia's largest dinosaur fossil, from the sauropod *mamenchisaurus sinocanadorum* (a type of diplodocus). Dinosaur Valley actually covers a huge 492-square-kilometre area, and fossils can be found across the entire 10,000-square-kilometre gobi region stretching east to Barkol County in Hami Prefecture, but the region near to Beiting and Qitai Ghost City has been particularly productive, in particular the areas of **Jiangjunmiao**, **Wucaiwan** and **Konglonggou**, collectively termed the **Shishugou Formation**. In 2002 the oldest tyrannosaur fossil was discovered in this area, and another *mamenchisaurus* bone became the largest dinosaur fossil in the world – the animal's neck was 15 metres long, allowing an estimation of its entire length of 35 metres. Superb specimens of the large, Tyrannosaurus-like theropods *Monolophosaurus* and *Sinraptor* have also been collected, and undoubtedly much more remains to be found.

In the same location is the **Qitai Petrified Forest Park** (Shishugou, or "stone tree valley"), which covers an area of 3.8 square kilometres containing up to 1,000 silicified trees, both standing (to a height of two metres) and lying horizontally on the ground (the longest is 26 metres in length). During the Jurassic Period, this region was warm, humid, and covered with thick jungle and wet marsh. During later tectonic plate movement many huge trees were buried underground, where the high silica content of the subterranean water combined with high temperatures and great pressure to silicify them, transforming organic matter into lifeless rock. You can still see the bark, grain and growth rings on massive, petrified tree trunks.

Wind erosion throughout the Junggar Basin creates fantastical rock formations, such as this giant toadstool-like creation at the Qitai Ghost City (Sun Jiabin).

THE ANCIENT CITY OF BEITING (BESH BALIK)

By Christoph Baumer

The ancient city ruins of Beiting are located 150 kilometres northeast of Urumqi and can be visited in one day with a hired car. An excellent highway follows the western and then northern edges of the Bogda Shan, offering spectacular views of its peaks, especially of ice-covered, 5,445-metre-high Bogda Feng. Upon reaching the town of Jimsar, instead of continuing straight on towards Mori and Barkol, turn northwards and after eight kilometres you arrive at the archaeological site of Beiting.

Beiting experienced a tumultuous history, for it was an intensely disputed border town. The region around Beiting, called "Chin Man" by the Chinese of the Western Han (206 BCE–9 CE), belonged at that time to the empire of the Xiongnu, but was conquered by the Eastern Han general Keng Ping in 74 CE. During the following decades it was attacked several times by both sides until the Chinese military governor Ban Yung, son of the famous General Ban Chao, managed to stabilize the borders in 123 CE. A few centuries later the

Excellent murals still exist in the subterranean rooms of Beiting's Xidasi, or "Big West Temple" (Sun Jiabin).

town belonged to the Western Turkic Khaganate and was called "Kagan Stupa", under which name it was mentioned by the itinerant monk Xuanzang. When China began, under the Tang Dynasty (618-907), to reconquer its former Central Asian territory, it subjugated first the Kingdom of Gaochang and then Beiting in 640, which was elevated in 702 to the rank of a Protectorate. Its local Turkic name by then was "*Besh Balik*", meaning five towns.

In 790 the Tibetans, who had already snatched the whole Tarim Basin from China, crossed the Tien Shan and conquered Beiting. Although the Uygurs, military allies of China, launched several counterattacks, they only succeeded in dislodging the Tibetans after the collapse of the Tibetan Empire in 842. The Uygurs occupied Beiting and made it their auxiliary capital after Gaochang (near Turpan); peace returned to the city, and Buddhism flourished until 1214, when the Muslim Choresm Shah Mohammed II crushed the Kara-Khitans and advanced on Beiting. Five years later Genghis Khan evicted the Choresmian troops from all of Eastern Turkestan and destroyed their empire: Beiting was then abandoned. In 1278 Kublai Khan created a Chinese garrison at Beiting as a bulwark against the rebellious Mongol Prince Khaidu. However, Khaidu conquered Beiting eight years later, putting an end to Chinese dominance in Eastern Turkestan for almost 500 years.

The archaeological site of Beiting is divided into two parts, the stupa and the city – the latter comprising an outer and inner city. The city walls, which are believed to date from the Tang Dynasty, are more than four metres high and in reasonable condition in the northern section of the site, but on the other sides the walls are crumbling. The walls of the inner city had a perimeter of less than 4,000 metres, but they have almost disappeared. You can, however, still see recognizable structures of some of the larger buildings.

About 700 metres west of the city stand the ruins of the stupa complex, around 1,970 metres long and 1,140 metres wide. The stupa has a rectangular ground plan of 50 x 75 metres, and consists on all but the southern side of three floors with eight niches on the lower level and seven each on the middle and top levels. (In this it resembles the three-tiered temple *Gamma* in Gaochang, which has six niches carved at each level and on each side.) Timber frames once supported the vault of each niche, and many remain, though some have been reconstructed. Each of the roughly two-metre-high niches contained one or several painted clay statues of a seated Buddha, or in a few instances a standing Buddha. Among the surviving, though rather damaged seated figures, you can recognize one large Sakyamuni Buddha wearing a red-and-white patchwork monk's robe, as well as several Maitreya Buddhas. All the niche walls were decorated with murals dating to the 9th–11th centuries and featured bodhisattvas, monks and nuns, palace scenes and princely attendants. The best-kept recesses are on the upper two floors of the eastern side of the stupa, but they are all locked, so you'll have to ask the keeper at the entrance to open them for you.

The southern side of the stupa consists of a complex of 17 subterranean rooms arranged on either side of a 16-metre-long, three-lane corridor leading to an underground chamber. As with the niches, the walls of these subterranean rooms were also covered with murals, but only two are accessible. The first, smaller mural is located at the entrance to the underground complex and features a male figure wearing a golden dress and holding a golden flower. He is framed by a roofed doorway on whose left vertical pillar a Uygur inscription is written, and he is surrounded by Buddhist worshippers. The best-preserved murals are to be found in subterranean room No. 105, in the eastern half of the underground complex. The chapel measures 17 x 4.5 metres and along its eastern wall are the remains of a 13-metre-long reclining statue of the Sakyamuni Buddha. This represents the death of the historical Buddha named *perinirvana*. Similar figures of the reclining Buddha were found at Adzhina Tepe in Tajikistan, in cave 158 of the Mogao Grottoes of Dunhuang, and in Zhangye, although that last is more than twice as long as the others. On the short northern wall are the remains of a huge teaching Buddha, most probably Sakyamuni again.

Opposite the reclining Buddha, well-preserved murals from the 9th–11th centuries cover the western wall. On the lower left part two main scenes show the siege of a large city attacked by archers, and in the centre and at the right a group of eight riders. The largest of these eight figures has a *mandorla*, an aureole, around his head, his right hand is raised in a blessing pose and he is riding a white elephant. His attendants are mounted on horseback and wear military dress and helmets. In the lower part of the mural two over-proportionally large figures of a royally dressed male and female appear, separated from the main scene by a mountain landscape. They are framed on both sides by vertical inscriptions in Uygur, and probably represent the princely couple donating the stupa; their clothing and headdresses are similar to those of donors featured in the murals of the Bezeklik caves of Turpan.

The interpretation of the two main scenes is not certain. The beleaguered city could represent the Indian city of Kushinagara, where the historical Buddha passed away. The Malla king of Kushinagara wished to keep the relics of the Buddha in his kingdom, but his claim was challenged by seven other rulers who laid siege to his city. To avoid an imminent war for the relics, the wise Brahman Drona – a non-Buddhist – divided the relics into eight parts which he handed over to the eight claimants. However, it is difficult to find a link from this sequence with the main figure seated with ankles crossed on the white elephant. He may represent Bodhisattva Samantabhadra (called *Puxian Pusa* in Chinese) and his retinue, or a Buddha with the Seven Historic Buddhas of the past. A third interpretation would see in the main figure the representation of a Uygur prince, the same as the one clad in a golden dress at the entrance and as the donor at the bottom of the main mural. If this were the case, the site could have been a funerary complex. However, neither a tomb nor a reliquary has so far been found.

An impressive stone bridge is actually a silicified tree trunk in the Petrified Forest Park (Hao Pei).

The Qitai Petrified Forest Park and Dinosaur Valley Park are being promoted together, and can be visited at the same time. A museum and new park facilities are being built, and current entrance fees cost around Rmb50 per person.

KARAMAY NATURE RESERVE

B ack on Highway 216, as you move north the road passes through a landscape of rocky hills and gravel plains punctuated by sparse shrubs and hardy hummocks of grass. This badlands scenery may appear unsuitable for much life, but in fact it encompasses the **Karamay Nature Reserve**, home to a surprising number of animal species. The 14,000-square-kilometre reserve, occupying a large chunk of the eastern Junggar Basin, provides habitat for eagles, Mongolian gazelles, wild ass, saiga antelope, even snow leopards and argali sheep in the highlands along the Mongolian border, as well as small numbers of Przewalski's horse, which have been slowly reintroduced to the habitat that once supported large herds of this earliest of wild horse breeds. This area was in fact where the Russian explorer Nikolai Przhevalsky first discovered the horse. In

1986, with help from the Worldwide Fund for Nature (WWF), the **Xinjiang Wild Horse Breeding and Research Centre** was established, acquiring 18 Przewalski's horses from the US, Britain and Germany. They now have a herd of approximately 290, 45 of which were released into the reserve in two batches in 2001 and 2004, and six more – a stallion and five mares – in 2007.

As vehicles motor up the road Mongolian gazelles can easily be seen at very close quarters, grazing on the slim plant pickings near the highway and only slightly put out by cars stopping to release excited tourists with their constantly clicking cameras. Rarely are large animals so easily viewed from the roadside.

THE COLOURFUL CITY SCENIC AREA (FIVE-COLOURED HILLS)

 s Highway 216 continues north it climbs and descends gently through undulating scrub desert lowland, punctuated by petrochemical and shallow mining operations. Huge concave chimneys pump out thick columns of smoke that smudge the otherwise cobalt-blue sky.

Located 220 kilometres south of Fuyun City, before the highway crosses the Ulungur River, is the **Colourful City Scenic Area** (also known as the **Five-coloured Hills**), in what was a huge lake basin during the Jurassic period (145–200 million years ago). The sedimentary rocks laid down by this lake have been weathered into an amazing landscape; softer sands, gravels and rocks were more quickly washed and blown away, leaving hundreds of rounded hills and gullies which, when

The Irtysh River flows broad and strong across the northern Junggar Basin, bringing life to the region (Sun Jiabin).

the sun is low in the sky in early morning or late afternoon, glow in differing shades of red, white and gold according to the varying amounts and types of minerals in each sedimentary layer. Agate is commonly found here, as well as examples of petrified trees and fossils.

FUHAI COUNTY

The Altai Mountains now come into view northeast of the road, and yurts begin to appear, snuggling up on the leeward side of low hills and sprouting thin tendrils of smoke, with herds of domestic animals scattered across the grassy plains. Horses, sheep, camels, cows and goats are kept and bred by Kazakhs and Mongols, a central component of the nomadic culture that still plays a significant role in far northern Xinjiang outside the urban centres.

Highway 216 veers away from the mountains a short distance before the local county seat of **Fuyun**, soon arriving at the **Irtysh River**, lined with poplar, elm and willow trees, and following it west towards **Beitun**. This rather plain town will be the railhead for a new rail link being built from Kuyten – on the Urumqi-Alashankou route – via Karamay and **Fuhai City**, located on the eastern shore of Ulungur Lake. Beitun is typical of many north Xinjiang urban centres, which were heavily populated by PLA soldiers in the 1950s to provide an easily mobilized force and safeguard China's remote border regions. To keep the men happy, young educated women were recruited from the central provinces and sent to be their wives; sadly, the harsh environment and difficult life so far from home was too much for many, and suicide rates soared, so in a rethink the central government switched to sending uneducated girls from poor peasant stock, who were more used to hardship, and dealt with their new lives in the remote western regions much better. The result is that today, northern Xinjiang's towns are primarily Han Chinese in their demographic, while the rural areas support a majority of Kazakhs and Mongols.

You are now in Fuhai County, which occupies an area of 31,800 square kilometres covering part of the Gurbantunggut Desert, the northern edge of the Junggar Basin, fertile grasslands through which the Irtysh and Ulungur rivers flow, and the forested mountain areas beyond Altay City up to the Mongolian border. It also harbours one of the 10 largest freshwater lakes in China: **Fuhai Lake**, as it is now named. Known as the "Pearl of the Junggar", this 900-square-kilometre body of water is actually split into two lakes – the larger **Ulungur Lake** and smaller **Jili Lake** – joined by a river channel. The lake is famous for its fish – more than 20 different types teem in its waters, including carp, bass and dace – and Fuhai fish is a renowned Ulungur product. Vast reed beds line the shores, but in recent years the lake has become a tourist attraction in its own right, and local authorities have encouraged this by creating a 10-kilometre-long sandy beach and building summer chalets, hostels and campsites to cater to tourists who come to swim, relax around barbecue fires or buzz over the water in pleasure boats and speedboats.

Opposite top: Rich pastures feed livestock in the foothills of the Altai (SC Keung). Opposite bottom: Reeds from riverbanks and lakesides in northern Xinjiang are used by locals for a multitude of purposes (Peter Hibbard).

CARVED IN STONE: ROCK ART AND
TURKIC TOMBS IN THE ALTAI
By Christoph Baumer

The mountain region of the Chinese Altai is a little-known El Dorado for enthusiasts of Neolithic and Palaeolithic rock art, as well as stone figures dating from the two Turkic empires. These sites are best reached by a one-hour flight over the spectacular Junggar Desert from Urumqi to the city of Altay, the administrative centre of Altay Prefecture, which comes within the administrative umbrella of the Ili Kazakh Autonomous Prefecture.

While ancient rock carvings, or petroglyphs, are not uncommon in China, polychrome rock paintings are scarce. However, three locations boasting ancient coloured paintings are to be found in prehistoric caves within Xinjiang's Altai Mountains. Most of the drawings are painted in red or reddish brown, a few in black or white; the dating of these polychrome cave paintings is open to debate – a comparison with similar paintings found in the Mongolian *aimag* (province) of Kovd may indicate their origin in the Late Palaeolithic period around 8000 BCE. Some paintings are located at the entrances of the caves, others deep in their interior, so visitors must bring a strong lamp with them. (Don't let local guides use torches as their smoke blackens the paintings.)

The largest of the three sites consists of seven caves at **Dugat**, located in the district of Sarbulak, Baihaba County, near the Sino-Kazakh border northwest of Buerjin. The most impressive rock painting shows a large hunting scene with relatively small hunters chasing large animals with spears; other hunters on the far right side of the painting lie in ambush waiting for the fleeing animals to come within reach of their spears. About five animals, cattle and horses, have already been killed and lie on the ground, pierced by spears. On top of the hunting scene are fences, traps and numerous foot- and handprints. The other six caves display

various geometrical patterns, dancing figures, men leading cattle and innumerable foot- and handprints. Petroglyphs from the Bronze Age are also to be found near the caves.

The second site is at a place called **Arktas** near Balibagai, about 25 kilometres northwest of Altay City. The paintings are found in a long, narrow cave, with representations of humans, cattle, horses and geometrical designs. In the vicinity of Altai City there are also two sites with rock carvings, located about 500 metres apart from each other. At the smaller one, called Telate, small mountain goats are carved in the rocks, as well as deer with huge antlers. About 60 metres higher to the northeast is the site of Duolate with rock carvings of mountain goats, antelopes, deer, hunters armed with bows and at least two birthing scenes.

The third site, which sports red and reddish brown rock paintings, is very close to the village of **Tangbaletas** at Kelabulegen, about 60 kilometres north of Fuyun. Tangbaletas is a Turkic name meaning "painted rocks". In the smaller of the two caves with paintings are drawings of deer, foxes and boars; in the larger, almost 12-metre-high cave there are large human faces wearing high caps, geometrical patterns and large ovals which could be interpreted as vulvae belonging to a fertility cult.

The Altai steppes are also home to numerous ancient Turkic tombs and stone figures representing humans. The Altai and the Junggar Basin were part of two Turkic empires 1,500 years ago. The First Turkic Khaganate was founded in 552 CE by the Turkic leader Bumin Khagan when he destroyed the federation of the Ruanruan, whose huge empire stretched from Xinjiang's Karashahr region in the west to northern Korea in the east. (The Ruanruan had even occupied Hotan in 471 CE.) After Bumin Khagan's death in the same year, the new empire was divided into two parts: Bumin's son Khagan Muhan (ruled 553–572) reigned over the Eastern Turkic Empire while Bumin's brother Khagan Ishtemi (ruled 553–575) controlled the Western Turkic Empire. When China regained its military strength under the Tang Dynasty (618-907), both Turkic empires collapsed, the Eastern in 630 and the Western in 659. However, when in the year 670 the Tibetans managed to conquer the four Chinese garrisons of Xinjiang – Kucha, Karashahr, Hotan and Kashgar – the Turks seized the opportunity to regain their independence. The Second Turkic Empire lasted from 682 to 745, when it was destroyed by the Uygurs.

The Turks venerated *Tengri*, or heaven, as a supreme deity, as well as the mother goddess *Umay* and numerous nature deities. As semi-nomadic people they built few durable constructions for the living, but many for the dead. In the Junggar Basin, the tombs of important warriors or leaders followed the same pattern as those in today's Mongolia, Kazakhstan and Kyrgyzstan, which also belonged to both Turkic empires. The burial mounds were marked by a rectangular or occasionally round arrangement of flat stones lying on the ground, and surrounded by smaller, standing stones (also flat faced) functioning as a stone fence. Within this marked area the deceased person, his most important belongings – commonly his weapons – as well as sacrificed animals or, in some cases humans, were buried in one or several underground chambers. Also within the area delineated by the outer stone fence, one or several large stone figures, known as *balbals*, were erected, often near the funeral chamber. These figures, with a more or less clear anthropomorphic shape, are said to either represent the dead man himself, or his defeated enemies. Many of the balbal figures hold a cup at chest level. This gesture is believed to symbolize the enemy's submission and an offer of service to their master in the next world.

A spectacular group of five balbals stands at **Qiemuer Qieki**, also called Kemuki, about 75 kilometres to the west of Altay City. On the way there, about 30 kilometres down the road leading towards the Kanas Nature Reserve, a single heap of large black boulders can be seen from the road, standing behind a farmhouse. Between the house and the heap of rocks stands a single balbal. After a few more kilometres a rectangular tomb arrangement measuring 10 x 10 metres appears next to the road. In front of the tombs two weathered black balbals are still standing, each around 80cm high. These are barely recognizable as human – they are coarse blocks with a face, arms and hands roughly chiselled onto them.

Qiemuer Qieki's tomb is the most interesting: after almost 70 kilometres on the main road, you have to drive cross country for another seven kilometres or so – a guide is necessary since this tomb is not visible from the road. The Altai range provides a spectacular background to the rectangular tomb, which covers an area of 25 x 25 metres with many small flat stones still standing in the grass. Here five balbals are gathered, probably originating from neighbouring tombs. These balbals don't have a clear anthropomorphic shape; their faces, arms and hands are simply cut into standing obelisks. Judging from the facial traits, they represent three women and two men, the tallest standing 150 centimetres above the ground, and this burial arrangement may be dated to the time of the Turkic empires in the 6th–8th centuries. The site itself lies at the ancient border between the Eastern and Western Khaganates.

Qiemuer Qieki is an important site, and even gave its name to a sub-culture. In certain tombs of this Qiemuer Qieki Culture bodies have been found in bent position, some of them decapitated. It is believed that they represent human sacrifices, the victims killed on the occasion of the burial. Chinese scholars have drawn parallels between the Qiemuer Qieki Culture and the Karasuk Culture of the Minusinsk Basin, which would imply a dating as early as the late second millennium BCE. However, since radiocarbon data are still missing for the Qiemuer Qieki Culture, this early dating remains a hypothesis. In addition, it is well known from Mongolian tombs that the Turks reused much older graveyards, so the Turkic balbals could be standing near much older tombs.

In winter a local fishing festival sees large groups of men carve a huge hole in the thick ice (the lake freezes solid to a depth of more than a metre in winter, and when strong winds blow huge icebergs are sometimes deposited on the lake shores) and cast a net in for an hour or two, before joining together to haul out the catch – which can reach dozens of tons in weight and require serious effort to land. Needless to say, a major feast and party follows. On the eastern side of Ulungur Lake are a number of yardang valleys – just in case you'd forgotten the unusual setting of this watery wonderland.

The **Alashan Valley**, in the mountains southeast of Altay City at an elevation of 1,400 metres, is another of this county's beautiful locations and is particularly popular with domestic tourists because of its 24 hot springs, which range in temperature from a relatively warm 34°C to a piping-hot 60°C, and have been named by the local people (who consider them sacred) according to their individual characteristics: Fountain Spring sends up a spout of hot water every few minutes; Heart Spring bubbles like a beating heart; and the Twin-Spring Bath is open to tourists – the trace elements found in the water are said to have curative effects on sufferers of arthritis, skin diseases and lumbago. Alashan in fact translates as "the valley of hot springs" in Mongolian, but it has more to offer than just the springs. The hiking in this area in summer is wonderful, with thick forests, flower-filled meadows and extraordinary rock formations. Nearby is **Butterfly Valley**, which, as its name suggests, is inundated with myriad multicoloured butterflies during the months of June and July. It remains a mystery why they gather in this particular location.

Weddings and akyn performances take place at a huge Kazakh gathering – a vibrant and joyous affair (Yan Xian).

The Qiemuer Qieki stone figures on the route from Altay City to Buerjin (Fan Shucai).

Fuhai mutton is said to be some of the best in Xinjiang – a bold claim given the ubiquity of this meat in the region. However, glowing reports in records dating from the Tang Dynasty, when local chieftains sent sheep as tribute to the royal court, seem to back this up – apparently the tenderness and sweet taste of the meat is a result of the fine pastures and pure mineral water the sheep graze on and drink. Just north of Alashan Valley is the 2,418-metre **Hongshanzui Port** border crossing, a remote entry/exit point for Mongolia and China, but open only to citizens of those countries.

ALTAY CITY AND THE NORTH

A ltay City stands at the foot of the Altai range astride the Irtysh River. It is 666 kilometres north of Urumqi, but only 90 kilometres from the Mongolian border, and has a population of around 166,000. Tourists generally only stop overnight in this small city, using it merely as a conduit to the more obvious attractions of Kanas Lake and its environs. However, it has its own interesting sites to offer: two kilometres outside town is **Hualin Park**, a pretty place based around the Kelan River, with small islands midstream covered in silver birch and poplar trees that are particularly beautiful in autumn, when their leaves blaze gold. Entrance costs Rmb5.

In the **Quer Gully** on the southeastern outskirts of town, the cliff walls are inscribed with petroglyphs dating back as a far as 1,000 BCE. The **Handega Cliff Paintings** (entrance Rmb10) show images of animals, people, and the daily lifestyle of the pastoral nomads and Saka horse warriors of that time. Ten kilometres farther south than Handega township is another petroglyph site in **Duolate Gully**; while the rock paintings are similar, this is a larger site than Handega, stretching a few kilometres up the gorge.

There are two flights a week to/from Urumqi. Buses connect the city with Buerjin, Habahe town, Fuyun, Fuhai, Jeminay, Karamay and Urumqi. The long-distance bus station is on Tuanjie Lu on the west bank of the river. Accommodation prices vary widely between high and low seasons; the **Jinqiao Hotel** (1 Jiefang Lu, tel: (0906) 212 7588, fax: (0906) 212 7519) has standard rooms from Rmb240, suites from Rmb420, or try the **Altay District Hotel** (205 Gongyuan Lu, tel: (0906) 212 3804) which has similar prices.

Stone Men

welve kilometres south of Altay City are a set of ancient tombs belonging to the nomadic tribes who populated the mountains in centuries past. Inside these tombs, along with the body were placed metal arrowheads and other weapons, clothing and items from daily life such as pottery. Placed facing east in front of the tombs are one or more upright stones, carved into the likeness of (predominantly) warriors. **Stone figures** (*balbals*) such as these have been found throughout the grasslands of the Altai and Ili Valley regions in Xinjiang, and exist in large numbers in Mongolia, Kazakhstan and Kyrgyzstan as well. Little is known for sure about these enigmatic anthropomorphic statues, which date from the Wusun period (sixth century BCE–fifth century CE) to the Turkic Khaganates of the latter half of the first millennium CE, but it is thought they are either effigies of the warriors buried in the graves below, or represent ancestral gods.

There are varying styles, some fairly basic with only facial features engraved and intaglio lines showing arms, hands and basic clothing outlines – these are typical of the Altai region. Others are more intricate, involving far greater skill and clearly showing arms, legs, weapons and other utensils (these figures are more commonly found in the Ili Valley). More than 80 stone figures have been discovered so far in the Altai region, but the most commonly viewed are the **Qiemuer Qieke** figures that stand side by side conveniently near the road from Altay City to Buerjin (the start of Highway 217). Consisting of three brown-stone and two black-stone figures, the rocks from which they are carved are large and rounded in shape; the faces carved into them are oval in shape, with large, curving eyebrows, and the figures' hands are tiny in comparison to the bulky bodies. Standing out from the surrounding steppe, they make a lasting impression – as no doubt their creators intended (*see* page 226).

Buerjin (Burqin)

The main town and administrative centre of Buerjin (Burqin) County is **Buerjin City**, the gateway to the mountains of the far north. Laid out in a grid pattern with wide streets, the town planner or government architect obviously had a penchant for European style since many of the buildings around town are decorated with Greek columns and fanciful porticoes, giving it a rather un-Chinese feel but also a refreshing if incongruous look. In summer Buerjin is packed with tourists, and regular buses take them north to the region's premier tourist site, Kanas Lake, which is 155 kilometres and 3–4 hours away by road.

The **Mystic Lake Grand Hotel** (Shen Hu Lu, tel: (0906) 652 0808, email: shenhuhotel@163. com, website: www.shenhuhotel.com) is a large, 256-room four-star hotel with an expansive front garden. This is the best accommodation in town, and acts as the top venue for important events. Rooms start from Rmb780, suites from Rmb1,680 (high season prices). The hotel shuts down completely out of season. A good alternative is the **Youyifeng Grand Hotel** (Xinjiang Youyifeng Road, tel: (0906) 652 6111, fax: (0906) 652 6008), rooms start from Rmb680 during high season, deluxe suites from Rmb1,680.

Food in this northern enclave tends towards hearty bowls of flat noodle soup with meat and vegetables, designed to warm you up when temperatures fall. Being close to Fuhai Lake, the grilled fish is recommended.

KANAS LAKE NATIONAL PARK

The road north from Buerjin crosses the Irtysh River, which is lined with birches and offers endless picturesque camping spots, before crossing an expanse of prairie land and fields. The landscape then turns to sandy hills, and the road cuts circuitously through a barrier of forbidding rock pinnacles and ravines before descending into a broad valley of forest and rich pastureland. Here, horsemen and their dogs watch over herds of sheep and goats; the men seem to favour ankle-length Chinese army trenchcoats with fur collars and fur-lined Russian-style caps with earflaps – it pays to stay warm when drops in temperature can occur at any time.

Crossing the valley floor, the road finally begins to wind into the mountains, up a typically sinuous road, well made but having to negotiate its way through steep ravines where rock falls are common. Roadside signs exhort visitors to "Protect rare species" and "Protect the environment, don't leave anything behind but your footprints". Emerging on a level plain the road passes **Kanas Airport**, still 80 kilometres from the lake itself. The pastures in this area are populated by Kazakhs whose cemeteries can be seen nearby, the tombstones topped by Islamic crescents. During summer this area is awash with lush meadows carpeted with wildflowers, but any time from October to May the entire region can be blanketed with thick snow overnight, and through the winter months it is a blank canvas of white dotted with animals huddling together and small groups of steep-roofed log cabins – a very Siberian landscape far from the conventional image of Xinjiang.

Finally the road reaches the entrance gate to the **Kanas Lake National Park**, where vehicles must be parked and the entrance fee paid. From here park-run shuttle buses take you up along the Kanas River, stopping at **Sleeping Dragon Bay** (*Wo Long Wan*), **Moon Bay** (*Yue Liang Wan*) and **Fairy Bay** (*Shen Xian Wan*) – the three most famous of the nine bends the river makes here – before reaching the Tuva Village, and stopping by the lakeside.

Initially the lake and its surroundings were designated as Kanas Nature Reserve, an area 2,500 square kilometres in size bordering Mongolia and Russia. However, in 2009 a much larger area of 10,300 square kilometres was officially established and called Kanas Lake National Park, incorporating much more of the wedge of land in this northern tip of the province, and including the Hemu and Baihaba valleys to the east and west. The park area is home to 798 types of plant (30 of which are rare species), 34 animal species (including snow leopards, stone martens and silver foxes), 75 types of bird, 124 insect species, and seven different kinds of amphibian (including the rare Altai frog). It contains the only belt of Siberian taiga forest in China, comprising Siberian larch, spruces, red pine, firs and birches.

Crescent-shaped **Kanas Lake** is the gem-like centrepiece of the park, approximately 1,375 metres above sea level, 24 kilometres long and between 1.6 and 2.9 kilometres wide, covering a total area of 37.7 square kilometres. With a maximum depth of 188.5 metres it is the deepest freshwater lake in China, fed – and drained – by the **Kanas River**, which in turn is fed by the glaciers around **Khuiten Peak** (4,374 metres) and **Nairamdal/Friendship Peak** (4,180 metres) to the north, which mark the Sino-Russian-Mongolian border. "Kanas" means "beautiful and mysterious place" in Mongolian – a deserved moniker.

The pristine beauty of the lake and its environs makes it a huge tourist draw, its lush forests, pure water and fresh air bringing increasing numbers of visitors every year. It is famous for changing its colour from season to season and even from morning to evening, turning from iridescent blue to mysterious green, moody grey or icy white. In the morning, fog often swathes the lake and lower valleys; if the sun appears later in the day the mountains are reflected in its smooth surface, their snowy peaks and the dark-green blanket of fir trees on their slopes mirrored perfectly – it is an inspirational sight.

Clockwise from top left: Sturdy wooden bridges are built to resist spring floods from glacial meltwater; Kanas Lake in turquoise mood, with the high peaks of the Altai to the north (Sun Jiabin x2); Kazakhs move their encampment loaded on camels (SC Keung); a Tuvan musician plays the limbe flute (Sun Jiabin).

Walking tracks and boardwalks around the lake's edge offer fantastic hiking opportunities; the farther you go, the fewer the tourists with which you will share the peaceful surroundings. Many hours can be spent simply wandering around, but horses are available to take you to small hamlets by the lake or up to the high pastures. The **Guanyu (Fish-Watching) Pavilion** stands on a bluff 2,000 metres above sea level, looking down on the curving, cerulean lake, and the views are simply stunning – on clear days you can see Friendship Peak off in the distance. Sunrise and sunset are the optimum viewing times, but the weather is always the determiner at Kanas, so there are no guarantees.

Kanas Lake has its own monster legend similar to Loch Ness in Scotland, UK. The Tuvans believe an ancient monster still lives in the lake, occasionally sending huge water spouts into the air. Needless to say, scientists have tried to solve the mystery, but with no success. The lake is certainly home to many varieties of fish, some of which, like the taimen (the largest of the salmon family), are said to grow more than two metres in length. There is even a folk tale of an enormous red taimen that reached 10 metres long and would drag drinking horses and camels into the water – more than likely it is from this story that the monster legend stems.

Kanas Lake and its surrounding valleys – in particular the **Hemu (Hom) Valley** just to the southeast, which is also popular with tourists for its rural villages with log houses and corrals to hold their animals in winter – are home to the **Tuva** ethnic group. Despite their small numbers, Tuvans have retained their own language and unique customs (they are shamanistic) through the centuries – a legend of their origin says they are descended from disabled and sick soldiers of the Great Khan's army, who were left behind on his campaign to conquer the West.

Tuvan elders in fact say that their ancestors migrated here 500 years ago from Siberia in the area around the upper Yenisey River now known as the Tuva Republic in Russia. Their language is part of the Turkic branch of the Altaic language family, and while their dress and culture is closer to Mongolian, their language is more akin to Kazakh. They combine pastoral practices with fishing, hunting and gathering in the rich forests that provide a treasure trove of natural products to those who know where and how to look. Spirit and nature worship stills holds strong here, and Tuvans are renowned for their forthright and hospitable nature.

One of the best things to do if you have the time is horse trekking. It is of course possible to head out for the day, but more adventurous – and rewarding – are multi-day treks either circumventing the lake itself, or journeying from Kanas Lake east to Hemu Valley, usually camping by Black Lake along the way, or west to **Baihaba** village. Treks are also possible in the other direction from both Hemu and Baihaba (entering Kanas Nature Reserve this way often means not having to pay the park entrance fee). At the wooden Kanas Lake jetty small speedboats are available for sightseeing trips around the lake and up and down the river – the farther you want to go, the more expensive the ride (plan on a few hundred renminbi at least).

KANAS LAKE PRACTICAL INFORMATION

Admission to the park costs Rmb230 (Rmb190 for students), and this includes the shuttle bus transport within the park. There are two flights per day to Kanas Airport from Urumqi during the summer, and coaches truck increasing numbers in from Altay City as well. This rise in popularity, while good for the local economy, brings with it inevitable risks to the environment and stability of local communities. As a result, where accommodation was previously available within the reserve at guesthouses and chalets, now you can only stay there in Tuvan homestays and yurts around the lake, because in 2009 the Xinjiang government moved all buildings (except the indigenous people's homes) out of the park 30 kilometres to the south, in order to protect the environment from damage and to bring the reserve into line with UNESCO requirements as a site of natural heritage (a designation to which it quite rightly aspires). The 658-room **Hongfu Lake Kanas Resort** (website: www.hongfuhotel.com) is an attractive four-star resort in the Jiadengyu scenic area where all hotel accommodation is now located, and this represents the face of tourism to come.

The Hemu River Valley to the southeast of Kanas Lake, and much of Habahe County to the west, have now both been incorporated into the national park area, in the hope that this will dissipate the ecological pressure of tourism in the region. Staying in Hemu village is still possible, but unfortunately a number of Chinese entrepreneurs have cynically married into local Tuvan families in order to bypass the law allowing only indigenous families to operate homestays in the park. The result has been building developments and tourism enterprises that are not traditional at all, but rather aimed purely at domestic China tourists. This dilutes the experience for many foreign visitors and causes bad feeling within the local Tuvan and Kazakh communities.

HABAHE COUNTY AND BAIHABA

Small but blessed by Mother Nature like Kanas to the east, **Habahe County** borders Russia to the north and Kazakhstan to the west. In this wedge of glorious, forested mountains lies the **Baihaba Scenic Area**, centred around the picturesque Baihaba Village. This beautiful rural village of 400 Kazakhs and Mongolians offers a chance to see lifestyle far removed from the modern, high-tech world. Autumn is the best time to visit, as the leaves of the many different trees turn different shades of brown and gold. The village houses are made from logs with high-pitched roofs to shed the heavy snow that falls during the long winters, and the large attics are also useful as ventilation rooms for drying meat. During the day cattle and sheep are driven slowly along dirt tracks beside tinkling streams to pasture; at night sturdy corrals constructed from rough-hewn wood protect them. Wood smoke wafts over the rooftops and birch trees, and the smell of pine sticks burning under cooking pots – themselves emitting a delicious fragrance of meat cooking – gives visitors a glimpse of a place where humans live in harmonious balance with the natural world surrounding them.

A Kazakh and his son load their yurt onto the back of a camel, preparing for the migration to wintering grounds (Sun Jiabin).

The residents of Baihaba can be very hospitable – if you are lucky you may be invited to share a meal inside a cosy house where walls are draped with blankets and the kang is covered with rugs of floral design. The Baihaba Folk Culture Village offers accommodation for visitors during the summer and autumn months, but these must be arranged through a travel agent.

About 100 kilometres west of Habahe town lies **Baisha Kol**, a small lake surrounded by desert with no visible watercourses running into it. Fed by underground springs, its shores are lined with reeds and thick growths of birch and poplar trees, and the surrounding sand dunes are dotted with hummock grass and ground cypress. Just south of the lake is a huge sand dune inevitably named **Mingsha Shan** (Singing Sand Mountain), but this one sees far fewer visitors than others in Xinjiang.

The Road South

Highway 217 heads south from Buerjin, cutting through ridges of black rock glistening in the sunlight like black diamonds, and crossing vast arid flatlands bounded in the west by snow-dusted mountains but to the east stretching into a hazy nothingness. The mountains are part of the **Tarbagatai** range, that runs southwest from the Altai and creates a natural boundary between Xinjiang and Kazakhstan. Situated at the mouth of a gap in the highlands is the town of **Jeminay (Jimunai)**,

Shafts of morning sunlight illuminate a valley in scenic Habahe County (SC Keung).

gateway to northern Kazakhstan. A frontier town with little to attract tourists, it nevertheless sees a trickle of adventurous travellers heading to the **Jeminay Port** border crossing 24 kilometres west of town, which is open to foreigners with a valid Kazakhstan visa. Across the border the road continues to Zaysan Lake and on across the steppe of the East Kazakhstan Region to Semey (Semipalatinsk), a full day's journey or more past Zaysan town.

Continuing south, after a few hours the highway enters a landscape of wind-eroded rock hills, and it is here that Xinjiang's most renowned yardang landscape can be found.

Uryhe Ghost City

A sign over the entrance gate claims it is the "Ghost City of the World". Supernatural status aside, the **Uryhe Ghost City** is actually a huge area of yardang rock formations 350 metres above sea level and covering 126 square kilometres. A hundred million years ago this area was – like the other "ghost cities" of the Junggar and Tarim basins – an immense lake surrounded by lush, primitive forests. Over the course of millions of years, the water dried up, leaving a lacustrine landscape of sedimentary rocks that was weathered away at different rates by the fierce winds and excessive temperature swings of the desert climate that developed.

OLD BELIEVERS AND ANCIENT INHABITANTS

*B*eyond Urumchi there comes a strip of land, interesting not only from an artistic, but also from a scientific and ethnographic point of view. Here we touch a region, with remnants of the great migrations of nations, such as kurgans and different burial places and stone images. On the other hand, these ranges of the Tarbagatai mountains, especially since the revolution, are infested with robbers. The Kirghiz, whose lands begin here, although outwardly resembling the Scythians and seeming like silhouettes from the vases of Kul-oba, are of little use in present day civilization. Their habitual robbing, "baranta," makes culture rather difficult. Besides, there is plenty of gold in the region of the black Irtysh and hence wandering masses of prospectors have invaded the place, and it is better not to sit round one camp-fire with them.

One is again surprised at the fertility of the country and how little it has been studied and exploited. Altai or, as it is now called, Oirotiya, is equally concealed and neglected. The Oirots are a Finno-Turki tribe, at a very low state of evolution. Their outworn kaftans of sheepskin and their unkempt hair compared with some of the Tibetans. The Old Believers, who settled long ago in this remote country, are of course, the only strong masters of the place. It was pleasant to see, that the Old Believers have considerably advanced, rejecting many of their old religious prejudices. They now think correctly of domestic affairs, of American machines, and they welcome foreigners, although this was not previously the case.

Of course, the old way of living, with its picturesquely carved wooden houses, with brocaded sarafans and old icons, has also disappeared. We wished that in the new forms of life, antiquity should not give way to the mediocrity of the bazaars. For in Siberia, where there is such mineral wealth and other natural treasures, the people have the heritage of highly artistic Siberian antiques, the heritage of Yermak and fearless pioneers. When we passed the place on the Irtysh, where Yermak—the hero of Siberia—was drowned, an Altayan said to us: "Never would our Yermak have drowned, if it were not for the heavy armor, which dragged him to the bottom!"

Meeting the Old Believers in the Altai, it was astonishing to hear of the numerous religious sects, which exist there even now. The Popovtsy, the Bezpopovtsy, the Striguny, the Pryguni, the Pomortsi, the Netovtse (not recognizing any of the beliefs, but considering themselves of "the old faith")—how many incomprehensible discussions they occasion! And toward Trans-Baikal among the Semeiski (Old Believers exiled to Siberia with their entire families), also are added the Temnovertsy and the Kalashniki. Each of the Temnovertsy has his own ikon, closed with little doors, to which he alone prays. If anyone else should pray to the same ikon, it would become unfit! Still stranger are the Kalashniki. They pray before the ikon through a little opening in kalach (a loaf of bread). We have heard much, but such obscure beliefs we have never seen nor heard of—and that in the summer of 1926! Here are also Hlysty, Pashkovtsy, Stundisty and Molokans—a great variety of different beliefs, which entirely exclude each other.

*B*ut even in these forsaken corners a new conception already begins to stir and the long-bearded Old Believer speaks with enthusiasm of agricultural machinery and compares the quality of manufactures of various countries. Although the beliefs have not yet been quite obliterated, in any case the prejudice against innovations has already evaporated and sound domestic principles have not diminished, but have encouraged new sprouts. This new building up of agricultural methods, the untouched riches, the great radio-activity there, the abundance of its grass (which is higher than a man on horseback), its streams, inviting electrification—all this gives to Altai an unforgettable meaning.

A family of Russians photographed in the Altai region by writer-painter-philosopher Nicholas Roerich during an epic journey through Xinjiang in the 1920s (Courtesy of the Nicholas Roerich Museum).

In the region of Altai one can also hear many significant legends connected with vague reminiscences of tribes that passed here long ago. Among these incomprehensible tribes, are mentioned the "Blacksmiths of Kurumchi." The name indicates these people as fine metal workers, but whence did they come and whither did they go? Perhaps the popular memory alludes to the creators of the metal objects, for which the antiquities of Minusinsk and Ural are so famous? When you hear of these blacksmiths, you involuntarily recall the legendary Nibelungen, who drifted far to the west.

In this melting pot of nations, it is most instructive to observe how sometimes under your very eyes, a language may be changed. In Mongolia, we heard of the most curious combinations of expressions, made up only recently from many languages. Chinese, Mongolian, Buriat, Russian and slightly modified foreign technical words, already afford quite a new conglomeration. A new problem will arise for philologists from this creation of new expressions and even entirely new local dialects.

Altai played a most important part in the migration of nations. The burial places of huge rocks—the so-called graves of Chud—as well as the inscriptions on rocks, all bring us back to the important epoch, when from the far south-east, impelled by glaciers, or at times by sands, nations collected themselves as an avalanche to over-run and regenerate Europe. From the prehistoric and historic point of view, Altai is an untouched treasure, and the ruler of the Altai, snow-white Beluha, who nurtures all rivers and fields, is ready to yield her treasures.

Nicholas Roerich, **Heart of Asia**, 1930

A huge rock tower at Uryhe Ghost City calls to mind ancient Egypt's famed sphinxes (Jeremy Tredinnick).

As a result of the constant wind assault, the conglomerate rocks have been effectively sandblasted into formations that look amazingly similar to man-made structures, from pagodas to watchtowers, castles, monumental sphinxes and massive fortresses. The gullies and gaps between them could be mistaken for streets and alleys, and this effect is helped by the tracks created by minibuses that follow a winding route through the most impressive formations, many of which have been given suitably dramatic names such as the Arabian Castle, Heavenly Horse, Twin Devils and Potala Palace. Viewing platforms around this circuit offer great photo opportunities – the rock towers are scattered over a wide area, and in the distance oil well gantries pierce the horizon. Late afternoon is the best time to visit, when the rocks turn a rich orange and the shadows stretch across the floor of the plain.

The Mongolian name for this spot is "*Sulumuhak*", and the Kazakh "*Shaytirkerse*"; both mean "ghost castle", and the reason for the superstitious moniker is the eerie sound produced by the wind as it blows sand particles over the buttresses and through the gullies, a moaning as if ghosts were sweeping through the city, or wolves were congregating in the shadows to howl. Its ethereal, monumental scenery and haunting atmosphere have made this a popular movie location among Chinese filmmakers – scenes for *Crouching Tiger, Hidden Dragon* and *Warriors of Heaven and Earth*, among others, were shot here.

Entrance to the Ghost City costs Rmb50 in the July–October high season. The minibus around the circular trail costs extra, and majestic sand-coloured camels are also on hand to give rides through the magical landscape. During summer special tour buses run to the site from Karamay 96 kilometres to the south. From April to July the winds are very strong, while winter is not really a time to be in the Junggar Basin; however, during the low season the ticket price drops to Rmb35, and it can still be a memorable experience – for a start you are more likely to have the place to yourself, rather than sharing it with the average 10,000 tourists who flock here every day in the peak period, and it is also possible to take your own 4WD around the trail out of season. Of course the process that created this phantasmagorical wonderland is still ongoing; beautiful smooth, multicoloured pebbles are everywhere, worn to a glossy sheen by the wind and abrasive sand; with luck, you may also find crystal carnelian, a flesh-coloured or reddish silica quartz stone of great beauty.

Just south of the Uryhe Ghost City, a **Dinosaur Park** has been built as an additional attraction for the tourists on their way to or from the ghost city. This area has also presented the archaeological world with a number of great prehistoric fossil finds, from ancient turtles and crocodilians to snake-necked plesiosaurs, carnivorous theropods and pterodactyls. Giant models of these creatures stand at the park's entrance, making it hard to resist.

The highway at this point becomes lined with a multitude of "**nodding donkeys**", small cantilevered oil wells all connected by underground pipes, sucking up the black gold that has made this region more famous – and valuable – than at any other time in its considerable history. You are now driving over a relatively thin crust of scrub desert land that covers a vast subterranean sea of oil.

KARAMAY (KELAMAYI)

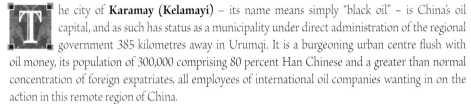he city of **Karamay (Kelamayi)** – its name means simply "black oil" – is China's oil capital, and as such has status as a municipality under direct administration of the regional government 385 kilometres away in Urumqi. It is a burgeoning urban centre flush with oil money, its population of 300,000 comprising 80 percent Han Chinese and a greater than normal concentration of foreign expatriates, all employees of international oil companies wanting in on the action in this remote region of China.

There is a story of the discovery of oil here and Karamay's subsequent rise in fortunes: In 1945 a Kashgari man fled the south after an ill-fated love affair with a girl whose father forbad their marriage. The girl committed suicide, and the man wandered north, crossed the Tien Shan and settled in a small, remote village, where he sang and played musical instruments for his living. Here he met a Kazakh who knew a place where a combustible black liquid seeped from the ground. The Kazakh showed him the location of the open well, and the Kashgari began extracting the oil and selling it in the local town.

In 1956 the People's Liberation Army (PLA) came on the scene, and immediately saw the well's potential. They promised the Kashgari that he could continue to own the well and they would help develop it, and the governor of Xinjiang gave him the "key to the region", so he would never have to pay for anything for the rest of his life. The Chinese sought Russian aid in developing the area, and the extent of the oil resources was soon established. The result is the growing metropolis of Karamay, and the districts around it that are covered with tens of thousands of small, bobbing oil rigs.

KARAMAY PRACTICAL INFORMATION

The city is modern and bustling, but offers little in terms of tourism, and is usually used only as a stopping point on tours travelling the huge distances between the attractions of the Altai and Tien Shan.

TRANSPORTATION

Buses run to Urumqi many times a day (four hours, Rmb91), as well as to Kuyten 126 kilometres to the south, and Buerjin or Altay City in the north. The Kuyten-Beitun rail line, with a stop at Karamay, began construction in 2007 and when completed will enhance the region's economic prospects even further.

ACCOMMODATION

New hotels are opening all the time here, but current favourites are the **Karamay Taole Hotel** (26 Guangming Dong Lu, tel: (0990) 698 8001, fax: (0990) 622 2982), a good centrally located three-star with rooms from Rmb258 and suites from Rmb358, and an excellent Uygur restaurant right next door. Alternatives are the **ZhenTian Landmark Hotel** (30 Youyi Lu), a new four-star business hotel with 114 rooms starting at around Rmb300, and the **Hongfu Zhungaer Hotel** (75 Zhungaer

Lu, tel: (0990) 698 9888, fax: (0990) 698 9868, website: www.hongfuhotel.com), a 74-room three-star 20 kilometres from the airport. All Karamay's hotels sport nightclubs with karaoke and plenty of "hostesses" – typical of oil town leisure pursuits worldwide! South of Karamay City in the Dushanzi District is the 213-room **Maitark Hotel** (11, Daqing Dong Lu, Dushanzi District, tel: (0902) 226 6859, fax: (0902) 226 6869, website: www.hongfuhotel.com), billed as a five-star establishment with all modern amenities; rooms begin at Rmb500.

TACHENG

The large wedge of land northwest of Karamay constitutes **Tacheng Prefecture**, a rural area of farms and pasture rising into the craggy Tarbagatai mountains. **Tacheng City** is the capital, only 10 kilometres from the border with Kazakhstan and historically an important link in trade and migration between the Junggar Basin and the open steppe of the Kazakhs, who call it **Chuguchak**. The town and surrounding area suffered horribly during the Qing army's destruction of the Junggar tribes in the 19th century. Today it is a commercial gateway between Xinjiang and Kazakhstan (12 hours by bus from Urumqi and connected also by air), but the border crossing at **Baketu Port** is intermittently closed to international travellers, and Jeminay and Alashankou ports to the north and south respectively are easier entry/exit points for cross-border travel.

CHANGJI, SHIHEZI AND KUYTEN

Driving south from Karamay, Highway 217 appears to be on a collision course with the Tien Shan, which rises massively directly ahead and makes a welcome change from the endless barren expanse of the Junggar Basin. Before it reaches the mountain slopes, however, it meets up with **Highway 312**, Xinjiang's major east-west artery, at **Kuyten**.

Highway 312, once the only major road north of the Tien Shan, has been augmented – at least as far as Kuyten – by Expressway 045, cutting travel time between the two cities from 6–7 hours to three hours. Since 1991, Urumqi has also been linked by rail to Russia via Kazakhstan along this route, passing north of the Tien Shan to Alashankou Port at the historically significant mountain gap known as the Junggar Gate. The result of this constant flow of trade and relatively easy accessibility to the outside world, as well as the military significance of the north-central Tien Shan corridor as a strategic point for maintaining Chinese control in the region, has been a drive to fast-track development in the area ever since the Communist Party took control in the 1950s. During that time, large numbers of PLA soldiers were organized into the **Xinjiang Production and Construction Corps** and settled in groups of hundreds and thousands on the plains beneath the mountains, creating state farms that have transformed the semi-desert landscape into a broad swathe of massive fields irrigated by the streams that emerge from the mountains.

Northwest of Urumqi, the first city the road meets is **Changji**, seat of the **Changji Hui Autonomous Prefecture**, which covers the Qitai, Manas, Jimsar, Hutubi and Mori Kazakh

The entrance to a Dinosaur park north of Karamay draws visitors on the road to or from Uryhe Ghost City (Jeremy Tredinnick).

TOLL WAVES AND SPEED TRAPS ON TODAY'S SILK ROADS

The old days of interminable travel on rutted, bone-jarring tracks from one remote Xinjiang town to the next are well and truly over. Today all the region's major towns are linked by smooth, meticulously maintained blacktop, along which Japanese saloon cars, German executive limos and huge articulated goods vehicles shoot at impressive speeds, their tires humming like swarms of angry bees.

The Chinese government has spent billions of renminbi on upgrades to Xinjiang's road network, mainly to facilitate the movement of petrochemicals and agricultural produce as the region's exports surge. However, this intricate new web of tarmacked highways benefits the general populace as well, taking much of the hardship out of travel between towns that historically have felt like disparate islands of habitation in an ocean of treacherous sand, but now find it easier to count themselves as part of a cohesive whole.

In true Xinjiang fashion, the expressways and larger highways have even developed a few of their own unique cultural idiosyncrasies – the modern "Silk Road" traveller may have it far, far easier than their predecessors, but there are still a few highway robbers to watch out for, and peculiar customs to make you smile.

Take the "tollbooth wave", for instance. Tollbooths litter the motorways and dual carriageways of Xinjiang's central corridor, with Urumqi at its hub; whether you're heading south to Turpan or Korla, west to Shihezi and beyond, or east and north towards Barkol or the Altai, every 10 kilometres or so a tollbooth appears in front of you.

You stop at a booth to pay the fee. The window slides open and a blank-faced man or woman receives your money. But then, as you are about to pull away, he or she raises a palm to offer an automated wave – like wiping a window – and utter a mantra-like phrase, which roughly translated means "We wish you a pleasant journey". This happens at every single tollbooth without fail – and if you're travelling by road, you will encounter many. It seems that staff must perform it for every vehicle they process, much like the American counter-staff goodbye-phrase of "Have a nice day!" Sadly, it is ignored completely by local drivers – who resent the mounting costs of any journey, despite the clear benefits of the superb road conditions – but for the visitor after a while it becomes fascinating in its monotonous repetition.

Another – less endearing – thing to look out for on Xinjiang's highways are speed traps. Speed limits can range from 30kph (19mph) on city and town roads to 80kph (50mph) on dual carriageways and up to 120kph (75mph) on expressways. However, any road approaching and passing towns (with turn-offs) can switch limits in swift and bizarre fashion; in general, 40kph is mandatory while passing a town, but it can be 60kph or 80kph just before or after that – and there are speed cameras hidden to catch the unwary. Sadly, police sometimes take down or hide the signs, then wait at the next tollbooth to demand a cash fine for speeding. While clearly nothing but modern-day highway robbery, drivers can do little else but pay up (anything from Rmb100–400). Some, however, mount radar and laser speed trap tracking devices on their dashboards to combat the problem – a suitably high-tech answer to the travails of travel on today's "Silk Road" routes.

Autonomous counties, as well as Fukang City and Miquan City. Three-quarters of the population of this prefecture is Han Chinese, although this is one of the main Hui centres in Xinjiang. Extensive farming occurs on irrigated land reclaimed from the scrub desert of the Junggar Basin's southern rim, with oil crops and cotton the major sources of revenue.

 outh of Changji City the upper valleys of the Tien Shan are home to Kazakhs who still practise animal husbandry and semi-nomadism, and these pasturelands see far fewer tourists than the Nan Shan area to the southeast. Farther west along the highway is Hutubi town, seat of Hutubi County; 75 kilometres southwest of here, cut into the red-rock cliffs of Keziletaxi Mountain, are the **Kangjia Shimenzi Rock Carvings**, a fascinating site consisting of Bronze Age petroglyphs dating back 3,000 years (*see* special topic on page 250). Only discovered by scientists in the 1980s, this site is famous for its explicit phallicism. Around 300 human figures and animals (horses, tigers, sheep, oxen and bears) are engraved into a vertical section of red rock nine metres high and 14 metres from east to west. The human figures – both male and female – are depicted with triangular bodies (broad shoulders and narrow waists) and egg-shaped heads; the site's main section consists of a group of nine female dancers who are separated from a male figure by two pairs of horses. The man is painted bright red, wears a hat and has an erect penis, and expert interpretation theorizes that this represents some kind of magical rite of fertility.

One hundred and fifty kilometres west of Urumqi on the road and rail routes is **Shihezi**, a large city of 560,000 people, almost 95 percent of whom are Han Chinese. Shihezi is surrounded by the military-structured farming cooperatives that typify China's determination to create productive agricultural land from a virtually lifeless wilderness. Its success in food processing and other light industries have seen it grow fast – it is a municipality under direct control of the regional government, and is home to Xinjiang's second largest university, boasting 40,000 students.

The Gurbantunggut Desert is no more than 100 kilometres to the north, and once stretched much farther south, but it has been turned to fields of cotton, sunflowers and other sturdy crops by huge irrigation works and the back-breaking labour of hundreds of thousands of Chinese soldiers turned farmers. The Daquangou Reservoir, 20 kilometres north of the city centre, was created by the regiments and divisions of the Production and Construction Corps to store water and irrigate farms, and is also used as a fish breeding centre as well as a leisure spot for fishing and boating. South of town in the green mountain valleys is the **Ziniquan Sheep Farm**, which breeds a type of sheep known as the Chinese Merino, famous for its thick, superior-quality wool and fine meat.

A hundred kilometres farther west is the city of **Kuyten (Kuitun)**, a crossroads for roads from the four compass points. As such it plays host to a large PLA garrison, stationed here to protect China's oil concerns. This is another relatively new town fuelled by the burgeoning oil and farming industries in the vicinity. If you need to overnight here, try the four-star **Kuitun Hyde Hotel** (56 Sheng Unity Street South) or the **Kui Tun Hotel**, a brand-new low-rise four-star hotel next to the army barracks.

The Tien Shan's northern foothills are home to the Chinese Merino sheep, whose fine-quality wool is much in demand (Sun Jiabin).

BORTALA MONGOL AUTONOMOUS PREFECTURE AND THE JUNGGAR GATE

West of Kuyten, Highway 312 continues parallel to the Tien Shan through dark fields of cotton interspersed with lighter strips of land sown with corn. On either side of the well-maintained highway – which seems to have a tollbooth every 10 kilometres or so – poplars line the side roads, skinny avenues down which donkey carts and tractor trailers piled high with produce vie for road space. In autumn, the cotton fields are polka-dot squares of land where migrant pickers form lines, baskets on their backs, and slowly work their way from one side to the other, towards trucks waiting to be filled up high with tons of the fluffy tufts.

At **Jinghe** the road and rail line finally part company. The railway turns north and passes Ebinur Lake on its way to **Alashankou (Alataw) Port**, otherwise known as the Junggar Gate, the strategic pass between the mountain masses of Central Asia that throughout the millennia of mankind's history has allowed human migration and conquering armies to bridge the Eurasian continent. Today, it remains vitally important as Xinjiang's only rail route into Kazakhstan, a border crossing that remains open year-round, in contrast to the seasonal nature of most of Xinjiang's other ports. The Kazakh side of the border is **Dostyk**, and from there the rail line skirts Alakol Lake and meets the **Turk-Sib Railway** at Aktogai, near the eastern end of Lake Balkhash – north from here the railway takes you across the Great Steppe to Semey and Russia, with Moscow the eventual railhead; south takes you to **Almaty**.

Ebinur (Aibi) Lake is a huge salt lake of roughly 1,000 square kilometres but with an average depth of only two metres, whose high level of salinity (100 times higher than seawater) precludes plant or fish life. However, the rivers that flow into it – the Bortala, Kuyten and Jinghe rivers, among many smaller streams – do harbour life, and its surrounding environment of diversiform-leaf poplar trees, saxaul and other scrub-desert species resulted in 2007 with its designation as the **Ebinur Lake Wetland National Nature Reserve**.

The lake and reserve lie within the **Bortala Mongol Autonomous Prefecture**, which occupies the southwestern corner of the Junggar Basin and has a 385-kilometre-border with Kazakhstan. Its prefectural capital is **Bole (Bortala) City**, 70 kilometres southwest of the Alataw Pass, and this region has historically been settled by Mongolian tribes who endured the harsh climate and brutal winds to raise their livestock on the broad plains between the mountain slopes to the north and south (Bortala means "green pastureland" in Mongolian).

In the 18th century, after the subjugation of the Junggar Basin by the armies of the Qing emperor Qianlong, the Bortala steppe became home to the **Torgut Mongols**, a tribe who in the 17th century had split away from the Oirat (Junggar) Mongol confederation that ruled the Junggar region, migrating across the Central Eurasian Steppe as far as the Volga River north of the Caspian Sea. Persecuted by tsarist Russia, on hearing that the Qing had destroyed the Junggar hordes and would accept them back, 400,000 Torgut Mongols began the epic journey east towards their traditional homeland, and the 80,000 who survived were given the Bortala region in return for their loyalty to the Qing throne. The American adventurer Owen Lattimore, who passed through this region in the 1920s and wrote of it in his book *High Tartary*, was inspired by their hardiness:

"These, then, were the people [Torgut Mongols] we saw in camp on the western side of Lao Feng K'ou, and on the next day in the deep snow of the pass, engaged in the ancient struggle of the nomad, which is as bleak and yet stirring as a saga; staking their children and their fortunes in the primal quest for grass, that their

A Mongolian woman ferments mare's milk in preparation for a feast (Sun Jiabin).

THE ROCK SANCTUARY OF
KANGJIA SHIMENZI
By Christoph Baumer

On the northern slopes of the Tien Shan, 147km west of Urumqi, lies one of the most spectacular rock art sites in China: **Kangjia Shimenzi**. Located at an altitude of 1,475 metres near the hamlet of Quergu in the district of Hutubi, the site is a full-day excursion from Urumqi by hired car.

About 20 minutes' easy walk from Quergu the rock carvings, or petroglyphs, are located in a slight indentation at the foot of a 100-metre-high cliff, with a total surface of 200 square metres. On the lower portion of the cliff wall and adjacent boulders small carvings can be seen of hunters armed with bows, mountain goats, antelopes, deer with large antlers and symbolic patterns such as a rising sun above waving lines. Petroglyphs like these are common throughout Central Asia and date from roughly the second millennium BCE – a nearby archaeological site has been discovered, dating from the late Neolithic period. There are also much later representations of camels and men on horseback which correspond to the Mongol expansion of the 12th–14th centuries CE.

However, more interesting are the carvings higher up, which cover an area of more than 140 square metres, more than 20 metres across the cliff surface and between 2.5 and 10 metres above the ground. The smallest of the approximately 300 figures measure only a few centimetres tall, while the largest are more than two metres high. The ancient carvers must have used scaffolding to work; binoculars or a strong telephoto lens are needed to see the carvings in detail.

Among the figures it's possible to differentiate at least three different periods where figures and sequences were carved over older ones. In the two elder epochs, at least 3,000 years ago, humans are featured almost exclusively. Many of the larger figures are fully depicted, their bodies painted in bright red and their faces in white. These two periods belong to the same culture, but the third period dates from the Scythian culture, around 600 BCE – two large tigers were carved on the left corner of the site in the typical "animal style" of the Scythian nomads.

The carvings of the two elder periods consist of at least five main scenes, displaying a strong sense of archaic energy and eroticism. In one scene, 18 figures of both sexes are dancing, the males each shown with a huge erect penis. Next to the dancers, two women lie on the ground on their backs, while in between the dancers and surrounding them, at least 24 masks are scattered. In another scene about 27 small figures dance in front of a male with an erect penis, while in a third scene nine women dance near an ithyphallic man. Within this group of nine dancing women, two kinds of tribal emblems were added in the later, Scythian period. They feature two ithyphallic horses facing each other and rearing up on their hind legs; this kind of tribal emblem, featuring paired animals, is well known in petroglyphs through the whole cultural realm of the Scythians, which stretched from Western Mongolia across Central Asia to the Black Sea during the first millennium BCE.

Also striking are several large dancers either with a mask carved on their chest or wearing an ape mask. From many of the figures' heads what appear to be feathers protrude, looking like antennae. One huge figure of a hermaphrodite with one body and two heads is very striking; in front of it at least 41 tiny figures dance, aligned in two rows. The general erotic impression of the carvings is further enhanced with five representations of sexual intercourse. It seems that Kangjia Shimenzi was a sanctuary dedicated to a cult of fertility, and given that in many places the carved figures deliberately overlap or cover previous ones, we can assume that this site was in use for a long time. Cult ceremonies similar to those featured on the carvings were probably performed at the foot of the cliff. However, it is still unclear which peoples created these expressive carvings. Chinese scholars believe that they were most likely related to the Indo-Iranian Saka people, or that they were early predecessors of the Mongol Xiongnu.

flocks might have plenty and increase. The world beyond their vision might change from the age of the nomad to the age of ploughed lands and walled cities, and then to the age of commerce and the railway and the conquest of sea and air; but for them the same pitiless wind blew over the same unforgiving snow, and they turned with the turn of the year between highland and lowland, as their fathers in the savage past had turned between Tarbagatai and Volga, the whole force of their desire still bound on one object – open pastures and free ranges. The sight of their caravans in the snow, cattle weakened by the winter and men and cattle equally suffering the cold, struggling but keeping inexorably on the move, tents packed up and children swaddled – all that, and the immensity of their hidden world, lost in the unconfined plains and locked in the uncatalogued mountains of Central Asia, was of a kind to pluck the spirit of man back into the dark, rich, violent past, where death gives vigour to the roots of the future; a most noble and healthy thing."

Bole City is a small, windy town without much appeal; a few kilometres southwest are the dilapidated ruins of an old fortress that controlled the pass during the Yuan Dynasty (1279–1368). More impressive is the **Mysterious Stone Valley**, 48 kilometres northwest of Bole, 26 kilometres from Alashankou Port and just to the west of Ebinur Lake. This 230-square-kilometre mountain valley is filled with truly bizarre rock formations, a result of severe wind erosion

For centuries Kazakhs have brought their animals to drink from the clear waters of Sayram Lake (Sun Jiabin).

coupled with the huge temperature differences this area is subject to. Huge circular bowls and holes have been gouged in the brown granite rock by swirling stone granules whipped up by the wind. The natural stone statues take on all sorts of strange appearances; many have been imaginatively named, such as "Rhinoceros Looking at the Moon", "Monkey Mother and Son" and "Sitting Camels". It comes as no surprise that this valley is rich in petroglyphs; early human inhabitants of the area must have thought the rocks had been created by superhuman beings or spirits.

Back at Jinghe town, an important new electric rail line now splits off from the main Urumqi-Alashankou Port line and cuts south through the mountains via tunnels to emerge in the Ili Valley, passing through Yining to the **Horgas Port**. This rail line opened for cargo in 2009 and passengers in 2010, allowing the already vibrant economy of the Ili Valley to reach even higher levels.

SAYRAM LAKE (SAILIMU HU) AND FRUIT VALLEY

ighway 312 leaves the Junggar Basin after Jinghe and climbs through the broad valleys into the Tien Shan. On the border of the Ili Kazakh and Bortala Mongolian autonomous prefectures lies the stunning expanse of deep-blue water known as **Sayram Lake**. Situated 2,073 metres above sea level, it is 30 kilometres long (from east to west) and up to 23 kilometres wide (north-south), covering a total of 458 square kilometres, which makes it Xinjiang's largest alpine lake. Formed 70 million years ago when tectonic movement caused the plate crust to drop, resulting in a "fault-trough" lake, it is around 90 metres at its deepest point (with a volume of 21 billion cubic metres) but still boasts a few small islands at the northeast end.

Sayram Lake (Sayram means "blessing" in Kazakh) is famous for its deep azure colour, said to be a result of the calcium carbonate rock strata of its surrounding hills, and the deep wellsprings that keep its water level constant despite evaporation. From January to April the lake freezes over, despite its slight salinity, and its mountain weather can be unpredictable, with storms and high winds turning it from a sapphire jewel to a slate-grey sea of choppy waves at any time. In summer, however, its surrounding mountain slopes and wide grassy fringes are a stunning setting for this gem-like lake, the broad meadows carpeted with yellow and purple flowers. Around the water's edge many yurts are raised, belonging to Kazakh (and Mongolian) herdsmen who bring their horses, cattle, sheep and camels to graze on the lush pasture.

The Sayram Lake area is a stronghold of Kazakh nomadic culture. Kazakhs are traditionally led by *begs* chosen for their strong leadership skills. As many as three generations live in a single yurt, hung with embroidered curtains to create rooms and provide privacy. Families rarely split up, for it takes many hands to tend the large herds of sheep and horses. Following the birth of a Kazakh child, the mother names her baby after the first thing that comes into her mind when she leaves the yurt on the second day, resulting in many beguilingly simple Kazakh names. The mobile Kazakh children are formally educated in one of three ways: roving schools that follow the nomadic households; horseback schools, where a teacher rides out to a group of children or they to him; and boarding schools for the older students. Most Kazakhs, however, finish their education at 15 years of age.

Every summer in July, 3,000 or more Kazakhs and Mongolians hold an outdoor *naadam* for six days, much like a summer fair with horse-racing, *kokpar* (a kind of no-holds-barred horseback rugby using a sheep or goat carcass, also known as *buzkashi*), wrestling (both on foot and horseback), "girl-chasing" riding competitions and much feasting, singing and dancing. Wherever there are large communities of Kazakhs and Mongols the naadam will take place (the Barkol and Altai regions, for example), but this is probably the best place for tourists to see the fair in all its colourful glory.

The highway runs along the south bank of the lake, and it is here that the tourist facilities are found. Near the water five or six hotels, and many sets of yurts and cabins (wooden and concrete) cater to the large number of visitors in the summer season; from here you can hike on foot around the lake or up into the mountains through the meadows and forests. Horse treks are of course popular, and motorboat trips are available around the lake – Rmb60 gets you four kilometres out, Rmb100 will cover 10 kilometres, etc. Trips are also possible to the lake's islands, one of which once housed a Qing Dynasty temple, but nothing now remains.

The regional government has recently decided to preserve as much of the lakeside area as possible from the rather ugly buildings that have arisen as tourism takes off in a big way. Therefore, by the end of 2008 they planned to relocate most of this tourism infrastructure to a point 40 kilometres or more south, in Fruit Valley. Locals' yurts will still be allowed to set up by the lake of course, as well as temporary yurts specifically for overnight stays, so the "nomad experience" will still be possible for those who want it, but hotel comfort will mean staying farther away and making day trips to the lake.

South of Sayram the road passes into a long, steep-sided valley known simply as **Fruit Valley (Guozi Gou)**. Rugged and beautiful with forests of dragon spruce blanketing the precipitous slopes and wild fruit trees farther down, this deep ravine is famous for its sweet Ili apples and the high-quality honey collected from the hives of bees that have a cornucopia of nectar to choose from in the rich valleys all around. As the road descends, twisting and turning next to the rushing river, many stalls are set up to sell the valley produce. Be warned, however: much of the honey on offer is simply sugar water, so take care and test anything carefully before buying.

After 28 kilometres the highway emerges from the mountains onto the Ili Valley plain close to the border with Kazakhstan at Horgas Port. Agricultural fields and orchards pattern the valley floor, and here, unless you are travelling into Kazakhstan, you must turn off Highway 312 and head east once more, towards Yining.

THE ILI VALLEY

The **Ili Valley** seems a world apart from the arid regions to the north and south, and it has the high peaks of the Tien Shan to thank for this. Surrounded by mountains that protect it from the worst extremes of continental weather patterns, draw moisture from the air and produce plentiful supplies of water, it has a warmer, more humid climate than the Tarim and Junggar basins. The mountain soils are fertile, and with the abundance of water create a foundation for a rich ecosystem that has attracted humans since prehistoric times. Central to the valley is the eponymous **Ili River**, which flows for 623 kilometres before crossing the border into Kazakhstan and emptying into Lake Balkhash (another 815 kilometres downriver). The river plain is so fertile that fruits, vegetables and grain crops grow easily, and by the side of the Ili's numerous tributaries – including the **Tekes**, **Kax** (Kasgar) and **Kunes** (Gonas) – fantastic pastureland is home to Kazakhs practising animal husbandry much as their forefathers did many generations ago.

The Ili Valley has, unsurprisingly, a rich history. In the second century BCE, clans of the **Yuezhi** tribe, driven westwards by the Xiongnu, attempted to settle here but were soon pushed southwest by the Turkic-speaking, nomadic **Wusun** tribe who, according to Chinese historians, had blue eyes and red beards. They established control over the Ili Valley and founded the Wusun state. In his second mission to the Western Regions in 119 BCE, Zhang Qian initiated diplomatic relations between the Wusun and the Han court, which eventually led to the introduction of the "heavenly" horse to China.

Above: Wildflowers carpet the shores of Sayram Lake in spring and summer. Left: Eagle hunting is an intrinsic part of Kazakh nomadic culture. Opposite: Warmly dressed nomads move their flock to more sheltered wintering grounds (Sun Jiabin x3).

258 XINJIANG: CHINA'S CENTRAL ASIA

Ili's rich pasturelands were trampled by almost every Central Asian power from the Xiongnu to the Chinese. In 744 CE, a Tang Dynasty army defeated the ruling Western Turkic Khanate, strengthening Chinese control of the new Northern Silk Road bypassing the Caspian Sea. In 1218, Genghis Khan (Chinggis Khaan) annexed Ili. Upon his death in 1227, his four sons inherited the great Mongol empire. Chaghatai, the second son, inherited the Tarim Basin, Ili Valley and most of Khorasan (southern Central Asia), and is thought to have made his capital in **Almaliq**, near Yining. The Mongols established strong East–West land communications, and a number of papal envoys from Rome eventually traversed the region, converting locals as they went. (In 1340, Richard of Burgundy and five other friars were murdered by Muslims at Almaliq, where a Catholic church had been built and a Nestorian community also existed.) In the latter part of the 13th century, Kublai Khan garrisoned troops here under the command of his son. Subsequently, the mighty Tamerlane, who claimed to be a descendant of Genghis Khan, inherited control over the area.

During the 16th century Kyrgyz and Kazakh hordes made frequent incursions into the Ili Valley, until they were ultimately defeated by the Oirat Mongols (Junggars). The Qing emperor **Qianlong** (reigned 1736–1796) defeated the Junggars in 1758 after an arduous campaign in the Junggar Basin, where tens of thousands of Mongols were massacred. The Qing government established the headquarters of the Ili General in **Huiyuan City** and founded a military colony at Yining, where large numbers

A GREEN, PLEASANT... AND DANGEROUS LAND

Around the lake of Sairam Nor, we were told, a man can ride in a day; but he would have to have a good pony. For several simple, striking reasons, the lake has an immemorial repute of holiness. It has no visible inlet or outlet, yet the water is drinkable; but although the water is good, no fish are found in it. Near the lake we saw a large flock of bustard; the only ones I saw in the province, though both the greater and the smaller bustard are said to be common in many places. No shooting is allowed within sound of the lake, for it is believed that any violence, and especially the sound of firearms, would bring a change in the weather. Near the shore where we passed is an island, with several smaller islets, and on the island is a temple, showing how the Chinese in their turn respect and do honor to this lake.

From the edge of the lake there is a climb of only a couple of hundred yards to the head of the Talki pass, where a Chinese shrine and an obo stand side by side. Then, in turning down the pass, one enters a new country, as through a gate. Instead of passing distant forests among dry hills, we rode under the shadow and through the fragrance of spruces, mixed with wild fruit trees, from which the Chinese call the pass the Valley of Fruits. The road, though carts can use it, was much more steep and stony, and every fold in the hills held its watercourse. A storm broke over us on the crest of the pass, but, after one strong burst of hail, held off for a while. We rode as fast as we could over the stones, down a valley that seemed to sing with water, looking up all the while to hanging copses and alps of pasture. In many places the spruces had been logged off, and a young second growth of birches was taking their place.

As we went down the valley it widened, the hills were not so steeply pitched, and the forests were broken by wide sweeps of mountain meadow, at the edge of which we passed many Qazaq yurts. The mouth of the valley closed in somewhat, giving the effect of another gate, and when we rode out of it we were in an open country of downs, where Qazaq camps could be seen widely scattered…

…Kulja, it may be seen, has an air of its own; but that air is rightly come by, for it is the capital of the Nine Cities of Ili. This is a frontier, and the most vulnerable and hazardous frontier for a journey of many hundred miles. All the contrasting peoples that congregate there are aware that the possibility of upheaval and terror underlies the prosperity and ease of life, and for that reason take on a spirit of recklessness and devil-may-care. The town populations especially are unruly and dissipated.

*T*he valleys of the Ili River and its tributaries are the richest ground in Central Asia. As we talk of "white man's country" in Kenya or some other territory that lies outside of our natural heritage, so the Chinese talk of the Ili, as a fat, desirable land, but one in which, in that phrase which has no parent language, "the natives must be kept in order." Not only is there an abundant supply of water in the streams, but there is also an ample rainfall, so that almost no true desert is to be found between the streams or between the towns. Bread is cheaper here than anywhere else in a province of cheap food. In the mountains, iron is easily accessible, besides gold and other metals, while coal is even more readily obtained, and there is a great supply of timber. All the materials of necessary clothing, and even the more solid comforts, are also produced in the sub-province, so that imports of Chinese origin are restricted to tea, silks, and articles of luxury requiring skilled manufacture. This tendency to be at the same time claimed by a ruling Chinese population and divorced from economic dependence on China explains much of its bloody and revolutionary history; but indeed, its modern history is only a pendant to a long and savage past of invasion and war.

Owen Lattimore, **High Tartary**, 1930

Above: In summer the shores of Sayram Lake are scattered with yurts as nomadic herders gather for the Naadam festival (Sun Jiabin). Right: The Ili Valley has been coveted for its fertility throughout the history of human habitation in Central Asia (Jeremy Tredinnick). Far right: The Naadam is a colourful, rambunctious event and the social highlight of the year for Kazakhs and Mongols alike (Sun Jiabin).

of settlers (Chinese convicts and exiles, Uygurs, Manchus and others) were brought in to farm and develop new land, a policy that successive Chinese governments were to emulate.

When Yakub Beg's rebellion spread to Ili in 1871, the Russians occupied the area and stayed for a decade, until the **Treaty of St Petersburg** was signed in 1881, giving Russia trade, customs and consular rights in Xinjiang (and a nine-million-rouble indemnity) in return for most of the territory it had seized, the new border line demarcated along the **Horgas (Korgas) River**.

In 1944, a Kazakh-Uygur independence movement established the East Turkestan Republic, which soon came under Soviet influence, and by 1949 Ili was, to all intents and purposes, Russian territory. The Chinese Communist government reasserted its control over the area by sending in large numbers of demobilized Chinese soldiers as production-construction corps, and in 1958 it established pastoral people's communes. By the 1960s, and the Sino-Soviet split, there was much dissatisfaction amongst the Kazakhs and Uygurs, resulting in a mass exodus of more than 60,000 to the Soviet Union before the borders were closed. Cross-border trade between the two countries resumed in 1984 at Horgas Port, and since the collapse of the Soviet Union and the creation of Kazakhstan trade has boomed.

YINING (KULJA)

The city of **Yining (Kulja** or **Ghulja** to Uygurs) is the capital of **Ili (Yili) Kazakh Autonomous Prefecture**, much of which borders on Kazakhstan. It is closer to the Kazakhstan city of Almaty (450 kilometres west) than to Urumqi (700 kilometres east), and is only 80 kilometres (50 miles) from the border with what was, until 1991, the Soviet Union. The majority of the city is on the north bank of the Ili River, but in recent years construction has spread across the wide river to the southern bank. Despite the influx of immigrants from the eastern provinces Yining still retains a unique but subtle, if fading, Russian – or more accurately Eurasian – atmosphere.

It also still has a rangy, almost wild frontier feel to it, a product of the millennia-old trading legacy that is as strong today as it ever was. Yining is now a booming city of close to 500,000 people, fast taking on the homogenized look of all Chinese urban centres with office blocks superseding many of the older Russian buildings, but traders from many different countries and ethnic groups still fill its streets; the faces you see as you walk around town are a mixture of Russian, Chinese, Kazakh, Mongol, Kyrgyz, Tajik, Uzbek, Tatar and others. The city is spread out but the centre of the old town revolves around **People's Square**, where paths crisscross between rose and tulip gardens. Lined on one side with excellent restaurants, this a popular spot in the evenings, when Uygur and Kazakh families have picnics, romantic couples stroll, and young and old men sit in groups, relaxing, playing chess and smoking *mohorka* and *nishee* tobacco.

Some of the buildings still show Russian influence, designed with grand mouldings and columns, often painted blue and white and crowned with red stars, like the old Yili Hotel on the post office square. Single-storey family residences are decorated with carved wooden window frames, painted bright colours, called *nalichniki* in Russian. Some households maintain flower gardens and often have orchards in their courtyards. Among the many minority peoples living in the city are a few hundred Russians, known as **Eluosi**, descendants of 18th-century settlers. They have their own Orthodox church, graveyard and primary school, which opened in 1985. A section of the Ili River was once reserved for the exclusive use of Eluosi fishermen – it's unclear if this remains the case.

SIGHTS

There are more than 100 mosques in Yining, frequented mostly by Huis and Uygurs. The largest is the **Uygur Mosque** (originally known as the **Baitula Mosque**) on the corner of Jiefang Nan Lu and Xinhua Lu a block west of People's Square. The original mosque was built in 1773 during the reign of Qing emperor Qianlong. At 1,800 square metres it housed a madrasa and was renowned across the Islamic world – a visiting Turkish mullah named it Baitula, "House of Heaven", and Muslims came here to study Arabic and Persian languages, Islamic scripture, medicine, philosophy and history. Over the years the mosque suffered but was repaired, enlarged, and eventually in 1996 rebuilt as a large, new, whitewashed building, blending Russian and Islamic elements with some style, its central dome and two enormous minarets all topped by golden

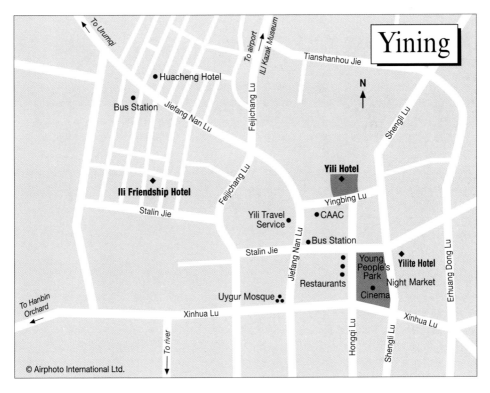

crescents. The current building is 6,950 square metres in area and can hold 3,000 worshippers. In front of the mosque stands the original 18th-century gateway, a classical three-tiered Chinese-style structure with flying eaves, preserved to remind visitors of the site's history, and still used to call the faithful to prayer. Another handsome building is the **Shaanxi Mosque** on Shengli Jie, No 1 Alley. Its ornate Chinese-style gateway is similar to that of the Grand Mosque in Xi'an, and its prayer hall dates from the 18th century.

Yining's earlier name, the Uygur word *Kulja*, means **"The Golden Roofed Temple"**; the city was named after a temple 3.6 kilometres northeast of the city, a famous lamasery built at the end of the Ming Dynasty. The temple was destroyed by Amursana of the Junggar tribe and a small fort was built here in 1762 by Emperor Qianlong. Nothing is left but a dirt terrace (the remains of the Qing fort) and to the north, Tibetan statues and tiles with animal designs at the site of the temple.

By the time the Ili River reaches Yining it has grown to substantial breadth, albeit shallow and strewn with sandbars in autumn and winter. However, during spring and summer when meltwater swells the river many times over, it presents a formidable barrier. It was not until the 1940s that Yining's first bridge was built over the Ili, and the city's residents had to wait until 2006 for a second bridge to be constructed in response to the booming economy. With a span of two kilometres the new **Yining Bridge** is said to be the second longest in China. A dual carriageway keeps traffic flowing easily, but the bridge is also used by herdsmen to bring their stock across the river to market, and the sight of hundreds of sheep or dozens of horses being driven over the gleaming bridge reminds one of the continuing traditions that exist side by side with modern progress in this remote corner of China.

The municipal authorities of Yining have recently set aside an area of the city traditionally inhabited by Uygurs, protecting its authentic buildings from demolition and creating a **Uygur Cultural Street** as a tourist attraction. Beyond an overhead sign reading "Uygur-Style Dwelling Houses Street of Yining", a single curving road is fronted by classic Uygur homes with ornate wooden courtyard doors and window frames, their lintels painted with colourful scenes of mountains, mosques and fruit orchards. Tiny side alleys off this road end at doorways hiding more courtyard homes, but you should never enter unless first invited.

The **Night Market** south of People's Square is a lively place to wander in the evening, extending down to the Uygur Mosque area, which is the most interesting part of town. Food stalls sell delicious poluo and noodle soups, and fruit and nuts of the highest quality can be had for ridiculously cheap prices. The Ili Prefecture is the main producer of fruit in northern Xinjiang and its fertile fields yield apples, peaches, pears, apricots, cherries and walnuts. There are several township communes located on the outskirts of Yining where visitors can pick their own fruit. The **Hanbin Orchard**, located two kilometres west of the city on Xinhua Lu, is an extremely peaceful commune suitable for pleasant walks and shady naps. Large plots of fruit trees are intermixed with small family plots of corn and squash interspersed with wild hemp.

Yining's Uygur Mosque, fronted by the original 18th-century Chinese-style gateway (Jeremy Tredinnick).

Another good spot to walk and enjoy a meal in the late afternoon is along the river near the old bridge a couple of kilometres south of the city centre. When the weather is balmy riverside cafés open and you can sit and watch children playing and animals being watered as the sun sinks, turning the sky a deep orange.

Ili Kazak Autonomous Prefecture Museum (Ili Kazak Zìzhìqu Bowuguan)

The small but excellent **Ili Kazak Autonomous Prefecture Museum** focuses solely on the prefecture's history and culture, but since this includes most of northwest Xinjiang, from the fertile Ili Valley to the Junggar Basin and Altai Mountains, there is plenty to see. There are English notes only on the main information boards, but this is enough to give you a good idea of what is on display, and the English introduction at the entrance next to a 3-D relief map of Xinjiang helps.

Three galleries cover the pre-history period, the rise of the great nomadic steppe cultures, and the ethnic groups that make their home here. The "**Gallery of History**" displays mammoth teeth from the Pleistocene era of a million years ago, flints, rock carvings and stone figures from Fuyun County in the Altai, and images of a cave at Tangbale that revealed simple concentric circles representing the vulva, an early fertility symbol, dating to 8000 BCE. Copper ingots illustrate early settlers' mining skills, and Bronze Age axes, sickles, chisels and arrowheads discovered in 1976 date from 2000–1000 BCE. Of note is a particularly well-wrought small bronze knife. Examples of "deer stones", a type of engraved stele used from the 13th–6th centuries BCE show how this type of artistic expression became an important element of steppe culture, as were petroglyphs – there are numerous rock carving and deer stone sites throughout the region.

The "**Steppe Culture in Nomadic Times**" gallery takes the visitor through the rich period from the Wusun (fifth century BCE–sixth century CE) right through to the Chaghatai Khanate of the 14th century. The Wusun left thousands of burial mounds scattered over the Ili steppe, and many of these have yielded skeletons, weapons and utensils, as well as beautifully designed gold work, from old cups inlaid with gems to a gold foil arm protector with finger sheath, a gold sword sheath inlaid with rubies, and in particular a superb fifth–sixth century CE gold mask unearthed at the Boma Tomb in the Ili Valley. These burial mounds were aligned south-north in groups, with the largest 80 metres in diameter and 10 metres high. A row of anthropomorphic stone statues, or balbals, from the Altai region stand in front of a huge photograph of the open steppe where typically these figures have been found. Iron stirrups, a helmet and chain armour from the Yuan Dynasty and the Chaghatai Khanate are next displayed, and the gallery ends with a collection of models of mosques and temples, which were built from the 14th century onwards after the region's ruler, Tughluq (Telug) Timur, converted to Islam.

The "**Gallery of Nations and Folkways**" displays mannequins clothed in the various traditional dress of the 13 indigenous ethnic groups (including the Han) of the region. The workmanship of the embroidery on silk, cotton, wool and felt is wonderful, the colours vividly emulating nature's hues. The centrepiece of the gallery is a glorious Kazakh yurt surrounded by animal furs, horse harnesses, musical instruments, houseware and handicrafts.

The museum is located a few kilometres north of the city centre at 122 Feijichang Lu (Airport Road), open daily from 9:40am–1:30pm and 4:30–8pm in summer, 10am–12pm and 3:30–5:30pm in winter. Entrance costs Rmb20; photography is permitted only in the Gallery of Nations and Folkways.

MUSEUM OF LIN ZEXU

Lin Zexu (1785–1850) was a talented and high-ranking official of the Qing government who, because of his vehement opposition towards the opium trade and high moral stance, has become a role model among Chinese people for the ideal of moral governance. Born in Fujian Province, Lin attained the highest degree possible in the imperial examinations, and went on to become the Governor-General of Hunan and Hubei, before being sent in 1838 to stop the opium trade instigated by the British in Guangdong Province. It was his stringent anti-opium policies in Guangzhou that led to the First Opium War. At first successful, at one point seizing and destroying 1.2 million kilogrammes of opium, he grossly underestimated the power of the British warships that eventually defeated the Chinese troops with ease, and as punishment was exiled to Ili in 1840.

As Governor of the Ili Valley, Lin built roads and developed the region's infrastructure, in particular opening 40,000 hectares of fertile land to agriculture through irrigation dykes, while studying and recording much about its Muslim inhabitants that was useful to the Qing government far away in Beijing. Because of the reverence in which he is held both within the prefecture and nationally, the **Museum of Lin Zexu** was opened in 1994 to highlight his extraordinary life. Located on Fuzhou Lu in the Ili Development Zone (tel: 0999 812 3131), the small museum has a pleasant garden in which stands a statue of Lin, robed from shoulder to feet and looking sternly off into the distance. Inside the museum the models and pictures of his campaign against the evils of opium are suitably vivid, but unfortunately there is no English translation to the many explanation boards. The museum is a popular excursion for schools, and classes of excited young students often buzz around; entrance costs Rmb15 and the museum's opening hours are the same as the Ili Kazak Autonomous Prefecture Museum (see above).

YINING PRACTICAL INFORMATION

 n spite of its reputation as a centre of political unrest, for international visitors Yining is a safe, friendly, easygoing city, definitely worth going out of your way to explore. Sadly, it struggles with an HIV problem linked to heroin use, accidental infection from shared needles, and rampant prostitution (see A–Z of Traveller's Tips section) due to its proximity to the Kazakh border and the large numbers of traders and business travellers who fuel the demand for their services.

TRANSPORTATION

There are twice-daily flights between Yining and Urumqi with China Southern Airlines, taking between 60 and 90 minutes (the CAAC office is on Jiefang Lu near the Yili Hotel, tel: (0999) 822 1505). The new electric railway line from Jinghe in the Junggar Basin to the north means that finally there is a convenient rail link into the Ili Valley. Two daily passenger trains run from Urumqi to Yining and vice versa, taking 10.5 hours and 11.5 hours – a hard sleeper berth costs about Rmb160. Daily buses operating to/from Urumqi, Kucha (continuing on to Aksu, Kashgar and Hotan) and other points within the Ili Prefecture depart from the main bus station on Jiefang Lu. It is possible to cross the border to Kazakhstan by road at Horgas Port, one hour from Yining. Visas for non-Chinese are available in Urumqi and Beijing, but not in Yining.

ACCOMMODATION

Yili Hotel (Yili Binguan)

8 Yingbin Lu. Tel: (0999) 802 2794; fax: (0999) 802 4964

Situated within the shaded park-like grounds of the former Soviet Consulate, this is Yining's most atmospheric, peaceful and relaxing place to stay. The older building's rooms are three-star and comfortable, but a new building was completed in 2007 offering a higher standard of facilities and décor in line with Yining's rising aspirations as a business hub (the new building's rooms have Internet access). Standard rooms cost Rmb388, deluxe rooms Rmb588 and suites start from Rmb1,088.

The colourful interior of a rich yurt, erected within the Ili Kazak Autonomous Prefecture Museum (Jeremy Tredinnick).

Twin Star General Hotel

23 Sidalin Jie (Stalin Street). Tel: (0999) 802 6666; fax: (0999) 802 2880.

This large, modern four-star business hotel has a curving blue-glass façade, 218 rooms, a spa fitness centre and business centre, and its lobby lounge is a popular meeting spot for Yining's smart set. Rooms from Rmb278, suites from Rmb644.

Yilite Hotel

98 Shengli Lu. Tel: (0999) 782 9666; fax: (0999) 802 1819

This good three-star hotel is ideally situated at the northeast corner of People's Square, and is popular with tourists. Standard rooms start from Rmb280, suites from Rmb380.

Hongfu Yiyan Hotel

Jiefang Lu. Tel: (0999) 823 4888; fax: (0999) 823 4999; website: www.hongfuhotel.com

Only five kilometres from the airport, this pleasant 74-room three-star is run by the Hongfu hotel group.

Ili Friendship Hotel (Youyi Binguan)

7 Stalin Jie, 3 Xiang (Third Lane). Tel: (0999) 782 3111; fax: (0999) 782 3222.

Also on display within the museum are extensive collections of ethnic traditional clothing, and examples of ancient Turkic stone figures known as balbals (Jeremy Tredinnick x2).

Located in the centre of Yining only 500 metres from the long-distance bus station up a side street, this is a two-star hotel with a good reputation. Rooms start from Rmb220.

FOOD AND DRINK

The Mie Xin Tian Chi Dian on Hongqi Lu (opposite the People's Square) serves large bowls of tea to accompany sweet breads, pastries, ice cream and tarts in a cool, spacious Russian-style teahouse. Next door is an even larger Uygur restaurant that offers the usual laghman, manta, samsa, kebabs and nan in a vibrant, bustling atmosphere – a great place to people watch. In front of the movie theatre (on the south side of the park), carts sell dried fruit, nuts and *kurut* – small, hard, dry cakes of goat's cheese with a strong flavour that resembles that of the Greek feta available in Yining. On the same street there are many food stalls that specialize in *apke*, cold noodles, and kebabs – there's a raucous night market atmosphere with lots of drinking. Do not forget to try *piwa*, the excellent local honey and wheat beer (usually in bottles with a rubber stopper) made by the old Russian women of Yining. Curbside refrigerators sell fresh or frozen yoghurt, ice cream, cold drinks and other refreshments. Kazakhs enjoy *kumis*, a mildly alcoholic drink made from fermented mare's milk – the flavour is sour-sweet and very palatable.

EXPLORING THE ILI VALLEY

QAPQAL (CHABUCHAER) XIBE AUTONOMOUS COUNTY

The **Qapqal (Chabuchaer) Xibe Autonomous County** lies 20 kilometres (12 miles) southwest of Yining. Among those Emperor Qianlong sent to settle in the Ili region were soldiers of the **Xibe (Xibo)** nationality, whose homeland is in present-day Liaoning Province, far away in northeast China near Korea. In 1764, the soldiers and their families, numbering over 3,000, set off on a westward trek that took them a year to complete; they travelled in small Mongol-style carts with tin-rimmed wooden wheels.

Originally these settlers were to stay for three years, but the emperor extended their tenure to six. Petitions to return to their homeland resulted in a further extension of 60 years, so the Xibe gave up all hope of returning and gradually established eight walled towns, opening up the land to agriculture and jealously guarding their cultural heritage. Their descendants (the eighth and ninth generations) now number 35,000. They have retained their language and script (similar to Manchu), unlike their 50,000 or so brethren in the northeast.

On the 18th day of the fourth lunar month, the Xibe commemorate the day their ancestors set off on their westward journey by holding picnics and archery and wrestling contests. The Xibe have a strong, sturdy physique, square jaws and flattish faces. Some of the old women continue to wear traditional dress, a long, dark-blue gown over black trousers and a white headcloth. They are expert archers and young athletes from this county often compete in China's Olympic team.

HUOCHENG COUNTY

Fifty kilometres (30 miles) northwest of Yining is Huocheng County and its several historical monuments. The road from Sayram Lake to Yining passes through the county, between fields cultivated with purple lavender, wheat, maize, hops, vegetables, sunflowers and other oil-yielding plants (Fruit Valley itself is also part of Huocheng County). The small Uygur-majority farming township of Huiyuan lies 30 kilometres west from Yining on the road to Horgas Port. Between 1762 and 1866, **Huiyuan City** was the military and political centre of Qing Dynasty authority in Xinjiang. Emperor Qianlong ordered the fortress of Huiyuan to be built during a local Muslim rebellion, and as the main stronghold of the "Nine Forts" of the Ili, Huiyuan was the seat of the Governor General of the region, the **Ili Jiangjun**, along with 20,000 Manchu troops.

Huiyuan suffered severe damage during the Muslim Rebellion of the 1860s, the besieged Jiangjun Mingxu blowing himself up in his palace rather than surrender to the rebels, and the fort fell into disuse during the Russian occupation that followed in 1871–81. The Treaty of St Petersburg (1881) saw the withdrawal of tsarist troops, and two years later the fortress and military-administrative town that accompanied it were rebuilt some 10 kilometres north of the Ili River. This included a three-storey **Bell Tower** dating from 1884, and the residence of the Governor General, both of which have been renovated at the Huiyuan site as a tourist attraction, often referred to as the "Huiyuan Old Town". The Bell Tower stands at the main intersection of this rather dusty town, and the "**Headquarters of the Ili General**" stands within a green garden containing a simple pavilion, grinning stone lions and four oak trees said to have been planted by Lin Zexu.

North of the town of Qingshuihe (where the road forks west to the Kazakhstan border and north to Sayram Lake) is a turn-off to the village of **Masar**. In this village stands the lovely turquoise-, purple- and white-tiled Persian-style **Tomb of Tughluq (Telug) Timur**, who was Khan of Moghulistan (part of the Chaghatai Khanate) from 1347 to 1363. He was decisive and energetic, and his circumcision and conversion to Islam, along with 160,000 followers, marked a religious turning point for the mainly Buddhist and shamanist herdsmen of the region. His military exploits took him as far south as the Hindu Kush. Telug Timur also named as his son's adviser the young **Tamerlane**, a fact which inaugurated the latter's meteoric rise to power.

T he high-arched entrance to the tomb is inscribed in Arabic; the tiles and decorations on the lower section of the façade are gone, baring the bricks. Inside are two small ante-rooms, and a series of niches supports a high, domed ceiling. Two memorial caskets stand in the centre, around which pilgrims kneel while praying aloud. An inside staircase leads to the narrow circular corridor on the upper floor and then up to the roof, where there is a view across a low mountain spur marking the border. The smaller, simple white tomb of Telug's sister stands alongside.

Ninety kilometres west of Yining, the **Horgas Port** is western China's largest highway port. The Horgas River demarcates the border between China and Kazakhstan in the Ili Valley, and this has been a significant way station along the Ili trade route since the Tang Dynasty. Horgas Port was opened as a trade port in 1983, and as an international border crossing in 1992 after Kazakhstan became an independent state. On both sides of the border massive trading markets thrive, and much construction is going on to increase market space; a frenetic frontier atmosphere exists, with Chinese and Central Asian products of all description being sold.

TEKES AND ZHAOSU COUNTIES

The Tekes River is the Ili's main tributary, flowing out of mountains to the south of the Ili Valley that are considered some of the Tien Shan's most spectacular, pristine terrain. In the upper reaches of the **Tekes Valley** the **Muzart Pass** crosses into what is now the southeastern corner of Kazakhstan, but in times past this was an important route between the Ili Valley and Issyk-Kul in modern-day Kyrgyzstan. (Muzart Port opened for commercial import-export in 1992, but unfortunately it is not possible for international travellers to cross this border.)

Young Xibe revellers dance up a storm during a local festival (Sun Jiabin).

J ust to the south of the pass is the Tien Shan's second-highest peak and its most revered mountain: the majestic 7,010-metre **Khan Tengri** ("Ruler of the Skies" or "Lord of Spirits"). The huge mountain massif that surrounds Khan Tengri and its near neighbour to the south, 7,439-metre **Tomur Mountain** (Tomur means "Iron", but it is more commonly known as Pobeda Peak in the West), is very rugged and remote, with multiple peaks spiking high ridges that fan out in all directions and are covered with thick alpine forest and high meadows. This superb area is home to exciting wildlife such as snow leopards, Tien Shan brown bear, ibex and argali sheep, as well as marmots, snowcocks, lammergeyers, golden eagles and much more. In the early 20th century rumours of the Tekes Valley's beauty and bountiful wildlife attracted Western hunters and explorers who made the long and arduous trek up from British India via Kashgar, but who were never underwhelmed. Trekking tours are now possible up the Tekes Valley and over passes to Aksu on the rim of the Taklamakan Desert.

The lower reaches of the Tekes River comprise Tekes County, a green and pleasant land for the pastoralist Mongolian and Kazakh communities who live here. Farther west and bordering Kazakhstan territory is the equally beautiful **Zhaosu County**, but Zhaosu's main claim to fame are the Wusun burial mounds on the Xiatai River plain, and the fine examples of stone figures – ranging from 0.6–3.1 metres high – placed in front of Turkic graves discovered across the broad grasslands. The county seat of Zhaosu town contains one of Xinjiang's best-preserved lamaseries, the **Shengyou Temple**, built in 1886 by craftsmen from Beijing at a cost of 100,000 taels of silver, paid for by the Mongol communities of the area. The temple faces south, and its five halls (front, main, rear, east and west) contain many Buddha figures and thangkas. Lamas are a constant presence in and around the lamasery's verdant grounds, as are worshippers who light votive candles and joss sticks to the Buddha.

THE NARAT GRASSLANDS

From Yining the road eastwards is designated Highway 218. At first it is lined by tall poplar trees but soon emerges to reveal the Ili Valley in all its verdant glory. Already very broad, the valley floor close to the various rivers that flow down to join the Ili is patterned with large, tilled fields; farther away are the sloping expanses of pastureland that for millennia have nourished the famed Ili horses (*see special topic on page 274*), and these are replaced by forests and craggy rock outcrops on the steeper slopes of the mountainsides. The fecundity all around makes it easy to understand why the Russians were so keen to control the Ili Valley in the late 19th century – and why the Chinese were so vigorous in reclaiming the best part of it.

The road follows the Kunes River as the valley begins to narrow and ascend to higher altitudes. Here the grassland is a sea of green in summer, a place where Kazakh horsemen canter around tending to their flocks of sheep and herds of cattle and horses. In autumn the grass turns yellow but is still good grazing for the animals, which stock up as much as possible as the snowline descends inexorably from the permanently white peaks. At 1,800 metres above sea level a log office marks the entrance to the **Narat Scenic Area**, where a Rmb65 entrance fee must be paid. The **Narat (Nalat) Grasslands** are particularly lush and picturesque, and this area has become a favourite place for sightseeing excursions among domestic Chinese tourists.

The nomads of Central Asia learn to expertly ride their sturdy horses from an early age (A Gai/Odyssey).

XINJIANG'S PRINCELY PONIES

*P*onies are bred in every oasis, as well as in every Qazaq, Mongol, and Qirghiz camp throughout Chinese Turkestan and Zungaria, but the three breeds of fame are those of Bar Kol, Qara Shahr, and the Ili valley. In spite of the way that tribes, nations, and peoples have been moving and shifting through these regions throughout history, their ponies have not merged into a common type any more than have the peoples themselves.

The Bar Kol ponies are named from the lake near which is the town of Barkol, whose official Chinese name for centuries has been Chen His – Controlling the West. These ponies are bred on stony, mountain pastures on which the grass is sweet and nourishing, but never lush. Even their wintering grounds are comparatively exposed. They are small, wiry, and tough, able to fast, able to forage for themselves, able to face any weather, and without equals in hill country. The average height is not more than twelve hands; but they are valiant weight-carriers. They have no end of bottom. The desert-going and hill-ranging Chinese of these regions are as knowledgeable as any nomads about horseflesh. They say that a good mount and a good man are equally matched so far as endurance goes, but that the strongest rider is ready to drop out of the saddle before he has ridden a Bar Kol pony to a standstill.

This, of course, does not refer to a straightaway gallop, but to a long ride at a well-judged pace. I am quite prepared to believe the tales I have heard of these ponies being ridden more than a hundred miles in a day... The Bar Kol ponies are big-hearted, in that they are hogs for work and distance; but, as the Chinese put it, "the holes in their hearts are crooked" – they are wily and vicious....

...The ponies of Qara Shahr are as much worth mention as those of Bar Kol. They get their name from being marketed at Qara Shahr on the road south of the Heavenly Mountains. They are bred by the Torgut Mongols who winter in the lowlands of the Qara Shahr oasis and spend their summers in the Yulduz plateau and contiguous valleys of the high T'ien Shan. The most remarkable thing about them is the formation of head and neck and the way that the ears, much longer than the stubby ears of the true Mongol pony, are set on top and in front of the crown of the head. The head, while heavy in proportion like that of the Mongol pony, is peculiar and striking in profile. The neck also is like that of the Mongol pony, in its heaviness at the joining with the shoulders; but the whole outline is astonishing in its resemblance – which, though heavy, and as it were debased, is undeniable – to the head and neck formation of the horses of Greek sculpture. One might also say that the Bucephalid or Macedonian strain should be sought here, not in Badakshan. Certainly there would be little hazard in pointing out these ponies as the type from which were drawn the "T'ang horses," modeled in clay, which are found in excavations in China, and which so little resemble the "China pony" of our time, which is drawn almost entirely from the markets of Eastern Inner Mongolia.

The Qara Shahr pony, while much valued for swank in town, is not so hardy a road-goer as the ponies of Bar Kol and the Ili. He is liable to shoulder lameness...

...The "Ili horses," which used occasionally to reach China, brought back usually along the Imperial High Road in the train of an official, were almost always ungainly half-Russian half-breeds, high-actioned trotters. The Ili breed had the reputation in China of being the finest of all those within the Chinese dominions, wherefore it was thought that any example brought back must be something at least bye-ordinary in size. The true Ili pony is something quite different; a most noble, gallant pony. He is bred more in such highland valleys as that of the Tekes than in the plains of the lower Ili, and the best herds are those of the Qazaqs. This indicates that the original strain must have come farther from the west, for the Mongols on the Qunguz, near as they are to the Qazaqs of the Tekes, have a true Mongol pony, which they must have brought with them from Zungaria, or rather from the Altai. They are fine, mountainy ponies, but not the same thing as the "Ili" pony. Probably the distinguishing strain of the Ili pony comes from Russian Central Asia. He looks a relative of the very fine breed of which I saw one or two examples at Kulja, which Russians told me came from Pishpek; and these Pishpek ponies, I am pretty sure, must be related to those of the Turkomans.

The Ili pony, in short, has much the character of a small horse. He has more of a pony head and neck, and is heavier in bone, than such a Badakshan horse as my noble bay stallion, but he can be seen at once to be more shapely than the true Mongol breeds. He is very sweetly gaited, has a nicer temper and finer spirit than the Mongol pony, is a tireless traveler, can forage under snow, and if handled constantly with understanding no better companion could be found. The breed undoubtedly has retained its excellence because, though not stall-fed, it ranges over such summer pastures as can hardly be equaled in Central Asia; and because it is easy to harvest enough wild hay to give him an extra ration in the winter. Thus he grows more freely, and escapes the stunting effect of winter cold and starvation during the first years of growth, which accounts for a great deal of the coarseness of the Mongol pony. In height there is not much to choose between the ponies of Qara Shahr and the Ili, unless the Ili ponies are a shade taller, averaging pretty nearly fourteen hands; but within that height the proportions of the Ili ponies are unmistakably sounder.

Owen Lattimore, **High Tartary**, 1930

The Kaidu River meanders in huge curves across the Bayanbulak Grasslands, home to nomadic Mongols (Sun Jiabin).

Mongols watch an archery competition on the Bayanbulak Grasslands during a festival (Sun Jiabin).

Near the road, which at this point is still sealed with tarmac, are red-roofed chalets and a new, modern hotel that cater to the tourist crowds, who usually drive in and stay a single night, allowing for one or two hiking tours through the meadows, past rustic wooden hamlets and into the forested mountains. More adventurous souls can arrange to make multi-day trips by foot or on horseback farther into the mountains – across the ridgeline south of the road is an even more picturesque grassland surrounded by gorgeous peaks. However, to wander around in this region usually requires a special permit that must be purchased in Urumqi through travel agents as part of a guided tour.

MOUNTAIN HIGHWAYS AND THE BAYANBULAK GRASSLANDS

Highway 218 leaves the Narat Scenic Area and continues east, becoming a dirt track that will eventually be metalled in its entirety by army construction crews. Following the river, which by now is more a rushing, stone-filled stream closely hemmed in by spruce and pine trees, the road comes to a crossroads where Highway 217 meets it on its way south from Kuyten in the Junggar Basin. That road cuts through the Tien Shan via the Hashlegen Tunnel, meets and crosses Highway 218, fords the river over a solid bridge and works its way south to Kucha on the northern rim of the Tarim Basin. Highway 217 is famous for its spectacular and varied mountain scenery; first it follows a river through a tight ravine, then crosses the lush Bayanbulak Grasslands, then twists and turns its way between the sheer cliffs of the southern Tien Shan.

The Bayanbulak Grasslands are located within **Hejing County** in the **Bayinguolin Mongol Autonomous Prefecture** and are the summer home for Mongol nomads, who tend vast herds of fat-tailed and Chinese Merino sheep, horses and yaks. Bayanbulak means "abundant spring" in Mongolian – it is a huge prairie of lush grass, one of the largest in China, watered by the Kaidu River, which winds through the ocean of grass like a giant gleaming serpent, making for fantastic pictures especially in summer, when the blooming of flowers such as the snow lotus presents a sight to live long in the memory.

This area is home to the **Bayanbulak Swan Reserve**, China's only protected area for this majestic bird. **Swan Lake** is in fact many small lakes situated within a 30 x 10 kilometre area; in April and May the swans arrive from southern climes to feed and breed, and their abundance draws ornithologists and tourists in large numbers too. As well as whooper and wart-nose swans, wild geese, ducks and egrets summer here. Even in summer temperatures can plummet at night due to the altitude, so warm clothes are necessary. In June every year a Naadam festival is held on the grasslands by the Mongol herdsmen, and this is an excellent time to visit and appreciate an ancient culture that has remained little changed for centuries. Visiting Bayanbulak requires a special permit, and entry costs Rmb30 – Rmb220 is charged for entrance to the Swan Lake area, but this includes a worthwhile environmental protection fee.

South of the grasslands Highway 217 enters mountainous country once again, and 70 kilometres north of Kucha County, at the 1026 distance marker, the road passes the **Tien Shan Grand Canyon**, a 5.5-kilometre-long canyon characterized by tall, thin pinnacles, massive buttresses, overhanging walls and heavily eroded red rock. The canyon is 53 metres at its

An obo is festooned with Buddhist Mongol prayer flags and kata scarves at a high pass in the Tien Shan (Jeremy Tredinnick).

widest point, but only 0.4 metres at its narrowest, and contains the ruins of a Tang-era Thousand Buddha Cave known as the **A-ai (Ayi) Grotto**, whose cave paintings bear a similarity to those of Dunhuang in Gansu Province.

Unfortunately, at time of print Highway 217 between Highway 218 and the southern limits of the Tien Shan was closed to traffic due to the danger of rock falls, but once Highway 218 has been sealed, it will be easier to bring materials into this remote area and Highway 217 will be rebuilt as a metalled and suitably protected road, allowing easier access to this beautiful region.

Meanwhile, the road from the crossroads east along Highway 218 is by no means unattractive. It climbs through a set of switchbacks up the northern side of the valley to reach its head at a pass just under 3,000 metres above sea level. Yaks wander along the road and the pass is marked by an *obo* or *ovoo*, a large cairn of stones covered in prayer flags and white *kata* scarves. This is a Buddhist Mongol structure, similar to the monuments gracing every pass in Tibet, and it serves as a clear sign that you have left predominantly Kazakh territory and are now entering Bayinguolin Mongol Autonomous Prefecture. The road from here crosses a huge high-altitude plain devoid of trees, a land of yaks, sheep, griffon vultures, eagles and lammergeyers. Off to the south the Bayanbulak Grasslands stretch away to mountain ridges in the distance that look deceptively small. At the eastern side the road suddenly drops into a barren defile cut by a rushing stream through precipitous cliffs of rock and dirt. Black-headed sheep and goats with twisted horns clamber about on the sheer rock faces, and farther down coal mining operations and tar factories pollute the air, pumping out fetid smoke that mixes with the dust. The highway now meets the main road from Urumqi to Korla, crosses the railway track twice, and finally shoots out of the mountains onto open plain that stretches to a hazy horizon: the Tarim Basin.

Two young Kazakhs ride a powerful Ili steed bareback in the Narat Grasslands (Jeremy Tredinnick).
Opposite: Camels roam free to graze in the shadow of Central Asia's mighty mountains (Peter Hibbard).

THE ROAD TO KASHGAR AND THE SOUTHWEST

The oases that lie along the northern rim of the Taklamakan Desert represented one of only a few possible routes for caravans transporting goods between China and the West in the early centuries of Silk Road trade, and as such became sizeable city-states that absorbed the cultural influences moving with the merchants from distant lands. After the collapse of the Loulan kingdom (*see* page 417) and the waning of the Southern Silk Road's importance in the fourth century CE, they controlled the major portion of caravan trade and became even more powerful and sophisticated.

In the 20th century this was still the main route connecting northern and southern Xinjiang, and today its highway and rail line keep tradition alive, following roughly the same course as the caravan trails of millennia past. As well as drastically reduced travel times between each oasis centre, a major development of only the last decade or so has been the opening of cross-desert highways, linking northern oases with their counterparts on the old Southern Silk Road, specifically Korla with Ruoqiang, Luntai (midway between Korla and Kucha) with Minfeng and Qiemo, and Aksu with Hotan. These roads now make travel across the infamous Taklamakan possible in a matter of hours, and increase the tour options for tourists substantially.

SOUTH TO KORLA

The old northern Silk Road route that skirted the Taklamakan Desert was still nothing but a dirt track until it was finally tarmacked in the 1970s. It weaves southwest from Turpan to the small oasis township of **Toksun**, which is sustained by the waters of the Baiyang and Ala streams. Soon the road enters the most dangerous stretch of its 1,500-kilometre (930-mile) run to Kashgar: the aptly named **Dry Ditch (Gan Gou)**; for 60 kilometres (37 miles) the road winds through the gorge of this barren spur of hills coloured blue, ochre, brown and grey. The road surface can be washed away by the frequent flash floods that sweep down the naked hillsides with amazing force and suddenness.

In *Journey to the West*, the angry husband of Princess Iron Fan, the Ox Demon King, aims to obstruct Xuanzang and company by casting down his long waistband, which turns into this dry, perilous gulch. The god of the Flaming Mountains, however, comes to their rescue by scattering pearls along the way, which turn into delicious, thirst-quenching fruit – the grapes of Turpan.

Today's road travel is far quicker, easier and less dangerous than yesteryear. Highway 314 sweeps south and west in a giant curve from Toksun to Hoxud, **Yanqi** and **Korla**, while Highway 216 cuts through the mountains south from Urumqi to Yanqi, where soda-whitened marshes, tall grasses and grazing cattle indicate the proximity of the vast **Bosten Lake**. These days, Yanqi is only the main town of the Yanqi Hui Autonomous County, where reed screens for fencing and roofing are produced. Historically, however, it was the very important oasis of **Karashahr** (Black Town), which in 11 CE revolted against Han domination by murdering the Chinese protector-general. The revolt was ruthlessly stamped out by the Han Dynasty general, Ban Chao, who sacked the town, decapitated 5,000 inhabitants and carried away 15,000 prisoners and 300,000 head of livestock.

By the Tang Dynasty, Karashahr was the capital of the Buddhist Kingdom of Agni (a Sanskrit word referring to the God of Sacrifice or Burnt Offerings), whose king, the monk Xuanzang noted, was boastful of his military conquests, but whose people were "sincere and upright". Xuanzang

Above: The twisted trunks of ancient diversiform-leaved poplar trees can be found in many locations around the rim of the Tarim Basin, as well as along the banks of its rivers (Li Yu De). Opposite top: Muslim faithful leave the Idkah Mosque in Kashgar, Xinjiang's most holy place of worship (Sun Jiabin). Opposite bottom: A mural detail of Buddhist pilgrims discovered in Karashahr (Image copyright The State Hermitage Museum, St Petersburg).

further observed that, "the written character is, with few differences, like that of India. Clothing is of cotton or wool. They go with shorn locks and without head-dress". Karashahr was the northernmost point of the Tibetan occupation of Xinjiang in the seventh century. Its Indo-European Tokharian population was gradually absorbed by the Uygurs after the ninth century, and the mighty Tamerlane sacked the city in 1389.

Sven Hedin described Karashahr as "the chief commercial emporium in that part of Chinese Turkestan" and "the dirtiest town in all Central Asia… consisting of a countless number of miserable hovels, courtyards, bazaars, and Mongol tents, surrounded by a wall". The British diplomat, Sir Eric Teichman, noted in the 1930s that it was "not a Turkic but a Chinese-Mongol city". The Mongols of Karashahr were in fact part of the Torgut Mongol tribe (also found in the Bortala region near the Junggar Gate) who returned from the Volga region during the Qing Dynasty and were granted rights to settle and live in the mountains to the north, where they summered in the Bayanbulak region and descended to winter in the grasslands around Bosten Lake. These nomads were famous for breeding superb horses, said to be capable of covering 300 kilometres (185 miles) a day.

BOSTEN LAKE

Twenty-four kilometres (15 miles) east of Yanqi and 57 kilometres northeast of Korla lies the largest freshwater lake in Xinjiang, **Bosten Lake** (also called **Baghrash Lake** or **Bositeng Hu**), more than 1,000 square kilometres in size but averaging only 9.7 metres deep. It is fed by the **Kaidu River** (which originates in the depths of the Tien Shan and snakes through the Bayanbulak Grasslands), and is a source of the **Konche (Peacock) River**, which flows across the northern wastes of the Taklamakan Desert in the direction of Lop Nor.

Known as the "Western Sea" during the Han Dynasty, Bosten Lake is rich in aquatic life, with carp, bullhead and bream all abundant; its fringing reed beds are also home to myriad water birds. (Legend tells that the lake once swarmed with water snakes, which attempted to bar the way to Xuanzang. But with a flap of his long sleeves he ordered them all back to the lake and turned them

The oil-enriched city of Korla has changed immeasurably in recent years, modernizing fast as the petro-dollars flood in (Michael D. Manning, Creative Commons Attribution 2.5 licence, creativecommons.org)

into fish.) There are 16 small lakes in the vicinity, one of which, called Lotus Lake, is a breathtaking mass of pink and white water lilies in the summer – a popular tourist destination.

Other areas of Bosten Lake have been developed for domestic tourism in recent years, including a fishing village at the western end of the lake, around the mouth of the Konche River, where visitors can gorge themselves at a fish banquet on one of the floating restaurants. Speedboat trips through the reed beds are also popular (Rmb500 and up). On the northeast shore of the lake, 23 kilometres south of Wushentala town in Heshuo County, a two-kilometre-long sandy beach has been created called **Golden Sand Beach (Jin Sha Tan)**, a leisure resort area with hotels and tourist yurts lining the shore, where you can play beach volleyball, waterski, sunbathe and take boats out into the middle of the lake for views of the snowy mountains to the north and desert sand dunes encroaching from the south.

KORLA

Although only around 250 kilometres south of Urumqi as the crow flies, the road distance to Korla is much longer. **Korla** is the capital of the **Bayinguolin Mongol Autonomous Prefecture**, the largest prefecture in all of China (at 462,700 square kilometres it is larger than France), encompassing the eastern half of the Taklamakan Desert and extending to the borders of Tibet, Qinghai and Gansu. The entire area has a population of 1.1 million, the majority of whom are Han Chinese, with about 350,000 Uygurs, 50,000 Hui Moslems and 45,000 Torgut Mongols (*see* page 249).

Korla was known as Weili during the Han Dynasty, but was subordinate to Karashahr and played no significant role in Silk Road trade. In 1934, Sven Hedin and his Sino-Swedish motor expedition undertook a journey under the auspices of the Chinese Ministry of Railways to survey road links between Chinese Turkestan and China proper. At Korla they ran into the desperate Muslim troops of the young rebel, General "Big Horse" Ma Zhongying. Their five vehicles were commandeered by the retreating soldiers, the expedition members were rounded up in a courtyard and their hands were tied as they awaited summary execution. General Big Horse spared the

expedition, but held them under house arrest while he sped away in their vehicles southwest towards Kashgar, fleeing bombing by Soviet planes undertaken at the request of the Governor of Xinjiang.

Today, Korla has grown to become one of Xinjiang's most important cities. It is the headquarters for PetroChina's oil concerns in the Tarim Basin, a meeting point for a number of highways leading to all corners of Xinjiang, and is a stop on the Nanjiang Railway line between Urumqi and Kashgar. The city's population of 430,000 (the large majority of whom are Han, with Uygurs a large minority) live by heavy industry and the export of such products as fragrant pears (for which Korla is famous), tomato paste (bought primarily by the Japanese), fish products, figs, mulberries and Korla cotton; its extensive surrounding farmland produces vast amounts of cotton, corn and sugar beet. Oil exploration and extraction, conducted with American and Australian expertise, is progressing at a rapid pace in the Taklamakan Desert south of Korla.

SIGHTS

As oil money floods into the city, Korla is emerging as one of Xinjiang's most modern urban centres. There appear to be more English signs on the streets even than the capital Urumqi, and the broad avenues and many small parks give it a relatively Western, cosmopolitan feel, perhaps a result of the avid interest and presence of international oil-related companies. However, there are no historical sites worthy of note in the city, and perhaps the best thing to do here is visit the park on a hill to the north of the city centre where a new pagoda and viewing tower offer a panoramic view of the city and mountains – this is a popular evening spot for locals. The **Korla Great Mosque** is worth a visit: large enough to hold 7,000 worshippers, its interior walls are covered with Islamic inscriptions and verses from the Koran, and its 25-metre arched gateway is suitably grand and imposing.

Seven kilometres (four miles) to the north of town is the historically important **Iron Gate Pass (Tiemenguan)**. This Silk Road gateway, a ravine wedged between the Huola and Kuluk mountains and known locally as Haman Gully, guarded the only ancient route connecting northern and southern Xinjiang. It was first stationed by soldiers during the Jin Dynasty (265–420 CE), and the Tang built a larger fortress-like gate and barracks where officers controlled and taxed trade caravans. Reduced to a pile of bricks during the Cultural Revolution, it was rebuilt in recent years and now receives plenty of visitors. Entrance costs Rmb11 and the slate-grey gate tower itself is a short walk from the office building along a small river lined with diversified-leaved poplars. The narrow, curving gorge beyond the Iron Gate is barren and almost lifeless – you can walk an undulating circuit of a few kilometres up the ravine, climbing to small, recently constructed viewing pagodas to get a sense of the harsh surrounding terrain.

A number of ancient Silk Road ruins are scattered around the area, including the earth-rammed walls of a city dating from the Han Dynasty, and two large Tang Dynasty Buddhist temples about 20 kilometres southwest of Yanqi, which are said to have once quartered 1,000 monks. Nearby are the **Qixing Buddhist Caves**, but they were thoroughly depleted by Japanese, British and German archaeologists, with only a few murals still recognizable in a few caves, and industry in the immediate vicinity has further ruined the area.

If you are in Korla in summer or autumn, try to visit a horticulture farm on the outskirts of town, where huge orchards of Korla pears are cultivated. The trees blossom with innumerable white flowers in summer, and when the pears ripen in autumn you can pick and taste them – like Xinjiang's grapes and melons, Korla pears are high in sugar content, extremely juicy and refreshing.

KORLA PRACTICAL INFORMATION

Though opened to foreigners in 1986, Korla, until recently, was not high on any visitor's list. But with the opening of the spectacular Tarim Highway, the oilfield access road that crosses the heart of the Taklamakan, Korla's strategic location at the northern edge of the desert suddenly increased in significance. It is now southern Xinjiang's largest and most modern city, boasting foreign-cuisine restaurants, nightclubs and oozing petro-dollars. The city's large main square, with its amusing decorations of multicoloured balls, arches and posts, gives some idea of how the authorities are trying to engender a modern outlook in its citizens.

TRANSPORTATION

There are daily flights to and from Urumqi, twice-weekly to Kucha, and three times a week to Qiemo; the airport is 11 kilometres outside town. The train station is four kilometres from the city centre; Korla is on the Nanjiang Railway line and daily trains travel in both directions – check with your

Above: The recently rebuilt fortress-gate at Iron Gate Pass guards a barren but once strategically vital trade route between north and south Xinjiang (Jeremy Tredinnick). Opposite: Korla pears have been renowned for millennia for their fragrance and sweetness (Sun Jiabin).

hotel for current arrival times and to book tickets. Buses run to Urumqi (approx eight hours) and Turpan (4–6 hours), across the top of the Taklamakan to Kucha (3–4 hours), Aksu (eight hours) and Kashgar (14 hours), and buses travel down Highway 218 on the desert's eastern edge to Ruoqiang, or via the Tarim Highway to either Qiemo, or Minfeng and on to Hotan.

ACCOMMODATION

The best accommodation in town can be found at the new five-star **Kangcheng Jianguo International Hotel** (618 Jiaotong Dong Lu, tel: (0996) 208 8888), a huge 322-room hotel with all mod-cons, including a swimming pool – rare in this part of the world. Rooms start from Rmb368 and suites from Rmb590. The four-star **Bayinguoleng Hotel** (12 Renmin Dong Lu, tel: (0996) 221 5000, fax: (0996) 221 5333, email: bzzbg-kr@mail.xj.cninfo.net) is situated in its own grounds and boasts Western and Muslim restaurants, a sauna, gym and piano bar – this is where Party members and VIPs used to stay when in Korla, though they may now prefer the presidential suite at the Kangcheng Jianguo International Hotel; rooms start from Rmb300. Another four-star option is the **Silver Star Hotel** (36 Renmin Dong Lu, tel: (0996) 202 8888) which offers similar prices. The three-star **Xinlihua Hotel** (Jiangguo Lu, corner of Jiaotung Lu, tel: (0996) 203 6588, fax: (0996) 201 7666) is in the south of the city, with good-value rooms from Rmb188.

FOOD AND DRINK

Korla has plentiful options for food, from market stalls and fast-food outlets like Dico's to quality Uygur and Chinese restaurants, while the new hotels offer increasingly sophisticated international fare.

LUNTAI AND THE TARIM HIGHWAY

The road from Korla to Kucha is typical of much of Xinjiang's desert-skirting highways. To the north, the view is of steep brown and grey hills and ridges etched with countless dry gullies showing as vertical lines on the rocky canvas. Scrub desert lies hard up against them, across which the well-maintained, two-lane highway extends endlessly. To the south, patches of poplar look grey with dust, and beyond them is a haze of featureless desert, flat, blank and uniform. The road passes periodic communities of concrete-block Chinese buildings and factories with belching chimneys.

The round leaves of the diversiform-leaved poplar turn a glorious yellow gold in autumn (Jeremy Tredinnick).

Diversiform-leaved poplars are reflected in the still water of the Tarim River (Fan Shucai).

After two hours the anonymous, dust-ridden town of Luntai materialises from the haze. It is here that the **Tarim Highway**, the longest desert road ever built, begins its 522-kilometre battle with the elements, 446 kilometres of which crosses pure desert (differentiated from the scrub desert that fringes the Taklamakan). A large archway frames the turnoff where Highway 312 – its official title – starts, and a monument stands beside it giving details of the amazing engineering feat accomplished from 1991, when planning began, until its opening in 1995 (*see* special topic on page 292). The Tarim Highway ends just north of Minfeng, and the only real town along the intervening stretch of road is **Tazhong**, named after the Tazhong Oilfield which was discovered in the very heart of the desert, and was the initial reason for the highway's construction.

Less than an hour's drive (70 kilometres) south from Luntai the highway crosses the Tarim River, southern Xinjiang's main watercourse, which flows from the west across the north of the Taklamakan Desert, eventually petering out in the western desert. Along the river's banks **diversiform-leaved poplars** (*populus euphratica*) grow in profusion; this hardy tree is one of Xinjiang's iconic images because of its gnarled, ancient trunks and its autumn foliage of golden leaves that create splendid panoramas framed by the deep-blue desert sky. The 100-square-kilometre **Tarim River Park**, the largest desert diversiform-leaved poplar park in China, is located around the area where Highway 312 crosses the Tarim River Bridge, and is possibly the best place to see these beautiful trees.

A report by the Tarim River Valley Administration in 1996 showed that in the 30-year-period between the 1960s and 1990s, the Tarim River had shortened by a quarter of its length (mostly due to the diversion of water from it and its tributaries for agricultural irrigation), and subsequently diversiform-leaved poplar forests declined by 67,000 hectares. In recent years this trend has been reversed by digging channels from Bosten Lake and allowing huge runoff flows at certain times of year to regenerate the "green corridor" of the Tarim River. (The consequences for Bosten Lake are unclear at this point.)

KUCHA (KUQA)

The seemingly endless *gebi* (stony wasteland) expanse west of Luntai is punctuated by low scrub, the occasional tree, and roadside shacks and straw-roofed shelters selling watermelons and Hami melons (you can buy them for Rmb1–2 per kilo in summer and Rmb4 in winter).

Kucha, the next major town along the Tarim Basin's northern rim, is a relatively small modern-day town of less economic importance than its city neighbours to east and west, but 2,000 years or so ago, it was the centre of the largest of the 36 kingdoms of the Western Regions. In the second century BCE, Zhang Qian passed through on his way west; in 91 CE, Kucha surrendered to General Ban Chao, who brought 50 Central Asian kingdoms under the suzerainty of the Chinese during his campaign against the Xiongnu. By the fourth century, the Kuchean **Kingdom of Qiuci** was one of the most important centres for Central Asian trade and Indo-European culture in the entire Xinjiang region. Trade routes running north to the Junggar Basin and south to Hotan across the Taklamakan intersected with the Silk Road at Kucha.

The city's most famous son was the linguist and scholar **Kumarajiva** (344–413), who earned a place in Chinese Buddhist annals as the "Nineteenth Patriarch of Buddhism". Kumarajiva's father was Kashmiri, and his mother was the sister of the King of Qiuci. He received his education in Kashmir, returning eventually to Kucha as a respected teacher of Hinayana Buddhism (among his disciples were grandsons of the King of Yarkand). In 383, Kumarajiva was taken to Liangzhou (modern Wuwei) in Gansu Province by General Lu Kuang, who had subdued the kingdoms of the Tarim Basin. There he lived for 17 years, gaining renown as a prolific translator of Buddhist manuscripts from Sanskrit into Chinese.

Prior to accurate translations of Indian Buddhist philosophy, the Chinese thought this new religion was a foreign barbarian form of their own Taoism, partly because both religions strive towards a state of salvation, and partly because the Chinese were unable to understand the essential doctrinal differences – the Chinese language is ill suited to the many subtleties and abstract reasoning in Buddhism that Sanskrit easily and gracefully accomplishes. Only after accurate translations appeared between the fourth and eighth centuries (begun by Kumarajiva) did the Chinese fully understand the nature of Buddhism. Still, the Buddhism introduced to China maintained only the simplest tenets of the religion; Chinese Buddhist sects of Chan (Zen) and Pure Land bear limited resemblance to Indian Buddhism.

During the Tang Dynasty the Qiuci kingdom reached its zenith as a centre of artistic achievement and cultural exchange. The wealth of the trade caravans subsidized the Buddhist monasteries, in which more than 5,000 monks worked and prayed, and where there are some of the finest examples of Gandharan frescoes. Kuchean music heavily influenced Chinese music: musicians and dancers from Kucha performed before the court at Chang'an, where their musical instruments (drums, lutes and reed-pipes) and notation were adopted.

When Xuanzang passed through the Kingdom of Kucha in the sixth century, there were two huge Buddha statues 27 metres high guarding the road. He wrote of Kucha's fabled dragon-horses, which despite their docility, were said to be offspring of lake-dwelling dragons and wild mares. Prior to 658, when the Chinese took control of the city, Kucha had its own style of painting, music and its own language. Archaeologist Paul Pelliot discovered Buddhist documents at Kizil that had been written in this lost, ancient Kuchean language.

The arrival of the Uygurs in the ninth century brought about the gradual absorption of Kucha's Indo-Europeans and their eventual conversion to Islam. Under the reign of the Mongols, Kucha formed part of the Chaghatai Khanate called Uyguristan and became embroiled in the power struggles and petty wars of neighbouring kingdoms, falling frequently under Kashgar's control. In 1864, Kucha joined in the Muslim rebellion against the Qing Dynasty and was incorporated into Yakub Beg's Kashgaria three years later. The Chinese regained control in 1877.

An archaeological free-for-all at the Kucha sites began in 1889, when local treasure seekers discovered a strange tower, probably an ancient Buddhist stupa, containing the mummified corpses of sacrificed animals and several piles of dusty manuscripts. In 1890, Lieutenant (later Sir) Hamilton Bower purchased a manuscript written on birch bark while in Kucha. Bower sent the manuscript to Dr Augustus Hoernle, an expert on Central Asian languages at the Asiatic Society of Bengal in Calcutta, who deciphered the script and dated the "**Bower Manuscript**" to 500 CE. The text was written in Sanskrit using the Brahmani alphabet, probably by Indian monks, and dealt with the subjects of medicine and necromancy.

This amazing find opened the floodgates of freelance exploration of the ancient buried cities of the Taklamakan, and a scramble for the treasures of the Kucha region. Japanese expeditions sponsored by Count Kozui Otani worked in the area in 1902 and 1908; in 1906, Albert von Le Coq was threatened by the Russian Beresovsky brothers during a squabble over sites. The French Orientalist, Paul Pelliot, spent seven months here during the same period. Aurel Stein followed in 1908, then the Russian Sergei Oldenburg in 1910. After that, not much was left.

Today, the local economy centres on agriculture (wheat, cotton, maize, and such fruits as smooth-skinned apricots, rose-pink plums, sweet figs and grapes) and small factories producing cement, agricultural implements, carpets and other household necessities. Kucha is an overtly Uygur city – only 25 percent of its 87,000 inhabitants are Han Chinese. It is divided into "old" and "new" cities, separated by two long roads and the Kucha River, as well as the remains of the old city wall, which once stretched

HIGHWAYS ACROSS THE SAND

Since early traders first guided their camel caravans along the Silk Road over two millennia ago, only a handful of intrepid adventurers and archaeologists, lured by the prospect of discovering ancient cities and buried treasure, have dared to penetrate the fearsome Taklamakan Desert.

Beyond Dunhuang, on the eastern threshold of Xinjiang's deserts, the Silk Road divided. Some travellers and merchants took the route north of the Taklamakan, others skirted the great void to the south. Indeed there was no reason to go into the world's second largest sea of sand.

But many centuries later, as socialist China's reforms took off, its economy thirsted for energy resources, particularly oil, and thus a thorough exploration of the Taklamakan began. After positive seismic surveys, wildcat wells were drilled, very expensively. Helicopters – normally used as a means of transport to service offshore wells – were used, together with surface access. Convoys followed a 1,200-kilometre detour around the north of the desert, with special desert motor vehicles (UNIMOGs) having to be used on the final leg of the route into the interior.

By this tortuous and costly means, the Tazhong-4 Oilfield was discovered in the heart of the Taklamakan. But the China National Oil Corporation, a state consortium that exploits all of China's oil

and gas resources, realized that an economical means of transport would be needed if the recovery of oil from the field were to be profitable. A road was the only viable option.

With a budget of US$60 million (Rmb423 million), the China National Oil Corporation organized 17 research institutes and more than 100 experts – engineers, geomorphologists and botanists – to build a tarmac route across the Taklamakan. Nowhere in the world had a road ever been built across such hostile terrain. Engineers faced two main problems: to build a

Although relatively low-tech, the checkerboard pattern of embedded reed stalks that comprises a major part of the desert highways' "shelter belts" are surprisingly successful at keeping the desert sand at bay (Jeremy Tredinnick).

Lights blaze in the empty desert at the Tazhong Oilfield in the remote centre of the Taklamakan (Sun Jiabin).

solid roadbed, and to protect it from being buried by the constantly shifting sand.

Experimentation began in late 1991. The most suitable roadbed formula was underlain with "geotextile", a heavy-duty weave of tough plastic that was laid on compressed sand. This was topped with a gravel-asphalt surface, approximately 30 centimetres in depth.

As the road inched its way south from Luntai, researchers focused their efforts on finding the best way to protect it from windblown sand. Lateral "shelter belts", consisting of two lines of defence, were built on both sides of the road. The first, about 100 metres from the road, was a 1.3-metre-high fence of interwoven reed stalks. The second line of defence lay alongside the road itself: a checkerboard pattern of reed stalks "planted" deep into the sand. This double defence proved effective because 90 percent of all windblown sand in the desert never rises more than one metre above the ground – even in the most powerful of desert storms.

In total, the road-building teams came up with 310 new desert-stabilizing and road-building techniques. Tens of thousands of labourers used thousands of square kilometres of geotextile and millions of tons of gravel. In summer they braved temperatures of 70°C (158°F), and in winter the mercury plummeted to minus 30°C (-22°F). Four sweating and shivering years of labour later, the 522-kilometre road, seven metres in width, finally linked Highway 314, to the north of the desert, with Highway 315 in the south.

Designated Highway 312 and dubbed the Tarim Highway, this road-building wonder – the world's longest metalled desert road drivable year-round – was opened to traffic in September 1995 by Chinese vice-premier Zhu Rongji on the eve of the 40th anniversary of the establishment of the Xinjiang Uygur Autonomous Region. The highway begins at Luntai's Lun Nan Oilfield, to the west of Korla, and emerges south of the desert just east of Minfeng. In 2002 another road opened, branching off southeast from the Tazhong Oilfield and running 200 kilometres to Cherchen (Qiemo).

The success of the Tarim Highway, and the ongoing exploration – and discovery – of oil reserves beneath the desert sands, also resulted in the improvement in 2000 of Highway 218 to the east, which extends from Korla southeast to follow the Tarim River before curving south to Charkhlik (Ruoqiang). Even more important, however, was the start of an Rmb834 million (US$118 million) construction project in 2004 to build another cross-desert highway farther west, linking Kucha and Aksu on the desert's northern rim, with Hotan (Hetian) in the south.

Officially opened in May 2007, this is Highway 217, an extension of the epic north-south road that cuts through the Tien Shan range and crosses the Junggar Basin via Karamay all the way to Altay town (Aletai) in the far northern Altai Mountains. Highway 217's southern section is equally impressive, running 425 kilometres through deep desert, roughly following the course of the Hotan River. Roads from Kucha and Aksu come together at the beginning of the desert road proper, which starts just south of the Tarim River near the town of Aral (Alar).

From there, it takes only 5–6 hours to cross the infamous Taklamakan and arrive in Hotan – an amazing feat, considering that only a few decades ago the same journey would require many weeks of extremely dangerous and uncomfortable travel. This new desert highway will not only benefit oil exploration in the western Tarim Basin, but will allow more comprehensive economic development of southern Xinjiang, which has been rather left behind in recent decades.

In 2001 anti-desertification plant species such as Chinese tamarisk, honey tree, diversiform poplar and saksaul were planted along a 30-kilometre section of the Tarim Highway to help hold off the sands, which constantly encroach despite the roadside shelter belts, and subsequently in 2003 a Rmb220 million (US$31 million) forestation project proceeded to create a green belt of desert plants on 3,128 hectares of land along 436 kilometres of the highway.

Of course the water these plants still require must be drawn from underground well stations as well as pumped through a network of pipes that run along the green belt. It is estimated that six million cubic metres of irrigation water is consumed annually, an average of less than 2,000 cubic metres per hectare – but of course this nevertheless places increased pressure on the water resources of the surrounding oases and mountain glaciers from which this most precious of Xinjiang resources originates.

There is no doubt that keeping Xinjiang's cross-desert highways open is a difficult, labour-intensive task. But one thing is certain: with so much oil beneath the sands, they will be maintained at whatever cost – at least until the oilfields run dry.

eight kilometres (five miles) from east to west. The new city, to the southeast, has a nucleus of modern Chinese buildings around People's Square, a typical quadrangle decorated with modern sculptures, flowerbeds and grape trellises. Around this the bulk of the city is low-rise brick houses. The old city is an atmospheric maze of narrow, unpaved alleys and high mud-brick walls, of mosques and market stalls.

SIGHTS

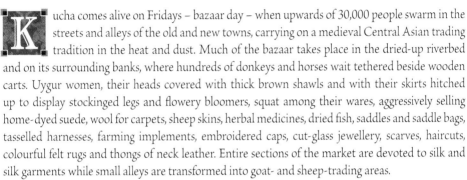

ucha comes alive on Fridays – bazaar day – when upwards of 30,000 people swarm in the streets and alleys of the old and new towns, carrying on a medieval Central Asian trading tradition in the heat and dust. Much of the bazaar takes place in the dried-up riverbed and on its surrounding banks, where hundreds of donkeys and horses wait tethered beside wooden carts. Uygur women, their heads covered with thick brown shawls and with their skirts hitched up to display stockinged legs and flowery bloomers, squat among their wares, aggressively selling home-dyed suede, wool for carpets, sheep skins, herbal medicines, dried fish, saddles and saddle bags, tasselled harnesses, farming implements, embroidered caps, cut-glass jewellery, scarves, haircuts, colourful felt rugs and thongs of neck leather. Entire sections of the market are devoted to silk and silk garments while small alleys are transformed into goat- and sheep-trading areas.

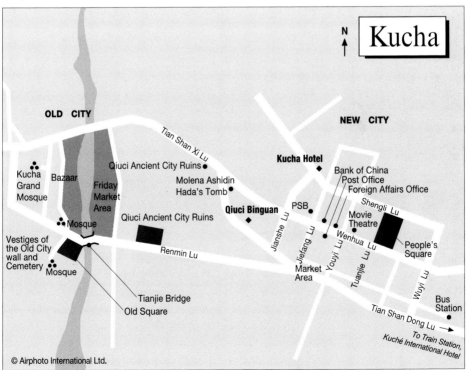

© Airphoto International Ltd.

Kucha's Grand Mosque is hidden in the back streets of old Kucha, where traditional stalls still hold sway (Jeremy Tredinnick x2).

T he bridge over the riverbed which marks the entrance into the old city, has two archways inscribed with the words "The Ancient Barrier of Qiuci". On the north side of the bridge is a small market square facing a Qing Dynasty mosque, whose muezzin appears from a trap door to call worshippers to prayer five times a day. The square is a constant hive of activity: white-bearded elders outside the mosque sell holy books; under large, makeshift umbrellas food stalls offer yoghurt, nan, mutton sausage stuffed with rice, *shashlik*, boiled mutton and ice cream; shops around the square's perimeter sell hats, clothing and dried fruits and nuts.

Horse carts and buses operate between the various markets in the old and new cities. In the broad tree-lined streets of the new town is an agricultural market with fresh fruit and vegetables, grains and seeds, soft sun-dried apricots, and fresh mulberry and pomegranate juice. A covered market area near to the bridge on the new city side is full with traders selling glittering lengths of spangled cloth, shoes and high boots in both colourful plastic and leather, and sheet metal utensils for house and farm use.

In the summer, when apricots, peaches, pomegranates and figs are in season, tourists can visit a family fruit orchard southwest of the old city and experience traditional Uygur hospitality in the form of the *dastarkhan* – a rich spread of local food and bowls of tea. For a nominal fee, you can pick your fill of fruit directly from the trees. Apart from vestiges of the ancient city wall, the old city contains Muslim cemeteries, several old mosques and narrow roads west and south of the main square that wind towards the surrounding fields and orchards. An hour or more can be happily passed simply wandering around, getting glimpses through beautifully decorated gateways into spotlessly cleaned courtyards; if you are lucky you may be invited in for tea.

KUCHA GRAND MOSQUE

Hidden away off a small street in the northern part of the old city, the **Kucha Grand Mosque** was originally built in 1580, when it was used as a religious court. A fire in 1931 destroyed it, but reconstruction of this handsome and imposing mosque began in 1923. It is Xinjiang's second largest mosque after the Idkah Mosque in Kashgar – the whole compound measures 14,398 square metres and includes prayer halls, smaller mosques, the moon-watching tower, religious court and dormitories. Its main gate façade has two tall, 20-metre-high minarets, and the interior dome is handsomely niched in arabesque brickwork. The large prayer hall, with its carved, inset ceiling and red, blue and green wooden pillars, is used for major Muslim festivals. Just to the west is a smaller mosque with honeysuckle roses in the courtyard, offering an excellent view of the old city and riverbed bazaar from its minaret. The mosque is closed to non-Muslims during prayer time.

MOLENA ASHIDIN HODJA'S TOMB

A 10-minute walk west from the Kucha Hotel on Wenhua Lu is the tomb of an Arabian missionary who arrived in Kucha 600–700 years ago. One day he thoughtlessly killed a pigeon and the next day he dropped dead. His tomb is now a local shrine with an attached mosque; green tiles adorn the simple entranceway. The sarcophagus, covered in white cloth, is inside a small hall of latticed wood. Strips of white cloth are tied to bare tree branches to indicate a holy site.

The ancient city of Subashi straddles the Kucha River as it emerges from the southern Tien Shan (Jeremy Tredinnick).

ANCIENT CITY OF SUBASHI

The extensive ruins of this ancient capital of the Kingdom of Qiuci lie 20 kilometres (12 miles) north of modern Kucha. They are divided by the Kucha River, which emerges from the mountains and immediately forms a broad riverbed – in flood it cuts off access to the eastern section (**Subashi** means "river's headwater"). The city dates from the third century CE and includes towers, halls, monasteries, dagobas and houses, all severely damaged by time but many still easily recognizable – this is Xinjiang's most extensive Buddhist temple site. The ruins of the large Zhaoguli Temple date from the fifth century. In 1978, after a flood unearthed a tomb at the foundation of the Western Subash Temple, excavation of the site revealed the corpse of a 20-something girl from the Qiuci era, intriguing because of her flattened forehead. Though not fully understood, this seems to confirm Xuanzang's claim that in Qiuci, "the children born of common parents have their heads flattened by the pressure of a wooden board". The city was sacked and burned in the ninth century, and by the 13th century had been abandoned.

Access to the Subash City site is by private car only. Entrance costs Rmb25 for each side of the river – called the Eastern Temple and Western Temple areas – although the western side may be the only section open to visitors. The ruins' location in the shadow of high, scarred mountains and its variety of easily identified buildings make it a worthwhile and interesting destination, although it is often windy and very dusty.

KIZIL KARA BUDDHIST CAVES AND THE KIZILGAHA BEACON TOWER

The **Kizil Kara Buddhist Caves** are a small complex of 47 caves hewn between the third and 10th centuries CE into a semicircular bluff of barren rock 16 kilometres (ten miles) northwest of Kucha by road and dusty track. Fragments of frescoes remain in 11 of the caves: in cave 21, the repeated small Buddha images in black, turquoise and white are quite powerful, while on the ceiling at the back of Cave 30 are paintings, still well preserved, of flying apsaras playing musical instruments. Cave 12 is carved in a highly unusual shape; it is a worshipping cave with a seven-sided flat roof, and a central pillar with side corridors and a tunnel at the rear for pilgrims to make circuits. To visit the caves you must make arrangements at the Kizil caves office, pay a fee and be accompanied by a special guide.

On top of the bluff, only 1,000 metres away but four kilometres closer to Kucha by road, stands the **Kizilgaha Beacon Tower**, dating from the third century, the original wooden struts that supported the crowning watchtower structure still protruding from its upper section. A lone rammed-earth structure, it is trapezoid at its base, rising 13.5 metres to a rectangular top, where fires were lit by Han Dynasty soldiers to warn of impending hostile incursions. Entrance costs Rmb15, and although there is nothing to see other than the tower itself, the location, once again, makes it a rewarding stop on travel itineraries.

Kumtura Caves and Simsim Caves

This famous site on the left bank of the Muzat (Weihe) River is 28 kilometres (17 miles) west of Kucha. A complex of 112 caves, on the eastern bank of the river and dating from the third to 11th centuries, the **Kumtura Caves** were extensively excavated by foreign archaeologists. Divided into southern and northern sections, the complex includes caves in which monk's lived and meditated, as well as places of worship. Three distinct periods of construction can be seen: first the classical Qiuci artistic style of the third to seventh centuries; then a period from the 8th and 9th centuries when styles attributed to inner China began to appear; and finally the Uygur era of the 10th and 11th centuries.

The Kumtura Caves are a significant cultural site illustrating a fascinating blend of Buddhist art from the Qiuci, Han and Uygur periods, and as with most of the historical sites in the Kucha area, are under state protection as historical and cultural monuments. Like Kizil Kara, a visit to these caves must be arranged through the authorities at the Kizil Thousand Buddha Caves site.

Another cave complex is located 45 kilometres northeast of Kucha. The **Simsim Caves** comprise 54 caves carved into a circular hill about 700 metres in diameter and dating from the Wei to Tang dynasties. The murals inside are similar to those at Kizil, but animal murals feature prominently. Simsim is not open to the general public, but special permission can be applied for. Access to both the Kumtura and Simsim cave complexes is by private car only – preferably a 4WD.

Kizil Thousand Buddha Caves

The Kizil Caves lie around 70 kilometres (43 miles) northwest of Kucha in nearby **Baicheng County**. Carved into a sheer cliff looking out over the broad, peaceful **Muzat River** valley, they contain some of the best fresco fragments to be found in Xinjiang. Of the 236 caves in this complex, 135 are intact, yet only 80 still contain fragments of wall paintings. No statuary remains. The earliest caves were hewn from the hillside in the third century CE, with the most artistically accomplished ones coming later during the Tang Dynasty. The cave temple complex was gradually abandoned with the spread of Islam to the Kucha region in the 14th century.

The Kizil Thousand Buddha Caves contained some of the finest examples of Hinayana Buddhist art in Central Asia. The earliest wall paintings show Gandharan (Indo-Hellenistic) influences overlaid with Persian elements; there is no trace of Chinese influence in the Kizil Caves. Some 70 Buddhist fables from the Jataka stories are illustrated in the murals – the Pigeon King burns himself to attain nirvana, the Elephant King sacrifices himself to help the poor, and the Bear King donates food to help the starving. In Cave 38 the song-and-dance tradition of the ancient Kingdom of Qiuci is vividly represented by paintings of celestial musicians and dancers. Donors – usually wealthy merchants or royalty – are richly and colourfully painted, providing good examples of Qiuci dress. Among the best remaining caves on show to the majority of visitors are Cave 27, which has many large and small alcoves with large Buddha figures in black, white, blue and ochre, and traces

of blue and white sky overhead; Cave 8, where the Buddhas on the intact ceiling have black, white or flesh-coloured faces; and Caves 32 and 34. Caves 10 and 15 show the placements of large statues – the marks in the walls show how they must have been chiselled out of place before being taken away. The caves served different functions: some were for religious ceremonies, others for teaching sutras, and still others were living quarters.

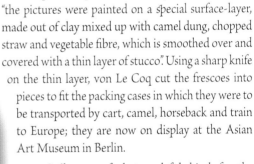

Of the numerous *fin de siècle* archaeological expeditions that came to Kizil, von Le Coq's probably made off with the most, the murals removed in a neat patchwork, as today the areas of the missing paintings reveal squares of the mud-and-stucco wall underneath. Von Le Coq wrote upon his discovery of the caves that,

"the pictures were painted on a special surface-layer, made out of clay mixed up with camel dung, chopped straw and vegetable fibre, which is smoothed over and covered with a thin layer of stucco". Using a sharp knife on the thin layer, von Le Coq cut the frescoes into pieces to fit the packing cases in which they were to be transported by cart, camel, horseback and train to Europe; they are now on display at the Asian Art Museum in Berlin.

Sadly, most of what was left behind after the archaeological frenzy of the first decades of the 20th century was defaced by local Muslims, and the majority of the caves are bare, with scratched graffiti on the walls and little else but dusty footprints. However, this should not put you off visiting, for such was the wealth within the caves that even the relatively poor remaining frescoes

Above: A flying apsara in the New No.1 Cave at Kizil (Liu Yu Sheng). Left: A deity with a musician from Cave 171 (Cave of the Painted Floor , 209 x 134cm, MIK III 8420), dating to the fifth century CE (Courtesy of the Asian Art Museum, National Museums in Berlin). Opposite: Dry and dusty, the extensive site of the Subashi ruins is nevertheless atmospheric, an impressive legacy of Buddhism's blossoming in the Tarim Basin (Jeremy Tredinnick).

still provide a fascinating insight into the artistic heights reached by the Qiuci craftsmen more than a millennium and a half ago.

The Kizil site itself is also very attractive, with its thick groves of mulberry and poplar trees along the left bank of the Muzat River. Birdsong can be heard all around, and the view from the cave entrances is stunning, looking across the wide valley that must be more than two kilometres across – it is easy to understand why this location would be attractive to monks with their minds bent on meditation.

Half a kilometre (a third of a mile) through an ever-narrowing gully behind the caves is the Spring of Tears, which flows from a semicircular rock face – this makes for a very pleasant walk in the early morning or late afternoon. A local legend tells of the daughter of the King of Qiuci, the beautiful Princess Zaoerhan, who went out hunting one day and met a handsome young mason whose love songs won her heart. The young mason, who came to the king for permission to marry his daughter bearing all the presents he could afford, was harshly received by the king, who said: "Since you are a mason carve out for me 1,000 caves. If you do not complete the task I will not give my daughter to you in marriage and shall punish you cruelly." The young man went to the hills around the Muzat River and began carving out the caves. After three years he had completed 999 caves, but had worked himself to death. The princess went in search of him only to find his wasted body. She grieved to death; her endless tears fall to this day upon this semicircular rock face.

To get to the Kizil Caves, cars must take the main road out of the city, Highway 217 which eventually leads to Yining, and pass through Salt Water Gully (Yanshui Gou), where the rock has been eroded by wind into weird, stark formations, the rock strata lying at steep angles in sharp relief to the surrounding terrain. A side road leads west to the oasis and village of Kizil, and another road branches off, winding down a steep pass that offers a spectacular view of the Muzat Valley. Much road construction was ongoing in 2007 to create a good sealed tarmac road to the Kizil Caves, but some of the trip is still currently on dirt road – keep your windows closed as it is *very* dusty.

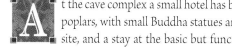t the cave complex a small hotel has been built, as well as a pond surrounded by reeds and poplars, with small Buddha statues and pavilions for shade and relaxation. It is a peaceful site, and a stay at the basic but functional hotel is recommended for the extra peace of early mornings and late afternoons before and after the coach and 4WD crowds have come and gone (the hotel requires advance booking in summer). There is also an artefact exhibit building and a small "tourism supermarket" in the complex.

Entrance to the Kizil Caves complex costs Rmb55, and this allows you to see 10 caves, of which six contain traces of frescoes, the others being completely bare. You can hire a guide to explain them; up to eight people will cost Rmb100, more than eight people costs Rmb200. Additional caves are available for viewing at varying prices, depending on the quality of the fresco – it usually works out at Rmb100–150 per cave. Photographers are also charged a fee of Rmb200–800 per picture, again depending on the size and quality of the fresco fragment, but permission must be sought for this, involving paperwork. Of course it is hard for guides and security guards to stop people with small digital cameras, but large cameras and camera bags must be left in lockers at the base of the cliff.

KUCHA PRACTICAL INFORMATION

ucha is divided into the new city (*xin cheng*), where hotels and the bus station are located, and the old city (*lao cheng*), where the lively Friday market takes place. As this town sees fewer visitors than Kashgar, the locals can be friendly and curious, often inviting you to eat and drink with them. In the new city, the Wenhua Lu area around People's Square comes alive in the evenings with the younger generation playing pool on outside tables and eating kebabs from the many food stalls. Beware, however, the many doorways with red lights along Tian Shan Dong Lu from the Kuche International Hotel into town.

TRANSPORTATION

The airport is five kilometres east of town; there are flights three times a week to/from Korla and Urumqi, the Nanjiang train runs north to Urumqi and south to Kashgar daily, and there are frequent buses to/from Korla (continuing on to Turpan or Urumqi), Aksu, Kashgar and Hotan. Sleeper buses do run to and from Yining every day (a spectacular 20–24 hour journey through the Heavenly Mountains and the Ili River Valley) when the road is open, but at time of writing (2008) the road was closed for repairs. The bus and train stations are at the eastern end of the new city.

ACCOMMODATION

Kuche International Hotel

Address: Tian Shan Dong Lu. Tel: (0997) 731 1000

The newest hotel in town, this large four-star block is located to the east of town on the main road to Luntai and Korla near to the railway station. Rack rates for rooms start at Rmb688, suites at Rmb1,680, but up to a 40 percent discount is possible.

Kuche Fandian

8 Tian Shan Dong Lu. Tel: (0997) 723 3158; fax: (0997) 713 1160

This pleasant three-star hotel, a few kilometres from the railway station and slightly closer to town than the Kuche International Hotel, is set at the back of its own compound, built around a lake and small orchard. The quiet rooms start from Rmb388, suites from Rmb880.

Qiuci Binguan

93 Tian Shan Xi Lu. Tel: (0997) 712 2005; fax: (0997) 712 4397

Another three-star situated in a compound set back from the main road that leads to the new bridge, with large, clean rooms at reasonable prices. Rooms start at Rmb180, suites from Rmb360.

A statue of Kumarajiva graces the entranceway to the Kizil Caves, once one of Xinjiang's – and Central Asia's – greatest depositories of religious art (Jeremy Tredinnick).

Kucha Hotel (Kuqa Binguan)

17 Jiefang Lu. Tel (0997) 712 2901

The Kucha Hotel is near the junction of Jiefang and Shengli Lu in the northern part of the new city; it has a handicrafts and bookshop, and rooms start at Rmb320.

FOOD AND DRINK

The Friday market in the old city is an orgy of food, fruit and drink. There are various small Uygur restaurants and teahouses that serve laghman, samsa, kebabs and nan. Local farmers stand beside mountains of melons and old market women sell fresh blackberries in natural syrup, which are exquisite when mixed with yoghurt or hand-churned maroji.

The night market area in the new city at the junction of Renmin Lu and Tian Shan Lu has many food stalls selling cold noodles and most other Uygur specialities, including apke, and Uygur restaurants abound. For Sichuan and other Chinese flavours, try the Wenhua Lu area.

AKSU

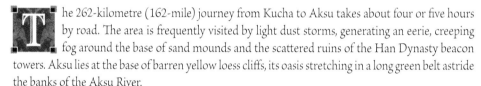

T he 262-kilometre (162-mile) journey from Kucha to Aksu takes about four or five hours by road. The area is frequently visited by light dust storms, generating an eerie, creeping fog around the base of sand mounds and the scattered ruins of the Han Dynasty beacon towers. Aksu lies at the base of barren yellow loess cliffs, its oasis stretching in a long green belt astride the banks of the Aksu River.

Neolithic artefacts from 5000 BCE have been discovered in the Aksu area. By the first century BCE, news reached the Chinese imperial court concerning the **Kingdom of Baluka** (as Aksu was formerly called), one of the 36 kingdoms of the Western Regions. Aided by the Xiongnu, the kingdom held out against a Chinese attack led by General Ban Chao, who finally marched upon the city in 78 CE and executed 700 inhabitants. Xuanzang wrote of the kingdom in 629: "With regard to the soil, climate, character of the people, customs and literature, these are the same as in the country of Qiuci. The language differs however a little. [The kingdom] produces a fine sort of cotton and hair-cloth, which are highly valued by neighbouring countries."

In the mid-14th century, Tughluq (Telug) Timur, Khan of Moghulistan, briefly made his capital in Aksu. Half a century later, an army led by Tamerlane the Great's grandson laid siege to the city, but by delivering the rich Chinese merchants to the troops in an effort to placate the Mongols, the people of Aksu ransomed themselves. Aksu was again the capital of Moghulistan during the reign of Esen-buqa (1429–1462) and a stage for murder and intrigue concerning the succession of the khanate. In the 1860s, Aksu became part of Yakub Beg's mighty state of Kashgaria; the city had joined the anti-Chinese rebellion and, like Kucha, was dominated by Yakub Beg, who maintained a fort on the bluff above the city. The Chinese re-established control a decade later.

ir Francis Younghusband, travelling along the northern Silk Road in the early 1890s, called Aksu "the largest town we had yet seen. It had a garrison of two thousand soldiers, and a native population of about twenty thousand, beside the inhabitants of the surrounding district. There were large bazaars and several inns – some for travellers, others for merchants wishing to make a prolonged stay to sell goods." During the same period, Sven Hedin stayed a few days in Aksu, noting fertile fields of grains, cotton and red opium poppies. Both he and Sir Aurel Stein enjoyed the warmth of local officials' hospitality and the cool of their fruit orchards. A less enchanted European traveller in the 1930s complained that "the swarms of flies are denser [and] the smell more concentrated and ranker than anywhere else", but conceded "there are not many places where the temples are more wonderful or the gardens of the rich Moslems more beautiful."

AKSU PRACTICAL INFORMATION

Han Chinese make up the majority of Aksu's 400,000 residents. The city has grown and modernized in recent years with money from cotton, corn, beet and other agriculture – much as it did as far back as Xuanzang's time – but also now from horticulture and mining, with cement and chemical industries also developing fast. The city is now centred around a multicoloured "flame" statue in People's Square, and another large open square a kilometre down the linking Dongda Lu (East Road). There is little of interest for the modern tourist apart from a cemetery for Muslims killed by Kuomintang soldiers a short way south of People's Square, and the inevitable bazaar.

TRANSPORTATION

There are air connections to Urumqi, Kashgar and Hotan daily. A few buses start from Aksu, but most pass through en route to Kashgar or Korla and Urumqi. The Nanjiang Railway passes through every day both northwards and southwards on its route between Kashgar and Urumqi.

ACCOMMODATION

The **Hongfu Jinlan Hotel** (32 East Road, tel: (0997) 228 3555, fax: (0997) 228 1555, email: jinlan@ hongfuhotel.com, website: www.hongfuhotel.com) on the corner of People's Square, is a surprisingly modern and impressive four-star property owned by the group who run the Hongfu Hotel in Urumqi. Rooms start from Rmb388, suites from Rmb588. A few hundred metres down East Road on the other side of the road is the **Aksu International Hotel** (1 Weng Zhouzhong Lu, tel: (0997) 214 8666, fax: (0997) 214 8000, email: mei28882002@yahoo.com.cn), a somewhat less modern four-star with rooms from Rmb580 and suites from Rmb1,080.

ARAL AND THE DESERT ROAD TO HOTAN

The landscape around Aksu is dominated by cotton fields and, during harvesting, enormous mountains of cotton in storage areas by the roadside. Cotton is planted in March and ready for harvesting by October, when the fields are picked by armies of migrant cotton pickers (90 percent of cotton workers are migrant Han Chinese, who come annually to find work that is in short supply in rural central China). After the first wave of picking, a field is left to rebud, then repicked – two or three harvests can be garnered in this way. The dead plants are cut down and used as fertiliser.

A road leads south from Aksu, running parallel to the Aksu River for 100 kilometres until it reaches the new town of **Aral** (also known as **Alar**) located on the north side of the Tarim River. Aral is also connected to Kucha to the northeast by Highway 217, which in recent years has been extended far beyond its original route from the Altai down through the Junggar Basin and bisecting the Tien Shan on its way to Kucha. This north-south highway now runs to Aral, then turns south and heads across the Taklamakan to finish in Hotan on the desert's southern edge.

Aral is a peculiar town; its People's Square is enormous, lushly green – despite its location on the edge of real desert – and fronted by a huge, gleaming municipal building. The town is home to the Tarim University of Agriculture, dedicated to developing knowledge related to farming in the arid conditions of the Tarim Basin, and boasting students from all over China. Just south of the square on Talinu Dadao Lu (Tarim Great Road) opposite the university's two modern buildings is the **Guangzhou Hotel**, a surprisingly good hotel where a huge deluxe suite can be had for only Rmb150. This six-year-old hotel seems to be waiting for an expected flood of business related to the new cross-desert highway that links it with Hotan and the southern Tarim towns.

South of town a long bridge crosses the Tarim River, which here is very wide, its riverbed fully filled from bank to bank in late spring and summer; in autumn and winter, however, water meanders down it in channels separated by piles of ultra-fine sediment – on windy days Aral must be a very dusty town.

Highway 217's cross-desert section was opened in May 2007, and very roughly follows the course of the Hotan River, which once provided water for caravans that crossed the mighty desert from the Kunlun oases towns to those of Aksu and Kucha. These days, only in years of uncommonly high snowfall in the Kunlun range, when the spring melt releases large volumes of water, does the Hotan River manage to run all its course to meet the Tarim River just west of Aral; in most years it peters out into the sand less than half way across the desert.

In order to prevent the desert sands from smothering it, Highway 217 uses the same ingenious methods of protection as the Tarim Highway far to the east (*see* special topic on page 292). As you drive south, away from the river and into the heart of the Taklamakan, on either side of the road a gridwork of straw squares has been lain for 20–30 metres, flanked by a 1.5-metre-high fence; this stops low-level sand movement. Beyond that the dunes extend beyond sight, not large but uncountable, dotted with ancient diversiform-leaved poplar trees, their gnarled trunks twisted and tortured by the hash environment, but their crowns golden-topped (in autumn).

A desert is often called a "sea of sand"; crossing the Taklamakan on Highway 217 you soon realize it is an ocean rather than a sea. But this is not an ocean of gigantic dunes; to take the water

BLOOD TIES

*A*fter an hour or so, our amiable bantering is interrupted by a loud bang. The Toyota lurches to one side and slows to a halt. All pile out to pinpoint the problem, which is not difficult: we have burst a front tyre, and it seems to have all but shredded itself in the process of stopping. There is silence while this sinks in, then someone remembers the spare wheel behind the back seat. A frenzy of activity breaks out; the stiff is removed from his position on the parcel shelf, and we open up the back of the vehicle. One by one the smiles disappear. There is no spare wheel; it has been left in Korla.

Minutes turn to hours. A lorry passes by, and a couple of army jeeps. One of the jeeps stops and we compare wheels, but they are not the same. Then, suddenly, from the north, we see approaching the unmistakable shape of a Toyota. Wild gesticulations from nine excited figures succeed in bringing it to a halt, and we explain our predicament.

The vehicle is carrying a spare wheel, but the Uyghur driver is reluctant to part with it for less than its full value, which is considerable. We bargain with gusto, offering all sorts of non-essential parts from our own vehicle in an attempt to beat him down. But our efforts are in vain. The man is about to drive off, and I have resigned myself to more waiting, when the conversation takes a surprising turn. His attitude visibly changes as it emerges that one of our passengers is engaged to his cousin. Kinship has been established! Instantly all monetary considerations are swept aside, and the man quickly hands over the precious wheel. Within minutes it has been fitted, hands have been shaken, and once more we are on our way.

John Pilkington, An Adventure on the Old Silk Road, 1989

analogy further, where the Sahara's mighty dunes appear to be the product of a fierce storm, the Taklamakan through which this road runs is more like a choppy sea. There are certainly areas within the Taklamakan where mighty dunes occur, but don't expect to see any on Highway 217. That said, the vista is still beautiful at first, mesmerizing and evocative, but after a few hours it becomes monotonous – what must it have been like for the early traders and explorers, who had to plod slowly through this harsh, sandy ocean week after week with no relief!

Thanks to today's road the trip from Aral to Hotan takes no more than 4–5 hours (caravans routinely took three weeks). A little over half way from north to south, a long, low ridge shows to the west – on top of this is the ancient fortress of **Mazar Tagh** (see page 391). Soon a line of trees in the distance shows where the Hotan River still flows on a regular basis, and the first signs of human habitation appear when you start passing lone men on donkey carts piled high with dead wood foraged from the desert for fuel in the Taklamakan's fringing villages. Fields finally start to appear, bordered by high poplar trees, and the road converges with the river and follows its eastern bank, where men pick their way over the rocks searching for jade. The cross-desert journey is over; you have reached the Southern Silk Road city of Hotan.

AKSU TO KASHGAR

O nce the green poplars of the Aksu oasis are left behind, the yellow void of the gebi reappears. Truckloads of horses, mules and donkeys, and convoys of long-distance buses head towards Kashgar. Ranged along the highway are rocky mountains in startling shades of jade green, red, orange, ochre and maroon. Telephone poles mark the distance. A young Scandinavian traveller on the Urumqi-Kashgar route in the 1930s wrote: "Out in the desert, up on the passes and in the narrow valleys – everywhere lie skeletons and skulls, grinning. Skeletons large and small, piles of bones and solitary femurs. Horse? Camel? Man? It is not easy to decide as you rattle past…" Mirages are common, and so are whirlwinds of sand, like dancing ghosts of the desert.

At the small town of **Sanchakou**, 214 kilometres (133 miles) southwest of Aksu, is a turnoff for **Bachu**, called **Maralbashi** in the records of 19th- and 20th-century European explorers. Sir Aurel Stein traced the wall of a fort and the structures of an extensive city here, both long abandoned. A direct desert route along the Yarkand River linked it with Yarkand (Shache), a journey accomplished by Stein in 1908 in five days.

ARTUSH

Forty kilometres before Kashgar is Artush (Artux), seat of the **Kizilsu Kirghiz Autonomous Prefecture**. Just outside town is the **Tomb of Satuq Bughra Khan**, the first ruler of Kashgar to convert to Islam. Legend tells how, while the young khan was out hunting one day, a hare he was pursuing suddenly transformed itself into a man. This apparition questioned the young man about his Buddhist beliefs and filled him with terror of the sufferings of hell. He convinced Satuq Bughra that by accepting the teachings of the Prophet Mohammed, he would unquestionably go to paradise. The boy unhesitatingly took the vow, and the wars against the Buddhist states of the Southern Silk Road began soon after.

egend aside, in 934 Satuq Bughra Khan did convert to Islam. As told in 12th century historian Jamal Qarshi's *History of Kashgar*, Satuq Bughra was first taught about Islam by Nasr, a wealthy merchant from Bukhara. Nasr was granted special dispensation by the ruler of Kashgar, Satuq's uncle, to build a mosque in the town of Artush. Satuq Bughra would often go there to watch the caravans arrive, and when he saw Nasr and other Muslims observing their daily prayers he became curious and was instructed by them in the Islamic religion. However, when Satuq Bughra's uncle discovered that his nephew had become a Muslim he punished him by forcing him to build a temple. But upon reaching the age of 25, Satuq Bughra overthrew his uncle and established Islam in Kashgar. He died in 955 and was buried in Artush in what must have once been a grand tomb; it was later destroyed in an earthquake, and the present tomb was built in the latter half of the 20th century. The **Sulitanjiamai Mosque**, beside the tomb, has a larger prayer hall and in front is a tree-shaded pool, providing a peaceful, contemplative atmosphere for the old Muslim men who gather here. Artush can be visited as a day trip from Kashgar, but the political sensitivity surrounding Satuq Bughra Khan's status as a venerated Islamic hero can cause problems, and only approved guides may accompany tourists there. There is an entrance fee of Rmb30.

THE KYRGYZ

The **Kizilsu Kirghiz Autonomous Prefecture**'s capital may be Artush, but its eponymous ethnic group live for the large part not in the towns and lowlands of the eastern Tarim Basin (dominated by Uygurs), but in the high mountain fastnesses of the Pamirs, Tien Shan and Kunlun ranges that surround them on three sides. The 120,000 nomadic **Kyrgyz (Kirghiz)** who inhabit these mountains are of Turkic origin, and speak a Turkic-Altaic language. Most Kyrgyz live across the border in Kyrgyzstan. The Kyrgyz were a powerful force in the ninth century, and were responsible for driving the Uygurs southwards from the Yenisey River region; they periodically moved south themselves, via the Zhetisu region of modern-day Kazakhstan, and by the 14th century they occupied their present highland pastures. In the last days of the tsarist empire, Russian peasants encroached on Kyrgyz pasturelands, which led to violent reprisals by both sides, and many Kyrgyz fled across the border into Xinjiang.

In the summer, Kyrgyz herdsmen set up their yurts in pastures 3,700 metres (12,000 feet) above sea level, just below the glacier level; in the winter, quarters are set up in valleys at around 2,700 metres (9,000 feet). Their white yurts, called *ak-ois*, are described by the former British consul in Kashgar, Sir Clarmont Skrine, as "looking like enormous button mushrooms on the wide meadow". The ak-ois are furnished with felt rugs and large reed mats decorated with bold designs of dyed woollen thread.

The Kyrgyz diet is simple and monotonous: curds, milk, sour cream, bread made from flour and mutton fat, sun-dried cheese balls, tea and *kumis* (wine made from fermented mare's milk). This fare is supplemented by hunting and hawking, but livestock is rarely eaten. The killing of a sheep or goat is reserved for special occasions – marriages, funerals and festivals – when feasts of boiled meat are enjoyed.

All Kyrgyz celebrations end in horseracing, wrestling and *buzkashi*, a type of very rough rugby on horseback played with the headless carcass of a sheep or goat. After the animal is slaughtered by a respected elder, a young man, gripping a whip in his mouth, mounts his horse, grabs the sheep and rides off shrieking. Hundreds of riders join in the game, trying to grab the sheep by the feet or any available part of its body. Whoever flings the carcass across the designated finish line is the winner. The Kyrgyz are closely related in custom and culture to Kazakhs.

KASHGAR (KASHI)

ashgar is still – at heart – a medieval city, a vibrant Islamic centre within Chinese territory. It is the largest oasis city in Chinese Central Asia and 70 percent of its population of over 350,000 are Uygur. Kashgar's historical importance derives from its strategic position at the foot of the **Pamir** and **Karakoram** mountain ranges, commanding access to the high glacial passes of the Silk Road routes into Central Asia, India and Persia. The weary trade caravans plodding west from China on the northern and southern routes met up at Kashgar, the desert hazards and demons finally behind them. Merchants bound for China thawed out after descending to Kashgar from the peaks of the Pamirs or the Karakorams, and exchanged their stolid yaks and exhausted packhorses for camels to convey their merchandise into the Kingdom of Cathay.

HISTORY

Kashgar's history spans more than 2,000 years; the earliest references appear in ancient Persian documents referring to an alliance of Tushlan tribes, who founded their capital here. In the first century CE, during the Han Dynasty, China lost its power over the Tarim Basin. The great General Ban Chao was dispatched to subdue the wild kingdoms of the Western Regions that had aligned themselves with the Xiongnu against the Chinese. He took the kingdoms of Kashgar, Khotan and Loulan either by brute force or cunning strategy, installed pro-Chinese rulers and reopened the Southern Silk Road to trade. Ban Chao remained in Chinese Central Asia for 31 years, crushing rebellions and establishing diplomatic relations with more than 50 states in the Western Regions. Accompanied by horsemen arrayed in bright red leather, he himself went as far west as Merv and made contact with Parthia, Babylonia and Syria.

Top: The square in front of the Idkah Mosque now sports periodic fountain displays and is a popular gathering place for both locals and out-of-towners. Bottom: Musicians play for customers in the Orda Palace Uygur restaurant (Jeremy Tredinnick x2).

Kashgar was possibly the first of the Buddhist kingdoms of the Tarim Basin. In the second century CE, Hinayana Buddhism flourished here and continued to do so until the ninth or 10th century. During this period Indian and Persian cultural influences were strong. Xuanzang noted that the Kashgaris had green eyes – perhaps a reference to Aryan origins – and that "for their writing they take their model from India... The disposition of the men is fierce and impetuous, and they are mostly false and deceitful. They make light of decorum and politeness, and esteem learning but little."

n the early seventh century, Kashgar recognized the suzerainty of Tang China, which garrisoned the city. However, the Chinese were soon forced to withdraw between 670 and 694, when Tibet expanded its territories throughout the southern oases of the Tarim Basin. Between the 10th and 12th centuries the **Karakhanid Khanate**, a loose nomadic alliance of the Uygur and Karluk Turkic tribes, controlled the area between Bokhara and Khotan from its capital in Kashgar. The Sunni Muslim, Satuq Bughra Khan, was the first of the Kharakhanid kings of Kashgar; he and his successors carried on bloody jihads against the still-Buddhist kingdoms of Yarkand and Khotan. These battles, along with fierce Kharakhanid internecine struggles, disrupted the caravan trade, and East-West trade was increasingly forced to rely on the sea routes.

Marco Polo wrote in the 13th century that the Kashgaris "have very fine orchards and vineyards and flourishing estates... [but] are very close-fisted and live very poorly... There are some Nestorian Christians in this country, having their own church and observing their own religion."

Following the death of Chaghatai, who inherited the region from his father, Genghis Khan, there followed numerous succession wars. Only briefly during the mid-14th century, when Tughluq (Telug) Timur held power in Kashgar, was a degree of calm and stability restored. But Tamerlane's armies were soon to lay waste to the Kingdom of Kashgaria.

In the 16th century, Kashgar came under the rule of a religious leader, or *khoja*, whose colleagues formed a powerful clique in Bokhara and Samarkand (*see page 61*). A theological split saw the formation of two opposing sects, the Black and White Hats, which began a bloody seesawing of power between Kashgar and Yarkand that ended only with Qing intervention two centuries later. The khojas attempted to return to power in Kashgar no fewer than six times, frequently backed by the Khokand Khanate and aided by Kyrgyz nomadic horsemen, bringing fearful reprisals on the citizens. An unfortunate observer of the khojas' last attempt in 1857 was a German, Adolphus Schlagintweit, whose throat was cut because of his arrogant comment that the three-month siege of Kashgar would have taken his countrymen a mere three days.

Kashgar was substantially fortified during the short but violent reign of **Yakub Beg**, who ruled Kashgaria from 1866 to 1877. This infamous boy dancer-cum-soldier from Khokand ruled most of Xinjiang, from Kashgar to Urumqi, Turpan and Hami, concluded treaties with Britain and Russia, and had the support of the Ottoman Empire. He was rumoured to have 300 wives and presided over a lavish court. In 1869, Robert Shaw, a British trader and unofficial diplomat, became the first Englishman to visit Yarkand and Kashgar, and was able to command two audiences with Yakub Beg, even though he was under virtual house arrest for the duration of his stay in the city. He wrote of Kashgar: "Entering the gateway, we passed through several large quadrangles whose sides were lined with rank upon rank of brilliantly attired guards, all sitting in solemn silence so that they seemed to form part of the architecture of the building... Entire rows of these men [were] clad in silken robes and many seemed to be of high rank judging from the richness of their equipment." After a leisurely three-year advance on Chinese Turkestan, the 60,000-strong Qing army of **Zuo Zongtang** suppressed the Muslim rebellions in Gansu and then moved southwest through the oasis towns, eventually ending Yakub Beg's rule in 1877. Yakub Beg died suddenly in Korla – rumoured to have either had a stroke or been poisoned by local leaders conspiring with the Qing. Gunnar Jarring, a Swedish diplomat and scholar who spent some months in the city in 1929, described it thus:

> The city of Kashgar was surrounded by a massive wall about ten metres high and built of sun-dried brick with mud filling in the spaces between. On top it was wide enough for a two-wheeled cart. Communication with the outside world was through four great gates which were closed at dusk and reopened at sunrise. Inside the walls were bazaars, the large mosques, and dwellings for both rich and poor. The Chinese authorities were outside the walls, as were the British and Russian consulates, and the Swedish mission with its hospital and other welfare establishments. Outside there was green nature, sunshine and light; inside it was always half dark.

As anti-Chinese Muslim rebellions broke out throughout Xinjiang in the 1930s, a pan-Turkic Islamic movement based in Kashgar declared an Independent Muslim Republic of Eastern Turkestan. Its flag (a white field emblazoned with a crescent moon and a star) flew over the walled city for two months in 1933. Chinese troops from Urumqi, aided by Russians, moved south in pursuit of Ma Zhongying and his rebel army. Ma held out at the Yangi Hissar (New Town) fortress of Kashgar for six months before mysteriously disappearing across the Soviet border in a truck he commandeered from the Swedish explorer, Sven Hedin.

Kashgar Prefecture administers 11 counties with a population of over 3.5 million. It is one of the main agricultural areas of Xinjiang, producing cotton, rice, wheat, corn, beans and fruit. However, in 2010 it was designated a Special Economic Development Zone, and the Kashgar city government is actively courting investment from abroad to develop it as a regional trading hub and a modern city modelled on special economic zones like Shenzhen near Hong Kong.

SIGHTS

Kashgar is the heart of Uygur Islam in China. Despite the many modern façades now appearing with increasing regularity throughout the town, arriving in this fabled city is still like a step back in time to an ancient Central Asian khanate; the traditional rhythms of the traders, worshippers and bakers seem unchanged amidst the mud-brick walls, horse carts and bazaars of the Old City, even though it is encircled by Russian-style administrative buildings erected in the 1950s and low concrete boxes from the 1960s and 1970s. Today the building vogue is for new apartment blocks, and increasingly large parts of the town are starting to look like a standard Chinese city. The much-publicised razing

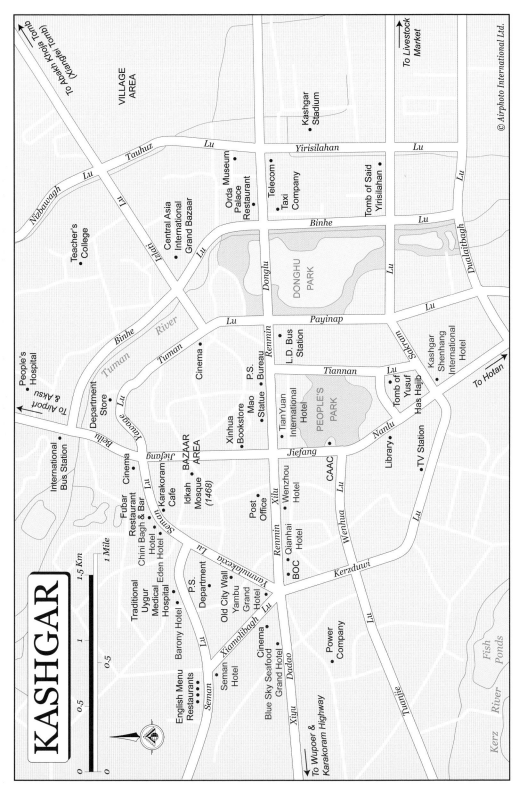

of large sections of the old Uygur part of the city that began in 2009 caused widespread outrage within various international circles, but as ever in Xinjiang the reality of the situation is far from black and white. Chinese officials insist they are bringing benefits to Uygurs by building new apartment complexes for them to replace unsafe, earthquake-prone mud-walled homes; in turn, Uygurs claim this is a deliberate attempt to undermine their heritage and culture. Politics aside, from a purely tourist-oriented viewpoint this translates to a diminishing of the "old Silk Road" atmosphere that is Kashgar's primary appeal.

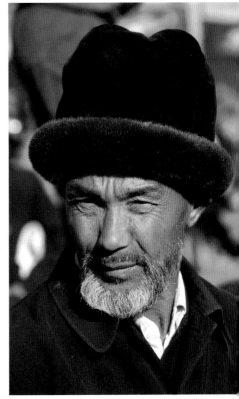

A carefully groomed Uygur presents a calculating but inscrutable face in a Kashgar market (Jeremy Tredinnick).

What is clear is that as the debate rages on, the rift between the two cultures is becoming more manifest in the city. The crossroads of Renmin Lu and Jiefang Lu is known locally as the "big cross" – it marks the border between the predominantly Uygur area to the north and the "department store and fast food" Chinese area to the south. An 18-metre-high (59-foot) steel-reinforced statue of Chairman Mao dominates Kashgar's main east-west street and People's Square. It is said to be the largest Mao statue in China – a symbolic fact given its position in the country's westernmost major city.

The heart of the Old City remains the **Idkah Mosque**, and the surrounding bazaar and alleys that extend east and west of it. Here, you can still see silversmiths, bootmakers, metalworkers and bakers labouring, and numerous teashops and stores selling jewellery, silk, and handsome wooden chests overlaid with strips of tin. In the remaining residential quarters high walls protect small courtyards encircled by two-storey houses with carved wooden balconies, window shutters and doorways executed in classical Uygur style.

You will rarely see a bare head here; a Uygur's head attire is a kind of fashion statement, and a wide variety of head coverings are available, including skull caps, prayer caps and fur-lined caps, as well as brown veils and colourful silk scarves for the women. Most older men tend to keep an extremely clean look; barbers set up throughout the bazaar and shave faces and scalps with an assortment of knives. The position of the cap or hat is also very important in achieving the desired carefree effect. Dress is conservative and meant to cover the entire body: long sleeves and pants for the men, dresses and stockings for the women. Wearing long brown veils over their heads to avoid exposure, the older women float by enigmatically.

KASHGAR THROUGH THE SEASONS

Diana Shipton was the wife of Eric Shipton, the last British Consul-General assigned to Kashgar from 1946 to 1948. The Kashgar of 60 years ago was far more remote a destination than today – where international tourists and business people now number in the tens of thousands annually, during their two years living in the oasis city, the Shiptons received no more than seven foreign visitors.

Before we reached Kashgar Eric and I had discussed the problem of how I should use my time in a place where there were no friends, no organized entertainments and very few obligations. With endless, empty days stretching ahead it is fatally easy to fritter away the time. Quite contentedly, and unnoticed, the days fade past with nothing accomplished. So we both set ourselves a mild routine and eventually became so attached to it that we resented any outside interference.

The day began with an hour's walk before breakfast. Later Eric bought a pony and I walked alone. We nearly always went the same way – down to the winding river, through the fields, past the groups of busy water-mills and back in a complete circle. The intial effort of getting up was always unpleasant, but once we were out it seemed worth the struggle. We followed the gradual change of the seasons and crops. On winter mornings we got up in the dark; the frozen earth, the bare trees, the bluffs of crumbling loess, all presented a uniform dust coloured picture. There were no evergreens in Kashgar and there was nothing to relieve the monotone except the gleam of the river and the frozen streams. Then the sun rose and for a short time flooded the scene with colour. In spite of the bleakness I enjoyed the winter walks. There was the sudden flurry of a wild duck from the river; the clouds of steam rising from the water as if it were boiling; the fantastic shapes of ice hanging from bridges and trees; and ice coating the mills with heavy patterns.

With the coming of spring, in March, there was a beauty more exciting than that of an English spring because of its suddenness and much greater contrast. The fruit trees broke into delicate pinks and whites. The willow trees, lining all the streams became a mist of subtle green. Looking down on the scene from our terrace, we watched this light mist develop into stronger colours, followed later by the tall slender poplars coming into leaf. In the fields we traced the wheat, cotton, rice, melons and tall ungainly maize through the seasons.

The melons were an important crop; they were larger, sweeter and more varied than I had ever dreamed of. The owners often slept out in the fields to guard their property; as I passed early on summer mornings I could see figures still fast asleep on their beds or on high platforms. After the harvest the fruit was stored underground and lasted almost until the small spring melons were ready once more.

Following the melons and the wheat, came the brilliant green of the rice fields standing deep in water. Then gradually, all the crops were harvested, only stubble was left and we were back to the bare brown of winter.

Diana Shipton, The Antique Land, 1950

The Sunday Bazaar and Livestock Market

Kashgar's markets are quintessentially Central Asian, a cacophony of colour, sound and smells on a scale found nowhere else in Xinjiang or any other Central Asian city. On Sundays, thousands of farmers driving carts flock from the countryside to the great Kashgar bazaar around Izlati Lu, east of the Tuman River. Officially named the **Central Asia International Grand Bazaar at Kashgar**, this enormous building has numerous entrance gates demarcating the many sections within the market: silk and cotton in aidelaixi patterns, knives, hats, pots and pans, fresh vegetables, mountains of stacked Hami and Xiang (fragrant) melons, heaps of dried fruits, baskets of peaches and apricots...

nside, the stalls are orderly; the lanes closest to the main entrances are filled with stalls selling tourist souvenirs such as knives, cheap musical instruments and the like. Farther back, the warren of alleys is packed with everyday items, from bolts of cloth and carpets to stoves and saucepans. There are many tourists, of course, but this is very much a working market for Kashgaris and indeed folk from much farther afield – you will see Uzbeks, Tajiks, Azerbaijanis, Russians and Turkish traders and shoppers here.

The overflow of people spills into the surrounding streets and wasteland, where uncured sheepskins, Karakul lambskins, boiled and dyed eggs, red twig baskets, glazed jars and water ewers, felt carpets, coloured cut-glass jewellery and fresh meat can all be found at makeshift stalls. Beyond these, horse and donkey carts jostle with each other, carrying people to and from the market, and shows of acrobats and magicians attract large crowds of shoppers.

Throughout the chaotic Sunday market are stalls selling noodles, poluo, samsa, boiled hunks of mutton and piles of fresh nan, yoghurt and maroji. To the loud cries from enthusiastic traders is added "*posh! posh!*", which means "get out of the way!" Those who ignore it risk being run down by a cart loaded with yellow carrots or freshly slaughtered sheep.

The livestock and horse section of the weekly market, which once added to the spectacle at the Sunday Market site, was moved six kilometres southeast of the city a number of years ago, and in October 2011 was relocated once again to nearby Hangdi village. The **Livestock Market** starts at dawn, when traders begin to bring the animals in – some walk in under their own steam, but these days trucks are often used to transport much of the stock to market. An entrance fee must be paid, and this gives access to a huge walled-in area of dust and stones perhaps two football pitches in size. Around the edge near the two entrances, stalls are set up selling horse tack, food and drinks, but everywhere else wooden posts are lined with yaks, cows, bulls, camels, fat-tailed sheep, goats, donkeys (with or without carts) and horses, all for sale at the right price.

By 1pm the market ground is heaving; dust is everywhere, and battling your way through the chaos can be almost claustrophobic – watch out for kicking camels or donkeys. Heated negotiations develop over purchases, and these are usually refereed by a middleman, the deal finally being sealed with a handshake and exchange of money. At the far end of the market area, where the crowd thins out, horsemen ride their mounts back and forth to show their worth, while small groups of potential buyers stroke their beards inscrutably, eying up each steed in turn. Like the Sunday Market in town, the Livestock Market spreads far outside the main arena, with fruit and vegetables laid out on the road, and men pulling lone sheep around trying to find a buyer. In all the heat and dust, a fresh slice of Hami melon is a godsend, sweet and refreshing, or if a small snack is needed try a bagel – both cost only Rmb2, and will invigorate you as you return for one last look at the pulsating crush of man and beast inside.

IDKAH MOSQUE

The Idkah Mosque is the largest mosque in China and the most holy site for Muslims in Xinjiang. Facing east across the Idkah Square, it is the religious and cultural centre of Kashgar – an average of 2,000–3,000 faithful come here to pray every day, and on Fridays this number rises to around 6,000–7,000. It was built in 1442 on the site of an ancient cemetery, but was damaged and rebuilt many times through the centuries until 1955, when it underwent a final extensive renovation.

The entire complex measures 140 metres from north to south and 120 metres from east to west, an area of 16,800 square metres. It consists of a Hall of Prayer, a Doctrine Teaching Hall, the Gate Tower, two ponds, a shady, 1.33-hectare poplar-lined inner garden and a few auxiliary structures. The yellow-and-white façade of the tall, rectangular entrance gate is a beautiful example of Uygur architecture; it is 4.7 metres high and 4.3 metres wide, and its two graceful minarets are 15 metres high topped by bronze crescent moons. Enter through this doorway and you must pass through the peaceful garden to get to the main prayer hall, which is held up by 140 round wooden columns carved in elaborate flower patterns and painted predominantly green.

Muslims come from far and wide to worship here, many dressed in traditional *chapans* (three-quarter-length coats of striped cotton), embroidered dopas and knee-length leather boots. Although the surrounding square is bordered by new shops and stalls, and a large fountain periodically shoots water 10 metres into the air right in front of the mosque in the afternoons, these signs of modernity do not stop veiled women and young children from standing outside the mosque in time-honoured fashion, holding teapots of water or pieces of nan in cloth. As the men stream out from prayers they bestow on these items their holy breath or spit, thereby blessing them; they will then be taken to feed a sick relative.

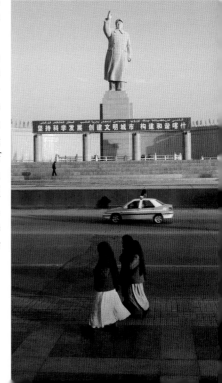

Right: The huge statue of Chairman Mao looks down on People's Square in downtown Kashgar (Jeremy Tredinnick). Opposite: Modern Kashgar architecture shows Islamic elements and styles consistent with traditional buildings still found in the Old City behind the Idkah Mosque (top, Magnus Bartlett; bottom, Jeremy Tredinnick).

At the time of the Korban Festival, 20,000–30,000 pilgrims fill the mosque, the square in front of it and surrounding streets; they kneel as one to pray, and afterwards the square is filled with singing and dancing – this is one of the liveliest places to be in Xinjiang during this special occasion for Uygurs.

n 2001 the Idkah Mosque was made a State Protection Site of Historical Relics. Entrance costs Rmb20. The old town streets south of the Idkah Mosque have been redeveloped in the last few years, with new Islamic-style façades going up all around, primarily for shopping and tourism ventures – the Kashgar Folk Custom Museum and the "Eidgah Folk Custom and Cultural Science Spot Visitor Service Centre" are just two examples. Faux "old" buildings now stand on either side of the mosque, but though some may baulk at this nod to commercialism, the overall effect is not at all unpleasant, and it only takes a minute's walk into the old town behind the mosque or across Jiefang Lu to find entirely authentic alleyways where mud-brick houses and old shops redolent with history still exist.

ABAKH KHOJA'S TOMB

Located five kilometres northeast of the city centre, this mazar (more commonly referred to as "Apakh Hoja") is the holiest place in Xinjiang for Sufis, and an architectural treasure. Built in 1640, it is reminiscent of the Central Asian artistic style of Samarkand or Isfahan. The mausoleum building is the largest dome-roofed structure in Xinjiang – its green-tiled dome is 17 metres in diameter and 26 metres high, with no support pillars within the spacious interior.

A COMMON LANGUAGE

I am still hurrying to the mosque when a dark, narrow shop, with caps of all kinds displayed by its doorway, catches my eye. I stop: I will need a cap to protect myself in Tibet from the rays of the sun. The interior of the shop is dingy. A sewing machine is clattering anciently away. Moons of cloth, strips of plastic, bobbins of thread, circles of cardboard lie on the floor, or on shelves, or hang from nails in the door. An old, bespectacled, bearded man, sharp-featured and dark, sits inside the shop talking in Uyghur to a boy of about twelve. When I enter, he addresses me in Uyghur. I shrug my shoulders. He repeats his sentence, but louder this time.

"I don't understand," I say in Chinese.

He understands this, but not much more, in Chinese. "Hussain!" he calls out in a thin and authoritarian voice.

Hussain, who must have learned Chinese at school, asks me what I want.

"A cap. Maybe one of those," I say, pointing at blue cloth caps hanging by the door. "How much are these?"

The boy speaks to the old man, who holds up three fingers.

"Three yuan. Are you travelling through here? Where are you from?"

"Yes," I answer, as I try on a couple for size. "I'm from India. This one fits. I'll buy this one." I take out a five yuan note.

"Yindu!" exclaims the boy. He exchanges a few excited words with the old man, who peers at me over his spectacles in annoyed disbelief. The boy runs out of the shop.

"Yes, Yindu. Hindustan," I say, hoping to convince the old man. In a flash of inspiration, I pull out my pen and write "Hindustan" on the palm of my hand, in Urdu.

The old man readjusts his spectacles, catches hold of my wrist tightly and peers at the writing. Urdu and Uyghur share the Arabic script; as he reads it his face lights up.

"Ah, Hindustan! Hindustan!" This is followed by a smiling salvo of Uyghur. He hands me three yuan in change.

"But the cap costs three yuan," I say, handing him back the extra yuan, and raising three fingers.

He refuses to take it, and I refuse to do him out of a yuan. Suddenly, with an exasperated gesture, he grabs the cap from off my head and begins to rip it apart. I am horrified. What is he doing? What have I done? Have I insulted him by refusing his gift? Fifteen young boys suddenly appear at the door with Hussain at their head. They gather at the open entrance in a jigsaw of heads and gaze unblinkingly at the man from India. They are all speaking at once, and I am even more concerned and confused than before.

The old man shouts "Hussain!" There is silence in the shop. He then fires rapid sentences off at me, which the boy translates.

"My father says he will make the stitching firmer for you because you will be travelling a long way."

With a few strong pulls of the needle and a few minutes at the sewing machine, the old man, now intent on his work and paying me not the slightest attention, stretches and stitches the cap into a tougher form. With a restrained smile, and a faint snort of satisfaction, he stands up to put it back on my head, gently, and adjusts it to the correct angle. He says a few more words, but I am too moved by his kindness to think of asking Hussain for a translation. As I nudge past the fifteen spectators at the door, I turn to say "salaam aleikum," knowing that he will understand this.

Vikram Seth, From Heaven Lake, 1983

Clockwise from top left: Goats stand tethered together at the Livestock Market (Jeremy Tredinnick); Uygurs set up shop on the streetside, hoping to sell homegrown melons (A Gai/Odyssey); testing a pony and cart at the Livestock Market before the bargaining begins; inside the Sunday Bazaar the negotiations for bolts of colourful silk can be just as protracted (Sun Jiabin x2).

In the 17th century, **Abakh Khoja** was the powerful ruler of Kashgar, Korla, Kucha, Aksu, Khotan and Yarkand. A leader of the White Hat Sect of Islam, he was revered as a prophet. The site was originally donated to Abakh's father, Yusup, a respected Muslim missionary who had travelled in Arabia and returned a greatly respected teacher of the Koran. Yusup set up his religious school here, and the mausoleum was built for him. But his son's fame was greater, and after Abakh's death in 1693 the tomb was renamed after him. All five generations of the family are buried within. There were 72 tombs until a 19th-century earthquake partially destroyed the tomb and it had to be rebuilt – now only 58 remain, lying on a raised platform and covered in colourful cloth.

Arriving at the tomb complex, the parking area is surrounded by a peaceful lily pond lined by poplar trees and a number of souvenir shops. The relatively small but beautiful front gate is inlaid with blue-glazed tiles with a white flower pattern. Passing through the gate a small mosque is on your left, fronted by a high platform with an intricately flower-patterned ceiling. The impressive domed mausoleum stands in its own walled compound with flowerbeds in front of its south-facing entrance; it is 35 metres wide by 29 metres deep, and covered entirely by green glazed tiles of varying shades.

To the west of the tomb is the **Jaman Mosque**, built in 1873 and still used on Fridays and special occasions, and the Doctrine Teaching Hall where religious lessons once took place. To the east is a large graveyard, where, it is said, Yakub Beg was brought and buried in an unmarked grave. The graves are coffin-shaped, above ground and made of packed mud. Many have a small hole in them that allows the soul of the dead to travel. Among the many devotees attracted to the mazar are women who come to pray for a child; they tie strings of coloured cloth – black, white and blue for a boy; red and floral for a girl – to one of the window frames. During the Korban Festival, Muslims from all over Xinjiang make the pilgrimage to the tomb.

The mausoleum is also known as the **Tomb of the Fragrant Concubine**. This refers to a legend that a descendant of Abakh Khoja, a lady named Yiparhan, was chosen to be one of the Qing emperor Qianlong's concubines, and was sent to Beijing. This lady was renowned for emitting a beautiful fragrance like a delicate flower, and she was thus known as Xiangfei, or Fragrant Imperial Concubine. When she died, her body was returned to Kashgar and interred at the mausoleum – it is said that the camel sedan chair inside the tomb is the very one that brought her home. Unfortunately, careful research has shown that Xiangfei was in fact Rongfei, another of Qianlong's concubines, and she was buried in Hebei Province. Entrance to the tomb complex costs Rmb30.

THE BRITISH AND RUSSIAN CONSULATES

The old **British Consulate** (**Chini Bagh**) was the home for 26 years of the most famous of British India's representatives in Kashgar, Sir George Macartney and his wife. The Macartneys' legendary hospitality was extended to weary foreign travellers on the Silk Road, including Sir Aurel Stein, Albert von Le Coq, Sven Hedin, Peter Fleming and Ella Maillart. Until 1948, its gates were guarded by turbaned soldiers of the Gilgit Scouts. Life at Chini Bagh is delightfully recalled in *An English Lady in Chinese Turkestan* by Lady Macartney, and *The Antique Land* by Diana Shipton, wife of the last

British Consul-General. The gardens were destroyed to make room for a large tourist hotel, behind which the house where the Macartneys lived still stands, somewhat the worse for wear; part of that building is now a restaurant, and part is available for rent through the Chini Bagh Hotel (although basic and neither a cheap nor comfortable option).

The once luxurious **Russian Consulate** (now the Seman Hotel) was the home of the powerful Nikolai Petrovsky, Macartney's chief adversary in the Great Game. During the years they were stoically positioned at this desolate outpost, the two consuls carried on an almost comic rivalry for political secrets as well as for antiquities dug up in the ancient buried cities of the desert. It is said that the extremely volatile Petrovsky did not speak a word to Macartney between November 1899 and June 1902. The consulate building, though now a rather run-down hotel, nevertheless still retains a faded grandeur in its large lobby, wide staircases and high-ceilinged rooms, and is worth a visit.

Tomb of Yusuf Has Hajib

usuf Has Hajib (also known as Yusuf Balasaguni) was an 11th-century Uygur poet, scholar and thinker originally from the city of Balasaghun (in today's Kyrgyzstan), the capital of the Karakhanid Empire. He moved to Kashgar, and wrote the *Kutadgu Bilig* (The Knowledge of Happiness), a masterpiece of compact rhyming, profound thought and philosophy. About 50 years old when he completed this work, Yusuf Has Hajib presented it to the prince of Kashgar, who awarded him with the title Khass Hajib, or Senior Advisor. When he died in 1085 at the age of 66, he was buried in Badige, outside the city of Kashgar. His tomb was moved to its present site when it was threatened by flooding from the Tuman River, and is now located on the grounds of the Twelfth Elementary School in the south of the city. Entrance costs Rmb30.

Kashgar Practical Information

Business hours can vary, but as a point of reference, the Bank of China usually closes for lunch 1:30–3:30pm in winter, and 1–4pm in summer, Beijing time. (Despite its location several time zones behind Beijing, the central government runs all of China on Beijing time. Much of Xinjiang, and Kashgar in particular, runs on an unofficial "Xinjiang time" that is two hours behind Beijing time, in order to make full use of daylight hours. This can be confusing to the traveller, so make sure you double-check all arrangements made regarding time schedules, to ensure you're not two hours early, or worse, two hours late!) Internet cafés are now booming throughout the city. A large one with 50 terminals is located 200 metres south of the Chini Bagh Hotel on the other side of the road. It charges low rates, but you must show your passport to get a login card, and a better option these days is to use Western-style establishments like the nearby Karakoram Café, which offer free wifi.

Transportation

In winter there are a minimum of two flights a day to/from Urumqi, while in summer frequencies can be up to five flights a day (Hainan Air, Shanghai Airlines and China Southern), and there are also regular flights to other Xinjiang cities such as Hotan, Kucha and Korla. At time of print there were no

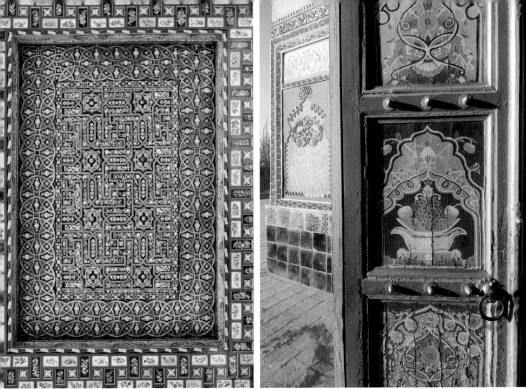

Clockwise from top left: Dawn lights up the many-coloured tiles of Abakh Khoja's Tomb; intricate ceiling painting in the Hall of Prayer within the Idkah Mosque; lush fruits colour the main door at Abakh Khoja's Tomb (Jeremy Tredinnick x3); musicians play merrily from the roof of the Idkah Mosque during the Korlan Festival (Sun Jiabin); giving alms is one of the Five Pillars of Islam; a modern Islamic-style building just south of the Idkah Mosque (Jeremy Tredinnick x2).

international flights to/from Kashgar, although a twice-weekly service between Urumqi and Islamabad that transited in Kashgar has operated in the past and may be restarted, while the Kashgar government is working hard to develop direct flights to major Chinese cities other than Urumqi, as well as direct international flights to Central Asian countries and beyond. A direct charter flight between Hong Kong and Kashgar is due to begin operation in late 2012.

Three trains per day operate to/from Urumqi, all running through Turpan Junction: K9786/K9787 leaves Urumqi at 9:50am and takes 26.5 hours; train 7556/7557 leaves at 12pm and arrives in Kashgar at 7:42pm (32 hours); and the new Urumqi-Kashgar-Hotan train (5826/5827) leaves Urumqi at 8:48am, arriving in Kashgar at 10:40am the next day (26 hours) and Hotan at 8pm after that.

BORDER CROSSINGS

he **Torugart Pass** is the most northerly of two passes connecting the Kashgar region to Kyrgyzstan. This is the quickest and smoothest way to Naryn (single day) and Bishkek (overnight trip), but you must arrange private transport through a tour agency, as the public bus is available only to Kyrgyz and Chinese citizens. The pass is closed on weekends and Chinese public holidays (eg May and October holiday weeks).

The **Irkeshtam Pass** to the south is an easier option; a weekly public bus is available through to the town of Osh. Private transport can also be arranged, but it is significantly more expensive for individual travellers. This pass is also closed on weekends and Chinese public

THE SILVER SCREEN

*A*t the Kashgar Odeon (or whatever name it went by) two films were currently being shown. One was advertised by pictures of the familiar "Happy Peasant" variety, and that film might well have been about manure collectors. But there was no mistaking the second film. It was Dr No. We bought two tickets and went inside. The film had just begun.

The auditorium was not large by English standards, but was packed full. The audience consisted entirely of Uigur men and all were in a great state of excitement. It seemed not to matter that very few had seats, and had to sit on a floor glazed with spittle. Going to the cinema was clearly a great treat, and everyone was determined to enjoy themselves whether or not conditions were perfect, indeed whether they could see or hear anything at all. I assume this because the Uigurs can in fact have understood almost nothing of what was going on. The film had been dubbed out of its original English, not into Turki but into French, which cannot have aided comprehension greatly. And, although there were subtitles, this also did not greatly help. The Uigur subtitles were placed at the bottom of the frame, beneath those in Tibetan and Chinese, and because of a technical error in the projecting box, all of these had disappeared below the screen and now rested on the backs of the heads of the people in the front two rows. This same error also deprived Sean Connery and Joseph Wiseman of their heads, which were projected beyond the screen and could just be seen, along with everything else from the top of the frame, wildly distorted at the front of the hall.

Despite all these irritations, the Uigurs were tolerant. There was an excited murmur every time a character bent down and his face could be fleetingly glimpsed on the screen, and the Muslim audience behaved with remarkable restraint during the sex scenes. Even Ursula Andress coming out of the sea, enough to craze the most worldly-wise Western audience, failed to move the Uigurs to any really dramatic behaviour, although this may have been because none of the audience had ever seen the sea (Kashgar is further from it than any other town in the world) and so were distracted from the more inflammatory aspects of the sequence. It may also have had something to do with the fact that the more inflammatory parts of Ursula Andress's body had missed the top of the screen and could only be seen indistinctly (if hugely enlarged) on the far wall.

There was, in fact, only one scene in the film which really impressed the Uigurs. This was when James Bond wakes up to find a large and very hairy tarantula crawling up his crotch and making for his torso. There cannot be many tarantulas in Kashgar, but the audience still got the gist of what was happening. They went berserk. As the spider crawled upwards the background murmur in the cinema got louder and louder. At the moment Bond tossed the beast off his chest and onto the floor, crushing it with his shoe, the cinema exploded. The Uigurs rose from their seats and bawled "Allah-i-Akbar" (God is all powerful). A very old man next to me took off his shoe and started thumping the floor with it. Hats were thrown in the air. Urchins made wolf whistles. It was like the winning goal in the Cup Final. After that, even the twenty-megaton nuclear explosion in the SPECTRE headquarters came as a bit of an anticlimax.

William Dalrymple, In Xanadu, 1989

holidays. There are persistent rumours that the **Kulma (Qolma) Pass** into Tajikistan will soon open to tourist traffic, but as of this book's publishing the pass – up a road off the Karakoram Highway just before Tashkurgan – is open to Tajiks and Uygurs only. There are always plans to open it to tourists "next year", but given this area's military sensitivity, there are no guarantees.

A daily bus departs from Kashgar to Sost (Sust), in Pakistan, via the **Khunjerab Pass**, although it is sometimes cancelled if there are not enough passengers. Private transport can also be arranged from Kashgar to Sost, Gilgit and/or Islamabad. The pass is officially closed from 31 October until 1 May, although the actual dates of opening are of course subject to the unpredictable weather conditions.

Strictly speaking, the route from **Yecheng** (Kharghalik) to **Tibet** by public transport is illegal for foreigners, but many do make it. A 4WD and driver can be organised through travel services in Kashgar, but it's not a trip for the budget traveller, costing up to US$2,000 just for passage to Ali. Travellers entering Tibet this way will need to pay a "fine" upon arriving in Ali.

ACCOMMODATION

Kashgar's hotel scene is finally shaking off its "run-down colonial" reputation, though the Chini Bagh and Seman Hotel are still going strong and worth considering for atmosphere alone. However, there are now better hotel options, more in keeping with the increasingly sophisticated requirements of many of today's Central Asian travellers. However, claims of being "four star" should sometimes be taken with a pinch of salt: service quality, maintenance of rooms and general staff attitudes can leave many guests frustrated or infuriated – even at the more expensive hotels – so be prepared .

TianYuan International Hotel

8 Renmin Dong Lu. Tel: (0998) 280 1111; fax: (0998) 280 2266

A gleaming four-star hotel located diagonally opposite the Chairman Mao statue on People's Square, and just five minutes south of the Idkah Mosque. A favourite of tour groups. Rooms from Rmb680.

The Barony Tarim Petroleum Hotel

224 Seman Lu. Tel: (0998) 258 6888; email: txn@baronyhotels.com; website: http://kashgartarim. baronyhotels.com

A foreign-owned four-star hotel with refreshingly clean, understated décor set in expansive grounds. Rooms from Rmb880, suites from Rmb1,680 (discounts possible out of season).

Kashgar Shenhang International Hotel

348 Jiefang Nan Lu. Tel: (0998) 256 8888

A new four-star, opened in 2011, that also gets good reviews from tour groups. Prices are similar to the TianYuan International Hotel (US$60–80).

Yambu Grand Hotel

West Region Square (corner of Yunmulakexia Lu). Tel: (0998) 258 8888; fax: (0998) 258 8882

A 128-room, Chinese-style four-star hotel boasting in-room internet and friendly service. Rooms start at Rmb330.

Chini Bagh Hotel (Wa-ke Binguan)

144 Seman Lu. Tel: (0998) 298 2103; fax: 298 2299

Located on the site of the former British Consulate a few minutes' walk from the Idkah Mosque, this is the best-known hotel in Kashgar. The old two-star building's rooms have been upgraded to three-star, but there is a cheaper hostel area too. Part of the original consulate building around the back of the complex can be rented, but it's expensive and rather basic. Three-star rooms start at Rmb300–400. However, in 2011 many guests complained of relentless construction noise as a new high-rise hotel is being built in the grounds, so check up-to-date internet feedback before booking.

Seman Hotel (Lao Binguan)

337 Seman Lu. Tel: (0998) 255 2129, 255 2147; fax: 255 2861

This three-star hotel in the former Russian Consulate is located 10–15 minutes' walk from the Old City. Currently a little run down, but the good food, faded splendour and helpful Info Centre keep it well frequented. Prices are similar or slightly lower than the Chini Bagh.

Blue Sky Seafood Grand Hotel

148 Xiyu Dadao (next to Law Courts). Tel: (0998) 290 0999/0888

A cheaper alternative to the Seman or Chini Bagh, but the quiet, clean air-conditioned rooms are of a similar standard. Double rooms with ensuite bathrooms start at Rmb120. No English is spoken but the staff are friendly.

Eden Hotel

148 Seman Lu. Tel: (0998) 266 4444; website: www.xjeden.com

A new 83-room business hotel close to the Chini Bagh with cheap, clean rooms for about Rmb200. Its restaurant serves good Turkish, international and Uygur food and Eden Coffee Shop has great fresh-brewed coffee and hookah pipes for those who like to indulge this Middle Eastern passion.

FOOD AND DRINK

One of Kashgar's top Uygur restaurants is the **Orda Palace** (167 Renmin Dong Lu, tel: (0998) 265 2777) just east of the Tuman River. Ornate and filled with local colour, it bustles with wealthy businessmen, families and tour groups; a small group of musicians entertain diners, and the open kitchen draws fascinated tourists to watch their food being prepared. While expensive by local standards, and very much part of the tour group itinerary, this is still an authentic establishment – and the food is excellent.

Small family-run Uygur restaurants are everywhere, serving spicy kebabs and nan, samsa, noodles, mutton and fresh vegetables. Stalls in the bazaar serve local specialities such as chickpeas (garbanzo beans) and potatoes in a hot chilli oil sauce. The **Uygur Teahouse and Restaurant**, located just east of the mosque at a busy intersection, serves pots of chai, laghman and chuchure eaten with a large wooden spoon. Spend a cool afternoon on the second-storey balcony watching the chaotic street market scene below. There are several Chinese restaurants with English menus opposite the Seman Hotel. Durap and maroji are popular on hot summer days.

For a change in flavour, try the **Pakistani Café** (50 metres northeast of Chini Bagh), where friendly Ugyurs serve excellent Pakistani cuisine. In the morning (afternoon, Beijing time), many of the Pakistani traders congregate for a leisurely breakfast of sweet milk tea, scrambled eggs and *prata*, fried dough dipped in sugar; a typical midday meal consists of chapatis with chicken or mutton curry, and fresh yoghurt served with a small plate of tomatoes, cucumbers and onions. If you crave Western food, **John's Café** in the grounds of the Seman Hotel is a good place to relax and chat with other travellers. The **Karakoram Café** (87 Seman Lu, opposite the Chini Bagh Hotel), has filled the gap created by the demise of the once popular Caravan Café, offering a selection of good pizza, homemade sandwiches, spaghetti, soups, breakfasts, takeaways and Korean *Kim Bab* (sushi) and *Bi Bim Bab* (Korean beef and vegetable rice). (Both the Karakoram Café and John's Café also provide travel information services, assistance in planning, organizing and booking trips – and free wifi.)

The latest newcomer is **Fubar**, a relaxed restaurant-bar right next door to the Chini Bagh Hotel, with Western food, foreign beer, free wifi, plenty of books and a pool table.

Around Kashgar

Three Immortals Buddhist Caves (Sanxian Dong)

The turn-off for these caves is close to the 10-kilometre (six-mile) mark along Wuqia Lu, northwest of Kashgar. After following the track for three kilometres (two miles) along the south side of the Qiakmakh River, the three caves are visible, hewn from the cliff face some 10 metres (30 feet) above the riverbed. Dating from the second or third centuries CE, they are the earliest Buddhist caves extant in China. Each has two chambers, and traces of wall paintings survive in the left-hand cave. The caves are virtually inaccessible, especially at high-water periods. However, if you are intent upon seeing them, arrangements must be made with CITS and the fire department, as they are the only ones with ladders tall enough to reach the caves.

Ancient City of Hanoi

Thirty kilometres (18 miles) east of Kashgar lie the ruins of the city walls of this Tang Dynasty town, which probably dates from the mid-seventh century, when the Shule military governorship was established in the region. Hanoi was abandoned after the 11th century. The remains of karez wells show how the city was supplied with water. A few kilometres north of the ancient city is the site of the **Mor Buddhist Pagoda**. The 12-metre-high pagoda comprises three square bases, the first with

12-metre sides, the second 10 metres and the third eight metres, with an oval shaped crown. Though weathered by time, it still presents an impressive vision of Buddhist power and devotion in this region before the coming of Islam. A huge terrace beside the pagoda was one of the central temple structures, and in its side walls carved niches once housed Buddha figurines. No statues remain, and even the niches themselves are barely visible, while darkened soil indicates that the dagoba and terrace were destroyed by fire. Entrance to the site costs Rmb15.

OPAL (WUPOER)

The tomb of the 11th-century Uygur philologist, **Mohammed Kashgeri**, is attractively situated in the rich agricultural oasis of **Opal** (**Wupoer**), a pleasant 45-kilometre (28-mile) excursion to the west of Kashgar. Kashgeri, a renowned scholar of Turkish culture in western Xinjiang and other parts of Central Asia, compiled a widely acclaimed Turkic dictionary in Arabic. The present mausoleum of Opal's native son was rebuilt in 1983, and several rooms are devoted to an exhibition of his works and local archaeological finds, including a large pottery shard showing a bearded foreign king crowned with vine leaves.

Kashgeri's tomb is so highly respected by Uygurs that many Islamic scholars have contributed books to the tomb; it has thus slowly become a kind of library, and Uygurs respectfully call it *Haiziliti Maolamu*, meaning the Tomb of Honourable Scholars. Monday is the village market day, and while it's much smaller than the Kashgar market, it's worth visiting for its less chaotic but equally authentic atmosphere. Entrance to the Kashgeri tomb costs Rmb30.

SHIPTON'S ARCH

Shipton's Arch is the largest naturally formed arch in the world, estimated to be around 500 metres (1,500 feet) in height, with the "hole" of the arch measuring 400 metres (1,200 feet) into a chasm below. Known locally as "*Tushuk Tash*", meaning "Pierced Rock" in Uygur, it became known to the Western world when it was discovered by the renowned mountaineer Eric Shipton, who was the last British Consul-General of Kashgar during World War II. An inveterate explorer of wilderness regions, Shipton and his wife, with the help of a local guide, were the first Westerners to reach the arch, although Shipton could not climb it because he did not have the requisite climbing equipment. It was not until 2000 that another Western expedition – sponsored by *National Geographic* magazine and including expert climbers – managed to locate the arch (again with local assistance), climb it, roughly measure it, and traverse the confusing and dangerous range within which it hides (*see* Literary Excerpt on page 336).

Shipton's Arch is notoriously difficult to find amongst the multitude of canyons that make up this eastern fringe of the Pamir range, even for locals. The arch can be visited as a long half-day or short full-day trip. A 4WD, guide and sometimes a ladder are necessary, but people have been known to travel to the Kashgar region from as far as England specifically to view the arch.

JOURNEY TO SHIPTON'S LOST ARCH

*E*ven from ten miles away, the arch was stunning the first time it came into view—an enormous Gothic window framed in stone, lit from behind by the afternoon sun. Five of us had arrived in a desert oasis called Mingyol in western China, having come halfway around the world on what some—including the jostling crowd of villagers around us—considered a curious quest: to reach, and then to climb, that tantalizing span of rock.

When we drove our dusty 4WD into their poplar-shaded village, people materialized from green fields and mud-walled homes, wondering who we were and what we wanted.

It was a pilgrimage of sorts that had brought us to this remote mountain range—a walk in the footsteps of the legendary British mountain explorer Eric Shipton. In his book *Mountains of Tartary* Shipton had described the "scores of bold pinnacles" we gazed at now, noting that one was "pierced by a hole . . . below its summit almost down to its base." Shipton tried to reach that arch, but three times a seemingly impenetrable maze of foothills, slot canyons, and sheer-walled towers stopped him short. After months of attempts he finally reached the arch but left it unclimbed.

We aimed to reach the arch too—and climb it in his memory. But we, like Shipton, would have to solve the riddles of this tortured terrain. Could anyone help us?

On the edge of the crowd an old, white-bearded man with a black hat and kind eyes gave a nod of recognition. He remembered an Englishman who was "about 40, not tall, but big," who had come to Mingyol by truck with his wife and friends. After 50 years of Chinese history, civil war, and revolution, we had found a living memory of Eric Shipton.

"Since Shipton," he added softly, "you are the first to come looking."

Even just looking, it was thrilling to be there. For years I had read Shipton's gripping accounts of mountain adventure from the Alps to East Africa, from Mount Everest to the untraveled glaciers of the Karakoram. I marveled at his achievements and admired his spirit.

*B*orn in 1907, by age 22 Shipton had logged the first ascent of Nelion, one of Mount Kenya's twin summits. In 1931 he and five companions were the first to summit 25,447-foot Mount Kamet in northern India, at that time the highest peak ever climbed. In 1933 he climbed within a thousand feet of the top of Mount Everest and later pioneered the route that Edmund Hillary and Tenzing Norgay used to reach the summit in 1953. He didn't make a big fuss—he just climbed and explored everything in sight. Before he died in 1977, he set standards and laid out dreams for others to pursue.

People liked Eric Shipton. He made friends easily and kept the ones he made. Although he married only once, many women were drawn to him. Admirer Beatrice Weir was just 17 when she met him at a garden party in India. "Suddenly," she later said, "there appeared this

Opposite: Shipton's Arch is an astonishing natural phenomenon that few have seen at first hand, even today (Magnus Bartlett).

extraordinary brown-faced man, fairly small, with strong legs and a strong body, a shock of hair and slightly weak chin. He had blazing blue eyes everyone used to talk about; he just sat and looked. It was indefinable. I melted like an ice cube."

*Y*et there was something distant about him, as if he held an important part of himself in reserve, as remote and wild as the mountains he loved so much. His greatest pleasure came from journeys into unknown, unmapped terrain, and he preferred to take the simplest way possible. Dismayed by the massive scale of a typical Everest expedition, he scorned the "small town of tents that sprung up each evening, the noise and racket of each fresh start, the sight of a huge army invading the peaceful valleys."

Instead, Shipton and his climbing partner, Bill Tilman, joked that they could "organise a Himalayan expedition in half an hour on the back of an envelope." Unusual in the 1930s, their no-frills style has since become the standard—lightweight, low impact, self-propelled, culturally sensitive, and motivated by the sheer joy of exploration.

All this was on my mind last May when Mark Newcomb, Nancy Feagin, Sam Lightner, Jr., Gordon Wiltsie, and I arrived in Kashgar, Xinjiang Province, with plans for our adventure—friends on a lighthearted, lightly ladened excursion to the far side of the planet. Our admiration for Shipton, and curiosity about his arch, had brought us together. We tried to imagine Kashgar as he would have seen it in 1940, when he arrived there to assume his post as British consul.

Among Britain's most remote diplomatic posts, Kashgar was Shipton's kind of place. Isolated, difficult to reach, steeped in the romance of Central Asia, the city lies on the edge of the vast Taklimakan Desert in the shadow of the continent's greatest mountain ranges. For some 2,000 years it served as a way station and trading center on the Silk Road. It was also a strategic vantage point for players in the "Great Game"—the political struggle for Asian dominance between Britain and Russia in the late 19th and early 20th centuries. At the junction of shifting empires, the region was controlled by China, but rebellions, civil war, and conquest often tested that control. During Shipton's time there was no telling who might win.

By all accounts Shipton was an effective diplomat. He led excursions into the surrounding country, where he climbed mountains and combined hunting with exploring and even some amateur spying. Every month he sent to India secret reports filled with political analysis and information on rebellions, intrigues, troop movements, and Soviet activities in the region.

On forays outside of Kashgar he occasionally caught glimpses of the formation that local people called Tushuk Tash, or Hole Rock. Intrigued, he set out to find it. Three times he and his wife, Diana, along with other companions, tried to approach it from the south side. Three times the labyrinthine fortress of eroded rock south of the arch thwarted their efforts. Finally they found a successful approach from the north. Shipton put his hand on the arch, but he lacked the modern climbing equipment that would have allowed him to ascend it safely.

If he could visit Kashgar today, Shipton would probably wince at its new Chinese-style business district, crowded with what he called "that great scourge of modern civilization, the internal combustion engine." He'd feel more at home, as we did, among the old rhythms beyond the city center. Kashgar grew up in a vast green oasis fed by the melting snows of surrounding mountains—a huge garden of barley, wheat, vegetables, and melons. The city still resembles Shipton's "curious, medieval land," where donkey carts haul goods and people along tree-lined lanes and where country people pour into the city once a week to attend the Sunday bazaar, said to be the largest of its kind in Asia. Graybeards in black robes and fur-trimmed hats head for the stock market—where they argue the merits of camels, horses, fat-tailed sheep, and cattle—while their wives stream through rows of bright fabrics, household goods, carpets, and jewelry.

As for the big arch, although it lies just 25 miles from Kashgar, it remains obscure. Our liaison in the city, Abdullah Hallick, had never been near it. Nor had his friends and neighbors. We had acquired a set of Russian topographic maps, but they were practically useless. The maps showed the mountains accurately, but in the core of the range, where it really mattered, their contour lines went haywire. The cartographers had simply given up. I called these areas Vales of Despair. The mapmaker's despair, that is—and our joy. Blank spots on the map are dishearteningly rare in these days of the global positioning system.

So to find the arch, we followed our imaginary companion Shipton—an expert in blank spots—to Mingyol, where we met the old man who remembered him. Entering the village that day, we found it a peaceful, shady place echoing with the sound of irrigation water, the soil damp beneath rows of poplars, cuckoos singing in the trees. It was home to some 50 Uygur and Kyrgyz families.

In Mingyol, Shipton had enlisted the help of a local villager to find the arch. His name was Usman Akhun, a man of "splendid physique and the easy rhythmical movements and self-assurance of an Alpine guide." Hoping that such an impressive character would be remembered, we asked around and were soon led to the home of Torogan Usman, the youngest son of Usman. He leaned on a shovel with a shy smile and told us that his father had died some years ago at an old age.

Curious neighbors gathered. I asked if anyone had been close to the arch, close enough to touch it. "Why would you want to?" one man replied, to laughter. I dug out one of Shipton's books and opened it to a picture of Usman. This caused a stir. People passed the open book with sad looks. Some of the men took off their hats as it came to them. One elderly woman pressed it to her forehead with a mournful, keening sound.

Usman's elderly brother-in-law, Juma Akhun, explained the sadness: Shipton's group had been cheerful people, he said. Usman liked them and enjoyed traveling with them. But some years later, in the hard aftermath of Mao's communist revolution, there had been trouble. Some local people with what he called "wrong ideas about foreigners" had punished Usman for associating with an Englishman.

In telling this, the old man's voice broke. Tears flowed into his beard, and I, mindful of Shipton's backcountry intelligence reports, did not press him for the painful details.

"I could take you to the arch," said a voice. I turned to see a slight, bald man. "Yes," said Arken Murat cheerfully. "I know the way."

It goes through deep canyons, he warned, dark and narrow and wet. We might have to swim. And when it rains, he added, "rocks come down!" He held his arms up and shook them to illustrate a flash flood. Then, grinning impishly, he asked his son to bring out his new green sneakers. He laced them tightly, then announced, "I can run like a deer. You'll never keep up!"

Piling into our 4WD, we drove three miles to a canyon at the base of the range, where I began to wonder if Arken was playing a joke on us. This canyon seemed wrong; it was too far west. On the other hand, this landscape had foiled one of mountaineering's great explorers. When Arken charged up the canyon in his green sneakers, we followed.

*S*tarting out, we could just see the pointed top of the arch but soon lost it behind high walls of unstable brown mudstone. For two hours we followed a small stream steeply uphill through a tangle of house-size boulders. We clambered over some and squeezed under others until we came to an abrupt change in the rock. Cliffs of hard gray conglomerate rose thousands of feet on either side of us. Our pulses quickened: Surely these were the "walls of the main massif" that Shipton had described five decades earlier in his book.

A few hundred yards farther, the cliffs closed in, blocking out the sky. As we picked our way upstream, twisting through shoulder-width narrows and scrambling up cold waterfalls, the canyon grew deeper and darker until it pinched down to a cavelike slit echoing with the sound of falling water. In a place like this in April 1947 Shipton encountered a frozen waterfall, a pillar of ice in a cul-de-sac so dark that he had to strike a match to see it. Unequipped for those conditions, he turned around.

So did we. It was getting late, and Arken said the first view of the arch was an hour away for him and three hours, he teased, for us. Either way we were out of time, stopped like Shipton at the bottom of a cold black pit.

We said farewell to Arken and the next day drove from Mingyol around to the north side of the range, hoping to find the route Shipton had finally taken to the arch.

To guide us, we had only the quirky Russian maps and a copy of Diana Shipton's book, *The Antique Land.* Her story of life in Kashgar includes more details than her husband's book of their successful attempt from the north.

To me this approach seemed just as difficult: The arch was completely hidden. The conglomerate rock was rugged and the country complex. The canyons and towers were jammed together so tightly that we began to think we could wander out there for days.

Suddenly we found our way blocked by a herd of sheep. They stared at us; we stared dumbly back. Only when a dog barked did we look up to see a young Kyrgyz shepherd perched on the slope above.

*T*he boy scrambled down, and we showed him a sketch of the arch from Diana's book. He studied it for a moment, then smiled and gestured for us to follow him—back the way we had come, over a low hill to another canyon, and up that for two miles through some tight narrows, until . . . well, let Eric Shipton tell it: "At last, emerging from one of these clefts, we were confronted with a sight that made us gasp with surprise and excitement. The gorge widened into a valley which ended a quarter of a mile away in a grassy slope leading to a U-shaped col. Above and beyond the col stood a curtain of rock, pierced by a graceful arch."

Now we too had a grandstand view of the arch, towering hundreds of feet above us. Its window opened on a turbulent scene of strangely sculpted towers and canyons. At our feet the ground fell away in a sheer gorge, its bottom too deep to see. A strong wind rushed through from the south, funneled by the arch, and in the distance, some hundred miles or so across a stormy sea of brown desert, rose the gleaming, ice-covered Pamirs.

The scene made me dizzy. I was not prepared for the grandeur of the arch, nor for the "buzzers"—rocks dislodged by the wind that plunged down from the upper reaches of the arch. They fell fast, too fast to see, ripping the air with a vicious vhzzzzzzz, followed long seconds later by the hard crack of stone on stone far below and out of sight. I couldn't help flinching every time one came by.

"Amazing," said Sam, standing beside me, "that this heaping pile of choss is standing at all." Choss, a climber's term, means loose, treacherous rock, the kind climbers avoid at all costs. The towers, consisting entirely of rounded cobbles in a poorly cemented conglomerate, seemed to be crumbling as we watched.

Despite the unstable nature of the rock, we had to climb it, as Shipton would have. So two days later we returned with climbing gear and set about getting to the top. The rock was too loose for any route except the skyline ridge, a narrow, rounded crest about two feet wide. Mark, Sam, and Nancy—all expert climbers—spent a day establishing a route to the summit. Gordon and I followed on their ropes. It was not difficult climbing, but we had to set our feet very carefully and never trust any one stone.

*F*rom the pointed summit I peered into a surreal landscape of twisted canyons and looming gray towers. I felt exposed and strangely vulnerable. Knowing that this chossy rock we stood on was suspended over open air made me queasy. Yet we still did not know how high the arch was. The world's biggest documented arches, all in the American Southwest, span voids of 300 feet, so we knew we were dealing with a formation of unprecedented scale. How could we measure it?

There was one way, and I think Eric Shipton's eyes would have gleamed at the prospect. Using our ropes as measuring tapes, we could lower ourselves below the arch to its base, then hike, slither, and climb through the dark and puzzling slot canyons back to

Mingyol. We would not only measure the arch but also cross the range and solve the mystery of the maze.

Fifty-three years earlier Shipton had peered into the chasm beneath the arch. "A mile away," he wrote, "the canyon was blocked by a massive tower . . . to pass it on either side or in either direction looked impossible." We weighed the hazards: falling rock, the chance of flash floods, uncertainty about the route ahead. In the end we gave in to the allure of the unknown, as I believe Shipton would have done.

Sam volunteered to take the upper section. The next morning he rappelled from the summit straight down the north face of the arch. I stood far below him on the facing hill as he worked carefully downward, a slow spider on a long thread, setting loose squadrons of buzzers. He made it to the edge of the opening, but there a strong wind set him swinging like a pendulum. Every time he swung under the arch, the rope would dislodge debris. A steady rain of pebbles hammered his helmet. Knowing that larger stones could follow, Sam scrambled back up the rope, having given us a ballpark measure of the arch's upper third—nearly 500 feet.

Tightening our helmets against buzzers, we dropped straight below the arch on doubled ropes. Reaching the ends of our lines, we anchored ourselves to the wall and then pulled the ropes down from the anchors above. After the first rope came down, we were committed; no going back now.

*D*irectly overhead, the arch split the sky. Sheer in places, embellished in others with mushroom shapes and wind-carved hollows, its underbelly was a Daliesque sculpture garden. After six rope lengths we were at the base of the arch, standing in a grotto and gazing up at what appeared to be an impossibly slender, impossibly fragile span of stone. We counted our rope lengths and were astonished: We had just dropped nearly a thousand feet. Added to the 500-foot upper section that we had measured earlier, it meant that Shipton's arch was about 1,500 feet high, with a 1,200-foot opening—far and away the tallest natural arch in the world.

When we were all at the bottom, Mark gave a tug. The ropes slipped through the last anchor and came whistling down around us. We coiled them, stuffed them into our packs, and turned to what we hoped was the way home—a dark slot angling into the cobbled bedrock of the labyrinth. Torn between anticipation and jitters over what lay ahead, we plunged into the slot. Above us soared Shipton's arch, but ahead lay undiscovered country, the kind that Shipton loved so well.

Jeremy Schmidt, National Geographic, December 2000

TOUR COSTS

Local tour agencies offer trips to the many interesting sights in the Kashgar region, but costs vary according to the quality of the vehicle and licensing of the driver, etc. The following prices are a guideline for a licensed, registered travel vehicle with driver, and don't include food, accommodation, gate tickets, etc:

Shipton's Arch day trip (4WD necessary) – approx Rmb1,300

Karakul Lake day trip (saloon car) – approx Rmb800

Oytagh day trip (saloon car) – approx Rmb900

Yarkand day trip (saloon car) – approx Rmb800

Tashkurgan, two days/one night (saloon car) – approx Rmb1,400

Overnight hire of a saloon car – approx Rmb200-250 per night

Overnight desert trips with camels, sleeping bags, tents, etc – approx Rmb600 per person for a group of four. (Cheaper rates for larger groups, more expensive for smaller groups.)

THE KARAKORAM HIGHWAY

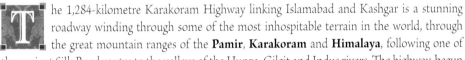

he 1,284-kilometre Karakoram Highway linking Islamabad and Kashgar is a stunning roadway winding through some of the most inhospitable terrain in the world, through the great mountain ranges of the **Pamir**, **Karakoram** and **Himalaya**, following one of the ancient Silk Road routes to the valleys of the Hunza, Gilgit and Indus rivers. The highway, begun in 1967, is an incredible feat of engineering by Chinese construction teams. The passage through the Northern Territories of Pakistan was blasted out of sheer rock faces that rise high above deep canyons carved by the rushing waters of the Indus River and its tributaries. In some places men suspended by ropes hand-drilled the holes for the dynamite. More than 400 lives were lost in building the road, and small stone cairns mark their graves. Travelling this road is still very unpredictable – rock slides and flash floods are a constant threat and frequently hold up transportation. The Pakistan Frontier Works Organization deploys 10,000 soldiers on the other side of the border for road maintenance and emergency clearance.

The Karakoram and Himalaya are the newest mountain ranges in the world; they began forming 55 million years ago, when the Indian subcontinent collided with the northern Asian landmass. The subcontinent is still shifting north at a rate of five centimetres per year and the young mountains are still growing, which results in earth tremors every three minutes (on average). Karakoram means "crumbling rock" in Turkish, an apt name for a highway that cuts through giant, snow-capped granite peaks, reaching 4,733 metres (15,524 feet) at the **Khunjerab Pass**.

Running south the Karakoram Highway heads on a collision course with the Karakoram and the High Pamirs (Magnus Bartlett).

OYTAGH

S outh of Kashgar the Karakoram Highway crosses gebi plain towards a line of intimidating mountains to the south. It approaches the rocky foothills and enters the narrow gorge of the **Gez River**, but at its mouth a side canyon turns off to the west, leading to the village of **Oytagh** (Oitagh), hidden within a gorgeous valley that boasts a glacier and alpine forest more representative of Tajikistan and Kyrgyzstan than the arid terrain of southwest Xinjiang (in fact both those countries are in close proximity at this point).

Kyrgyz nomads migrate here during the hot summer months with their livestock, but access is very often impossible for vehicles due to the constant washout of roads by flash floods. In 2007 work began on a 30-kilometre sealed tarmac road that will provide a surer connection between the Karakoram Highway and Oytagh, and when it is finished in 2009, tourism should increase rapidly. The official line is that the residents of the valley will be given control over how tourism develops – hopefully this will result in a type of low-impact ecotourism that ensures Oytagh's resources and great natural splendour are not ruined.

Access to Oytagh can be difficult at times due to heavy rains and flash floods, and a 4WD may sometimes be required if the new road has been damaged. Late July till late August is usually a time of significant rainfall high in the mountains along the Karakoram Highway – typically in the afternoon, so take this into consideration if you travel there, as you may be forced to turn back, or be stuck there for longer than you intended.

KARAKUL LAKE AND MUZTAGATA

Back on the Karakoram Highway the road enters the Gez River gorge, a majestic and slightly intimidating defile that remains a dangerous road to travel, despite the advances of modern-day engineering. The two-lane highway hugs the sheer western face of the gorge; falling rocks and accidents caused either by poor driving or unroadworthy vehicles can result in catastrophe, and since there are no phones or other means of signalling for help in this area, help is a very long way off if you need it.

Still in the lower end of the gorge all vehicles must pass through a checkpoint where passports are scrutinized and your destination – on to Pakistan or back to Kashgar – is checked. The road continues, heading towards a wall of jagged rock that seems to present an impenetrable barrier. At this point it is still following the swift river, only a matter of five metres or so above it – during the spring flood the Gez River becomes a raging torrent that frequently washes the road away, requiring a huge rebuilding effort by the work crews charged with keeping the highway open. The road then begins to ascend and turns southeast, rising to a pass that is just under 4,000 metres above sea level, then dropping slightly to skirt a vast high-altitude plain where a salt lake is watched over by giant sand dunes. Here, a few hardy Kyrgyz live, supplementing their income by selling semiprecious stones, necklaces and other local handicrafts to the occupants of the cars and buses that stop to take in the panorama.

Less than an hour farther south, 196 kilometres from Kashgar and at an altitude of 3,500 metres (11,480 feet), the road reaches the shores of **Karakul Lake**, another watery gem in a stunning mountain setting. The high, windswept plateaus between the parallel ranges that constitute the Pamirs, the "Roof of the World" (called the Onion Mountains in early Chinese records), are home to a nomadic branch of the Kyrgyz people known as the **Kara-Kyrgyz**, who live in encampments of round *ak-ois* (yurts covered in thick felts of goat or camel hair). In summer, horses, yaks and camels graze on the rich pasturage around this high-altitude lake, which is surrounded by majestic peaks on all sides.

A magical spot, Karakul Lake has become something of a must-see destination in Xinjiang, and it now boasts concrete yurts and wooden hotel buildings between the road and the water's edge, catering to the tourists who come to trek on foot, horse or camel around the lake and into the surrounding valleys. It is of course possible to stay in a real yurt (for a fee) belonging to the Kyrgyz nomads who live here in summertime, but in recent years they have become somewhat militant in their handling of the "Karakul tourist industry", and have been known to demand Rmb50–100 "permit" fees for staying by the lakeside. Construction of a large Chinese hotel right on the lakeshore has not helped matters. However, if you do stay overnight, make an effort to hike around or away from the easiest access to the lake and into the rugged scenery, and you are guaranteed a memorable experience.

The views around Karakul Lake are dominated by the massive **Muztagata Mountain** (Muztag Ata), the "Father of the Ice Mountains" at 7,546 metres (24,756 feet), and to a lesser extent 7,719-metre **Kongur Tagh** to the north, which is the westernmost peak of the Kunlun Mountains but is also considered part of the Pamirs (some sources claim its height at 7,649 metres). Muztagata appears to have three separate summits, cleaved by mighty glaciers – it is aptly named – and it is a treacherous peak for mountaineers; first summited in 1956, it took the lives of three climbers in 2007 alone. Kongur Tagh proved even more difficult, and was only successfully climbed in 1981 by a UK expedition including legendary British mountaineer Chris Bonnington.

Past the lake, the Karakoram Highway rises in a series of hairpin bends to around 4,100 metres (13,450 feet), where a closer view of Muztagata reveals its awesome glaciers and snowfields in all their glory. It then drops gradually to a broad valley at 3,200 metres (10,240 feet), and arrives at Tashkurgan, the county seat of **Tajik Autonomous County**, 260 kilometres from Kashgar.

TASHKURGAN

In the second century CE, Ptolemy spoke of Tashkurgan as the extreme western emporium of the Land of Seres (China), for it stands on the trade route over the Taghdumbash Pamirs and the Karakorams to the ancient Buddhist kingdoms of Taxila and Gandhara. The inhabitants, then known as Sarikolis but today called **Tajiks**, are regarded as pure Homo alpinus stock, the occupiers of High Asia since

AN EXCURSION TO OITAGH

The rough desert seemed interminable. The sun baked into us and the foot-hills which were our goal never seemed to get any nearer. After an hour's walking we curved round to the river again, where we drank endless cups of water and ate some of the battered remains of yesterday's lunch. Soon after this halt our way lay up a valley to the right. It was no less hot or stony, but narrower, than the main valley and more steep. At the first bush we came to we stopped again and had tea made. For nearly two hours we lay under the scanty shade of the only shrub in sight, and that a very prickly one, waiting for the cool of evening.

The cliffs of this valley were in high, complicated shapes, resembling mighty cathedral walls, giant organ pipes, or slender towers. In some places they were a deep red colour, glowing even more deeply in the sun. Rounding a bend, the quite unexpected green of a flourishing oasis spread before us; like a Shangri La hidden in the rugged hills. This was Oitagh. Unknown to us, a traveller who had joined our party for tea, lower down, had invited us all to his house for the night. We should have preferred a peaceful camp of ur own choosing, but could not refuse this kind hospitality. Passing by a deep gorge, with a muddy river racing far below us, we waded through a brilliant carpet of irises, the air heavy with their scent. Then towards the end of the village we stopped, and under an ancient willow rugs were spread for us, while our host disappeared into his house to make hurried preparations.

In his small noisy courtyard, surrounded by stables for ponies, camels and sheep, we found a raised platform. Two wooden beds and a table furnished it and there we had to sit, in high state, like royalty or perhaps a side-show in a circus. The servants, our host, the local school-master and various interested neighbours sat below and watched our every movement. Mysterious women flitted past shyly and they also enjoyed the free entertainment...

It was very disappointing to find on the following day, that a heavy dust haze was creeping up from the plains and firmly blotting out the view. In the curious suffocated light Eric and I began walking up the valley. The cultivated fields soon ended in thorny bushes; out of the gloom a camel suddenly appeared, contentedly munching this harsh diet...

We came to a small, rocky hill covered with stunted pines. These tended to increase our unenthusiastic state of mind, as we had been expecting tall, handsome trees. But as we went on the pines developed and high above we could just see fringes of trees on the hill-sides. I was persuaded to pass a delightful glen of trees, green grass and a sparkling stream, with promises of even better camp sites farther on. Feeling very unconvinced I followed the crowd. Our party had now swollen to a motley collection of cattle, sheep, donkeys and camels, all being driven up to the summer pastures. This procession was enlivened by harassing attacks from Sola.

At last we could go no farther, our way was effectively blocked by a forbidding, black glacier. But we found ourselves in such a beautiful place that we had no desire to go on. Although visibility was still poor, immediately around us were tall pines and slopes of soft, brilliant grass; in such startling contrast to the wide, hot severity of the desert and the barren hills we had passed, that we felt we had entered another world...

After tea we began to explore a little and walked on to the glacier. The dust haze persisted but we could just define faint shapes far above and around us. One pointed peak, a little clearer than the rest, hung so high and isolated in the air that I thought I must have imagined it. There was something exciting about this dimness, exasperating though it was; there was a promise of unknown beauty when the curtain was lifted, like a woman hiding behind a heavy veil.

Early the next morning the veil was lifted. Running out in my pyjamas I saw Chakragil shining in clear, cold majesty. From the floor of the valley a semi-circular wall of ice swept 10,000ft, up to the line of peaks and buttresses, with the two main peaks of the mountain dominating them all. To our disappointment the miserable dust haze was once more creeping up from the plains. But for a long time yet Chakragil remained unclouded and graceful.

Diana Shipton, The Antique Land, 1950

Clockwise from top left: A Kyrgyz yurt sits on the high plains of the Pamirs near the border with Tajikistan; the Karakoram range presents a wall of rock as the highway passes up the Gez River gorge (Jeremy Tredinnick x2); on its way towards Tashkurgan, the Karakoram Highway skirts a huge high-altitude plain that boasts a wide salt lake and huge sand dunes – an esoteric landscape (Sun Jiabin); a glacier flows down from Muztagata, the "Father of Ice Mountains"; Tajik women in Tashkurgan still wear their attractive traditional headwear, even for an afternoon stroll down the main street (Jeremy Tredinnick x2).

earliest times. Their language belongs to the Persian group of Indo-European languages, and they are followers of the Ismaili sect of Islam.

The Tajiks in Xinjiang number more than 26,000 and, apart from a small number in the cities of the Southern Silk Road, live in their traditional homeland in the High Pamirs. Unlike their nomadic neighbours, the Kyrgyz and Kazakhs, the Tajiks engage in both animal husbandry and agriculture; they are semi-sedentary, building houses of stone and wood. Barley, beans, wheat and vegetables are planted during springtime, but at altitudes of over 3,000 metres crop yields are low. They become yurt-dwellers during the summer grazing season, when they tend flocks of sheep, goats and horses in the higher valleys, and return to their stone homes in autumn. Hawking and buzkashi are popular among the Tajiks, as are dancing and music. One of their traditional musical instruments is a three-holed flute made from the bones of eagles' wings.

Tashkurgan is Tajik for "Stone City", referring to the **Stone Fortress** perched on top of a hill at the northeastern edge of town that was first built in the sixth century. The present ruins date from the Yuan Dynasty and the fort was restored during the Qing. At the base of the wall is a narrow dirt road, said to be the ancient Silk Road itself. Xuanzang, laden with 570 Buddhist sutras, spent 20 days here on his return journey. Inside the fortress ruins there is little to see, and the truth is it is most impressive from a distance. Very early in the morning or late afternoon is the time to see it; make a short trip down the dirt road at its eastern base and out onto the valley floor, turn and you will have a marvellous view of its outer walls with the serrated mountain peaks as a backdrop.

Modern Tashkurgan is a delightful town, compact and easy to navigate. Government buildings have been constructed with Graeco-Roman style columns, and curiously there is an abundance of orange and pink in the façades of many of the town buildings – Tajiks are a colourful lot both in their traditional clothing and it seems their architectural preference. A large, attractive eagle statue – symbol of the Tajiks – stands in the centre of town, and the main shopping street, which runs north from here, has recently been reworked, and now sports a central promenade complete with shady trees. Also facing the eagle statue is the **National Culture and Art Centre**, a small but interesting museum detailing Tajik customs and culture (open 11am–5pm, closed Saturdays and Sundays, entrance Rmb30).

On top of a high mountain by the Tashkurgan River, about 80 kilometres southwest of the town, are the ruins of the **Princess's Castle**. The tamped-earth walls are crumbling, but piles of stones within are evidence of inner rooms. It was already in ruins when Xuanzang told its legend. Once, the King of Persia became betrothed to a Chinese princess, but during her long journey to join him wars broke out, confining her to the Pamirs. Her escort built a temporary fortification on top of a steep mountain and guarded it night and day, and here she lived until peace was restored six months later. But, to the horror of the accompanying ministers, the princess had become pregnant, and an exhaustive investigation was demanded. The trusted handmaiden of the princess came forward: "I know only that every day at noon a handsome young man comes from the sun to meet the princess. Afterwards, he mounts the clouds and departs." Afraid to relate this to the court, the ministers decided to stay where they were and built a palace on the mountaintop for the princess. The boy she bore was beautiful and intelligent. The princess established rule in the region, and her son eventually became king.

Tashkurgan Practical Information

Today, Tashkurgan is a small border town of 5,000 residents, and despite the thin air is best explored on foot. It is the site of Chinese customs for travellers to/from Pakistan. **Tagharma** village, a short drive north of Tashkurgan, boasts natural hot springs, and there is excellent hiking in the surrounding valleys. Daily buses run to/from Kashgar (six hours), Pirali and Sost, Pakistan.

Accommodation

The **Crown Inn** (Pamir Road, tel: (0998) 342 2888, fax: (0998) 342 2018, e-mail: enquiry1@ crowninntashkorgan.com, website: www.crowninntashkorgan.com) is a two-storey, three-star hotel at the southern end of town 10 minutes' walk from the town centre. Efficiently run by a Singaporean company, it offers modern, comfortable rooms (Rmb350–480) with spectacular views of the surrounding mountains, and a Silk Road Restaurant providing excellent food. The hotel can provide guides and assistance with sightseeing and other tour options in the area.

A new hotel opened in late 2007 on the northern edge of town. The **Ben Lei Xin Hotel** (China Friendship Road, tel: (0998) 342 3488, fax: (0998) 342 2555) is a single-storey property built in colourful, traditional style, with good, well-equipped rooms from Rmb288. Rooms are also available at either the **Bus Station Guesthouse** or the **Pamir Guesthouse** (tel: (0998) 342 1085).

The Khunjerab Pass

 ustoms and immigration formalities take place at the checkpoint before leaving Tashkurgan. Thirty kilometres south of town the road forks near a stone bridge, one route leading to the Wakhan Corridor of Afghanistan, only 80 kilometres away but off limits to international travellers, the other heading for the **Khunjerab Pass**.

The Khunjerab Pass and the simple stone Sino-Pakistani frontier marker are another 50 kilometres farther on, about one hour's drive across a barren, treeless landscape. Though Sir Aurel Stein dismissed the crossing of the 4,733-metre pass as "an excursion for the ladies", its name means "Valley of Blood" in the Wakhi language, referring to the murderous raids on caravans and travellers staged from the neighbouring Kingdom of Hunza.

At this altitude both man and beast suffer altitude sickness, with nosebleeds a common occurrence. The traditional method of relieving horses of pain was to jab their muzzles with sharp iron spikes so that the blood ran. A young Scandinavian travelling this route in the 1940s was appalled: "Along the whole pass there are dark-brown splodges on the stones. Once they were fresh streaming blood. Each drop is a message from the trembling horses that have foundered there."

The Stone Fortress, on the northeastern outskirts of Tashkurgan, presents an evocative image at dawn, with the majestic peaks of the Pamirs towering behind (Jeremy Tredinnick).

Over the pass, the road descends via hairpin bends to 2,500 metres, and then continues 86 kilometres through the closed Pakistan border zone to the checkpoint at **Sost**, where Pakistan entry formalities take place. Good accommodation is available here at the **PTDC Motel** (Rmb175). The complete overland journey down the Karakoram Highway from Kashgar to Islamabad can be arranged in Kashgar and is becoming popular; the trip can be made comfortably in 7–10 days.

The Khunjerab Pass is Xinjiang's highest border crossing, and is officially open from 1 May to 31 October, but exact dates are impossible to predict, as it is subject to very unpredictable weather and snowstorms can close it later in spring and earlier in autumn. The best way to check if it is open is to ask in Kashgar as soon as you arrive, but as with so much in Xinjiang, at the end of the day, Mother Nature will have the last word.

Top: The clear waters of Karakul Lake, looking north towards the Kongur massif, where the Pamirs and Kunlun range come together (Jeremy Tredinnick). Above left: During festivals and on special occasions, Tajik men play flutes made from eagles' wing bones. Above right: A centrally located mud-brick oven keeps a Tajik family's house warm, and allows large feasts to be prepared for guests (Sun Jiabin x2).

THE SOUTHERN SILK ROAD

The trail along the southern oases of the Taklamakan Desert – the oldest Silk Road route – wound its way westwards between the foothills of the Kunlun Mountains and the southern rim of the Taklamakan, from **Miran** to **Endere**, **Niya**, **Keriya**, **Khotan** (Hotan or Hetian) and **Yarkand** (Shache), where it turned to meet the northern route at Kashgar. Today's Highway 315 follows roughly the same route, with allowances for the shifting of the desert sands through the centuries. Historically, from Kashgar one route continued over the High Pamirs, and thence to the famous towns of Khokand, Samarkand, Bokhara and Merv, before making its way through Persia and Mesopotamia to the Mediterranean Sea, where the exotic produce from the East ended up in the markets of Rome and Alexandria.

Another Silk Road route branched off at Yarkand, continuing south to the Karakorams, over the Five Great Passes to reach **Leh** (Ladakh) and **Srinagar** (Kashmir), then on into the Indian subcontinent. Sadly this route has been closed since China's occupation of Tibet in 1950 and the ongoing political – and actual – fighting between China and India over the correct demarcation of their mutual border.

A classic Xinjiang image: a camel caravan crosses a sea of sand dunes – even today these hardy beasts are usually the best way to traverse the remote regions of the harsh but beautiful Taklamakan Desert (Christoph Baumer).

The Southern Silk Road was the shortest connection between central China and Kashgar, the combined gate to Central Asia and to India. A second advantage of this route was the virtual absence of robbers (the northern Silk Road trails were infested by bandits). The flip side of this coin, however, was the very reason why robbers shunned it: the climatic conditions on the Southern Road were much harsher than on the northern routes; sandstorms often raged, except in autumn and winter, and between Dunhuang and Miran there was no potable water. Furthermore, the Southern Silk Road was, from the seventh century CE on, the target of both regular Tibetan troops and renegade Tibetan gangs. The Chinese called it "*Nan Shan Bei Lu*" or "Northern Road of the Southern Mountains".

Today, the cities along the present southern road (known as Highway 315) are officially open to foreigners, including – from west to east – **Shache** (Yarkand), **Yecheng** (Karghalik), **Hotan** (Khotan or Hetian), **Yutian** (Keriya), **Minfeng** (New Niya), **Qiemo** (Cherchen) and **Ruoqiang** (Charklik). The 510-kilometre road journey from Kashgar to Hotan once took several weeks, but can now be accomplished in 10 hours by Landcruiser – and the metalled road continues all the way to Ruoqiang. There are several flights a week from Urumqi to Hotan via Aksu, and to Qiemo via Korla; both flights take about 3.5 hours, and in winter the flight frequency is reduced. Three cross-desert highways now span the Taklamakan from north to south: Highway 218 in the east, connecting Korla with Ruoqiang; the Tarim Highway – the longest – from Luntai to the oil town of Tazhong in the depths of the desert, where it continues south to Minfeng but also branches off southeast to Qiemo; and Highway 217, the newest, which only opened in spring 2007 and runs from Aral (Alar), south of Aksu by the Tarim River, to Hotan – a journey that takes only five hours or so.

Despite this opening up of a once famously hostile and remote region, however, access to major archaeological sites such as **Dandan Oilik**, **Karadong**, **Yuan Sha**, **Niya**, **Endere** and **Loulan** – which are all still off the beaten track – is forbidden. To visit these places, a special permit issued by both the Cultural Relics Bureau *and* the Public Security Bureau PSB in Urumqi is required. To visit some areas like Lop Nor, a permit from the PLA may also be needed. The permit must be applied for at least three months prior to leaving Urumqi; they are seldom granted and include a fee of hundreds or even thousands of US dollars, depending on the site. All visitors to these sites are accompanied by an official liaison officer.

Permits to visit sites of secondary archaeological importance, however, like **Mazar Tagh** or **Rawak** near Hotan, may be obtained within one or two days for a modest fee at the local Cultural Relics Bureau, or with the help of the Hotan Museum. Places that are near cities, like **Yotkan** and **Melikawat**, which are close to Hotan, or **Miran** near New Miran, are open to anyone. Regardless of where you go, however, remember that picking up ancient objects and carrying them out of China is strictly prohibited.

There is neither public transport to nor accommodation at any of the most important archaeological sites along the Southern Silk Road, and should you be intent on visiting them, it is mandatory to plan expeditions well ahead in cooperation with a Chinese travel agent. Equipment like tents, cooking gear, etc can be rented in Urumqi. To get to Mazar Tagh, Rawak, Niya and Miran, 4WD vehicles are sufficient, but the other sites require either UNIMOG trucks, camels, or special Chinese-made trucks called "*Shato*", used by the oil drilling companies. These trucks can be rented in Korla at a cost of US$280 per day including a driver; a UNIMOG costs about US$240 per day. Camels must be arranged a few days in advance since they may have to be collected from different owners and locations. The only feasible season for desert expeditions is from mid-September to the end of December. In December, however, the days are very short. January and February are very cold and from March to June strong sandstorms can rage, sometimes lasting for a week. Spring also brings thick fog, which can restrict visibility to 10 metres or even less. In summer, the temperature climbs so high that even camels struggle to work if loaded.

YENGISAR

Sixty-eight kilometres southeast of Kashgar lies the small town of **Yengisar**, whose 400-year history of knife-making has made it famous throughout Xinjiang and Tibet. A Yengisar knife is essential for every Uygur man, who usually wears it slung around his waist (this practice is discouraged in towns and cities). A knife is especially important during the melon season, when it is produced with ceremonial flair and thoroughly cleaned before cutting off the base of a melon. Knives are carefully chosen; hand-made ones encrusted with stones and inlaid with silver are highly valued, but just as effective are the sturdy types with bone or horn handles and intricate carvings on the blade.

Most knives now found in the markets of northwest China are factory produced, but Yengisar has a plethora of small, locally owned workshops, where men hand-operate the simple lathes and decorate the handles with various metals, horn or plastic. You can purchase knives directly from these micro-factories, or from any of the dozens of shops that line the streets of the town. Traditionally the skill of knife-crafting was handed down from father to son, but today it is kept alive through these small workshops, employing half a dozen master knife-makers and apprentices. The best knives were made before 1968, when silver was still readily available and fine craftsmanship was employed in honing the wide blade, and decorating and inlaying the handles with mother of pearl. These old knives are now rare and cherished by their makers, who will only part with one – reluctantly – for Rmb2,000 or more. A perfectly good new knife of similar style will cost around Rmb500, while more basic horn- and bone-handled varieties can be had for as little as Rmb100.

Each craftsman creates his knives in their entirety, first heating and beating the blade into shape, sharpening it, engraving and polishing, then designing and creating the handle's ornamentation using his own personal stock of materials, which can include silver plate, mother of pearl and various different-hued semi-precious stones such as lapis, turquoise, garnet, etc. A tour of a workshop is a fascinating experience – one of the best in town is **Enjisa Knife** (tel: 0098 362 2377, e-mail: badamguli@hotmail.com), whose showroom displays the full gamut of knife styles and sizes.

It's important to remember, though, that the carrying of knives on trains is strictly forbidden, so if you are travelling by train north from Kashgar, your precious souvenir will be confiscated; the smart option is to post your souvenirs home from Kashgar – they will take quite some time to make their way through China's postal system, but can be relied upon to arrive eventually.

There is little else to see in Yengisar. There are several guesthouses in town that offer basic Chinese accommodation. The road continues southeast towards Shache through flat, dry country, but just past Yengisar the road skirts a huge reservoir, home to water birds such as coots and seagulls. Men line the shore fishing, and the backdrop is stunning, with the huge white peaks of the Pamirs off to the southwest.

SHACHE (YARKAND)

U ntil recent decades, the historic town of **Yarkand** was larger than Kashgar due to its extensive commercial trade with India via **Leh**, in Ladakh. Silk Road caravans carried silks, tea, precious stones, gold, furs and skins and, during the Qing Dynasty, opium from India. Kashmiri merchants taught the Yarkandis to clean and treat wool fleeces, and soon the quality of Yarkand's shawl wool surpassed that even of Kashmir. Hindus, Pathans, Tibetans, Baltis, Afghans, Khokandis and even Armenians were among the many foreign traders who swelled the city's population.

By the beginning of the first century BCE Yarkand was already under Chinese control. However, during the Wang Mang interregnum

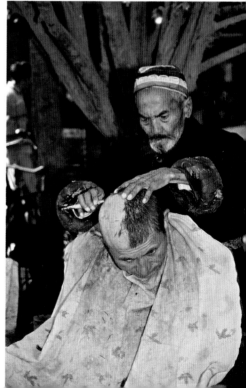

Top: A knife maker in Yengisar hones the blade of a new knife prior to adding its handle (Jeremy Tredinnick). Bottom: Roadside haircuts are possible throughout southern Xinjiang (Christoph Baumer).

Titled Approach to Yarkand, *this finely drawn picture was created by artist Robert B. Shaw in 1868, and published in his 1871 book* Visits to High Tartary.

(9–23 CE) China lost its grip over the states along the Southern Silk Road and Yarkand, like other small states, seized the opportunity to regain independence. It even rose to the status of a regional power in 33–61 CE when it subjugated Khotan, Shanshan and even Kucha in the northern part of the Tarim Basin. It could not maintain control for long, though, and by 63 CE all these vassal states had managed to regain their independence. By the end of the century, the Chinese General Ban Chao had forced all the states of the Tarim Basin to acknowledge Chinese suzerainty.

A brief flowering of creative culture occurred in the 16th and 17th centuries, when Sultan Saiyid (Said), a descendant of the Chaghatai Khanate, founded the Yarkand Kingdom. Influenced by his grandfather, who had previously sought refuge in Samarkand, Saiyid set about building a dynasty along the lines of that great city-state, encouraging the building of fine architecture, and the development of musical and artistic thought. Both Saiyid and his son, Abud Rushitihan, were poets and musicians, but sadly their kingdom could not withstand the onslaught of the theocratic regime of Abakh Khoja (Khoja Afaq) from Kashgar, which engulfed it in 1682 (see page 62).

On a perilous journey in 1895, Sven Hedin set out on an expedition to chart the southwest Taklamakan between the Yarkand and Hotan rivers. Twenty days out of Merkit, the point of departure 60 kilometres to the north of Yarkand, his expedition ran out of water and struggled through the Taklamakan for six days. Hedin finally crawled to the Hotan River and brought back

Andijani taifurchis of the Yarkand Governor's Guard, *sketched by T.E. Gordon in 1870, and published in his 1876 book* The Roof of the World.

water to save the life of his one remaining expedition member. In his travel memoir *Through Asia*, Hedin remembered:

> How sweet that water tasted! Nobody can conceive it who has not been within an ace of dying of thirst. How delicious! The noblest wine pressed out of the grape, the most divine nectar ever made, was never half so sweet... Then my thoughts flew back to [my servant] Kasim, whom I had left lying alone in the forest, fighting against death and unable to move a yard. How was I to carry him a sufficient quantity of the life-giving elixir? My boots! Of course my Swedish waterproof boots. Plump they went into the pool. Then I threaded the spade shaft through the straps, and carrying it like a yoke over my right shoulder, hastened back... When I came to Kasim, he was lying in the same position in which I had left him [more than twelve hours before]... I placed one of the boots near him, and shook it so that he might hear the splashing of the water. He started, uttered an inarticulate cry; and when I put the boot to his lips, he emptied it at one draught without once stopping; and the next moment he had emptied the second.

Two of Hedin's servants, and all but one of his camels, died of thirst and exhaustion. It was a tragedy caused by human error, and by the unforgivable theft of water: first, the leader of the camel drivers, called Yollchi, disobeyed Hedin's order to take 10 days' water supply on the expedition and only took water reserves for four days; this was bad enough, but when Hedin discovered after two days' marching that the expedition had only two days' water left, he refused to turn back and instead severely rationed the daily supply. But this measure couldn't save the situation, because Yollchi, the main culprit, stole water during the night. Hedin admitted 30 years later, "It would have been more judicious to return in our own tracks; the caravan would have been saved and no lives lost."

Hedin's most famous discoveries came on later expeditions, when he found the ancient cities of Dandan Oilik, Karadong and Loulan, and charted the Yarkand River and its continuation, the Tarim River, when he discovered the secret of the "wandering" lake of Lop Nor (*see special topic on page 420*).

Visiting Yarkand in 1923, the British consul-general in Kashgar, Sir Clarmont Skrine, was amazed by "the size and spaciousness of the long roofed bazaars, far better-built than those of Kashgar... courtyards of houses, weeping willows drooping over them, eating shops and groceries, smithies and old-clothes shops and carpenters' shops, and everywhere masses of picturesquely garbed people."

In *News from Tartary* (1936), Peter Fleming wrote of a tenser city in the wake of a Muslim rebellion:

> Parts of the bazaar were still in ruins; the bastions of the New City were pockmarked with bullets, and the walls of the houses round it with loop-holes; Chinese inscriptions were defaced. Here a Chinese garrison held out with some gallantry against the fanatical insurgents from Hetian, and after a siege of several weeks was granted a safe-conduct; in the desert they were massacred almost to a man. The incident is typical of a Province whose whole history stinks with treachery.

Today known officially as **Shache** (though the Uygur majority still call it Yarkand), the town is 126 kilometres southeast of Yengisar, and its character is more subdued than in previous times. The town is surrounded by an oasis of trees, fields and rice paddies; on Sundays, a large market sprawls over the streets and alleys of the east (old) end of the city – make sure you try a delicious cold bottle (no label) of the locally made plum soda (*meigui xiangjiu*).

Of most interest to visitors is the Imperial tomb complex of the **Altun (Aletun) kings** who ruled the Yarkand kingdom from 1514 until 1682. Situated in the old town a hundred metres north of the town's main street, the "Altun Historical and Cultural Square" is fronted by the façade of the Imperial Court, or "Cultural Palace", where once the kings would inspect their troops and pass judgement on their people from a balcony above the entrance gate. The palace was built in the mid-16th century, but was destroyed and the façade alone was rebuilt in the 1980s – pass through its huge doors and, incongruously, immediately behind are simple houses with household bric-a-brac strewn all around.

A resident of Yarkand in the 1920s, accompanied by his Tibetan mastiff guard dog (Courtesy of the Nicholas Roerich Museum, www.roerich.org).

Facing the Cultural Palace across the open square is the **Tomb of Amanisa Han** (Amanni Shahan), the wife of Sultan Abud Rushitihan. She is credited with collating and composing much of the epic **"Twelve Muqam"**, the most significant collection of music in Uygur culture. Known as the "mother of Uygur music", the Twelve Muqam comprises large-scale sets of sung poetry, stories, dance tunes and instrumental pieces. To play all of them together would take days, so usually one or two are chosen and performed at festivals and special occasions. In late 2005, UNESCO recognized the importance of the Twelve Muqam by designating it as a "Representative Work of Human Oral and Intangible Cutural Heritage".

Amanisa Han died during childbirth in 1560 at the age of only 34, and was buried near her late husband in the main tomb area. Her body rested there until 1992, when the present tomb was erected in the square next to the **Altun Mosque** and tomb area to honour her contribution to Uygur culture. The mosque entrance is a beautiful example of Islamic architecture in the Samarkand style – it was built by Abud Rushitihan in honour of his father after his death in 1533; an entrance ticket costing Rmb10 allows entrance to Amanisa Han's pretty tomb, the mosque's calm, classical interior, and the mazar area between and behind them, which contains some beautiful, intricately carved tomb structures.

A hundred metres south of the square a road leads east into the old town area; here the constant sound of craftsmen tap-tapping away at sheets of metal in open shopfronts creates an evocative atmosphere that could as easily belong to the centuries-old era of Yarkandi sultans as to the modern day. Everything from household necessities such as pots, pans and ovens to farming implements is made and hung up on display – it's well worth a wander.

Unsurprisingly, Shache is a centre of Uygur musical culture; it holds an annual **Muqam (Mukam) Festival** in September which ranks as one of the best places to see major sections of the Twelve Muqam performed by experts in an authentic and vibrant setting. Also, with its location next to classic Taklamakan Desert territory, Shache is a popular day and overnight trip from Kashgar with a private vehicle. If you are staying overnight, you will trek out into the sand dunes with camels carrying your luggage and camp under the desert sky – an inspirational experience.

Above: The entrance to Altun Mosque uses an architectural style borrowed from Samarkand. Opposite top: The wood-columned prayer hall of Altun Mosque. Opposite bottom: The attractive Tomb of Amanisa Han, built in 1992 to commemorate her contribution to the rich musical heritage of the Uygur people (Jeremy Tredinnick x3).

Shache Practical Information

Options for accommodation in all the Southern Silk Road's towns are increasing fast – new hotels are opening as the economy grows. Traditionally foreigners stay at the **Shache Hotel** (4 Xincheng Lu, tel: 998 851 2365, fax: 998 851-2356) south of the bus station, but good alternatives are the **Delong Hotel** (2 Chini Bagh Lu, tel: 998 851 6666, rooms Rmb220+) and the **Yarkan Queen Grand Hotel** (*Yarkan wang hou da jiu dian*, tel: 998 852 9999, rooms Rmb228+) at the Old City Road crossroads. Excellent Uygur restaurants are everywhere, and inexpensive. Shache is now connected to Kashgar and Yecheng/Hotan by a new rail line – see Kashgar and Hotan sections for details.

Zepu (Posgam)

From Yarkand the highway turns south and heads for **Zepu** (**Posgam**), a well-watered agricultural zone courtesy of the Yarkand River, which courses down from its source near the Karakoram Pass, bringing meltwater from the mighty Karakoram mountains. Before reaching Zepu, the road crosses the Yarkand via a long bridge; depending on the time of year you will either see a broad expanse of fast-flowing water (spring and summer), or a wide rut of rocks and sand, with shallow water channels meandering randomly down it (autumn and winter). Zepu is a productive region for farming, especially cotton, but its development and increasing numbers of modern buildings are a result of oil revenues in the region, as with so many other towns flanking the Taklamakan.

A 30-minute drive south of the main road brings you to the **Jin Hu Yang Golden Diversiform Poplar Park**, a newly created area alongside the upper Yarkand River that contains fine examples of this colourful tree, whose leaves shine gold in the bright sunshine. Small hamlets still farm within the park, and it can be marvellously peaceful wandering down the leafy avenues. A pedestrian cable suspension bridge provides entrance to the park (there is another gate for vehicles), and it is three kilometres from the bridge to the river.

Yecheng (Karghalik)

The town of **Yecheng (Karghalik)** is another fast-developing oasis. Historically Karghalik was the point at which merchant caravans and travellers heading for India would turn southwest into the mountains, trading the parched pathways of the desert for the freezing, torturous track that led over the **Five Great Passes** route to Leh and thence to Srinagar in Kashmir. The month-long journey to Leh traversed the Kunlun and Karakoram ranges and crossed five passes over 4,800 metres (16,000 feet) above sea level, with the apex at the Karakoram Pass (5,540 metres), followed by a three-day march across the 5,400-metre Drepsang Plain, which was strewn with the skeletons of pack animals. However, despite its terrible hardships this was still the best supplied and most used route between the Tarim Basin and the Indian subcontinent – until the British finally created a safer and faster route in the second quarter of the 20th century via the Hunza Valley and the Kunjerab Pass.

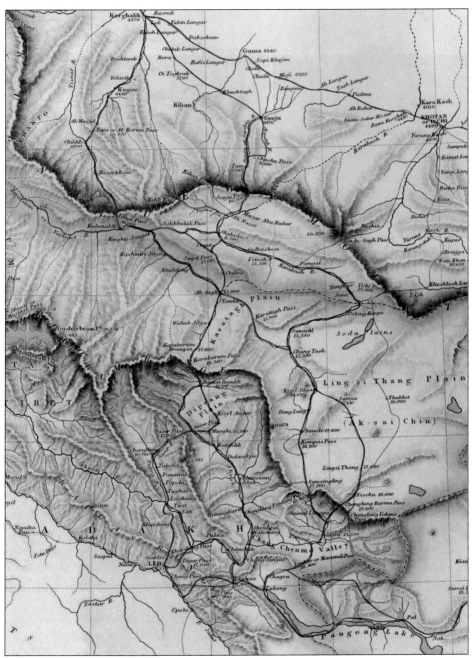

First appearing in H. Trotter's article "On the Geographical Results of the Mission to Kashgar, under Sir T. Douglas Forsyth in 1873–74," printed in the Journal of the Royal Geographical Society of London in 1878, this map shows the Five Great Passes mountain route between the Southern Silk Road towns of Karghalik and Khotan (at top) and Leh in Ladakh – the favoured trading route to the Indian subcontinent through most of the Silk Road's long history.

Today Yecheng is generally known as the assembly point for mountaineering expeditions planning to climb up the Chinese side of **K2**, which was opened to foreigners in 1980. The base camp is a journey of two days by car and a further nine days by camel from Yecheng (the ascent usually takes two to three months). Highway 315 curves around the north side of town after passing the bus station and crossing the river, and the mosque and bazaar are in the southwest, but compared to Shache and Hotan, Yecheng has relatively little to offer. The **Yecheng County Mountain Climbers Hotel** (Tuan Jie Lu, tel: 998 728 2652) offers accommodation to foreign nationals, but just east of town at the junction where Highway 219 begins a large hotel has been built, the **Yecheng K2 Hotel** (*Qiao Ge Li Binguan*, Ling Gong Lu, tel: 998 748 5000, rooms Rmb360–880, with seasonal discounts available).

Highway 219 is reputed to be the highest road in the world (though others make the same claim). Whether this is true or not, along its long, winding route south to the **Ali** region of **Western Tibet**, it crosses a number of passes approaching or more than 5,000 metres above sea level, and it is therefore a route not to be considered lightly. Travel agents in Kashgar can arrange 4WD tours into Tibet without any problem, but travellers making the trip on their own should take spare food provisions, carry suitably warm clothing, and check the current situation vis-à-vis Alien Travel Permits, "fines" for foreigners entering Tibet without the proper paperwork (up to Rmb450 fines have been reported), or the possibility that they may be turned back and have to retrace their steps and make alternative travel arrangements (a potentially big problem in this remote corner of China). Nevertheless, the chance to ascend to the Tibetan Plateau and cross such a starkly beautiful landscape, visiting the ancient **Guge Kingdom** and sacred **Mount Kailas** on the way to Lhasa, keeps a steady stream of travellers passing through Yecheng.

Back on Highway 315, the verdant strip gives way to stony desert, and the road, subject to severe damage from flash flooding, leads to **Pishan (Goma)**. Skrine wrote of this oasis:

> Goma is on the very verge of the Takla Makan . . . It is a great place for the treasure seekers known as "Taklamakanchis", who are to be found all along the fringe of the great desert; ragged, ever-hopeful men of the tramp type who spend their lives ransacking the remains of ancient Buddhist tombs and temples far out among the sands of the Takla Makan. Occasionally these

men find a few coins or seals, one of them becoming rich in the process. From the archaeological point of view, the activities of the ubiquitous Taklamakanchis cut both ways; Stein acknowledges many debts to them including assistance, direct or indirect, in the discovery of his chief sites; but he had far oftener to deplore the damage done by them to tombs and temples, stupas and dwelling-houses.

Thirty kilometres before Hotan, the road passes the small town of Moyu. In 1989, a farmer chanced upon fragments of Buddhist statues near **Zhawa**, which lies 15 kilometres southwest of Moyu. Subsequent archaeological excavations brought to light the ruins of a Buddhist temple which included murals and broken pieces of small Buddhist statues in clay and gypsum; these were originally covered by thin gold leaf. In the vicinity of the monastery, the remains of some houses and a graveyard were found. This settlement existed during the Tang Dynasty (618–907) and was destroyed at the very beginning of the 11th century, at the same time as Khotan.

HOTAN (KHOTAN OR HETIAN)

The oasis town of Hotan (historically called Khotan, and known as Hetian in Chinese) is famous for its jade, carpets, silk and embroidery. Indeed, its fame predates the blossoming of the Silk Road as we know it, since its wealth in precious nephrite, or jade, brought it to the attention of China's earliest dynasties centuries before the start of concerted trade between the cultures of West and East.

For almost 2,000 years the Kingdom of Khotan was the principal supplier of nephrite jade – much cherished by the Chinese – to the dynastic courts of the Middle Kingdom. White jade came from the bed of the Yurungkash (White Jade) River, dark-green jade came from the Karakash (Black Jade) River, and the precious stones were transported by caravan to the heartland of China where they were carved by master craftsmen into exquisite sculptures, jewellery pieces and numerous other items. Khotan's gem markets also dealt in cornelian and lapis lazuli.

Today, Hotan is a collection centre for the raw white jade still found by individuals along the river; however, finds of good jade amount to only a few kilos annually. Some mining is carried out in the Kunlun Mountains during the summer months, but the yield is also very low. The relative scarcity of the precious stone, however, does not deter men from all over Xinjiang and beyond, who converge on the town in the hope of finding that one piece of superb "mutton fat" jade that will make their fortune.

Opposite top: Three Uygurs pass the time of day on the road between Hotan and Pishan. Opposite below: A cotton "bud" awaits a picker's expert hand – cotton is one of Xinjiang's most important crops (Jeremy Tredinnick x2). Right: A jade prospector cradles a rock in his hand, hopeful that he has found a valuable piece of nephrite jade (Sun Jiabin).

A couple practise traditional sericulture in Hotan, the man pulling skeins of 25–30 silk threads from the cocoons, the woman spinning the thread onto a reel (Christoph Baumer).

A ccording to a legend narrated by the famous Chinese pilgrim-monk Xuanzang, sericulture was introduced to Khotan more than 1,500 years ago by a canny Chinese princess betrothed to the King of Khotan. The king had tried in vain to acquire the secret of silk manufacture, so he asked for the hand of a Chinese princess. When his request was granted, he informed his future spouse that in Khotan there was neither silk, silkworms or even mulberry trees. If she wanted to have those at her future domicile, she would have to bring them along. She therefore concealed the eggs of the silkworm and the seeds of the mulberry tree in her headdress to avoid discovery by border officials instructed to zealously guard this national secret. Interestingly, in Dandan Oilik in the winter of 1900–01, Sir Aurel Stein unearthed a painted wooden tablet that accurately illustrated this story. (Today it resides in the British Museum, London.)

The silk industry thrived in ancient Khotan, and examples of the city's magnificent silks can be seen in Xinjiang's museums. Modern Hotan is still the centre of the traditional hand-woven *aidelaixi* silk that is produced by small family units and is a favourite of Uygur women. The rich natural colours and designs of Hotan carpets have also been treasured all over Central Asia for centuries. They are especially valuable because of the long, thick wool the local weavers use. Villagers make carpets as a sideline, selling them at the bazaar or to private buyers from other parts of Xinjiang. Pieces of chain-stitch embroidery made with a hooked needle are also much prized.

THE SILK SECRET

Chinese legend gives the title Goddess of Silk to Lei Zu (Lady Xiling), wife of the mythical Yellow Emperor, who was said to have ruled China in about 3000 BCE. To her is attributed the introduction of silkworm rearing and the invention of the loom. Rituals and sacrifices to Lei Zu were made annually by the imperial court. Court regulations of the Zhou Dynasty decreed that "the empress and royal concubines fast before making their offerings and gather mulberry leaves in person in order to encourage the silk industry". During the Han Dynasty, the heyday of the Silk Road, the annual celebration of Lei Zu was held in splendid style during the third lunar month. The empress and the ladies of the court rode in

grand procession to the Temple of Silkworms in horse-drawn carriages, accompanied by "tens of thousands of horsemen" carrying dragon banners and silk pennants to the Altar of the Silkworms. In Beijing's Beihai Park, once part of the Forbidden City, stands a temple to the Goddess of Silk built in 1742. The age-old annual silk ritual continued until the fall of the Qing Dynasty in 1911.

Half a silkworm cocoon unearthed in 1927 from the loess soil astride the Yellow River in Shanxi Province, in northern China, has been dated between 2600 and 2300 BCE. More recent archaeological finds – a small ivory cup carved with a silkworm design and thought to be between 6,000 and 7,000

Spinning silk is an ancient art perfected in Khotan and still practised in local homes today (Wong How Man).

years old, and spinning tools, silk threads and fabric fragments from sites along the lower Yangzi River – reveal the origins of sericulture to be even earlier. Some Shang Dynasty (1600–1027 BCE) oracle-bone inscriptions bear the earliest known pictographic characters for "silk," "silkworm" and "mulberry."

The fifth-century BCE *Book of Annals* catalogued tributes to Emperor Yu of "lengths of silk of blue or red" from six provinces of China. At that time, not only was the production of silk widespread, but the colours and designs were rich and varied. By the Han Dynasty sericulture was practised from Gansu in the west, where painted tomb bricks show scenes of silkworm breeding and silk weaving, to Sichuan in the south, where the ancient capital of Chengdu was dubbed "Brocade City," and to Shandong on the east coast, which was famous for its wild silk.

From about the fourth century BCE, the Greeks and Romans began talking of Seres, the Kingdom of Silk. Some historians believe the first Romans to set eyes upon the fabulous fabric were the legions of Marcus Licinius Crassus, Governor of Syria. At the fateful battle of Carrhae near the Euphrates River in 53 BCE, the soldiers were so startled by the bright silken banners of the Parthian troops that they fled in panic. Within decades Chinese silks were widely worn by the rich and noble families of Rome. Its production remained a mystery, however; Pliny, the Roman historian, believed that silk was obtained by "removing the down from the leaves with the help of water."

The flimsy transparency of the silken "glass togas" so loved by the Roman elite was soon to bring moral condemnation. Seneca, the Roman philosopher, wrote in the first century: "I see silken clothes, if one can call them clothes at all, that in no degree afford protection either to the body or the modesty of the wearer, and clad in which no

woman could honestly swear she is not naked." Silk drained the Roman Empire of its gold, and by the fourth century one-third of the Byzantine Empire's treasury went to imports of luxury items from the East. High court and church dignitaries dressed lavishly in imperial purple silk, and important personages were buried in silk winding sheets.

The Chinese zealously guarded their secret, but around 440 CE (according to legend) a Chinese princess hid silkworm eggs in her headdress and carried them to Khotan upon her marriage to the king, bringing the art to present-day Xinjiang. Around 550 CE, two Nestorian monks introduced the silkworm to Byzantium, where the church and state created imperial workshops, monopolizing production and keeping the secret to themselves. By the sixth century the Persians, too, had mastered the art of silk weaving, developing their own rich patterns and techniques. It was only in the 13th century – the time of the Second Crusades – that Italy began silk production with the introduction of 2,000 skilled silk weavers from Constantinople. By that time silk production was widespread in Europe.

In the Tang Dynasty the main silk centres were south of the Yangzi River around Taihu Lake, where factory looms produced exquisite brocades highlighted with gold thread. To stock the wardrobe of Yang Guifei, Precious Consort of Emperor Xuanzong, 700 weavers were employed full time. While in Beijing, Marco Polo noted that, "every day more than 1,000 cart-loads of silk enter the city." Bolts of silk and silken robes were essential gifts to political envoys, princes and tribute missions to the Tang, Ming and Qing courts. A mission of 2,000 men to the Ming Dynasty capital of Beijing returned laden with 8,000 bolts of coarse silk, 2,000 lined satin robes and 2,000 pairs of boots and leggings, as well as many other presents.

The breeding of silkworms is a sideline of the Chinese peasant – one that has remained unchanged through the ages. During the summer

A Uygur weaver creates a vibrant, beautiful length of aidelaixi *silk on a basic loom (Wong How Man).*

families take care of large round rattan trays of voracious **bombyx mori** caterpillars, which feed day and night on fresh, handpicked mulberry leaves. Around Tai Lake and the Grand Canal – China's main silk-producing area – the mulberry tree grows to about a man's height, making it easy to pick the leaves.

The newly hatched silkworm, like a tiny piece of black thread, multiplies its weight up to 10,000 times within a month, changing colour and shedding its whitish-grey skin several times. After 30-odd days the silkworms are placed on bunches of straw or twigs, to which the worms attach the cocoons they spin from a single thread

of silk about a kilometre (half a mile) long. The cocoons are then heated to kill the pupa and sent to the silk-reeling mills. There, they are sorted by hand and boiled at 48°C (120°F) to soften and release the thread. The workers plunge their hands continually into the hot water, plucking the threads from about eight cocoons and feeding them into the reeling machine to form a single strand. The rewinding process, resulting in skeins of pure white silk, is usually automatic. The silk from rejected cocoons is made into floss silk, and the pupae are used as a source of protein for animal fodder.

HISTORY

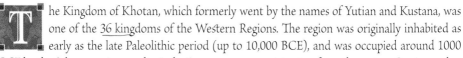

The Kingdom of Khotan, which formerly went by the names of Yutian and Kustana, was one of the 36 kingdoms of the Western Regions. The region was originally inhabited as early as the late Paleolithic period (up to 10,000 BCE), and was occupied around 1000 BCE by the Saka, a semi-nomadic, Indo-European group originating from the eastern Persian realm. Around 300 BCE, immigrants from India moved into the region and probably founded the city of Khotan. In order to enhance its authority, the princely house associated itself not only with the mighty Indian king Ashoka, a famous supporter of Buddhism, but also to the Buddhist tutelary deity Lokapala Vaishravana, the "Lord of the North". Legend tells that the first king of Khotan was a son of Ashoka who had been banished by his father. Having no son of his own, he went to the temple of Vaishravana and implored him to help, whereupon a male child emerged from the head of the statue and became the king's successor.

At the beginning of the second century BCE, Khotan became a vassal state of the Xiongnu, but around 75 CE General Ban Chao drove the Xiongnu out of the oases of the Tarim Basin. During that time the King of Khotan was under the influence of a Xiongnu court shaman. The king and the shaman plotted the humiliation and death of Ban Chao; they demanded that he surrender his prize warhorse to be sacrificed to their gods, to which Ban Chao consented if the shaman himself would lead the horse away. When the shaman appeared, Ban Chao had him decapitated and sent the head to the King of Khotan, who immediately surrendered to the general.

During the second century CE, Khotan was ruled by the Indo-Scythian kingdom of the Kushans, whose King Kanishka I was revered as a devout Buddhist, although he also supported other religions such as Hindu and Iranian faiths. Khotan flourished as an important centre of Mahayana Buddhism in the fourth and fifth centuries, although it was forced to accept the overlordship of, in turn, the Hephthalite Huns, Western Turks, Chinese and twice the Tibetans (663–691 and c. 790–850). Its inhabitants remained Buddhist until the early 11th century when it was conquered – in 1006 – by the Muslim Karakhanids of Kashgar.

The Buddhist pilgrim Fa Xian left a vivid account of the Kingdom of Khotan when he passed through in 399 CE: "This country is prosperous and happy; its people are well-to-do; they have all received the faith and find their amusement in religious music. The priests number several tens of thousands." Fa Xian stayed in Hotan for three months and visited the king's new monastery, which had taken 80 years and three reigns to build. He noted: "It is about 250 feet in height, ornamentally carved and overlaid with gold and silver, suitably furnished with the seven preciosities [gold, silver, lapis lazuli, crystal, ruby, emerald and coral]. Behind the pagoda there is a Hall of Buddha which is most splendidly decorated."

Fa Xian recorded that there were 14 large monasteries, as well as a number of smaller ones. During his visit he attended an important Buddhist festival in which the royal court took part.

"Beginning on the first day of the fourth moon, the main streets inside the city are swept and watered, and the side streets decorated. Over the city gate they stretch a large awning with all kinds of ornamentation, under which the king and queen and court ladies take their places." A procession followed, led by the Buddhist priests. Outside the city was a float "over thirty feet in height, looking like a moveable Hall of Buddha and adorned with the seven preciosities, with streaming pennants and embroidered canopies." A figure of the Buddha was placed on this "image car," followed by two bodhisattvas "all beautifully carved in gold and silver and suspended in the air," Fa Xian noted. The parade halted before the city gate and the king exchanged his royal robes for simple clothes. "Walking barefoot and holding flowers and incense in his hands, with attendants on either side, he proceeds out of the gate. On meeting the images, he bows his head down to the ground, scatters the flowers and burns the incense." The festival lasted for 14 days, with each monastery assembling a Buddha float on a different day, after which the king returned to his throne, and Fa Xian continued northwest to Kashgar.

During the early Tang Dynasty (618–907) Khotan paid tribute to the Chinese court, on one occasion sending 717 pairs of polo ponies to Chang'an. Having been summoned to the imperial presence in 648, the King of Khotan returned home laden with titles and gifts, including 5,000 rolls of silk.

In 643, Xuanzang passed through Khotan on his return from India and reported a strange legend. West of the town was a range of small hills that locals said had been formed by a tribe of sacred rats. These precious vermin and their rat king were protected and fed by locals because they had once saved the Buddhists of Khotan from an army of Huns by gnawing their leather harnesses and armour, thereby rendering them helpless in battle.

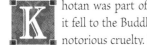 hotan was part of the Muslim Kharakhanid Kingdom between 1006 and 1165, when it fell to the Buddhist Kara-Khitan rulers, whose last ruler, the usurper Küchlüg, was of notorious cruelty. Küchlüg was a Naiman Mongol who had snatched power away from his father-in-law. He was born a Christian Nestorian, but converted later, under the influence of his wife, to Buddhism. When the leading Imam of Khotan refused to convert to Buddhism, he had him crucified on the door of the main mosque. As Khotan was the only oasis in Kashgaria to defend itself against Genghis Khan, it was consequently razed to the ground to set an example to other recalcitrant states. Wars raged between Buddhist and Muslim rulers during the late 10th and early 11th centuries, and the kingdom was enmeshed in all the power struggles of the next eight centuries, including those of the Chaghatai Khanate and the *khojas* of Kashgaria. Marco Polo travelled through the kingdom in 1273, noting that it was "eight days' journey in extent."

In the 19th century, the kingdom became part of Yakub Beg's Kashgaria after a desperate stand against the army by the proud women of Khotan; offerings of packhorses laden with silver bullion, 70 camel-loads of gifts and 14 racing camels were subsequently made to placate Yakub Beg.

ENTER THE ARCHAEOLOGISTS

Khotan was one of the first cities to be excavated by foreigners in the late 19th century. One of the first Western explorers to visit Khotan was William Johnson. A civil servant with the British Survey of India, he was following up on the report of a native who had been conducting surveys in Khotan in 1864 and had run across some old ruins. According to the native, "Khotan... was long ago swallowed up by the sand," and now the local inhabitants were digging out artefacts from those houses left uncovered. The man reported that, "it would appear as if the city had been buried suddenly before the inhabitants had time to remove their property". Johnson braved the territory of the wild Kyrgyz nomads to visit the Khan Badsha of Khotan (who held him hostage in the hope that the British government would send him troops with which to fight the encroaching Russians). Johnson learned of tea bricks "of great age", of gold coins weighing four pounds that had been dug up, and of buried cities whose locations were "known only to a few persons who keep it secret in order to enrich themselves".

As fantastic as Johnson's information was, scholars did not venture into Chinese Turkestan for another 20 years or more. This was partly because archaeologists were occupied at that time with rich finds in Greece, Palestine, Mesopotamia and Egypt, partly because the area was considered dangerous and risky to travel in, and also because of the assumption that any buried cities beneath the Taklamakan were likely to be "only" Islamic rather than Buddhist. The murder of a British citizen in 1888 changed everything.

In 1889, the British lieutenant Hamilton Bower was dispatched to East Turkestan to track down the murderer of the British explorer Andrew Dalgleish, who had been killed by an Afghan from Yarkand. While Bower's agents caught the assassin in Samarkand, Bower purchased an ancient manuscript which had been found by local treasure hunters near Kucha. The manuscript was handed to the Anglo-German philologist Hoernle, who identified the text as being Sanskrit, written in the Indic script Brahmi, and dated it to the fifth century CE. This find was sensational, for it was the very first proof of Indian cultural influence in the pre-Islamic Tarim Basin.

After the discovery of the Bower Manuscript and other finds by Xinjiang treasure seekers, foreign travellers and scholars became more intrigued with the Taklamakan region. In 1892 two Frenchmen, Jules Dutreuil de Rhins and F. Grenard, came to Khotan where they bought an ancient Buddhist manuscript written on birch bark in the Indian Kharoshthi script and dating from the second century CE. Then, in 1895, Sven Hedin arrived in Khotan determined to be the first European to explore the lost Silk Road cities. Hedin was taken to an ancient village called Borasan (Yotkan), where he discovered – and bought from local treasure hunters – manuscripts, coins, terracotta images of the Buddha, figurines of people and camels, a copper cross, and other antiquities. He then went on to explore a city located more than 100 kilometres northeast of Khotan, simply called "Taklamakan" by locals, a collection of ruins in the dunes; today it is called Dandan Oilik. Hedin discovered images of the Buddha and Buddhist deities on one of the walls protruding through the sand. He

ISLAM AKHUN

On Aurel Stein's first expedition, he wanted to verify the validity of certain ancient books the Anglo-German oriental scholar, Rudolf Hoernle of Oxford University, had obtained through Islam Akhun, a local Kashgar trader. Soon after the discovery of the Bower Manuscript, local treasure seekers became acutely aware of British and Russian interest in old books and artefacts, and realized a small fortune could be made in delivering them. Islam Akhun and his partner provided both George Macartney and Nikolai Petrovsky, the consul-generals in Kashgar, with several manuscripts that had baffled scholars because the texts were written in an unknown language. Suspecting a hoax, Stein found his proof in the desert between Khotan and Goma, where Akhun's supposed source contained nothing more than empty ruins in sands.

Upon confronting the spurious historian with his artificially discoloured paper and a fictitious report of the site, the terrified Islam Akhun admitted to having falsified the book prints. He and his partner were desperate to find more manuscripts to sell to the foreign collectors and decided to write their own. The first was handwritten, a collection of odd characters that learned scholars believed to be related to ancient Greek. Realizing the foreigners couldn't distinguish the fake characters from authentic ancient scripts, Akhun stopped imitating actual ancient letters and symbols and invented his own (which explained the odd discrepancy in the texts). As this method proved time-consuming, Akhun eventually came up with the idea of block printing. Using local paper stained yellow, the two entrepreneurs then block-printed books, hung them over a fire to give the paper an authentic, ancient look, then washed them with desert sand, suggesting that the texts came from a buried site.

Although Akhun was not prosecuted by the Chinese, his enterprise caused considerable embarrassment to the academic world, as all 90 volumes of his forgeries had been bound and now rest, forgotten, in the British Library's Oriental department. To be fair to the deceived academics, the texts were amazingly authentic and sophisticated; the neat script seemed scholarly or at least artistic. Some of the blame must lie with the two consul-generals of the time, who indiscriminately bought up all offered books in their eagerness to procure artefacts for their respective nations.

wondered if he had discovered the ancient city that Fa Xian had described in such detail. He said of his discovery, "The scientific research I willingly left to the specialists. For me it was sufficient to have made the important discovery and to have won in the heart of the desert a new field for archaeology." Hedin's digging produced the remains of apricot trees in the barren desert, houses, and a temple that contained wall paintings with Indian, Greek, Persian and Gandharan influences.

Subsequently, Sir Aurel Stein explored the sites of Yotkan, Niya, Dandan Oilik, Endere and Rawak. In 1901, he unmasked the forger, Islam Akhun, whose "ancient scripts" had caused many a Western orientalist in India and Russia – Hoernle for one – to waste years in attempting to decipher his "old books" (*see* page 375). An old treasure hunter showed Stein pieces of fresco with Indian Brahmi characters and Buddhist designs. Stein determined that these were from Sven Hedin's "Taklamakan", which locals called Dandan Oilik. Subsequent work at the site produced Sanskrit texts of the Buddhist canon from the sixth and seventh centuries, and administrative and financial documents in Chinese from the eighth century CE. He also found several paintings on wood in a few temple complexes. One of them, a human figure, is depicted with the head of a rat, flanked on either side by attendants. Stein realized this was the sacred King of Rats who had saved Hotan, a story that Xuanzang had heard about 1,300 years earlier.

In 1935, when Peter Fleming and Ella Maillart arrived in Khotan on their daring overland journey to India, the city was hand-printing its own currency on paper made from mulberry trees. They had the delightful experience of witnessing the arrival by mule of the British Indian postman with documents for the local Indian merchants and three-month-old copies of *The Times* brought all the way from Kashmir.

The Hotan region consists of seven counties with a population of 1.2 million, of whom 96 per cent are Uygur. Twenty-four rivers flow during the summer months when the snows from the Kunlun Mountains melt to

Atop a column in the centre of Hotan's Unity Square, a statue depicts a smiling Uygur man shaking hands with Chairman Mao (Jeremy Tredinnick).

PAPER MANUFACTURING IN HOTAN

By Christoph Baumer

"Paper is one of the four greatest inventions that have contributed to developing the civilizations of the world."

Shaanxi Provincial Museum, Xi'an

Traditionally, the honour of having invented paper has been credited to the state official Cai Lun around the year 105 CE. However, this view has been revised in recent decades. The oldest piece of paper known today was brought to light in 1957 at Pa-chhiao, near Xi'an. There, in a grave from the time of the Han emperor Wudi (140–87 BCE), archaeologists found a felt-like paper sheet 10cm x 10cm in size behind a bronze mirror. Another paper fragment from the Western Han Dynasty (206 BCE–9 CE) was discovered in Xinjiang, in the ruins of a watchtower in the Lop Nor desert. It has been dated to 49 BCE. The pulp for the first paper made in China was made from hemp (*cannabis sativa*) and similar plant fibres mixed with silk waste. At this time, paper had a rather rough surface; its texture was very similar to that of felt, and it was chiefly used as packaging material, for instance for medicines.

Cai Lun did not invent paper, but he did refine its production. He was born in the present province of Hunan around 50 CE. In 75 CE, he entered the service of the imperial court and was promoted to imperial advisor in administering state affairs. At that time, books were made of thin bamboo boards bound together, with shorter texts written on silk. But bamboo was difficult to process, and silk was expensive, so neither material was particularly suited for books. Cai Lun had the idea of improving the quality of paper by manufacturing it from tree-bark, hemp fibre, textile waste and the remains of fishermen's nets. In the year 105 he submitted his invention to Emperor Ho Ti, who took the idea up with enthusiasm.

Thanks to an improved breaking down of the raw materials, the subsequent finer fibrous substance produced paper with more regular fibre distribution and strength over the whole surface of the sheet. These relatively smooth paper surfaces were thus easier to write on. At the same time, paper could now be made thinner and lighter – and it was several times cheaper than woven silk. Reed fibre was also used as a raw material for paper during the Jin Dynasty (265–420 CE), when paper replaced wood as a writing medium. The fibre of the mulberry bush (*Broussonetia papyrifera*) and daphne plants were first processed for paper pulp during the Tang Dynasty (618–907), and bamboo during the Song Dynasty (960–1278).

In some ancient oasis cities along the Southern Silk Road – Niya being an example – virtually no paper fragments have been found at all; however, in 1901 Sven Hedin unearthed paper documents dated between 252 and 310 CE in Loulan, while in 1914 Sir Aurel Stein discovered hundreds of paper documents and paper scraps dating from 263 to 280 CE in the same region.

These earliest examples of paper documents in Xinjiang were most likely imported from central China, but it seems local paper production was active in Khotan from the eighth century onwards, as it served as a paper production centre for the countless manuscripts from the eighth and ninth centuries that Stein discovered in Khotan, Mazar Tagh, Endere and Miran. These manuscripts were written in Chinese, Tibetan and Sanskrit using the Brahmi script as well as in Khotanese, an Iranian language also written in Brahmi. As Khotan was part of the Tibetan empire or within its zone of influence from 670 to about 860, with brief interruptions, it is conceivable that paper also reached Tibet via Khotan.

As well as inventing paper, China also developed block printing. The motivation for the introduction of a reproducible script is to be found in Buddhism, which spread throughout China from the 2nd–3rd century CE onwards. In the popular form of Mahayana Buddhism, it was meritorious to repeat short, sacred prayers, called *mantras*, as many times as possible – whether audibly in the form of a recitation, visually by the repeated writing down of the mantra as so-called *dharanis*, or by the supplicants commissioning monks to copy prayers or whole sutras several times over. The copying of lengthy texts or even short prayers hundreds or even thousands of times by hand took a great deal of time and was inefficient. By the invention of the block printing process during the Tang Dynasty (618-907), the reproduction of texts and pictures was considerably accelerated. Even though the manufacture of the wooden printing plate is time-consuming, it can, once made, be used hundreds of times. With the use of the block printing procedure, the individuality of handwriting was lost, but the uniformity and precision of the text were guaranteed.

The oldest preserved printed book in the world, which also contains the oldest printed illustration, is the famous *Diamond Sutra* dating from 868. It was kept in Cave 17 of the Mogao Caves at Dunhuang, and bought by Sir Aurel Stein from the local Abott Wang in 1907, together with 7,000 other documents. The text

was printed on seven white sheets of paper glued together in a roll approximately five metres in length. On the picture at the start of the roll one sees Buddha enthroned, flanked by bodhisattvas and servants. In front of him the monk Subhuti is kneeling, asking Buddha the meaning of life – the answer being given in the following text. The final lines of the colophon read: "Presented by Wang Jie, in reverence of the names of his parents for universal dissemination on the 15th day of the 4th month of the 9th year of the Xiantong Period" – that is, 11 May 868.

In contemporary Hotan, a papermaker named Mesum Apiz continued the roughly 1,250-year-old local tradition of paper manufacturing right up until 2003. This last papermaker of the Southern Silk Road made paper out of mulberry-bush fibres, using the traditional pouring technique handed down by his ancestors. For almost half a century, he made up to 100 small sheets (45cm x 55cm) and 10 large sheets (60cm x 70cm) per day, depending on weather conditions. Until illness prevented him in late 2003, he beat the mulberry-bush fibres by hand before cooking the mass in a wooden stove. Another hard and time-consuming task was changing the cotton cloth of the 100 small and 10 large pouring screens, which had to be done every two years.

Apiz sold the small paper sheets for Rmb1 and the large ones for Rmb5. Among his last customers were hat-makers, who used the strong, tear-proof paper, which was unsuitable for writing purposes, to line felt or fur hats. In the 1960s and 70s his paper sheets were also glued onto window frames as a cheap replacement for glass. Sadly, in 2003, with debilitating illness and age creeping up on him, the paper manufacturing work become too strenuous for Mesum Apiz, and the tradition of papermaking in Hotan finally came to an end.

fill them, and ample water is available to grow maize, wheat, rice, cotton and oil-bearing plants. Mulberry and fruit trees are also abundant.

SIGHTS

T he modern-day town of Hotan (population 114,000) contains no historic structures except a few sections of the crenellated city wall that once surrounded the "New City" or Chinese cantonment (the Uygur "Old City" had no fortification). The centre of town is the enormous **Unity Square** (*Tuanjie Guangchang*) boasting a large plinth on top of which stands a golden statue of Chairman Mao shaking hands with a Uygur gentleman. At the southern end of the square a huge new shopping centre has been constructed, topped by a golden dome, and this is indicative of the way Hotan is developing. Surrounding the square and to its west are the banks, newer hotels and business centres; the eastern part of town is more traditional, and it is here you'll find the market area. Hotan's **Sunday Bazaar** is a large, vibrant affair to rival Kashgar's, and in atmosphere is more traditional and authentically Uygur. The area devoted to carpets (*gillam*) is predictably colourful.

On the eastern outskirts of town the main road can get packed with hundreds of men milling about, cradling small and large pieces of raw jade rock in their arms. All of them are hoping that they will make a good deal with one of the buyers who drive up in Japanese cars – there is big money to be made in the jade trade, though not often for the thousands of hopefuls who flock to Hotan each year from all over China and fossick in the dry riverbeds, dreaming of unearthing a horse's head-size rock that will be hiding the highest quality jade under its cold, dark outer surface. Sadly for the vast majority this is only a dream – but it is a powerful one, and visiting tourists happily buy into it for half an hour too, scrambling around the rocky floor of the White Jade River picking up shiny pebbles and rocks with no understanding of whether what they are holding is worthless or priceless (apparently good jade is heavier and colder than plain rock).

The **China Xinjiang Hetian Arts & Crafts Jade Carving Factory** (1 Gujiang Beilu, tel: (0903) 203 5281) is a small place hidden away on the first floor of an unprepossessing building. Inside its single room you'll find six or so craftsmen and women casually carving beautiful jade pieces of varying shapes and sizes. The process involves a designer, who studies a stone's size, shape and colour variations before painting lines on the rock for the cutters to follow; the cutters use diamond or hard-steel lathes to cut the jade into its planned shape under a small tap of softly dripping water, then it is passed to the polishers, who use a soft stone to bring out the jade's colour. The factory's gift shop (across the landing from the craftsmen) has an excellent selection of carving, from small, affordable pendants to exquisite necklaces and superb statuettes of different colours. There are said to be seven different types of jade found in the Hotan region, but the best known are the dark-green jasper jade, and the creamy, opaque "mutton fat" jade that is the most prized of all – the best pieces sell for more than Rmb1 million.

lso in the eastern part of town is the **Xin Jiang Hotan Nakixwan Carpet Factory** (tel: (0903) 209 1113, email: nakixwan1113@126.com), which, despite the dishevelled appearance of its building, masks a cottage industry employing local women who make wonderful carpets of every size and design – many people bring their own designs and have their carpet custom-made. A superb 2" x 4" 100-percent silk rug can be had for Rmb4,000-5,000 (bargaining is *de rigueur*), while large, high-quality wool carpets can cost anything from Rmb15,000 up to Rmb100,000 plus – still much cheaper than the comparative price you'd pay in Western countries. Major credit cards are accepted, and international shipping is also claimed to be possible (although this would be a long process, with inherent risks).

Despite its growing modernity, the pace of life in the city is pleasantly relaxed; the unpaved lanes of the residential "suburbs" on the town's outskirts afford glimpses of daily life lived in tree- and vine-shaded courtyards. The lanes are covered with wooden trellises supporting grape vines – it is said that Hotan County contains 5,000 kilometres of these roads – and this gives blessed shade to those walking the dusty tracks or riding one of the ubiquitous donkey carts. The grapes on each road's trellis belong to the families who live on that road – an extra resource for residents. West of town, up one such long, trellis-tunnelled road, is a garden dedicated to the "**Millennium-old walnut tree**" –

Below: The Hotan Museum is an attractive new building well worth a visit (Jeremy Tredinnick). Opposite: An ancient, ship-like coffin still shows the artistry of its decorative painting at the Hotan Museum (Liu Yu Sheng).

the so-called King of Walnut Trees, which is huge and ancient, and whose gnarled trunk and main branches are now supported by wooden beams. The surrounding garden is lovely, with walnut trees, apple trees, rose beds and sitting-out areas. A shop by the entrance sells inexpensive walnut products like bowls, spoons, combs, etc, beautifully grained and coloured by nature. Entrance to the garden is Rmb10.

HOTAN MUSEUM (HOTAN BOWUGUAN)

The Hotan Museum is now located in an attractive new building facing a roundabout on Beijing

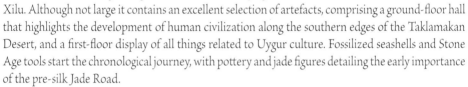

Xilu. Although not large it contains an excellent selection of artefacts, comprising a ground-floor hall that highlights the development of human civilization along the southern edges of the Taklamakan Desert, and a first-floor display of all things related to Uygur culture. Fossilized seashells and Stone Age tools start the chronological journey, with pottery and jade figures detailing the early importance of the pre-silk Jade Road.

Highlight exhibits include an amazingly well-preserved carved pillar from the Han-era Niya ruins, a particularly emotive Tang Dynasty jade monkey from Mazar Tagh, coins from 60 BCE (eastern Han period) clay figures and clothing, silk and brocade fragments of the Han–Jin era Udun people, showing intricate patterns, animal motifs and Chinese writing. There are household artefacts from the Sampul cemetery, engraved leather bags, a bow carved from bone, and a beautiful tasselled shirt piece from the Udun period whose workmanship is of an astonishingly high quality.

Wooden doorposts, bed frames and brickwork stupas are given a photographic background setting of desert sands and ruins; pieces of frescoes and wall paintings from Karadong are accompanied by fine clay and bone sculptures from the Yotkan ruins; jade lamps, Tibetan bronzes, jewellery, chased silver and gold utensils, and ancient documents of Khotan script on parchment continue the rich display. Of special note, however, are two Five Dynasties period (907–960 CE) mummies from the Imam Musa Kazim cemetery. The well-preserved corpses – an adult man and young woman or girl – rest in wooden coffins (assembled without nails), their feet tied together, symbolic of achieving a final peace without further wandering. The man is clad in finely embroidered slippers, while the girl has an intriguing flattened head. A ship-like wooden coffin, still graced with colourful paintings of birds, dragons, snakes and tigers even after more than 1,000 years, stands in the middle of the floor allowing close-up inspection of its superb decoration.

uddhism spread to China along the Southern Silk Road and the museum has a section devoted to this, with many clay Buddha statues in the Indian style from the Rawak stupa site, as well as carvings of flying apsaras and a Ganesh head. A copper Buddha statue found at Damiku Topilik Dong Temple in Qira County is particularly beautiful. Finally, an Islamic Art section displays copper jugs, trays and fire-makers from the Song Dynasty, copper and wood pencil boxes embellished with tiny decorative detail in the Central Asian style, and three Qing Dynasty books, one of which details Uygur medicine of the time.

Upstairs, a huge ewer and basin stand in front of the ornate doors that lead into a large room filled with every item of cultural importance to the Uygur people. Rows of *dopas* (embroidered skullcaps) and traditional robes are displayed in glass cabinets; a wooden weaving loom shows how silk is made, and there are displays of Uygur medicinal products, household goods, mulberry paper, foodstuffs, carpets, musical instruments, and both raw and carved jade.

The Hotan Museum (342 Beijing Xilu, tel: (0903) 251 9286, website: www.htww.gov.cn) is open 9:30am–1pm and 4–8pm (in summer), 10:30am–1:30pm and 3:30–7pm (in winter), and stays open an hour later on weekends; ticket price is Rmb20, and photography is permitted in the upstairs room only.

SHATUO SILK FACTORY

The **Shatuo Silk Factory** (previously called the Silk and Mulberry Research Centre), located five kilometres north of town, operates between April and October. In spite of substantial support from the local government, however, the output from sericulture is only slowly approaching the figures achieved prior to the Cultural Revolution, since during that chaotic time about 80 percent of all mulberry trees within the Hotan Prefecture were cut down. The factory employs over 1,000 workers and produces 150 million metres of silk a year. The compound has dorms, cafeterias and schools, and houses workers from all over Xinjiang. Products include raw or dyed spun silk for the international market, velour and velvet-patterned comforters

Right: A craftsman draws multicoloured silk thread from a massive spool as he carefully weaves an exquisite bolt of aidelaixi silk at the Hotan Atlas Silk Workshop. Opposite: Women gather to pray at the Tomb of Imam Asim on the very edge of the vast Taklamakan (Jeremy Tredinnick x2).

shipped to the CIS, and synthetic fabrics for domestic use. Silk pupas are brought in from the countryside and boiled; the silk thread is extracted with the use of machines and then wound. The thread is taken to other buildings to be spun, dyed and woven, all by heavy machinery. Tours of the centre can be arranged, or it is possible to go yourself; take bus 1 to the end of the line.

The weaving of the *aidelaixi* (Atlas) silks favoured by Uygur women remains very much a cottage industry, and the Jiya township, 25 kilometres northeast of Hotan, is a centre for the production of this traditional hand-woven silk. At the **Hotan Atlas Silk Workshop** (*Atlas Karakhana*), a family-run business employing over 30 local craftsmen and women, visitors can walk around the mill and watch the cocoons being boiled, the silk reeled, and the fabric woven and dyed using traditional techniques. Atlas silk requires much more time to produce than machine-woven silk – even the most skilled weaver can only produce three metres per day. The finished fabric is 40 centimetres wide and up to seven metres long – it is most often black and white, with splashes of crimson red, sky blue and golden yellow. The workshop produces both mixed silk (a combination of synthetic materials and silk) and pure silk products such as scarves and dresses, as well as full silk bolts, and both artificial and natural dyes are used – predictably the priciest items in the colourful shop are pure silk coloured with natural pigments (approx Rmb200 for a scarf), but they are without a doubt wonderful souvenirs, and make exquisite gifts. Entrance to the workshop is only Rmb10.

The Tomb of Imam Asim

Drive 30 kilometres northeast of Hotan, beyond Jiya township down long, straight, dusty poplar-lined roads, and eventually the road and trees peter out into desert dunes. Here you will find the **Tomb of Imam Asim**, a spiritual and military leader of the Kashgari army that came to conquer and convert Khotan to Islam in the 11th century. He died during battle, and was buried here on the edge of the desert, along with many of his soldiers. The tomb became a pilgrimage site for Muslims, and a mosque was built next to it, but as climate changes the desert has encroached, swallowing the site, which is now surrounded by high sand dunes – it is now a 10-minute walk through the dunes from the road's end. (Locals say that every year the desert moves 5–10 metres further south, covering all in its path.)

The mosque and the large, square tomb itself – which is topped by dozens of long poles festooned with pieces of colourful cloth and, curiously, the inflated skins of sheep – are kept as clear of the bullying sand as possible by constant sweeping and digging; the tomb is an important pilgrimage site even today, with up to 10,000 people at any one time congregating here between April and June, when a huge bazaar develops nearby. The tomb is especially popular with barren women, who come to pray for children, sitting in lines on the far side of the tomb away from the mosque. Although a problem for those who maintain the site, its desert location makes it an evocative destination for tourists, a modern-day illustration in miniature of the natural forces that spelt doom for so many of the Taklamakan's great cities.

Ancient City of Yotkan

The remains of this ancient city, believed to be the capital of the Kingdom of Khotan between the third and 10th centuries, are 10 kilometres (six miles) west of present-day Hotan, under four metres of accumulated mud, now planted with rice. Lovely shards of decorated red pottery and pieces of jade can still be found sticking out of the sides of the water channels cutting through the site.

Historical records say the city once covered 10 square kilometres. Both Sven Hedin and Aurel Stein visited **Yotkan**, and Hedin devoted a chapter to it (calling it Borasan) in his mammoth book *Through Asia*. In the late 19th century, finds of great value drew teams of local treasure hunters more interested in the gold and silver objects than in the richly varied shards of pottery, which depicted animals and figures in a style heavily influenced by Indo-Hellenistic and Persian styles (some of these can be seen in Hotan Museum). Stein noted that much of the gold found was actually gold leaf, and concluded that the statues and some of the buildings must have been lavishly coated with it. Among the coins he found were "bilingual pieces of the indigenous rulers, showing Chinese characters as well as early Indian legends in Kharoshthi, struck about the commencement of our era, to the square-holed issues of the Tang Dynasty."

ANCIENT CITY OF MELIKAWAT

Thirty-five kilometres (22 miles) south of Hotan by the banks of the White Jade River lie the broken walls of this ancient city. In 1977, the remains of what are believed to have been an imperial hall and a collection of pottery were excavated. Archaeologists, referring to historical records, think that the site was the capital of the Yutian Kingdom during the Han Dynasty, and was inhabited until the Tang. The desert surface is covered in shards – a playground for small lizards. The sites of Yotkan and **Melikawat** are accessible by car, but very little remains.

ANCIENT STUPA OF RAWAK

hile archaeological sites such as **Balawaste** or **Farhad Beg** – located a few dozen kilometres to the east of Hotan and excavated by Sir Aurel Stein – offer little to see above the ground today, the site of **Damagou**, about 100 kilometres east of Hotan, revealed an important discovery in 2005. Here, a cattle breeder chanced upon fragments of murals that belonged to a tiny Buddhist temple, only 2.25 metres long, two metres wide and 1.3 metres high. It is not only one of the best-preserved Buddhist temples of the entire Southern Silk Road, but also has the best-preserved murals; they date from the seventh century CE, and depict large standing Buddhas, small sitting Buddhas, unidentified bodhisattvas, lay donors and also wild animals. The influence of Persian culture is highlighted by the depiction of a dove within a ring made from pearls, a well-known Sassanian motif. Interestingly, no other finds were made within a radius of 100 metres of the shrine. The present name of "Damagou" is believed by Chinese scholars to derive from the Sanskrit word "dharma", meaning "Buddha's teachings", and "kho" being a locative used as suffix. The name "Dharmakho" would hence mean "place of Buddha's teachings". The murals have not been detached and are still *in situ*, and some Buddhist figures are also still preserved here. It is possible to visit the shrine; the entrance fee is Rmb500 per person. The shrine is about three kilometres south of Highway 315; a 4WD is needed to reach it.

This small shrine is not an isolated find, since Aurel Stein had already found important Buddhist murals from the sixth and seventh centuries CE at the sites of Balawaste and Farhad Beg in the same area. These depict a meditating Buddha, most probably the supreme Tathagata Buddha Vairocana, then an ithyphallic, three-headed male deity holding the symbols of sun and moon, and the goddess Hariti surrounded by five small children. They exemplify the school of Khotanese art, influenced by the art of the Indian Kushan and Persian Sassanian empires. The Khotanese syle of painting had itself great influence on early Buddhist art in China and Tibet.

Probably the most rewarding single-day excursion from Hotan is to the large **Rawak Stupa**. It stands 32 kilometres to the northeast of town, and is accessible by 4WD vehicle but for the last five kilometres, which must be tackled on foot or by camel. A permit and a local guide are needed. The nine-metre-high stupa, dating from the third to fifth centuries, is one of the best-preserved Buddhist sanctuaries on the Southern Silk Road. From each of the four cardinal points, stairs lead

A SIDE TRIP TO RAWAK

A day's march into the sands, I knew, a lonely relic of the kingdom had survived: a great Buddhist stupa discovered by Aurel Stein over a century ago. I found a jobless guide who had once been there, a Uighur woman who knew where to hire a Land-Rover and camels. Gul had once been handsome, and even now, in middle age, her eyes glittered vivid under strong brows, and she dressed for the desert as if for a party.

For an hour we drove over grasslands beyond the oasis, until we came to brushwood shelters disintegrating round a well. No one was in sight. A misted sun lit up the desert beyond. Then, from far away, out of the scrub-speckled dunes, a herdsman came driving camels – huge, moulted beasts with lax humps and chewed ears – and an hour later we were swaying through the May heat into a purer wilderness. Perched on felt blankets lashed over a wooden frame, I watched the salinated scrublands thin away. The sun – a frosted lamp when we set out – burnt away the haze and blazed down over amber dunes crumpled to the horizon. Ahead of me the camel-driver rode in silence, and Gul, under a white sunhat sashed in muslin, her skirts overlapping leather boots, sat her beast delicately and fanned herself with a lilac handkerchief.

Around us was utter silence. The camels' plate-like feet went noiseless over the sand. Only the saddle-packs beneath us, where the beasts' humps drooped like empty bags, creaked in uneasy rhythm with their stride. All about us the dunes were scored with concentric ripples, as if a giant comb had been run down them, and flowed together in a sculptural peace. But here and there, where water lay deep underground, a red willow blew, or a tamarisk tree sent up a tangle of startling green, clotted by hawks' nests, and over the lifeless-seeming sands a snake or lizard had left its feathery track.

*T*hen a weird delusion gathered. Far into the distance, the slopes and valleys of the intersecting dunes, and the punctuation mark of tamarisks, started the fantasy that a landscape of hedged fields and hamlets had been petrified here long ago, and that we were riding through a once-Arcadian land.

Momentarily I could believe the Uighur legend that this was anciently a country of lakes and cities. Taklamakan – Gul called back at me – might in Uighur mean "homeland", and its civilisation was said to have drowned in a great hurricane which raged for forty-nine days. Now they called it "the Sea of Death".

Our way grew emptier, starker. The tamarisks disintegrated into bleached twigs like chicken bones, littering the humps where they had stood. The pulverised gravel along the dunes glinted with quartz. Into this wilderness the camels pushed easily, as if padding back into prehistory. Rearing in front of me, my beast's wrinkled neck had moulted upward to the mauve crown of its head, tufted with leftover auburn curls, like the skulls of the Cherchen mummies.

Suddenly the camel-driver pointed – "Rawak!" – and we all squinted into the glare. A mile away, perhaps, paler than the pale sands around it, a building shone in isolation. The tributary that nourished it had long ago gone underground, and its oasis disappeared, leaving this champagne-coloured sanctuary to disrupt the desert with its tiers of etiolated brick. Even in decay, it was gracefully simple: a circular shrine mounted on a star-shaped base, ascended on four sides by tapering stairways.

As we drew close, a broken drum rose from the debris of its terraces, its cupola crashed in, and the rectangle of an enclosing rampart undulated over the sand. We passed the brushwood hut of its watchman, who had gone, and our camels slumped to their knees.

We walked through the walls by a vanished gate. The whole enceinte was half drowned under the dunes, which overflowed the ramparts or poured through their breaches. Above me the stupa too was blurred by coagulated sand, and its stairways crumbled; but its upper tiers shook clear in bulwarks of creamy brick, and pushed their bright, domeless cylinder into the sky.

Colin Thubron, Shadow of the Silk Road, 2007

to the uppermost room of the stupa. The stupa has a cruciform base platform and is surrounded by a rectangular wall 3.5 metres high and 50 x 45 metres long. The stupa and its wall are understood to represent a gigantic three-dimensional mandala.

In 1901 Aurel Stein excavated along the outer walls enclosing the stupa and discovered about 100 man-sized stucco statues featuring the Buddha and bodhisattvas, some of them still adorned with their original red paint. Tragically, when Stein returned in 1906, he found that local treasure hunters had smashed the statues, hoping to find gold inside them. In 1928, the German Emil Trinkler and the Swiss Walter Bosshard conducted further excavations. Among the statues, two different styles can be distinguished: the first is of classical uniformity and almost exclusively features Buddhas. The heads of the larger figures have stereotyped traits showing that they were made with moulds (one such mould is on display in Hotan Museum). The absence of bodhisattvas suggests that these figures of the first period were created in a Hinayana environment concurrently with the stupa. The sculptures of the second period are more mannered and include bodhisattvas, a clear indication of a Mahayana environment. It is assumed that there was a monastery attached to the stupa.

Even as recently as 1994 and 1998, newly found torsos of figures have been vandalized by local treasure seekers. Fortunately, most of the statues excavated by Trinkler and Bosshard are protected by a huge sand dune, putting them out of reach of local treasure hunters and fanatical iconoclasts. But regardless of damage done, Rawak is still a very impressive site. Just near the stupa, reeds growing out of the sand show that an underground water source is close to the desert surface here.

Worthy of an excursion too is the ruined, brick-built fort of **Aksipil** dating from the fifth to sixth centuries, about 18 kilometres to the east of Hotan. Although less impressive than Rawak, Aksipil gives a fair impression of how other, less accessible sites located deep in the desert look.

Also to the east of Hotan, at a location called **Shanpula** (also known as Sampul), between 1983 and 1996 archaeologists discovered three graveyards, and excavated 69 tombs dating from the third century BCE to the fourth century CE. Some of the tombs were mass burials, with more than 200 dead bodies inside a single tomb. Here unique, colourful woollen textiles were found featuring hunting scenes and animals such as winged stags, camels and birds of prey. The motifs seem to be influenced by the culture of the Saka people – who lived in the Pamir and Tien Shan mountains – and inspired by ancient Persian mythology.

At the excavation's start in 1983, a fantastic 120-centimetre-long woollen wall hanging was discovered, depicting in its upper portion a centaur playing his flute, and in the lower part a warrior with almond-shaped eyes, a large, long nose and full lips. He holds a lance in his right hand. The influence from the Hellinistic world, probably from Bactria, is obvious; such wall hangings were often cut by Saka riders and transformed into leggings. The wall hanging dates from the last centuries BCE; at that time the people of Shanpula were nomadic cattle breeders who also practised modest agriculture. There is not much to see above ground, and the excavated objects are now in the

The Rawak Stupa is an evocative remnant of Xinjiang's Buddhist heyday (Christoph Baumer).

museums of Hotan and Urumqi. Unfortunately, the best and by far most spectacular pieces have been smuggled abroad.

River rafting

Hotan can be used as a base for expeditions into the Kunlun Mountains. For the seeker of rare experiences, it's possible to raft down the Black or White Khotan rivers; however, special permits are required and the logistics are complicated, so this is an adventure for the intrepid – and deep-pocketed – explorer only.

Hotan Practical Information

Hotan is a sprawling town struggling to modernize without ruining its dusty charms. The town centre revolves around Unity Square, and coffee bars and Internet cafés are springing up in this area, with new hotels boasting nightclubs as proof of their modern sophistication. For those without their own transport, most sights in and near the town are accessible by foot or bus. A fairly up-to-date city map can be found at www.centralasiatraveller.com.

Transportation

There are daily flights to/from Urumqi with China Southern Airlines and Shanghai Airlines (the airport is nine kilometres southwest of town), and frequent daily buses to/from Yecheng, Shache, Yengisar and Kashgar to the west, and Yutian, Minfeng, Qiemo and Ruoqiang to the east. Now that the cross-desert Highway 217 links Hotan with Aksu to the north, buses should start making that trip soon – a journey of only around seven hours thanks to the quality of the new road.

However, the new rail line from Kashgar that opened in 2011 has made it even easier to visit Hotan – train No 5826/5827 operates between Urumqi and Hotan via Kashgar every day, arriving at 8pm at Hotan Station and leaving Hotan at 9am each morning. The journey from/to Kashgar takes 9–10 hours.

ACCOMMODATION

Hotan has seen some welcome additions to its hotel options in recent years. The **Hotan Zhejiang Grand Hotel** (75 Beijing Xilu, tel: (0903) 202 9999) is a new four-star hotel just northeast of Unity Square; rooms range from Rmb458 for a standard to Rmb988 for a deluxe suite (20 percent discounts available out of season). The **Hotan Muztagh Hotel** (11 Beijing Beilu, tel: (0903) 202 7777) is also new, offering rooms from Rmb388 to Rmb888.

For a more traditional-style hotel, try the **Hotan Hotel** (Urumqi Nanlu, tel: (0903) 251 3564), whose rooms cost Rmb380–880. Its entrance building and gardens with grape trellises and orchards make for a pleasant retreat after a day's dusty exploration.

FOOD AND DRINK

All the above hotels have restaurants offering traditional Uygur dishes and approximations of Western fare. However, Hotan is replete with small, local eateries – particularly near the bazaar – and this is an ideal way to taste Uygur food at its best. Don't miss trying a *goushnaan*, a Hotan speciality like a large *sumsa*, or baked dumpling, which tastes much like a fragrant Cornish pasty and is just as nourishing.

BEYOND HOTAN

In the desert east of Hotan, a metalled road leads towards Yutian (Keriya), Minfeng (New Niya), Qiemo (Cherchen) and Ruoqiang (Charkhlik). There is not much to see along the way – fields and reed marshes are interspersed with large tracts of barren desert – and the small intervening towns offer little attraction but for their lively and colourful markets. However, some of these small towns are starting points for expeditions to explore the ancient ruined cities buried in the desert (most only open to expedition members who have paid the considerable permit fees). While an expedition's main equipment has to be brought from Urumqi or Kashgar, the necessary food supplies, including livestock such as sheep and chicken to be slaughtered on the trip, can be purchased in the markets of these small towns.

Both north and east of Hotan are some 15 rivers, which once flowed more than 80 kilometres farther into the Taklamakan than they do today; the Hotan and Keriya rivers once even crossed the entire Taklamakan Desert to reach the Tarim River at its northern edge. Today, only in years with exceptionally rich snowfall in the Kunlun Mountains – and high subsequent snowmelt – does the Hotan River reach the Tarim. Many of the once prosperous towns watered by these rivers were abandoned to the sands between the third and ninth centuries due to climatic change, rivers shifting their courses, and political disturbances which caused irrigation channels to be neglected and fall into decay. Over time the towns became buried treasure troves.

MAZAR TAGH

bout 160 kilometres north of Hotan as the crow flies stands the old fortress of **Mazar Tagh**, which controlled the north-south trade route following the Hotan River and linking Hotan with Aksu. The well-preserved fortress sits on a rocky ledge at the very eastern end of a 95-kilometre-long, 200-metre-high range of hills that was probably once linked to another line of hills to the northwest near **Maralbashi**, and which together would have formed a single 260-kilometre mountain massif that, over millions of years, was eroded by the abrasive action of the constant desert windstorms down to its current much reduced size.

The fortress of Mazar Tagh was built out of sun-dried brick in the seventh century by the Chinese; it was occupied by Tibetan troops from 790 until about 850 and was thereafter abandoned. Thirty metres northwest of the fortress, a massive, six-metre-high tower protects the only access point to the fortress, steep rock faces on the other three sides offering natural protection. This tower looks similar to those built during the Eastern Han (25–220 CE) and Jin (265–420 CE) dynasties, and could well date to an earlier period than the fortress. In 1908 and 1913 Aurel Stein found numerous documents here written on wood and paper in Chinese, Khotanese, Indian Brahmi, Sogdian, Tibetan, Arabic and Uygur.

Below the fort, but still on the western side of the Hotan River, stand the modest ruins of a Buddhist temple. The quadrangular ground pattern is easy to see, with the outer wall and the pole above the cella, or inner temple area. Three more rooms are attached to the shrine, and a few metres to the north stand the rectangular pedestals of two small stupas.

Access to Mazar Tagh is much easier now that much of the distance from Hotan can be covered on Highway 217. However, the fortress is still some way from the road, which runs along the Hotan River's east bank, and a 4WD is still essential, while if the river cannot be crossed then you are in for a long day's drive up the western edge of the river, so make sure the car is in perfect condition for there are a few "minor" sand dunes to cross on the way!

It's possible to trek eastwards from Mazar Tagh with camels to the small village of **Tunguzbasti**, located near the dry riverbed of the Keriya River – a 100-kilometre-trip (as the crow flies) taking six or seven days. The actual distance covered will more likely be about 150–170 kilometres, since you must bypass the higher dunes and avoid having to climb soft lee sides with possible quicksand, which can be dangerous for heavily laden camels. This is a relaxing and relatively popular desert trek offered by both European and Chinese expedition agencies, but a wonderful experience nevertheless. It is easy to obtain a permit for this trek, but for topographical reasons the journey is usually made in the other direction, starting in Tunguzbasti and ending at Mazar Tagh.

DANDAN OILIK

The Southern Silk Road continues from Hotan eastwards to Qira. About 115 kilometres to the north, in the desert between the Hotan and Keriya rivers, lies **Dandan Oilik**. This large archaeological site, whose centre covers an area of 4.5 square kilometres (the total oasis measured approximately 22 square kilometres) is also accessible via a six-day camel trek from Mazar Tagh, or by a three-day trek from the western shore of the Keriya River.

This site was discovered in 1896 by Sven Hedin, who was overwhelmed by his discovery. In his book *Through Asia* he wrote: "Who could have imagined that in the interior of the dread Desert of Gobi... actual cities slumbered under the sand, cities wind-driven for thousands of years, the ruined survivals of a once flourishing civilization? And yet there stood I amid the wreck and devastation of an ancient people, within whose dwellings none had ever entered save the sand-storm... there stood I like the prince in the enchanted wood, having awakened to new life the city which had slumbered for a thousand years, or at any rate rescued the memory of its existence from oblivion."

Four years later, Aurel Stein started his first Central Asian expedition with *Through Asia* in his luggage. He hired the two hunters who had previously led Sven Hedin to Dandan Oilik and excavated parts of the city in the winter of 1900–01. Stein identified 16 ruined structures within the centre of Dandan, most of them Buddhist shrines or monasteries. The city was not on any main travelling route, but on a road of secondary importance connecting those that ran along the Keriya and Hotan rivers. It may have been a religious centre that bloomed in the 6th–8th centuries and was abandoned in 790 due to marauding Tibetan troops and lack of support from Hotan. Therefore the last agriculturalists left the oasis, and the formerly fertile land lay waste forever after, engulfed under shifting sand.

Top: A Sogdian mural at Dandan Oilik's Temple 13 depicts worshippers making offerings of lotus flowers (U. Möckli). Above: Another mural at the same site shows, from the left, the Hindu deities Shiva, Hariti and Brahma. Opposite bottom: Temple 13 at Dandan Oilik, excavated from its centuries-long immersion by sand. Opposite top: A young Uygur boy and his hawk get ready to hunt for hares at the desert's edge (Christoph Baumer x3).

Such catastrophes were, in a similar way to those in other religions, worked into myths in which the traumatic event was reinterpreted as a divine punishment. Such a myth, which is reminiscent of the Biblical story of the end of the cities of Sodom and Gomorrah, fits the decline of Dandan perfectly; in Stein's book *Ancient Khotan* it is told by Xuanzang: Once upon a time, a Buddhist saint was treated with disdain by the citizens of Ho-lao-lo-chia, situated about 150 kilometres east of Khotan, because he had pilloried their sinfulness. When he was refused drinking water, he cursed the city and while the inhabitants mocked him, "sand began to rain from the skies and continued for seven days and nights until the whole of the buildings were buried."

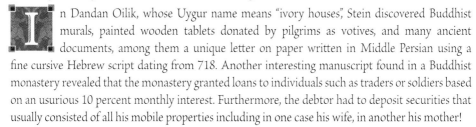

I n Dandan Oilik, whose Uygur name means "ivory houses", Stein discovered Buddhist murals, painted wooden tablets donated by pilgrims as votives, and many ancient documents, among them a unique letter on paper written in Middle Persian using a fine cursive Hebrew script dating from 718. Another interesting manuscript found in a Buddhist monastery revealed that the monastery granted loans to individuals such as traders or soldiers based on an usurious 10 percent monthly interest. Furthermore, the debtor had to deposit securities that usually consisted of all his mobile properties including in one case his wife, in another his mother!

Stein's rich finds were divided into two parts: the removed murals, including those from Miran, Balawaste and Farhad Beg, and some figures were given to the National Museum in New Delhi, which now displays them in a new, exclusive gallery. The painted wooden tablets, all manuscripts and other finds are kept in the British Museum, London. Some of the highlights are on permanent display, as are those finds from Niya.

This remote site was next visited briefly by Huntington in 1905 and again in the spring of 1928 by Trinkler and Bosshard. In 1998, on his second Sino-Swiss expedition the Swiss explorer Christoph Baumer discovered three additional ruins, among them a small temple with murals featuring Sogdian and Buddhist deities, dating from the eighth century CE. They depict a white deity sporting an aureole and riding a red camel, which can be identified as the Sogdian god of victory Washagn, called Veretragna in Persia. As well as the representations of devotees holding lotus buds and lotus flowers – a traditional symbol expressing the wish of Buddhist believers to be reborn in the "Pure Land", the paradise of Buddha Amitabha – two groups of three deities each are highly remarkable. In the centre of both trios of haloed deities sits a goddess holding one or two babies in her arms. She is Hariti, who in Buddhist mythology was originally a child-devouring ogress, but who was converted by Buddha into a child-protecting goddess. To achieve this conversion, Buddha hid the youngest of her own 500 children to make her realize the pain she was causing to those mothers whose children she had stolen. Her cult expanded from India to Central Asia, China and Japan. Within a Sogdian context Hariti was probably associated with the goddess of fertility, Anahita.

On the left of the first trio sits a three-headed, ithyphallic deity. Stein had already found in 1901 a similar representation on a wooden votive board in another temple of Dandan Oilik as well as on a mural from Balawaste. The comparison with Sogdian paintings from Penjikent, in today's Tajikistan, suggests that the figure represents the Sogdian wind god Weshparkar in the shape of the Hindu god Shiva. Weshparkar was a Sogdian adaptation of the ancient Aryan god Vayu who, like Shiva, appeared as creator and destroyer of life, providing not only breath to all living creatures, but also withholding it from them at the moment of death. As per Hindu tradition, Weshparkar/Shiva is shown in the mural with his mount Nandi, a black bull. On the right side of this triumvirate sits another three-headed, ithyphallic deity who holds with his upper hands the sun and moon, or both cosmic eggs. The figure probably represents the Sogdian god of time and fate, Zurvan, but with the traits of the Hindu god Brahma (see picture on previous pages).

In the second group of three deities, a three-headed male deity sits on the left. He holds three arrows in his upper left hand and a bow in his upper right, while his lower left hand holds a cockerel. Close to his left knee stands a peacock. Since the peacock was the attribute of the Indian war god Kartikeya, this figure can be interpreted also as the Sogdian god of victory, Washagn. On the right side sits a boar-headed deity wearing a royal crown in the style of the Persian Sassanians (224–651 CE). It is probably a benevolent medicine deity called "Graha", belonging to the retinue of Washagn/Kartikeya, and a protector of children. Although all these murals were executed in a rough manner, almost as sketches, they clearly belong to the important painting school of ancient Khotan.

The discovery of Sogdian deities is not really unexpected, since Aurel Stein found documents in Chinese and Kharoshthi which not only mentioned Sogdian traders in Dandan, but also indicated that in the last decades of the eighth century the political leader of Dandan was a Sogdian, or, at least, bore a Sogdian title. While the Sogdian religion had a pantheon of its own, its deities were often portrayed with the traits of Buddhist and Hindu deities.

A low sand dune divides the city into northern and southern halves, while a ditch 15–30 metres wide and 3–6 metres deep, presumably a former riverbed, separates the western part from the eastern. Thus the site can be divided into three distinct groups of ruins: a northeastern one with seven complexes, a central one consisting of three ruins and a southwestern group with all other ruins. In one of these latter ruins, Stein discovered a unique clay statue of the Buddhist tutelary god Lokapala Vaishravana, standing on a dwarf flying on the ground, and undamaged except for its head. Vaishravana was the Buddhist adaptation of the Hindu deity Kubera, the god of wealth. Vaishravana was worshipped as the cosmic guardian in the North, as the protector of traders and also of the Kingdom of Khotan to which Dandan Oilik belonged. Just beside Vaishravana, Stein also found a painting of a lightly clad woman bathing in a pool between lotus blossoms, to whose left thigh a cupid is clinging. Beside the pool, a horseman was visible. Aurel Stein connected the curious scene with a legend told by the pilgrim monk Xuanzang, according to which the widow of a river god, thirsting for love, dried out the Khotan River, which was essential to the survival of the oasis city. When the King of Khotan besought her to allow the water of the river to flow again, she insisted to be given a new husband. For this, a minister sacrificed himself; he rode into the river, whereupon the goddess drew him down into her subterranean palace.

Left: A fragment of a Buddhist mural from Karadong, dating from the third century CE. Above: The eastern gate of Karadong is flooded by sand – the beams and pillars showing are part of the second storey of the building. Opposite: A quintessential scene in southern Xinjiang – a Uygur drives a small flock of sheep down a poplar-lined lane near the Keriya oasis (Christoph Baumer x3).

The Sino-Swiss expedition of 1998 also made an interesting discovery in a rubbish heap near a group of small houses: a paper document 30 centimetres long and seven centimetres wide, inscribed with 27 lines on both sides in the middle-Khotanese language written in cursive Brahmi script. This text from the 7th–8th centuries is a Buddhist spell against disease. The spell is formulated as a dialogue between the Buddha and seven *Nagas*, archaic deities in the shape of snakes who provoke terrible diseases such as typhus or leprosy. In a meeting with the Buddha, they regret the meanness of their doing and promise to protect humans from disease; thus they become medicine demigods. While such texts explaining the roles of the nagas are known from documents in other languages, this is the only one found in Khotanese. It is now kept at the Archaeological Institute of Xinjiang in Urumqi. Some of the murals discovered in 1998 were removed by Chinese archaeologists in 2002 and also brought to the Archaeological Institute in Urumqi. A full survey of the ruins was conducted in 2006, but so far there is no plan for a systematic excavation of the ruins. Unfortunately, Dandan Oilik is strictly off-limits for general travellers.

Travelling east from Qira on Highway 315, less than halfway to Yutian the road passes through Damagou (Domoko) township. Seven kilometres southeast of here is the site of the **Tuopuklun (Tuopulukedun) Temple**, discovered in 2002 and said to be the world's smallest ancient temple. Located on top of a large sedentary sand dune covered in reeds and tamarisks, the site measures a mere 2 x 1.7 metres and 1.45 metres high, but contains some exquisite fragments of wall paintings belonging to the "Khotan School of Painting," as well as a 0.65-metre Buddha statue in its centre. A museum building has now been constructed around and over the site to protect it and allow visitors to view it safely.

YUTIAN (KERIYA)

The small town of **Yutian** (**Keriya**) does not have any specific tourist attractions, but as the seat of Yutian County, which has a population of 220,000 people, it often bustles with life, and can be interesting to wander around. A lot of new construction has occurred in recent years, the result of Chinese immigrants moving in as part of Beijing's "Go West" programme. The new look of the town is somewhat incongruous – a plaza just west of the mosque has a Graeco-Roman colonnade – but the main mosque in the southeast is impressive, with beautiful geometric ceiling decoration. In the middle of the roundabout where Highway 315 enters town is a statue of Chairman Mao greeting a Uygur, a smaller version of the one in Hotan's Unity Square. The **Zhe Jiang Hotel** (Da Jiudian, just northeast of the plaza) has rooms from Rmb288, suites Rmb598.

A major earthquake (7.2 on the Richter scale) in March 2008 was centred south of the town in the Kunlun Mountains, but only four villages were affected, and amazingly there were no reported casualties. Nevertheless, this event puts into sharp relief the fact that the Altun and Kunlun ranges to the south of the Southern Silk Road accommodate a major fault line that is the result of the continuing movement of the Tibetan Plateau eastwards in relation to the Eurasian Plate.

KARADONG AND YUAN SHA

Following the ancient Keriya River 170 kilometres north from Yutian, you reach the small village of Tunguzbasti. From here it's a leisurely one-day camel ride to the ancient fortified caravanserai of **Karadong**. Like Mazar Tagh, Karadong controlled a north-south traverse through the desert, but this site is much older, for it was already abandoned in the fourth century CE when the Keriya River changed its course eastwards and its water volume dropped. However, we know from the autobiography of Mirza Haidar, a prince and historian from Kashgar, that the Keriya River still reached the Tarim River in the early 16th century. Like Dandan Oilik, Karadong was initially explored by Hedin in 1896 and then excavated by Stein in 1901 and 1908.

The most impressive ruin at Karadong is the large fort or fortified caravanserai from the Eastern Han Dynasty (25–220 CE). The ground plan is roughly square (the longest side is 68 metres long and the shortest 58 metres), with slightly rounded corners. On the clay walls, which were at least five metres thick and of the same height, there once stood numerous wooden structures plastered with clay. Inside the fortress are the ruins of a large, two-storey residential house. On the eastern side of the fort stand huge pillars which once formed the two-storey main gate.

In 1993/94, a Sino-French team of archaeologists found Buddhist murals in a temple within a complex of more than 20 houses, located a couple of hundred metres from the fort, which had already been noticed by Hedin but was twice missed by Stein. These murals, which show standing and seated Buddhas, probably date from the first half of the third century CE, and display a noticeably Indian influence. The remaining murals were found near the temple's floor, and with a surface area of four square metres they represent only a tiny fraction of the whole painted surface, which was about 70 square metres. They are slightly older than those found in Miran and, in fact, one of the world's oldest extant painted representations of the Buddha. Some of the fragments are on display at the Xinjiang Uygur Autonomous Region Museum in Urumqi. Agricultural tools and huge pottery jars were also found within the complex of houses, while to the north of this area are huge sand dunes that have resisted excavation but could be hiding more treasures.

In 1994 the same Sino-French team discovered the site of **Yuan Sha** (Jumbula Kum in the Uygur language) about 40 kilometres north of Karadong. Both the Chinese and the Uygur names mean "round desert" – the town was given this name because it was protected by a circular clay wall with a circumference of almost 800 metres. On both the northern and southern sides stood a seven-metre-high fortified gate. Dating from the Iron Age, Yuan Sha was the predecessor to Karadong and was already abandoned at the latest by 130 BCE, when the Keriya River shifted its course eastwards next to Karadong. Neither silk nor Chinese coins were excavated – a clear indicator that the town had been abandoned before the Chinese presence began. However, maritime cowries were found which suggests that these people had trading contacts with China. The residents of Yuan Sha were able to grow millet, barley and wheat based on a complex irrigation network.

About 500–1,000 metres outside the city, four graveyards were situated at each of the four cardinal points. Naturally mummified corpses were discovered here, of which about half are of Indo-European stock. In a few tombs, two men were buried together head to foot, with their skulls pierced by five arrows each. Were they executed or sacrificed? No one knows. Even further north, two burial grounds dating from the Bronze Age (2000–900 BCE) were uncovered. The Sino-French archaeological exploration of the Keriya River and its many deltas was officially closed at the end of 2006, having identified about 50 archaeological sites.

LIUSHUI

About 95 kilometres south of Yutian and 35 kilometres south of Aqiang, deep in the Kunlun Mountains, a graveyard was discovered in 2003 near the village of **Liushui**. Its excavation, lasting till 2005, brought 52 graves to light. Inside the tombs, metal ornaments were found, crafted in the Scythian "animal style", as well as the earliest jadeware so far unearthed in Xinjiang. The graves are about 3,000 years old, but virtually nothing is to be seen above ground, except for a few heaps of flat stones.

MINFENG (NEW NIYA)

The next oasis town after Yutian is **Minfeng**, also called New Niya. While Minfeng offers nothing of special interest, the Muslim pilgrimage site at the *mazar*, or tomb, of the saint **Imam Jafer Sadik** is worth seeing, especially in the latter part of summer and autumn when it is visited by thousands of pilgrims. The tomb is popularly called the "Mecca of Turkestan" and is located next to the settlement of **Kabakasgan**, 70 kilometres north of Minfeng up a road that roughly follows the Niya River. Although legend tells that Imam Jafer Sadik was a descendant of the Prophet Mohammed, the shrine is no older than the 16th or 17th century.

On the walk to Imam Jafer Sadik's tomb you pass numerous graves, each consisting of a small mound of clay with a rectangular wooden fence about 120 centimetres high around it. Stuck into the sand next to each one are wooden poles up to three metres high, to which are affixed colourful scraps of cloth. There are also larger subterranean graves that have burial chambers made from tree trunks. Through a wooden gate decorated with many flags, horses' tails and animal skins, you arrive at the

Above: The imam of the tomb of Imam Jafer Sadik at the mazar entrance (Christoph Baumer). Opposite: A skull at the Niya site acts as a reminder of the harshness of this region, both past and present (J.D. Carrard).

saint's tomb, which is a simple wooden structure. It is, however, completely covered by a forest of red, yellow, white and green flags with sayings from the Koran written on them. Inside the mausoleum, an equally colourful sight greets the eye: dozens – if not hundreds – of coloured wimples, and at the centre the great sarcophagus, covered with a dark red cloth. On this are printed views of Mecca, the Muslim creed, and the names of Mohammed and his son-in-law Ali.

Minfeng Practical Information

A daily bus goes west to Hotan (six hours), but buses heading there from Urumqi and Korla also pass through. There are a number of buses every day east to Qiemo, and one daily bus north to Korla (8–9 hours) and on to Urumqi (18 hours). East of the traffic circle opposite the China Post building is the **Lu Zhou Guesthouse** (tel: (0903) 675 2999) with rooms from Rmb120 up. The **Niya Gong Yu Hotel** (tel: (0903) 675 1111) is the best place in town, with good rooms from Rmb180 and suites Rmb470. To get there, go south from the traffic circle, turn left into a tree-lined street and take the third driveway on the left. The hotel also has a good Chinese restaurant. Just west of Minfeng's main traffic circle is the entrance to its covered bazaar – there are Uygur restaurants on the street here.

Niya

About 45 kilometres north of the Imam Jafer Sadik shrine is the ancient site of **Niya**, whose former name was **Jin Jüe** and which formed part of the **Kingdom of Shanshan** till the fifth century CE. In its heyday in the second and third centuries CE, the kingdom encompassed the whole southeast region of the Tarim Basin, stretching from Loulan in the east to Niya in the west. In those days its official name was Cadota. Nevertheless, it had to recognize Chinese suzerainty each time China stressed its claims by sending an army eastwards, for example when General So Man reconquered Loulan around 260 CE and three years later forced Shanshan's ruler, King Amgoka (ruled 246–277) to replace his honorific Indian titles with Chinese ones, thus recognizing China's supremacy. The discovery in Niya of tablets written in the early Indian scripts of Kharoshthi and Brahmi lent weight to the argument that the Southern Silk Road had until the middle of the third century CE been mainly under the cultural influence of northern India, despite the fact that from the first century BCE it had fallen most often within the political and military zone of influence of China.

The latest document found in Niya is dated to the end of the fourth century CE. Around this time, the final abandonment of Jin Jüe took place and the Silk Road was diverted farther south. The reason for this dramatic event was, as with Karadong, a combination of political change – the crumbling of the Kingdom of Shanshan – and ecological factors, namely an acute water shortage due to a shift in the course of the Niya River. A manuscript from the fourth century highlights this dramatic incident, saying that "at the time when the river dried up, Kampila abandoned his wife."

A place called "Ni Jang", mentioned by Xuanzang in the year 644, cannot therefore be ancient Jin Jüe, but must relate to a settlement between Kabakasgan and today's Minfeng – that is still called

"Niya" or "New Niya" by locals. This mysterious seventh-century settlement of Ni Jang has still not been found, though the search is ongoing.

Stein led three expeditions – in 1901, 1906 and 1913 – to the site which he called "my little Pompeii". There he found hundreds of huge wooden tablets (up to two metres long) inscribed on both sides in the Indian Brahmi and Kharoshthi scripts. (Since paper was scarce at that time, ordinary letters and public records were written on wood.) Stein's work on a nearby rubbish heap ("I had to inhale its odours, still pungent after so many centuries, and to swallow in liberal doses of antique microbes luckily now dead") yielded wooden tablets sealed with the figures of Pallas Athene, Zeus, Herakles, a sitting Eros and other Greek deities. The cultural links with the Hellenistic world were further enhanced by the 1959 discovery of a linen fragment depicting a naked goddess with a nimbus, wavy hair, crescent-shaped eyebrows, almond-shaped eyes, a long, large nose and full lips. She holds a large cornucopia in her hands and is probably the Graeco-Gandharan tutelary goddess Tyche or the Greek goddess of harvest, Demeter. Stein found no paper manuscripts in Niya at all, and only a few fragments have been found since then. This is noteworthy, for the earliest paper manuscripts found in the Taklamakan are those from Loulan dating from the third century CE. Although paper was widely used in the eastern region of the Kingdom of Shanshan, it seems that it remained virtually unknown in Niya.

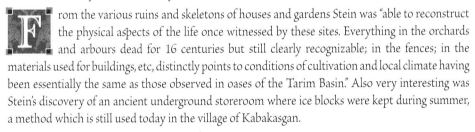 rom the various ruins and skeletons of houses and gardens Stein was "able to reconstruct the physical aspects of the life once witnessed by these sites. Everything in the orchards and arbours dead for 16 centuries but still clearly recognizable; in the fences; in the materials used for buildings, etc, distinctly points to conditions of cultivation and local climate having been essentially the same as those observed in oases of the Tarim Basin." Also very interesting was Stein's discovery of an ancient underground storeroom where ice blocks were kept during summer, a method which is still used today in the village of Kabakasgan.

The ruins of Niya are scattered far apart over the oasis, which covers about 50 square kilometres. In contrast to Dandan Oilik, where most remaining ruins are from temples and monasteries, Niya's buildings were clearly residential. The majority were on small, terrace-like platforms of clay or loess, from which it is concluded that the terrain was formerly marshy. Stein provided further evidence of a previous abundance of water, or at least of larger irrigation channels, when he found an almost intact wooden bridge in the city's southern section. Quite a gruesome find was made later by Chinese archaeologists in 1959 in a tomb, wherein a man and a woman were buried together in the same coffin: there were clear signs that the man had died in great pain and that the woman was buried alive alongside him.

Between 1995 and 1997, a Sino-Japanese archaeological team not only found more than 60 additional ruins on top of the 40 ruins identified by Aurel Stein, but also discovered a large fortress, Buddhist murals dating from the late third to early fourth centuries, and even a princely graveyard. The fortress was surrounded by three oval-shaped earthen walls, the inner wall having a circumference of 150 metres and the outer of 185 metres. This discovery fits perfectly with an ancient chronicle saying that Jin Jüe had round city walls – the text must have referred to the fortress and not the vast city situated to its north. The excavated fragments of Buddhist murals are the only ones found in Niya and a few of them are on display in the Xinjiang Uygur Autonomous Region Museum in Urumqi. The Sino-Japanese team also found several wooden boards with a dancing female figure carved on both sides. Whom the figures depict is unknown.

The discovery of the two graveyards was quite sensational. The larger one contained 13 mummies and is located close to the stupa, while the smaller one is situated north of the city boundaries and housed eight mummies. All but two of the 21 mummies had Indo-European characteristics. Most interesting was the discovery of a double tomb with two coffins lying on top of each other. Both contained a richly clad couple with two special pieces of textile, one found in each coffin. The first, from coffin M3, was a silk quilt with an inscription in Chinese saying "marriage of families of the King and the Marquis". This inscription, together with the discovery of a pitcher marked in black ink with the Chinese character for "*wang*", which means "king", suggested that the corpses were a princely couple, probably a king of Jing Jüe and his wife.

The second textile, from coffin M8, was a silk arm protector manufactured in central China between the second and third centuries CE, with an inscription declaring: "The five planets all appear in the east. This is very auspicious for China, and the Qiang will be defeated." This fascinating text refers to a rare astronomical event, namely when the planets Jupiter, Mars, Mercury, Saturn and Venus appear at the same time in the East, and such a constellation is confirmed in an edict by Emperor Xuandi, who ordered General Zhao to attack the Eastern Tibetan Qiang. Such a prestigious inscription could only have been granted to a king, implying that the couple in coffin M8 must also have been regal. Interestingly, this arm protector was made using the five standard colours – white, black, blue, red and yellow – which not only correspond to the five planets, but also to the five elements (metal, wood, water, fire and earth) and the five directions (north, east, south, west and centre).

In the following years a much older site dating from the Bronze Age (2000-900 BCE) was discovered some 40 kilometres north of Niya – it also contained Neolithic tools and weapons such as sickles and swords that were pre-2000 BCE. Excavations of this new site, called **Niya North**, have yet to be started (as of summer 2007), and based on the findings along the Keriya River, more sites could very well be discovered farther north. For these reasons, access to Niya and Niya North is strictly restricted, as with Dandan Oilik.

Minfeng to Qiemo

About 170 kilometres east of Minfeng the road passes through the village of **Hortang**, the starting point for an easy two-day camel ride to the ancient site of **Endere**. From the hamlet of **Andier**, the distance is reduced to a single day. If you have an official permit to visit Endere, you will be accompanied by an archaeologist from the Cultural Relics Bureau, either from Hotan, Ruoqiang or Korla. Try to hire the local warden to accompany you and show you the important ruins.

ENDERE

When the Buddhist monk Sung Yun passed through Endere in 518 CE he noticed a large monastery with more than 300 monks where a six-metre-high golden Buddha statue was kept. But towards the end of the sixth century CE, the city was abandoned. When Xuangzang returned from India to central China via the Southern Silk Road in 644, he found the stretch between Minfeng and Cherchen depopulated. His mention of a long since abandoned desert town called **Tuhuoluo** must relate to Endere. However, when the Tang rulers regained control over the Southern Silk Road towards the end of the seventh century, they re-established an administrative centre and built a fortress in Endere, as shown by a Chinese graffito of 719, reporting the death of a Chinese commander-in-chief, and battles between China and the "Great Tibetans". While the Chinese managed to repel the Tibetans in the short term, they came under renewed Tibetan pressure in the Tarim Basin following their defeat by the Arabs at Talas in 751 and the An Lushan rebellion (755–63).

By 791, all Chinese strongholds in the Tarim Basin had capitulated. When the Endere River changed its course in the ninth century, Endere was abandoned for the second – and final – time. However, in the 11th century a new settlement, **Bilel-Konghan**, was established on the western bank of the river as it was then. The visual impression of this site, protected by a defensive wall, is no different to Endere, but the absence of shards and of any indication of Chinese or Tibetan occupation shows that Bilel-Konghan cannot have been founded before the 10th or 11th century, and would have been of a low cultural level. When the Endere River once again changed its course, this time moving three kilometres to the east, this settlement was also abandoned.

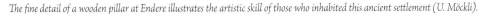

The fine detail of a wooden pillar at Endere illustrates the artistic skill of those who inhabited this ancient settlement (U. Möckli).

The main buildings of the huge site of Endere (not including neighbouring Bilel-Konghan) are 1.5 kilometres apart and cover an area of about 16 square kilometres. In the northwestern section is the first group of settlements. This older part, dating from the first few centuries CE, is dominated by a stupa eight metres in height and made of clay bricks. About 300 metres to the northeast of the stupa are the archaic-looking ruins of a nine-metre-high wall, which forms a rectangle 170 x 110 metres in size. On the way to the fortress, located 1.5 kilometres farther east, you pass two more stupas, standing alone in the desert, bearing witness to the omnipresence of Buddha. The fortress, which was built around 630, had a circular groundplan 100 metres in diameter. The walls, up to 12 metres thick, still rise seven metres into the air. In the centre of the complex is a forest of slender poplar pillars buried in the sand; these are the ruins of the main Buddhist temple, which had been founded during the first period of Endere's settlement in the 4th–5th centuries CE. Here, in 1901 and 1906, Stein discovered not only several dozen documents written on paper, which served as amulets or were presented by the faithful as small votive tablets, but also three almost life-size figures of red- and white-painted clay. Unfortunately, when the Sino-Swiss expedition surveyed Endere in 1998, it was obvious that this temple had been vandalized, as well as a small shrine nearby where Stein had found ancient murals that he didn't remove.

In the eastern part of the fortress stand clay-brick walls up to three metres high, as well as great wooden poles 60 centimetres thick, which once supported the roof of the building. As in Loulan, the sole brick building in Endere served as a residence for the military commander, and consisted of 12 rooms. On a wall in one of these rooms, Aurel Stein discovered two inscriptions: one short, vertical inscription in Chinese, and a horizontal Tibetan inscription of three lines, 2.8 metres long. Both relate to the history of the fort, the Chinese one mentions the imperial ambassador Xin Lizhan, and the Tibetan one reads as follows: "At Pyagpag in the province of Upper Jom Lom this army was outwitted, and a tiger's meal was obtained. Eat until you are fat." Stein interpreted this text as recording a Chinese defeat with many enemies killed. Its probable date of 790 or 791 coincides with the assumed abandonment of Dandan Oilik and the retreat of the last Chinese troops from the Tarim Basin.

At the end of his 1906 excavation, Aurel Stein concluded that the fortress had been built in the seventh century at the site of the already three- or four-century-old settlement. This conclusion was confirmed in 1998 when Baumer's Sino-Swiss expedition discovered a Kharoshthi administrative text, written on soapstone (steatite), at the foot of a small stupa in the immediate vicinity of the citadel. The text is a proclamation listing the titles of a king of Shanshan who prides himself on being a "crusher of his enemies". Although the king's name and the date are lost, the ruler referred to is most probably King Amgoka (ruled 246–277 CE), although his predecessors Pepiya and Tajaka cannot be totally ruled out.

Since the list contains titles usually applied to Indian Kushan rulers, we can infer that Shanshan was at that time a kind of semi-independent vassal of the Kushan Empire of northern India and southern Central Asia. This suggests that the inscription predates the 17th year of Amgoka's reign around 263 CE, when the king had to yield to Chinese overlordship. After this date, Amgoka and his successors discontinued the use of almost all Indian titles. Another interesting clue is provided by the word "*hinargami*", since the ending "*mi*" is a locative, and "*hinarga*" a toponym. Hinarga was most probably the ancient and hitherto unknown name of Endere. The most important conclusion stemming from this inscription's discovery concerns the introduction of Mahayana Buddhism into Shanshan, for it also includes the title "*mahayana-samprastida*", the one "who has set forth the Great Vehicle", namely Mahayana Buddhism. This is the earliest official proclamation of this title in Shanshan, and it demonstrates that Mahayana Buddhism already benefited from royal support during the first half of Amgoka's reign, several decades earlier than previously assumed.

QIEMO

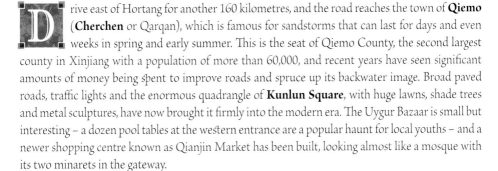

Drive east of Hortang for another 160 kilometres, and the road reaches the town of **Qiemo** (**Cherchen** or **Qarqan**), which is famous for sandstorms that can last for days and even weeks in spring and early summer. This is the seat of Qiemo County, the second largest county in Xinjiang with a population of more than 60,000, and recent years have seen significant amounts of money being spent to improve roads and spruce up its backwater image. Broad paved roads, traffic lights and the enormous quadrangle of **Kunlun Square**, with huge lawns, shade trees and metal sculptures, have now brought it firmly into the modern era. The Uygur Bazaar is small but interesting – a dozen pool tables at the western entrance are a popular haunt for local youths – and a newer shopping centre known as Qianjin Market has been built, looking almost like a mosque with its two minarets in the gateway.

The ancient sites of **Neleke** – next to the Muslim cemetery, or Yulghuz Tugh Mazar – and **Lalulik** offer little to see, and the small folk museum in the western suburb of Qiemo called **Toghraklek Manor**, which is located in a large Uygur villa built in 1911, includes only a modest collection of objects found at the Bronze Age necropolis of Zaghunluk, Qiemo's main attraction.

ZAGHUNLUK

The small museum of **Zaghunluk** itself, located two kilometres north of Lalulik and about five kilometres southwest of Qiemo, is a 15-minute drive from Toghraklek Manor and much more interesting. Here about 1,000 tombs were excavated between 1985 and 1999, many containing several bodies. Most of the people buried between the 12th and seventh centuries BCE were cattle-breeding farmers of Indo-European stock, whose ancestors originally came from eastern Persia. For the burial of higher-ranking people, horses, goats and even humans were sacrificed. Such a gruesome find was made in the tomb of an elderly woman, in whose honour three people had been sacrificed: the first was a one-year-old boy who had been strangled, his mouth wide open as if in a frozen scream; the second was a small baby, and the third a young woman whose arms and legs were amputated while she was still alive. The graveyard was used until the Eastern Han Dynasty

(25-220 CE). The site's small museum, the only building in the vicinity, is built directly above a pit containing 14 corpses and their ritual offerings, all left in place. The museum is usually closed; get the key from the small District Museum in Toghraklek Manor. Photography is strictly prohibited.

WHERE IS ANCIENT QIEMO?

In spite of the fact that the ancient city of Qiemo is described in several documents dating from the first century BCE to the ninth century CE, the site has not yet been found. Qiemo belonged to the Kingdom of Shanshan and its population numbered about 1,600 civilians and 320 soldiers. When the Chinese dynasty of the Former Liang attacked Shanshan around 443 CE, its ruler King Bilong fled to Qiemo, which became the last capital of Shanshan. About 50 years later Qiemo was conquered by the Tuyuhun, a people of Turkic stock related to the Xianbei. But when Xuanzang returned in 644 from his pilgrimage to India, he recorded that its high city walls were crumbling and that it was abandoned. The riddle starts less than two decades later in 659, when a Chinese garrison was again stationed at Qiemo, which was renamed Po Xien in 674. Six centuries later, Marco Polo mentioned a city called Qarqan located at the site of the modern town of Qiemo. The puzzling question is whether Po Xien and Marco Polo's Qarqan are in fact the same as Ancient Qiemo.

While some European explorers such as Aurel Stein, who visited Qarqan in 1907 and 1914, believed that Ancient Qiemo was located near the modern city, several Chinese archaeologists doubt that theory. Between 1978 and 1996, three Chinese expeditions searched for the site without success, while Christoph Baumer's 2003 Sino-Swiss expedition, which followed ancient riverbeds of the present Cherchen River deep into the desert, also failed to find the site despite using modern equipment such as satellite photos and air reconnaissance. Their only find was an Upper Neolithic era black flint blade and a rough piece of flint the size of a fist out of which knives or arrowheads had been cut. The two finds were 5,000–6,000 years old and the first artefacts of the Upper Neolithic found in this part of the desert.

TRIPS FROM QIEMO

Qiemo is the closest town to the **Tazhong Oilfield** in the centre of the Taklamakan Desert, courtesy of the spur road of the Tarim Highway that turns northwest from Highway

A local Uygur from the Andier oasis near Endere dresses in timeless fashion, his appearance probably no different to that of his ancestors of many centuries ago (Christoph Baumer).

The main Buddhist stupa at Endere endures, harshly treated by sandstorms, but still recognizable (Christoph Baumer).

315 just west of town and cuts through the desert for 188 kilometres to connect with the main cross-desert highway at the mining town named Tazhong. The Qiemo County Travel Bureau can arrange full-day trips to tour an oilfield should this be of interest, but there are no English guides so you should bring your own translator if one is available.

"**Wildlife safaris**" are also said to be possible in the Kunlun Mountains 230 kilometres south of Qiemo, beyond the village of **Kulamlak** in a designated wildlife park. While it is difficult to speculate how much wildlife you would actually see, this remote region is home to Tibetan antelopes (chiru) and gazelles, wild ass, wild yaks, brown bear, red fox, argali sheep, eagles and snowcocks, to name but a few species. Another park with a very different purpose is located 150 kilometres southeast of Qiemo and at an altitude of 3,000 metres; this is the 100-square-kilometre **Altun International Hunting Park**, where both domestic and foreign hunters can pursue certain species such as red deer and Tibetan gazelle.

Bronze Age **petroglyphs** can be seen 180 kilometres southwest of Qiemo near the village of Serikule on the eastern bank of the Molcha (Moleqie) River. Thousands of rock carvings etched into the black sandstone cliff face show scenes of hunting with bows and arrows, grazing livestock and horse riding, as well as handprints, images of the moon and stars, and abstract designs.

OASIS FOUND

*P*eter Fleming was a British journalist who delighted in exploring remote parts of the world – the farther from "civilization" the better. In the 1930s, along with the like-minded Swiss journalist-explorer Ella Maillart he made an astonishing journey – without the knowledge or approval of the Chinese government – of more than 5,600 kilometres from Peking to India via Xi'an, Xining, the desolate regions of the Altun Mountains and the Southern Silk Road oasis towns. It is conjectured that Peter Fleming's exploits may have influenced his younger brother Ian Fleming in the creation of his famous fictional character: 007, James Bond.

Next morning, exactly four months after leaving Peking, we entered the oasis of Cherchen.

For two hours we slanted expectantly across the wide and sprawling riverbed. We could not keep our eyes off the wall of vegetation which crowned its further bank. It looked extraordinarily dense, like the jungle. We could see as yet no signs of human life: only this opulent but non-committal screen, concealing what? Concealing, it was certain, the arbiters of the expedition's fate, the outposts of the rebel Tungan armies. What would they take us for? How would they treat us? We had plenty of food for speculation.

But as we came in under the trees we ceased to speculate. Wonder and joy fell on us. I suppose that the earth offers no greater contrast—except that between land and sea—than the contrast between desert and oasis. We stepped clean out of one world into another. There was no phase of transition; we slipped into coolness and delight as smoothly

and abruptly as a diver does. One moment we were stumbling in the open riverbed, plagued by glare and a grit-laden wind; the next we were marching down a narrow path under the murmurous protection of poplar and mulberry and ash.

Trees lined the path, which threaded a patchwork of neat little fields of hemp and rice and barley. Men of gentle appearance in white robes lent on their mattocks to watch us pass. Here and there an acquaintance of Tuzun's came forward with a soft cry of "Yakshi kelde"; hands were pressed, beards stroked, curious glances thrown at us. Everywhere water ran musically in the irrigation channels. A girl in a bright pink cap, washing her baby in a pool, veiled her face swiftly at the sight of infidels. Low houses with mud walls and wooden beams stood under the trees round courtyards half roofed over; women peered, or scuttled into the shelter of their doorways. A cock crowed....

A crock crowed. The familiar sound, unheard for nearly three months, asserted definitively our return to a world where men had homes; we began to think gloatingly of eggs. I think it was the sounds that were, for me, the most vivid part of a strange and unforgettable experience. The wind in the leaves, the gurgling water, a dog barking, men calling to each other in the fields—these noises, and especially the wind in the leaves, changed the whole texture of our environment, filled the air with intimacy, evoked forgotten but powerful associations. Then a cuckoo called, lazily; the essence of the spring that we had missed, the essence of the summer that we had suddenly overtaken, were comprehended in its cry, and I had a vision of lawns picketed with great trees, young rabbits scampering into gorse, a wall of ivy loud with sparrows: a vision that the cuckoo made oddly substantial, oddly near.

We wound deeper into the oasis in a kind of trance. The gaunt camels strode ahead; the little echelon of donkeys followed patiently. Cynara, with Kini up, stepped delicately, twitching her ears and blowing down her nostrils; she had never seen a tree before and was gravely disconcerted by these monstrous growths.

Presently, for no apparent reason, we halted at a poor house where we were welcomed by friends or relations of Tuzun's, who installed us on a dais in their courtyard and brought us bread and sour milk and unripe apricots, our first fruit since March. Half a dozen women flocked, giggling, to stare at Kini, and held animated debate upon her sex. Tuzun, with touching courtesy, presented her with a rose. He was an extraordinarily nice man; two days before I had given him an iron fireplace for which we had no further use, and ever since he had carried it, with true delicacy, on his back, refusing to burden our tired donkeys with something that was no longer ours.

Among the men there was much talk of an aksakal. The word means "white beard" and may be applied to any venerable head of a community; there had, for instance, been an aksakal at Bash Malghun. But it is also the official title given to the local agents of the British Consul-General in Kashgar, one of whom had formerly, as we knew, been stationed in every important oasis to deal with matters affecting the interests of British subjects—mostly traders from India—in the Province. We hardly expected, after two years of bloody civil war, to find a British aksakal as far afield as Cherchen; nor could I discover whether the aksakal into whose hands they proposed to deliver us was a British aksakal or just a local worthy. Still, here was a ray of hope from an unexpected quarter.

Peter Fleming, News from Tartary, 1936

QIEMO PRACTICAL INFORMATION

The largest southern Xinjiang town east of Hotan, Qiemo is still fairly compact and can easily be explored on foot. Motorbike taxis cost only a few yuan, with car taxis not much more. The Qiemo County Travel Bureau (tel: (0996) 762 8574) publishes a basic map of the town and its surroundings, available in hotels for Rmb2. Banks do not have ATM machines and it is advisable to stock up on cash in Hotan if you are coming from the west.

TRANSPORTATION

The airport is only a kilometre north of town. There are regular flights linking Qiemo with Korla and Urumqi, three times a week in summer and once in winter. Given the long distances involved in going anywhere from Qiemo, most buses are of the "sleeper" variety. There are daily buses to Korla and Urumqi (via the spur road meeting the Tarim Highway at Tazhong), to Minfeng, Yutian and Hotan farther west, and to Ruoqiang to the east.

ACCOMMODATION

For years the only acceptable accommodation in town was the **Muztag (Muzitage) Hotel** (Yinbing Lu, near the entrance to the airport, tel: (0996) 762 2687/1499), with extensive grounds and good rooms ranging from Rmb170 to Rmb300 – a bonus is an English-speaking member of staff, very useful in Qiemo. However, in late 2006 a new hotel opened, the **Kun Yu Binguan** (corner of Sichou Lu and Tuanjie, tel: (0996) 762 7666), offering an expansive two-storey lobby with circular staircase, and suites sporting impressive bathrooms and flat-screen TVs. Rooms start from Rmb198 with suites a bargain at Rmb388 – however, there are no English-speaking staff.

NB: Water is a precious resource in Qiemo, and therefore running water may not be available 24 hours a day in your hotel room, while hot water may be available for only a few hours each day.

FOOD AND DRINK

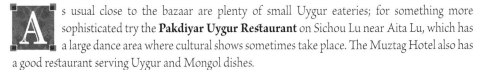

As usual close to the bazaar are plenty of small Uygur eateries; for something more sophisticated try the **Pakdiyar Uygur Restaurant** on Sichou Lu near Aita Lu, which has a large dance area where cultural shows sometimes take place. The Muztag Hotel also has a good restaurant serving Uygur and Mongol dishes.

RUOQIANG (CHARKHLIK)

The highway continues east towards **Ruoqiang (Charkhlik)**, edging closer to the mountains as the Altun range curves northeast away from the Kunlun Mountains. Eventually the village of Waxxari appears, close to the ancient site of **Washixia**, Stein's Vash Shari from the time of the Tang (618–907) and Northern Song (960–1127) – this site was occupied right up to the 12th century. Stein, who explored the ruins in 1906 and 1914, noticed the absence of artefacts related to any non-Chinese

A vast alluvial fan bursts forth from the Kunlun Mountains – the blue lines are the current streambeds, an intricate network of braided channels whose water disappears quickly upon entering the desert. Older, grey lines show how fickle and ever-changing the mountain meltwater's course can be (Image provided by the USGS EROS Data Center Satellite Systems Branch as part of the Earth as Art II image series).

culture, and concluded that it was a much more Chinese town than the others along the Southern Silk Road. Since China had lost control of the Tarim Basin at the end of the eighth century, Washixia must have maintained close commercial and cultural ties with central China.

The town of Ruoqiang is the most important in this vast region – Ruoqiang County is the largest in Xinjiang at 198,000 square kilometres, but boasts a population of only 30,000 or so since so much of its land is uninhabitable desert or protected mountain reserve. Within its remit lies the salt bed of the dried-up lake Lop Nor, and in the first century BCE it formed part of the **Kingdom of Loulan**, which was later called Shanshan. At Ruoqiang the road divides, one branch becoming Highway 218 and heading 490 kilometres north to Korla, for much of its route following the old southernmost watercourse of the Tarim River, which divides the sandier Taklamakan Desert to the west from the more rocky **Lop Desert** (today called the **Kumtag Desert**) to the east.

CROSSING THE ALTUN

*O*n my map the Altun looked like nothing: a thin outcrop of the ranges shielding Tibet. But now they erupted about us to eighteen thousand feet in sheets of inky rock. They made a fearful, sombre violence. All their intersecting ridges were picked out by snow, so that they engulfed us skyward in a chiaroscuro of blackly shining precipices. No shrub softened them. Soon we were running along five-hundred-foot chasms. As we ascended, they plunged and hacked their way into constricted valleys where nothing was, while high above them the mountains hung like wrecked stencils for hundreds of feet. The snow soon banked around us. It had fallen overnight, and lay virgin over our track. We all craned forward. Three times we clambered down to dig out the Cruiser, and once it slewed out of control altogether, landing at right angles to the verge two yards away. I went to the edge and stared down into nothing.

For hours we wound on more slowly, while the track coiled dizzily under us. The Chinese women fell silent, and the old Hui beside me turned his face to the steel frame of the window and fixed his gaze on it. The afternoon was waning before we left the snowline, but our path was now slashed by avalanches and mudslicks. For hours longer we picked our way gingerly between boulders, and sometimes followed a stream's course while its waters lapped our axles.

Then suddenly we were released, purring over sand. Before us stretched a plain where the horizon levelled to a purplish line, and dusk was falling. An old excitement welled up. I was on the rim of the Taklamakan, one of the largest deserts on earth, and the most bitter: the heart of Xinjiang. The Tian and Kun Lun mountains curl north and south like pincers upon Kashgar and the Pamirs, but the desert separates them in a vast, advancing oval and eats their rivers. Before India merged with Asia, this was the Tethys Sea.

I sat in a half-lit restaurant, among a different people. A heavy woman with large, soft eyes and hennaed fingernails served me kebabs on sesame-sprinkled bread. From the room beyond rose an ornate, liquid song, and the plunk of a native lute. I had forgotten people sang. Sometimes outside, a horse- or donkey-cart trotted by in the night, driven by grizzled men in skull-caps, whose wives dangled their thick-stockinged legs over the side. And once a blind man came in, led by a child, and was given bread. This was the Muslim world. I was in another nation, only half acknowledged by my map.

Colin Thubron, Shadow of the Silk Road, 2007

Highway 315 continues east, then curves south on a route that takes it through the Altun Mountains and into Qinghai Province at **Huatugou**, then across the fearsome **Qaidam Basin** southeast to **Golmud** or northeast to **Dunhuang**. Buses are available for this "backdoor" route into Tibet or Gansu, but they are neither frequent nor reliable, and unpredictable delays should be considered (and provisioned for). Officially a permit is required for this trip, which should be arranged in Ruoqiang at the PSB office.

By taking this road you will actually be following the ancient **Qinghai Route**, a lesser-known silk trade route that bypassed the Hexi Corridor and instead struck off southeast from Miran towards Koko Nor and Xining. This route was most popular between the fifth and ninth centuries CE, when much of modern Qinghai and the southern Tarim Basin was under the control of, or heavily influenced by, Tibetan tribes such as the Tuyuhun and Tubo. It also provided a valuable conduit to southern China at a time when the Middle Kingdom's north and south were divided.

In Golmud, you can catch the new train to **Lhasa**, a 15-hour journey over the high Tibetan Plateau known as **Chang Tang**, the highest point on the route being the station of Tanggula at 5,072 metres. (All foreigners require an "Alien's Travel Permit" to enter the Tibetan Autonomous Region.)

RUOQIANG PRACTICAL INFORMATION

Ruoqiang is a small oasis town with little to boast of; it too has a large main square, around which the main Chinese business offices are centred, with the Uygur suburbs spreading out behind. The bus station is a block north of the square. The **Tian Ran Ju Guest House** (just northeast of the main square, tel: (0996) 710 5566) is the best accommodation option, with rooms starting at Rmb120 and suites Rmb260 (running water may only be available for a few hours of the day). A number of good restaurants can be found between the bus station and the main square.

ARJIN MOUNTAIN NATIONAL NATURE RESERVE

To the south of Ruoqiang the Altun and Kunlun mountains diverge; encompassing parts of their high peaks and the high-altitude desert plateau between is the vast, 14,800-square-kilometre **Arjin Mountain National Nature Reserve** (also known as the Altun Mountain Nature Reserve), which, lying contiguous with other reserves in Qinghai and Tibet, combines to form China's largest protected area. Established as a national reserve in 1985, its grasslands and salt lakes are home to large herds of the endangered Tibetan antelope, as well as wild yak, Tibetan wild ass and gazelle; preying on these are wolves, lynx and Tibetan brown bear, while on the slopes of the snow-capped peaks snow leopards hunt ibex and blue sheep. The wild yak herds here are especially important because they represent the purest stock of any population throughout Tibet and Central Asia – elsewhere wild yaks often interbreed with domestic yaks, but this has not happened in this most remote of regions.

It was here in the 1880s that the great Russian explorer, Nikolai Przhevalsky, discovered the only existing species of the original horse, which was named *Equus Przewalskii*. Driven to extinction

A mural from a shrine at Miran shows Buddhist pilgrims and cherubs carrying garlands (National Museum of New Delhi).

in the wild, Przewalski's horse is now being reintroduced from stocks bred in zoos. The best time to visit the reserve is during the brief summer from June to August; special permits must be arranged (at a high price), and 4WD vehicles are essential – this is a very remote region with a harsh, unforgiving environment, and it is rarely visited. The reserve also encompasses the peak of **Muztagh Ulugh** (6,973 metres), which can be climbed by suitably experienced mountaineers with the correct permits.

MIRAN

Northeast of Ruoqiang lies another archaeological site, **Miran**, which Stein visited in 1906, 1907 and 1914. Ancient Miran is 25 kilometres north of the village of New Miran, itself 75 kilometres away from Ruoqiang. The site is situated in a pebble desert, is easy to reach by 4WD vehicle, and consists of the ruins of a huge circular fort – occupied between the eighth and ninth centuries by Tibetan troops – a stupa, a temple and a few other structures. When the town was abandoned at the end of the ninth century, there was no protective sand to cover the buildings so they were exposed to the impact of the strong winds. For this reason there are no traces of wooden structures there, but only the more resistant clay buildings. Miran is now an official tourist site (tickets are Rmb350 from the Cultural Relics Bureau, tel: (0996) 710 2909).

Tibet constructed, or rebuilt, the rectangular fortress around the year 760 to control three strategically important trade routes: the Southern Silk Road from Dunhuang to Khotan and Kashgar, a direct route to Lhasa over the Qiman Tagh Mountains, and another route southeast through the

Qaidam Basin. Thanks to Miran and other forts in the Tarim Basin, around Turpan and in the present-day province of Gansu, Tibet was able to interrupt China's trade connections with Sogdia, thus robbing the Middle Kingdom of an important source of income. At that time, Tibet, which was twice the size of the present Autonomous Region, waged war on China for almost two centuries. Despite a small population, Tibet was able, thanks to general conscription, to put large armies in the field.

Inside the fort, Stein made the richest finds in the rubbish heaps left by the Tibetan garrison. Their odour was, even after a full millennium, fetid. In *Ruins of Desert Cathay, Vol. I*, Stein remembered: "I have had occasion to acquire a rather extensive experience in clearing ancient rubbish heaps, and know how to diagnose them. But for intensity of sheer dirt and age-persisting smelliness I shall always put the rich 'castings' of Tibetan warriors in the front rank. The recollection of these Miran fort perfumes was fresh enough a year afterwards to guide me rightly in the chronological determination of another site." Here Stein unearthed manuscripts written in Tibetan, Chinese, Brahmi, Kharoshthi, and even in a Turkic runic script.

Stein's most important discovery at Miran were magnificent Buddhist murals dating from the late third century CE, which he uncovered at and around the stupa. Stylistic influences include Gandhara and the Eastern Mediterranean area. Stein noted: "When the digging had reached a level of about four feet below the floor and a delicately painted dado of beautiful winged angels began to show on the wall, I felt completely taken by surprise. How could I have expected by the desolate shores of Lop Nor, in the very heart of innermost Asia to come upon such classical representations of Cherubim! And what had these graceful heads, recalling cherished scenes of Christian imagery, to do here on the walls of what was beyond all doubt a Buddhist monastery?"

Stein also found a Kharoshthi inscription from the late third century CE within a painted frieze featuring 28 portraits surrounded by a garland carried by putti (cherubs). This inscription recorded the painter of the murals as "Tita", which corresponds to "Titus". This Titus may have been an itinerant painter from the Eastern Mediterranean region. Another mural depicts a princely disciple of Buddha Shakyamuni. Some of the paintings that Stein removed are displayed in the National Museum of New Delhi; others were destroyed around 1912 by the Japanese spy Tachibana, who pretended to be an archaeologist and tried to remove them, but with no real skill succeeded only in ruining them. A few are still *in situ*, buried under the earth.

Lop Nor and Loulan

Lop Nor (Lop Nur), to the north of Ruoqiang, was until the last century a shallow salt lake fed by the Tarim River and surrounded by salt marshes and a salt-encrusted plain. Since the 1960s, the area around Lop Nor has been a prohibited military zone, as China's **nuclear testing grounds** are situated about 145 kilometres northwest of the Loulan site. The testing grounds are divided into four zones. Between 1964 and 1980, 23 plutonium and hydrogen atmospheric bombs were detonated; from 1975 a further 22 underground tests were carried out.

As well as much dessicated wood, the site of Loulan boasts a number of ruined buildings, such as the Governor's palace and a stupa (Christoph Baumer).

Yardangs form twisting, turning corridors at Lop Nor, south of Loulan (J.D. Carrard).

Just west of Lop Nor once stood the important caravan trading city and military garrison of **Loulan**. All foreigners hoping to visit Loulan must obtain special permits from the Cultural Relics Bureau, the Public Security Bureau and, depending on the chosen route, from the PLA as well. These are all mandatory, and very expensive. A permanent guard ensures that no illegal visits take place, and there is a rather modest guesthouse for the rare guests, who are virtually all Chinese.

Due to the harsh nature of the terrain and the lack of potable water – unlike many other areas of the Taklamakan there are no wells – using camels for transport is not recommended. In the past, pioneers like Hedin and Stein were forced to travel in winter and load frozen blocks of ice onto their camels. Their camel drivers also had to sew pieces of ox hide onto the animals' hooves, to stop them being cut to ribbons by the sharp salt crystals that littered the terrain. The best choice of transport is UNIMOG trucks, which can be rented from the oil companies based in Korla. Strong 4WDs can also make the trip, but they run a high risk of getting stuck, while the ride is very uncomfortable since many obstacles have to be mastered at high speed.

If you start from Ruoqiang, the drive brings you first to Miran, then continues along the ancient dirt road eastwards through a stony desert in the direction of Dunhuang. After about 160 kilometres you reach a place called **Hongligugou**, where you turn northwards into the bed of the Lachin Darya (River), which is now a mere trickle. After another four or five hours' slow drive, the narrow ravine opens out and you reach the floor of the former **Lake Karakoshun**, which both Przhevalsky and Hedin once explored in small boats.

Alternatively, a new road runs from Donglik to the southern edge of Karakoshun, avoiding Hongligugou and the drive through the valley of the Lachin Darya. Today, the former lake offers nothing but an endless desert of shimmering white salt deposits, which present a particular danger. Salt rises to the surface of the lake floor by the action of water lying below the floor itself. This means that, beneath the stony-hard but thin crust of earth, a marshy morass is lying into which heavy trucks sink – a Sino-Swiss expedition experienced exactly this in 1994. It's therefore wise to avoid any really salty surface and bypass this area by heading northeast. After a few days' drive, the low sand dunes give way to *yardangs*, the clay deposits – up to a metre high – of the former Lop Nor lake bed. Wind erosion has dug long, deep furrows between the yardangs (the Uygur word actually means "steep bank"). In an area of sand, large numbers of shells cover the ground – the last evidence of the dried-up lake of yesteryear.

The earliest mention of Loulan dates from the year 176 BCE, and is to be found in a letter from Motun, king of the Xiongnu, to the Chinese emperor Wen-Ti. In it, Motun exalts his victories over the Yüeh-chih and the conquest of Loulan, together with 28 other states. But Loulan misused its strategic location on the Central Silk Road to plunder Chinese trading caravans, which led to a Chinese reprisal under General Cao Ponu in 108 BCE. When Loulan once more turned to the Xiongnu, China sent a second punitive expedition in 77 BCE, installing a Chinese commander.

Lop Nor: the Riddle of the Wandering Lake

By Christoph Baumer

One of Sven Hedin's most interesting achievements in the field of geography was to once and for all solve the famous mystery of Lop Nor ("*Nor*" means "lake"). The lake and its tributaries, the Tarim and Cherchen Darya rivers, were first mentioned at the time of the Warring States (475–221 BCE) and the Western Han Dynasty (202 BCE–9 CE). In the West, it was the Greek geographer Marinos of Tyre, who lived towards the end of the first century CE, who was the first to speak of Lop Nor, which he called "Öchardes", and the Tarim, which he named "Bautisus". He had his information from a merchant named Maes Titianus, who was active in the China trade. Around two millennia later, in 1876, the Russian explorer Colonel Nikolai Przhevalsky followed the course of the Tarim southeastwards, starting from Korla, until he came upon the sweet-water Lake Karakoshun, which he identified with the mysterious Lop Nor.

This was contradicted by the geographer Ferdinand von Richthofen (who coined the phrase "Silk Road" in 1877), because Przhevalsky's supposed Lop Nor was located one degree of latitude farther south than indicated in Chinese sources from the 17th century. Furthermore, the ancient Chinese sources mentioned a salt lake, whereas Przhevalsky described a sweet-water lake, and in addition the Chinese sources showed a tributary of the Tarim flowing eastwards, while the main river flowed southwards for its last few hundred kilometres. Von Richthofen concluded that Przhevalsky had discovered not the original Lop Nor, but a different, newly formed lake,

and that the original Lake Lop must be located farther north, at the end of the eastward-flowing tributary. To this, in 1878 Przhevalsky raised the objection that there were no more lakes north of Karakoshun. However, when he returned to Karakoshun in 1885, he was struck by the shrinkage of the lake.

The young Sven Hedin, who studied under von Richthofen from 1889 to 1892, was eager to test the validity of his teacher's theory. In 1896, he followed the Tarim and the Konche Darya, running parallel to it, as far as the western shore of Lake Karakoshun. This short journey confirmed von Richthofen's view that Lake Karakoshun must be a recent stretch of water, and could not be identical with the historical Lop Nor. Conversations with native peoples also led Hedin to suppose that this recent lake had existed at its present site only since about 1725. Hedin, too, noted a rapidly progressing shrinkage of Lake Karakoshun. It was tragic for Przhevalsky pupil P.K. Kozlov, the future discoverer of Karakhoto in the delta of the Etzin Gol, that he missed his chance to solve the riddle three years before Hedin. In the winter of 1893–94 he had been on the right track when he followed the Kuruk Darya, but he didn't recognize the importance of his find when he reached traces of the ancient shore of Lop Nor where it was before 330 CE, and he continued to defend Przhevalsky's theory.

On returning to the Tarim Basin in 1899, Hedin undertook a journey by raft of about 900 kilometres on the Tarim River. During the course of this, he was struck, as he had already been in

1896, by the completely dried-up bed of the Kum Darya, running off eastwards to the left of the Konche Darya, near the town of Tömenpu. Kum Darya means "Sand River", and is also known as Kuruk Darya – "Dry River". Hedin had already guessed in 1896 that the historical course of the Tarim was located here, in this so-called tributary, and that the classical Lop Nor had been situated in an extension of it. Now, in early 1900, Hedin followed the Kum Darya eastwards until he did indeed come upon traces of the ancient Lop Nor, and then discovered Loulan by chance. Although Hedin could not know at the time that the ancient garrison town of Loulan had been abandoned around 330 CE because the Tarim near Tömenpu suddenly ceased flowing eastwards through the Kum Darya, and turned southwards, thus robbing Loulan and the existing Lop Nor of their water supply, he realised in early 1900 that: "Anyone who has followed the course of the river [Tarim] as far as its dissolution and annihilation understands that its final point, Lop Nor, must be a wandering lake, a lake that periodically migrates from north to south and from south to north, just like the brass weight on the end of an oscillating pendulum, the pendulum in this case being the Tarim." (*Central Asia and Tibet*, Vol. I.) With the Tarim's change of course, shortly before the year 330, the ancient Lop Nor lost the inflow of water necessary to compensate for its high evaporation rate, and disappeared quickly. Lop Nor had, metaphorically speaking, "wandered" over the centuries from Loulan to the location of Lake Karakoshun.

Having found some marshes of recent date northeast of Lake Karakoshun, Hedin ventured the forecast: "I am convinced that in some years we shall find the lake back in the place where, according to Chinese reports, it used to be and where, as von Richthofen acutely proved in theory, it must in fact have been located." (*Ibid.,Vol. II.*) Hedin was lucky enough to witness

the return of Lop Nor to the north that he had predicted 28 years before. When he was in Turpan in February 1928, his former collaborator Tokta Akhun reported to him that the Tarim had since 1921 been again flowing through its old bed of the Kuruk (Kum) Darya, and that Lop Nor had returned into a depression northeast of Loulan. Hedin at once dispatched his collaborator Erik Norin to the area referred to; Norin confirmed Tokta Akhun's report, and also found a number of small, shallow sweet-water lakes in the delta of the new Tarim. However, the Tarim had not returned to its ancient basin southeast of Loulan, but had formed a new lake in another, deeper depression farther north.

The main reason for these "pendulum movements" of the Tarim is the very shallow gradient of its lower course, resulting in its bed filling up with transported sediment, so that it meanders markedly. The resulting sluggish bends in the river results in the formation of small lakes or ponds, which lead to a change in direction of the river current. Therefore Lop Nor changes its location as a result of the changes in direction of the Tarim, of which it is the terminal lake.

Six years later, Hedin unexpectedly had the opportunity to make an excursion into the Lop Nor area. On 5 April 1934, he set off for the last time on a river journey, allowing himself to drift down the Konche and then the Kuruk Darya, until on 9 May he reached the new Lake Lop. On the way, near Tömenpu he passed the place where the Konche Darya had taken its new course eastwards in 1921, and where the authorities had tried in vain to force the river to return to its old bed by building a dam. Sadly, this new Lop Nor, which came into being in 1921, dried up again in 1972–3, because of the many irrigation systems along the Tarim that deprived its tributary, the Kuruk Darya, of its water.

At the same time, Loulan, whose local name was **Kroraina** – the Chinese name Loulan is a phonetic adaptation of Kroraina to Chinese – had its name changed to Shanshan. The garrison was further strengthened in 124 CE by General Ban Yung, the son of the famous Governor-General Ban Chao. The final flourishing of Loulan began with the coming into office of General So Man around the year 260 CE. The so-called *Classic of the Waters* reported: "So Man took over the office of the general; at the head of 1,000 soldiers he came to Loulan, in order to set up an agricultural colony there. He built a white house." This "white house" is identical to the large clay-brick building which stands near the huge stupa in Loulan, and was once whitewashed with chalk.

But the small garrison town fell into oblivion, for the last dated document, from 330 CE, was written in the name of the last Western Jin emperor, whose rule had ended in 316. By 330 Loulan had probably been isolated from the central government for 14 years. Around this time Loulan was finally abandoned for good, because of the drying-up of the Kuruk Darya and of Lop Nor.

Sven Hedin's greatest archaeological discovery came in the Lop Nor region in 1900. His expedition was financed by the King of Sweden and the millionaire Emmanuel Nobel, and originally planned to survey and map the **Tarim River**. After three months of travelling along the river, it froze over. Hedin's expedition marched on foot across the desert to Qarqan, then towards Marco Polo's "Desert of Lop" in the eastern part of the Taklamakan.

Hedin had the misfortune of a Uygur worker to thank for his success. Towards the end of March 1900, in the northeastern part of Lop Nor he came across the ruins of three houses and a small stupa. The following evening, it was discovered that the worker, Ördek, had left his spade at the site of the ruins. Ördek returned to fetch it, but got lost in a night-time sandstorm, and as a result, on 30 March found Loulan. He reported to Hedin that he had seen several ruined houses and "richly carved planks of wood". Hedin's water supply was beginning to run out, and the hot summer was approaching, so he resolved to postpone the return to "Ördek's town" until the next year, which Stein later called "L.B." In March 1901, 10 kilometres east of "Ördek's town", the Swedish explorer found the actual garrison town of Loulan, named "L.A." by Stein.

The fortified town was fairly small; the four-metre-high encircling walls form a rectangle only 340 x 310 metres in size. It was densely populated, as is evidenced by the poplar pillars now lying all around on the ground. Loulan is dominated by two buildings, a 12-metre-high tower of clay bricks that Stein interpreted as a stupa and Hedin as a watchtower, and a 12-metre-long brick building, the seat of the Chinese military commander. It was here that Hedin made his most important archaeological find in Lop Nor. In a rubbish heap, he discovered hundreds of Chinese documents written on wood, paper and silk, which helped reconstruct Loulan's history. Stein's excavations in 1906 and 1914 brought many coins and documents written on both wood and paper to light. The international scope of Loulan's involvement was highlighted by the discovery of a fragment of a woollen textile featuring the Greek god Hermes that was used as a shroud, and had probably been imported from the West.

few kilometres south of Loulan stand hundreds of almost 2,000-year-old trees that once formed a large orchard. About 30 kilometres northeast of L.A. are the ruins of two ancient Chinese fortresses, the larger one named L.E. by Stein and the smaller L.F. From here the Silk Road led to **Dunhuang**, the eastern section being marked with more than 60 beacon towers from the Han and Jin dynasties (206 BCE–420 CE). The distance from L.E. to Dunhuang is around 500 kilometres; some sections of the trek pass through moonlike landscapes marked by endless huge yardangs. About 150 kilometres before reaching Dunhuang, the trek meets the eastern end of the ancient Great Wall of Han and Jin times. Ninety kilometres before Dunhuang, the trek passes **Yumenguan**, the "Pass of the Jade Gate", dating from the Han Dynasty (206 BCE–220 CE). Yumenguan symbolized for the westbound traveller the end of the civilized world and the entry into the barbarian world of Central Asia.

In recent decades, Chinese archaeological teams have worked at this site and others nearby and unearthed lengths of tamped walls and timbers of an ancient roadway. Coins, jewellery, inscribed wood strips, wooden figures and pottery shards have also been recovered. In the winter of 2002–03, tombs almost 2,000 years old were found north of L.A., their walls decorated with murals. They feature banquet scenes, a standing red-brown horse, a charging bull, and a fight between two camels, one painted golden and the other silver. Unfortunately, the archaeologists arrived only after the tombs had been looted by tomb raiders, who had torn the mummies and seriously damaged some murals.

Marco Polo took 30 days to cross the "**Desert of Lop**" to reach Dunhuang. This was the worst stretch of the southern caravan route. Apart from the lack of water, strange voices misled travellers, causing them to wander off:

> And there were some who, in crossing the desert, have seen a host of men coming towards them and, suspecting that they were robbers, returning, they have gone hopelessly astray... Even by daylight men hear these spirit voices, and often you fancy you are listening to the strains of many instruments, especially drums, and the clash of arms. For this reason bands of travellers make a point of keeping very close together. Before they go to sleep they set up a sign pointing in the direction in which they have to travel, and round the necks of all their beasts they fasten little bells, so that by listening to the sound they may prevent them from straying off the path.

For those adventurous enough to complete the overland journey to Dunhuang from Ruoqiang, there are two routes now open, each offering very different experiences. A fairly good southern road – skimming the Xinjiang-Qinghai border – now links Ruoqiang with Dunhuang via the small settlements of Hongliugou, Shorköl, Lapeiquan and Hongliuwan. More in keeping with the Silk Road ethos however, is the northern desert track following the southwestern edge of the former Lake Karakoshun, passing Han Dynasty ruins before reaching Yumenguan, and approaching Dunhuang from the north. This off-road route requires a special permit and a certain hardiness, but offers a chance to really experience travel on the Silk Road as it once was.

LOULAN: LOST CITY OF THE GOBI

By John Hare

The lake of Lop Nur, surrounded by the Gashun (Bitter) Gobi and the Desert of Lop in Xinjiang Uygur Autonomous Region, will always be associated with the great Swedish explorer Sven Hedin. For 1,600 years the lake had lain in two separate depressions to the northeast of Charkhlik (Ruoqiang) and had, in 1876, been revealed to the outside world by the Russian explorer Nikolai Przhevalsky. When the first telegram containing his story was flashed around the world the geographer, Dr. E. Behm wrote:

"So at last the darkness which surrounded Lop Nur is put to flight . . . Our ideas of the Gobi desert are about to be revolutionised."

But it was Hedin who was responsible for the revolution. In 1900 he walked west to Aksupe, a junction point on the Konche Darya, a tributary of the Tarim River, and discovered that an ancient riverbed led off it to the east. Using camels as pack animals, he followed this dry riverbed, called the Kuruk Darya, for over 500 kilometres, until his guide Ördek, while searching for a mislaid spade, suddenly came across the abandoned ancient city of Loulan (originally spelt Lou Lan), an important former staging point on the middle Silk Road.

In 1901 he returned to Loulan, carried out a survey to the south of the old city and discovered a huge, dried-up lakebed. He concluded from these discoveries that in about 330 CE there was a shift in the course of the Tarim and subsequently in the position of Lop Nur. After having flowed to the east for many centuries and formed its terminal lake in the northern part of the desert, the lower Tarim or the part of it called the Kuruk Darya, had left its old bed and broken a new course for itself through the desert to the southeast where, in the southern part of the Gashun Gobi, it formed two new lakes. It was these lakes that Przhevalsky had discovered in the 1870s. At the same time, the old river course and lake dried up, and the town of Loulan was abandoned by its inhabitants and consigned to oblivion.

Hedin concluded that the lake swung like the pendulum of a clock approximately every 1,600 years as each tributary in turn became silted up by the winds, sands of the desert and decomposing vegetable and animal remains. As the filling-up process was going on in the south, the arid desert regions to the north were being eaten away by the extraordinarily violent east-northeasterly storms, and while the level of the ground in the northern parts of the Gashun Gobi was falling, the bottom of the southern lake rose and became higher and higher. The ultimate effect of this alternation between north and south is that the river and lake must eventually return to a location near their old, previously dry beds. In 1901 Hedin predicted:

"In the light of the knowledge we now possess of the levels that exist in the Lop desert, it is not too daring to affirm that the river must some day go back to the Kuruk Daria."

It is seldom given to a man that an improbable theory that he formulates is proven in his lifetime, but in 1921, the Kuruk Darya suddenly filled with water. The lower Tarim which flowed to the then Lop Nur silted up, and Hedin's pendulum swung just as he had predicted. What Hedin could not predict was the development of the nuclear bomb. Nor could he have foreseen that the Chinese would select the Lop Nur area as their nuclear testing site.

He could also not have known that the Tarim River would eventually be dammed many kilometres away upstream for irrigation projects, out of the range of the testing area. In 1976 the Kuruk Darya dried up once again, after an all-too-brief awakening from its 1,600-year-old sleep. There was to be no rebirth of the ancient city of Loulan. Both the new and the old Lop Nur lakes have disappeared.

*   *   *

I had long wanted to establish the critically endangered wild Bactrian camel's migration route from the winter grazing area south of Lop Nur, to the summer grazing in the foothills of the Arjin Shan (also known as the Altun Mountains) which together with the Kunlun Mountains form the northern frontier of the Tibetan Plateau. Although I had managed to squeeze out more dollars for wild Bactrian camel survey than previously, the truck that stood mournfully in front of the Xinjiang Environmental Protection Institute looked dilapidated.

I stared gloomily at the rusting, pale blue, wooden-sided truck with its two bald tyres and sagging exhaust. Even my unmechanical eye could see that it hovered on the brink of permanent consignment to a scrap heap. By the time we reached Tikar south of Turpan some 200 kilometres from Urumqi, the truck had broken down a second time, our jeep was leaking oil and all my earlier premonitions about the vehicles were fully justified.

To reach the wild camel migration route, south of Lop Nur, meant crossing an unknown expanse of metre-high, treacherous calciferous salt called *shor*. Even our guide, Lao Zhao, had not been there before. In addition, there was an added complication to our journey that could prove to be as hazardous as anything that we had risked so far. Professor Yuan Guoying had suggested that when we got to Lop Nur, we should make an attempt, either by vehicle or on foot, to reach the ancient city of Loulan to the west of the lake. Hedin, Aurel Stein and other early explorers and archaeologists had struggled across a pitted and broken Mars-like landscape to reach the abandoned city from the west. We were planning to approach Loulan from the east. If we succeeded, we would be the first expedition to have done so in recorded history. It was one thing to do this with sound and proven equipment, but quite another with a vehicle that had been patched and mended to the point of redundancy.

The repairs to the truck took longer than anticipated and we were forced to spend our third desert night at a spring that was crisscrossed with wild camel tracks. It was cold, at least -8°C, and the jeep's engine froze. Driver Liu applied a blowlamp to the iced-up engine. Then he lit a fire under the radiator. Eventually, with the failure of flame and fire, it was a tow from the truck that freed up the engine and at midday we were at last under way. Next evening, at a spring named Aka Bulak, the truck sank up to its axles in salt sludge. This time it was the jeep's turn to do the towing. We followed a riverbed that led from Aka Bulak, which gradually widened until it merged into a vast, dried-up floodplain north of Lop Nur. After two hours in the floodplain, we reached a bewildering maze of hundreds of 10-metre-high, weird and wonderful eroded landforms called *yardangs*. We drove south in failing light for a further two hours. Still we were not out of the maze. Our truck took a wrong turn and for half an hour all contact with it was lost. We were all relieved when we finally linked up again – trucks in the Gashun Gobi have been known to disappear completely.

We were frustrated by the constant hold-ups, tired and hungry. The temperature was well below freezing and a biting, bitterly cold wind was blowing from the east. We struggled to erect our unruly tents with numb fingers, only to discover that just below the sandy surface was granite rock. Tent pegs buckled and we were forced to collect rocks to secure our guy ropes.

Next morning, our guide Lao Zhao called out to me in a state of great excitement. My team-mate Leilei explained: "This morning, Lao Zhao got up early and went for a walk. He discovered that we've pitched camp near Tu-ying, an ancient outpost of Loulan on the middle Silk Road. Zhao says that none of the early explorers discovered Tu-ying."

I was, of course, thrilled with this news, but later research revealed that unfortunately it was not wholly true, for although Stein and others had certainly not been to Tu-ying, the incredible Hedin had, if only for an hour. Hedin had written of his 1934 expedition:

"The scouts had been out, and when we got up in the morning they reported that they had not been able to find an arm of the river with any current, but that they had found the ruins of a fair-size house on the mainland to the north-west. Chen [Hedin's Chinese expedition scientist] suspected at once that this was the fort T'u-ken, discovered by the

archaeologist Hwang Wen-pi in 1930."

I suspect that our "find" of Tu-ying was Hedin's T'u-ken, but whether this is true or not, we did find remarkable artefacts in and around Tu-ying: coins, jewellery, jade, beads and a sizable piece of cloth and felt. These latter objects could not have been woven or made later than 1,600 years ago – a testament to the dryness of the climate. However, our greatest discovery was an ancient grave, marked with upright posts that had been missed by earlier explorers. The coffin contained bones and a skull. Over the last 100 years, explorers and archaeologists have discovered magnificently preserved mummies in the deserts of the Gashun Gobi and the Taklamakan, whose features and characteristics point incontrovertibly to the fact that the people were not Han Chinese. Who were these ancient people and from whence did they originate? According to Elizabeth Barber, a noted expert on ancient textiles, the cloth in which some of these mummies were wrapped was constructed by using exactly the same weave as those binding Celtic mummies that were discovered in the latter part of the last century at Salzburg in Austria. From this she constructed the theory that the people who occupied Loulan as far back as 1500 BCE were Celts – an intriguing possibility.

At 1pm we resumed our southward journey to the lake and before long, had reached the complex delta of the Kuruk Darya, dry by the hand of man since 1974. Here and there a tamarisk bush struggled to survive. Occasionally there was a pathetic flash of green, a signal of struggling life from among the dry, dusty, brittle clumps of reed. But it was desolate, a land of death, in striking contrast to Hedin's description 61 years earlier when he had canoed through this exact spot:

"Tamarisks and reeds looked up out of the water. It was a delicious place! I sat with my sleeves rolled up and dabbled my hands in the cool, rippling water ..."

After an hour of grinding travel we reached Lop Nur. There was no rippling water – the grey, dusty surface of the lakebed stretched to the skyline. To the east, a row of black lumps, possibly hillocks on a tongue of land, appeared to hover above the horizon. To the west, more black objects, shaped like horsemen, quivered in the rising currents of hot air. But apart from these slightly ominous features, the prevailing colour was grey. Even the blue sky had disappeared behind the dust thrown up by the howling wind. We drove slowly down the lake for a further hour. The truck was frequently bogged down in sand, which meant arduous work with pick and shovel.

Then at last, following a compass bearing worked out by Lao Xiao, we turned due east. We were now attempting to pioneer a route from the east to Loulan. After another hour of snail-like progress we hit rough shor. The engines of both the truck and the jeep boiled almost every 10 minutes, necessitating frequent stops. Travelling at a speed of no more than 6kph, we eventually crossed the shor. We passed a group of sentry-like yardangs, indicators of the western boundary of the old lake, and entered a landscape so utterly dead and barren that we all fell silent. Before us lay mound after mound of soft grey clay, covered with scattered roots of ancient poplars and interspersed with eroded gullies lined with shale.

Occasionally, the trees themselves, petrified into a rock-like hardness, would lie twisted and tangled in our path, forcing us to change direction. We snaked through these impediments, made

frequent stops to cool our engines, and regularly resorted to picks and spades to extricate ourselves. As dusk fell, I called a halt and as my journal relates:

"...we pitched camp on the surface of the moon in the middle of nowhere. Freezing wind. A rotten campsite. It did occur to me in the middle of the night that if we broke down here we would have a problem. No one knows we are here. Twenty kilometres to the north is the nuclear test site. Ahead lies 400km of sand. Behind us a further 400km of sand, dry lake and desert. I try to banish these unwholesome thoughts."

The next day, Good Friday, 5 April 1996, I wrote in my journal:

"Freezing wind. We start to go in the wrong direction (east) over one of the countless and totally misleading tributaries of the Kuruk Darya. I feel that the risk of trying to reach Loulan with these two unpredictable and nearly clapped-out vehicles is too great. Gently persuade Professor Yuan Guoying, whose ambition it has been to drive to Loulan, that it would be more prudent to walk. So, after travelling just under four km in three hours, we pitch camp on a windy knoll. It is planned to attack Loulan on foot tomorrow."

Early the next morning, Professor Yuan erected a long wooden pole on the back of the truck, which we carried to extricate us from sand. He tied a light bulb on the top, attached it to our generator, and Driver Li was left behind to guard our camp and given strict instructions to start the generator at dusk and keep it going until we returned.

At nine o'clock, with full water bottles, a compass, maps, torches and stomachs packed with noodles, we launched ourselves into a featureless wasteland that stretched in every direction. Our plan was to try to find the main tributary of the dried-up Kuruk Darya. The river had formerly flowed quite close to the ancient city, and as long as we stuck to the main riverbed, we should eventually spot the Buddhist tower or the city watchtower, two prominent features of Loulan. The problem was that the river had flowed into a network of small tributaries as it neared Lop Nur and in their dried-up state, it was difficult to pick up the main artery. After numerous false starts and dead ends, we eventually reached a wide, deep-sided riverbed that we felt must be the main tributary of the Kuruk Darya.

We set off, our faces to the west, trekking along the twisting sand river, and taking turns to climb up the steep bank to see if we could spot either of the two landmarks. After four hours of trudging though soft sand, with a freezing wind blowing strongly on our backs, there was still no sign of a tower. By this time we had all realized that Lao Zhao's calculations were wrong. Loulan was much more than 15 kilometres from our campsite.

Soon we were all picking up pottery shards and I noticed with interest that a few seemingly dead tamarisk bushes by the side of the river had sprouted long, twisting roots that sprawled metres over the riverbed in a desperate attempt to find moisture. Then at long last, there was a shout from the top of the bank. Lao Zhao had spotted the Buddhist tower. We all scrambled excitedly out of the riverbed and stared at a tiny triangular hump just discernible on the horizon. It was a very long way away. When the outline of the watchtower came into view, we saw to our dismay that it was a good way to the left of the triangular tower.

We had now entered the remains of an ancient oasis. In nearly every gully between the hummocks of decayed poplar and tamarisk roots, the ground was littered with broken pottery. Spurred on by the sight of the shards and the tower, and propelled forward by a stiffening wind that caused dust to swirl around us, we at last reached our destination. It was four o'clock and we'd been walking non-stop since nine that morning.

The dimensions of a number of the ancient houses can still be identified by the woven tamarisk and reed building material that once formed the base of their external walls. Many of the buildings could also be accurately plotted by the distance between their upright support poles. A large building near a market square had been the city's municipal centre or *yamen*, and within it, individual rooms could quite clearly be seen. One building had a door lintel, firmly positioned between two upright posts, and another large construction had a massive end wall which had splayed out on either side to form a huge "V". Man-made square notches could also be seen in a number of collapsed crosspieces. The early explorers had unearthed manuscripts and letters written on paper and wooden staves, which accurately dated the abandonment of the city at about 330 CE. They show that Loulan had an inn, a hospital, a post office building and a temple.

Our team searched hard among the ruins for gems, earrings, coins, spoons, tweezers, hairpins and Roman and Syrian glass – trinkets and necessities that earlier explorers had unearthed. But apart from numerous pieces of pottery, only Xiao Yuan found a fragment of a bronze mirror and a coin.

We stayed in Loulan for as long as we dared. Without provisions or water it was dangerous not to return to our camp that night, especially as Lao Zhao had grossly underestimated the distance. If a sandstorm sprang up and we were marooned in Loulan we could find ourselves in considerable difficulty. All of us felt a growing sense of unease as the watery sun, half hidden by dust, started to dip towards the horizon. None of us wanted to remain in the ancient city after dark.

My journal again reads:

"We set off in a setting sun which provides a spectacular backdrop for this ghostly city. We head directly for the riverbed and avoid the Buddhist tower. The sun disappears as we reach the river and our torches light up footprints left on our outward journey. Fortunately, as our batteries fade, a watery moon rises. If there had been no moon and if the wind had not changed direction to blow from behind us, it would have been much more difficult. Professor Yuan tires but keeps going. It's too cold to rest. If we do, we stiffen up with cold. We leave the riverbed as our torches 'die' and to our great relief see our 'star in the east,' the light from the bulb on the truck. As we walk towards it, the moonlight fades away. The going becomes more and more difficult and we stumble around yardangs and through crumbling shale for over three hours. Suddenly, our 'star' disappears!"

At this point our situation was serious. We spread out in a long line as far as we dared. The shadows ahead of us played constant tricks. What appeared to be a truck turned out to be yet another hummock of twisted wood. We constantly stopped to call out, hoping that Driver Li would hear us. There was no response. Apart from the howling wind, it was as silent as a tomb. And then unexpectedly, just as our hearts were sinking into the sand, Xiao Zhao gave a great shout. He had spotted the truck. It was 1.30am on Easter Sunday and we had walked non-stop for 16 hours and covered 55 kilometres.

Let Professor Yuan Guoying have the last word on our journey to Loulan. In 1997, he published a paper in Chinese on our discoveries at both Loulan and Tu-ying. The quaint English translation reads like a piece of prose from the 17th century, yet in its final three descriptive sentences, it captures poignantly the hazards of our trek:

"Former archaeological and touring teams had to start at the March bridge on the bank of the Konche Daria and walk 27km to the Lou Lan town from the west. We initiated a new eastern route and also walked 25km to get to Lou Lan because it was hard for automobile to travel. The rode [sic] is so rugged and rough, and so wriggling tortuous for walk, with no fresh water for camel and horse, that it is terribly hard to make tour of Lou Lan town from the east for archaeology."

John Hare runs the Wild Camel Protection Foundation, established in 1997 to protect the critically endangered wild Bactrian camel, which winters in the Lop Nur region. He has helped the Chinese to establish a 65,000-square-kilometre Lop Nur Wild Camel National Nature Reserve in the area surrounding the dried-up lake. Hare was awarded the Ness Award by the Royal Geographical Society for raising awareness on wild Bactrian camels and the Lawrence of Arabia Memorial Medal for exploration under extreme hazard by the Royal Society of Asian Affairs. In October 2006 the Royal Scottish Geographical Society awarded him the Mungo Park medal for distinguished contributions to exploration. For more information on his work visit **www.wildcamels.com**

SITES ALONG THE KONCHE RIVER (KURUK DARYA)

At ancient Loulan, trade caravans had two options: they could either head southeast to Miran, continuing on the southern route to Kashgar; or they could proceed eastwards, following the course of the **Kuruk Darya**, now called the **Konche River**, past the fortress and monastery of **Yingpän** (southeast of modern-day Korla) in the direction of Kucha, from where they travelled on to Kashgar. Since the discoveries of isolated tombs and small graveyards by Aurel Stein (1915) and Sven Hedin (1934), spectacular finds have been made (from 1979 on) at various graveyards along the Konche River.

QÄWRIGHUL

About 70 kilometres northeast of Loulan L.A. lies the ancient necropolis of **Qäwrighul (Gumugou)**, excavated by Chinese archaeologists in 1979. Here, mummies believed to be up to 4,000 years old and showing early Indo-European characteristics were unearthed (*see* special topic on page 148). There

are no monuments above ground, but instead arrangements of concentric rows of wooden stakes, jutting only a few centimetres from the earth. One year later, the very well conserved mummy of a young woman was found at the neighbouring site of **Töwän (Tieban).** Believed to date to 1800 BCE (although some experts believe she could be up to 1,000 years younger), she has been nicknamed the "**Beauty of Loulan**", becoming a symbol of national identity for the Uygur population despite the fact that she lived up to two millennia before the arrival of Uygurs in the Tarim Basin.

Another 130 kilometres east of Qäwrighul lies the site of **Yingpän**, which was first visited by Hedin in 1896 and then by Stein in 1915. It consists of the ruins of one large and at least nine small stupas, a Buddhist shrine and a fortress. Here, as in Miran, the Japanese spy Tachibana, masquerading as an archaeologist, broke several Buddhist clay figures while attempting to remove them from the shrine. However, in 1995, Chinese archaeologists made a sensational discovery when unearthing a tomb. Inside a painted wooden coffin was the mummy of a 1.8-metre-tall man dating from the third or fourth century CE. He lay flat on his back, and his red woollen robe was decorated in an obviously Hellenistic style with woven yellow designs of paired, naked putti fighting like Roman gladiators, and paired goats around pomegranate trees. This garment was probably not imported, but made locally by artists familiar with Western patterns. The mummy also wore a mask of white painted hemp paste on which the eyes, the eyebrows and moustache were painted black. A thin leaf of gold covered

the forehead. Both this spectacular mummy and the "Beauty of Loulan" are today on display in the Xinjiang Uygur Autonomous Region Museum in Urumqi. The route along the Konche River leading northeast to Korla is lined with ancient beacon towers from the same period as Yingpän.

XIAOHE

When Sven Hedin returned in 1934 to the Kuruk Darya, his old camel man Ördek – the discoverer of Loulan 34 years earlier – came to greet his former boss. He informed him that around 1910 or 1911 he

Above: Human remains at the Bronze Age necropolis of Xiaohe, prior to its excavation. Left: A dessicated wooden figure at Xiaohe dates to approximately 1800–1700 BCE – these effigies were buried in place of bodies, perhaps as representations of family members who had died while travelling far away (Lixue Liang x2). Opposite: Wonderful detail on a woollen robe, discovered at Yingpän covering a Han-era mummy; two naked putti, or cherubs, are shown fighting in a distinctly Hellenistic style (Christoph Baumer).

had found a graveyard of "one thousand tombs" near a secondary river to the Kuruk Darya. Hedin dispatched the expedition's archaeologist Folke Bergman (1902–1946) to investigate with Ördek. Following the dry bed of the Xiaohe River (which means "Little River") in a southerly direction for 60 kilometres, they eventually found "Ördek's necropolis", today called **Xiaohe**.

Lying about 170 kilometres to the west of Loulan L.A., this was a graveyard consisting of an eight-metre-high artificial hill of sand, out of which more than 100 stakes – painted red – jutted, with almost the same number lying on the ground. Also 140 arc-shaped boards were scattered on the ground – the remains of burst canoe-shaped coffins – as well as large wooden oar-shaped posts. A wooden palisade divided the graveyard into two parts. Bergman opened an intact tomb and examined 11 others that had already been disturbed, either by natural elements or by tomb raiders like Ördek himself. Bergman also found two almost life-size wooden figures of a man and a woman; raiders had taken them out of their coffins and thrown them to the ground, considering them of no value. Bergman noticed the absence of silk in the coffins and concluded – due to a lack of comparable finds – that the graveyard dated from the third or second century BCE, the period prior to the Chinese cultural influence that began in 108 BCE.

fter Bergman's departure, political turmoil made further investigation impossible and "Ördek's necropolis" fell into oblivion. However, once his archaeological report (published in 1939) was translated into Chinese in 1998, interest was reignited for Chinese archaeologists, who rediscovered the necropolis in December 2000 and excavated it in the years 2002–2005. Unfortunately, the archaeologists left the site unguarded after their first preliminary excavation campaign in the winter of 2002, whereupon tomb raiders seized the opportunity and ransacked about 50 square metres of the necropolis's centre. Only then did Beijing's State Cultural Relics Bureau approve a plan for Xinjiang-based archaeologists to complete excavation and remove all important finds to Urumqi.

Those finds proved to be sensational. Archaeologists discovered 330 tombs stacked on top of each other in layers up to five deep, suggesting that the necropolis was used over a long period of time. The coffins and mummies of the lowest two layers had rotted away due to the relatively high humidity of the ground. In total, 163 burials were excavated – the remaining 167 were either damaged or destroyed by robbers or ground moisture. From 33 well-preserved coffins 15 intact mummies were recovered, plus one female and six male wooden figures, looking like mock corpses. These wooden figures had been buried as replacements for an absent corpse, the person having probably died far away. The mummies show clear Indo-European traits and date from 1800–1700 BCE, based on C-14 measurements. They are thus contemporary with the mummies of Qäwrighul and Töwän.

The dead were buried in wooden, canoe-shaped coffins made out of poplar, similar to certain coffins in Niya, and most tombs were marked by a wooden stake, up to three metres high. In front of many tombs containing female bodies stood a torpedo-shaped stake, obviously a phallic symbol, while in front of male burial sites a large wooden oar-shaped post was driven into the ground. The combination of canoe-shaped coffins and oars placed in front of them suggests the hypothesis that these ancient people may have associated the journey from this life to the beyond with the crossing of a river that both separates and connects the two spheres. All coffins were oriented to the northeast, and consisted of two long, arcing wooden boards, covered with small boards placed in cross directions. The coffins had no bottom section, but were wrapped in an ox hide.

The corpses wore woollen garments and moccasin-style slippers made out of leather. Next to them a small basket containing millet was laid – an indication that these Bronze Age people practised agriculture. The millet may be symbolic food for the afterlife, or represent the regenerative power of nature, similar to the symbol of maize in ancient Meso-American cultures. This second theory is supported by small phallic wooden pegs placed inside the coffin, and by the large red phallic stakes marking the tombs above the ground.

Wooden masks and small wooden figures of humans or snakes were placed in some of the coffins, and in certain cases up to seven ox skulls, painted red and white, were stacked on top of each other and placed upon the coffin. In some female burials, golden earrings and pieces of bronze mirrors were found; these suggest that the people from Xiaohe had trading contact with central China; however, neither pottery nor bronze vessels were found. As at Qäwrighul and Töwän, branches of the evergreen shrub ephedra were placed on or beside every dead person – the alkaloid ephedrine was an ancient traditional medicine used to decongest nasal or bronchial passages. In the western sector of the graveyard was a sacrificial area with two altars, on whose wooden stakes ox skulls or horns were attached by ropes made of grass.

What is puzzling is the total lack of any contemporaneous settlement in the neighbourhood of the graveyard. Since these ancient people practised agriculture and weren't pure nomads, they must have had permanent dwellings somewhere. Either these settlements have been totally destroyed, or have not yet been found, or perhaps Xiaohe was an isolated necropolis where the dead were brought from an unknown distance. Discoveries made about 10–12 kilometres to the east and west of Xiaohe belong to a much later time period, namely from the Han and Jin dynasties (206 BCE–420 CE). Most probably, an ancient caravan route followed the Xiaohe River, linking the main trade route with the small circular fortress of Merdek, dating from the Eastern Han Dynasty (25–220 CE), and from there on to Miran.

Xiaohe is a closed area for tourism, but there are plans for the Archaeological Institute in Urumqi to organize one excursion each year in the autumn for selected persons. The necropolis looks less spectacular today than it appeared prior to the excavations. Access is either from the start of the former Xiaohe River on the southern shore of the Konche River, 88 kilometres east of Yingpän, or from the village of Argan, situated on the road from Korla to Ruoqiang, 140 kilometres to the north of the latter. From Argan it is a 33-kilometre trek to Xiaohe. A small-scale replica of the graveyard has been built in the Xinjiang Uygur Autonomous Region Museum in Urumqi.

A–Z FACTS FOR THE TRAVELLER

ACCOMMODATION

The quality of accommodation options in Xinjiang covers the whole gamut from luxurious international five-star hotels such as the Yin Du and Sheraton in Urumqi, to stark guesthouses in remote mountain towns where the sheets are rarely changed.

Cheap, basic lodging at *lushe/luguan* (traveller's hostels with communal toilets and no showers) is usually not possible – or indeed acceptable – to foreigners. *Zhaodaisuo* (guesthouses) are often the only places for foreigners to stay in small, remote towns; these are inexpensive, with communal toilets and public showers. Cleaner and more comfortable are *binguan* (hotels), a term that can cover a range of establishments, from two-star to five-star properties. Some English may be spoken (but don't count on it), and there will be at least one restaurant; binguan are patronized by foreigners, Chinese businessmen and senior cadres. The word *Fandian* (hotel or restaurant) is also used, usually referring to the higher end of Chinese accommodation. In cheaper and some mid-range hotels, a thermos of *kai shui* (boiled water) is placed in every room, and every floor has a *fuwuyuan* (attendant) who looks after your needs.

Specific locations and details of hotels are contained in the Practical Information section for each city in chapters 2–6 (quoted prices are subject to change and should only be used as a reference). They generally include a small selection of the best accommodation for those adventurers who like their comforts away from home too. However, for those independent-minded souls with the instinct to enhance their travel experience by experimenting when looking for a place to stay, the following websites will open the door to a wider range of hotel options:

www.smarttravel.com	www.asiahotels.com	www.orientaltravel.com
www.zuji.com.hk	www.tripadvisor.com	www.sinohotel.com
www.travelchinaguide.com	http://english.ctrip.com	www.hotelclub.net
www.chinaplanner.com		

AIRLINES AND AIR TRAVEL

Only in recent decades has Xinjiang become easily accessible by air – it remained very much a vast but remote backwater until its economic value to China (oil, agriculture and renewed trading potential with Central Asia) brought it firmly under the gaze of the central government. All flights into Xinjiang, whether domestic or international, currently fly into **Urumqi Diwopu International Airport** (although plans are being made for direct domestic and international flights to Kashgar in the near future). Urumqi Airport has undergone extensive enlargement and improvement in the last decade, and is now considered one of the five major airports of China. Flights around the Xinjiang region mostly originate from Urumqi; more details of its flight schedules to Yining, Karamay, Tacheng, Altay City, Korla, Kucha, Aksu, Kashgar, Hotan and Qiemo can be found in the "Urumqi Practical Information" section. (Kashgar now also operates flights to main towns such as Hotan, Kucha and Korla.)

The following international airlines serve Xinjiang from the listed cities:

Ariana Afghan Airlines (**www.flyariana.com**) – Kabul

Azerbaijan Airlines (**www.azal.az**) – Baku

China Southern Airlines (**www.csair.com**) – Almaty, Ashkhabad, Baku, Bishkek, Dushanbe, Irkutsk, Islamabad, Jeddah, Khabarovsk, Moscow-Sheremetyevo, Novosibirsk, Osh, Samarkand, Sharjah, Tashkent, Tehran-Imam Khomeini

Dalavia (**www.dalavia.ru**) – Khabarovsk (Russia)

Dragonair (**www.dragonair.com**) – Hong Kong (seasonal charters only)

Hainan Airlines (**www.hnair.com**) – Astana (Kazakhstan)

Korean Air (**www.koreanair.com**) – Seoul-Incheon (seasonal)

S7 Airlines (**www.s7.ru**) – Novosibirsk (Russia)

Somon Airlines (**www.somonair.com**) – Dushanbe

Tajik Air (**www.tajikair.tj**) – Dushanbe

Uzbekistan Airways (**www.uzairways.com**) – Tashkent, Fergana

Domestic airlines connect the following Chinese cities with Urumqi:

Air China (**www.airchina.com.cn**) – Beijing, Chengdu, Jinan

China Eastern Airlines (**www.ce-air.com**) – Kunming, Lanzhou, Nanjing, Shanghai-Hongqiao, Xi'an

China Southern Airlines (**www.csair.com**) – Aksu, Altay, Beijing, Changsha, Chengdu, Chongqing, Dalian, Guangzhou, Hangzhou, Kashi, Kunming, Lanzhou, Qingdao, Shanghai-Hongqiao, Shenzhen, Xiamen, Xi'an, Xining, Yinchuan, Zhengzhou

Hainan Airlines (**www.hnair.com**) – Beijing, Chengdu, Guangzhou, Hangzhou, Kashi, Kunming, Sanya, Xi'an

Shandong Airlines (**www.shandongair.com.cn**) – Yinchuan

Shanghai Airlines (**www.shanghai-air.com**) – Shanghai-Hongqiao

Shenzhen Airlines (**www.shenzhenair.com**) – Shenyang, Shenzhen, Xi'an, Zhengzhou

Sichuan Airlines (**www.scal.com.cn/en**) – Chengdu, Chongqing

Spring Airlines (**www.chinaspringtour.com**) – Shanghai-Hongqiao

ALCOHOL

Xinjiang's main ethnic groups – Uygur, Kazakh, Hui, Kyrgyz, Uzbek and Tajik – are Muslim, but although the precepts of Islam forbid the consumption of alcohol, the form of Islamism practised in Xinjiang, like that across the border in Kazakhstan, has been diluted to the extent that it is acceptable to the majority to drink beer and hard liquor. Indeed, for many this is an intrinsic part of any social function, especially in large cities, and if you dine out with newfound friends you may find yourself having tumblers of local firewater or Russian vodka forced on you in a friendly but persistent manner. You will be applauded if you take up the challenge, but a firm and gracious refusal will be accepted without rancour. It is wise not to draw attention to this apparent flouting of Islamic code, since this may be perceived as a questioning of your dining partners' faith, which is highly rude and, in some situations, can be dangerous.

The Chinese of course are great drinkers, and you will find bars, drinking clubs and KTV bars everywhere. In the cities and towns of southern Xinjiang, which are predominantly Uygur and more traditional in outlook, there is far less overt drinking; it still exists, but is hidden away and not trumpeted so loudly as in the northern cities.

BARGAINING

With the exception of state-run stores with fixed prices, always bargain in markets and shops, and occasionally hotels. Even state-run stores will sometimes give discounts on expensive items like carpets. Bargaining in Xinjiang can be good-humoured or it can be infuriating; it is a game won by technique and strategy, not by anger or threats. Thus, it should be leisurely and friendly, and not be seen as a one-way process at all, since the local traders expect and enjoy it.

It is bad manners to continue to bargain after a deal has been struck, a service rendered, or an item purchased. Ask around before you buy to try and determine what the "correct" price is. When you have offered the highest price you are willing to pay, do not budge, and as a last resort walk away as a feigned lack of interest may make for a good deal. Your position is strongest when you appear not to care. You can save a lot of money and make friends more easily if you know how to bargain in Chinese or Uygur. It can be a challenge to get the same price as the locals, yet coming close is almost as satisfying.

CLIMATE AND CLOTHING

Xinjiang, one of the most landlocked regions on the planet, has an extreme continental climate, meaning very hot summers and very cold winters. Nevertheless, conditions vary substantially, from the severe desert aridity and massive swings in temperature of the Taklamakan Desert to the milder, wet alpine climate of the Altai Mountains and Ili Valley. The former entails an extremely hot and arid summer, a short, barely noticeable autumn and spring, and a relatively cold winter, with snow on high ground; the latter are more temperate, with plentiful precipitation but very cold winters when huge snowfalls block access to many areas. The oases have their own microclimate similar to conditions in the hot Mediterranean areas, with moisture provided from underground channels and wells.

lthough the hottest, the summer months are the most rewarding time to travel: the oasis towns are full of life, flowers are in bloom, fruit is in season, and the smell of sweet melons and hemp resin fills the air; in the mountains the meadows are carpeted with glorious, colourful wildflowers, and hiking trips to the camps of nomadic herdsmen are extremely rewarding. June is already very hot, with summer temperatures averaging 30°C (86°F) in Urumqi and rising to the mid-40s°C (110°F) in the Turpan area. Precipitation is minimal and the air is very dry in the deserts and around their rims, but for a break move up into the mountains where the temperature and humidity is idyllic.

In deference to Muslim sensibilities, trousers or long skirts should be worn whenever possible – shorts are disapproved of for both women *and* men. Visitors would do well to imitate the locals by staying in the shade around midday. Shoes should be solid and comfortable; even in the summer it is advisable to have thick-soled shoes, not thin sandals, since the ground temperature can get extremely hot, especially at sites in the desert.

Winters are raw and severe. By late October there is a risk of mountain passes being snowed in, so plan routes carefully. During December and January, the average temperature in Urumqi is -10°C (14°F) and is considerably lower in the Pamir, Kunlun and Tien Shan mountains, as well as the northern Junggar Basin and Altai. Wool and fleece layers, topped with a coat or jacket of down or *thinsulate* with a wind-breaking shell, should constitute your main defence against the cold. Pay attention also to extremities: hats, scarves, gloves and good socks in thick-soled boots are essential. Even in spring and autumn, the most comfortable seasons for travel, one's feet can freeze to numbness while sitting motionless on a long-distance bus or 4WD trip. Two thin pairs of all-wool socks are better than a thick pair of acrylic ones.

Travellers should also be prepared for dust storms, especially in Turpan, which often begin in the early afternoon and last for several hours: abrasive, blasting sands whipped up by strong winds, bringing all activity to a halt. The dust is particularly bad news for cameras – protection in the form of a sealable zip-lock plastic bag is often a good idea. It is important to carry a good torch, especially when visiting unlit Buddhist caves. A sturdy pair of sunglasses, broad-brimmed hat and water bottle are also highly recommended. The ideal time for visiting the Southern Silk Road is autumn (late September to November) – in spring and early summer there is often fog and powerful sandstorms, and temperatures in high summer and winter are too extreme.

CRIME

injiang, like the rest of China, is generally a very safe place to visit. Foreigners are treated with respect or plain indifference, and scams or major criminal activity is rarely focused on international visitors. However minor crime, principally theft by pickpockets, is not uncommon, so caution should be taken in crowded public areas like bazaars, bus and train stations, where razor slashers can empty your daypack in seconds and pickpockets use surgical tongs to ingeniously "fish" in pockets for wallets, phones or cameras. The best prevention against theft is a money belt worn inside your clothing. The annoying practice by some taxi drivers and guides of stopping at shops where you will be pressured to buy souvenirs (for which they earn a commission) is present in Xinjiang though not as common as in other parts of China. In truth, conflicts between tourists and tour companies over what was promised and what was actually provided on a day trip or tour are probably the most frequent problem to expect. Though it may seem criminal in some cases, this is not how it is perceived by Chinese, and there is rarely any recourse to the authorities.

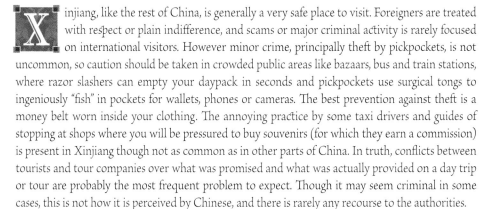

CURRENCY AND CREDIT CARDS

The Chinese currency is called **Renminbi** (meaning people's currency) and this is abbreviated to **Rmb**. It is denominated in *yuan*, referred to as *kuai* in everyday speech. The yuan is divided into ten *jiao* (colloquially called *mao*). Each jiao is divided into 10 *fen*. There are large notes for 100, 50, 10, 5 and 1 yuan, small notes for 5, 2 and 1 jiao, and coins for 1 yuan, 5 and 10 jiao, and 5, 2 and 1 fen. In January 2012, US$1 was worth Rmb6.3 and £1 was worth Rmb9.77.

There is no limit to the amount of foreign currency you can take into China, but amounts over US$5,000 should be declared. In the major cities, all freely negotiable currencies can be exchanged for Rmb at branches of the Bank of China, in hotels and large stores. Traveller's cheques are changed at a slightly better rate than cash.

All major European, American and Japanese traveller's cheques are accepted, although there are no facilities to exchange these en route so travellers are advised to change these for cash at major cities. International credit cards are accepted in only the most upmarket shops and hotels, and a limited number of ATM machines in major cities (showing the appropriate sign). In other places only Chinese Visa and Mastercards may be used. Cash may be drawn with a four percent service charge at larger branches of the Bank of China in major cities.

Clockwise from above: The different shades and colours that permeate a piece of jade are often used cleverly by jade carvers in its design (Jeremy Tredinnick); modern-day desert travellers hike up towards the crest of a wave of sand dunes near Qiemo (Christoph Baumer); organized chaos at Kashgar's Livestock Market (Jeremy Tredinnick); Yengisar knives come in many shapes, sizes and colours (Sun Jiabin).

CUSTOMS AND CULTURE

As few Chinese are able to leave the country, they travel extensively and in great numbers within China, with Xinjiang an increasingly popular "exotic" destination. Contact with the domestic tourists can be rewarding as they are friendly and interested in meeting foreigners. Men are constantly offered cigarettes, beer and rice wine as a token of friendship or merely as a standard act of courtesy. Spoken English is generally poor, but you will find that a few words of Mandarin or Uygur go a long way and are greatly appreciated – in particular a *"Salaam Aleikum"* greeting, with a handshake, to Muslims will be well received. Chinese women are less outgoing than the men and more hesitant in approaching foreigners. While Uygurs, Kazakhs and other ethnic groups will be most interested in your religion and whether you are Muslim, the Han Chinese will ask where you are from and how much money you make. Questions considered personal in the West are fair game for the Chinese.

Standards of hygiene in China are not perceived in the same way as in the West. Although the Chinese as individuals are clean, their public habits may lead you to think otherwise. Most significant is the habit of hawking and spitting regardless of whether in a restaurant, train, bus, waiting room or on a crowded street corner. Spitting has been a recent government hygiene issue, resulting in many public signs banning the habit. Hygiene in most restaurants is not up to Western standards but most are safe and offer disposable chopsticks, the result of another government hygiene campaign.

Away from the better hotels (three-star and up), "squat "toilets are the norm and you will need to get used to them. Public toilets consist of long rows of holes in the ground, which are sometimes separated by low walls. Buy your own toilet paper and carry some around with you.

When visiting mosques, it is important to show the right attitude. Shoes must be removed and appropriate clothing worn – women should have legs and arms fully covered, and a scarf to cover the head. Visiting during prayers and on Fridays is usually forbidden or highly frowned upon, and cameras should always be used with utmost discretion, preferably with the subjects' permission. (To put this in perspective, imagine a group of Japanese tourists entering a church in the UK or US and beginning to snap close-up pictures of the priest and congregation during a sermon – the reaction would be one of rightful indignation and anger, of course.)

Uygurs mark special events such as festivals, weddings or the birth of a child with a *meshrep*, essentially a huge celebration or party where enormous amounts of food are eaten, and much singing and dancing takes place. If you are lucky enough to be invited to one, be sure to attend, as this is where you will see Uygurs at their most vibrant and traditional.

DINING ETIQUETTE

The *dastarkhan* (literally "tablecloth", and used by both Uygurs and Kazakhs) is a term meaning a full meal prepared for a special occasion, usually centred around a low table spread with a wide assortment of fruits (fresh and dried), nuts, nan bread, rice and meat dishes. If invited to a Uygur household for dastarkhan, traditionally the host will greet you, and you should wash your hands three times under water poured by him from a ewer into a basin.

When entering a Kazakh yurt, do not step on the doorstep, enter with your right foot first, and always wait to be seated –honoured guests will be given the positions farthest from the doorway. Toasting is part of a Kazakh feast, and a member of the household, acting as the *tamada* or toastmaster, will begin proceedings, inviting individuals to make toasts – you will be expected to make a toast if asked, and should ask permission from the tamada if you wish to make a toast at a certain point in the meal – your request will never be refused. Never finish all the food on your plate, as it will be refilled on the assumption that you haven't had enough. When you are replete, leave a small amount on your plate to show that you have had your fill.

ELECTRICITY

Voltage in Xinjiang is 220V and 50Hz. Electrical outlets vary widely depending on the age of the building, so it is recommended to take a good multiple adaptor set with you. In the newer hotels square three-pin plugs are becoming more common, but older outlets are still the most frequently available, with sockets for both round two-pin and flat blade two-pin plugs, as well the angled (oblique) three-pin variety.

EMBASSIES AND CONSULATES

Embassy and consulate addresses within China can be found at **www.embassiesinchina.com**, while Chinese embassies and consulates around the world can be sourced at the Ministry of Foreign Affairs of the People's Republic of China website at **www.fmprc.gov.cn/eng/wjb/zwjg/2409** or **www.embassyworld.com**.

FOOD AND DRINK

Food and drink in Xinjiang is wholesome and tasty, if perhaps sometimes simple and repetitious. Although the main cities boast restaurants specializing in Sichuanese or Cantonese cuisine, you will immediately be aware of the Islamic influence on eating habits in the region – pork, the staple meat of the Han Chinese, disappears to be replaced by mutton or lamb.

Night markets (*ye shi*) and small restaurants (*xiao chi*) are by far the tastiest places to eat. Each night around dusk, street vendors set up stalls and tables on prearranged streets throughout the various cities. These lively night markets provide an excellent opportunity to stroll and sample from the various cauldrons, woks and grills that line the street. Small restaurants are best for authentic local dishes and distinct regional flavours. The best way to order is by pointing to what others are having or by going into the kitchen and picking out various meat and vegetable combinations. With some exceptions, hotel restaurants offer relatively expensive and unexciting meals, a last resort when deciding where to eat. The "Practical Information" section for each city contains useful information on night markets, small restaurants and local specialities.

One of the most popular foods in Xinjiang is barbecued mutton on skewers (*kebab*, *shashlik* or *kao yangrou*), which is placed on the table piping hot – use a knife, fork or chopsticks to strip it from the spiral metal skewer and eat the lumps of lean meat, leaving the lumps of fat and gristle on the table (these are interspersed on the skewer during cooking to add flavour, but generally not eaten). Kebab is commonly eaten with a wide variety of nan flatbreads (*bing*) that can be sweet, salty or plain. Boiled mutton dumplings (*yangrou shuijiao*) are served either in soup or with a spicy soy/vinegar sauce.

Most meals consist of noodles or nan bread served with mutton in one form or another. The most common dish is *laghman* – fresh noodles served with sautéed lamb, tomatoes, aubergine and hot green peppers. Another popular dish is *poluo*, rice mixed with finely chopped vegetables and topped with mutton. Nan bread is sold from street stalls everywhere, and the smaller Rmb2 size makes a great snack, especially when topped with herbs or spices, as does the bagel-like *girde nan*. Don't throw unwanted bread away, however, as this is a cultural no-no – and anyway, the bread keeps indefinitely so can be saved for later.

Xinjiang produces a wide variety of fruit (*shuiguo*), which is in season in the summer months – apricots (*xingzi*), plums (*meizi*) and mulberries (*sangshu*) in June; melons (*gua*) in July; peaches (*taozi*), figs (*wuhuaguo*) and grapes (*putao*) in August; pomegranates (*shiliu*), apples (*pingguo*) and pears (*lizi*) in September. There are over 50 types of Hami melon and many different varieties of watermelon (*xigua*, or western melon), which first came to Xinjiang from Africa via the Silk Road.

Above left: A Tajik wedding is a major event, and cause for much celebration (Hao Pei). Above right: More conservative Uygur women cover their heads and faces with scarves, though colour and style often still come into the equation (Sun Jiabin). Opposite: The entrance to the Abakh Khoja mausoleum garden (Jeremy Tredinnick).

Tea (*cha*) is taken with meals or just bread. In Xinjiang people mainly drink a strong black tea resembling sticks and twigs, rather than the smoother green tea of the east. Beer (*pijiu*) and rice wine (*baijiu*) are popular, particularly among the Han, and often accompany meals. Most types of refreshments that you may desire in the desert heat – from Coca-Cola to flavoured water, thick fresh yoghurt to fruit juice as well as ice cream, frozen yoghurt and popsicles – are available from vendors with refrigerators on almost every street corner.

HEALTH AND ALTITUDE

There are no mandatory vaccination requirements, but make sure your basic immunizations are up to date: polio, diphtheria and tetanus. Many foreign doctors recommend vaccinations against the following, although the need may vary according to time of year: meningococcal meningitis, cholera, hepatitis A and B, and Japanese B encephalitis. Contact your nearest specialist travel clinic or tropical medicine hospital, and plan well ahead.

Trekkers to the high regions of Xinjiang's mountain ranges, as well as travellers crossing the Khunjerab Pass and overnighting at Tashkurgan, where the altitude is over 3,300 metres (10,800 feet), may suffer altitude sickness. This is caused by an insufficient flow of oxygen to the brain and other vital organs. It can affect anybody at above 3,000 metres (10,000 feet).

The symptoms of altitude sickness include headache, nausea and shortness of breath. In 99 percent of these cases, rest and two aspirins relieve the discomfort. However, the serious, sometimes fatal conditions of pulmonary and cerebral oedema also begin with these same symptoms. Overexertion and dehydration contribute to altitude sickness, so drink plenty of fluids, do not smoke, and avoid sleeping pills or tranquillisers, which tend to depress respiration and limit oxygen intake. Diamox (acetozolamide), a mild prescription diuretic that stimulates oxygen intake, is used by doctors of the Himalayan Rescue Association in Kathmandu for climbers making sudden ascents.

Chinese pharmacies carry Eastern and Western medicines and are the best places to go for basic stomach disorders, colds and headaches. Most Western health and sanitary products should be brought with you; items such as tampons are expensive and often hard to find.

INTERNET

The world-shrinking phenomenon that is the Internet has found its way into towns throughout Xinjiang, but only in the major cities are connections reliable and fast enough to be practical. The best four- and five-star hotels have Internet cable connections in their rooms, and there are business centres in the others, as well as most three-star properties. Connection speeds can vary dramatically, even in Urumqi, but basic email communication and web searching is possible most of the time. Internet cafés have sprung up even in smaller towns, with charges as low as Rmb5 per 30 minutes, while some Western-oriented cafés offer free wifi. Bear in mind, however, that a number of mainstream sites, the BBC in particular, are often not available in China.

Maps and Books

rumqi is the only place where you will easily be able to buy English language maps of Xinjiang. On the street of Xinhua Bei Lu just south of the Xinjiang Grand Hotel street hawkers sell a range of surprisingly good maps of the entire region, as well as of Urumqi city. Hotel book shops will also stock maps, and limited selections of English language publications, including coffee table books on Xinjiang with excellent photography (but somewhat suspect English text).

Post and Telecommunications

Post offices in Xinjiang are much like in other provincial Chinese areas – slow, frustrating, but ultimately efficient in that you can be reasonably sure your letter or package will eventually arrive at its destination. The major hotels also provide postal services, but any item under customs control, such as antiques, must be sent from a city's main post office.

IDD service is provided in hotels and post offices of all major towns and cities. Phone cards can be bought at post offices, in some hotels, and from street newsstands. However, a much less expensive option is to bring your mobile phone and buy a prepaid SIM card (Rmb100 minimum), which will work throughout the region – China's regional network connections are excellent, and relatively inexpensive. There are mobile phone shops scattered throughout Urumqi and the other large cities.

Potential Danger of Illegal Pastimes

Minutes after entering your hotel room, your room phone is likely to ring and a sultry voice will ask if you would like a "massage". Though it is possible to order and have a simple massage and no more, your masseuse will not be qualified; in Xinjiang, as in other parts of China, Central Asia and indeed most of the world, this is a euphemism for sexual services rendered. Prostitution is a problem in Xinjiang's cities, which is hardly surprising given its recent growth as an oil industry centre, its status as a frontier region with increasing cross-border trade, and the consequent rise in businessmen travelling to its urban centres. Cities like Urumqi, Karamay, Yining and Korla all suffer, and Yining in particular is said to have a related drug problem due to its proximity with the Kazakhstan border, across which heroin is allegedly smuggled from southern Central Asia.

The advice is simple: drug use is illegal and highly dangerous in this distant corner of China, and penalties are harsh; equally, the use of prostitutes carries its own high risk of contracting STDs. The best policy is to steer well clear of both.

Public Holidays

In contrast to the long calendar of traditional Chinese festivals, the modern Chinese calendar now has only four official holidays: 1 January (New Year's Day); 1 May (Labour Day); 1 October

Clockwise from top left: In the High Pamirs, yaks take the place of camels as the beast of burden of choice; poluo, a rice dish served with mutton and vegetables, is a popular meal; an intriguing machine outside Kashgar's Sunday bazaar turns out to be a pomegranate juicer (Jeremy Tredinnick x3); once one of the most remote cities in the world, Kashgar is now more accessible than ever, with regular flights from Urumqi and beyond (Magnus Bartlett); the Uygurs of the Tarim oases are generally a long-lived people, possibly due to their healthy diet – this man is Kumran Banyas from New Miran, who was born in 1886 and worked for both Sven Hedin and Aurel Stein during their explorations of the Taklamakan in the early 20th century (Christoph Baumer); despite its march into the modern world, Xinjiang still sees cars sharing space with more traditional forms of travel; mutton and nan bread are staples of the Xinjiang diet (Sun Jiabin x2).

(National Day, commemorating the founding of the People's Republic of China); and Chinese New Year, also called the Spring Festival, a three-day holiday in late January or early February celebrating the Lunar New Year. As offices usually close for several days around major holidays it is essential to book travel arrangements well in advance, especially as this is a popular time for the Chinese themselves to travel.

In Xinjiang, Islamic festivals are celebrated, though not officially classified as national holidays. These include the **Bairam** or "Minor "festival (immediately after Ramadan) and **Korban** or "Major "festival (in the final lunar month of the Islamic calendar). The month-long Ramadan fast, during the ninth Islamic lunar month, is also observed. (As these festivals follow the Islamic calendar, there are no fixed dates in the Western calendar, and they therefore take place at different times each year according to the Gregorian calendar.) Visitors should avoid travelling during public holidays, when all forms of public transport are filled to bursting.

RED TAPE

You will often come up against seemingly absurd rules and regulations governing foreign travel in Xinjiang that can be extremely frustrating, especially when enforced by power-starved minor officials. With decades of whimsical official policy, the Chinese are reluctant to take matters into their own hands: "Never take the initiative in making decisions – you may be held responsible for the consequences," reads a maxim from an old civil-service manual. When dealing with bureaucratic problems, do not raise your voice or become visibly upset, and above all never give the person you are dealing with a reason to refuse you. In most cases a compromise is usually possible with neither party losing face.

ROADS

ou will probably be astonished at the quality of Xinjiang's road network. There are sealed two-lane highways between all major towns, and these are maintained better than many Western countries' roads. Even secondary roads are of good quality, and it is usually only in the most remote regions, or in small village back roads, that tarmac gives way to dirt track. There is a price to pay for such good roads, however: the major highways are sectioned by tollbooths that charge Rmb10–25 for cars, making a long journey (few trips in Xinjiang are not of the lengthy variety) more expensive than you planned. Prearranged tours have this expense factored into their prices, but if you are travelling independently, be prepared. Watch out for speed traps as well (see special topic on page 246) – speed limits can be relatively low, even in open stretches, and a 40kph limit is usually enforced when passing a town. The driving standard in Xinjiang is generally very good, and other road users will help vehicles in breakdown situations – an unwritten law that ensures no one is left stranded in the region's many harsh environments.

TIPPING

lthough tipping is not part of traditional Chinese culture, Western influence has infiltrated even as far as Xinjiang, and travellers will now find that upmarket hotel staff, particularly bellboys, and guides and drivers often expect tips. Whether you give a gratuity or not is entirely up to you, but if excellent service is rewarded, it can only result in a raising of standards.

TIME

China is eight hours ahead of Greenwich Mean Time (London) and 13 hours ahead of Eastern Standard Time (New York). Since time is standardized throughout China, Xinjiang finds itself with dawn at 7:30 or 8am and dusk around 10:30 or 11pm (even later in the summer). Though all official government facilities, as well as air and rail timetables and bus schedules use **Beijing standard time**, locals often follow an unofficial "**Xinjiang time**", which is two hours behind. It is therefore essential to determine whether departure or meeting times are Beijing or Xinjiang time. Office hours in Xinjiang are generally 10am–2pm and 4–8pm, Beijing time, but this can vary from city to city; the farther south and west you go the more lax the adherence to official hours becomes. Beijing time is three hours ahead of Pakistani standard time, and two hours ahead of Kazakhstan's Eastern standard time and Kyrgyz time.

TOURS AND TOUR AGENCIES

An increasing number of visitors to Xinjiang use prearranged tours as the best way to see as much as possible within their time limits and minimize potential problems through use of experienced guides and established tour companies. Many are journeying along the Silk Road and passing through Xinjiang as part of a broader pan-Central Asia trip, and the oases of the Taklamakan – with their archaeological treasures and rich culture – remain the greatest draw for tourists. But as the region opens up and the potential of areas such as the far north and Ili Valley begins to be realized, new itineraries are being offered, for example circumnavigating the Junggar Basin with stops at Uyrhe Ghost City, Kanas Lake, Altay City, Ulungur Lake, and the Petrified Forest and Dinosaur Valley parks; or perhaps east from Urumqi to the ancient city of Beiting, then on to the Barkol Grasslands and down to Hami, returning via the Turpan Depression. Other options are an exciting loop through the central Tien Shan via the Bole region, Sayram Lake, the Ili and Tekes valleys, and the Narat and Bayanbulak grasslands; tracking wild antelope and yak in the Altun Nature Reserve; climbing Muztagata; or for the truly daring a 70-day trek along the Southern Silk Road by camel.

Listed in alphabetic order below is just a sampling of some of the tour companies offering excellent trips and adventures throughout Xinjiang:

XINJIANG-BASED AGENCIES

Silk Road Adventures, 10/F, 8 Jianshe Lu, Urumqi, tel: (0991) 230 8318, email: info@silkroute.cn, website: www.silkroute.cn

SERVICE ALONG THE SILK ROAD

Adventur
Culture,
History,
Nature,
and
much
more
...

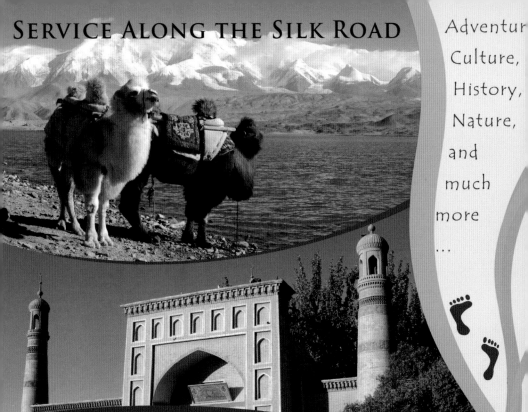

CARAVAN TRAVEL SERVICE . CHINA

Head Office (Kashgar)

Tel   : 0086-998-2838988
           0086-998-2828809
Mobile : 008613909989088
Fax   : 0086-998-2829019
Email : caravan_travel@yahoo.com.cn
Address : #18, North Jiefang Road
           Kashgar China.

Urumqi Office

Tel   : 0086-991-6118292
         : 008613609921805
Mobile : 008613309918801
Fax   : 0086-991-2605700
Email : info@caravan-travel.com
Address : #108, 34fr, Office G1
           New Century Building
           North Xinhua Road
           Urumqi . China

Tashkent Office

Tel   : 00998712679646
Fax   : 00998909577628
Mobile : 00998712679646
Email   : gulnura@travel-caravan.com
         caravantravel.cn@mail.ru
Address : Street Buyuk Ipak Yuli
          dom 1 office 9
          Tashkent , Uzbekistan

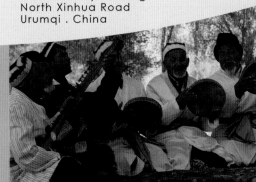

China Xinjiang Nature International Travel, 17/F, Tianji Mansion, 90 Jiefang Bei Lu, Urumqi, tel: (0991) 233 3891, website: www.china-adventure.com

CITS, 33 Renmin Lu, Urumqi, Xinjiang 830004, tel: (0991) 282 1426, email: oumei@xinjiangtour.com, website: www.xinjiangtour.com

Crown Inn @ Tashkorgan, Karakoram Café (opposite the Chinibagh Hotel), 87 Seman Lu, Kashgar, tel: (0998) 342 2888, fax: (0998) 342 2018, email: enquiry1@crowninntashkorgan.com, website: www.crowninntashkorgan.com

CYTS, 3rd Floor, Hong Yuan Building, 2 Wen Yi Lu, Urumqi, Xinjiang 83002, tel: (0991) 281 8634, fax: (0991) 283 2331, email: info@cytsxj.com, website: www.cytsxj.com

Uighur Tour & Travel Service, tel: (0998) 298 4042, fax: (0998) 298 0487, email: alitash22@yahoo.com, website: www.kashgartour.com

Xinjiang Caravan International Travel Service, 18 Jiefang Bei Lu, Kashgar, tel: (0998) 283 8988, fax: (0998) 282 9019, email: caravan_travel@yahoo.com.cn, website: www.caravantravel.cn

China-based Online Agencies

ChinaTour.Net, 802 Tower B, RunFengDeShang, 60 An Li Lu, Beijing, tel: (10) 8260 0771, website: www.chinatour.net

Travel China Guide, Suite 508, Yu Yuan Mansion, 65 Nan Er Huan Xi Duan, Xi'an 710068, tel: (029) 8523 6688, website: www.travelchinaguide.com

Wild China, Room 801, Oriental Place, 9 East Dongfang Road, North Dongsanhuan Road, Chaoyang District, Beijing, 100027, tel: (10) 6465 6602, fax: (10) 6465 1793, email: info@wildchina.com, website: www.wildchina.com

International Agencies

Abercrombie & Kent International, USA, website: www.abercrombiekent.com

Asia Transpacific Journeys, USA, website: www.asiatranspacific.com

Audley Travel, UK, website: www.audleytravel.com

Exodus, UK, website: www.exodus.co.uk

Explore, UK, website: www.explore.co.uk

Geographic Expeditions, USA, website: www.geoex.com

Golden Bridge International, Hong Kong, website: www.goldenbridge.net

GW Travel, UK, website: www.gwtravel.co.uk

Helen Wong's Tours, Australia, website: www.helenwongstours.com

MIR Corporation, USA, website: www.mircorp.com

Peregrine Adventures, Australia, website: www.peregrineadventures.com

Regent Holidays, UK, website: www.regent-holidays.co.uk

Steppes Travel, UK, website: www.steppestravel.co.uk

Sundowners Overland, UK and Australia, website: www.sundownersoverland.com

TCS & Starquest Expeditions, USA, website: www.tcsandstarquestexpeditions.com

Travelsphere Ltd, UK, website: www.travelsphere.co.uk

Voyages Jules Verne, UK, website: www.vjv.co.uk

Wild Frontiers Adventure Travel, UK, website: www.wildfrontiers.co.uk

World Expeditions, USA and UK, website: www.worldexpeditions.com

Travel To and Within Xinjiang

Only in the last two decades has Xinjiang begun to open its borders to foreigners and permit wider-ranging travel within its vast territory. Road and rail networks have been radically improved – and continue to be developed – while both domestic and international air travel are now taking off as never before. Details of routes, connections, timetables and booking offices are contained in the "Practical Information" section for each city, and airline websites in the "Airlines" section of this chapter. However, take note that China is experiencing a burgeoning demand from domestic travellers eager to see the more remote parts of their own country, so availability of seats can be an issue, and where possible booking well ahead is advised.

By Air

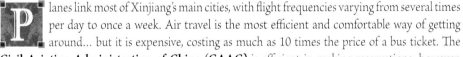

Planes link most of Xinjiang's main cities, with flight frequencies varying from several times per day to once a week. Air travel is the most efficient and comfortable way of getting around… but it is expensive, costing as much as 10 times the price of a bus ticket. The **Civil Aviation Administration of China (CAAC)** is efficient in making reservations; however, tickets are in short supply, so book as far ahead as possible. **CITS** and **CYTS** (*see* listing on previous pages) can also make reservations, and you can book air tickets from any reputable travel agency, for example those attached to the best hotels. Direct Internet booking is becoming a favoured method of arranging flights, but booking domestic tickets this way can be troublesome, and it may be better to go through a Xinjiang-based agency.

By Rail

The **Lanxin Railway** line linking **Lanzhou** with Urumqi (the "Iron Silk Road") was completed in 1963. This is a very popular way to access Xinjiang from eastern China, and there are also stops in Hami and Liuyuan in Gansu Province, from where a spur rail line continues to **Dunhuang**.

The **Beijiang Railway** line from Urumqi to Alashankou Port on the (then Soviet) border was completed in 1990, and passenger traffic began in 1992 into a newly independent **Kazakhstan**. You can now book a ticket in Urumqi all the way through to **Almaty** (and vice versa) via Alashankou Port and Aktogay on the **Turk-Sib Railway** line (subject to having a valid Kazakh visa). This journey takes around 40 hours. A spur of the Lanxin Line, from Turpan to Korla, came into use in 1984, and the **Nanjiang Railway**, the 975-kilometre westward extension of this, reached Kashgar in 2000. In 2011 an extension came into operation from Kashgar along the Southern Silk Road towns as far as Hotan. Trains leave every day between Urumqi and Kashgar, the faster morning train taking around 26.5 hours, a slower afternoon train 32 hours, and the Hotan-bound train 26 hours (with an additional 9–10 hours to Hotan).

 new electric rail line now runs from **Jinghe** – on the Beijiang Line – to **Horgas Port** via Yining in the Ili Valley, while another line is under construction from **Kuyten** – also on the Beijiang Line – to **Beitun** in the far north near the Altai Mountains. This will provide additional options for exploration at a fraction of the cost of air travel and in more comfort than a bus or car. China has also signed an agreement with **Kyrgyzstan** to build a rail line from **Kashgar** to **Tashkent** in Uzbekistan, via the Irkeshtam Pass, Osh and Andijan, creating an exciting new link to West Asia from Xinjiang. When this will be ready, however, is anybody's guess.

    Hard seat tickets can be bought easily, and are perfectly acceptable for mid-range daylight travel – especially since they allow interaction with Xinjiang residents, whose conversation and kindness can result in marvellous experiences. However, **sleeper tickets** are recommended for travellers taking longer, overnight journeys. Sleeper carriage berths, both hard and soft, are perfectly comfortable, but may sometimes need to be booked months in advance. Travellers making long journeys should bring provisions of both food and drink, though thermos flasks of boiled water are provided for each carriage, and some food is available onboard. All ticket prices are now standardized, which means foreigners and Chinese pay the same fare. An extremely useful site to check out is **www.seat61.com**, devoted solely to train travel and packed with information.

BY ROAD

There are now a number of ways to enter or exit Xinjiang by road. Highway 312 is the main route from eastern China, crossing into Xinjiang from **Gansu**, with Hami the first major town on its route. Buses ply this road constantly, with long-distance sleeper buses travelling between Urumqi and Lanzhou (the train is a better bet though), and many others catering to shorter legs along the way. To the south, the "back door" into Xinjiang from **Qinghai Province** is on Highway 315, from **Golmud** to the southeast or **Dunhuang** to the northeast – Ruoqiang is the first major town on the Southern Silk Road. It is also possible to cross the **Tibetan Plateau** and descend into southern Xinjiang on Highway 219 at Yecheng, though strictly speaking this is not allowed for independent travellers and should only be as part of a registered group tour (individuals do, however, often get through).

    The opening of the **China–Pakistan** border at the **Khunjerab Pass** in 1986 opened the door to what has become a popular road trip from the subcontinent into China along one of the Silk Road's most dramatic routes. A public bus runs from May to November, depending on the weather,

For Nicholas Roerich and his retinue, the journey from Kashgar to Urumqi was a long and arduous affair taking many weeks, with plenty of stops along the way (Courtesy of the Roerich Museum).

and vehicles of various size can be chartered for the remainder of the year. A public bus now also runs across the **Irkeshtam Pass** between Kashgar and **Kyrgyzstan**, and private vehicles can use this route or cross the **Torugart Pass** to the north. At some time in the future the road border into **Tajikistan** at the **Kulma Pass** near Tashkurgan may open to foreign travellers, but as of spring 2012 it was still closed to all but Chinese and Tajik citizens. It is now possible to cross between Xinjiang and **Kazakhstan** by road in a number of places: these include the border crossings at the **Horgas** (near Yining), **Alashankou**, **Tacheng** and **Jeminay** ports. There are currently no land border crossings between Xinjiang and **Mongolia** open to foreigners.

Within Xinjiang, improved road conditions and new highways have made bus travel much faster and more pleasant than in years past. Sleeper buses from either Urumqi or Turpan make the run southwest to Kashgar via Korla, Kucha and Aksu (about 30 hours – again, the train is a better option); they also now cross the Taklamakan on the Tarim Highway to cities on the Southern Silk Road, skirt the northern slopes of the Tien Shan then cut into the Ili Valley to Yining, and head north to Altay City in the Altai Mountains. Fitted with berths rather than seats, they drive non-stop through day and night. There are now express buses along the highway between **Turpan** and Urumqi throughout the day; they take about 2.5 hours.

The best way to see Xinjiang by road is to hire a 4WD or minivan, enabling you to visit sites far from cities or towns that would otherwise be inaccessible. Costs can be minimized if you are in a group, and bargain the price down to a reasonable level. Travel agencies and many hotels have cars or minivans for hire. Prices should be based on the number of days hired and kilometres travelled, an average of perhaps US$80–100 per day.

CYTS 中青旅 中青旅新疆国际旅行社有限责任公司
CYTS XINJIANG INTERNATIONAL TOUR CO.,LTD

Discover Xinjiang with the Experts
Specialists in Cultural, Ethnic and Historical Tours

- Silk Road Highlight Tours
- Xinjiang Landscape Tours
- Adventure Tours
- Tailored Trips for Businessmen or Backpackers
- "Inbound" and "Outbound" Tours
- Charter Flights
- Multilingual Guides

CYTS Xinjiang International Tour Co. Ltd has been organizing quality tours since 1987, and is one of the three largest travel agencies in Xinjiang. A member of the CYTS Share Holding Corporation, it was listed as one of the "Top 100 International Travel Agencies in China" in both 2006 and 2007. With a policy of "Opening the market with outstanding service", our "Human Resources First" strategy has helped us build a strong team who work in a harmonious atmosphere, and strive constantly to make sure you will remember your Xinjiang experience with pleasure forever.

Address: Third Floor, 2 Wen Yi Road, Urumqi, China 830002
Tel: +86-991-2818634; Fax: +86-991-2832331
E-mail: info@cytsxj.com; Website: www.cytsxj.com

USEFUL WEBSITES

Although by no means a fully comprehensive list of useful online sources related to Xinjiang, the following selection will hopefully help to broaden your knowledge and understanding of the region:

REGIONAL GOVERNMENT SITES

www.aboutxinjiang.com: An excellent authorized online guide to Xinjiang (the English version of Tianshannet's website), with comprehensive news, travel and business information.

www.china-embassy.org/eng: Chinese Government site for visa information.

www.egi.ac.cn: The Xinjiang Institute of Geography and Ecology.

www.fmprc.gov.cn/eng: Official foreign-policy information and news.

www.xinjiang.gov.cn: Official website of the Xinjiang Uygur Autonomous Region Government.

NEWS SITES

www.chinadaily.com.cn: Online version of China's only English daily national newspaper. Features national and business news, as well as weather and sport.

www.china.org.cn/english: Authorized state portal with daily updates of general and business news. Contains topical features and a travel guide section.

www.chinatoday.com: Huge amounts of information collated from global sources by InfoPacific Development Inc.

www.chinaview.cn: News from China's official news agency, Xinhua, in English.

SILK ROAD-RELATED

http://idp.bl.uk: The British Library's International Dunhuang Project contains excellent links to aspects of Silk Road history related to Xinjiang sites.

www.chinapage.com: Contains information on Silk Road art and culture in Chinese and English.

www.silkroadfoundation.org: The Silk Road Foundation, Saratoga, California has a vast amount of useful information.

www.silkroadproject.org: The Silk Road Project, an organization founded by classical cellist Yo-Yo Ma, aims to "illuminate the Silk Road's historical contribution to the diffusion of art and culture".

www.silkroadstudies.org: The Central Asia-Caucasus Institute Silk Road Studies Program.

GENERAL

wwwnc.cdc.gov/travel/destinationchina.htm: US Center for Contagious Diseases website, giving up-to-date information on potential health hazards in China.

www.centralasiatraveler.com: A personal but highly informative site about locations in the Southern Silk Road area, with useful maps.

www.cers.org.hk: The China Exploration and Research Society, which documents and undertakes the preservation of many of Xinjiang's most important wildlife species, natural wildernesses, ethnic nationalities and archaeological sites.

www.chinaexpat.com: Offers a huge amount of information on cities and regions throughout the country, including Xinjiang.

www.chinaplanner.com: Contains comprehensive information on the region.

www.chinatt.org: An invaluable English-language Chinese Railway Timetable available to download online.

www.discoverkashgar.com: A brand-new, comprehensive site by the Kashgar Research Institute for Strategic Development.

www.farwestchina.com: The best personal website about Xinjiang, containing comprehensive travel, cultural and historical information presented in a laudably measured fashion.

www.lonelyplanet.com: Its Thorn Tree Travel Forum can be a good source of up-to-the-minute travel information.

www.odysseypublications.com: Information on its wide range of historical and cultural guides.

www.pingtianresorts.com: PingTian Resort's website, giving update news on the opening and progress of this huge international skiing and leisure development near Urumqi.

www.uighurdictionary.com: Contains useful Uygur-English and English-Uygur translations.

www.who.int/countries/chn/en: World Health Organization.

http://wikitravel.org: A constantly updated database of info on all aspects of tourist travel.

Visas and Customs

All visitors arriving at Xinjiang ports of entry must have a valid passport and China visa, but this is usually a straightforward process. Tourists travelling in a group are listed on a single group visa issued in advance to tour organizers. Tourist visas for individual travellers can be obtained directly through Chinese embassies and consulates around the world (see **www.fmprc.gov.cn/eng** for your nearest Chinese embassy). Certain travel agents and tour operators can arrange individual visas for their clients. Visa fees and their duration vary considerably, depending on the source of the visa and the time taken to issue it. Single-entry and double-entry tourist visas valid for three months are currently available, and six-month multiple-entry visas are also possible. However, check with your local travel agent or nearest Chinese embassy for the latest information. In Hong Kong, visas can also be obtained directly from the **China Travel Service (HK) Ltd** (4/F CTS House, 78–83 Connaught Road, Central, tel: 2853 3533) or the **Visa Office of the Foreign Ministry of the PRC** (7th Floor, 26 Harbour Road, Wanchai, Hong Kong, tel: 3413 2424).

Most nationalities require a visa to cross the Khunjerab Pass into Pakistan. For a while it was possible to get a transit visa for Pakistan on arrival in Sost, valid for 30 days and at varying costs according to what passport you held. However, in late 2011 this service was stopped, with no word as to if or when it will be reactivated, so it is advisable to get one either before leaving home or if already in China at the **Embassy of the Islamic Republic of Pakistan** (1 Dongzhimenwai Dajie, Sanlitun, Beijing, tel: (010) 6532 2504). During the tourist season the border is open daily. The Torugart and Irkeshtam passes into Kyrgyzstan are becoming increasingly popular. Kyrgyz visas can be obtained at the **Kyrgyz Embassy** in Beijing (2-4-1 Tayuan Diplomatic Office Building, Beijing, tel: (010) 653 24180, email: kyrgyzch@95777.com or kyrgyzch@public2.east.net.cn) or in Urumqi at the **Visa Department of MF KR** (Free Economic Zone "High and New Technology", Urumqi, tel: (0991) 383 9117). Although the Kulma Pass into Tajikistan is still closed, it may open in the foreseeable future, while flights to Dushanbe are available from Urumqi. A Tajik visa can be arranged in China at the **Embassy of Tajikistan** (LA 01–04, Liangmaqiao Diplomatic Compound, Beijing 100600, tel: (10) 653 22598, fax: (10) 653 23039, email: tjkemb@public2.bta.net.cn). **Kazakhstan** visas can be arranged in Beijing (Kazakhstan Embassy, N9, Dong 6 Rd, Sanlitun, Beijing 100600, tel: (010) 653 26182, fax (010) 653 26183) or in Urumqi at its **Passport & Visa Service** office (31 Kunming Lu, 830011 Urumqi, tel: (0991) 381 5796, fax: (0991) 382 1203, email: kazpass@mail.xj.cninfo.net).

Travellers can have their China visas extended for 30 days up to three times at Public Security Bureaus in most open towns and cities, although the third extension can be difficult. The service is only granted up to four days before an existing visa or extension expires. At some offices extension charges vary according to nationality; at others there's a flat fee.

A Kazakh on horseback herds his flock of sheep and goats across a hillside in northern Xinjiang's Altai mountains – a timeless scene that has changed little in centuries (SC Keung).

A China visa permits visits to all "open" locations in Xinjiang, but a full list of "closed" places is almost impossible to acquire, even from Chinese embassies abroad, since it may change at any time according to political events and sensitivities (usually in border regions). In theory, closed areas can only be visited if you procure an **Alien's Travel Permit**, normally in Urumqi. These are not granted for a third category of places deemed "forbidden". The PSB in Urumqi is currently located a short distance north of South Lake Square on Nanhu Nan Lu; for information try the Xinjiang Uygur Autonomous Region Government website at **www.xinjiang.gov.cn**.

Except where otherwise mentioned, all cities and sites described in this book are open to foreign tourists, while the territory in between them may be closed. One might be able to travel through but not stay overnight in such areas. (All major archaeological sites along the Southern Silk Road – including Dandan Oilik, Karadong, Niya, Endere and Loulan – are off-limits. To visit these sites a special permit is required, issued by the Cultural Relics Bureau in Urumqi. These are seldom granted and may carry a fee of several hundreds or even thousands of US dollars.)

If you have purchased antiques in Xinjiang you will be required to show the official Export Certificate to customs officials. A limited quantity of duty-free goods is allowed to be brought into the country. This includes two bottles (0.75L) of alcohol, 400 cigarettes, a "reasonable" amount of perfume, and prescription medicine for personal use. Firearms and illicit drugs are strictly forbidden, but there is no limit to the amount of foreign currency you can bring into China.

The Chinese Language

Explanation of Pinyin

In 1958, the Chinese government adopted pinyin as the official system for romanizing Chinese characters, now used by the Western press and most phrase books. Previously the Wade-Giles system was the most common way for English speakers to phoneticize Chinese, and can still be found in many old history and art books on China. Throughout this book, the spellings of people, places and things follow the pinyin transliteration. Despite the large percentage of Uygurs living in Xinjiang, the most useful language to know is Mandarin (*putonghua*, or common speech) the official language of China; in Beijing the most standard form of *putonghua* is spoken, and pinyin follows that pronunciation. Signboards and restaurant names are often written in pinyin, mostly for a foreign look, which many Chinese themselves have difficulty reading. Nowadays, however, Chinese schoolchildren begin learning pinyin from the age of seven. Letters in pinyin correspond closely to standard English pronunciation, although some letters have different sounds.

Initials (Word Beginnings)

c   like the *ts* in 'fits'

q   like the *ch* in 'cheese'

x   somewhere between *sh* and *s*, an aspirated sound

z   like the *ds* in 'lads'

zh   like the *j* in 'judge'

Finals (Word Endings)

a   like *ah* in 'cheetah'

ai   like the *ie* in 'tie'

e   like 'her' without the *r*

ei   like the *ay* in 'ray'

i   like *ee* in 'wheeze' except after c, ch, r, sh, z and zh when it becomes a short sound, like the *i* in 'sir'

ian like 'yen', or the *ien* in Vienna

ie   sounds like ieh, or the *ye* in 'yes'

o   like 'oh', slightly drawn out

ou   like *o* in 'mow'

u   like the French '*tu*' or the German '*ü*'

uai   sounds like 'why'

uan   like *uan* in 'iguana', sounds like 'wan'

ue   like the *ue* in the Spanish '*fuego*'

ui   like *ey* in 'hey'

Every Chinese character has only one syllable with its own tone and meaning; words consisting of several characters will take on a variety of different meanings (each syllable retains its own tone and pronunciation):

Pinyin		English Approximation
Beijing	=	Bay-Jhing (not zhing)
Cixi	=	Ts-shee
Mao Zedong	=	Mao Ds-dong
Qianlong	=	Chien-lohng
Xi'an	=	Shee-Ahn
Zhou Enlai	=	Jho En-lie

Chinese has four tones, which are marked above the word and used primarily in language texts. The tone of a word corresponds with its meaning; the same word pronounced with a different tone takes on an entirely different meaning. The four tones are: flat (ˉ), rising (´), falling-rising (ˇ) and falling (`). Although difficult to learn at first, they are essential to being understood in China. If you ask for something as simple as tea (*cha*) in a restaurant, using the wrong tone, the waiter will either give you a blank look or a fork.

Vocabulary

One of the best ways to learn "street Chinese" or basic "market Mandarin" is by listening and repeating. When making a purchase, ask the name of the item (*zhège jiào shénme míngzi?* 这个叫什么名字?) before asking how much it is (*duoshao qián?* 多少钱?) , and if five kùai is too expensive offer him two (*Wu kuài tài guì le! Liang kuài hao bù hao?* 五块太贵！两块好不好?). Within a few weeks, with a keen ear, you can pick up a surprising amount, which is particularly satisfying if you plan to spend several months in China. There are many dialects spoken in China, which vary widely in their proximity to putonghua. In Xinjiang, spoken Chinese is fairly standard with some local flavour and regional variation. In order to make something a question add "ma" to the end of the sentence. The following is a relatively simple list of phrases and words broken down into four sections: basics, getting around, food and drink, and numbers.

BASICS

Hello, how are you?	*Ni hao ma?*	你好吗?
Very good, thank you	*Hen hao, xièxiè ni*	很好，谢谢你
Yes/no	*Dùi / Bù*	对/不
Goodbye	*Zàijiàn*	再见
I do not speak Chinese	*Wo bù huì shuo Zhongwén*	我不会说中文
Can you speak English?	*Ni huì shuo Ying yu ma?*	你会说英语吗?
I understand / don't understand	*Wo dong / bùdong*	我懂/不懂
I know / don't know	*Wo zhidào / bù zhidào*	我知道/不知道
OK?	*Xíng bù xíng / hao bù hao?*	行不行/好不好?
Is it possible? / Not possible	*Keyi ma? / Bù keyi*	可以吗? /不可以
Sorry / Excuse me	*Dùibùqi*	对不起
What's the problem?	*You shénme wèntí?*	你有什么问题?
No problem	*Méi you wèntí*	没有问题
Big problem	*Dà wèntí*	大问题
It doesn't matter / Forget it	*Méi guanxi / Suàn le*	没关系/算了
Are you crazy?	*Ni húlihútu ma?*	你胡理胡涂吗?
Was it fun?	*Hao wánr ma?*	好玩吗?
It was very interesting	*Hen you yìsi*	很有意思
OK, so-so	*Mamahuhu* (horse horse tiger tiger)	马马虎虎
What does this mean?	*You shénme yìsi?*	有什么意思?
I am a student	*Wo shì xuésheng*	我是学生
What is your name?	*Ni jiào shénme míngzi?*	你叫什么名字?
How old are you?	*Ni ji sùi?*	你几岁?
Where are you from?	*Ni shì cóng nali lái de?*	你是从那里来的?
I am (American)	*Wo shì (Mei guó rén)*	我是（美国人）
British	*Ying guó rén*	英国人
Australian	*Aò dà lì yà rén*	奥大利亚人
Canadian	*Jia ná dà rén*	加拿大人
Chinese	*Zhong guó rén*	中国人

Uygur	*Wéizú* (Uygur minority)	维族
What is your monthly salary?	*Ni de gongzi yi ge yuè duoshao qián?*	你的工资一个月多少钱?
I don't smoke	*Wo bù chouyan*	我不抽烟
Let's go	*Zou ba*	走吧

GETTING AROUND

Where is the (toilet)?	*(Cè suo) zài nar?*	(厕所)在那儿?
Do you have (a double room)?	*Nimén you méi you (shuangrén jian)?*	你们有没有(双人间)?
Single room	*Danrénjian*	单人间
Dormitory	*Sùshè/duorénjian*	宿舍/多人间
I want/don't want (a bed)	*Wo yào/bù yào (yi gè chuáng wèi)*	我要/不要(一个床位)
Too expensive!	*Tài guì le!*	太贵了!
Do you have something cheaper?	*You méi you piányi yi dian?*	有没有便宜一点的?
Hot water	*rè shui*	热水
Shower	*línyù*	淋浴
Where is the bus station?	*Qiche zhàn zài nar?*	汽车站在哪儿?
How much is a ticket to (Kashgar)	*Dào (Kashí) de piào duo shao qián?*	到(喀什)的票多少钱?
I want two tickets to Hami	*Wo yào liang zhang dào Hamì de piào*	我要两张到哈蜜的票
Now, what time is it?	*Xiànzài, ji dian zhong?*	现在几点钟?
What time is the next (bus)?	*Xià tàng (qiche) ji dian zou?*	下趟(汽车)几点走?
Bus Station	*qiche zhàn*	汽车站
Train Station	*huoche zhàn*	火车站
Airport	*fei ji chang*	飞机场
I want to leave at (6 o'clock)	*Wo yào (liù dian) zou*	我要六点走
one hour	*yige xiaoshí*	一个小时
one minute	*yi fenzhong*	一分钟
half an hour	*bànge xiaoshí*	半个小时

I want a hard sleeper	*Wo yào yìngwò*	我要硬卧				
soft sleeper	*ruanwò*	软卧				
hard seat	*yìngzuò*	硬座				
Excuse me, can you please buy a ticket for me?	*Máfan ni, ni keyi tì wo mai yizhangpiào ma?*	麻烦你，可以替我买一张票吗？				
East	*dongbian*	东边	West:	*xibian*	西边
North	*beibian*	北边	South:	*nánbian*	南边
left	*zuobian*	左边	right:	*yòubian*	右边
Yesterday	*zuótian*	昨天	Today:	*jintian*	今天
Tomorrow	*míngtian*	明天			
Museum	*bówùguan*	博物馆			
Post office	*yóudiànjú*	邮电局			
Stamp	*yóupiào*	邮票			
Post card	*míng xìn piàn*	明信片			
I'd like to make a phone call	*Wo yào da diànhùa*	我要打电话			
Collect call	*duìfang fùqián*	对方付钱			
Public Security	*gonganjú*	公安局			
Bank of China	*Zhongguó yínháng*	中国银行			
Change money	*huàn qián*	换钱			
Travel agency	*luxíngshè*	旅行社			
CAAC	*Zhongguó Mínháng*	中国民航			
Bookstore	*Shudiàn*	书店			

FOOD AND DRINK

I don't eat meat	*Wo bù chi ròu*	我不吃肉
I like/don't like spicy food	*Wo xihuan / bù xihuan chi làde*	我喜欢/不喜欢吃辣的
I'm full	*Wo chibaole*	我吃饱了
Do you have (vegetables)?	*Nimén you méiyou (shucài)?*	你们有没有（蔬菜）？
I would like egg fried rice	*Wo yào dàn chaofàn*	我要鸡蛋炒饭

aubergine	*qiézi*	茄子		bean curd (tofu):	*dòufu*	豆付
bean sprouts	*dòuyá*	豆芽		beef:	*niú ròu*	牛肉
chicken	*ji ròu*	鸡肉		Chinese cabbage:	*báicài*	白菜
chopsticks	*kuàizi*	筷子		cold beer:	*bing píjiu*	冰啤酒
eggs	*jidàn*	鸡蛋		fish:	*yú*	鱼
fried noodles	*chao miàn*	炒面		fried rice:	*chaofàn*	炒饭
garlic	*dà suàn*	大蒜		ginger:	*jiang*	姜
hot peppers	*làjiào*	辣椒		mushrooms:	*mógu*	蘑菇
mutton	*yáng ròu*	羊肉		noodles:	*miàntiáo*	面条
oil	*yóu*	油		peanuts:	*hua sheng*	花生
pork	*zhu ròu*	猪肉		raisins:	*pútáo gan*	葡萄干
rice	*mifàn*	米饭		soda:	*qì shui*	汽水
soup	*tang*	汤		stir fried:	*chao de*	炒的
string beans	*jiangdòu*	江豆		tomatoes:	*fan qié*	番茄
wine	*pútáo jiu*	葡萄酒		yogurt:	*suan nai*	酸奶
a little bit	*yi diandian*	一点点儿		a little more:	*duo yidianr*	多一点儿
one bowl	*yi wan*	一碗		cup:	*beizi*	杯子
small	*xiaode*	小的		big:	*dàde*	大的
tea	*chá*	茶		black tea:	*hóng chá*	红茶
green tea	*lù chá*	绿茶		coffee:	*kafei*	咖啡
boiled water	*kaishui*	开水		ice cream:	*bing qílín*	冰淇淋

popsicle	*binggùnr*	冰棍儿
waitress	*(fúwùyuán) xiaojie*	(服务员)小姐
waiter	*fúwùyuán*	服务员
the check	*jié zhàng*	结账
great food / delicious	*hen hao chi*	很好吃
terrible food	*feicháng bù hao chi*	非常不好吃
I am uncomfortable / unwell	*Wo bù shufu*	我不舒服
headache	*tóu tòng*	头痛
cold	*ganmào*	感冒

diarrhoea	la dùzi	拉肚子
doctor	yi sheng	医生
hospital	yi yuàn	医院
rest	xiuxi	休息

NUMBERS

1	yi	一	one kilo	yi gong jin	一公斤
2	èr	二	half a kilo	yi jin	一斤
3	san	三	quarter kilo	bàn jin	半斤
4	sì	四			
5	wu	五	Monday	xingqi yi	星期一
6	liù	六	Tuesday	xingqièr	星期二
7	qi	七	Wednesday	xingqi san	星期三
8	ba	八	Thursday	xingqi sì	星期四
9	jiu	九	Friday	xingqiwu	星期五
10	shí	十	Saturday	xingqiliù	星期六
11	shí yi	十一	Sunday	xingqitian	星期天
12	shí èr	十二			
19	shí jiu	十九	January	yi yuè	一月
20	èr shí	二十	February	èr yuè	二月
21	èr shí yi	二十一	March	san yuè	三月
22	èr shí èr	二十二	April	sì yuè	四月
29	èr shí jiu	二十九	May	wu yuè	五月
30	san shí	三十	June	liù yuè	六月
50	wu shí	五十	July	qi yuè	七月
100	yi bai	一百	August	ba yuè	八月
101	yi bai ling yi	一百零一	September	jiu yuè	九月
125	yi bai èr shí wu	一百二十五	October	shí yuè	十月
500	wu bai	五百	November	shíyi yuè	十一月
1000	yi qian	一千	December	shíèr yuè	十二月

RECOMMENDED READING

Abulat Abdulreshit, *A Grand View of Xinjiang's Cultural Relics and Historic Sites, China* (Suntime Intl. Cooperation Group, Urumqi, 1999)

Barber, Elizabeth, *The Mummies of Ürümchi* (Macmillan, London, 1999)

Baumer, Christoph, *Southern Silk Road: In the Footsteps of Sir Aurel Stein and Sven Hedin* (White Orchid Books, Bangkok, 2004)

Bergman, Folke, *Archaeological Researches in Sinkiang* (Sven Hedin's Reports, Publication 7, Stockholm, 1939)

Blackmore, Charles, *Conquering the Desert of Death: Across the Taklamakan* (Tauris Parke Paperbacks, 2008)

Bruce, C.D., *In the Footsteps of Marco Polo* (Blackwood, Edinburgh, 1907)

Boulnois, Luce, *Silk Road: Monks, Warriors & Merchants on the Silk Road* (Odyssey Books & Guides, Hong Kong, 2008)

Bovingdon, Gardner, *The Uyghurs: Strangers in Their Own Land* (Columbia University Press, 2010)

Cable & French, *The Gobi Desert* (Hodder & Stoughton, London)

Chen, J., *The Sinkiang Story* (Macmillan, New York, 1977)

Clarke, Michael E., *Xinjiang and China's Rise in Central Asia – A History* (Routledge, 2011)

Dabbs, J.A., *History of the Discovery and Exploration of Chinese Turkestan* (Mouton, The Hague, 1963)

Dalrymple, William, *In Xanadu* (Harper Collins, London, 1989)

Debaine-Francfort Corinne and Abduressul Idriss, *Keriya, Mémoires d un Fleuve* (Editions Findakly, Paris, 2000)

Dubbs, Homer H., *A Roman City in Ancient China* (The China Society, London, 1957)

Feng Zhao and Zhiyong Yu, *Legacy of the Desert King* (China National Silk Museum, Hanghzou, 2000)

Fleming, Peter, *News from Tartary* (Jonathan Cape, London, 1936)

Foltz, Richard C., *Religions of the Silk Road* (Griffin Trade Paperback, 2000)

Gifford, Rob, *China Road: A Journey into the Future of a Rising Power* (Random House, 2007)

Giles, H.A., *The Travels of Fa-hsien* (Cambridge, 1923)

Härtel, Herbert, *Along the Ancient Silk Routes* (The Metropolitan Museum of Art, New York, 1982)

Hedin, Sven, *Across the Gobi Desert* (Routledge & Sons, London, 1931)

　— *Central Asia and Tibet*, 2 vols (Hurst and Blackett, London, 1903)

　— *My Life as an Explorer* (Cassel, London, 1926)

　— *Scientific Results of a Journey in Central Asia, 1899-1902* (Lithographic Institute of the General Staff of the Swedish Army, Stockholm, 1904-1907)

— *The Silk Road* (Butler & Tanner, London, 1938)

— *Through Asia,* 2 vols (Methuen, London, 1898)

History of Civilizations of Central Asia, six volumes (UNESCO Publishing, Paris, 1992)

Holdstock, Nick, *The Tree That Bleeds* (Luath Press, 2011)

Hopkirk, Peter, *Foreign Devils on the Silk Road* (Oxford University Press, Oxford, 1986)

— *The Great Game: On Secret Service in High Asia* (John Murray, London, 1990)

— *Setting the East Ablaze: Lenin's Dream of an Empire in Asia* (John Murray, London, 1984)

Huc, Evariste-Régis and Gabet, Joseph, translated by William Hazlitt, *Travels in Tartary, Thibet and China 1844–1846* (Routledge)

Israfel, Yusufu, (editor), *Xinjiang Uigur Autonomous Region Museum* (Catalogue of the new Xinjiang Regional Museum in Urumqi), (Xinjiang Uigur Autonomous Region Museum and Xinjiang Baishiyuan Craft and Art Co, Urumqi, 2005)

Knauer, E.R., *The Camel's Load in Life and Death* (Akhanthus, Zurich, 1998)

Lattimore, Owen, *High Tartary* (Little, Brown and Company, 1930)

Lattimore, Owen, *Pivot of Asia: Sinkiang and the Inner Asian Frontiers of China and Russia* (Little, Brown and Company, Boston, 1950)

Li Kangning, *The Mystical Tarim* (Xinjiang People's Publishing House, Urumqi, 1998)

Lin, Yongjian, *Niya: Paradise Regained* (Minzhu Publishing House, Beijing, 1995)

Macartney, Lady, *An English Lady in Chinese Turkestan* (Oxford University Press, Oxford, 1985)

Macleod, C. and Mayhew, B., *Uzbekistan: The Golden Road to Samarkand* (Odyssey Books & Guides, Hong Kong, 2008)

Maillart, Ella, translated by Thomas McGreevy, *Forbidden Journey* (Century, London, 1987)

Mair, Victor, *The Bronze Age and Early Iron Age Peoples of Eastern Central Asia* (Institute for the Study of Man Inc, Washington, 1998)

Mallory J.P. and Mair Victor, *The Tarim Mummies* (Thames & Hudson, London, 2000)

Mannerheim, C.G., *Across Asia* (Suomalais-Ugrilainen Seura, Helsinki, 1940)

Millward, James A., *Crossroads of Eurasia: A History of Xinjiang* (C. Hurst & Co, London, 2006)

Millward, James A., *Beyond the pass: economy, ethnicity, and empire in Qing Central Asia, 1759–1864* (Stanford University Press, 1998)

Mitchell, George, Vicziany, Marika and Yan Hu Tsui, *Kashgar: Oasis City on China's Old Silk Road* (Frances Lincoln, 2008)

Montell, Gösta, *Sven Hedin's Archaeological Collections from Khotan* (Museum of Far Eastern Antiquities, Stockholm, 1935)

Mooney, Maudsley and Hatherly, *Xi'an, Shaanxi and the Terracotta Army* (Odyssey Books & Guides, Hong Kong, 2005)

Mu Shunying, *The Ancient Art in Xinjiang, China* (The Xinjiang Art and Photography Press, Urumqi, 1994)

Neville-Hadley, Peter, *China: The Silk Routes* (Globe Pequot Press, 1997)

Perdue, Peter C., *China Marches West* (The Belknap Press of Harvard University Press, 2005)

Pilkington, John, *An Adventure on the Old Silk Road* (Random Century, 1989)

Piotrovsky, Mikhail, *Lost Empire of the Silk Road* (Electa, Milan, 1993)

Polo, Marco, *The Book of Ser Marco Polo*, edited by Sir Henry Yule (Scribner's Sons, New York, 1926)

Polo, Marco, translated by R.E. Lathan, *The Travels of Marco Polo* (Penguin Books, London, 1958)

Przhevalsky, Col N., *Mongolia*, 2 vols (translated from Russian, 1876)

— *From Kulja: Across the Tian Shan to Lob-nor* (translated 1879)

Puri, B.N., *Buddhism in Central Asia* (Banarsidass, Delhi, 1993)

Saha, Dr Kshanika, *Buddhism and Buddhist Literature in Central Asia* (Calcutta, 1970)

Seth, Vikram, *From Heaven Lake* (Chatto & Windus, London, 1983)

Shaw, Robert, *Visits to High Tartary, Yarkand and Kashgar* (Oxford University Press, Oxford, 1984)

Skrine, C.P., *Chinese Central Asia* (Methuen & Co, London, 1926)

Skrine, C.P. and Nightingale, P., *Macartney at Kashgar* (London, 1973)

Snellgrove, D. (editor), *The Image of the Buddha* (Kodansha International, Japan, 1978)

Starr, Frederick S. (editor), *Xinjiang: China's Muslim Borderland* (M.E. Sharpe, 2004)

Stein, Sir Aurel, *Ancient Khotan* (Clarendon, Oxford, 1907)

— *On Central Asian Tracks* (Macmillan, London, 1933)

— *Innermost Asia* (Clarendon, Oxford, 1928)

— *Ruins of Desert Cathay* (Macmillan, London, 1912, republished as facsimile reprints by Dover Publications, New York, 1987)

— *Sand-Buried Ruins of Khotan* (Clarendon, Oxford, 1904)

— *Serindia* (Clarendon, Oxford, 1921)

Sugiyama, Jiro, *Central Asian Objects Brought back by the Otani Mission* (Tokyo National Museum, 1971)

Sumner, Christina, *Beyond the Silk Road: Arts of Central Asia* (Museum of Applied Arts and Sciences, 2000)

Sykes, Ella and Sir Percy, *Through Deserts and Oases of Central Asia* (London, 1920)

Talbot Rice, Tamara, *Ancient Arts of Central Asia* (Thames and Hudson, London, 1963)

Teichman, Sir Eric, *Journey to Turkistan* (Hodder & Stoughton, London, 1937)

Thubron, Colin, *Shadow of the Silk Road* (HarperCollins Publishers, 2007)

Tucker, Jonathan, *The Silk Road: Art and History* (Philip Wilson Publishers, London, 2003)

Tyler, Christian, *Wild West China: The Taming of Xinjiang* (John Murray, 2003)

Vincent, Irene V, *The Sacred Oasis* (London, 1953)

von Le Coq, A., *Buried Treasures of Chinese Turkestan* (Oxford University Press, Oxford 1986)

Walker, Annabel, *Aurel Stein: Pioneer of the Silk Road* (J. Murray, London, 1995)

Wang Binhua (editor), *The Ancient Corpses of Xinjiang: The Peoples of Ancient Xinjiang and their Culture* (CIP, Urumqi, 1999)

Wang, Gang, *English* (Viking Penguin, 2009)

Warner, Langdon, *The Long Old Road in China* (Arrowsmith, London, 1927)

Wei, Cuiyi and Luckert, Karl W., *Uighur Stories from Along the Silk Road* (University Press of America, 1998)

Whitfield, Roderick, *The Art of Central Asia,* The Stein Collection in the British Museum (Kodansha International, London & Tokyo, 1982)

Whitfield, Susan, *Life along the Silk Road* (University of California Press, 2001)

Wood, Frances, *Did Marco Polo Go to China?* (Westview Press, 1998)

Wood, Frances, *The Silk Road* (The Folio Society, London, 2002)

Wriggins, Sally Hovey, *Xuanzang: A Buddhist Pilgrim on the Silk Road* (Westview Press, Inc, 1996)

Wu, Aitken, *Turkistan Tumult* (Oxford University Press, Oxford, 1984)

Wu Ch'eng En, *Monkey,* translated by Arthur Waley (Penguin Books, London, 1961)

Wu, Dunfu, (editor), *Footprints of Foreign Explorers on the Silk Road* (China Intercontinental Press, Beijing), 2005

Xia Xuncheng, *The Mysterious Lop Lake* (Science Press, Beijing, 1985)

    — *Wondrous Taklimakan* (Science Press, Beijing, 1993)

Xuan Zang, *Buddhist Records of the Western World translated from the Chinese of Hsuen Tsiang (629 CE) by Samuel Beal* (Reprinted, Chinese Materials Centre Inc, San Francisco, 1976)

Yue Feng, *Archaeological Treasures of the Silk Road in Xinjiang Uygur Autonomous Region* (Shanghai Translation Publishing House, Shanghai, 1998)

INDEX

User's note: Page references to illustrations are printed in **bold** type, ie **362**.

A-ai (Ayi) Grotto   280
Abakh Khoja   62, 326, 359
Abakh Khoja tomb   62, 322, **328**, **329**, **443**
Abdureyin, Molla   122
Abud Rushitihan, Sultan   363
Afanasievo culture   148
Afaqiyya   62
Aidelaixi (silk)   **1**, 99, 141, 368, 383
Aiding Lake (Moon Lake)   36, 48, 166, 194
air travel   153, 329, 389, 434
Aksipil   388
Aksu
    City   96, 294
    Prefecture   106
    River   306, 308
Alakol Lake (Kazakhstan)   248
Alashankou Port   78, 96, 244, 248, 454
Alashan Valley   228
alcohol   436
Ali Khan Tore   75
Almaliq   258
Almaty   153, 248, 453
Altai Mountains   36, 39, 42, 48, 50, 58, 213, **215**, **225**
Altay City   216, 226-229
altitude sickness   444
Altun
    International Hunting Park   409
    Kings   361
    Mosque (Yarkand)   **362**, 363
    Mountains   37, 40, 42, 398, 410, 414, 415, 425

Amanisa Han   114, 363
An Lushan   55, 405
April 18th Festival   111
apsara   124, **301**
Aral (Alar)   294, 308
Archaeological Research Institute of the Xinjiang Academy of Social Sciences   90, 398
archery   111
argali (wild sheep)   42, 409
Argan village   433
Arjin Mountain National Nature Reserve   37, 425
Arjin Shan, *see* Altun Mountains
Arktas (rock art)   226
Artush   310
Artux City   146
Asian Art Museum   12, **88**, 186, **188**, **192**, **301**
Astana Tombs   147, 151, **172**, 174, 187

Bachu   310, 391
Bactria   52,
bactrian camel   **24-25**, **29**, 41, **42**, 233, **236**, **425**, 429
Baicheng County (Kucha)   299
baiga (horse race)   111
Baihaba Scenic Area   216, 226, 231, 234, 235
Bairam Festival   99, 448
Baisha Kol   236
Baishitou   208

Baitula Mosque (Yining)   263, **265**
Baiyang Gou, *see* White Poplar Gully
Baiyanggou Temple   203
Baketu Port (Tacheng)   244
balbal   227, **229**, 230
Baluka, kingdom   306
Ban Chao, General   52, 79, 80, 199, 219, 283, 290, 306, 313, 359, 372, 422
Banjin Festival   110
banner troops   63
Ban Yung, General   422
Baojiacaozi   163
Baren Incident, the   77
Barkol
    (Balikun) Kazakh Autonomous County   199, 211
    Grasslands   208, 274
    Lake   203, 211
    town   211, 219
Bartus, Theodor   186
Batu Khan   58
Baumer, Christoph   148, 250, 377, 394, 406, 408, 420
Bayanbulak
    Grasslands   **276-277**, 278-280, 284
    Swan Reserve   44, 48, 279
Bayinguolin Mongolian Autonomous Prefecture   103, 279
begs   63
Beiting City   204, 216, 219
Beitun   224, 453
Bergman, Folke   89
Bezeklik Caves   88, 123, **124**, **125**, 186, **188**
Bilel-Konghan   405, 406
bingtuan (farms)   76, 78, 93, 97

bird life   44

Black Jade (Kurukash) River   367

Bleisch, William   12, 41, 45

blue sheep   42

Bogda
Peak (Feng)   138, 156, 162, 163, 216, 219
Shan   36, 133, 219

Bogeda Biosphere Reserve   162

Bokhara   52, 58, 70, 142, 209, 311, 314, 355

Bole City   249

bolsheviks   73, 108

Boma Tomb (Ili Valley)   266

Bortola Mongolian Autonomous Prefecture   103, 248, 249, 284

Bosten (Baghrash) Lake   **30-31**, 37, 44, 48, 51, 97, 283, 284, 290

Bower Manuscript   291, 374, 375

Bower, Captain Hamilton   84, 291, 374

Brahmi Script   148, 374, 378, 391, 402, 403, 417

British Consulate (Kashgar), *see* Chini Bagh

British Empire, the   65, 411

British Indian Agency   67

British Library, the   12, **87**

Bronze Age, the   49, 148, 226, 247, 265, 400, 407, 409, 433

Buddhism
Hinayana   290, 314
Mahayana   54, 126, 372, 378, 407
spread of   56, 70, 82, 122, 124, 167, 190, 205, 394
texts   117
Tibetan   106

Buerjin City   230

Bukhara, *see* Bokhara

Butterfly Valley (Altai)   228

buzkashi   102, 111, **112**, 255, 313

Byzantium   55

Cable, Mildred   169, 212

Caceres, Fausto   113

Cai Lun   377

Central Asia International Grand Bazaar of Kashgar   319, **324**

Central Jade Market (Urumqi)   142

Centre of Asia, the   **161**, 163

Chaghatai   58, 258, 314

Chaghatai Khanate   58, 60, 167, 200, 266, 271, 291, 359, 373

Chang'an   40, 52, 55, 113, 126, 167, 210, 291, 373

Changji City   244

Changji Hui Autonomous Prefecture   103, 211, 217, 244

Chang Tang Plateau (Tibet)   415

chapan   99

Charkhlik, *see* Ruoqiang

Charwighul   150

Cherchen, *see* Qiemo

China Xinjian Group   93

Chinese Communist Party, the   68, 76

Chinese dynasties (chronology)   50

"Chinese Turkestan"   64, 66, 69

Chinggis Khaan, *see* Genghis Khan

Chini Bagh (Kashgar)   326, 333

chiru, *see* Tibetan antelope

Chuguchak, *see* Tacheng

climate   436, 437

coal reserves   48, 93

Colourful City Scenic Area (Junggar Basin)   223

Commonwealth of Independent States (CIS)   68, 78, 95

Confucian Temple (Urumqi)   **145**

cotton farming   93, 307, **366**

Cultural Relics Bureau (Urumqi)   459

Cultural Revolution, the   77, 194, 286, 382

Dabancheng   163, 164

Daheyan   164, 195

Dalrymple, William   331

Dalgleish, Andrew   84, 374

Dandan Oilik   84, 123, 356, 361, 368, 374, 376, 392, **393**, 394, 398

dap (musical instrument)   114

Daquangou Reservoir   247

dastarkhan   **13**, 101, 296, 440

Daur, people   110, 117

Dawaz (tightrope walking)   111, **112**, 142

de Goes, Benedict   59

Deng Xiaoping   77, 78

Dihua   133

Dinosaur Park (Karamay)   240, **245**

Dinosaur Valley   217

dombra (musical instrument)   102, 115

dopa (cap)   99, **104**, 139, 171, 382

Dostyk (Kazakhstan)   248

Drepsang Plain   364

Dry Ditch (Gan Gou)   282

Dudin, Samuil   88

Dugat (rock art caves)   226

Dughlat (emirs)   58, 60

Dunhuang   56, 86, 87, 88, 91, 203, 205, 221, 356, 378, 415, 419, 423, 452

Duolate (rock art site)   226, 229

dutar (musical instrument)   114

eagle bone flute, *see nay*

eagle hunting   102

East Turkestan Islamic Movement (ETIM)   92

East Turkestan Republic
  first   71, 74
  second   75, 262

Ebinur Lake   249, 251

Elias, Ney   83

embassies   441

Emin Khoja   63, 175

Emin Minaret   171, 175, **176**

Endere   40, 355, 356, 376, 377, 404, **405**, 406, **409**

Erdaoqiao Market (Urumqi)   138, **141**

ethnic nationalities   98, 151

Etzina   205

Eurasian Land Bridge   78, 96

Fairy Bay (Kanas River)   231

Farhad Beg   385, 394

Flaming Mountains   **26-27**, 36, 177, 183, **184-185**, 187

Fleming, Peter   361, 376, 410

Ferghana   52

Fa Xian   82, 126, 372, 376

Five-coloured Hills   223

Forsyth Mission, the   83

falconry   107, 111

Fa Xiang, artistic school   126

Five Great Passes, the   355, 364, **365**

food   128, 141, 155, 198, 208, 269, 441, 442

Fruit Valley (Ili)   255, 258

Fuhai
  City   224
  Lake   224

Fuyun
  City   223, 224
  County   265

Gai Si's Tomb   202

Galdan (Junggar chief)   62

Gaochang   **26-27**, 40, 55, 56, 113, 126, 147, 166, 167, **173**, 174, 182, 186, **189**, 190, **192**, 204, 220

Gashun (Bitter) Gobi   424, 426

gazelle, goitred (black-tailed)   41

General of Ili   63

Genghis Khan   57, 71, 167, 205, 220, 258, 314, 373

Gez River (Gorge)   344, 345, **349**

Ghandara
  art   124, 128, 147, 190, 291, 299, **301**, 417
  kingdom   124, 126, 346

Gobi bear   44

Golden Sand Beach (Bosten Lake)   285

Golmud   415

Goma, *see* Pishan

Gongnaisi Grasslands   **6-7**

Grand Canyon (Tien Shan)   279

grapes   **129**, **165**, 166, 179, 191, 442
  growing and drying   128, **181**, 182
  mare's nipple   179

Grape Valley (Turpan)   179

Great Development of the West programme   78, 138

Great Game, the   65, 66, 82, 338

Great Hall, the (Urumqi)   139

Great Leap Forward, the   77

green corridors   **95**, 97, **292**, 293

Grenard, Ferdinand   150, 374

Grunwedel, Albert   88, 186, 190

Guanyu Pavilion (Kanas)   234

Guge Kingdom   366

Gumugou, *see* Qawrighul

Gurbantunggut Desert   **34**, 36, 213, 216, 224

Hami
  ancient kingdom   33, 55, 56, 61, 65, 167
  Ghost City   203
  mausoleums of the kings   **201**
  modern city   199
  Prefecture   199

Hami Rebellion   73, 74

Handega Cliff paintings   229

Han Dynasty   28, 48, 51, 79, 113, 133, 146, 166, 182, 194, 203, 204, 209, 211, 216, 219, 284, 298, 369, 377, 385, 391, 399, 407, 420, 423, 433

Hanoi, Ancient City of   334

Hare, John   41, 45, 424, 429

Heaven Lake, *see* Tianchi

Hedin, Sven   84, 89, 128, 149, 200, 207, 217, 284, 285, 307, 315, 359, 360, 374, 376, 377, 384, 392, 399, 419, 420, 421, 422, 424, 425, 426, 430, 432

Hemu Valley   216, 231, 234

Hephthalites   54, 372

Hetan Expressway (Urumqi)   **135**, 138, 144

Hetian, *see* Hotan

Hexi Corridor   40, 52, 56, 79, 80, 415

Highway
  216   216
  217   278, 294, 302, 308
  218   278, 294
  312   244, 254, 289, 294, 453
  314   283, 293
  315   293, 356, 366, 398, 409, 415, 453

Himalayan griffon vulture   44

Hoernle, Rudolf   291, 374, 375, 376

Hongshan Park (Urumqi)   138, 144, **145**

Hongligugou   419

Hopkirk, Peter   134

Horgas Port   95, 96, 153, 254, 262, 271, 453, 454

horses   52, 102, 209, 273, 274, 275

Hortang village (Endere)   404

Hotan
   Atlas Silk Workshop   383
   City   49, 65, 96, 147, 148, 294, 308, 310, 356, 367, 379
   Museum   356, **380**, 381, 384, 388
   River   **30-31**, 294, 308, 359, 390, 391, 392, 395

hotels   153, 154, 197, 208, 332, 364, 412

Hualin Park (Altay City)   229

Huang Wenbi   85, 89, 90

Huatugou   415

Hui, people   102

Hui-He, *see* Hui

Huiyuan   63, 258, 270

hunting   111

Huth, George   88

hygiene   440

Iagnaki, Ahmed   128

ibex, long-horned   42, 415

Ibn Battuta   82

Idkah Mosque   **8**, 48, 99, **120-121**, 297, **312**, 317, 320, **328**, **329**

Ili
   General, the   258, 270, 271
   Kazakh Autonomous Prefecture   216, 262
   Kazakh Autonomous Prefecture Museum   116, 264, **268-269**

River   256, 259, 262
   Valley   33, **46-47**, 50, 58, 60, 62, 69, 75, 102, 106, 110, 213, 215, 255, **260**, 274

Imam Asim Tomb   **383**, 384

Imam Jafer Sadik Tomb   **400**

Imam Musa Kazim cemetery   381

International Dunhuang Project   12, 90, **91**

International Grand Bazaar (Urumqi)   115, 138, 139, **142**, 152

Irkeshtam Pass   330, 453, 454

Iron Age, the   49

Iron Gate Pass   286, **287**

Irtysh River   36, 58, 97, 214, **223**, 224, 231, 239

Ishaqiyya (sufi sect)   61

Islam
   spread of   56, 82, 127

Islam Akhun   375, 376

Islamic Party of Turkestan   77

Ismaili (Islamic sect)   128, 350

Ismail Khan   62

jade (nephrite)   142, 151, 367, 379, **438**

Jahangir Khoja   63

Jaman Mosque (Abakh Khoja's Tomb)   326

Jarring, Gunnar   315

jasak   63

Jeminay   236, 454

Jiangjun Gobi   216, 217

Jiangjunmiao   217

Jiang Xiaowan   89

Jiaohe   40, 166, 174, **180**, **181**, 182

Jili Lake   224

Jimsar   216, 219

Jin Dynasty   286, 377, 391, 433

Jinghe   96, 248, 254, 453

Jin Hu Yang Golden Diversiform Poplar Park   364

Jin Jue, *see* Niya

Jin Shuren   73

Jiya township (Hotan)   384

Johnson, William   83, 374

Junggar
   Basin   32, 33, 36, 49, 58, 96, 102, 133, 213, **214**, 222, 249
   Empire   61, 62
   Gate   153, 213, 244, 248
   people   **46-47**, 61, 62, 103, 167

junxian   72

K2 (mountain)   37, 366

Kabakasgan   400, 402, 403

Kaidu River   37, **276-277**, 284

Kailas (mountain)   366

Kalmyk, people   116

kalpak (hat)   102

Kanas
   Lake   216, 229, 230, **232-233**
   River   **16-17**, 231 232

Kanas Lake National Park   231

Kangjia Shimenzi Rock carvings   247, 250

Kangxi, Emperor   199

Kara Bator   206

Karadong   84, 356, 361, 381, **397**, 399, 402

Karakhanid Khanate   56, 314, 327, 372

Kara-Khitan, people   57, 58, 71, 101, 116, 373

Karakhoto   85, 87, 204, 204, **205**, 207, 220

Karakoram
    Highway   343, **344**, 346, 354
    Pass   364, **365**
    mountain range   37, 66, 126, 313, 343, 346, 364
Karakoshun Lake   419, 420, 421, 423
Karakul Lake   **24-25**, **35**, 343, 345, **354**
Karamay
    City   95, 97, 213, 243
    Nature Reserve   42, 44, 222
Karashahr   41, 150, 274, 283
karez (irrigation)   36, 166, 176, **177**
Karghalik, *see* Yecheng
Kashgar
    City   39, 41, 54, 67, 84, 92, 313-334, **321**, 453
    Prefecture   315
Kashgeri, Mohammed   56, 117, 335
Kax River (Ili)   256
Kazakh, people   62, 101, **105**, 115, 160, **161**, 163, 203, 211, **228**, 231, **36**, **252-253**, 254, **257**, **260-261**, 275, **280**
Keriya
    people   **13**
    town   83, 355, 356, 398
    River   390, 391, 392, 399, 400, 404
Khaidu   58, 220
Khan Abdullah   62
Khantengri Mosque (Urumqi)   **140**
Khan Tengri (mountain)   272
Kharakhoja, *see* Gaochang
Kharakhoja, warrior   183
Khara-Khoja, confederation   56, 60, 167
Kharoshthi script   54, 70, 86, 374, 384, 395, 402, 403, 406, 417
Khizr Khwaja   60
Khocho, *see* Gaochang
Khoja Afaq, *see* Abakh Khoja
Khoja Buzurg   65
Khoja Ishaq Wali   61

Khoja Muhammad Yusuf   62, 63
Khoja Niyaz   74
Khoja Wali Khan   63
Khokand kingdom   63, 65, 314, 355
Khunjerab Pass   332, 343, 351, 444, 453
Khotan
    ancient kingdom   40, 54, 56, 74, 79, 83, 84, 86, 313, 314, 355, 370, 372, 375, 377, 395, 398
    modern city, *see* Hotan
Khuiten Peak   213, 232
Kizilgaha Beacon Tower   298
Kizil Kara Buddhist Caves   298
Kizilsu Kirghiz Autonomous Prefecture   106, 310, 311
Kizil Thousand Buddha Caves   82, 87, 125, 147, 291, 299, **304-305**
kobyz (musical instrument)   115
kokpar, see buzkashi
Kok Turks, people   55
komuz (musical instrument)   115
Konche (Konqe) River   37, 97, 150, 284, 420-422, 424-431, 433
Konglonggou   217
Kongur Tagh   346
Koran, the   127, 140
Korban Festival   99, 322, 326, 448
Korla   283, **284-285**, 309, 315, 413, 419, 420, 430, 431, 433
Koros, Csoma de   83
Kozlov, Pyotr   87, 128, 206, 420
Kroraina, *see* Loulan
Kublai Khan   58, 220
Kucha
    ancient kingdom   41, 54, 55, 87, 88, 113, 126, 147, 148, 209, 290, 298, 430
    Grand Mosque   **296**, 297
    modern city   291
Kuchluk   57
Kulamlak village (Qiemo)   409

kulan (wild ass)   42
Kulja, *see* Yining
Kulja Incident, the   78
Kulma Pass   332, 454
Kumarajiva   54, 82, 290, **304-305**
Kum Darya (River)   149, 150, 421
kumis   313
Kumtura Caves   299
Kumul, *see* Hami
Kumtagh Desert   **2-3**, 198, 413
Kunes River (Ili)   256
Kunlun Mountains   36, 37, 40, 42, 355, 364, 376, 390, 398, 400, 409, 412, 414, 415, 425
Kunlun Square (Qiemo)   407
Kuomintang (KMT)   73, 74, 75, 76, 307
kurgan (tombs)   51
Kuruk Darya (River)   420, 422, 424-428, 430, 431
Kuruk Tagh   36, 42
Kushan Empire   51, 53, 54, 79, 209, 372, 385, 406
Kuyten   244, 247, 278, 453
Kyrgyz, people   56, 106, 115, 311, 344, 345

L

Lafuqueke   203
laghman (noodles)   131
Lalulik   407
lammergeyer   44
language   132
Lattimore, Owen   64, 71, 123, 170, 249, 259, 275
Le Coq, Albert von   **88**, 128, 134, 169, 186, 189, 190, 191, 194, 200, 291, 301
Liao Dynasty   57

Li Kun   52, 53
Liushui   400
limbe (flute)   116, **232**
Lin Zexu   266
Liu Jintang, General   69, 72
Livestock Market (Kashgar)   319, **324, 325, 439**
Loayemiao Port (Barkol)   212
Lop Desert   41, 53, 85, 86, 150, 377, 413, 422, 423, 424
Lop Nor   37, 40, 48, 53, 77, 83, 84, 89, 90, 97, 149, 151, 284, 356, 361, 413, 417-422, **418**, 424, 425, 427-429
Lop Nur Wild Camel Nature Reserve   48, 429
Loulan   41, 49, 53, 80, 84, 86, 146, 166, 282, 313, 356, 361, 377, 402, 403, 406, 413, 417, **418**, 419, 421, 424-429, 430, 431
Loulan Beauty   **147**, 151, 430
Lunnan Oilfield   95
Luntai   52, 133, 289, 293

M

Macartney, George   67, 84, 89, 327, 375
Mair, Victor and Mallory, JP   49
Manas (epic poem)   106, 116
manaschi   115
Manchu, people   109, 117
Manichaeism   56, 70, 82, 117, 122, 126, 167, 190
Mannerheim, Baron   88
Mao Zedong   75, 76, 93, 138
Mao Zemin   75
Maralbashi, *see* Bachu
Marco Polo   58, 59, 82, 86, 127, 167, 200, 205, 206, 314, 373, 408, 422, 423
Marco Polo sheep   42

maroji   131
Mathura, artistic school   125
Mazar Tagh   310, 356, 377, 381, 391, 392
Ma Zhongying   73, 74, 135, 201, 285, 315
Melikawat   356, 385
melons
   Hami   128, 131, 198, 199, 442
   water   **129**, 131, **325**
Merdek   433
Meshrep   99, **104**, 114, 440
Mesolithic sites   49
Mesum Apiz   378
Miao'er Gully   163
Millennium-old Walnut Tree (Hotan)   380
Millward, James   12, 45, 92
Minfeng   294, 356, 400
Mingdi, Emperor   124
Ming Dynasty   60, 82, 167, 206, 210, 264
Mingsha Dunes (Hami)   211
Mingsha Shan (Baihaba)   236
Miran   40, 86, 123, 355, 356, 378, 394, 399, 415, **416**, 419, 430, 433
Mirza Abu-Bakr   60
Miyim Haji Karez Museum (Turpan)   176
Moghulistan   60, 69, 271, 306
Mohammed-i-Hamed   83
Molcha (Moleqie) River   409
Molena Ashidin Hodja's Tomb   297
money   438
Mongke Khan   58
Mongol
   Empire   57, 182
   people   57, 103, **104**, 116, **249**, **278**
Mongolian gazelle   42
Moon Bay (Kanas River)   **34**, 231

Mor Buddhist Pagoda   334
moriin khuur   116
Mori Kazakh Autonomous County   211
Mu, Emperor   79, 160, 199, 210
Muhammad Emin Bughra   74
Muhammed, the Prophet   127
mummies   148, **149**, 151, **173**, 175, 432
Muqam (Mukam)   **113**, 363
Muqam Festival (Yarkand)   363
Murtuk River   186
music   113-117
Muzart Pass   271
Muzat River   299, 302
Muztagata (mountain)   **35**, 346, **348**
Muztagh Ulugh   416
Mysterious Stone Valley (Bortala)   251

N

Nadaam   103, 255
Nairamdal Peak   213, 232
nan (bread)   **130**, 131, 442
Nanjiang Railway   96, 153, 286, 287, 307, 453
Nan Shan   **160**, 162
Naqshbandiyya (sufi sect)   61
Narat Grasslands, *see* Narat Scenic Area
Narat Scenic Area   **6-7**, 273
Nawruz   103
nay (eagle bone flute)   107, 117
Neleke   407
Neolithic sites   49, 202, 250, 408
Nestorian Christianity   70, 82, 122, 126, 167, 190, 205, 258, 314, 370, 373

New Niya, *see* Minfeng

Ni Jang ancient settlement   402

Niya   40, 86, 123, 146, 294, 355, 376, 377, 381, 394, **401**, 402, 404, 432

"nodding donkey"   242

Northern Wei Dynasty   54, 166, 182

nuclear testing   41, 77, 417, 425, 427

obo (stone cairn)   106, 280

Ogedei   58

oil
  industry   75, 78, **94**, 95
  reserves   48, 93, 242, 286

Oirats, people   61, 62, 103, 167, 200, 249, 258

Old Believers   238, **239**

Oldenburg, Sergei   87, 291

Opal (Wupoer)   335

Orthodox Eastern Church   108

Osman Batur   75, 76

Otani, Count Kozui   89, 128, 291

Otkur, Abdurehim   122

ovoo, see obo

Oytagh   343, 344, 346

Pamirs   **24-25**, 36, 66, 106, 313, 343, 345, 346

paper manufacturing   376, 377, 378

Parthia   52, 53

peaches   **129**, 442

pears   131, **286**, 442

Pelliot, Paul   128, 291

People's Liberation Army (PLA)   76, 243, 247, 356, 419

People's Park (Urumqi)   **139**, 144, 162

People's Republic of China (PRC)   76

People's Square (Kashgar)   317, **320**

People's Square (Urumqi)   138, 139

People's Theatre (Urumqi)   139, 140, **145**

petroglyphs   226, 229, 247, 250, 409

Petrovsky, Nikolai   68, 84, 327, 375

Pilkington, John   309

Pillars of Islam   127

PingTian resort   163

Pishan   366, 375

Pobeda Peak   272

poluo   131, 142, 442, **447**

pomegranates   129

poplar, diversiform-leaved   **283**, **288**, **289**

Posgam, *see* Zepu

Potanin, GN   206

Princess's Castle (Tashkurgan)   350

prostitution   445

Protectorate of the Western Regions   52

Przewalski (Przhevalsky), Nikolai   83, 87, 206, 222, 415, 419, 420, 424

Przewalski's horse   44, 222, 415, 416

public holidays   445

Qaidam Basin (Qinghai)   415

Qamar ad-Din   60

Qapqal Xibe Autonomous County   110, 270

Qarshi, Jamal   311

Qäwrighul   150, 430, 432, 433

Qianlong, Emperor   **46-47**, 62, 134, 249, 258, 263, 264, 270

Qiemo   40, 90, 148, 151, 294, 356, 407, 408, 410, 412

Qiemuer Qieki   227, 229, 230

Qing Dynasty   **46-47**, 62, 65, 134, 140, 151, 157, 163, 200, 201, 270, 284, 296, 382

Qinghai Route, the   415

Qinghe County   215

Qin Shihuangdi, Emperor   51

Qira County   382, 392

Qitai Ghost City   203, 217, **218**

Qitai Petrified Forest Park   217, **222**

Qiuci, *see* Kucha

Qixing Buddhist Caves   287

"Queen Mother of the West"   79

Quer Gully   229

Qu Wentai   166

Ramadan   99

Rawak Stupa   125, 356, 376, 382, 385, 386, **389**

rawap (musical instrument)   114

religious art   122, **125**, **282**

reptiles   44

Rhins, Jules Deutreuil de   83, 150, 374

Richthofen, Ferdinand von   32, 83, 84, 420, 421

river rafting   389

rock art, *see* petroglyphs

Roerich Museum, the   12

Roerich, Nicholas   39, 239

Roman Empire, the   52, 53, 80, 127

Ruanruan, tribe   54, 226

Ruoqiang   294, 356, 412, 413, 415, 419, 423, 433

Russian
  Consulate (Kashgar)   327, 333
  Empire   65, 73, 108, 109
  people   **108**, 117, **239**
  Revolution   135

Saban Festival   109

Sabir, Zordun   122

Sabit Damulla   74

saiga (antelope)   42

Saiyid, Sultan   359

Saka, people   50, 70, 148, 251, 372, 388

Samarkand   52, 58, 70, 126, 190, 209, 314, 322, 355, 374

Samedi, Ziya   122

Sampul, *see* Shanpula

Sanchakou   310

Sand Therapy Health Centre (Turpan)   183

Sarikol kingdom   107

Satuq Bughra Khan   310, 314

Saypidin Azizi   76

Sayram Lake   96, **252-253**, 254, **257**, 258

Schmidt, Jeremy   342

Schuyler, Eugene   83

Scythian culture   49, 101, 250, 400

Seman Hotel, *see* Russian Consulate (Kashgar)

Seres   53, 370

Serindian art   124, 128

Seth, Vikram   323

Shaanxi Mosque (Urumqi)   140

Shaanxi Mosque (Yining)   264

Shache, see Yarkand

Shah Yari   122

Shang Dynasty   49

Shanghai, connection with   77, 95

Shanpula   **90**, 148, 150, 381, 388

Shanshan
   County   191
   kingdom   53, 55, 402, 406, 408, 413, 422
   town   198

Shatuo Silk Factory   382

Shaw, Raynor   33

Shaw, Robert   314

Shengjinkou Thousand Buddha Caves   187

Sheng Shicai   71, 73, 74, 135

Shengyou Temple (Zhaosu)   272

Shia (Islamic sect)   128

Shihezi   247

Shipton, Diana   318, 327, 347

Shipton, Eric   318, 335, 336

Shipton's Arch   335, 336, **337**, 343

Shishugou Foundation   217

silk production   **368**, **369**, 370, **371**, 382, 383

Silk Road Ski Resort   163

Simsim Caves (Kucha)   299

Skrine, Sir Clarmont   32, 311, 361, 366

Sleeping Dragon Bay (Kanas River)   **16-17**, 231

snowcock   44

snow leopard   42, **43**, 44, 415

snow lotus   160

Sogdians, people   53, 54, 56, 70, 82, 117, 391, 394

So Man, General   422

Songyun, military governor   83

Sost (Sust)   332, 354

Southern Silk Road, the   28, 32, 40, 53, 54, 83, 355, 356, 385, 410, 416, 437

Soviet Union   74, 75, 78, 135

Srinagar (Kashmir)   355

Stein, Aurel   85, **87**, 89, 128, 149, 169, 189, 204, 207, 291, 307, 310, 368, 375-378, 384-386, 388, 391, 392, 395, 399, 403, 406, 408, 412, 416, 417, 419, 422, 425, 426, 430

Stone Fortress (Tashkurgan)   350, **352-353**

Subashi, ancient city of   **297**, 298, **300**

sufis   61

Sui Dynasty   55, 147, 209

Sulitanjiamai Mosque (Artush)   311

Sunni (Islamic sect)   128

swinging games   111

Tacheng   65, 103, 110, 244, 454

Tagharma village (Tashkurgan)   351

Tajik, people   106, 117, 346, **348**, **354**, **442**

takhi, *see* Przewalski's horse

Taklamakan Desert   **14-15**, **30-31**, 32, 37, **38**, 39, 40, 48, 84, **94**, 97, 149, 282, 292, 308, 310, 338, **355**, 413, 414, 419, **439**

Talas River, Battle of   55, 405

tambur (musical instrument)   114

Tamerlane   60, 65, 167, 258, 271, 284, 306

Tangbaletas   226

Tang Dynasty   41, 55, 70, 113, 122, 126, 133, 147, 167, 182, 207, 209, 210, 220, 227, 258, 271, 283, 291, 299, 314, 367, 370, 373, 377, 378, 381, 405, 412

Tangut, people   57, 87, 204

Tarbagatai range   36, 58, 213, 236, 238

Tarim
   Basin   33, 36, 49, 89, 133, 148, 402, 413, 417
   Highway   96, 289, 294, 454
   River   **20-21**, 37, 85, 97, **289**, 294, 308, 361, 417, 420, 422, 425

Tashkurgan   49, 50, 92, 107, 343, 346, 350, 444

Tashkurgan Tajik Autonomous Country   106, 346

Tatar Mosque (Urumqi)   140

Tatar, people   **109**, 117, 140

Tazhong Oilfield   289, 292, **293**, 408

Tekes River Valley   106, 256, 271, 275

Telate (rock art)   226

Temujin, *see* Genghis Khan

Thorner, Alice   123

Three Districts Revolution   75

throat singing   116

Thubron, Colin   387, 414

Tianchi   156, **157**, **158-159**

Tianchi Nature Reserve   162

Tibetan
  antelope   42, **43**, 409, 415
  brown bear   42, 415
  Empire   55, 56, 182, 204, 216, 220, 314, 372, 378, 391, 392, 405, 415, 416, 417
  Plateau   42, 332, 366, 425
  wild ass   42, 415

Tien Shan   28, **30-31**, 33, 42, 82, 93, 106, 133, 162, 213, 254, 278, **279**

Toghraklek Manor   407, 408

Tokharian, people   49, 51, 56, 70, 148, 166, 284

Toksun   282

tollbooths   246

Tomb of the Fragrant Concubine   326

Tomenpu village   421

Tomur Mountain, *see* Pobeda Peak

Torgut Mongols   63, 103, 249, 274, 284

Torugart Pass   330, 454

tour agencies   449, 451, 452

Töwän (Tieban)   150, 151, 430, 432, 433

trade routes   38, 40, 52, 56, **81**

Transoxiana   54, 60

Trans-Siberian Railroad   72

Treaty of Kulja   65

Treaty of Livadia   69

Treaty of St Petersburg   69, 262, 270

Treaty of Tsientsin   83

Tsarist Russia, *see* Russian Empire

Tuhuoluo   405

Tughluq Timor   60, 266, 271, 306, 314

Tuman River (Kashgar)   319, 327

Tungan
  people   65, 103, 410
  rebellion   65

Tunguzbasti   391, 399

tuntian system   53, 63

Tuoming   134

Tuopuklun Temple   398

Turfan, *see* Turpan

Turkic Khaganate
  Eastern   55, 56, 227
  Western   55, 200, 202, 204, 216, 220, 226, 227, 258, 372

Turk-Sib Railway   78, 96, 248, 453

Turpan   40, 41, 48, 63, 65, 67, 87, 88, 123, 126, 147, 166, 170, 203, 425

Turpan Bazaar   171

Turpan Depression   28, 33, 36, 48, 49, 89, 164, 166, **168**, 194

Turpan Prefecture Museum   169, 174

Turpan Silk Road Grape Festival   174

Tushuk Tash, *see* Shipton's Arch

Tuva, people   116, 216, **232**, 234

Tu-ying (Loulan)   426

Tuyoq   191, **193**, **196**

Tuyugou Hojamu Tomb   191

Tuyuhun, people   408

Twelve Muqam   **10-11**, 113, 114, 363

Ulungur
  River   215, 223
  Lake   215, 224

underground water reserves   97

UNESCO   113, 162, 235

UNIMOG (vehicles)   292, 357, 419

Unity Square (Hotan)   **376**, 379, 389

Urumqi   48, 65, **94**, 96, 133-156, **134**, **135**, 215

Uygur
  clothing   99, 101
  Empire   56, 58, 106, 167, 216
  Khaganate   55
  literature   117
  medicine   101
  music   99
  people   98, **104**, 148, **169**, **173**, **282**, **358**, **366**, **367**, **396**, **408**, **442**, **447**
  script   117, **173**
  weddings   **100**, **101**

Uygur Cultural Street (Yining)   264

Uyguristan, *see* Khara-Khoja

Uygur Mosque (Turpan)   174

Uyrhe Ghost City   203, 217, 237, **240-241**

Uzbek, people   107, 117

visas   457

Wang Enmao   77

Warring States period   51, 420

Washixia   412, 413

Water Mill Ditch Park (Urumqi)   145

websites 456

Wei, Cuiyi and Luckert, Karl W 119

Weili (ancient Korla) 285

West-East Gas Pipelines 95

Western Regions, the 36 kingdoms 69, 372

White Jade (Yurung Kash) River 367, 385

White Poplar Gully 162

White Russians 73, 108, 135

Wild Camel Protection Foundation 45, 429

wildlife 41-45, 82, 409

wolf, Eurasian 42

wrestling 111

Wucaiwan 217

Wu Cheng'en 183

Wudi, Emperor 51, 52, 209, 377

Wupu (Wubao) 202, 203

Wusun, people 51, 101, 216, 256, 265, 272

Xiaohe 89, 150, 151, **431**, 432, 433

Xibe, people 110, 117, 270, **272**

Xingzhou 205

Xinjiang
  administrative regions 92
  climate 33
  economy 92-96
  environmental issues 96-97
  GDP 96
  geology 33
  population 32
  "time" 152, 449

Xinjiang Karez Research Association 176

Xinjiang Production and Construction Corps (XPCC) 63, 76, 77, 93, 244, 247

Xinjiang Uygur Autonomous Region Museum 90, 139, **146**, 150, 189, 431, 433

Xinjiang Wild Horse Breeding and Research Centre 223

Xinxingxia 202, 212

Xiongnu, people 51, 52, 54, 80, 166, 182, 199, 204, 209, 211, 216, 219, 251, 290, 306, 313, 372, 419

Xixia kingdom 57, 204

Xuanzang 82, 126, 166, 183, 190, 200, 212, 220, 283, 291, 298, 306, 307, 314, 350, 368, 373, 376, 394, 395, 402, 405

Xu Song 83

Xu Xusheng 89

yak 42, 107, 111, 409, 415, **446**

Yakub Beg 65, 67, 84, 134, 163, 167, 200, 262, 291, 306, 314, 326, 373

Yang Chung-chien 217

Yanghang Mosque, see Tatar Mosque

Yanqi Hui Autonomous County 283

Yang Zengxin 72, 134

yardang **418**, 419, 426

Yarkand
  Khanate 60, 62, 114, 359, 361
  modern city 343, 356, 361, **362**
  oasis kingdom 40, 41, 54, 55, 67, 74, 83, 310, 314, 355, 358, **359**, 374
  River 37, 310, 361, 364

Yengisar 74, 357, **358**

yeti 44

Yingpän **430**, 431, 433

Yining
  Bridge 264
  City 48, 62, 65, 69, 75, 82, 96, 254, 259, 262, 275

Yiwu
  City 202
  County 199, 208

Yotkan 356, 376, 381

Younghusband, Sir Francis 167, 200, 307

Youyi Feng (Peak) 213

Yuan Dahua 72

Yuan Dynasty 58, 71, 151, 182, 186, 198, 206, 210, 251, 350

Yuan Sha 356, 399

Yu, Emperor 370

Yuezhi, people 51, 52, 80, 256

Yumenguan (Jade Gate) 423

yurt 102, 103, **268**, **348**, 441

Yusuf Has Hajib 56, 117, 327

Yutian 113, 356, 385, 398, 399

Zaghunluk 148, 150, 407

Zeng Jize 69

Zepu 364

Zhang Qian 51, 52, 79, 256, 290

Zhangye 56

Zhawa 367

Zhang Zhizhong 76

Zhaoguli Temple (Subashi) 298

Zhaosu County 106, 271, 272

Zhenglong Pagoda (Urumqi) **143**, 144

Zhenguan, Emperor 133

Zhou Dynasty 199, 202, 210, 369

Zuo Zongtang, General 67, 69, 200, 315